Toasting *Cheers*

Toasting *Cheers*

An Episode Guide to the
1982–1993 Comedy Series,
with Cast Biographies
and Character Profiles

DENNIS A. BJORKLUND

McFarland & Company, Inc., Publishers
Jefferson, North Carolina, and London

British Library Cataloguing-in-Publication data are available

Library of Congress Cataloguing-in-Publication Data

Bjorklund, Dennis A.
    Toasting *Cheers* : an episode guide to the 1982–1993 comedy
series, with cast biographies and character profiles / by Dennis A.
Bjorklund.
        p.   cm.
    Includes index.
    ISBN 0-89950-962-2 (library binding : 50# alkaline paper) ∞
    1. Cheers (Television program)   I. Title
PN1992.77.C473B56   1997
791.45'72—dc20   96-31359
                                                                CIP

Manufactured in the United States of America

McFarland & Company, Inc., Publishers
  Box 611, Jefferson, North Carolina 28640

Table of Contents

Acknowledgments

There can never be enough commendation and adulation of everyone who partook in the preparation of this manuscript. First and foremost, the highest veneration must be given to Rochelle A. Theroux for her meticulous research, scrupulous perfectionism, infallible editorial assistance, constructive criticism, and forbearance. Thank you for everything. In addition, due reverence must be given to Sarah Brandt for her dedication, succor and ardor (not to mention tolerance). Next in line is Mark J. Madden for his research assistance and authoritative opinion as a "Cheers" zealot and entertainment guru. Lastly, Julie Dolezal for last minute assistance, and Steve Marquardt (wherever you are).

A special acknowledgment goes to James Gehrke, my Alpha Phi Omega brother, for your procrastination. For it was your indolence on January 24, 1985, in preparation for an evening of barhopping, that forced me to wait patiently and watch a television show you lauded. That remarkable "Cheers" episode (#59) ignited an obsession which culminated with this book.

In addition, acknowledgment is given to J & J Construction and the three idiots and a dog (they know who they are) for the memorable weekend in June 1995; James L. Bjorklund for creative genius, trustworthiness, and silence; James Anthony Martin for long-suffering; Thomas L. Harbit for pleasurable deviations into inane discourse and daily banter; and Robert C. Schwartz and Rose Bjorklund because they would love to see their names in print.

Introduction

When "Cheers" debuted on national television on September 30, 1982, it had the smallest viewing audience for the entire week. Despite the poor ranking, critics expressed nothing but accolades—praising the quality and sublime humor of the script, and the commendable performance of the cast. These strengths proved to be the foundation for the show's longevity, but "Cheers" owes its early success to the subsequent influx of other quality programs on Thursday night. Thereafter, "Cheers" began a slow but steady ascent toward the top of the Nielsen ratings, and by the fourth year it was an anchor of Thursday night prime-time programming and well on its way to years of unbridled prosperity.

The unremitting success and popular appeal of "Cheers" had many facets. First, the script quality was unsurpassed. The scripts were perfectly suited for each character's persona; this fused the cast into a cohesive, almost family-like unit. It also appealed to a diversified viewing audience—the physical appeal, sexual innuendoes and double entendres coalesced with humorous badinage, character comedy and candid malevolence. In addition, the script was further strengthened by the writers' boldness in successfully tackling controversial issues such as alcoholism, homosexuality, and adultery.

Second, the cast was impeccable. Ted Danson (Sam Malone), Shelley Long (Diane Chambers), Rhea Perlman (Carla Tortelli), Nicholas Colasanto (Coach), and the supporting cast of George Wendt (Norm Peterson) and John Ratzenberger (Cliff Clavin) provided a well-balanced and diversified ensemble. As the show evolved, the addition of lead actress Kirstie Alley (Rebecca Howe) and supporting actor Woody Harrelson (Woody Boyd) presented an effective transition with comparable synchronicity. The other successful additions included the intellectual duo of Kelsey Grammer (Frasier Crane) and Bebe Neuwirth (Lilith Sternin). Thus, credit must be given to the creators for effectively exploiting the comedic niche within each character.

Third, the combination of the script and cast made the characters authentic and credible, and thereby accessible to the viewing audience. The owner of the bar, Sam Malone, was an attractive, macho ex-athlete and male-chauvinist philanderer. Rebecca Howe, later added as the bar's manager, was the success-minded, power-driven corporate guru hindered by insecurities and neurotic tendencies.

The bartender, Ernie "Coach" Pantusso, represented the befuddled employee who was so convincing and adorable that you could not help but love him. When Coach passed away, he was capably replaced by Woody Boyd—a young, naive hick from Indiana with a childlike innocence.

Cheers had two waitresses, Diane Chambers and Carla Tortelli. Diane was an attractive barroom misfit who prided herself in intellectual enlightenment but often succumbed to her hedonistic desires. Carla, on the other hand, served more insults than drinks, represented the bar's uncensored dose of reality, and used her scorned-woman demeanor to vent sardonic wit (and through each sadistic and odious comment often revealed the unspoken truth).

The supporting cast of bar regulars (more like bar fixtures) cannot be forgotten. Norm Peterson and Cliff Clavin provided their own brand of raillery and unique idiosyncrasies. Norm was a beer-guzzling patron who made Cheers his home, whereas Cliff represented an oddball postal worker with numerous psychological problems (like an Oedipus complex) and was a self-proclaimed know-it-all and trivia expert. The appearance of Frasier Crane and Lilith Sternin brought a new type of drollery to the show enabling the writers to prey upon their yuppie mentality and the psychiatric profession.

The characters all possessed their own personality and individuality, and each actor worked with true professionalism and realism. Which leads to the final reason "Cheers" was so successful: the comedy was frequently based on character persona and actor delivery, rather than one-liners. The actors used their talents to mold the script to fit their characters' personas. The net result was continuous humor based upon the viewer's perception of the characters' personality traits, and not solely upon the script. This created a broader forum of comedy for the writer and the viewer, and was a significant factor in the program's longevity (11 years) and achievement.

As a reference source, this book is a monument to one of television's most successful programs—one that is sure to withstand the test of time (watch for it on Nickelodeon in the year 2014). The show garnered an unprecedented 118 Emmy nominations (winning 28 Emmy awards), and maintains a consistently large viewing audience through syndication, which further evinces its timelessness.

The book commences with a detailed reflection on the history of "Cheers" ranging from biographies of the creators, to show concept and evolution, to major cast changes, and then to the reasons for its vast success. In addition, this foundational section delves into ratings, awards, advertising, and syndication.

The following section contains detailed biographies of pertinent cast members and provides an in-depth examination of all aspects of their personas.

Following a smaller section on the Cheers bar itself, a large portion of the book is then devoted to narratives of each character (as if they were real people), analyzing their personas.

Well over a third of the book is then devoted to a recapitulation with detailed summaries of all 275 episodes in chronological sequence based upon air dates, from 1982 to 1993, providing technical credits, writers, directors, guest actors (with their noteworthy accomplishments), and the most humorous episodic quotes (ranging from Norm's famous one-liners to Cliff's most insightful dialogues).

The concluding section lists all Emmy nominations and awards bestowed upon the television series during its 11 years of prime-time television programming.

An exhaustive index to persons (real and fictional), places, things, and themes or topics completes the book. I am especially interested in the reader's reactions to this book. Please direct your correspondence in care of the publisher.

I. "Cheers": A Historical Overview

Background—Creators

James Burrows (b. 1941), son of Abe Burrows (Pulitzer Prize–winning writer, librettist, and legendary Broadway writer and director), learned from his masterful father, which became the foundation to a prolific directorial career. Raised in the then-unfashionable Upper West Side of Manhattan, James was a shy, introverted boy who rarely spoke but enjoyed singing, especially for the Metropolitan Opera Children's Chorus and downtown in *Carmen* and *Boris Godunov* for $3 a show.

Although college did not pique any interest, James attended the Yale School of Drama to avoid the draft. After taking an inspirational directing class, and utilizing this knowledge in the summer musical theater and off-Broadway, James was hired as a stage manager for *Holly Golightly* (an adaptation of *Breakfast at Tiffany's*) which was directed by his father and starred Mary Tyler Moore. The show bombed, but James impressed the star and her then-husband Grant Tinker, who subsequently recruited the younger Burrows to apprentice at their production company, MTM Enterprises, Inc. Despite lacking knowledge about television directing, James was hired for his skill at relating to and motivating actors. (MTM became a comedy factory for writers in the 1970s and 1980s, and spawned such television successes as "The Mary Tyler Moore Show," "Rhoda," "Lou Grant," and "The Bob Newhart Show.")

While working for "The Mary Tyler Moore Show," James learned from experienced director Jay Sandrich, and together they captured most of the directorial awards in the 1970s. In 1978, four MTM veterans left to create their own television show, "Taxi," and recruited Burrows as their director. After four years, two of the "Taxi" creators (Glen and Les Charles) teamed up with Burrows to create a new comedy show, "Cheers." James' success and experience has made him a prime candidate to direct a multitude of television pilots with the expectation that his talents and skills will elevate each show to unprecedented

1

success. He has launched many successful series, such as "Dear John," "Night Court," "Wings," "Frasier," and "Friends."

The Charles brothers, Glen (b. 1943) and Les (b. 1948), were raised in Las Vegas and spent a considerable amount of time sneaking into comedy lounge acts. Glen was an advertising copywriter and Les a substitute teacher in Pomona, California, but their occupations changed when a script they wrote for "M*A*S*H" opened new avenues for them in television. In 1975, the pair began their television careers at MTM Enterprises, Inc., writing for "Phyllis" and then "The Mary Tyler Moore Show." They subsequently wrote for "The Bob Newhart Show" and then "Taxi."

The Charles brothers achieved notoriety as comedy writers while penning scripts for "Taxi." Together with their most frequent director, James Burrows, "Taxi" became a highly successful and critically acclaimed show on ABC. After three years the trio abandoned "Taxi" before ABC axed the show (and NBC picked it up). In 1981 the triumvirate discussed another workplace comedy with a more appetizing environment, and a year later "Cheers" debuted. (Despite the success of "Cheers," the trio created other television comedies that were not nearly as prosperous, such as "The Tortellis," "All Is Forgiven," "Flesh 'n' Blood" and "Buck and Barry.")

Throughout the duration of "Cheers," the Charles brothers maintained offices on the Paramount lot across from the set. However, in 1990 they distanced themselves from the daily grind of producing the show and confidently passed the reins to director James Burrows, who handled the bulk of the production during the final years. Burrows has been credited for being the most indispensable person (on and off the set) and personally responsible for the show's success and longevity. He not only directed most of the episodes, but also supervised the overall production. Despite numerous movie offers, Burrows remained with "Cheers" because he loved the show.

The Model Tavern

The "Cheers" set was a replica of Boston's real-life Bull & Finch Pub right off the Commons on 112½ Beacon Street. The pub occupies the basement of the red brick and granite Hampshire House, and was named after architect Charles Bulfinch, who designed the nearby Statehouse and a considerable amount of the local architecture. The "Cheers" replica included 28 red vinyl barstools, a wooden bar with brass rails, an old Wirlitzer jukebox, a wooden Indian (Geronimo, owned by Nicholas Colasanto) by the front door, a photograph of Red Sox pitcher Jim Lonborg (chosen to represent Sam Malone because of his lantern jaw) and, in the sports bar tradition, posters of Babe Ruth, Ty Cobb, and a dog-eared picture of ex–Red Sox shortstop Rick Burleson. The creators also added personal mementos, such as a picture of the

Charles brothers which hung above the jukebox, an award from the Harvard Alcohol Project for scripts cautioning against drinking and driving, and a Boston Bruins hockey stick presented to Rhea Perlman.

The Bull & Finch, capacity 130, opened in 1969 under the ownership of Tom Kershaw, and earns $7 million annually (half from the gallery upstairs selling "Cheers" memorabilia—caps, T-shirts, sweatshirts, beer mugs, shot glasses, coffee mugs, ashtrays, Bloody Mary Mix). The pub is currently Boston's third most popular tourist attraction (behind Faneuil Hall and Freedom Trail) pulling in an estimated one million visitors annually (the peak is 16,000 per week) with an estimated economic impact on Boston of $125 million.

The primary disappointment of visitors to the Bull & Finch is its size. The actual pub is considerably smaller and less spacious than the Cheers replica, is overcrowded with tables, and the bar is set against the back wall. As for parking, a locals-only rule forbids non-locals from parking after 6 p.m., but they are allowed to plug the meter during the day.

When Glen Charles originally set foot in the Bull & Finch and asked the owner (Kershaw) for permission to shoot exterior and interior photographs of the pub, Kershaw agreed, charging $1. Since then he has made millions. Under a licensing agreement with Paramount, he made a fortune and owns two companies, one of which merchandises "Cheers" souvenirs and made *Inc.* magazine's list of the 500 fastest-growing firms in 1990. It all began by selling a handful of shirts from behind the bar, but now Kershaw owns and operates four satellite shops around Boston. He has more than 100 employees, and has the 42nd busiest outlet in the United States food and beverage industry.

Show Concept

Conceptually, the creators wanted a working environment that functioned as a family unit. This is certainly not a novel concept, but an effective one. "The Mary Tyler Moore Show" is probably the closest cousin to "Cheers" in envisioning a familial working environment. Despite personal insults amongst the characters (though more acrimonious on "Cheers"), they always appeared more happy at work than at home, and closer to coworkers than to family.

The creators also wanted an Americanized version of John Cleese's British series "Fawlty Towers" which is set in a country inn. Original ideas included Cheers being a hotel, a California country club, or an inn near Las Vegas. As the concept evolved, they settled on a saloon, which began to resemble an old radio drama called "Duffy's Tavern," written by Abe Burrows. A tavern setting had appeal because it opened the door to a never-ending supply of persons who could randomly wander into the bar, and was an ideal means of introducing new characters. Furthermore, it represented a place where people frequently go during important or problematic times of their lives, thus creating built-in drama and stories.

The tavern location became the next topic of debate. At first it was Barstow, California, but then the East Coast became the primary target. Boston was chosen partially because only five short-lived television shows claimed the city ("Banazak," "Beacon Hill," "James at 15," "Paul Sand in Friends and Lovers" and "The Young Lawyers"), and the East Coast pubs were real neighborhood hangouts. To ensure authenticity, the Charles brothers traveled to Boston searching for the right tavern. They settled on the Bull & Finch Pub after Glen Charles' wife came across the bar while thumbing through the Yellow Pages. The creators subsequently sent their set designer to take pictures.

Thus evolved the concept of a neighborhood bar. Judy Hart Angelo and Gary Portnoy then joined forces to create the music and lyrics for the pithy theme song, "Where Everybody Knows Your Name" (sung by Gary Portnoy), to capture the essence of the East Coast pub scene. However, the lyrics were not original, but from the Broadway musical *Carnival* (1961). In the production, the heroine Anna Maria Alberghetti sang about her hometown, Mira. The song "Mira" was subsequently released as a single and peaked at No. 83 on the Billboard charts.

The show concept also strived for a Spencer Tracy–Katharine Hepburn relationship, mixing antagonism and romance between two highly competitive people. "Cheers" became the first sitcom to stage sexual tension as its central premise, and in the first year thrived on it. Furthermore, the show concept created desirable character personas that would not be intellectually elevated above the average American, and ones who had their own idiosyncratic flaws.

Sam was the aging lothario representing the typical macho demeanor; Diane was the pretentious waitress with suppressed sexual impulses; Rebecca was the neurotic corporate executive and resident gold digger; Carla was the caustic, abusive, say-anything waitress; Woody was the ingenuous, addlepated farm boy; Norm was the affable, chronically unemployed beer guzzler with a life nobody envied; Cliff was the blowhard mailman and chronic loser with women; Frasier was the socially misfit psychiatrist; Lilith was his robotic, overbearing psychiatric wife; and Coach was the pleasantly absentminded bartender.

Despite all the conceptual refinements, timing remained a central issue. The creators used an old-fashioned bar setting at a time when this remnant of Americana was on the decline; they flaunted sexual promiscuity when AIDS was becoming an epidemic; and emphasized a male chauvinistic sex-addict when feminists were beckoning for equality. The primary question of timing involved a setting that encouraged alcohol consumption when the national consciousness was moving toward abstinence. To combat this concern, the creators assured an anti-alcoholism message on a regular basis, i.e., no

The "Cheers" cast in the early years. Standing (from left): John Ratzenberger, Nicholas Colasanto, Rhea Perlman, George Wendt; seated: Ted Danson, Shelley Long.

intoxicated patrons being allowed to drive home, stressing the negative effects of alcohol as a means of escaping problems, and eliminating humor that lauded intoxication, such as slurred speech or falling down. Toward that end, rarely did the patrons (except Norm) do anything but sip their drinks, and even less frequently was anyone intoxicated.

One final concern of NBC executives was the willingness of the creators to ensure authenticity on the set by stocking the bar with brand name alcohol and having the taps pour near-beer into salt-laced mugs to augment beer foam. Additional complications arose when the show began prominently displaying alcohol brand names. NBC became concerned about only promoting certain products, so the "Cheers" creators appeased everyone by agreeing to serve a different brand to each customer.

The one conceptual difference from the rest of the television programs was that "Cheers" never forced societal causes upon its viewers. Most successful programming since the late 1960s, beginning with "All in the Family," advanced some social cause. "All in the Family" and "M*A*S*H" advocated anti-war campaigns; "Family Ties" focused on the abomination of Reaganomics and the "Me Generation" of the 1980s; "The Cosby Show" always had a moral; and "Roseanne" stressed class divisions. Then each show would air the obligatory social campaign against drug abuse, illiteracy, or teenage pregnancy to raise societal consciousness or to teach viewers a lesson about life.

In contrast, "Cheers" had no social causes, no lessons to be learned, no role models; it was pure, unadulterated comedy that was sophisticated and intelligent, not pretentious. The characters never groveled for viewer affection nor overemphasized cuteness, because the creators insisted on maintaining the same level of comedic genius. It was a show that did more than entertain, it extended the viewers' circle of friends without forcing a viewpoint upon the audience.

Casting

In an uncommon maneuver, the creators chose a cast of relatively unknown actors, rather than having one premier draw to attract an audience. After auditioning over 300 actors, the male and female lead roles were narrowed to three actors for each. The male lead possibilities were Ted Danson, ex–football star Fred Dryer ("Hunter"), and William Devane ("Knots Landing"). The female lead was narrowed to Shelley Long, Julia Duffy ("Newhart"), and Lisa Eichhorn (*Yanks*).

The show's concept was sold to NBC executives as a 22-minute Miller Lite beer commercial, which was immensely successful at the time. The Sam Malone character was based upon a real-life bartender whom Glen Charles knew in Los Angeles. To mimic a Miller Lite beer commercial, the creators were being pressured into hiring a retired professional athlete for the part of Sam Malone (ergo, Dryer became their immediate preference), but they wanted someone who could act, not just a known personality. Thus, Sam Malone was originally inked as an ex–football player, but when lanky Ted Danson received the part, they transformed him into an ex–baseball player.

The female lead was originally envisioned as a business executive, but as the concept evolved she became a pretentious college student. The producers wanted Long for the lead, but she was hesitant; it took several meetings just to persuade her to read for the part. Coincidentally, after reading the script, Long told the producers it reminded her of a bar she knew in Boston Commons. (In 1980, she was in Boston filming *A Small Circle of Friends* and happened upon the Bull & Finch Pub.) In a wake of deafening silence, the creators paused with dumbfounded expressions on their faces because Long had envisioned the exact bar as replicated for the "Cheers" set.

Each of the six finalists were paired to audition for NBC executives. They were all funny, and even though Fred Dryer was the ideal Sam Malone and Julia Duffy had a phenomenal audition, the Danson-Long chemistry was instantaneous and undeniable. After signing the lead roles, the creators still had to cast the supporting actors.

The role of Norm (who at that point was named George) was an acting battle between George Wendt and John Ratzenberger. Although Ratzenberger did not earn the role, he suggested the producers include a bar know-it-all. They agreed to an audition where Ratzenberger was given a chance to resurrect a stage character he had played years earlier. He earned a guest spot for seven episodes, but became such a delightful and amusing character that it evolved into a regular role.

The part of Coach was originally given to Robert Prosky ("Hill Street Blues"), but when he backed out at the last minute, they followed a suggestion to give Nicholas Colasanto an audition. Colasanto immediately projected the ideal image of who Coach should be, and was signed as a regular cast member.

Weekly Filming

Nearly 100 crew members partook in the Tuesday night filming before a live studio audience on Paramount's Stage 25. However, the actors and the rest of the ensemble began preparing for their performance a week earlier. New scripts were issued on Wednesday with a no visitors allowed read through. The following day the director blocked shots using extras wearing cardboard placards of characters' names. Friday was a rehearsal, and a final script was issued on Monday. Each afternoon the executive producers-creators, staff writers and story editors listened to their material, and after the cast departed, they spent the evening rewriting the script.

Tuesday afternoons were run-throughs, and at 7:45 p.m. the cast was introduced. When the actors' names were announced, James Burrows hugged each cast member before they descended the steps and went through the front door for the obligatory applause. The cast then huddled for a group handshake and a united cheer before proceeding to their acting positions.

When filming ended, the actors took their bows and the audience was removed. Then began hours of pick-ups where the cast would re-shoot scenes needing work or requiring a different angle from the four huge cameras wheeling about the set. Pick-ups were physically exhausting and emotionally draining because each actor was required to bolster the same emotions repeatedly, on cue, out of context, and without externalizing the tedium on camera.

The predominate "Cheers" director, James Burrows, is one of the few directors who insists upon using film rather than tape. He believes that film fully affects the ambiance and gives everything a warmer appeal. One other trademark of Burrows' directorial techniques is his attempt to interject movement into the show; the cast and extras were constantly moving, never staid or static.

Early Years—The Struggle to Survive

The first episode craftily introduced the characters by stating their names within seconds of their appearance on the set. As with nearly every sitcom, the first episode had a heartwarming finish that drew the two principal characters together. In essence, "Cheers" parallels the first episode of "The Two of Us" (canceled by CBS), where the perceived lout offered a supercilious woman a job, and their repulsion changed to instant liking.

The critics lauded "Cheers" as the most substantial comedy series since "Taxi" with the potential of becoming an all-time classic. The scripts were sharp and lively, the direction comedically timed to perfection, and the cast contained a first-rate repertoire. However, few people were aware of this because "Cheers" was the least watched television program of the week and spent most of the entire season in the ratings basement. Despite remaining a critical success and having a faithful, albeit small audience, there were times when the creators did not expect the series to survive (but they knew it still would look good on their resumés).

With such a dismal ranking at the end of the first season, the future of the show seemed questionable. Nevertheless, NBC was compelled to renew the series for a second season for several reasons: it was desperate for quality programming, "Cheers" earned 13 Emmy nominations (winning five) in its freshman outing, it was one of the few NBC programs receiving praiseworthy press coverage, and the NBC executive in charge of entertainment (Brandon Tartikoff) was a fan of the show. Having written many of his own one-liners and considering himself a comedic writer (but not in the same league as the writers for "Cheers"), Tartikoff appreciated the comedic genius and insisted the show remain on the air.

To bolster ratings, the "Cheers" cast made an across the country talk show tour to promote the series. When NBC discovered "Family Ties" and then

"The Cosby Show" and placed both shows on Thursday nights, a huge influx of viewers tuned in and the residual audience quickly discovered and loved "Cheers." Thursday night soon became the powerhouse night of prime-time television comparable to the awesome 1973 CBS Saturday night lineup of "All in the Family," "M*A*S*H," "The Mary Tyler Moore Show," "The Bob Newhart Show" and "The Carol Burnett Show."

Cast Changes

The first cast change was in 1984 with the introduction of Kelsey Grammer as psychiatrist Dr. Frasier Crane, who was intended as a temporary ploy to reintroduce Diane Chambers to the bar. The creators soon realized the talent of Grammer, and enjoyed writing for his character, so they retained him as a regular. Frasier received the pretentious intellectual discourse previously confined to Diane. Similarly, the introduction of Bebe Neuwirth was intended to be a one time only role as Dr. Lilith Sternin. However, the episode was so hilarious the writers kept bringing Lilith back to lock intellectual horns with Frasier, and eventually Neuwirth became a cast regular.

The saddest cast change occurred when Nicholas Colasanto died in 1985. Late in 1984 the cast learned he had an incurable heart disease, and the doctors advised he had anywhere from five weeks to five years to live (it turned out to be the former). Despite his illness, the producers labored to accommodate Colasanto's health in the scripts, but he was visibly ill and often in the hospital. Moreover, it became increasingly difficult because Colasanto frequently forgot his lines, so he wrote them down on napkins, the wall or his hand. For weeks after his death, the crew found his lines scribbled everywhere and disseminated throughout the bar.

The most significant cast change was in 1987 when Shelley Long notified the producers of her intent to leave the show. Despite claiming new career opportunities as the reason for leaving, she was a source of constant friction with the cast and crew. Long's departure created a panic on the set out of concern the series would fail without her. Those fears were quickly allayed with the introduction of Kirstie Alley, who gave the other characters an opportunity to expand their roles, thereby re-energizing the show with new actors and a new story line.

Show Evolution

The original concept of "Cheers" was based upon the Tracy-Hepburn sexual tension, which actually existed in the series' nascence. Unfortunately, when Sam and Diane began dating in the second season the series lost that tension; the show changed from the "will they, won't they" sexual tension to simply endless bickering. Originally there was an equal emphasis on the character roles of a womanizing bartender and a pretentious barmaid; however, the on-screen chemistry of Danson and Long irreparably transfigured the direction of the show to highlight the *nexus* between them. For the next three seasons, Sam and Diane fluctuated in this cycle of sexual tension, which ended when Long exited the show after its fifth season.

When Kirstie Alley arrived, the show recaptured the essence of its original concept by creating a business-minded executive. However, her character also underwent a metamorphosis from a no-nonsense martinet to a neurotic, mediocre corporate manager. The show's emphasis returned to a 50-50 (half bar/half relationship) split, thereby allowing the producers to rejuvenate the sexual tension of whether Sam and Rebecca would ever begin a relationship. Nevertheless, the chemistry between Danson and Alley was not equal to the sexual tension that existed between Danson and Long. Thus, the producers chose to emphasize Rebecca's vulnerability and neurotic tendencies, and even though she and Sam delved into a sexual relationship, it was never serious and did not evolve beyond friendship. This opened the door for each of them to become involved in different romantic relationships and expand the scope of the show.

Essentially "Cheers" can be divided into three distinguishable parts. First, the Shelley Long era, which concentrated on the sexual tension between Sam and Diane during their intermittent dating relationship. The crafty writing for this tandem molded them into one of the hottest and funniest sexual couples on television. The second, the Kirstie Alley era, redefined the sexual tension in a different context. Sam never was seriously in love with Rebecca, rather their relationship evolved into friendship. Similar to the first era, the emphasis was on character comedy. The last era, the final three seasons, was an emphasis on physical comedy rather than character comedy. A classic example is Woody and Kelly's farcical wedding. Although character comedy was not entirely abandoned, an increasing number of episodes emphasized physical comedy which had not been present in the preceding eight seasons.

One interesting aspect of "Cheers" is that the creators always strove for a season-ending cliffhanger. This was quite uncommon at the time, and "Cheers" became the first non-serial show to introduce such a method. The only exception was at the end of the seventh season (1988–89). The creators developed an entire profile for the following season which revolved around Sam marrying a woman he met on the spur of the moment. However, the first show was a disaster and never aired, so the entire idea was abandoned. The producers then scrambled to assemble an episode in a few days to air in its place, and that makeshift episode received an Emmy nomination. Since the producers were undecided which direction Sam's life would take after that one disastrous episode, the season ended without a cliffhanger.

The cast in the later years. Standing (from left): Kirstie Alley, Rhea Perlman, Woody Harrelson, John Ratzenberger, George Wendt; seated: Ted Danson, Kelsey Grammer.

The most interesting occurrences that affected the direction of the show and required smooth script maneuvering were the concurrent pregnancies of Shelley Long and Rhea Perlman. Both divulged their impending motherhood to the producers within days of each other, with a due date of April 1, 1985. Rather than depicting two pregnancies out of wedlock, the creators wrote Perlman's pregnancy into the script (which they did for three of her actual pregnancies) and hid Long's pregnancy with camera and wardrobe tricks (using trays, towels, aprons, flat shoes, sinking floorboards, and putting her behind the bar whenever possible).

"Cheers"—The Final Episode

The series finale was promoted as "the television event of a lifetime" and "the greatest night of television." On May 20, 1993, NBC devoted most of their Thursday night programming to "Cheers." Following the hour-long season finale of "Seinfeld," there was a 22-minute "Cheers" retrospective, "Last Call! A 'Cheers' Celebration," hosted by Bob Costas; a 98-minute series finale; and a live television broadcast from the Bull & Finch Pub starring the "Cheers" cast on "The Tonight Show with Jay Leno."

The final episode was further hyped when Shelley Long was invited for a special guest appearance, as well as President Clinton (though scheduling difficulties made it impossible for him to appear). Additional intrigue came from the secrecy of taping the final seven minutes of the episode with only the cast and crew present. Similar to when Long left the series in 1987, the creators taped three different endings to ensure nobody could predict which version would air.

As part of the hoopla, NBC executives parked themselves on barstools as set extras. The stiff-suited extras included Grant Tinker, former NBC chairman; John Pike, Paramount Network Television president; Warren Littlefield, current NBC Entertainment president; Kerry McCluggage, Paramount Television group chairman; and Lilly Tartikoff, wife of former NBC executive in charge of entertainment, Brandon Tartikoff.

Other television stations joined the "Cheers" bandwagon of media sensationalism by offering programs to cater to the viewing public. The cable station Comedy Central, still in its teething years, offered a "Cheers" salute between the series finale and "The Tonight Show."

The creators—infallible James Burrows as director and the Charles brothers as writers (even though they had not written a "Cheers" episode since 1987)—masterminded the final episode. The finale became the first live sitcom to film an entire 90-minute episode in one night, on Wednesday, March 31, 1993. The cast rehearsed in the afternoon, and filming began at 7:20 p.m. and did not finish until 2:15 a.m., making it extremely difficult to have the specially selected audience remain seated. When the audience was absent, the final seven minutes for each of the three different closures were taped, and a wrap party was held April 8, 1993, at Santa Monica's Museum of Flying with 825 guests dancing to the music of Los Lobos.

As for the cast's most memorable "Cheers" episodes, George Wendt loved the Thanksgiving food fight at Carla's house (episode 104); and Ted Danson had two favorites, one when Rebecca had sexual dreams about Sam (episode 169) and another when the gang took Diane to the opera (episode 91).

"Cheers"—Relationships

The on-air camaraderie paralleled the backstage harmony. Everyone was well-liked (except Shelley Long) and quite rambunctious on and off-screen. For example, in Carla's Thanksgiving dinner episode, the cast engaged in a food fight lasting one-half hour after filming stopped. In the Gary is dead episode, the actors hid a naked actress in the casket to surprise Ted Danson in front of the camera and live audience.

Rehearsals were equally raucous. The cast attacked one another with spitballs and water pistols, dumped buckets of water on one another, and raced around the bar on the barstools. The most memorable ribaldry was between

Danson and Harrelson. Knowing Harrelson's propensity of not wearing underwear beneath his clothing, Danson pulled down Harrelson's pants in front of 100 extras. In retaliation, Harrelson took a polaroid of Danson in the shower and inserted it on the yearly gag reel so 250 people could see it.

The only exception to the unity was Long. Although she asserted several legitimate reasons for her departure, it was undeniable that her acting style was problematic to cast and staff, and her temperament was intolerable to nearly everyone associated with the show. Reports cited backstage fits, fights, and clashing egos as the reason for Long's departure. (The endless bickering on the "Cheers" set reportedly paralleled that on "Moonlighting," with Bruce Willis and Cybill Shepherd, and "Remington Steele," with Pierce Brosnan and Stephanie Zimbalist.)

Ending the Series

It is quite unusual for a production company to cancel its own highly successful show, but that is exactly what happened with "Cheers." The only other television hits to do the same in recent history have been "The Cosby Show" (though it was on a slow decline at its expiration), "M*A*S*H" (though the story line was degenerating) and "The Mary Tyler Moore Show."

When Ted Danson decided not to return for another season, the production team immediately discussed their various options: ending the series, continuing without a leading man, finding a new leading man, or emphasizing one of the other current "Cheers" characters. The discussion was short-lived since Danson was the center of the show; without him there could be no series.

Another compelling reason for canceling "Cheers" after Danson's departure was a unique clause in the syndication contract that committed television stations to purchase all new episodes, but only if Danson was the star. Gauging the precariousness of success without Danson and the financial instability of having no guaranteed syndication revenue, the producers chose to forego another season.

Success—The Reasons Why

Since its debut in 1982, "Cheers" immediately impressed the critics with its quality writing and talented cast. However, the foundation of success began when the creators followed their training and established track record of success by tailoring "Cheers" to the long-standing tradition of ensemble character comedies perfected by MTM Enterprises, Inc. The first ingredient was good, solid comedy writing, and then relying upon strong performances by a cast who could vividly portray the characters in a realistic manner.

Over the years "Cheers" amassed a stable of more than 50 writers, many of whom came from a literary background with fresh ideas (so the show would not belabor or rehash old television plot lines). Moreover, they were well-recognized and successful in the industry, with established writing credentials on other hit television sitcoms. For instance, a sampling of their extensive resumés include: "M*A*S*H" (Glen and Les Charles, Tom Reeder, Ken Levine, David Isaacs); "The Mary Tyler Moore Show" (Charles brothers, David Lloyd, Earl Pomerantz); "The Bob Newhart Show" (Charles brothers); "Taxi" (Charles brothers, Lloyd, Pomerantz, Sam Simon, Ken Estin); "Rhoda" (Pomerantz, Lloyd); "Barney Miller" (Reeder); "Newhart" (Pomerantz, Dan O'Shannon, Tom Anderson); "The Jeffersons" (Peter Casey); "The Golden Girls" (Jeff Abugov); "Roseanne" (Abugov); "The Cosby Show" (Pomerantz); "Night Court" (Reeder); "Bob" (Phoef Sutton, Cheri Eichen, Bill Steinkellner); "The Simpsons" (Simon); "Wings" (Casey, David Angell); and "Phyllis" (Charles brothers).

The "Cheers" comedy writing machine is often but inaccurately compared to feature film comedy writers. "Cheers" unequivocally mass-produced more laughs in four 22-minute episodes than any two-hour film comedy. Moreover, movies take months to produce and studios pay $20-30 million per film, whereas each "Cheers" episode was produced weekly on a budget of less than $1 million. (However, by the tenth season the stars' inflated salaries pushed production expenses to unprecedented levels, requiring NBC to pay Paramount $2.8 million per episode.)

The "Cheers" writers crafted irrepressible humor. First, "Cheers" was unique because its fine-tuned comedy compounded multiple jokes (one upon the other). If they devised a quality joke, the writers would continue to add another line, another laugh. Second, the humor was often based on the lead up, a casual aside or the character's reaction, rather than the punch line itself. Third, much of the humor hinged on dialogue, actor delivery and viewer perception of the character, rather than slapstick comedy (as some of the latter episodes portrayed). Writing that would fail on other television shows thrived on "Cheers" because of a combination of the writers' tailor-made lines that meshed with the characters' personae, and then the corresponding quality of the actors' delivery, physical presence or expression. Finally, the writers did not condescend to the viewers, and allowed Diane to say "pomme de terre" rather than potato, and if the audience caught on, then fine. (This proved problematic for NBC because they were dumbfounded on how to promote a television show that made Schopenhauer jokes.)

The producers further bolstered the show's humor by creating considerable conflict among the many diversified characters and emphasizing different types of humor. Everything can be funny—stupid, weird, pompous, cruel—if the character is properly developed and the delivery is sound. The writers were fortunate to have a vast and talented group of regulars to portray broadly diversified characters and to create seemingly endless plot lines. The success of "Cheers" prompted at least nine former "Cheers" producers to participate in their own prime-time shows during the 1994-95 television season.

Part of the staying power of "Cheers" was the stability of its characters. Unlike many successful television shows, like "M*A*S*H," there were no abrupt evolutions in the characters' personae, and they never imposed their own personalities on the characters (nor did they create grandiose heroism). "Cheers" did not use sentiment or heartwarming sermons to court audiences, and relied upon writing, not the likability of the stars to propel the show to success.

There is no denying the success of "Cheers" was further enhanced by the sound leadership of James Burrows and the Charles brothers. First, Burrows personally directed 243 episodes and maintained a loose rehearsal with a watchful eye on quality. Second, Burrows and the Charles brothers must be commended for their superb effort in effectively replacing the departing actors and finding the perfect niche to exploit within the ensemble. Third, they were open to suggestions. The cast was frequently involved in the characters' development and freely shared their ideas with the director throughout rehearsals. Finally, and most importantly, the network maintained a distance. Although NBC executives frequently consulted with the "Cheers" producers to suggest new character and show ideas, NBC was quite obliging in not getting involved in the day-to-day production or the headaches associated with the show.

Ratings—Eleven Seasons

In 1982, heralded as what could be the best night of television since CBS' Saturday night in 1973, NBC Thursday had "Fame," "Cheers," "Taxi" and "Hill Street Blues." However, the first episode of "Cheers" was ranked 77th among 77 shows—dead last. It continued to flounder in the Nielsen ratings and remained in the cellar by season's end with a rating of 71st. In fact, all the shows on NBC Thursday in 1982 were at the bottom of the ratings.

The following year, the demise of "Cheers" was thwarted when NBC signed "Family Ties" which boosted "Cheers" to the mid–20s in the ratings. The greatest hoist came the following year (1984-85), with the signing of the instantaneously successful family program, "The Cosby Show." With the addition of both flourishing sitcoms to Thursday night and positioned in the time slots preceding "Cheers," there was an inevitable residual effect of viewers staying tuned to "Cheers," and consequently its ratings immediately spiraled upward, ending the third season (1984-85) ranked 13th.

The following season, "Cheers" became a top-five show partially due to the addition of Woody Harrelson (replacing Nicholas Colasanto after his death). Since "Cheers" followed "Family Ties" (starring Michael J. Fox), the younger viewing audience was better able to relate to Woody Boyd, and consequently the "Cheers" demographic ratings soared in this category. "Cheers" finished the 1985-86 season ranked fifth, and remained a top-five show for the next seven seasons. In 1987, "Cheers" had its greatest ratings success to date by ending the year ranked third in the Nielsen ratings (behind "The Cosby Show" and "Family Ties," respectively).

The next three seasons, "Cheers" was ranked third, fourth and third, respectively, behind "The Cosby Show," "A Different World," and "Roseanne" in various years. During the latter of these three seasons (1989-90), "Cheers" commanded unprecedented success by capturing the No. 1 position in the Nielsen ratings for seven weeks. In the previous seven seasons, "Cheers" had never occupied the No. 1 position more than once per season. Remarkably, in the history of television, "Cheers" and "Lou Grant" are the only two series to have finished both first and last in the weekly ratings.

According to the Nielsen ratings for the 1990-91 season, "Cheers" was the highest-rated program in television. In another rating system, the Q-ratings, which measures viewer preference based on familiarity and popularity, "Cheers" ranked 10th behind many shows receiving mediocre Nielsen ratings. The import of both surveys solidified "Cheers" as a crossover success with advertisers and viewers. "Cheers" was not only watched frequently, it was well-liked by the public.

During the 10th season (1991-92), by being ranked fourth (behind "60 Minutes," "Roseanne" and "Murphy Brown," respectively), "Cheers" tied a television record for being a top-five show after a decade of airing. This astonishing ratings feat has only been matched by "Bonanza" (which was also ranked fourth in its 10th season). In the final season, "Cheers" slipped to eighth place. However, by placing in the top 10, "Cheers" made a string of eight consecutive seasons in single-digit ratings, and is often compared to "M*A*S*H" because of its longevity and late-blooming success. With an 11-year reign, "Cheers" became the longest running comedy in NBC history.

Ratings—The Final Episode

The final episode was so hyped commercially that it failed to attain the inflated expectations of being the most-watched program in television history. However, it was the most-watched program for the 1992-93 season; the second highest-rated episodic program; and the 11th highest-rated entertainment show in television history. "Cheers" had 93.1 million viewers, 64 percent of the viewing audience, and 40 percent of the entire nation watching the epic finale. (In contrast, the highest-rated episode of all time, the "M*A*S*H" series finale on February 28, 1983, had 121.6 million viewers and 77 percent of the viewing audience.) Experts agree it will be nearly impossible for any episode to overcome the ratings success of "M*A*S*H" because of the prolific increase in television options and cable competition that was practically nonexistent in 1983.

"Last Call! A 'Cheers' Celebration" was rated second with nearly 70 million viewers, and even the live broadcast of "The Tonight Show" from the Bull & Finch Pub tripled its viewing audience, despite critics berating Jay Leno for a dull monologue that dampened the crowd's spirits and bored the "Cheers" cast (who resorted to blowing spit wads at one another). The encore presentation of the series finale which aired three days later was rated 42nd. Although "M*A*S*H" had the largest viewing audience, it was reported that the telecasts of the "Cheers" finale on Thursday and Sunday had a combined unduplicated audience that surpassed the final "M*A*S*H" episode.

Impact on Television

"Cheers" has been labeled by many critics as an all-time classic, and frequently referred to as the wittiest, most intelligent, most sophisticated television comedy of its time. Moreover, it changed the typical sitcom focus by combining a group of friends linked by locale, not family.

One television show labeled as the kissing cousin of "Cheers" is the sitcom "Wings" (NBC, 1990–present), which happens to have several commonalities in personnel—technical advisors, script writers, and creators (David Angell, Peter Casey and David Lee). The one slight difference is that "Cheers" premised a story on sexual tension and conflict between friends, whereas "Wings" is based on sexual history and a contrast of brotherly differences.

"Cheers" has had two television spin-offs, "The Tortellis" (NBC, 1987) and "Frasier" (NBC, 1993–present). "The Tortellis" was a short-lived series based on Carla's ex-husband Nick Tortelli's family—Loretta (wife), Anthony (son) and Annie (Anthony's wife). Although this series endured abysmal Nielsen ratings (ranked 50th) in its only season of airing and suffered a rapid demise, the spin-off "Frasier" achieved immense success. This series is based on the idiosyncratic psychiatrist (Dr. Frasier Crane) relocating to Seattle to become a radio talk show therapist. It remains a highly rated and critically acclaimed show. Interestingly enough, after "Cheers" wrapped up in 1993, NBC considered creating three spin-offs, with at least one costarring George Wendt and John Ratzenberger as bar buddies, but it never materialized.

Awards

From the day "Cheers" premiered on national television on September 30, 1982, it received critical acclaim, which culminated in 13 Emmy nominations during its first season—more nominations than any comedy series in the history of television. "Cheers" won five Emmys that year en route to becoming the most nominated show in television history with 118 Emmy nominations. "Cheers" also amassed 28 total Emmy awards, second only to "The Mary Tyler Moore Show" which seized 29 awards. "Cheers" also received a Golden Globe award for Best Television Comedy Series in 1991.

Advertising

"Cheers" had overwhelming success, but part of the credit was its affluent viewing audience. The show appealed primarily to yuppies with disposable income, which was ideal for advertisers, as well as producers when setting advertising rates.

"Cheers" was one of the most expensive shows for advertisers, commanding $300,000 for a 30-second commercial. The season finale, marketed as "the television event of a lifetime," garnered an astonishing $650,000 for the same amount of airtime, a figure usually limited to the Super Bowl. But many claim that NBC undersold the time slot, which may explain the encore presentation on Sunday, May 23, 1995. The Sunday telecast remained exorbitantly priced, charging $175,000 per 30-second commercial (normal rates for Sunday night were $50,000-$80,000). NBC grossed $13 million on the season finale, $5 million on the half-hour retrospective, and $7 million on the encore telecast.

Syndication

The success of "Cheers" translated into a strong national syndication market. By the time the series concluded, it was syndicated in 38 countries with 179 U.S. television markets and 83 million viewers. Moreover, "Cheers" earned over half a billion dollars solely in syndication revenues. Part of its syndication success was due to the lack of quality television sitcoms and the shortage of reruns for a fast-growing independent television market. As networks wield the ratings numbers, fewer and fewer shows are renewed and many freshman shows are quickly canceled. For instance, during the 1995-96 television season, the networks introduced 34 new shows. A similar trend existed five years earlier and during the mid–1980s. Thus, to capitalize on the lack of quality programming available, the "Cheers" producers wisely ushered their show into syndication a year before any rerun episodes could air.

The other impetus was financial. Due to the lack of syndicated programs, "Cheers" was commanding lofty syndication prices comparable to the hour-long "Magnum, P.I." series which was the highest priced syndicated show (at the time), earning $115,000 per episode. Paramount wisely guaranteed the buyers of "Cheers" a minimum of 94 episodes and, if the show was canceled before its sixth season, Paramount, the "Cheers" creative team and the new station partners would immediately begin production of additional episodes.

When "Cheers" entered its 11th season, Paramount had grave reservations whether the show would continue to sell in syndication. The show already had a voluminous and exorbitantly priced library of episodes that stations were required to purchase. Moreover, the prospective 12th season had additional quandaries because the "Cheers" syndication contract only committed television stations to purchase new episodes if Danson was the lead. Syndication of "Cheers" without Danson would have been even more financially perilous in the absence of a guaranteed syndication revenue.

Post–"Cheers" Activities

The cast and crew went through numerous changes during the 11-year run of "Cheers." In this time frame, 10 members of the cast and crew died, and 50 children were born. For the cast, Ted Danson, Shelley Long, Kirstie Alley, Kelsey Grammer and Woody Harrelson had one child apiece; John Ratzenberger had two; and both Rhea Perlman and James Burrows had three.

"Cheers" also inspired Host International, a subsidiary of Marriott Corporation, to install 46 bars modeled after Cheers in their hotel and airport terminal lounges. Marriott's catering division signed a deal with Paramount Picture Television to open the first bar in the Minneapolis–St. Paul International Airport. By 1993, the hotel chain had seven Cheers replica bars from Anchorage to New Zealand.

The replicas are complete with Sam's Red Sox jersey framed and hanging on the wall, a wooden Indian, a jukebox, two robotic regulars (Bob and Hank) perched at the end of the bar, souvenirs for sale, and menu items named after the characters. In 1993, John Ratzenberger and George Wendt filed a lawsuit in federal court claiming the robots infringed upon their image, and requested Marriott to remove the mechanical barflies. Three years later the lawsuit was judicially dismissed as meritless.

II. The Cast

Kirstie Alley
(Rebecca Howe)

Childhood

Born January 12, 1955, in Wichita, Kansas, Kirstie was named after a film heroine nun portrayed by Loretta Young. Kirstie hated the name (a Scottish version of Christine or Christina) because it was frequently the object of childhood ridicule. She also loathed her appearance—a tall, lanky body and dark auburn hair. Kirstie describes her suburban family life as a relatively peaceful, serene and conventional middle-class environment (but she was forbidden to own pets because of her family's allergies).

The desire to be an actress was apparent when Kirstie was three years old and traipsed around the house with pictures of actress Linda Darnell. Kirstie loved to make people laugh, and not only had her first taste of acting at age six when she debuted as the sun in a school play, but also recalls watching Patty Duke in *The Miracle Worker* (1962) and thinking she could do better. Nevertheless, close friends contend the nearest Kirstie came to expressing an interest in acting was reading movie magazines.

Despite a serene childhood, Kirstie was an artsy, troubled, inquisitive, and obnoxious child who always worried the family. Although she was insecure and had difficulty competing with siblings for attention, most of the problems arose during high school. Unlike her siblings, Kirstie was rebellious. She was not predictable and was never satisfied with stability and simplicity.

Kirstie's rebelliousness inevitably created a disputatious relationship with her mother. They fought continuously. Kirstie's mother had little hope for her daughter and, in fact, was primarily concerned about Kirstie dying of a drug overdose or becoming a whore. Of course, Kirstie's behavior appeared worse when compared to a brother and sister who were model children.

21

As a child, Kirstie had an insatiable appetite to win, whether it was swim meets or arm wrestling with the boys. In high school, her brash personality alienated her from the popular crowd—the attractive, buxom, blonde-haired, blue-eyed cheerleaders—so Kirstie veered toward a more radical appearance and demeanor. She opted for the Bohemian beatnik image—smoking, drinking and swearing, using fake IDs to get into bars, breaking curfew, sporting provocative black outfits and outrageous microminis, and dating boys who owned fast cars and loud motorcycles.

Kirstie idolized James Dean and Kris Kristofferson, and admits having a long-standing weakness for football players and men of danger—bikers, truckers, cowboys—men to use for a 30-day affair and then move on down the road. She loved the excitement and danger in their lives. During adolescence Kirstie would sneak out of the house in geeky clothes and no makeup, and in the backseat of a car transform herself into a provocative creature who scoured the Dairy Queens searching for boys.

Kirstie also experienced the wild life of Wichita. She and her friends would sit around drinking sloe gin and using their tongues to tie cherry stems into knots. She was wild, but not promiscuous; the pranks were mild—often including toilet paper, eggs, and crepe paper dipped in water.

Family and Relatives

Kirstie was the middle child with two siblings, an older sister and younger brother. Her biology teacher sister (Colette) was the perfect child—a straight-A student who practiced sexual abstinence until marriage, and their brother (Craig) was similarly predictable as a youth, and works as a lumber company manager. Both siblings live in Wichita, and remain relatively close to Kirstie. Robert Alley, the family patriarch, owned a prosperous lumber company and is currently retired. His wife, Mickie, a German-Irish homemaker, had a wonderful sense of humor.

Tragically, in 1981 Kirstie's parents' car veered into a telephone pole after being hit by another car. Her mother was crushed to death, and her father suffered a collapsed lung and crushed chest, and was unconscious in the intensive care unit. Although she was saddened by her mother's death, the trauma helped draw Kirstie closer to her father.

Personal Characteristics

Kirstie is 5'8" and averages 120 pounds, though she battled a weight problem and soared to 151 pounds (contributing factors included a miscarriage and quitting a two pack a day smoking habit). Kirstie has opalescent emerald eyes, a luxuriously dusky auburn mane, and a husky, brassy alto voice. She is acrophobic and has an unusual diet of coffee, barbecue pork rinds, Big Macs, pasta pastries, and Bacardi cocktails.

Kirstie's charm is a mixture of tough-minded realism and self-deprecating humor; a blend of down-home, girl-next-door kindness and lowbrow, down-to-earth rebelliousness. At times she is stable and in control, and other times neurotic and out of control. Although Kirstie is perceived as a self-confident, down-to-business, hard-core woman, she readily admits that her insecurities and self-doubt occasionally get the best of her. Usually once or twice a year she stores her emotions for a tumultuous session of long, dramatic weeping.

Kirstie is a devout member of the Church of Scientology, a religious sect founded by L. Ron Hubbard. Other sect members include John Travolta, Kelly Preston, Tom Cruise, Nicole Kidman, Anne Archer, Karen Black, Priscilla Presley and Lisa Marie Presley; and former members include Jerry Seinfeld and Patrick Swayze. Kirstie is also a firm believer in reincarnation.

Education

Kirstie skipped the fifth grade, and graduated from Wichita High School Southeast in 1973. She continued her education by attending Kansas State University, majoring in art and English literature. During the second year she transferred to the University of Kansas, but attended only briefly before dropping out of college. She frankly admits attending college merely as an excuse to follow her boyfriend, and when the relationship ended, so did her formal education. At this period of her life Kirstie became riddled with self-doubt and self-pity, so she gravitated toward cocaine as an escape because it allayed insecurities and alleviated her fear of failure.

Employment and Career Opportunities

Kirstie's first serious career was working as an interior decorator in Kansas City. Inspired by Doris Day, who played a successful interior decorator in the movie *Pillow Talk* (1959), the inexperienced Alley applied for a position at a local design firm, and in 1977 was hired to cater to the city's most elite. A friend promptly introduced her to cocaine, and within two years she was addicted. What began as a weekend routine, Thursday night through Saturday, quickly consumed every day and at one point became a $400 per week addiction. Despite maintaining employment for another two years, she decided to abandon cocaine after an humiliating experience where her sister visited unexpectedly, and Kirstie was too stoned to play with her niece.

Kirstie Alley

Realizing that drugs were affecting her job and alienating her family, Kirstie made the decision to quit, and sent letters of apology penned with the utmost sincerity to her family and interior decorating clients. Kirstie found the strength to overcome her addiction through the teachings of Scientology as outlined in the book *Dianetics: The Modern Science of Mental Health* (1950) by L. Ron Hubbard. The Church of Scientology provided the strength Kirstie needed to overcome her overwhelming fear of failure and pursue her dream of becoming an actress. Accordingly, Kirstie quit her job, broke up with her boyfriend and, despite having only $2,000 and lacking both experience and training, drove to Los Angeles with her clothes and her dog to fulfill that dream. Of course it took 30 days to drive from Kansas to Los Angeles because she had to score drugs. After arriving at her destination, but before pursuing an acting career, Kirstie spent the first month in Narconon, the Church of Scientology's drug rehabilitation program.

As an aspiring actress in Los Angeles, Kirstie had no employment prospects, so she used her past experience and talents to survive. She worked as an interior decorator, cleaned houses, and won $6,000 on "The Match Game" and $1,000 on "Password" (with Lucille Ball giving the clues). Despite lacking formal dramatic training or experience, Kirstie continued hunting for acting parts and going to auditions, and eventually found an agent by using her game show appearances as a selling feature. She enrolled in acting classes but after three weeks abandoned formal training because she was beginning to receive acting roles.

Hollywood—Early Years

In late 1981, within one year of arriving in Los Angeles, Kirstie was on the brink of landing a significant role in a feature film—she was invited to read for the part of Lieutenant Saavik (Mr. Spock's sidekick) in *Star Trek II: The Wrath of Khan* (1982). Despite her jubilation, this was also a time of deep sorrow. During the fifth and final audition Kirstie learned her mother had died in an automobile accident and her father had suffered life-threatening injuries. Kirstie insisted on rescheduling the audition, and the day after the funeral she was given the part. Kirstie's deepest regret is that her mother never lived to see her succeed, as *The Wrath of Khan* became one of the most successful *Star Trek* movies. This role led to many movie offers as a space alien, but Kirstie rejected them (including a recurring part as Lieutenant Saavik in the third *Star Trek* movie) because she did not want to be typecast. Instead, she opted for television.

The following year Kirstie was cast in the television pilot "The Highway Honeys." This led to guest appearances on "The Love Boat" and "The Hitchhiker," and a regular role in the short-lived series "Masquerade." (Kirstie was particularly upset with ABC because they would not release her from the series when she was offered another television role.) Kirstie also forged a career path with the television movies "Sins of the Past," "The Prince of Bel Air" and the miniseries "North and South, Book I" and its sequel "North and South, Book II."

"Cheers"—Getting the Part

James Burrows, co-executive producer of "Cheers," recalls being impressed with Kirstie's seductiveness and great voice during her performance in the role of Maggie in a local theater production of *Cat on a Hot Tin Roof* (1984). Iron-ically, three years later, Kirstie, who lacked comedy experience and training, was the first actress to audition for the role of Rebecca Howe, a strong-willed, business-minded, career-oriented woman. Kirstie gravitated toward the role for several reasons. First, her feature film offers were limited to alien roles. Sec-ond, although she preferred comedy, Kirstie lacked comic acting experience, so the excellent writing and talented cast could offer her invaluable experience. Finally, she figured a comedic role would broaden her character roles and fea-ture film options.

Since Burrows questioned Kirstie's comedic abilities, he consulted Carl Reiner, who worked with her in *Summer School* (1987), and watched footage of the movie. Although the producers were mesmerized by Kirstie's audition, they felt obligated to audition other actresses. After ushering scores of other actresses, they went back to their original choice, Kirstie.

The departure of Shelley Long left a major void in the cast. To lighten the mood, on the first day of work Kirstie appeared on the set cloaked in a blonde wig and clothes resembling those of Shelley Long. Despite her initial jocularity, the next few weeks were intensely pressured, though the cast made every effort to make her feel at home. Kirstie overcame the anxiety, nervous tremors and elevated expectations by delivering a sound performance. She proved to be comedically talented and added depth to her character. She became the rejuvenating force the show needed to ascend to a higher level, as well as higher ratings.

"Cheers"—The Rebecca Years

Interestingly enough, the role of Rebecca Howe was originally cast as a tough no-nonsense martinet. But after the first few episodes, the executive pro-ducers and writers realized Kirstie's vulnerability and comic rhythm, and began writing her part as an amiable neurotic who was in and out of control. Actu-ally, Kirstie's own wacky disposition helped shape the character. Due to her nervousness during the first few weeks of taping, the producers decided to incorporate her neurotic twinges beneath a facade of self-confidence.

A similar metamorphosis took place with regard to Kirstie's image and physical appearance on the show. When Rebecca was introduced as the seri-ous-minded businesswoman, her makeup was very simple and her outfits were conservative and businesslike. As Rebecca began to expose her vulnerability and infatuation with her boss, Evan Drake (Tom Skerritt), she began power dressing in shapely suits with brighter colors, and wore additional lipstick and blush.

Miraculously, "Cheers" had a smooth transition from Shelley Long to Kirstie Alley. The viewing audience actually increased, the ratings remained consistently high, and Kirstie earned five Emmy nominations for Outstanding Lead Actress, winning in 1991. The success of "Cheers" translated into financial rewards, and by the final season Kirstie was earning $115,000 per episode ($3 million per year). Despite a huge salary, her dressing room, positioned two floors above the "Cheers" set in Paramount Studios, was an indistinguishable, unadorned, closet-sized room.

Kirstie was liked by everyone and immediately jelled with the entire cast, especially Rhea Perlman, who was Kirstie's closest real-life friend on the set. In addition, she easily matched wits with the raucous behavior of Ted Danson and Woody Harrelson during their backstage ribaldry. She was like one of the guys, but also a favorite among the crew. Kirstie was quite jocular on and off the set, a sharp and pleasant contrast to Shelley Long, who was inordinately serious and intolerable at times.

Movies

Kirstie's silver screen debut was playing the part of Lieutenant Saavik (Mr. Spock's sidekick) in the highly successful *Star Trek II: The Wrath of Khan* (1982). Although she did not have a significant role, the film gave Kirstie enough exposure to receive several movie offers, mostly as an alien. Kirstie rejected those roles, instead accepting small roles in *Runaway* (1984), Tom Selleck's sci-fi thriller about robotic killers, and *Champions* (1984), starring John Hurt in a true story of a British jockey overcoming cancer.

Kirstie had a more significant role in *Blind Date* (1984), in which Joseph Bottoms portrays a blind man who has a visual computer implanted in his brain to aid police in tracking a psychopathic killer. Unfortunately, the movie was not well-received by critics or audiences.

After a three-year hiatus, Kirstie appeared in two movies with Mark Harmon. In *Summer School* (1987) she plays a dedicated history teacher who assists a gym teacher (Harmon) alternating as the remedial summer school English teacher. *Prince of Bel Air* (1987), originally a made-for-television movie, involves a pool cleaning playboy (Harmon) who exchanges a string of one-night stands for the love of a good woman. Both movies received mixed reviews and had average box office success.

In *Shoot to Kill* (1988), Sidney Poitier and Tom Berenger are FBI agents on the trail of a kidnapped cutie (Alley). The film was a moderate financial success, and the critics viewed the movie with disdain (though crediting the actors for upgrading the weak script).

The following year Kirstie appeared in a pair of mediocre films, the much forgotten *Daddy's Home* (1989) and *Loverboy* (1989). In the latter film, Kirstie plays an affluent sex-crazed housewife who seduces a teenage pizza delivery boy (Patrick Dempsey). Both films were denigrated by critics, but later that year Kirstie's movie career was resuscitated with a blockbuster hit.

In *Look Who's Talking* (1989), Mollie (Kirstie) is an unwed accountant who gives birth to a wisecracking infant (dubbed with the voice of Bruce Willis). While searching for a live-in father, she falls in love with a taxicab driver (John Travolta). The movie was lambasted by critics, but the public flocked to it in droves, making it one of the most profitable movies of the year, earning over $140 million. The movie's success bolstered Kirstie's marketability as a feature film star (and rejuvenated costar John Travolta's ailing film career). Almost instantly she received more film offers and demanded a higher salary.

Kirstie continued in the comedic vein with *Madhouse* (1990), in which she plays an upwardly mobile television news reporter married to a successful financial planner (John Larroquette) and living in a state house that is invaded by unruly houseguests. (Ironically, this movie closely resembles Kirstie's own open-door policy for the penurious.) Once again, the movie was panned by critics, but the public made it a box office success. By the turn of the decade, Kirstie's multiple box office successes made her one of the highest paid actresses in Hollywood.

That same year, in *Sibling Rivalry* (1990), Kirstie plays an aspiring writer and neglected housewife who has a one-night stand with a stranger (Sam Elliot) who not only dies during their multi-orgasmic tryst but also happens to be the long-lost brother of her husband, Harry (Scott Bakula). The story then revolves around a farcical concealment of the sexual rendezvous from her relatives. Critics and moviegoers alike thought the movie had less life than the corpse, though Kirstie was received in a more favorable light.

The movie *One More Chance* (1990) represented Kirstie's first top-billed role but became one of the least successful movies of her career. Fortunately, her next movie was the sequel *Look Who's Talking Too* (1990), which again resurrected her faltering film career. In the sequel, Travolta and Alley undergo the stress of pregnancy and experience marital turmoil resulting from the financial constraints of supporting a family of four. Kirstie reportedly earned $2.5 million plus a percentage of the gross revenues and a $500,000 retroactive bonus for her performance in its predecessor. Once again, the critics expressed insolence toward the film and Kirstie was given mixed reviews; nevertheless the general audience made the feature immensely successful at the box office. The pair of *Look Who's Talking* movies have a combined gross revenue of more than $380 million in worldwide ticket sales, with additional prosperity in movie rentals and video sales. It even spawned the short-lived ABC television series "Baby Talk."

One noteworthy television movie is "David's Mother" (NBC, 1994), in which Kirstie stars as Sally Goodson, the plump and slobby mother of David, an autistic and retarded child. Her commitment to being the sole caretaker for her son destroys her marriage and ruins the relationship with her daughter. Kirstie was uncharacteristically lauded by critics for an awe-inspiring performance, and earned an Emmy for Outstanding Lead Actress in a Special.

In the sequel to the sequel, *Look Who's Talking Now* (1993), the Alley-Travolta tandem returns in a story line revolving around a pedigree poodle (the voice of Diane Keaton) smitten by a street-smart mutt (the voice of Danny DeVito). Despite a delightful cast, the movie was vilified for a dreadful script, yet once again the general audience made the feature a box office success.

In *Village of the Damned* (1995), a remake of the 1960 sci-fi thriller, costarring Michael Pare, Kirstie plays a research scientist amidst a group of small-town women who give birth to emotionless demonic children. After receiving unfavorable reviews and reeling at the box office (earning only $9 million), the movie was quickly ushered onto video. Her follow up, *It Takes Two* (1995) costarring Steve Guttenberg, had moderate reviews and box office success.

Despite mostly mediocre silver screen success, Kirstie is still a popular favorite, and her movies thrive financially on video. As for Kirstie's missed opportunities in feature films, there are two: losing to Glenn Close for the female lead role in *Fatal Attraction* (1987) and falling short to Kathleen Turner for the female lead in *Body Heat* (1981). Kirstie also lists one acting disappointment—not being selected for a small part on the television series "B.J. and the Bear."

Relationships—Romantic

Despite an attraction toward masculine men who exhibit danger and excitement, Kirstie wanted a man who had never loved before, so he could learn the aspects of love from her and never want anyone else. In the 1970s she gravitated toward dangerous men, and during "the drug years" (her cocaine addiction), Kirstie had two memorable relationships.

The first relationship is referred to as the "the Wyoming years," when she dated a man named Jake. He was the son of a wealthy oil businessman, and bought Kirstie anything and everything. They lived together for a few years, until she reached "the holistic years" by dating a rich hippie who ran a juice bar. However, when the cocaine ended, so did this phase of her existence. Although Kirstie wanted a man who would take charge, she ultimately married a sensitive male.

Kirstie first saw Parker Stevenson at a Los Angeles restaurant. After ogling him from a distance, she told actress friend Mimi Rogers (before she married Tom Cruise), "For him I would die." Mimi knew Stevenson, and although he was on a blind date, she arranged for him to meet Kirstie at a disco later that evening. Stevenson tried to impress Kirstie by paying for all the drinks, but she took the initiative by asking him to dance and then kissing him.

Stevenson is best remembered as the blond-haired, blue-eyed teen idol of the 1970s costarring in "The Hardy Boys" opposite Shaun Cassidy. Despite striving to shed the image with more serious roles, Stevenson lacked respect until he appeared in the movie *Stroker Ace* (1983), in which he plays Aubrey James, Burt Reynolds' villainous foe on the stock car circuit. He subsequently earned a recurring role on "Melrose Place" (directing one episode), and is a regular on "Baywatch." Stevenson has also entertained offers to direct various television episodes and to act in movies.

The relationship between Kirstie and Parker had a rather precarious start, and seemed destined for demise. She was the wild vixen, and he was a straight-laced Princeton graduate, but he was cute, so Kirstie reluctantly agreed to another date. When Stevenson arrived on a motorcycle, she knew he was the ideal mate—a Renaissance man on a motorcycle. Despite dating other people, within three months Parker proposed marriage to Kirstie at a restaurant by having a waiter hand deliver the note. They wed on December 22, 1983.

According to Kirstie, their marriage is based on mutual admiration and the fact that they elicit the uninhibitedness of each other. Moderation and commitment are two other essential ingredients. In the first year of their marriage Parker was likely to sulk in the corner, whereas Kirstie was likely to throw pots and pans. Since then they have reached a happy medium.

Parenthood

Kirstie and Parker tried for years to conceive a child, and their wishes were answered in 1990. Ecstatic about impending motherhood, Kirstie spent $23,000 on maternity clothes, baby clothes and decorating the nursery. Her jubilance was quickly dampened by tragedy when she suffered a miscarriage eight weeks into the pregnancy. In a spontaneous abortion her body rejected the egg, which would have become a baby with Down's syndrome. Kirstie contends the miscarriage was not related to her demanding work schedule, and since the fetus was only weeks along, she did not suffer the physical loss but rather the emotional loss associated with the expectation of birth.

Determined to have a family, Kirstie and Parker decided to adopt a child. They opted to bypass the typical agency adoption process for the more expeditious independent adoption. Of course, the latter route is much more expensive, approximately $25,000 (covering medical expenses, legal fees, and the birth mother's living expenses), but this was not a deterrent.

On October 12, 1992, Kirstie and Parker adopted a baby boy, William True (born October 5, 1992). He was named William after Kirstie's grandfather and great-grandfather, and True in honor of a Stevenson family name (though she often refers to him as "Bud" or "The Intruder"). In early 1995, Kirstie and Parker added another child to their family, an adopted daughter, Lillie Price.

Kirstie always planned to have children as a stabilizing force in her life—to give her a fulfilling existence. Although she and Parker have only two children, Kirstie intimates she would like to tackle pregnancy again, but the prospect is unlikely with career commitments and recent adoptions.

Pets

Kirstie is fanatical about animals, and has a house overflowing with a multitude of various species. The menagerie of over 40 pets includes dogs, marsupials, chickens, rabbits, turkeys, raccoons, possums, cockatoos, geese, a crow, parrots, mice, a miniature horse, koi fish and at least a dozen cats. Some of her feline friends are named Trixie, Monkey, Wild Dog, Tar Baby, Black Top, Lolly, and her famous cat is named Elvis (his claim to fame was being featured on the Purina Cat Chow calendar). Since she loves animals, Kirstie willingly opens her doors to stray animals or nurses them back to health.

Home Life

Kirstie and Parker live in Encino, California, in the San Fernando Valley in a 32-room, 8,000 square foot red brick mansion situated on two and one-half acres. The home was built by Al Jolson for his wife Ruby Keeler in the 1930s. The gravel driveway meanders through a grove of lemon and orange trees, past the guest house, Olympic-size swimming pool, and lush flower garden. Inside is a formal entrance hall, a cavernous living room, chaise lounge, and aviary. Kirstie used her special talents to redecorate the entire estate with eclectic and high-tech furniture, antiques, and an extensive art collection. The bathrooms have painted murals and *trompe l'oeil* effects reminiscent of movie stars' tastes of the 1930s and 1940s. Naturally there is an animal motif—oil paintings of dogs, porcelain rooster figurines and statues of deer strategically placed among the bright red-and-green plaid and chintz. (Unfortunately many of the rooms were damaged by the earthquake of 1994.)

Kirstie and Parker also have vacation hideaways in Oregon and Isleboro, Maine (population 600). The Ashland, Oregon, compound is a ranch estate, including four houses, two log cabins and stables, located in a forest. The East Coast abode is a sprawling estate on an Atlantic Ocean upper-crust island resort south of Bangor. This summer residence is a remote 20-bedroom, two-story New England Colonial Inn with an interior that mixes classical and whimsical decor. The inn was built in 1915 for a Philadelphia rubber baron.

Sister Parrish, who helped Jackie Kennedy redecorate the White House, assisted with the redecoration. The inn consists of animal figurines and lamp bases amongst Grecian friezes, with botanical motifs everywhere. Kirstie's goal is to capture romance by infusing nature into every room—colors in harmony with the environment, natural textures (wicker, wood, bamboo), and leaving windows bare to eliminate barriers with the outdoors. Their winter hideaway is a refurbished 1870 farmhouse near the Bangor inn. Despite the influx of celebrities to the remote island resort, Kirstie easily wooed the residents of Isleboro by contributing generously to their local library and civic organizations, and playing softball with neighborhood children.

Charitable Contributions

Kirstie is active in charities, and often volunteers to assist those in need. As the owner of over 40 animals, it is not surprising that she is fiercely devoted to animals rights and an active member of PETA (People for the Ethical Treatment of Animals). She is also funding a chimpanzee refuge in Africa with her longtime idol, zoologist Jane Goodall. Kirstie is a board member of the Earth Communications Office (Hollywood's leading environmental group), and her own organization, the Alley Foundation, was instrumental in publishing *Cry Out*, an ecological cartoon booklet printed in English and Spanish (on recycled paper) aimed at recruiting grade school children as junior environmentalists. She works with children exposed to drug abuse, and is the international spokesperson for Narconon Chilocco, a drug rehabilitation facility in Oklahoma founded by the Church of Scientology for drug addicts of all or no denominations. Kirstie's involvement in Narconon is due to a personal obligation to make amends for past misdeeds of turning some non–drug users into cocaine addicts.

Kirstie has always been a devout environmentalist, and practices what she preaches. She totes canvas shopping bags for her groceries, recycles paper, glass and aluminum, and refuses to use aerosol cans or purchase produce tainted with pesticides. Kirstie's advocacy has permeated her employment as well. She insists upon recycling bins on her movie sets, urges the caterers not to use polystyrene containers, and once convinced the "Cheers" producers to include a pitch for recycling on one episode.

The Future

Kirstie signed a multi-year contract with Universal Pictures for television and feature film projects. In addition, she signed with the film company Castle Rock, which bought *Hold on Tight*, a script she co-wrote with friend Doc Lawrence after being inspired by a love song he had written. She would love to work with rock icon Prince, and did appear as a pushy reporter in his sexy hit video "My Name Is Prince." Kirstie has recently established a production company, True Blue Productions, which is named after her son.

One acting tandem that is unlikely to materialize is Kirstie and Parker.

They played the parts of sister and brother in "North and South" but have since decided against such endeavors because they are too cocky about their own work and too critical of each other's. According to Kirstie, a romantic lead with her and Parker would be boring—there is nothing they could bring to the screen that is not already there.

Although she still perceives herself as a dramatic actress, Kirstie loves comedy and is tentatively slated to reappear in an NBC sitcom in 1997.

Acting Credits

The following is a comprehensive list of Kirstie's acting accomplishments since her arrival in Hollywood in 1981.

TELEVISION: "The Highway Honeys" (pilot) 1.13.83 (NBC); "The Love Boat" episode "Don't Take My Wife, Please" 11.26.83 (ABC); "Masquerade" (series) 12.15.83 to 4.20.84 (ABC); "Sins of the Past" (telefilm) 4.2.84 (ABC); "A Bunny's Tale" (telefilm) 2.25.85 (ABC); "The Hitchhiker" episode "Out of the Night" 10.29.85 (HBO); "North and South, Book I" (miniseries), 11.3.85, 11.5.85, 11.7.85, 11.9.85, 11.10.85 (ABC); "The Prince of Bel Air" (telefilm) 1.20.86 (ABC); "North and South, Book II" (miniseries), 5.4.86 to 5.8.86, 5.11.86 (ABC); "Stark: Mirror Image" (telefilm) 5.14.86 (CBS); "The Hitchhiker" episode "The Legacy of Billy B." 3.31.87 (HBO); "Infidelity" (telefilm) 4.13.87 (ABC); "Cheers" (series; episode "Home Is the Sailor") 9.24.87 to 5.20.93 (NBC); "Mickey's 60th Birthday Special" (special) 1.13.88 (NBC); "Friday Night Videos" (host) 4.21.89 (NBC); "Cutting Edge with Maria Shriver" 8.14.90 (NBC); "Saturday Night Live" (host) 10.12.91 (NBC); "44th Annual Primetime Emmy Awards" (cohost) 8.30.92 (FOX); "Wings" episode "I Love Brian" 2.25.93 (NBC); "Saturday Night Live" (host) 4.24.93 (NBC); "Christmas in Washington" (special; host) 12.15.93 (NBC); "Comic Relief VI" (special) 1.15.94 (HBO); "David's Mother" (telefilm) 4.10.94 (CBS); "The Wonderful World of Disney: 40 Years of Television Magic" (special) 12.10.94 (ABC); "Peter and the Wolf" (special) 12.8.95 (ABC); "Radiant City" (telefilm) 3.31.96 (ABC); "When Somebody Loves You" (telefilm) (forthcoming).

MOVIES: *Star Trek II: The Wrath of Khan* (1982); *Blind Date* (1984); *Champions* (1984); *Runaway* (1984); *Summer School* (1987); *Prince of Bel Air* (1987); *Shoot to Kill* (1988); *Loverboy* (1989); *Look Who's Talking* (1989); *Daddy's Home* (1989); *Madhouse* (1990); *Sibling Rivalry* (1990); *Look Who's Talking Too* (1990); *One More Chance* (1990); *Year of the Comet* (1992); *Look Who's Talking Now* (1993); *Village of the Damned* (1995); *It Takes Two* (1995); *Nevada* (forthcoming, 1997).

THEATRICAL PRODUCTIONS: *Cat on a Hot Tin Roof* (1984); *Answers.*

GAME SHOWS: "The Match Game"; "Password."

EMMY NOMINATIONS: Outstanding Lead Actress in a Comedy Series, NBC ("Cheers," 1988, 1990–93); Outstanding Lead Actress in a Miniseries or Special, NBC ("David's Mother," 1994).

AWARDS: Emmy: Outstanding Lead Actress in a Comedy Series, NBC ("Cheers," 1991); Emmy: Outstanding Leading Actress in a Miniseries or Special, NBC ("David's Mother," 1994); Golden Globe: Best Actress in a Musical/Comedy Series, NBC ("Cheers," 1991).

Nicholas Colasanto
(Ernie "Coach" Pantusso)

Nicholas Colasanto was born January 19, 1924, in Providence, Rhode Island, where he eventually worked as an oil company accountant and bookkeeper. In 1951, he was on the verge of accepting a new position with an oil company in Saudi Arabia when he saw the theatrical production *Mister Roberts*, starring Henry Fonda and Charles Boyer. Nicholas was immediately captivated and enthralled by the stage and, at age 28, abandoned everything to pursue a career in the theater. He applied to the American Academy of Dramatic Arts, but after being rejected, joined a small theater company in Phoenix.

Nicholas returned to New York City, and like most struggling actors, supplemented his income—in Nicholas' case by working as a bartender, waiter and dishwasher. Despite brilliant performances, Nicholas only had a few parts during a 10-year stint in mostly Off Broadway productions. At age 39, his annual income from acting was only $90.

During an Off Broadway road tour production, Nicholas befriended fellow actor Ben Gazzara. At the time, Nicholas was handling the laundry of the production company, though he occasionally appeared onstage as a standby for minor parts. By 1956, he appeared opposite Gazzara in the Broadway production *A Hatful of Rain*, and continued to receive critical acclaim on the stage, earning an Obie nomination in 1962 for his role as a befuddled cab driver in *Across the Board on Tomorrow Morning*.

The following year, Nicholas received national exposure for the first time in a television commercial for "White Knight," an Ajax laundry detergent. This was his first and last performance in a commercial. Nicholas was financially destitute at the time, so Gazzara was preparing to co-sponsor a personal loan to help him survive the next six months. When Nicholas checked the mailbox before leaving the apartment that day, he found the first residual check from the television commercial. Whooping with laughter, he shredded the loan application and accompanied Gazzara to a champagne breakfast at the Loggia Room. Each morning thereafter, Nicholas kissed the mailbox before opening it.

In 1965, Nicholas moved to Hollywood after receiving an invitation from Gazzara to direct an episode of his dramatic television series "Run for Your Life." Nicholas accepted the generous offer (and plane fare to Los Angeles), and in his directorial debut, discerned a preference for being behind the camera because there was more action.

The residuals from the Ajax commercial were enough to keep Nicholas afloat while commencing a directorial apprenticeship. After directing an episode of "Run for Your Life," he spent a considerable amount of time with directors Mark Rydell and Leo Penn learning the nuts and bolts of filmmaking en route to personally directing over 100 television drama episodes for series such as "Bonanza," "Columbo," "The Streets of San Francisco," "Name of the Game," and "Hawaii Five-O." Nicholas became so successful at directing he all but gave up acting. Consequently, little is known about this beloved actor-director because most of his life was spent behind the scenes, and not in the public eye as an actor.

Although directing was his true vocation, Nicholas did not abandon acting as an avocation. Despite a relatively sparse number of roles in the 1970s, he appeared in dozens of television shows and a handful of mostly forgettable television movies. His most noteworthy motion pictures were *Fat City* (1972) and *Family Plot* (1976), where Nicholas performed under the tutelage of such accomplished directors as John Huston and Alfred Hitchcock.

A decade of scarce employment opportunities sent Nicholas to the bottle. He began drinking alcohol heavily, which further limited his marketability. After joining Alcoholics Anonymous, Nicholas returned to acting as a fight-fixer in *Raging Bull* (1980), under the superb direction of Martin Scorsese. Two years later, after Robert Prosky declined the part, Colasanto and Sid Caesar were asked to audition for the role of Coach Ernie Pantusso on "Cheers." Ironically, Nicholas was a reformed alcoholic and member of Alcoholics Anonymous at the time he auditioned for the part of a bartender.

Oddly enough, even though "Cheers" was Nicholas' first attempt at television comedy, he landed a role as a regular cast member. Nicholas is best known for his popular portrayal of Coach Ernie Pantusso, the endearingly addlepated bartender on "Cheers." In each of the three seasons he appeared on the show, Nicholas received an Emmy nomination for Outstanding Supporting Actor, though he never won. (The winners were Christopher Lloyd for "Taxi" in 1983; Pat Harrington, Jr., for "One Day at a Time" in 1984; and John Larroquette for "Night Court" in 1985.) Nicholas successfully portrayed his character by perceiving everything through the eyes of a 12-year-old child, listening intently to every word and interpreting them literally.

During the taping of the third season of "Cheers," friends and coworkers became concerned about Nicholas' significant weight loss. At Christmas time, the elderly actor was diagnosed with congestive heart failure. He immediately told his friends the prognosis gave him anywhere from five weeks to

Nicholas Colasanto

five years to live. Nicholas spent the next couple of weeks in the hospital and then a few weeks convalescing at home. Naturally, the illness prevented his appearance in several "Cheers" episodes, so the producers and writers had the other characters make references to Coach, who was conveniently visiting his sister in Minnesota, taking a driver's test in Vermont, and attending a family reunion in Ohio.

While attending a "Cheers" rehearsal, Nicholas told the cast he felt fine and anticipated returning for the season finale. Four days later, on Tuesday, February 12, 1985, he died of a heart attack while watching television in bed at his Los Angeles home. The cast was notified of Nicholas' demise shortly before Tuesday night's scheduled taping at Paramount Studios. The cast was heartbroken because Nicholas had been a beloved and popular friend on the "Cheers" set. Filming was suspended for several days, and in a tributary rebroadcast, NBC aired an episode which featured Nicholas prominently. As a personal tribute, the cast and coworkers inserted a full-page ad in Hollywood trade papers stating, "Nicky, we're going to miss you—Everyone at 'Cheers'." Nicholas was 61 years old at the time of his death, and the most surprising fact about him is that he never married or had children.

The show's co-creator and co-executive producer, James Burrows, described Coach as a father figure to everyone in the cast. The producers made a conscious effort not to replace him with another elderly gentleman; they did not want to create another Coach or anything like that character. Nicholas was irreplaceable, so a young Woody Harrelson was cast as the replacement bartender.

In Harrelson's first episode of the 1985-86 season, the characters sorrowfully referred to the death of Coach. The producers wanted to pay homage to their friend, but did not want to exploit his death to boost ratings. Thus, no episode was devoted specifically to exorcising the grief; rather, Nicholas was endearingly remembered in several episodes through characters' thoughtful references to Coach. In the series' finale, over eight years after his death, the cast paid their respects to Nicholas by having Sam Malone adjust the picture of Geronimo that was hanging on the balcony wall. (The picture was originally hanging in Nicholas' dressing room prior to his death and was placed on the upstage wall in remembrance.)

Acting Credits

The following is a comprehensive list of Nicholas Colasanto's television, movie and theatrical credits, including acting and directorial endeavors.

TELEVISION: "Fame Is the Name of the Game" (telefilm) 11.26.66 (NBC); "Lassiter" (telefilm-pilot) 9.8.68 (CBS); "Toma" (telefilm) 3.21.73 (ABC); "Baretta" (series; episode "The Secret of Terry Lake") 4.16.75 (ABC); "The Return of the World's Greatest Detective" (pilot) 6.16.76 (NBC); "Westside Medical" (series; episode "Red Blanket for the City") 3.31.77 (ABC); "Martinelli: Outside Man" (telefilm-pilot) 4.8.77 (CBS); "Lou Grant" (series) 10.23.78 (CBS); "Cheers" (series) 9.30.82 to 3.28.85 (NBC).

MOVIES: *The Counterfeit Killer* (1968); *Fat City* (1972); *Family Plot* (1976); *Mad Bull* (1977); *Raging Bull* (1980).

THEATRICAL PRODUCTIONS: *A Hatful of Rain* (1956); *Across the Board on Tomorrow Morning* (1961).

DIRECTING CREDITS: "Run for Your Life" (1965, NBC); "Bonanza" (NBC); "Felony Squad" (ABC); "Hawaii Five-O" (CBS); "Name of the Game" (NBC); "Columbo: Etude in Black" (telefilm) 9.17.72 (NBC); "Hec Ramsey: The Detroit Connection" (telefilm) 12.30.73 (NBC); "Columbo: Swan Song" (telefilm) 3.3.74 (NBC); "Nakia" ep No Place to Hide 10.19.74 (ABC); "Police Story" ep Across the Line 11.12.74 (NBC); "Nakia" ep A Matter of Choice 12.7.74 (ABC); "McCoy: New Dollar Baby" (telefilm) 1.25.75 (NBC); "The Streets of San Francisco" ep The Programming of Charlie Blake 2.6.75 (ABC); "McCoy: Bless the Big Fish" (telefilm) 10.5.75 (NBC); "The Family Holvak" ep Crisis 12.21.75 (NBC); "S.W.A.T." ep Soldier on the Hill 3.13.76 (ABC); "S.W.A.T." ep Any Second Now 3.16.76 (ABC); "Logan's Run" ep NA 10.17.77

(CBS); "CHiPS" ep Highway Robbery 12.1.77 (NBC); "Kaz" ep NA 10.15.78 (CBS); "Kaz" ep Which Side You On? 11.5.78 (CBS); "Starsky & Hutch" ep The Groupie 11.28.78 (ABC); "The Contender" ep no title 4.17.80 (CBS); "Lobo" ep The Fastest Ladies Around 1.27.81 (NBC); "Lobo" ep The French Follies Caper 3.3.81 (NBC); "Lobo" ep The Fastest Women Around 3.10.81 (NBC); "Fitz and Bones" ep To Kill a Ghost 11.7.81 (NBC); "Today's FBI" ep Kidnap 4.19.82 (ABC)

EMMY NOMINATIONS: Outstanding Supporting Actor in a Comedy Series, NBC ("Cheers," 1983–85).

OBIE NOMINATIONS: *Across the Board on Tomorrow Morning* (1962).

Ted Danson
(Sam Malone)

Childhood

On December 29, 1947, Edward and Jessica Danson rejoiced at the birth of their only son, Edward (Ted) Bridge Danson, III. Of British ancestry, Ted was born in San Diego, California, but lived most of his childhood outside Flagstaff, Arizona, because of his father's employment commitments. Ted spent most of his youth playing outdoors in the canyons, rummaging through archaeological digs, riding horses, and going to the reservation with the Native Americans (Hopi and Navajo tribes) and ranchers' kids. He would leave the house at nine in the morning and return at dark, living a childhood devoid of pop culture— his family did not even have a television. Ted also recalls the family taking an annual pilgrimage to the California coast, which prompted his love for the ocean.

Ted describes his youth as idyllic, but with a family wrapped a little too tight. There was a lot of love in the family, but there remain some serious issues and secrets that need to be resolved. Although refusing to divulge specifics, Ted intimates they were significant enough to require intense family therapy. Part of the problem was the Danson family's inability to share their emotions with one another. Everything was kept inside and they never told the truth about their feelings of grief, pain, or sadness. In addition to repressed emotions, Ted was very insecure about his masculinity. He felt gawky and unattractive and was very shy. Ted is currently involved in psychotherapy to cope with these personal problems.

In 1961, Ted, then 13, was sent to Kent School in Kent, Connecticut, one of the nation's most selective all-boys college preparatory boarding schools. Kent is affiliated with the Protestant Episcopal Church, and known for having trained some of our country's political and social elite. In this Spartan school, every student is required to enroll in at least five classes, work a school job (such as sweeping, cooking or serving meals), and be involved in at least one of 89 intramural teams. Televisions are not allowed in the students' rooms, and attendance at the chapel is mandatory.

During his tenure at Kent, Ted played the cello but was more interested in athletics than academics. He dreamed of becoming a professional basketball player, and this burning desire for the sport was the only motivation which kept him from dropping out of school. Already 6'0" and weighing 120 pounds, Ted was a member of the school basketball team, and within two years he reached his current height of 6'2". It was also at Kent where Ted had his first acting role in Martin Duberman's *In White America.*

Ted had few youthful romances. Naturally, attending an all-boys school severely curtailed dating; however, once every two months the school held a dance with an all-girls school in Connecticut. The girls were bused to Kent on Saturday morning, and by the time they attended a football game, dinner, and a sock hop in the gym, it was nine in the evening and they were heading home.

The dances were designed to inhibit opposite sex relationships. Holding hands was considered risqué, and chaperons used rulers to separate couples who were dancing too close. Moreover, dates were assigned by height, so Ted was always dating someone six feet tall. Thus evolved the Moose Pool, where 60 boys pitched in 50 cents apiece and whoever had the ugliest date, by mutual consent, won $30 (which was a substantial sum in the mid–1960s).

At one memorable dance, Ted was paired with a large six-foot lacrosse player with whom he had nothing in common. Although depressed, after looking at the other boys' dates, Ted realized he would probably win the pool. At the end of the evening he apologized for his sophomoric behavior, but she just smiled and said it was okay because she won the Moose Pool. The girls had the same pool, and Ted was the moose!

Family and Relatives

Ted's parents were Episcopalian, but in 1989 converted to Catholicism after meeting an impressive group of Carmelite monks. His father, Edward (Ned) Bridge Danson, II, was a university professor, archaeologist, anthropologist, and museum director. Ned was the director of the Museum and Research Center of Northern Arizona (outside Flagstaff) which is dedicated to the natural history of the Southwest, including the arts and crafts of the Hopi and Navajo tribes. Ted's relationship with his father was such that it took him 28 years to finally assert his independence. Ted's mother, Jessica D. Danson, is a housewife and an avid reader. Ted also has an older sister who is married to Lauren Haury, an oceanographer at Scripps Institute of Oceanography.

Personal Characteristics

Ted has a lanky but well-molded 6'2" muscular frame and an athletically lean 195-pound physique. His wavy pompadour of brown, collar-length hair is graying at the sideburns, with wiry silver and sable strands from the temples and forehead flowing to an exposed bald pate. (Ted only wears a hairpiece when filming is involved.) Below an overhanging forehead are lugubrious, deep-set blue eyes, occasionally recessed behind gold-rimmed reading glasses. His perfect teeth are encompassed within a lantern-square jaw, chiseled face, and a devilishly enticing smile.

The nutrition-conscious Danson does not drink coffee and has quit cigarettes and a four cigar per day habit. He enjoys chess, is terrible at remembering names, and candidly admits having been emotionally immature until the birth of his daughter Kate (he was nearly 30 years old). Parenthood accentuated the areas he needed to change and the ways in which he needed to mature.

Ted is incredibly amiable and relatively temperate. He has a slow, pensive speaking style when discussing such subjects as his career and childhood, and a firm, impassioned tone on subjects dear to his heart—the environment and his family. Ted's rigid exterior masks deep feelings and emotions that are often conveyed in his speech. He frequently interjects self-deprecating witticisms into the conversation. A veritable class clown, Ted has the unique quality of being attractive and humorous.

In acting, Ted is intensely self-motivated to give the best possible performance; he is extremely self-critical and rarely satisfied with the end result. In life, Ted is goal-oriented with specific well-compartmentalized priorities—family, environment, and then his career. At times he is self-assured and confident, and other times insecure and neurotic (especially about his appearance). In an attempt to be interesting, Ted used to act out his insecurities. Acting became a safety valve to externalize the fearful, insecure side of his personality. Although still present, the insecurities incrementally dissipated primarily because his role as the libidinous bartender created an illusion among the public that he was sexy (and soon he began to believe it).

Education

In 1966, after graduating from Kent, Ted pursued higher education at Stanford University in Palo Alto, California. For two years he floundered in academia, uninspired by the educational world. He rarely studied, had no academic major, and did not even contemplate acting as a profession. His introduction to this art form at the collegiate level occurred rather fortuitously. Ted was attracted to a waitress and accompanied her to an audition for a Bertolt Brecht play. To impress her, Ted also read for a part. After unexpectedly winning a non-speaking role in the play, Ted was instantaneously consumed by the theater.

In 1968, after two years at Stanford, Ted transferred to Carnegie Tech (presently Carnegie-Mellon University) in Pittsburgh, Pennsylvania, a renowned school with a prestigious drama program. For 15 hours a day he did nothing but act or study acting, and work on his dancing and voice. Although he had no social life, he loved it. After four laborious years of intensive study, he graduated with a B.F.A. in theater/drama.

While attending Carnegie, Ted met his first wife, Randall Lee Gosch. Ted and Randy married, and after graduation, they and several other aspiring graduates moved to New York to help one another survive the early, struggling years of acting. The newlyweds rented a one-bedroom apartment on West 90th Street.

Employment and Acting Philosophies

Ted Danson is one of the few actors who has had the luxury of being able to concentrate on his trade without the distraction caused by having to take non-acting jobs. Having come from a family of considerable financial means, Ted spent much of his academic career studying, instead of working, and any employment he did accept was related to acting. However, as with nearly every actor, Ted was not famous overnight and willingly accepted small roles to develop a name for himself in the industry.

For Ted, choosing a project is usually based upon finding a quality script and an inspired director with a strong point of view, regardless of reputation. Similarly, Ted enjoys working with quality actors to elevate his performance. Despite their past difficulties, Ted commends Shelley Long's quality acting skills for having elicited his best performances. Ted is not an egomaniac. All reports depict him as a caring individual who goes out of his way to help other actors by willingly agreeing to assist with their problems at extra rehearsals. Ted emanates energy on the set, and is well-focused, but not an obsessive actor. According to Ted, part of his success must be credited to the motivational self-help group est for changing his perspective on life. As a member of the group since his acting career began, Ted has overcome internal feelings that his life and career were a total failure.

Acting Career

After arriving in New York, Ted was chosen to act in a few Off Broadway productions while continuing his theatrical education at the Actors Institute. In his stage debut at the Off Broadway Theatre Four on April 23, 1972, Ted was hired as an understudy in *The Real Inspector Hound*. He subsequently joined the regular cast with a small speaking role as Reginald for an 18-month tour.

Ted's Broadway debut occurred on February 18, 1973, at the Brooks Atkinson Theatre, where he played the wealthy bartender Paul Regents, III, in *Status Quo Vadis* (1973). Although Ted was praised by several critics, the play opened and closed on the same night. Ted's first Shakespearean role was as a bodyguard in the New York Shakespeare Festival's production of *The Comedy of Errors*, which opened on July 24, 1975, at the Delacorte Theater in Central Park.

The progression of Ted's acting career included television commercials. His most notable advertisement featured him marching down a New Jersey street as a dancing box of Duncan Hines lemon chiffon pie mix. Ted gradually became successful, appearing in two now-defunct NBC daytime dramas, "The Doctors" (1974) and "Somerset" (1974–76), in which he played Tom Conway, a womanizing lawyer.

Prior to moving to Los Angeles, Ted befriended Dan Fauci. They both studied at the Institute in New York, and in 1986 became partners in a production company, Danson/Fauci Productions. (Ted has another production company, Anasazi, which derives its name from a Navajo term meaning "the ancient ones.") After relocating to California, Danson and Fauci cofounded an est-inspired Actors Institute in Los Angeles. For two years, Ted doubled as manager (with wife Casey's assistance) and acting teacher.

Hollywood — Early Years

Ted moved to Los Angeles in 1978, and within six months was given a small role as a Los Angeles police officer in the highly successful movie *The Onion Field* (1979). Ted then directed his attention to television. From 1980 to 1982, he appeared in two telefilms, two series pilots (which were never picked up), and made several guest appearances on successful television shows.

In 1981, Ted had a successful year in film and advertising. He had a somewhat larger role as a prosecuting attorney in the mega-hit *Body Heat* (1981), and landed a popular and prestigious advertising job as the Armani man in cologne ads (earning $40,000 the first year and $60,000 the following year). The next year was equally successful. Ted appeared in *Creepshow* (1982) and canceled the Armani advertisement contract to accept the role of Sam Malone in "Cheers."

"Cheers" — Getting the Part

Prior to auditioning for "Cheers," Ted auditioned for a role in the pilot series "The Best of the West" but did not receive the part. Unbeknownst to him, series director (and future cocreator of "Cheers") James Burrows was impressed with Ted's acting abilities. After viewing Ted's exemplary performance in a "Taxi" episode a few months later, Burrows asked Ted to audition for the part of Sam Malone in "Cheers."

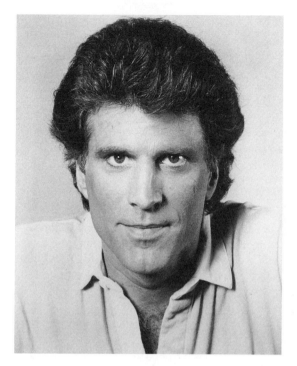

Ted Danson

At the audition, the producers recognized there was a special intangible chemistry between Ted Danson and Shelley Long, so they were paired in the audition for Paramount and NBC executives. NBC loved the concept and immediately signed Ted to a five-year deal (but only guaranteed 13 episodes). Despite Ted's athleticism in basketball, he had no baseball knowledge, so the producers had to teach him the game. (Ted was also sent to bartender school in Burbank for two weeks.)

"Cheers"—The Eleven Year Stint

The most publicized relationship, because of its disputatious nature, was between Ted Danson and Shelley Long. Although only recalling one insignificant incident where they fought, Ted acknowledges tension existed. Notwithstanding this relationship, Ted fit in well with the rest of the jocular, prankster cast, especially Woody Harrelson (they became immediate friends on and off the set). Ted's self-deprecating humor is one of the laudable characteristics that attracts friends and coworkers, and qualified him for the role of peacemaker on the "Cheers" set.

Despite lasting 11 years on "Cheers," the departure of Shelley Long seriously threatened Ted's livelihood. At the end of the fifth season, the contracts of both Danson and Long expired. In December 1986 Long refused to renew her contract, but Ted made a courageous decision to continue with the show. He had every neurotic thought imaginable, primarily fear that Shelley was the sole reason for the show's success.

Besides his own insecurities, Ted was angry. At times he felt Shelley had made the right decision, and then the next minute he felt enraged that she had abandoned everyone for purely selfish motives. There were a lot of hurt feelings. Despite their differences, after filming the season finale, the cast and crew held a party to air a memorable and nostalgic montage of scenes highlighting Shelley's character. At the end of the celebration, Ted made a toast that he would miss his partner very much.

Ted's successful portrayal of Sam Malone did not go unnoticed. He received an Emmy nomination all 11 years, winning the coveted award twice (1990, 1993), and won two Golden Globe Awards (1990, 1991). Ted's popularity also translated into financial rewards. He was earning $40,000 to $50,000 per episode in 1987, and within five years became one of the highest paid actors in television history, earning $450,000 per episode ($12 million for the season, including salary, future residuals, and a producing fee to develop other television projects for Paramount). Moreover, he reportedly turned down an unprecedented $20 million offer to return for a 12th season.

Although the entire cast talked about ending the series, Ted made the ultimate decision. After seeking therapy, and spending weekends with his family in profound soul searching, Ted decided to leave "Cheers." On Thanksgiving weekend of 1992, he informed the entire cast of his decision, and the news was officially reported a few weeks later (after the producers concluded that another season without Ted would be futile).

Ted wanted a creative challenge and the opportunity to experience something new and unknown—to take chances and change the direction of his career and life. Ironically, a few years earlier he was singing a different tune, and expressed contentment with his life, career, goals and ambitions. Ted insists he did not leave "Cheers" as a career move and it certainly was not for money. In 1994, Ted was reportedly worth an estimated $80–$100 million, and canceling "Cheers" cut his earning power in half.

Movies

In his early years, Ted's success steadily increased as his roles expanded. In his debut film *The Onion Field* (1979), a true but brutal crime story, Ted plays Ian Campbell, a melancholy, Scottish-American, bagpipe playing police officer who is murdered. This paved the way for a larger role in *Body Heat* (1981), starring Kathleen Turner and William Hurt, in which Ted plays Peter

Lowenstein, a wisecracking, tap dancing, Fred Astaire–like prosecuting attorney. The performance was praised by critics and audiences alike, convincing Ted to become a leading man (reminiscent of his idol, Cary Grant).

In his third film, the Stephen King thriller *Creepshow* (1982), Ted (in the segment titled, "Something to Tide You Over") plays an adulterous lover who is buried up to his neck in sand by a jealous husband. Ted and his lover are emotionally tortured by having to watch each other drown when the tide comes in, but they return from the dead covered with seaweed to haunt their murderer.

Interestingly enough, after being cast for "Cheers," the industry showed little interest in Ted as a feature film star. He continued accepting roles in television films with an eye on feature films, but it took three consecutive Emmy nominations for his performance as Sam Malone on "Cheers" before the movie industry began calling. By 1985, Ted was able to begin developing a movie career during the annual five-month break from "Cheers."

After a three-year feature film hiatus, Ted returned with a substantial role in the comedy drama *Little Treasure* (1985), in which he plays a former seminary student who helps a woman (Margot Kidder) search for $20,000 buried by her father (Burt Lancaster) in a Mexican ghost town. Ted received the highest praise of all the actors, although the film itself was a commercial failure and received a lukewarm critical reception. Ted agreed the off-screen battle between Kidder and Lancaster was more interesting than the film itself.

The following year replicated Danson's silver screen mediocrity with *Just Between Friends* (1986) and *A Fine Mess* (1986). In *Just Between Friends*, Ted plays a seismologist whose wife (Mary Tyler Moore) becomes best friends with his lover (Christine Lahti). The entire ensemble was praised, with Lahti winning the most accolades, but the directing was denounced. *A Fine Mess* was a slapstick comedy inspired by the Laurel and Hardy short films *The Music Box* and *Helpmates* (both 1932). Danson and Howie Mandel star as Hollywood losers who win a fortune at the racetrack and are pursued by two inept hit men. The film was vilified by critics, and Ted was criticized as being miscast from his true talents in dramatic acting.

Despite a moderate track record, Ted continued receiving movie offers, primarily due to his critical and popular acclaim in "Cheers." His unbridled popularity was evidenced by a marketing firm which rated Danson as one of the top 10 most familiar and popular performers. In 1987 Ted proved his worth with the biggest box office success of his career, *Three Men and a Baby* (1987), a remake of the 1986 French film *Three Men and a Cradle*. Ted cannot accept full credit for the movie becoming the fourth highest-grossing film of the year ($170 million), since he was paired with two heavyweight commercial draws, Tom Selleck and Steve Guttenberg. In *Three Men*, Ted plays Jack, an egomaniacal actor and the father of a child abandoned on his doorstep. Selleck earned the accolades, while Ted was given mixed reviews for his performance.

The financial success of *Three Men* made many people wonder why Ted did not abandon "Cheers" and make the transition from the small screen to the big screen. Ted's explanation: if his movies were not well received, he may have abandoned "Cheers" to perfect the art, but since he was attaining movie and television success, he wanted to enjoy the best of both worlds—rather questionable reasoning, considering most of his films prior to 1987 were box office bombs with limited critical acclaim.

At this juncture in his movie career, Ted had the following insight to explain its progression. Early in his film career, he lacked selectivity in the roles chosen and had little regard to carefully building a strong film career. Fortunately, he was given parts in quality films. Once "Cheers" pushed him into the limelight, Ted felt the pressure to be successful and began selecting feature film roles to compete with Shelley Long. It was only after *Three Men and a Baby* that the pressure subsided, and he was more selective in choosing his roles.

Ted's follow-up to *Three Men and a Baby* was *Cousins* (1989), another remake of a French film, the romantic comedy *Cousin, Cousine* (1975). In this comedy drama, which features Ted as a leading man for the first time, he plays a laid-back ballroom dance instructor who becomes involved in an adulterous liaison with a distant cousin after it is revealed their spouses are having an affair with each other. *Cousins* earned roughly $25 million and was mostly extolled, but Ted's performance, once again, received mixed reviews. (Interestingly enough, for this film Ted was required to shave the back of his head to affix a hairpiece, which prompted him to begin wearing it on "Cheers.")

The same year Ted was involved in the heart-wrenching drama *Dad* (1989) costarring Jack Lemmon and Olympia Dukakis. Ted plays a successful Wall Street investment banker returning home to care for his septuagenarian father (Lemmon) when his mother (Dukakis) has a mild heart attack. The film earned a modest $10 million and was met with derision, with Danson receiving disparate reviews. Ted originally accepted the role as an embodiment of love for his father—a way to say, "I love you, Dad."

Ted began the next decade with a sequel to his most successful movie, *Three Men and a Baby*. In *Three Men and a Little Lady* (1990), the three bachelors try to enroll their child in a New York school, and when her mother (Nancy Travis) moves to England to be wed, the trio flies to London to convince her to marry someone else. Most movie critics were insulted, and Ted was given moderate reviews; however, the film became a box office success, earning $30 million in gross sales in the first two weeks.

In *Made in America* (1993), Ted plays an abrasive, hedonistic Caucasian car dealer who discovers his donated sperm was used to impregnate an African-American bookstore owner (Whoopi Goldberg). While attempting to reconcile this horrendous misfortune, they become lovers. The movie was a critical and box office fiasco.

In 1994 Ted appeared in two more feature films. In *Getting Even with Dad*, he plays an ex-con blackmailed by his son (costar Macauley Culkin) into being a good father for one week in exchange for information about the where-abouts of money he had stolen. Although a moderate box office success (earn-ing $18 million), the movie was panned by critics as lacking everything—humor, emotion, energy—and for exposing the weaknesses of both actors.

In *Pontiac Moon*, a black comedy set in 1969, Ted plays an eccentric schoolteacher with an agoraphobic wife (Mary Steenburgen), in a story which revolves around a four-day primal journey to prepare for the first landing on the moon. Once again, Ted was associated with a feature film that failed to appeal to critics or moviegoers.

Despite silver screen mediocrity, Ted has never had difficulty being accepted as an actor playing many divergent roles. Public perceptions have not stereo-typed him as a one-character-only actor, something which has indelibly tar-nished Shelley Long's career. However, he still shoulders the burden shared by many television stars—translating television stardom into feature film success.

Relationships—First Marriage

While attending Carnegie-Mellon University, Ted had a serious rela-tionship with a fellow college student, Randall Lee Gosch, whom he married in August 1970. Two years later they moved to New York. They endured the hard times as struggling actors, but as Ted achieved a higher degree of noto-riety, the marriage slowly dissolved. Success intensified his love of acting and escalated his immaturity—he developed an oppressive ego and constantly prated his success. However, the split was not bitter. In fact, they separated without ever saying a word. Randy was learning sign language, and they had this life-changing conversation in 45 minutes of silence. The marriage lasted seven years, and in early 1977 they were divorced. (Randy is currently an actress and retains the surname Danson.)

Relationships—Second Marriage

Prior to the divorce, Ted met interior and environmental architecture designer Cassandra Coates (a Greek-American from Long Island) at the est seminar Headgames Lite (a cultic motivational training and self-help pro-gram). It was love at first sight for Ted, and part of Casey's appeal was her not being an actress. He invited the down-to-earth woman to a Mexican restau-rant, and they talked until four in the morning. She told him up front she wanted a serious commitment in a relationship and wanted to get married. When they began dating, Casey taught Ted to overcome his "me only" atti-tude and to absolutely commit to their relationship. Within six months, on July 30, 1977, they were married in New York.

Although Casey is 10 years his senior, Ted adamantly states their age difference was never a problem. However, in the mid–1980s he concealed their age discrepancy as merely six years, and then staunchly refused to discuss the topic. Despite years of marital bliss, relationship strains occurred when Casey was recuperating after a near-fatal stroke in 1979. During her first pregnancy, Casey was bedridden for nearly one month with high blood pressure, but doctors told them there was no reason for alarm. On Christmas Eve, she went into labor and was given drugs to lower her blood pressure and help facilitate the labor. Casey had a stroke right before giving birth but nobody realized it until she tried to get off the gurney and onto the delivery table. It all happened within a minute. Fortunately their daughter, Katherine (Kate) MacMaster Danson, was born without complications. The Dansons also have one other child, Alexis Lane, who was adopted as an infant in 1984. A decade later, in 1994, there were reports the family might lose Alexis when the birth mother threatened to sue for breach of contract. This matter has not been resolved.

The stroke Casey suffered was not only physically debilitating, but also emotionally draining. Casey left the delivery room temporarily paralyzed on the left side. Despite doctors advising she would never walk or use her left arm again, Casey was optimistic and began three years of intensive physical therapy to overcome the paralysis. Within eight months, both she and Kate were walking. The hard work paid off (the only remnant of the stroke is a slight limp), but the stress of the ordeal nearly dissolved their marriage.

Ted described this as a 2½-year emergency. He spent the first three weeks of Casey's convalescence sleeping on the floor in her hospital room, and took a six-month hiatus from acting to concentrate on her rehabilitation. The most arduous aspect of her recuperation was enduring the suppression of emotions. Overcoming her physical limitations was the only task for nearly three years, so neither spouse expressed their innermost feelings. When Casey was sufficiently recovered, they unleashed their raw emotions—she was disconcerted that Ted was never there for her, and he was upset because there was no more passion between them.

Ted considered leaving Casey, but counseling temporarily solidified their marriage. According to Ted, the passion was inexplicably reignited, which elevated their relationship to a higher plane—from the physical to the spiritual. Their spiritual love was an all-encompassing passion that enabled them to build toward a better future.

Despite having a spiritual love with Casey, in 1992 Ted found physical love when he was romantically linked with Whoopi Goldberg. In the midst of Ted's adulterous relationship, Casey was hospitalized for depression, and in October 1992 she separated from her husband. They retained joint custody of their two children, and on June 3, 1993, she filed for divorce in Superior Court in Santa Monica, California, ending their 16-year marriage. She reportedly settled for $80 million.

Relationships—Recent Romances

Ted and Whoopi first fell in love in April 1990 as guests on "The Arsenio Hall Show": Ted blazoned that he thought she was very sexy and funny; Whoopi was flattered because it was the first public pronouncement that she was feminine and pretty. Thereafter they costarred in *Made in America* (1993), and by the time they toured to promote the movie, their union was apparent. Rumors continued in April 1993 when Whoopi requested Ted as the Head Roastmaster at the Friar's Club (a private club with 3,000 famous members), where she was the guest of honor.

Despite the speculation, their relationship was officially confirmed a few months later, but the Friar's Club incident on October 8, 1993, precipitated their breakup. Ted appeared on the dais with his face painted black, like the 1930s version of Al Jolson, and delivered a monologue laced with racial epithets and crude sexual references. The audience had mixed opinions, but public opinion and media commentaries were decidedly outraged. In defense of Ted, it was a bold effort to dispel the Sam Malone image in a forum that encouraged the unspeakable. (The Friar's Club has a long history of X-rated topics and raucous humor.) Some prominent producers opined the Friar's Club incident may have rejuvenated Ted's career because it was one of the few interesting things he ever did.

Of course, Whoopi publicly defended Ted's actions and accepted joint responsibility for creating the monologue. But the negative publicity failed to subside until their publicists issued a public statement announcing their breakup two months later. Prior to the breakup, Whoopi and Ted agreed to a *Made in America* sequel and to costar in *Pink Vodka Blues*, though it is unlikely these projects will materialize.

The combination of a career in the balance, his marriage on the rocks, and the public reaction to the Friar's Club monologue sent Ted's world into a tailspin. On October 16, 1993, thoughts of anxiety, confusion, and the emotional distress of recent events culminated in a near-fatal automobile accident. Ted was driving too fast on a winding California highway when his Lexus spun into an embankment (rather than off the cliff) and into the path of an oncoming truck. The impact with the truck crushed him into the embankment. Physically, he was relatively unscathed, but emotionally he learned the preciousness of life and the need to regroup.

Ted met his current paramour, Mary Steenburgen (b. 1953), during the filming of *Pontiac Moon* (1994). The actress and activist from Little Rock, Arkansas, has two children (Lilly, b. 1981, and Charlie, b. 1984). Mary was previously married to Malcolm McDowell, whom she met while costarring in *Time After Time* (1979) and divorced in 1989. Ted and Mary bought a house together; and on February 8, 1995 (her birthday), she accepted Ted's proposal of marriage. They were married on October 7, 1995.

Public Interest Activities

Ted's interest in the environment was spawned during his youth. Being raised in the Southwest among Native American tribes and having a father who preached environmental preservation genuinely influenced Ted's earthy views (though he claims to be an activist out of guilt for being overpaid for "Cheers"). Whatever the reason, he became aggressively involved in environmental and charitable causes, most notably American Oceans Campaign (AOC) and the Futures for Children organization. Ted's activism arose primarily out of a sense of family responsibility. When he moved to California in 1978, his wife Casey became involved in a community organization called No Oil which was attempting to prevent Occidental Petroleum from drilling off the coast. Casey was a member of the advisory board and prompted her husband to attend a meeting. Although only six people attended, Ted was so impressed with the presentation he immediately donated $5,000.

One particular incident induced Ted to campaign for oceanic causes. In 1987 the Danson family went to a Santa Monica beach, but were prohibited from swimming by a sign that read, "Water Polluted, No Swimming." Shortly thereafter, he and Casey hired an environmental lawyer, who in turn hired the best ocean lobbyist in Washington, D.C. After speaking with Ted's brother-in-law, the Dansons wrote a check for $250,000 to start the American Oceans Campaign (AOC), a Santa Monica–based lobbying organization committed to formulating a responsible coastal resource policy.

Ted became the president and chief spokesperson while Casey was the highly active vice president teaching society to change behaviors and stressing individual efforts to enhance the environment. Ted utilized his celebrity status to gain access to microphones and cameras to espouse the tenets of the cause, and volunteered for a series of public service announcements and a television documentary. He even solicited the support of fellow "Cheers" stars Kirstie Alley, Rhea Perlman, George Wendt, and John Ratzenberger, as well as other Hollywood stars such as Danny DeVito, Ally Sheedy, Sally Field, James Garner and Jeff Bridges.

For the first three years the AOC was entirely funded by the Dansons, but through active involvement, nearly half of the $500,000 budget, which supports nine staff members in Santa Monica and Washington, D.C., was acquired through fund-raising activities. (By 1994, the Dansons had paid nearly $2 million, and still provide much of the funding and nearly all of the publicity.) Through their active involvement, the AOC has written legislation to prohibit offshore oil and gas drilling.

His commitment to the environment is not merely lip service for the benefit of publicity. Ted actually practices what he preaches. At home he recycles, conserves water, and refuses to use plastics or toxic cleaners. He even fasts three days a month to rid his body of toxins.

Ted is also involved in charities for children. He is a member of the board of directors of Futures for Children, a New Mexico–based organization raising money for the education of Native American children in New Mexico and Arizona. In addition, Ted participated in the "For Our Children" (1993) television benefit concert to raise money for the Pediatric AIDS Foundation, a nonprofit organization that researches the effects of HIV/AIDS on children.

Home Life

When Ted and Casey moved to California in 1978, they bought a home in Los Angeles. Their ascendancy into wealth began with rather modest living accommodations in a house redesigned by Casey. The Danson family forewent the extravagance and ostentatious displays of Hollywood opulence, and were content driving a Jeep and a Volvo wagon. However, within time they became more accustomed to wealth. Ted purchased a Learjet and a white Lexus, and the Dansons bought homes in Santa Monica, Brentwood and Malibu, and Casey was designing a getaway retreat in New Mexico. After the divorce, Ted and Mary Steenburgen purchased a home in Martha's Vineyard.

Ted's home life consists mainly of spending quality time with his family—horseback riding with the kids or shooting hoops in the driveway. Other pleasures include inviting friends over for pasta and classical music (such as Puccini). Ted loves wasting endless hours watching television, especially basketball games, and engaging in biweekly yoga and weight lifting sessions.

The Future

Acting remains Ted's true passion, and he always dreamed of becoming a movie star, but after 14 films in 17 years, his priorities are slowly changing. The silver screen is no longer the only aspiration because it infringes on his personal life, requiring monthly isolation from family, friends, and society. Conversely, a television series is alluring because he can see his family in the morning for breakfast and in the evening for dinner.

At this juncture, Ted does not have the clout to choose feature films, but he does have influence in television. Since he owns a production company, Ted is quite capable of procuring lead roles in television, such as the miniseries "Gulliver's Travels" and the sitcom series "Ink." In addition, his production company is developing and producing various projects (including additional episodes of *When the Bough Breaks* and Aldrich Ames' story as a CIA-KGB double agent). Other projects include developing the movie *Ghost*, a love story between a 10-year-old runaway con and a professional basketball player, and, in conjunction with Disney Studios, the movies *One Fine Day* and *Meet John Doe.*

Although Ted's feature film future is uncertain, it was reported that he is considering the role of a scientist distraught over whether to reveal scientific evidence that debunks the myth of the Loch Ness monster in the movie *Loch Ness.*

Acting Credits

The following is a comprehensive list of Ted's television, movie and theatrical accomplishments.

TELEVISION: "The Doctors" (daytime drama) 1974 (NBC); "Somerset" (daytime drama) 9.74 to 12.31.76 (NBC); "Kate Loves a Mystery" episode "Love on Instant Replay" 10.18.79 (NBC); "B.J. and the Bear" episode "Silent Night, Unholy Night" 12.15.79 (NBC); "B.A.D. Cats" episode "I Want It or You Die" 1.18.80 (ABC); "Family" episode "Daylight Serenade" 3.10.80 (ABC); "Laverne and Shirley" episode "Why Did the Fireman…?" 4.4.80 (ABC); "The Women's Room" (telefilm) 9.14.80 (ABC); "Once Upon a Spy" (telefilm-pilot) 9.19.80 (ABC); "Benson" episode "The Fireside Chat" 2.13.81 (ABC); "Benson" episode "Marcy's Wedding" 2.20.81 (ABC); "Magnum, P.I." episode "Don't Say Goodbye" 3.28.81 (CBS); "Comedy Theater" (pilot) episode "Dear Teacher" 7.17.81 (NBC); "Our Family Business" (telefilm-pilot) 9.20.81 (ABC); "Taxi" episode "The Unkindest Cut" 2.25.82 (ABC); "Cheers" (series) 9.30.82 to 5.20.93 (NBC); "Tucker's Witch" episode "The Good Witch of Laurel Canyon" 10.6.82 (CBS); "Cowboy" (telefilm) 4.30.83 (CBS); "Allison Sidney Harrison" (telefilm-pilot) 8.19.83 (NBC); "NBC All-Star Hour" (special) 9.17.83 (NBC); "TV Censored Bloopers No. 6" (special) 11.12.83 (NBC); "Quarterback Princess" (telefilm) 12.3.83 (CBS); "Something About Amelia" (telefilm) 1.9.84 (ABC); "An American Portrait" episode "Chief Joseph" 11.9.84 (CBS); "NBC's 60th Anniversary Celebration" (special) 5.12.86 (NBC); "When the Bough Breaks" (telefilm) 10.12.86 (NBC); "We Are the Children" (telefilm) 3.16.87 (ABC); "Saturday Night Live" (host) 2.11.89 (NBC); "Friday Night Videos" (host) 4.21.90 (NBC); "The Earth Day Special" (special) 4.22.90 (ABC); "Challenge of the Seas" (special) 4.22.90 (A&E); "Line of Fire: The Morris Dees Story" (telefilm) 1.21.91 (NBC); "Fifth Annual American Comedy Awards" (special) 4.3.91 (ABC); "National Audobon Society" episode "Danger at the Beach" 7.9.91 (PBS); "Rock the Vote" (special) 9.23.92 (FOX); "For Our Children" (special) 2.16.93 (DISNEY); "TV's All-Time Classic Comedy" (special) 5.1.94 (FOX); "The Simpsons" episode "Fear of Flying" (voice) 12.18.94 (FOX); "Frasier" episode "The Show Where Sam Shows Up" 2.21.95 (NBC); "The 9th Annual American Comedy Awards" (special) 3.6.95 (ABC); "Deadly Whispers" (telefilm) 5.10.95 (CBS); "Gulliver's Travels" (miniseries) 2.4.96, 2.5.96 (NBC); "Ink" (series) (forthcoming 10.21.96).

MOVIES: *Chinese Web* (1978); *The Onion Field* (1979); *Body Heat* (1981); *Creepshow*—"Something to Tide You Over" (1982); *Little Treasure* (1985); *Just Between Friends* (1986); *A Fine Mess* (1986); *Three Men and a Baby* (1987); *Cousins* (1989); *Dad* (1989); *Three Men and a Little Lady* (1990); *Made in America* (1993); *Getting Even with Dad* (1994); *Pontiac Moon* (1994); *Loch Ness* (forthcoming).

EXECUTIVE PRODUCER: "When the Bough Breaks" (telefilm, 1986); "We Are the Children" (telefilm, 1987); "Down Home" (series, 1990-91); "Walk Me to the Distance" (telefilm, 1989).

THEATRICAL PRODUCTIONS: *The Real Inspector Hound* (1972); *Status Quo Vadis* (1973); *Comedians; The Comedy of Errors* (1975).

EMMY NOMINATIONS: Outstanding Lead Actor in a Comedy Series, NBC ("Cheers," 1983–93); Outstanding Lead Actor in a Limited Series or a Special, ABC ("Something About Amelia," 1984).

AWARDS: Emmy: Outstanding Lead Actor in a Comedy Series, NBC ("Cheers," 1990, 1993); Golden Globe: Best Television Actor, Miniseries or Made For TV Movie, ABC ("Something About Amelia," 1984); Golden Globe: Best Actor in a Television Series, NBC ("Cheers," 1990-91).

Kelsey Grammer
(Frasier Crane)

Childhood and Education

Kelsey Grammer was born on February 21, 1955, in St. Thomas on the Virgin Islands, the first child of Allen and Sally Grammer. Kelsey was only two years old when his parents separated and divorced. Although the family remained in St. Thomas, a few years later they moved to New Jersey to live with his grandparents.

Kelsey spent the next half-decade with his grandfather, Gordon, an Army colonel and oil executive characterized as a liberal conservative and situation philosopher. He had the greatest influence on Kelsey's early life because he treated the youngster, not as a child, but like a male companion. Kelsey has fond memories of dinnertime, where they discussed the day's events and what Kelsey had learned at school that day. His grandfather had such a profound impact that Kelsey initially considered a career in the armed forces. However, his vision of attending naval school in Annapolis, Maryland, quickly dissipated once he began reading poetry.

In 1967 Kelsey's family (including his grandparents) moved to Pompano Beach, Florida, and one week later his beloved grandfather died. This event forced the 11-year-old Kelsey, who had lost the only male figure in his life, into a reclusive state. While attending Pine Crest High School (a private school in Fort Lauderdale, Florida), Kelsey had few friends and spent most of his time alone. Originally ostracized by peers who ridiculed his name (he was called Elsie the Cow and Graham Cracker), Kelsey lost interest in seeking new friendships and deliberately separated himself from his peers. Surfing, meditation, and music became his sanctuary. Although Kelsey was always a smart, witty student, for most of his adolescence he was a rebel, social outcast, and recluse. Moreover, he felt suffocated and uninspired with education, and ultimately renounced academics, extracurricular activities, and social functions.

In 1972, an English teacher at Pine Crest introduced the 16-year-old Kelsey to acting and convinced him to accept a role in the school production of *The Little Foxes*. Kelsey immediately fell in love with acting because it possessed the same qualities as surfing—it was all at once exciting and engaging with a moment to moment type of freedom. After his first performance, Kelsey knew this was the one pleasurable occupation that he could enjoy for a lifetime.

Family and Relatives

Kelsey's father, Allen Grammer (b. 1930), was an eccentric expatriate who ran a bar and grill, published the *Virgin Island View* magazine, had a radio talk show, and gave music lessons in St. Thomas. After divorcing Allen in 1957, housewife Sally Grammer was awarded sole custody of Kelsey and his younger sister, Karen (b. 7.15.57). Since Sally never really cared for life on the Virgin Islands, in the early 1960s she relocated the family to her parents' home in New Jersey. Once in the United States, Kelsey rarely saw his father.

Allen subsequently remarried, and with his wife, Elizabeth (b. 1935), had a daughter (Betty) and three sons (Stephen, Billy and John). In 1968, when Kelsey was 13 years old, his father was shot to death in his St. Thomas home by a mentally ill intruder. Just before midnight on April 22, 1968, Allen Grammer heard a marauder on the grounds of his lagoon-front home. He went to investigate, and was shot twice and died. The assailant was a cab driver who was subsequently found not guilty by reason of insanity.

In 1975 Kelsey suffered his most devastating family tragedy when his sister Karen was murdered. On the night of June 30, 1975, Karen was sitting on a curb outside a Colorado Springs Red Lobster restaurant where she worked as a waitress. Three men who had been planning a robbery approached and then forced her into a car. According to police records, they took her to an apartment where she was raped by at least one of them. After being discarded in an alley, she was stabbed 42 times and her throat slashed. Karen managed to crawl to a nearby trailer park where her body was found the next morning. A few months later three men were arrested, and one ultimately received the death sentence for her murder.

It was Kelsey who identified his sister's body, claimed her belongings, and brought her back to Pompano Beach for burial. For years he was haunted by the terrible memory, feeling numb, violent, and often angry because he blamed himself for her death—for not being there to protect her (as he had when they were children). Karen's death made him lose faith in the world and in God.

Five years after Karen's death, Kelsey faced the loss of two more family members. On June 1, 1980, his half-brothers, Stephen and Billy, drowned in a scuba diving accident off the coast of St. Thomas. When Billy failed to surface, Stephen plunged into the depths and suffered a fatal embolism during an improper ascent. Billy's body was never recovered; his mother remains convinced he was eaten by sharks.

Personal Characteristics

The 6'2" Kelsey has sandy-brown, thin hair, receding considerably in the front with hair tufting wildly behind his ears. (During adolescence he wore a short-haired wig to hide his long, curly locks to conform with high school regulations.) His complexion is puffy and well-defined when he projects a smirky-smile, with signs of age wrinkling around his blue eyes. Although he looks 10 years older than he is, Kelsey certainly acts 20 years younger.

Unlike Dr. Frasier Crane (his character on "Cheers" and "Frasier"), Kelsey is not refined and conservative looking. He often relaxes barefooted and in shorts, or dons worn-out blue jeans and a tennis shirt. The contrast of their personae is equally diverse. Kelsey is an eccentric, rebellious man, which is sharply divergent to his pompous, straight and narrow television character. As for similarities, both have a tendency toward pomposity, but beneath Kelsey's ostentatiousness is an ingenuous vulnerability.

Kelsey has many interests, such as playing billiards, darts, golf and tennis, cruising in his sailboat, and singing. He is also a skilled jazz pianist (mostly playing for meditative purposes), loves tropical climates, and is a zealot about gardening. The fixation with gardening originated in his youth when Kelsey and his revered grandfather planted flowers annually. He continues to garden today because an allergy to food additives makes a fresh food diet essential.

Despite repeated tragedies, Kelsey maintains an optimistic attitude toward his life, career, and future, a tribute to his resiliency and strong character. However, the years of repressed emotions commencing with a troubled childhood and proceeding through multiple family tragedies certainly perpetuated his self-destructive tendencies. Kelsey turned to drug and alcohol abuse that peaked with formal criminal charges in 1987 and 1988, and culminated in a 1990 jail sentence.

Substance Abuse Problems

By the late 1970s, Kelsey began experimenting with cocaine. After landing the "Cheers" role in 1984, his frequency of drinking increased along with cocaine usage. Kelsey admits turning to alcohol and cocaine as an escape, and in 1987 was arrested for drunk driving. Initially, Kelsey was put on probation and ordered into a rehabilitation program (a typical sentence for a first offender) but in October 1988 he failed to appear in court to establish compliance with the terms of probation. Consequently his probation was revoked, then reinstated 10 months later. In February 1988 he missed another hearing and was sentenced to 30 days in jail, which eventually was changed to 90 days house arrest with an electronic transmitter.

Kelsey followed a similar pattern of behavior with his drug charge. After being arrested in April 1988 for possession of approximately $25 worth of cocaine, Kelsey missed two arraignments and was ordered into a drug rehabilitation program, but again failed to provide a progress report to the court. Despite a plea from Kirstie Alley, and Kelsey's self-serving justification (i.e., his girlfriend Cerlette Lamme's seizures and sinus pressure medical condition), in 1990 the unsympathetic judge sentenced him to 30 days in jail and 300 hours of community service (which included picking up garbage along a roadside) for violating the terms of probation. Most recently Kelsey admitted himself to the Betty Ford Clinic for rehab therapy, September 25, 1996, to October 20, 1996.

There were times in the late 1980s when his addiction nearly cost him the role on "Cheers" (arriving to the set glassy-eyed and puffy faced). He remains reluctant about discussing his recovery from drugs, but intimates it helped reestablish his sense of faith. Kelsey demurs at the idea of becoming a poster boy for recovering addicts, and refuses to do public service announcements warning about the evils of drugs. The actor does not believe in self-righteous preaching on the subject because everyone has to make this decision on their own.

Acting Career

When Kelsey was 18 years old he was offered $10,000 to star in a porno film, *The Bermuda Triangle*. Despite being desperate for work and financially destitute, he rejected the offer because it was the wrong thing to do (though a friend boldly accepted). Kelsey decided long ago he would never get very far on his looks, and resolved it was best to maintain his dignity and reject such offers, even in times of despair.

After graduating from Pine Crest High School in 1973, the talented young drama student (who idolized Jack Benny) was accepted into the theater program at New York City's prestigious Juilliard School. At Juilliard, Kelsey maintained a reputation as an eccentric—arriving at school on sub-zero days in sandals, cutoff shorts, and a Hawaiian shirt. However, as at Pine Crest, Kelsey soon felt constrained and uninspired with formal education. He wanted to be an actor, but was disgusted by having to prove it to instructors through recognized formulas. After two years of study at Juilliard, Kelsey was expelled for lack of discipline.

Thereafter, Kelsey ricocheted across the East Coast accepting odd jobs— unloading fishing boats in Rhode Island, painting roofs in Florida, and waiting tables in New York. His professional career changed in 1976 when a casting director, whose office he was painting, found him a position at the Old Globe Theatre in San Diego. Grammer tuned up his old motorcycle for an exhausting four-day cross-country trip to California.

Kelsey had an enjoyable two-year stint at the Globe, but feared going stale in the same locale, so he departed to pursue regional theater employment in Minneapolis and Buffalo. After gaining experience, Kelsey returned to New York to conquer the theater. In New York City, he worked steadily onstage in the Broadway and Off Broadway hits *Othello*, *Macbeth*, and *Sunday in the Park with George*, with an occasional foray into television. In 1984, Kelsey was playing a doctor on the soap opera "Another World" when he was asked to read for the part of Dr. Frasier Crane on "Cheers."

Television— "Cheers"

After two seasons of "Cheers," the role of Dr. Frasier Crane was created, but the producers were very secretive about the new character, and no actors were allowed to read the script before the auditions. Since Kelsey never saw the show, he had no notion about the part or character for which he was auditioning. As soon as Kelsey saw the "sides" (excerpts with his dialogue), he knew he could play the part. Kelsey understood the character so well that he protested when the script depicted Frasier dating Diane Chambers despite his being her therapist; such a great psychiatrist would never act so unethically and unprofessional. So instead, the producers devised the humorous story of Frasier intervening when Diane was about to hit another patient with a croquet mallet.

In the Boston bar, Frasier was initially the subject of the patrons' derision or a prop who rolled his eyes in contempt. His sole function was to reintroduce Diane (who had a nervous breakdown after breaking up with Sam) as a waitress at Cheers by advising her that confrontation was the only means to affect an emotional catharsis. Despite Frasier's being a wonderful supporting

Kelsey Grammer

character, Kelsey never expected the role to last longer than the scheduled seven episodes. He had the distinct feeling that Shelley Long did not approve of his character because he was apportioned some of her intellectual discourse.

However, the "Cheers" staff quickly recognized Kelsey's comedic talent and how much they liked to write for his character, so he was signed as a regular cast member. Frasier not only survived the first few episodes, he became a breakthrough character as one of the funniest, most likable characters on "Cheers." He began as a typical television intellectual—a pompous, condescending cerebral psychiatrist, scorned by patrons (with whom viewers were supposed to identify)—but quickly became a sympathetic, complete character capable of shenanigans like his barfly counterparts. Kelsey's successful portrayal of Dr. Frasier Crane on "Cheers" earned him two Emmy nominations for Outstanding Supporting Actor (1988, 1990).

Television—"Frasier"

After spending nine years as part of an ensemble on the colossal hit "Cheers," in 1993 Kelsey graduated to his own television series. He initially balked at the producers' conceptualization of a spin-off of Frasier's character, and staunchly opposed a Frasier-Lilith series because he believed that quarreling spouses have no value. When Frasier was ultimately chosen as the spin-off character, the producers attempted to capitalize on his popularity by isolating him from the rest of the "Cheers" characters and relocating his exploits to misty Seattle. There Frasier would practice psychiatry as a radio talk show host dispensing advice to interested listeners.

In the series premiere on September 16, 1993, Frasier was recovering from a recent divorce from Lilith, and burdened with the unenviable task of caring for his acrimonious and cantankerous ailing father, Martin (John Mahoney). When his brother, Niles (David Hyde Pierce), refused to provide any assistance, Frasier hired a live-in English caregiver, Daphne (Jane Leeves). The series swiftly became a highly rated and critically acclaimed television show (and is filmed in Paramount's studio 25, the same locale as its predecessor).

While hosting the radio call-in show, Frasier's pacifying trademark salutation is, "This is Dr. Frasier Crane—I'm listening." The creators envisioned various famous actors offering their voices as callers. However, when the show debuted, the producers had to beg famous personalities to commit to a cameo (Linda Hamilton agreed first). After the series had become a smash success, the tables turned and agents eagerly requested cameo appearances, which have included Christopher Reeve, Judith Ivey, John Malkovich, Joe Mantegna, Jeff Daniels, Matthew Broderick, Teri Garr, and Eddie Van Halen.

The success of "Frasier" was all but foreordained when NBC cushioned the show in the coveted Thursday night position following the hit "Seinfeld." Thus, in its freshman season, "Frasier" became NBC's highest-rated new series (rated sixth overall) and a critically acclaimed show, earning ten Emmy nominations and winning five awards. Kelsey, who had previously received four Emmy nominations, finally won the coveted award in 1994 for Outstanding Lead Actor.

Since NBC dominated Thursday night in the ratings during the 1994-95 season, the following year the network shifted "Frasier" to Tuesday night in an effort to expand its ratings domination. NBC wanted to build another solid evening of hit comedies around the show, so it purposely matched "Frasier" against ABC's strong but aging heavyweight, "Roseanne." In an interesting twist, ABC moved "Roseanne" to Wednesday to avoid a potentially fatal ratings game, and aligned "Home Improvement" (the no. 1 rated entertainment show on network television) head-on with "Frasier." Consequently, "Frasier," the one-time top 10 show on Thursday night, was struggling to remain in the top 20 on Tuesday night. However, "Frasier" held strong and over the next two seasons was ranked 16th and 12th, earning another 21 Emmy nominations and winning 9 awards with Kelsey coveting the trophy for Outstanding Lead Actor. Despite dipping in the raings, "Frasier" stole some of the viewing audience from "Home

Improvement" and remains one of the most critically acclaimed programs on television.

The success of "Frasier" made it ripe for syndication in 1997, so Kelsey, reportedly earning $200,000 or more per episode, will become quite wealthy since he negotiated a portion of the $300 million syndication rights. According to Kelsey, the most pleasing aspect of the show's popularity is its independent success, and not just as an extension of "Cheers."

Acting—Recent Roles

Despite playing the immensely popular Dr. Frasier Crane for over a decade, Kelsey devoted part of his busy schedule to theatrical work at the Mark Taper Forum in Los Angeles. In April 1992 he gave an acclaimed performance in Shakespeare's *Richard II* despite a rocky performance during an earthquake registering 6.1 on the Richter scale. The theater seats were rumbling, but everyone sat quietly, entranced and captivated by the actor onstage.

In March 1994 Kelsey starred in *J. Edgar*, a radio musical-comedy about the life and romance of the late FBI director. Kelsey plays Hoover and John Goodman ("Roseanne") plays his longtime assistant Clyde Tolson. In addition, Kelsey stars as an assistant district attorney in the television movie "The Innocent" (1994), and has a recurring voice role as sinister Sideshow Bob in the television series "The Simpsons."

Home Life

Despite a successful acting career, the Hollywood lifestyle has always made Kelsey apprehensive and he initially resisted falling prey to ostentatious displays of wealth. In the late 1980s, Kelsey, already famous as Dr. Frasier Crane, lived in a forlorn Van Nuys abode deep within the San Fernando Valley, in a neighborhood of sprawling passé properties avoided by developers due to its dilapidation.

The one-story, four-bedroom rental property exemplified a lack of concern for details, and a rather precarious habitat for a successful actor. Outside was an unkempt yard of overgrown weeds, with six dogs and twelve cats swarming about, a mound of bricks reclining against the exterior, windows propped open, and tattered bamboo shades dangling awry. The interior was as equally disheveled as the yard. The only touch of elegance in Fort Grammer (an appellation used by Kelsey's friends), was a well-stocked bar comparable to his dressing room stock at Paramount. In the rear was an armada of remnant vehicles he collected—an aging Oldsmobile, a battered Cadillac, a well-seasoned truck, and his favorite, a 1972 Triumph.

Kelsey finally succumbed to the affluence of Hollywood in the 1990s when he purchased a home in the exclusive Agoura Hills suburb. His four-bedroom, Spanish style hilltop canyon domicile is located on rustic, expansive ranch property. It is a typical Southern California villa with huge windows and capacious ethereal rooms, but personalized with eclectic African and Asian antiques, a surfeit of foliage, and a Jacuzzi with stone lion fountains.

Relationships—Romantic

Labeled an oddball ladies' man, Kelsey does not gravitate toward physical beauty, rather his attraction is to uninhibited women who are very needy and difficult to please. His grandmother, mother, and sister best illustrate this characteristic. At a young age Kelsey assumed the burden of caring for a family of three unsatisfiable women who never offered gratification to the man of the house. Consequently, after years of socialization in a deleterious home environment, Kelsey became accustomed to and gravitated toward similar unhealthy relationships.

Kelsey's domestic relationships further exemplify this pattern of conduct. He had two failed marriages, first to dance instructor Doreen Alderman, and then to Canadian exotic dancer Leigh-Anne Csuhany. In 1982, Kelsey met Doreen while performing with a touring company. They were married three months later, and on October 9, 1983, had a daughter, Spencer Karen (her middle name honoring his slain sister). The marriage was precarious almost from the start, and in 1990, after a six-year separation, they were officially divorced.

In 1985, while separated from his wife, Kelsey met Cerlette Lamme, a former professional skater with the Ice Capades. While performing in the Mark Taper Forum production of Shakespeare's *Measure for Measure* (1984), Kelsey noticed her in the audience and had the house manager deliver a personal note. After years of drug abuse, mostly cocaine, Kelsey and Lamme's seven-year relationship faltered when Lamme learned of his affair with Barrie Buckner, a bartender and part-time movie makeup artist. The following year Buckner gave birth to Kelsey's second daughter, Kandace Greer (b. 1992). Since Kelsey was still living with Lamme at the time, the unexpected birth drove an irreversible wedge between them.

After breaking up with Lamme in the spring of 1992, Kelsey began dating Leigh-Anne Csuhany (b. 1971), a former exotic dancer he met at Pelican's Retreat, a restaurant in Calabassas, California. She promptly moved in with him and within five months Kelsey proposed marriage. This relationship was no less turbulent than Kelsey's previous ones. In August 1992 police responded to a hysterical call from Kelsey and arrived at his home to find the actor with a shiner, courtesy of Csuhany. However, Kelsey refused to press charges, and less than three weeks later, on September 11, 1992, the couple eloped. Nine months later, on June 2, 1993, he requested an emergency restraining order against Csuhany, who insinuated she was going to shoot him and burn the house.

The next day Kelsey importuned an annulment of their marriage, accusing Csuhany of fraud and having an unsound mind. She was three months pregnant at the time, so Kelsey demanded custody in the hope of raising the child himself. That same day, under court order to vacate Kelsey's home, Csuhany checked into the Malibu Beach Inn about 10 miles away. Five days later, she attempted suicide and lost the unborn child in the process. Los Angeles County Sheriff's deputies found her in the hotel room, sprawled on the floor semiconscious, with five empty Tylenol containers, a half-empty bottle of red wine nearby, and a suicide note intimating Kelsey did not love her.

Their interminable feuding continued over the legitimacy of the marriage and the division of property in the divorce settlement. Kelsey's attempt to have the marriage annulled was resisted because it infringed upon Csuhany's claim to community property. In 1993 he sued, claiming she broke a promise to sign a prenuptial agreement, lied about her mental illness, and menaced him with a kitchen knife. Csuhany countered by claiming Kelsey pressured her into having an abortion. The divorce became final in December 1993.

The afflictions continued when later that year Kelsey was accused of having sex with a 15-year-old baby sitter in New Jersey and Arizona, and leaving 21 telephone messages showing a romantic link between them. He denied touching the girl, claiming the allegations were a blackmail attempt. Criminal charges in New Jersey and Arizona were labeled unsubstantiated when a grand jury failed to indict Kelsey. However, in July 1995 the teenager's parents filed a $20 million lawsuit charging Kelsey with having sex with a minor and inflicting mental distress. The teen has been in drug rehabilitation and lives in Phoenix.

Kelsey also had a long-term relationship with Tammi (Baliszewski) Alexander (b. 1966), a slender, bubbly, Kansas-bred former model and bit actress. Alexander was a partner in the company Lifespan, which uses blood tests to diagnose food allergies and offers recommendations for a proper diet, and currently is the spokesmodel for a Los Angeles insurance company. They met in June 1993 at the Southern California restaurant and bar Harry O's in Manhattan Beach, just days after he separated from Csuhany. They continued dating throughout the summer, and she even accompanied Kelsey to the fall premiere party for "Frasier" in September 1993. A moderate scandal occurred when tabloids revealed that as a fledgling model Alexander submitted nude photographs to *Playboy* in the expectation of posing for a pictorial. The headlines quickly subsided and their relationship remained untarnished.

At Alexander's insistence, Kelsey began working out, shedding 15 of his 210 pounds, and began attending St. Monica's Roman Catholic Church in Santa Monica. In February 1994 he proposed marriage in a limo by crouching on one knee in the backseat. Then, before a Tuesday night taping of "Frasier," he summoned Alexander from the audience and proposed again, this time offering her a 2-carat diamond engagement ring. She answered "Yes" both times. The wedding will be held at St. Monica's; however, there remains the obstacle of having Kelsey's two previous marriages annulled (which is a time-consuming process).

They have undergone relationship therapy because Kelsey does not want to make another marital gaffe. Their biggest problem is finding time for one another because of Kelsey's busy schedule of acting, singing, and producing.

The Future

Kelsey is basking in the success of his hit sitcom "Frasier," and has no plans of abandoning this endeavor despite landing the lead role in the comedy *Down Periscope* (1996), in which he stars as a commander overseeing a motley crew aboard a tottering World War II submarine. In addition, Kelsey penned the autobiography *So Far*, a candidly open and sincere account of his life. After the success of his singing the "Frasier" theme song, "Tossed Salad," there is also discussion of Kelsey preparing an album of standards. Finally, he is appearing in a national television advertising campaign to promote McDonald's Value Meals, and has his own company, Grammnet, Inc.

Acting Credits

The following is a comprehensive list of Kelsey's television, movie and theatrical credits.

TELEVISION: "Kennedy" (miniseries) 11.20.83 to 11.22.83 (NBC); "Another World" (daytime drama) 1984 (NBC); "Kate and Allie" (premiere) 3.19.84 (CBS); "George Washington" (miniseries) 4.8.84, 4.10.84, 4.11.84 (CBS); "Cheers" (series; episode "Rebound") 9.27.84 to 5.20.93 (NBC); "Crossings" (miniseries) 2.23.86 to 2.25.86 (ABC); "Dance 'til Dawn" (telefilm) 10.22.88 (NBC); "The Tracey Ullman Show" 1.7.90 (FOX); "The Simpsons" episode "Krusty Gets Busted" (voice) 4.29.90 (FOX); "Baby Talk" episode "One Night with Elliot" (voice) 4.12.91 (ABC); "Wings" episode "Planes, Trains and Visiting Cranes" 2.13.92 (NBC); "Star Trek: The Next Generation" episode "Cause and Effect" 3.29.92 (SYND); "The Simpsons" episode "Black Widower" (voice) 4.9.92 (FOX);

"Roc" episode "To Love and Die on Emerson Street" (Part 2) 5.9.93 (FOX); "Frasier" (series) 9.16.93 to present (NBC); "The Simpsons" episode "Cape Feare" (voice) 10.7.93 (FOX); "The Return of TV Censored Bloopers II" (special) 10.30.93 (NBC); "Beyond Suspicion" (telefilm) 11.22.93 (NBC); "The Tenth Annual Soap Opera Digest Awards" (special; cohost) 2.4.94 (NBC); "Saturday Night Live" (host) 4.9.94 (NBC); "The 46th Annual Primetime Emmy Awards" (special) 9.11.94 (ABC); "The Innocent" (telefilm) 9.25.94 (NBC); "The Simpsons" episode "Sideshow Bob Roberts" (voice) 10.9.94 (FOX); "The Second Annual Comedy Hall of Fame" (special) 10.29.94 (NBC); "The 1994 Clio Awards" (special; host) 10.31.94 (FOX); "The Barbara Walters Special" (special) 11.9.94 (ABC); "The American Revolution" (telefilm) 11.27.94 to 11.29.94 (A&E); "An Affectionate Look at Fatherhood" (special; host) 5.6.95 (NBC); "The 47th Annual Primetime Emmy Awards" (special) 9.10.95 (FOX); "The John Larroquette Show" episode "More Changes" (Part 1) 9.30.95 (NBC); "The Simpsons" episode "Sideshow Bob's Last Gleaming" (voice) 11.26.95 (FOX); "Kelsey Grammer Salutes Jack Benny" (special) 11.30.95 (NBC); "Tony Bennett: Here's to the Ladies, A Concert of Hope" (special) 12.1.95 (CBS); "Christmas in Washington" (special) 12.13.95 (NBC); "Stars in the Making" (special) 12.13.95 (CBS); "Second Annual Blockbuster Entertainment Awards" (special; host) 3.6.96 (UPN); "London Suite" (telefilm) 9.15.96 (NBC).

MOVIES: *Down Periscope* (1996); *Galaxies Are Colliding* (1996).

THEATRICAL PRODUCTIONS: *Macbeth; Othello; Troilus and Cressida* (1976); *Too Good to Be True* (1977); *Plenty; Month in the Country; Sunday in the Park with George; Mary Stuart; Hurly Burly* (understudy); *Quartermaine's Terms; Measure for Measure* (1984); *Richard II* (1992); *The Third Man* (1995).

DIRECTORIAL CREDITS: "Frasier" episode "Moon Dance" 2.6.96 (NBC).

AUTHORIAL CREDITS: *So Far* (autobiography), 1995.

EMMY NOMINATIONS: Outstanding Supporting Actor in a Comedy Series, NBC ("Cheers," 1988, 1990); Outstanding Lead Actor in a Comedy Series, NBC ("Wings," 1992); Outstanding Lead Actor in a Comedy Series, NBC ("Frasier," 1994–96).

AWARDS: Emmy: Outstanding Lead Actor in a Comedy Series, NBC ("Frasier," 1994–95); Golden Globe: Best Actor in a Television Comedy Series, NBC ("Frasier," 1996).

Woody Harrelson
(Woody Boyd)

Childhood

Born in Midland, Texas, on July 23, 1961, Woodrow Tracy Harrelson had a disruptive early childhood. By age 7, his father had abandoned the family, he had been removed from kindergarten and first grade twice, and was diagnosed as hyperactive, dyslexic, and psychologically disturbed. Woody's phase of violence and hyperactivity prompted his mother to enroll him in Briarwood School, a private school in Houston for children with learning disabilities. This became a dramatic turning point in his development. Woody discovered unconditional love from people outside his immediate family. The following year Woody overheard a radio report announcing that his father was imprisoned on a murder for hire charge.

Woody insists his violent tendencies were not related to a rough childhood. Instead he blames the media, especially television, as the disruptive influence. However, Woody admits that his troubled childhood, which included ridicule by other kids for being perceived as weird, generated considerable tension and rage.

The second half of Woody's childhood was filled with regular attendance at church, giving sermons, and holding weekly youth group meetings at his mother's house. In 1974 the family of six moved to Lebanon, Ohio, where he was raised by his mother, grandmother Polly, and great-grandmother "Sweetie Pie." In Lebanon, Woody used the stage as a focal point to release all his foolishness, and his first high school musical, *Li'l Abner*, was his best performance, according to his mom. Other extracurricular activities included track, football, and pickup games of basketball at Pleasant Square (the predominantly black section of Lebanon). Upon graduation, the bible-toting, "goody two shoes" attended college.

Family and Relatives

Woody's father, Charles Voyde Harrelson (b. 1939) is the most newsworthy and notorious of all Harrelson relatives. His exploits were dramatized on an ABC reality-based series titled "FBI: The Untold Stories." Charles, described as charming, brilliantly articulate and well-read, was an encyclopedia salesman, debt collector, professional hit man, and cardsharp banned from Las Vegas casinos. He was a fugitive from an indictment for possessing an unregistered shotgun in Kansas City, and in 1968 was convicted as a hired assassin in Texas. He was released in 1978, but one year later was arrested for murdering federal judge John H. Wood, Jr., in San Antonio, Texas. A local drug dealer in El Paso, Texas, facing trial with the austere judge, hired Charles and then reported the murder to attain a lighter sentence.

In his trial, Charles testified the only reason he confessed to the killing was based upon an agreement with his lawyer that Harrelson's three sons would receive $100,000 each. (He also confessed to killing John F. Kennedy but has since recanted.) Charles was convicted and is serving a double life sentence in an Atlanta federal prison for murder and conspiracy to commit murder. The drug dealer was found not guilty of these crimes on retrial.

Woody insists the trial was not fair because of prejudicial pretrial publicity and is not convinced his father is guilty. For example, Charles' lawyer was the brother of the drug dealer accused of hiring Charles to assassinate Judge Wood, and the presiding judge at Charles' trial was a pallbearer at Judge Wood's funeral. It was reported that while in prison, the elder Harrelson bribed inmates with cigarettes so he could watch episodes of "Cheers," and on July 4, 1995, he and two other inmates unsuccessfully attempted to escape by climbing over a wall. They surrendered after a tower guard fired a warning shot.

Divorce and prison kept Woody from seeing his father when he was younger, though now he writes and visits the prison once a year. Woody even functioned as the stand-in groom for his father's 1987 wedding when Charles married his third wife, Gina Adelle Foster, by proxy from prison. Although Woody sometimes questions his loyalty to a man who abandoned his family, he views his father more as a friend rather than a father.

Woody's mother, Diane, is a paralegal and secretary for James D. Ruppert, an attorney in Franklin, Ohio, who specializes in medical and legal malpractice and insurance law. She is a devout Christian who eventually divorced Charles and moved to Ohio. Woody's family was destitute and endured a great deal of suffering over the years. Consequently, Woody spent his youth fantasizing about being rich and famous, and longed to be the center of attention.

As for siblings, Woody remains distant from his brothers. He and his older brother used to be the best of friends, but now they see each other once a year at most. There had always been considerable friction between Woody and Brett, his younger brother by two years. They were radically different and went opposite directions with their lives. As adults, they see each other more frequently, primarily because Brett became a regular bar extra on the "Cheers" set and has been Woody's roommate since they moved to Los Angeles. All things considered, however, Woody considers George Wendt and Ted Danson as closer kin than his own brothers.

Personal Characteristics

The 5'11" actor normally weighs 170 pounds, but recently lost to an emaciating 153 pounds during an "80 percent-living diet," which involves fasting for one week out of every six; in one weeklong fast he lost 15 pounds. He plans to maintain this diet regimen for three years to purify his body of harmful toxins. Woody's skeletal frame is muscular, not rippling, and his supple athletic build nicely conforms to his interest in sports, especially basketball. Woody has blond hair, receding at the temples and thinning on top. At times handsome and other times unremarkable, the extroverted Harrelson has an innocence and charm he can turn on like a spigot, commencing with an insouciant, gap-toothed grin. Woody's primary avocations include playing the guitar, playwriting, and writing poetry and songs, though he also has an interest in playing the piano, juggling, chess, and reading Faulkner, Nabokov and Krishnamurti.

Woody has an irresistible appeal that combines a cockiness and machismo that women adore with a solid comedic sense and indelible savvy. Although he has his own peculiar idiosyncrasies—he is spacey, his mind wanders (he is often called Mr. Tangential), and is frequently tardy—Woody is still adored by friends. Behind his unique blend of surfer dude and philosopher is a string of sex, drugs and rock 'n' roll. Woody dated numerous Hollywood personalities, is an openly admitted sex addict, and is notorious for never missing a party. He is always testing his limits, whether they are spiritual or physical.

Woody has a macho element that inhibits the expression of his feelings or emotions. His approach to sex is purely recreational, without feelings, emotion or love. But it was not always this way. After attending Briarwood, Woody became more in tune to his feminine side, but upon reaching puberty, he began emphasizing masculinity, which still remains predominate. According to Woody, part of the problem is the dichotomy in male and female perceptions of a relationship—women want commitment in a monogamous relationship, whereas men want conquest. Woody hopes the learningexperience of life will eventually allow him to love freely and unconditionally.

This machismo is also exhibited through Woody's uncontrollable violent streak that originated during childhood. Mere rudeness can create a Jekyll-Hyde metamorphosis within Woody from serenity to fury—an immediate snap and loss of control. Of course, Woody believes all individuals have the capacity for violent tendencies and credits ex-lover Carol Kane for helping him learn to control his rage. However, the old wounds of youth were unleashed when he portrayed a serial killer in *Natural Born Killers* (1994). Woody delved deep into the psyche of the role and unleashed a rage he is still trying to control.

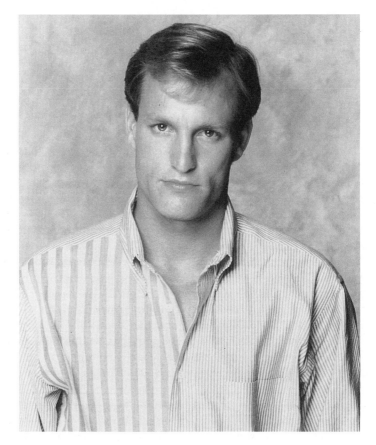

Woody Harrelson

Woody is staunchly environmentally conscious and imbibes holistic medicine. In 1990, he spent 2½ weeks in spiritual development in a commune with the Incas in Machu Picchu, Peru, and is now a devout yoga participant (he even taught classes in New York). He returned from his experience a vegetarian (eating nothing but fruit before noon), sold his gas-guzzling Corvette and began actively pursuing environmental causes. Woody even constructed a teepee in his backyard as a New Age dwelling to conform with his belief in communal living. In Africa he learned the simplicity of existence while sleeping in a tent, and he has been to an ashram in the Himalayas where he sat before a swami.

Woody's favorite rock group is Pink Floyd, and he listens to the Indigo Girls when he needs to be reminded of the dysfunction in his life. Woody has his own musical aspirations as a member of the 10-piece rock group Manly Moondog and the Three Kool Kats (naturally he is Manly, the lead singer), formed in 1991.

Personal Beliefs

Woody has long been outspoken on various topics of personal importance, and his trenchant positions on sensitive issues have sometimes been at odds with his commercial success. When Woody publicly denounced the United States' military involvement in the Persian Gulf, he was dropped as a commercial spokesperson for Miller Lite Beer. Similar views and his participation in anti-war rallies cost him the position as Grand Poobah of the Mardi Gras.

Woody's beliefs have also reaped positive results. He has donated time to children's crusades, such as the "For Our Children" (1993) benefit concert to help the Pediatric AIDS Foundation. He also donates money and time to the Earth Communications Office, Christic Institute, and Ted Danson's American Oceans Campaign.

As for his family, Woody consciously avoids discussing current feelings toward his mother and father. He also avoids any discussion of why he cannot sustain a long-term relationship with a woman, but denounces traditional psychotherapy explanations for his fear of commitment. He credits his father's injustice as one explanation for his personal reservations and inability to wholeheartedly trust another individual. In addition, Woody has a definite distrust and disrespect for the legal system. His father's experience has left an indelible impression which instilled dismal feelings about society, particularly government and its abundance of politics and bureaucracy.

Woody describes himself as having his heart and mind on a parallel course but never meeting. One of his favorite lines in an Indigo Girls song involves the dichotomy of childlike innocence and cynical reality. This defines Woody's internal conflict as he struggles with aging, fatherhood, and commitment, which sharply contrast with a desire for youthfulness, sexual conquests, and independence. It is a constant struggle between the spiritual and the physical, masculine and feminine, right and wrong.

Education

After graduating from Lebanon High School in 1979, Woody attended Hanover College in Hanover, Indiana, on a Presbyterian scholarship. He began his college education as a pure-hearted Christian. After receiving a bachelor of arts degree in theater arts and English in 1983, he began studying theology, which changed his perception of our existence and opened his eyes to the notion that the bible is merely man-made, philosophical rhetoric.

Woody's entire belief system—religion, family, the infallibility of his mother, and his staunch Republican views—was turned upside down. By the 20th year of life, he began a period of agnosticism, cynicism, and self-destruction. His senior year as a Sigma Chi fraternity member was laced with drinking, smoking marijuana, fighting and doubting everything. When a college friend was accepted at the Juilliard School, a prestigious school of the arts in New York, Woody also headed East.

Acting—Early Years

In New York, Woody spent 14 months trying to find stage work, and at one point held 17 jobs in one year (and was fired from most of them). His selection of employment was equally varied, from waiter to cook to workout trainer. After failing to find acting work or an agent for more than a year, Woody spent an inordinate amount of time in his room, depressed, stoned, and out of control. He smoked marijuana daily, frequently engaged in physical altercations, and lived off his friends. Finally, in 1984 he became an understudy in Neil Simon's Broadway hit *Biloxi Blues*, but received no stage time. Despite having very few acting credits, the following year he auditioned for and landed the role of Woody Boyd on "Cheers."

As for his one regret in life, Woody claims it was when he was leaving a production and had to tell the director, John Cassavetes. Woody was departing at his agent's insistence to pursue a film project in Italy. Despite knowing it was the wrong thing to do, Woody did it anyway.

"Cheers"—Getting the Part

When Woody auditioned to replace Nicholas Colasanto, the creators had already envisioned a naive farm boy named Woody (though Harrelson did not actually fit the image of Woody Boyd when the part was originally cast). Woody Boyd was supposed to be a skinny farm boy with big teeth—a real yokel. Harrelson was too attractive, more rugged, and definitely not naive. He displayed his uniqueness and bold appeal when he first auditioned for the part—his first action was to blow his nose!

Naturally, after being offered the part on "Cheers," Woody was also offered the part in a Broadway production he had been waiting months to land. He ultimately opted for the television exposure associated with a successful sitcom series. Once earning the part, Harrelson strived to portray Woody Boyd as naive and extremely literal, but not dumb.

"Cheers"—Relationships

Whereas Nicholas Colasanto was the father figure on the "Cheers" set, Woody became the son or younger brother. Woody added a dimension of raucousness to the set that had previously been missing, which especially impacted Ted Danson. They became very close, and Danson reverted to his juvenile ways. In one incident, Danson, knowing Woody's propensity not to wear underwear, dropped Harrelson's trousers in front of the cast and crew. Besides practical jokes on the set, they actively engaged in arm wrestling, basketball, and Ping-Pong. Woody is also off-screen friends with George Wendt, and they frequently go to concerts and play basketball.

Employment and Theater Productions

Woody is quick to note he is a performer, not an actor; he has no special technical abilities, he just needs to be on stage performing, being a showman. Whether it is acting or music, Woody craves the limelight.

Woody's first professional acting job was working as an understudy for the Broadway production of *Biloxi Blues* (1984). He also starred in the Off Broadway productions of *The Boys Next Door* (1987) and *The Zoo Story* (which he also produced), as well as writing, producing, and acting in *2 on 2*, a one-act play of camaraderie in a macho talkathon about existence and the human condition.

Despite being involved in a successful sitcom, Woody was still involved in theatrical endeavors, such as *Brooklyn Laundry* (1991), a comedy drama directed by James L. Brooks in which he costarred with Glenn Close and Laura Dern. This acting stint sparked a romance between Harrelson and Close, who was then scheduled to appear on "Cheers" as Frasier Crane's ex-wife. When the romance with Harrelson faded, Close was replaced by Emma Thompson.

Woody considers the screenplay *Furthest from the Sun* (1993), which he wrote, directed and produced, to be the most important project he has ever undertaken. Based on a real-life experience which occurred one summer after college, it involves personal reflections and an expression of Harrelson's dark repressed feelings. The story line involves three roommates, one black and two white, living in Houston, with scenes unveiling violence, sex, racism, and repressed fear about these topics.

Woody's agent and close friend, Bryan Lourd, has molded and finely tuned Harrelson's career to facilitate the transition from television sensation to movie star. Woody began his movie career with small roles (in *Doc Hollywood* and *L.A. Story*) that were memorable though comparable to his television persona, and then began rejecting Woody Boyd–type roles. Harrelson wanted to avoid being typecast, so he accentuated his talents, humor, and irresistible charm onstage in high profile productions (*Brooklyn Laundry*, *The Zoo Story*, and *2 on 2*). The result has been remarkable, as Harrelson is one of Hollywood's highest paid actors, earning over $5 million per feature film.

Movies

Woody's silver screen debut in *Wildcats* (1986), originally entitled *First 'n' Goal*, stars Goldie Hawn as the female football coach of rowdy high school jocks, one of whom is Harrelson. The movie was a box office hit. He followed up this role with a few small and less than noteworthy movies, such as *Eye of the Demon* (1987) and *Cool Blue* (1988). However, his cameos in *Casualties of War* (1989) and *L.A. Story* (1991) led to a more substantial role in *Doc Hollywood* (1991).

In *Doc Hollywood*, Michael J. Fox stars as Ben Stone, a big-city doctor who inexplicably meanders into a hick town and is subsequently sentenced to community service after driving his Porsche into a judge's white picket fence. Woody plays a small role as Hank, an insurance salesman, who becomes jealous about Lou's (Julie Warner) affections toward Ben. The movie was critically acclaimed for its brilliant acting and supporting cast, though it was not as successful at the box office. The same year, Woody had a small role as a homeless Vietnam veteran living in a box in *Ted and Venus* (1991). The movie had mixed reviews and was not financially successful.

In *White Men Can't Jump* (1992) Woody costars with Wesley Snipes as two basketball hustling cons, Billy Hoyle and Sidney Deane, who use the playground courts to earn a living. Both actors were given positive reviews as a comedic duo with credible basketball talent, despite a mediocre script that lacked originality. The movie was one the year's biggest successes, grossing $70 million.

Indecent Proposal (1993) costars Woody Harrelson, Demi Moore and Robert Redford in a movie asking the ageless question: "Would you sell your wife to another man for one night in exchange for $1 million?" Architect David Murphy (Harrelson) and real estate agent Diana Murphy (Moore) ponder the question posed by billionaire John Gage (Redford). Since the Murphys are financially constrained, they agree, and as the torment of her affair destroys their marriage, Gage does the noble act of discarding Diana, knowing she truly loves David. Despite the absurdity of the plot, and some critics being offended by the story's demeaning depiction of women, the acting was commendable, and audiences flocked to see the perennial box office stars shine, shelling out more than $93 million ($270 million internationally).

The movie actually entangled Harrelson in a lawsuit. He was sued by MGM for breach of contract when he abandoned the movie *Benny and Joon* to accept the more lucrative deal offered by *Indecent Proposal* after Charlie Sheen rejected the part. (Sheen also rejected the lead role in *White Men Can't Jump*.) After Harrelson met with Alan Ladd, Jr., the suit was settled when Paramount paid MGM $400,000. *Benny and Joon* was subsequently released starring Adrian Quinn and Mary Stuart Masterson and earned $20 million.

In *The Cowboy Way* (1994), Pepper Lewis (Harrelson) and Sonny Gilstrap

(Kiefer Sutherland) are two New Mexico roping champions who wind up in New York City to battle white slavers who kidnapped the daughter of their best friend. The movie provides some amusement, and Harrelson was praised for his comedic talents and sensuous performance, but critics were mostly appalled.

That same year, Woody starred in *Natural Born Killers*, in which two maniacs, Mickey Knox (Harrelson) and his co-conspirator wife, Mallory (Juliette Lewis), go on a killing spree that propels them into the limelight as heroes and media demigods. Critics alternately lauded and lambasted the film, though Harrelson was given good marks for breathing variety and color into his performance. Originally, Michael Madsen was cast for the part but Warner Brothers doubled Oliver Stone's budget specifically to cast Harrelson. Stone knew of Harrelson's troubled youth and notorious father, and after their meeting he immediately noticed the rage within the actor.

This movie actually cost Harrelson the lead role in John Grisham's autobiographical movie, *A Time to Kill*. Despite director Joel Schumacher urging the signing of Harrelson, Grisham, who has casting approval, vetoed the deal after watching *Natural Born Killers*. Grisham did not want a psycho-killer portraying him.

Relationships—Romantic

Woody began dating Glenn Close while they appeared in the play *Brooklyn Laundry* (1991). The relationship was short-lived and ended when they had emotional differences about him spending a vacation in Hawaii surfing with his friends. Other paramours have included Brooke Shields, Moon Unit Zappa, and Ally Sheedy. On a whim, in 1984 he traveled to Tijuana, Mexico, to marry Nancy Simon, Neil Simon's daughter, though two days later they returned to Los Angeles to divorce. One of Woody's longest relationships was with Carol Kane. It lasted 18 months but ended because of their conflicting views on monogamous relationships—Woody had a less traditional view of this moral issue.

Woody has always been outspoken about his views on sex. However, he has recently toned down the public pronouncement of his promiscuity to maintain a more private sex life. He is an admitted sex addict who needs immediate physical gratification in a romantic relationship. (He claims this is to compensate for shyness during his youth.) Though not absolutely ruling out the possibility of marriage in the future, Woody is not currently inclined towards matrimony; he cannot fathom being attracted to the same person for 20 years.

Woody's most recent love and current paramour is the mother of his children. Laura Louie (b. 1965), a former personal associate in Woody's production company Children at Play Productions for 2½ years, is a round-faced Asian woman who has a calming influence on Woody. She is serious-minded, spiritually inclined (some say she is psychic), and equally environmentally conscious. On February 26, 1993, Woody became a father for the first time with the birth of a daughter, Denni Montana Harrelson. Laura gave birth to their second child, Zoe, on September 22, 1996.

With a new relationship, Harrelson has somewhat modified his promiscuous behavior. Following the wisdom of the Orient, Harrelson has maintaned three-month periods of celibacy, due to the belief that releasing the seed reduces vitality.

Home Life

Woody, his younger brother Brett, Louie, and Denni currently reside in the chic Malibu Colony, bordering neighbors such as Johnny Carson and John McEnroe. Their three-bedroom beach house has a contemporary beige interior with a foot-high crystal amethyst, oriental statuettes, an oversize white couch, and abundant foliage towering into the open spaces. A Foosball table is strategically placed in the center of the entryway, and the floors are decorated in Mexican tiles. Outside is a large pool, a huge white teepee (to which friends are invited to drum and chant around a big crystal) and an abundance of barbells. He also owns homes in Paris, the mountains of Big Bear, and Beverly Hills, where a personal staff caters to his every need.

The Future

Woody remains busy as an entrepreneur of his company, Son International, which he established in 1986. The company produces and sells quirky items, such as water-powered wristwatches and round beach towels. He has also invested in the Hempstead Company of Costa Mesa, California, a business manufacturing hemp clothing, baggage, and additional essentials. Other avenues he is exploring include possibly opening a school for troubled children, but not in the Los Angeles area because he cannot tolerate breathing the air.

As for his forte, Woody recently contemplated leaving show business, but decided to continue making movies—movies that will shock people's emotions and awaken their hearts. *Natural Born Killers* (1994) represented such an out-of-character endeavor. With the success of "Cheers" and recent box office prosperity, Harrelson is poised to continue perusing an abundance of scripts with the luxury of being discerning before taking his next course of action.

Harrelson recently starred in three moderately successful movies within the last year: *Money Train* (1995), in which he plays an undercover decoy cop and costarring friend and regular feature film partner, Wesley Snipes; *Kingpin* (1996), a comedy costarring Randy Quaid; and *The People vs. Larry Flint*, a controversial account of the *Hustler* magazine founder.

Acting Credits

The following is a comprehensive list of Woody's career accomplishments.

TELEVISION: "Cheers" (series; episode "Birth, Death, Love, & Rice") 9.26.85 to 5.20.93 (NBC); "Bay Coven" (telefilm) 10.25.87 (NBC); "Killer Instinct" (telefilm) 11.22.88 (NBC); "Showtime Coast to Coast: All-Star Edition" (special) 4.21.90 (SHOWTIME); "Mother Goose Rock 'n' Rhyme" (special) 5.19.90 (DISNEY); "Showtime Comedy Club All-Star IV" 6.23.90 (SHOWTIME); "Back to School '92" (special) 9.8.92 (CBS); "In Concert" episode "Halloween Jam at Universal Studios" (cohost) 10.31.92 (ABC); "For Our Children" (special) 2.16.93 (DISNEY); "Saturday Night Live" (host) 5.14.94 (NBC); "The Simpsons" episode "Fear of Flying" (voice) 12.18.94 (FOX).

MOVIES: *Wildcats* (1986); *Eye of the Demon* (1987); *Cool Blue* (1988); *Casualties of War* (1989); *L.A. Story* (1991); *Doc Hollywood* (1991); *Ted and Venus* (1991); *White Men Can't Jump* (1992); *Indecent Proposal* (1993); *I'll Do Anything* (1994); *Natural Born Killers* (1994); *The Cowboy Way* (1994); *Money Train* (1995); *Kingpin* (1996); *The People vs. Larry Flint* (forthcoming); *Sunchasers* (forthcoming).

THEATRICAL PRODUCTIONS: *Biloxi Blues* (understudy, 1984); *The Boys Next Door* (1987); *The Zoo Story* (also producer); *2 on 2* (also writer and producer); *Brooklyn Laundry* (1991); *Furthest from the Sun* (also writer and director, 1993).

EMMY NOMINATIONS: Outstanding Supporting Actor in a Comedy Series, NBC ("Cheers," 1987–91).

AWARDS: Emmy: Outstanding Supporting Actor in a Comedy Series, NBC ("Cheers," 1989).

Shelley Long
(Diane Chambers)

Childhood

On August 23, 1949, Ivadine and Leland Long celebrated the birth of their only child, a daughter they named Shelley. Shelley was born in Fort Wayne,

Indiana, and attended Kekionga Junior High School and Southside High School. She liked the city's family-oriented structure and was particularly fond of its sense of history—the fort was named after "Mad" Anthony Wayne, a general during the French and Indian Wars, and her junior high school was named after a Native American village.

As an only child, Shelley never had to compete for her parents' love. Instead, she was their sole emotional focus, which put a great deal of pressure on her. Both parents provided positive reinforcement for her involvement in extracurricular activities (Brownies and Girl Scouts), so Shelley felt obligated to participate to please them.

Shelley's childhood was sprinkled with feline pets, which seem to be one of the few things that do not elicit an allergic reaction from her. Her allergies include household dust, wool, and many foods, such as dairy products, onions, mushrooms, garlic, chocolate, and very spicy foods.

One of Shelley's earliest childhood recollections is of an incident which occurred at the age of two or three. A woman visitor asked Shelley what she wanted to be when she grew up, and Shelley immediately responded she wanted to be a clown. Shelley believes children know what they need and want to be the moment they come into the world, and are inspired by the things around them. Naturally, she was inspired by the movies and theater, and dreamed of becoming a movie star.

Shelley often frequented the movies on weekend afternoons with her mother, and her father took her to plays at the Fort Wayne Civic Theater. At age 10, she was impressed by a production of *Othello*, and followed up this interest by playing the title role of Mama in the senior class production of *I Remember Mama*. Shelley's other artistic pleasures included singing, dancing, and performing puppet shows.

Although Shelley was only involved in one high school production, she was active in other theatrical endeavors. She worked on holiday assembly programs, wrote skits, and even performed skits in the school gymnasium. She was also involved in various competitions, such as public speaking, and dramatic and humorous interpretations. One of Shelley's most cherished moments in high school was during her senior year when she won a national title in Girls' Extemporaneous Speaking on a sex education topic.

Besides excelling in the arts, Shelley was an outstanding student academically, and enjoyed reading biographies on accomplished women such as Elizabeth Barrett Browning and Clara Barton. Academics even took precedence over social gatherings. Shelley did not have a serious romantic relationship until the end of her senior year.

Family and Relatives

Shelley's Presbyterian parents were elementary and junior high schoolteachers in Fort Wayne, Indiana, and are currently retired. The Longs lived in a nice residential section called Indian Village, which had been an actual Native American village named Kekionga. Most of the streets have Native American names, and residents often found artifacts while planting flowers.

Shelley had several relatives who lived nearby. Her aunt and uncle lived in Fort Wayne, and Shelley was especially close to their four children. Her grandmother lived in Lagro, a small town on the Wabash River, and on at least one Sunday every month, Shelley and her cousins would meet there for dinner.

Personal Characteristics

Shelley is 5'7" and weighs 115 pounds, with immense azure eyes and blonde, shoulder-length hair. Her features are near perfect, with a cameo face and complexion. She speaks slowly and collectedly in a tutorial-like manner, with a tone that can be simultaneously cordial and patronizing. Shelley has a sprightly disposition that is pragmatic, self-focused and controlled, yet she describes herself as anxious and worrisome (especially about offending others). For instance, after leaving "Cheers," Shelley had an overwhelming feeling that she had abandoned the cast and began fretting about negative fan reaction and the future success of the show.

Shelley has an internal drive and a self-determination to make things work. She is extremely independent and assertive, and has a clear sense of the priorities in her life. An obsessive compulsive about everything—clothes, hair, scenes—Shelley strives for perfection through endless practice and even records her interviews to improve her speech. Shelley has the ability to ad-lib under pressure and still remain spontaneously funny. She uniquely combines the qualities of warmth, humor and pretentiousness. For pleasure, Shelley enjoys watching movies and television, walking, and hiking; her vices include cigarettes, hot-fudge sundaes and caramel corn.

Several people have been influential in Shelley's life, especially her parents, who preached equality between the sexes. Other influences include Katharine Hepburn and Lucille Ball. Shelley most admires women who balance motherhood and a career. As a parent and schoolteacher, Shelley's mother proved that a woman can have a family and a career. Shelley admired Lucille Ball for the same reason; she was a marvelous actress and a wonderful comedienne, and still maintained a family. Moreover, Shelley admired actresses who could perform both drama and comedy, such as Hepburn, Ball, Thelma Ritter and Irene Dunne.

Shelley does not believe in a god figure but has many spiritual beliefs. She believes in existences beyond our own and that there is some very powerful energy force functioning in the universe. She believes individuals orchestrate their own lives, and the book *A Course in Miracles* has been influential in Shelley's spiritual evolution and the improvement of her "spiritual sight." Since spiritual well-being is the key to happiness, she seeks solace in the spiritual realm to manage her two loves: work and family.

Shelley is also active in self-improvement and self-knowledge techniques. In 1974, she began transcendental meditation as a release from the anxiety of her failed first marriage and exhaustion from working too hard. She practices relaxation techniques for 15 to 20 minutes, three times a day. In addition to meditation, Shelley is an ardent believer in visual programming. She believes there is good in the world, and a positive approach to life can generate more of the positive aspects. She receives part of this positive affirmation through psychotherapy which helps her deal with the dangers of success and how to interpret her dreams. Shelley is also an avid reader (especially of Carl Jung and psychological theories).

Another self-improvement technique Shelley practices is Reiki (pronounced rakey). This is a Japanese healing technique that energizes those who are tired, and is especially helpful for acute illnesses (cuts, headaches or stomachaches) and chronic illnesses (allergies and backaches). Shelley attests that Reiki alleviates the severity of her allergic reactions.

As for her personal philosophy, Shelley realizes professional success is not the same as happiness. She has achieved professional success—including Emmy and Golden Globe awards—but does not believe awards are the true measure of success. To achieve both professional success and happiness there must be people she cares for and people who care for her.

Education

After graduating from high school in 1967, Shelley followed the advice of a speech teacher who encouraged her to enroll in special acting classes at Northwestern University in Evanston, Illinois. The classes went well and she was subsequently accepted into the school's prestigious drama program. Her parents disapproved of this college major because they wanted Shelley to earn a teaching degree as an occupational safety net if her acting career did not materialize. However, the encouragement of professors gave Shelley the courage to pursue this career, notwithstanding her parents' disapproval.

While attending Northwestern, Shelley worked various on-campus jobs to pay for her education, but also enjoyed many extracurricular activities. She wrote poetry, accepted many theatrical roles, and even participated as a peaceful activist against the Vietnam War. However, after two years of academia,

Shelley felt suffocated and uninspired so she dropped out of college. She was tired of sitting in the classroom listening to people talk about acting—she wanted to be onstage.

Employment and Career Opportunities

In the summer of 1968, after one year at Northwestern, Shelley commenced an acting career by joining a summer stock company in western Illinois. Upon discovering the troupe was not very good, she returned for one more year of college, where campus roommate Ann Ryerson introduced Shelley to a modeling career posing for catalogues and magazines. After leaving Northwestern, Shelley continued searching for employment in the theater, primarily dramatic roles. Within a year she appeared in television commercials and became the television and radio spokesperson for Homemaker Furniture. During this time she was cast in the play *Jimmy Shine* and appeared in plays at Chicago's Candlelight Dinner Theatre and Ivanhoe Theatre.

Shelley's diversified interests and experience gave her a natural predilection toward television and film occupations, and her first husband, Ken (b. 1940), was instrumental in introducing her to the business. Ken started a business which created educational films for *Encyclopædia Britannica*, and solicited Shelley's writing skills for the endeavor. She began writing educational films, and eventually produced, wrote, and directed a series of industrial and educational films.

Shelley's film experience paved the way for her guest appearance on "Sorting It Out," a local television news magazine program (Chicago NBC affiliate station WMAQ, channel 5). In 1974, she was offered a job as the associate producer for the program, and by age 25 was the writer, associate producer, and cohost of the show. One illustration of Shelley's youthful ambition occurred when the producer asked her to find a poem to include with film footage about fall foliage. Shelley did not have time to locate a poem in the library, so she wrote one herself. She told the producer she had the perfect poem. When he asked who wrote it, she said "Shelley" (implying Percy Shelley), and the poem was aired. He eventually discovered the identity of the true poet, but was not too upset because he loved the verse.

As cohost of "Sorting It Out" for over two years, Shelley functioned as a television journalist—going on location to speak with people and then writing stories about them. The show became very successful and won three local Emmys (1974–76). The station then offered Shelley a permanent position as a newscaster.

In 1975, while Shelley was cohosting "Sorting It Out," producer-comedian Jim Fisher asked her to act in *The Graduates* (a minor film made by Second City comedians). At his and Ryerson's suggestion, Shelley joined a one-year weekend improvisational workshop, and eventually auditioned at Second City at the request of her improvisation teacher, Jo Forsberg. The founder and director of Second City, Bernie Sahlin, described Shelley's audition as "splendid"—she was poised and confident, did not exhibit stage fright, and was not afraid to attempt bold, outrageous things. Shelley performed well enough to be offered employment with the troupe.

This became a pivotal point in her career. Shelley was in her mid-twenties and had to reconcile a potentially successful career in broadcasting (because many women were achieving success in news) with the personally rewarding but financially constraining career with a theatrical company. In addition, Shelley had reservations about television because she was a familiar face around Chicago, and other stations around the country were mimicking her format. The station gave Shelley a grace period to decide her career path, so she flew to New York and Los Angeles to investigate career opportunities in broadcasting.

Shelley ultimately accepted the employment offer at Second City along with a significant pay cut. The primary reason for choosing this career path was the reputation of Second City as a prestigious stepping stone for many successful actors. Bernie Sahlin was known for having nurtured the careers of Bill Murray, Gilda Radner, John Belushi, and Alan Arkin. Other Second City alumni include Jim Belushi, Joan Rivers, George Wendt, Ed Asner and John Candy. The other reason was employment satisfaction. Since money was never the primary purpose for becoming an actress, Shelley was content knowing she would probably never become a millionaire but could still attain success.

Acting Career

In August 1976 Shelley replaced Ryerson (who moved to Los Angeles) and debuted in the troupe's 53rd revue, *North by North Wells* (deriving the title from Second City's address at 1616 North Wells in Chicago). Second City was a time of personal growth for Shelley. She experienced sibling rivalry for the first time in her life. As an only child she never had to compete for attention, but at Second City she found herself battling other actors for the adoration of Bernie Sahlin and his wife, who were like parents to the group. Shelley felt threatened and uncomfortable, but described it as one of the fullest years of her career because she sang, played comedy, and developed the character Mildred (an eccentric bag lady with a squeaky Midwestern voice).

Will, one of Shelley's friends, named the Mildred character. Whenever Shelley would begin speaking in that Midwestern tone, Will would say, "Now, Mildred!" In Shelley's life, Mildred represents the spirit of Indiana and a combination of several women she knew as a child, but mostly her late grandmother. Shelley describes Mildred as more than a character, almost an alter

Shelley Long

ego. Ever since Second City, Shelley has used Mildred in her work and would still like to develop a screenplay featuring the character.

As for Shelley's acting methodology, she has a well thought-out approach. She asks numerous questions, especially about character motivation, which drives everyone, including herself, crazy. However, this allows her to give the best performance—to attain perfection.

Second City was also the place where Shelley was "discovered." In late 1977, two producers saw a tape of her performance and went to see her live at the Second City Theater. They were impressed and offered Shelley a long-term contract with ABC, which she willingly accepted.

Hollywood—Early Years

When Shelley signed with ABC in 1978, she drove her Honda to Los Angeles to begin working on a television pilot—two musical comedy-variety programs titled, "That Thing on ABC" and "That Second Thing on ABC." Interestingly enough, one of the scenes featured a character vaguely resembling Diane Chambers. She also made a guest appearance on "The Love Boat."

One year later, Shelley appeared in many successful television programs, two television pilots, and one television movie. After a barrage of exposure at the end of the decade, ABC put Shelley on hold, so she began focusing on feature films. Her silver screen debut was in *A Small Circle of Friends* (1980), which led to her sophomore appearance in *Caveman* (1981), and then a more significant role in *Night Shift* (1982). It was during the filming of *Night Shift* that Shelley was offered the part of Diane Chambers on "Cheers."

"Cheers"—Getting the Part

In 1981, the producers of the successful and critically acclaimed television show "Taxi" were casting a new series, "Cheers." Shelley's manager, Marty Mickelson, sent her the "Cheers" script, and she read for the part. Although impressed with the script's quality and superior writing, Shelley was hesitant to commit to a television show because her movie career appeared to be taking off, and she did not know whether television was the direction she wanted her career to go. But when she read for the part, the producers laughed in all the right places, and it just felt right.

After the audition Shelley told the producers she preferred reading with Ted Danson because there was a special chemistry between them. James Burrows (a producer of the show) agreed so they were paired for the audition for Paramount and NBC executives. Shelley was signed by NBC to a long-term contract; however, credit billing was another issue. To give equal billing, Long and costar Ted Danson were placed on the screen concurrently with his name at lower-left and her name at upper-right.

"Cheers"—In the Beginning

The typical television contract runs for seven years, so Shelley had to fight for a five-year deal. She had mixed emotions about such a long-term commitment with a series she knew nothing about. Her movie career was gaining momentum and she wanted to continue that aspect of her career. The producers assured her they would work around her schedule, and they did, but it was not easy.

The success of "Cheers" was partially due to the quality writing to which Shelley also contributed. When the writers had problems with the scripts, they often consulted Shelley to smooth out the trouble areas. Unfortunately, her perfectionism often entailed line by line discussions, pondering minute details of the script, and creating an inordinate amount of additional work for the producers and writers.

"Cheers"—Diane Chambers

Shelley has made certain observations and comments about her "Cheers" character. She considers Diane to be a likable character, but aggravating at times. On the positive side, Shelley has increased her vocabulary tremendously—there are very few words Diane did not use.

One interesting corollary is the striking similarity between the actress and the character. Shelley cringes whenever she is compared to Diane Chambers, but it is an intriguing topic worthy of discussion. Both stress the thinking element of being, are intelligent, and strive for precision in thought. Both are bright, well-educated, and highly articulate (and give paragraph-size answers to simple questions). Their work, lifestyles and attitudes are neatly compartmentalized, and they are well-groomed (Shelley has every strand of blonde hair meticulously in place—even during rehearsals). In addition, they also participate in psychotherapy and meditation.

Shelley prefers to stress the differences between her and Diane. First, she was never a waitress. Second, her career, love life and family are stable, whereas Diane's life was out of control as she floundered in work and love. The most significant difference is that Shelley has a sense of the real world; she is better able to balance her intellect and emotions, and is more in touch with her feelings, intuitions and sensations. In contrast, Diane often confused intellect and emotion by allowing the former to stimulate the latter. Although she strived for an objective analysis of her feelings, intuitions and sensations, Diane often allowed her logical, rational and analytical mind to be overcome by her hedonistic desires.

Shelley has long endured comparisons to Diane Chambers, but was particularly upset when certain writers decided both identities were exactly alike. As the years passed, the other actors, and maybe even herself, confused Shelley with the character Diane. Shelley admits some of Diane's mannerisms may have carried over into her own life, but stresses she always tried to maintain an identity separate from her character. This became even more apparent when Shelley tried to abandon the Diane persona. She spent years trying to lose the voice of Diane and to modify her mannerisms. According to Shelley, regardless of how many showers you take per day, when you go home it is very difficult to divorce yourself from the character.

The striking resemblance between Shelley and Diane even parallels their childhoods—feline pets, high school and college acting credits, and a preference for cultural activities, such as the opera and theater. In sum, there may be differences between Shelley and Diane, but the two identities coalesced to the point where Shelley had to make a conscious effort to create a separate and distinct identity.

"Cheers"—Leaving

Although Shelley mentioned the possibility of not renewing her contract at the end of the fifth season, in July 1986 she and Ted Danson interrupted a writing session (something they did only once or twice in five years) to find out when Sam and Diane were going to be married. The producers reminded Shelley that she might be leaving the show, but then arranged for Sam and Diane to wed.

In December 1986, shortly after taping the engagement episode, Shelley officially notified the producers she was leaving the series and would not renew her contract. The timing of her notice proved problematic because they had only three weeks to decide on an ending for the season finale before taping commenced. The producers offered her a $500,000 salary increase to stay, but she declined.

Shelley had several legitimate reasons for leaving "Cheers." First, she did not want to be typecast or identified as one character. And she saw no future for Diane as a character except going to the altar. Second, Shelley began acting like Diane and acquiring her mannerisms. When people on the street began treating her like Diane, Shelley knew it was best to abandon that persona.

Third, she wanted to pursue other projects (especially movies) that she did not have time to develop while costarring in "Cheers." Earlier that year, Shelley signed a three-year film contract with Walt Disney to develop, produce, and star in various projects. The opportunity to pursue feature films appealed to her because it represented a new challenge and an opportunity to broaden her life. However, Shelley did not abandon the idea of another television series role, she merely wanted to wait until one came along that felt right.

Finally, Shelley wanted to spend more time with her family. She worked year round in a very hectic schedule—on "Cheers" full-time for seven months and in movies during the five-month off-season. She resolved not to have work interfere with her health, family, and personal relationships. Shelley did not thrive on pain and suffering, and strived to minimize re-experiencing the turmoil that plagued her first marriage.

One of the most difficult aspects of leaving "Cheers" was saying goodbye. Thoughts of missing the cast and crew were legitimate because of the wonderful work they did together. But like any family, she felt the need to do her own thing (though have a reunion now and then). In addition, Shelley experienced tension and hostility from the cast. At times they treated her like she was going to die, and near the end she was treated like she *was* Diane. In one incident, Shelley was trapped behind a piece of furniture. When someone attempted to assist her, Ted Danson said, "Hey, guys. Let's think about this." Danson was furious, and admits his reaction was out of fear that Shelley was irreplaceable and the show would fail without her. Even though they rarely socialized off the set, Shelley still considered him a friend, but felt she knew Sam Malone better than Ted Danson.

"Cheers"—The Final Episode

When the creators of "Cheers" invited Shelley to participate in the show's finale, she gladly accepted and enjoyed the opportunity to reconnect with the cast. For years, however, she had tried to lose the voice of Diane, and now she had to recapture it again. A critical review of her performance in the final episode indicates she needed more practice because Diane Chambers too closely resembled Susan DeRuzzo (Shelley's "Good Advice" character). Notwithstanding this review, Shelley received an Emmy nomination for her performance. Although insisting that her departure from "Cheers" in 1987 was positive, Shelley admits her return to the final episode provided a better sense of closure.

Movies

Shelley has been involved in many movies since arriving in Los Angeles in 1979, but few have been successful at the box office. Her laudable performance as Diane Chambers and the acclaim that accompanied it was not enough to solidify Shelley as a box office attraction. One of the primary reasons was her abandonment of the "Cheers" persona which was the critical basis for her public image and recognition.

In her early years, Shelley's success steadily increased as her roles expanded. The small role as a militant college student in *A Small Circle of Friends* (1980) launched her movie career. Then came the limited auditory role as prehistoric cavewoman Tala, love mate of the tribe leader (Ringo Starr) in the financially successful spoof *Caveman* (1981). Shelley thought *Caveman* would propel her forward, but instead she spent the following 11 months without work because the industry went on strike. She used this time to reflect upon her life, goals, and priorities, and also met her second husband.

After the 11-month hiatus, Shelley expanded her range of acting abilities in *Night Shift* (1982), in which she plays a sweet hooker working out of a morgue with Michael Keaton and Henry Winkler as her pimp. Shelley's appearance in "Cheers" prompted more substantial movie roles. In *Losin' It*

(1983), she continues the sexually provocative theme as a horny housewife who drives a carload of teens to Tijuana, Mexico, and seduces Tom Cruise's character. During this time, Orion pictures hired her to cowrite a sorority version of *Animal House,* but the film was never produced.

The following year Shelley costarred with Ryan O'Neal and Drew Barrymore in the most difficult role of her career. In *Irreconcilable Differences* (1984), Shelley plays a writer who undergoes radical personality changes within a 10-year period, and is sued by her daughter for a legal separation. The movie had limited financial success, but the critics applauded Shelley's performance as a combination of Meryl Streep and Mary Tyler Moore—an intellectual girl next door with humor and heart-warming charm.

Two years later, Shelley costarred with Tom Hanks in Steven Spielberg's *The Money Pit* (1986). This film had box office success, earning over $30 million, but the critics thrashed David Giler for writing an incredibly weak script. Shelley was praised for her comedic ability and was described as coyly cute, even when the script left her stranded.

The ensuing feature film *Outrageous Fortune* (1987) became Shelley's most successful movie to date, earning over $60 million, though this was partially due to costar Bette Midler. Shelley was initially signed with top billing, but everything changed when Midler joined the cast. The billing had to be renegotiated; the resolution was for Shelley to have top billing west of the Mississippi River and Midler in the eastern half of the country.

In this movie, two dichotomously opposed actresses team up to find their two-timing lover, Michael (Peter Coyote), who mysteriously disappears. Shelley plays a snobby New York actress, and Midler plays a streetwise, soft-core porn star. Critics were divisive in their reviews, but agreed that Shelley's range was being restricted by playing another straight-laced intellectual. Shelley disliked making the movie because it was physically exhausting (including mountain climbing, fencing and ballet), but was pleased with the end result.

Shelley had her first lead role in *Hello Again* (1987), which was part of her contractual obligation with Walt Disney Studios. In this sophisticated comedy, she plays a housewife who dies but gets another chance at life. The critics were merciless in their scalding criticism of the film, and it faltered financially.

In *Troop Beverly Hills* (1989), Shelley's character, Phyllis Nefler, is a ditsy Beverly Hills princess who functions as the leader of her daughter's pampered troop of wilderness girls. Once again the movie was berated by critics and floundered at the box office, grossing approximately $10 million.

Shelley's follow-up movie, *Don't Tell Her It's Me* (1990), costars Steve Guttenberg and Jami Gertz. Shelley plays a romance novelist who transforms her nerdy, overweight, but endearing brother (Guttenberg) into a gorgeous biker named Lobo. The physical, attitudinal, and identity reconstruction is a combined effort to help him win the heart of an attractive journalist (Gertz).

Critics praised the acting for salvaging humor out of a senseless story line, but the movie waned at the box office.

Two years later, Shelley was paired with another big-name actor, Corbin Bernsen, in *Frozen Assets* (1992), but it also represented another feature film disappointment for Shelley. She plays a strait-laced manager of a sperm bank whose new boss (Bernsen) is a dumb junior bank executive from Los Angeles. Shelley's character, Dr. Grace Murdock, is appalled at the corporate executive's idea to hold a contest for the largest sperm count in order to fill a sales order, but subsequently falls in love with him. Critics reacted with derision to the bad taste, ludicrous plot twists, and overly abundant absurdities.

Shelley's latest films, *The Brady Bunch Movie* (1995) and *A Very Brady Sequel* (1996), are part of a recent Hollywood trend to revive classic television programs from a prior generation. Shelley plays the role of the mother, Carol Brady, and although receiving top billing and favorable press, her roles were somewhat limited because the story lines concentrated on the time-warp exploits of the Brady children. The movies received favorable reviews and were box office successes, grossing over $50 million and $20 million, respectively.

Career—Television

After her departure from "Cheers," Shelley had various sitcom offers which she rejected because they seemed like variations of her previous role. It took six years before she agreed to do another sitcom. "Good Advice" was her own creation, an idea she had in 1991 when thinking about a therapist in need of some advice herself. Shelley took the idea to Jeff Sagansky, a CBS entertainment chief, who had given her a standing offer for a series if she devised one she liked. Shelley involved her production company (Itzbinso Long Productions) in the series, hired her manager (Marty Mickelson) as executive co-producer, and became active in selecting the cast.

"Good Advice" debuted Friday, April 2, 1993, and revolved around a troubled marriage counselor and best-selling author, Susan DeRuzzo, who catches her husband (Christopher McDonald) cheating on her. More problems arise when a divorce attorney (Treat Williams) rents office space across the hall from her office, and they take turns stealing each other's clients. Despite a healthy debut (ranking 35th), the show's remaining five episodes plummeted to the depths of the Nielsen ratings. Nevertheless, "Good Advice" was signed for another 13 episodes for the 1993-94 season. To bolster sagging ratings, the show added Teri Garr to play the role of Shelley's sister-in-law.

The second season was hindered and delayed by Shelley's relapse of the flu and an allergic reaction to antibiotic medication. Some sources claim she collapsed because of an inability to handle the daily rigors of a weekly series. Other sources speculated about a nervous breakdown, money battles with the network, and an ego clash with costar Teri Garr. If delays were not enough, the critics panned the show for its strained acting, writing, and humor. "Good Advice" was perceived as Shelley's fatal attempt to resurrect the death of her movie career—illustrative of either the lack of movie offers or a career in a tail-spin. After a disastrous second season in the ratings, and only 17 episodes in two years, "Good Advice" was canceled.

Relationships—Employment

Shelley earned a reputation as being a difficult coworker, and as she pre-pared to depart from "Cheers" there were rumors of backstage tantrums, cast disputes, and clashing egos. However, some people who have worked with her claim this allegation was overblown. Gary H. Miller, a creative consultant for "Good Advice," claimed the series was never smooth, but Shelley was not an egomaniac and was quite amenable and resigned as an actress. But the rumors continued.

One of the most publicized contentions was her working relationship with Bette Midler. In *Outrageous Fortune* (1987), Long and Midler were specifically cast for the parts because they were complete opposites which cre-ated a natural antagonistic chemistry. They undoubtedly had contradictory act-ing methods, but Long denied reports they were acrimonious offscreen. She claims they did not have time to become friends during the filming, but did so afterwards. Long blamed the stress of filmmaking—the bad weather, Midler's pregnancy, and the physical exhaustion of acting in the scenes—as the hinderance to their bonding.

Relationships—Romantic

Shelley has had very few romantic relationships in her life. Her first seri-ous relationship did not develop until the end of her senior year of high school, and during college there was only one man she thought she loved. After col-lege she moved to Chicago, where the 20-year-old aspiring actress met and married Ken, a 30-year-old local director and producer. They collaborated on educational and industrial films, but divorced after a few years. It was a brief marriage, and one she describes as a mistake.

Shelley is extremely hesitant to discuss this time of her life, but acknowl-edges she and Ken remain friends. She admits the marriage failed due to their work commitments and inability to reserve time for one another. They loved working, but their dedication and long hours impeded the marital bond. Some-how the marriage was lost among all the films and other projects.

Another significant factor was Ken's inability to cope with Shelley's career aspirations of working on television and in theater. She always supported his career, but when she wanted to go forward with hers, Ken did not reciprocate. Their marital difficulties escalated after she accepted employment with a local television station. During their separation she became cohost of the show "Sorting It Out," and continued in that position after the divorce was finalized.

Shelley's second husband and current paramour is Bruce Tyson (b. 1953). They met in 1979, during Shelley's embryonic but burgeoning acting career. Shelley's college friend, Ann Ryerson, was involved in arranging Shelley's romance with Bruce. After winning dinner for four at a Los Angeles restaurant on a charity benefit roulette wheel, Bruce invited Ryerson and her husband to accompany him. They in turn brought Shelley as a blind date.

Shelley thought Bruce was stunning the moment she met him and noticed a profound emotional attraction resonating between them. The connection hit like bells ringing. He matched her image of the perfect man—an image she never realized she had developed before that night. Although Bruce did not have the same earth shattering experience when he first met Shelley, within two years, on October 16, 1981, they exchanged wedding vows on the steps of Beverly Hills City Hall in a legal ceremony for their immediate families. They reenacted another wedding ceremony the next day at Santa Monica Park in a spiritual (nondenominational) service for their friends. (Embossed on the cover of their wedding scrapbook is the phrase "An Entyson Shellebration.")

Bruce is 6'6", a financial analyst, and the father of Shelley's only child, Juliana (b. 3-27-85). Shelley loves his sense of humor and describes Bruce as witty, handsome, self-confident, intelligent, quietly spoken, easygoing and patient. Bruce is not a womanizer or a braggart, and is very romantic—he loves giving flowers, gifts and jewelry. Bruce was an athlete, which is a type of man Shelley did not usually gravitate toward; she was more interested in the lean, suffering types—the poets.

Motherhood

One of Shelley and Bruce's first arguments was about having children. Bruce wanted children from day one, but Shelley was against the idea at first. All her life she had wanted a career and by 1981 it was starting to take off, so she did not want to give it up to have a baby. They compromised by delaying parenthood for several years. When they finally agreed on starting a family, Shelley planned her pregnancy around her work schedule. She did not want the birth to interfere with the taping of "Cheers" or her film career, so she tried to schedule a March birth. This would coincide with the season finale of "Cheers" and give her two months before the start of her next movie.

Unfortunately, Shelley's scheduling of the birth was not an exact science.

Juliana was born one month after the season finale of "Cheers," but only two and one-half weeks before the filming of *The Money Pit*. Juliana accompanied her mother on location in New York, and upon returning home to Los Angeles, attended a neighborhood Presbyterian church nursery school. Juliana continues to accompany Shelley on location for the filming of her movies.

Shelley treasures motherhood. The experience has heightened her awareness and understanding about living, her body, and being a woman. She is now able to feel things on a deeper level, which has expanded her range as an actress. Shelley believes the most important aspect of motherhood is the quality (not quantity) of time spent with Juliana—the feelings and connections to her child. Despite her deep love for Juliana, Shelley still insists on having a family *and* career. She believes they are compatible, and that acting enables her to bring her best energy to Juliana—more love, more magic, more energy. In 1989, Shelley attempted parenthood one more time, but the pregnancy tragically ended with a miscarriage.

In 1990, Shelley and Bruce paid $3 million for a 7,000 square foot, two-story, four-bedroom Pacific Palisades home resting on a half-acre of land with an ocean view. It is complete with seven baths, a tennis court, pool, spa, and fountains. In terms of household chores, Shelley does not clean or do laundry and only cooks occasionally. Their activities are centered around a family-oriented lifestyle, like picnicking or casual strolls to a nearby park that overlooks the ocean. They entertain at home for friends and family and occasionally host an industry gathering.

Balancing Career and Family

Shelley and Bruce both want successful careers, but also desire a successful relationship and family. Shelley strives to balance these seemingly conflicting activities and feels the absence of either component would leave a huge, unfulfilled gap in her life. Accordingly, each component must take priority at different times—sometimes Bruce, sometimes Juliana, and sometimes her career.

Shelley learned from the mistakes of her first marriage. Although work is important, she no longer does it day and night, and makes a conscious effort to devote time exclusively to her marriage. Every Wednesday is date night. She and Bruce reserve this night to get away from their daily routine to spend quality time together—at the ballet, a restaurant, or the movies. The dating ritual is a vital means of rejuvenating their relationship, since they rarely see each other during the week.

Relationship tensions reach an apex when Shelley is on location filming a movie. While in New York filming *The Money Pit*, she and Bruce tried to develop intimacy through telephone conversations (which was not easy), and

Bruce flew to New York every other weekend. According to Shelley, they were able to establish an emotional connection through silent moments on the telephone that was better than holding hands, kissing or hugging. The filming experience of *Hello Again* paralleled *The Money Pit*, and created the same relationship problems. The stresses of their Hollywood lifestyle has forced them to attend marriage improvement seminars, attempt active listening techniques, and undergo therapy to solidify their relationship.

Shelley realizes success is addictive. When things are going well, it is difficult to stop, and the abundance of opportunities compels further pursuit. She also realizes success is satisfaction from work, whatever you do, and it is especially important to stop and rest—to tune into your inner experiences, otherwise you will die spiritually or physically.

The Future

As for her career, Shelley maintains a production company (Itzbinso Long Productions) at Walt Disney Studios and will continue to develop, produce, and star in various projects. With the success of the *Brady Bunch* movies, she is likely to star in additional feature films, and will probably increase her exposure with more substantial headlining roles.

As for her family, Juliana's birth in 1985 represented a major decision in Shelley's life. She always said if she was going to have children, she would have a lot. However, Shelley was 35 years old when Juliana was born, and over 10 years have passed since. Thus, it is likely that Juliana will remain an only child. Since Shelley remains genuinely career-oriented, it is likely she is content with one child and a handful of career options.

Acting Credits

The following is a comprehensive list of Shelley's television, movie and theatrical accomplishments.

TELEVISION: "Sorting It Out" (news magazine show) 1974–76 (NBC); "That Thing on ABC" (special) 1.4.78 (ABC); "The Love Boat Valentine Special" episode "Computer Man" 2.13.78 (ABC); "That Second Thing on ABC" (special) 3.8.78 (ABC); "Family" episode "Sleeping Over" 2.1.79 (ABC); "The Cracker Factory" (telefilm) 3.16.79 (ABC); "Young Guy Christian" (pilot) 5.24.79 (ABC); "The Dooley Brothers" (pilot) 7.31.79 (CBS); "Trapper John, M.D." episode "The Shattered Image" 10.28.79 (CBS); "M*A*S*H" episode "Bottle Fatigue" 1.7.80 (CBS); "Ghost of a Chance" (pilot) 7.7.80 (ABC); "The Promise of Love" (telefilm) 11.11.80 (CBS); "The Princess and the Cabbie" (telefilm) 11.3.81 (CBS); "Cheers" (series) 9.30.82 to 5.7.87 (NBC); "TV Censored Bloopers—No. 5" (special) 2.14.83 (NBC); "NBC All-Star Hour" (special) 9.12.83 (NBC); "All-Star Party for Lucille Ball" (special) 12.9.84 (CBS); "Second City 25th Anniversary Special" (special) 4.13.85 (NBC); "An American Portrait" episode "Richard Outcault" 3.27.86 (CBS); "NBC's 60th Anniversary Celebration" (special) 5.12.86 (NBC); "Secrets Women Never Share" (special) 12.14.87 (NBC); "Happy Birthday, Bob" (special) 5.16.88 (NBC); "Bob Hope's Super Bowl Party" (special) 1.21.89 (NBC); "The 75th Anniversary of Beverly Hills" (special) 2.26.89 (ABC); "Friday Night Videos" (host) 3.17.89 (NBC); "Smothers Brothers Comedy Hour" episode "Fun and Games" 8.2.89 (CBS); "Voices Within: The Lives of Truddi Chase" (miniseries) 5.20.90 to 5.21.90 (ABC); "Cheers" episode "Cheers 200th Episode Celebration" 11.8.90 (NBC); "The Best of Disney: 50 Years of Magic" (special) 5.20.91 (ABC); "Memories of M*A*S*H" (host) 11.25.91 (CBS); "Fatal Memories" (telefilm) 11.9.92 (NBC); "A Message from Holly" (telefilm) 12.13.92 (CBS); "Good Advice" (series) 4.2.93 to 8.10.94 (CBS); "Cheers" episode "One for the Road" 5.20.93 (NBC); "Basic Values: Sex Shock & Censorship in the '90s" (special) 9.10.93 (SHOWTIME); "Shelley Duvall's Bedtime Stories" episode "Ruby the Copy Cat" 10.20.93 (SHOWTIME); "Scene Screen" with Angela Stribling 10.21.93 (BET); "Frasier" episode "Adventures in Paradise" (Part 2 of 2) 11.22.94 (NBC); "Women of Spring Break" (telefilm) 1.10.95 (CBS); "Freaky Friday" (telefilm) 5.6.95 (ABC); "Comic Relief VII" (special) 11.11.95 (HBO); "Lois & Clark: The New Adventures of Superman" episode "Ultra Woman" 11.12.95 (ABC); "Murphy Brown" episode "Dick and Dottie" 11.27.95 (CBS); "Frasier" episode "The Show Where Diane Comes Back" 2.13.96 (NBC).

MOVIES: *A Small Circle of Friends* (1980); *Caveman* (1981); *Night Shift* (1982); *Losin' It* (1983); *Irreconcilable Differences* (1984); *The Money Pit* (1986); *Outrageous Fortune* (1987); *Hello Again* (1987); *Troop Beverly Hills* (1989); *Don't Tell Her It's Me* (1990); *Frozen Assets* (1992); *The Brady Bunch Movie* (1995); *A Very Brady Sequel* (1996).

THEATRICAL PRODUCTIONS: *Jimmy Shine; The Woolgatherer* (1981).

PRODUCING CREDITS: Associate producer: "Sorting It Out"; Co-producer: *Hello Again* (1987); *Outrageous Fortune* (1987); *Troop Beverly Hills* (1989); "Good Advice" (Itzbinso Long Productions, 1993–94); "Voices Within: The Lives of Truddi Chase" (miniseries, 1990).

WRITING: "Sorting It Out."

EMMY NOMINATIONS: Outstanding Achievement for Entertainment Programs for a Series, NBC, WMAQ-TV (cohost "Sorting It Out," 1974–76); Outstanding Lead Actress in a Comedy Series, NBC ("Cheers," 1983–86); Outstanding Guest Actress in a Comedy Series, NBC ("Cheers," 1993); Outstanding Guest Actress in a Comedy Series, NBC ("Frasier," 1996).

AWARDS: Outstanding Achievement for Entertainment Programs for a Series, NBC, WMAQ-TV (cohost "Sorting It Out," 1974–76); Emmy: Outstanding Lead Actress in a Comedy Series, NBC ("Cheers," 1983); Golden Globe: Best Television Supporting Actress, NBC ("Cheers," 1983); Golden Globe: Best Television Actress in a Comedy, NBC ("Cheers," 1985).

Bebe Neuwirth
(Lilith Sternin-Crane)

Childhood

On December 31, 1959, Beatrice "Bebe" Neuwirth was born in Newark, New Jersey, the daughter of Lee Paul and Sydney Anne Neuwirth. Her German-American father is a mathematician who taught periodically at Princeton University. He also worked for the Institute of Defense Analysis where he developed an encrypter used to ensure information safety. Her Russian-American mother is a painter and former amateur dancer with the Princeton Regional Ballet. Bebe's brother, Peter, is a Harvard University graduate and a mathematician currently working as an actuary.

Bebe was raised in Princeton, New Jersey, and admits to being a problem child. Her days were filled with indolence and youthful disobedience. Bebe's moderately wild adolescence included being arrested for smoking marijuana when she was 13 years old and coasting through school (learning some French in the process). Her father agreed that raising Bebe was occasionally difficult because she was very independent, fierce, and determined. Her mother also remembers Bebe exerting independence through ballet. She was a willful little ballerina who would commence with a very graceful bourrée step and then radically shift to a jazz flourish finale.

At age four, Bebe fondly remembers accompanying her mother to see *The Nutcracker*. She was mesmerized by the dancing and desperately wanted to begin ballet lessons. The following year, Bebe started ballet classes and has danced onstage since age seven. She always dreamed of becoming a ballet dancer, and the only other career she seriously contemplated was being a veterinarian on the side.

Unfortunately, at age 13 or 14 Bebe realized her ballerina dream would never materialize. Despite having a petite ballerina's body and being fast and light onstage, Bebe's level of strength and technique was limited, her training outside of New York restricted her development, and she definitely had flat feet. Although crushed emotionally, she quickly found a comparable career in dance. When Bebe was 15 years old, she accompanied a friend to Manhattan to see Bob Fosse's musical *Pippen*. The intriguing production helped Bebe realize that dancing was an attainable field of study. Although it could never replace ballet, the musical *Pippen* helped Bebe make the transition from ballet to Broadway.

Personal Life

Bebe is much more multifaceted than her austere character Lilith, but describes herself in colors a shade closer—an innocent, very cerebral intellectual with limited social and interpersonal skills. Although she appears unapproachable and radiates callousness from behind a wall of reserve, Bebe is actually a loving, giving person.

Since her introduction to pottery by a costar in 1986, Bebe has immersed herself in this craft and continues taking lessons. She thoroughly enjoys pottery because she loves working with the earth to create personal masterpieces. Bebe eats from self-made dishes, and around the home unabashedly displays her favorite creations—plates, pitchers, bowls, and vases. Besides this hobby, Bebe remains true to her trade by dancing daily, which has been her ritual since she was a child. In addition, she rarely drinks alcohol, though occasionally has champagne at an opening, anniversary or birthday party.

As for her philosophy for a happy life, Bebe advocates following your heart when pursuing individual interests and desires; and to avoid entrenchment in a lifestyle or occupation lacking personal satisfaction. In other words, live your own life, and not the life of other people. According to Bebe, if you fail to be true to yourself and do not pursue your love, everything will be altered by choosing the wrong path. And she speaks from experience. Bebe does not want other people to sabotage their lives as she has had a tendency to do with her own.

Education and Career

In 1976 Bebe was accepted to study modern American dance at the prestigious Juilliard School in New York City. She immediately hated the school and only lasted one year because there was absolutely no Broadway training. According to Bebe, the Juilliard instructors denigrated Broadway as an artistic outlet and fostered a stifling creative environment. Her parents supported her decision to leave Juilliard and recommended that Bebe live in New York City to acquire a degree from the school of hard knocks. After leaving Juilliard in 1977, Bebe moved into a YWCA and enrolled in singing lessons and jazz classes.

Within a year, at age 18, Bebe landed a chorus spot in an international company production of *A Chorus Line* (1978–81), and in 1980 performed the show on Broadway. Other musicals followed: *West Side Story* (1981), *Little Me* (1982), *Upstairs at O'Neal's* (1982–83), and *The Road to Hollywood* (1984). Bebe was the principle dancer in *Dancin'* (1982), and the choreographer and lead dancer in *Kicks* (1984).

"Cheers"—Getting the Part

In 1985, Bebe was in Los Angeles awaiting the commencement of her Tony award–winning role in *Sweet Charity*. Despite lacking acting experience in a play or stage comedy, she used the spare time to audition for the one-time-only role of Dr. Lilith Sternin on "Cheers." Although Bebe never envisioned acting in a television series, she received the part. Irrespective of her reluctance to do television, Bebe resolved that playing Lilith was not much different than acting on the stage—it was just another character.

Dr. Lilith Sternin was first introduced to "Cheers" while on a date with Dr. Frasier Crane. The entire evening was disastrous, and they parted ways, but not without indulging in outrageously humorous, intellectually acrimonious banter. Bebe's character perfectly complemented Frasier's self-indulgent pomposity, and the writers so thoroughly enjoyed writing her lines that Lilith was repeatedly reintroduced into the script. Thus, she returned the following season to debate Frasier on a televised psychology program during which their repressed physical attraction to one another manifested itself in discourse laced with sexual metaphors. In 1987 Bebe joined the popular television series as a recurring regular, playing the obdurate, sensual psychiatrist with the dour, deadpan delivery. In time she and Frasier luxuriated in cohabitation, marriage (with a brief separation after seven years), and parenthood.

Bebe was fond of her character's honesty and sincerity, and could relate to Lilith's innocence and social ignorance. She thought Lilith was incapable of anything malicious, and abhorred people classifying Lilith as a yuppie, because that had nothing to do with her persona. Lilith was a scientist with feelings, and if she appeared cool and hard, it was not intended.

Although Bebe played the robotic-voiced, ghostly-complexioned psychiatrist for seven years, she left the cast as a regular at the beginning of the final season (though she returned briefly in 1993 for two guest appearances). A script was written for Lilith to have an affair and depart with her lover to live in an Ecopod. During her reign as the formidable doctor, Bebe earned two Emmy awards for Best Supporting Actress (1990, 1991).

Bebe claims to have left the show because it was time for a change, but emphasizes it was not based on discomfort with any cast members or the desire to entertain film or stage offers. Bebe saw her career as having a natural progression, and it seemed appropriate not to commit to another year on the show. Her lifelong goal has been to be a dancer, and since a dancer's career longevity is limited, Bebe wanted to be onstage and not forego another year's worth of performances.

Bebe Neuwirth

Other Acting Endeavors

After leaving "Cheers" Bebe continued working on television. Besides involvement in M & M advertisements, she appeared in the television miniseries "Wild Palms" (1993). In 1994, Bebe revisited her role as Lilith by making guest appearances on the NBC hit sitcom "Frasier" (a "Cheers" spin-off) starring Kelsey Grammer. Lilith was reintroduced in "Frasier" because the producers and writers wanted to provide a sense of closure to prove she and Frasier had both gone on with their lives. In the February 3, 1994, episode, Lilith shared a romantic evening with her ex-husband, which became the highest rated "Frasier" episode for the entire season.

The success of this episode prompted the producers to have Lilith return the following season for a two-part episode on November 15 and 22, 1994, in which she inadvertently met Frasier as he shared a romantic weekend on an island paradise with a new girlfriend. Frasier spent the remainder of the vacation trying to prove he was over Lilith and having a fabulous time. Once again, Bebe's appearance was one of the highest rated "Frasier" episodes of the season, and she earned an Emmy nomination for Outstanding Guest Actress in a Comedy Series for her role.

During her time at "Cheers," Bebe continued acting in feature films, mostly as a supporting actress. She had small roles in *Say Anything* (1989), *Penny Ante* (1990), and *Pacific Heights* (1990). In *Green Card* (1990), starring Andie MacDowell and Gerard Depardieu, Bebe had a larger role as an artsy, lusty friend, in a movie about a mutually fraudulent marriage arrangement designed to obtain a Manhattan apartment that only accepted married couples and to help a Frenchman become a United States citizen. Bebe received favorable reviews, and the movie was a critical and financial success.

The following year Bebe landed the role of the well-heeled Countess di Frasso, who has an affair with mobster Benjamin "Bugsy" Siegal (Warren Beatty), in *Bugsy* (1991). This film documents the life of the notorious mobster whose desert casino put Las Vegas on the map. Bebe performed admirably, and the movie received critical acclaim and numerous nominations and awards.

In *Malice* (1993), a mystery-thriller of murder, lust, and greed starring Alec Baldwin and Nicole Kidman, Bebe was praised for offering an excellent supporting role. The movie was moderately successful at the box office, and received mostly positive reviews. The same year, Bebe earned her only lead role to date in *The Paint Job* (1993), a black comedy and odd psychological thriller about an uninspired wife inexplicably attracted to a neighbor. The movie was a financial failure and received mixed reviews.

Bebe also appeared in the feature film *Jumanji* (1995). In this film, starring Robin Williams, a young boy is engulfed within an ancient, magical jungle board game, and when he returns to reality 26 years later, the jungle follows him. The following year she appeared in two feature films, *The Adventures of Pinocchio* (1996) and *The Associate* (1996).

Despite appearances in several films, Bebe has concentrated primarily on the stage. In 1986, she won a Tony award for Best Supporting Actress in a Musical for portraying a tough-tootsie dancer in the revival of *Sweet Charity*. Bebe subsequently appeared in *Showing Off* (1989) and *Chicago* (1992). When her "Cheers" role ended, Bebe assumed Chita Rivera's role in the London West End production of *Kiss of the Spider Woman* (1993).

In March 1994 Bebe starred in the Broadway production *Damn Yankees*. It was the first Broadway revival of the 1955 musical about a middle-aged real estate man who sells his soul to the devil to regain his youth as a baseball hero for the Washington Senators. The reborn hero wants to return to his wife, so the devil sends chief seductress Lola (Neuwirth) to lead him astray. Although much leaner and sultrier than Gwen Verdon in the 1955 version, Bebe sported a short and sassy platinum-blonde wig, making her the physical opposite of her popular characterization of Lilith. She received mostly favorable reviews, despite giving a performance decidedly inferior to the original.

In her latest Broadway production, *Pal Joey* (1995), Bebe had a supporting role as Melba Snyder, and not only sang, but also did a modified striptease. Reviews were praiseworthy for this revival of the 1940 version.

Relationships—Romantic

Bebe was married for seven (mostly unhappy) years to occasional theater director Paul Dorman. They met in New York City in 1982. Dorman was a bartender at O'Neal's restaurant, and Bebe was there performing in a cabaret revue. In 1984, they married in Bebe's hometown, and after seven years the relationship ended in divorce.

Bebe's latest paramour, an actor and writer, qualified for a tryout as an Olympic pole-vaulter. He has taught skiing, studies martial arts, and is an Eagle Scout, Order of the Arrow. They met during *A Chorus Line* (1978) and remained friendly acquaintances for about 13 years before he asked her for a date (the first time she had ever been asked out on a date). The two are now taking their relationship slowly and enjoying each other's company, with no immediate plans for marriage or children.

Future

Since she never felt comfortable in Los Angeles, Bebe has permanently relocated to New York City with her cat, Frankie (named after Frank Lloyd Wright). Bebe is delighted with her achievements onstage and in films, and will continue to emphasize this aspect of her career. In addition, she has left the door open to reappear in subsequent "Frasier" episodes to reprise her Lilith role. Bebe's ultimate goal is to do quality work with quality people, regardless of whether it is a production on Broadway or in a small theater.

Acting Credits

The following is a comprehensive list of Bebe's television, movie and theatrical accomplishments.

TELEVISION: "Cheers" episode "Second Time Around" 2.6.86 (NBC); "Cheers" episode "Abnormal Psychology" 10.16.86 (NBC); "Cheers" episode

"Dinner at Eight-ish" 2.26.87 (NBC); "Cheers" episode "The Crane Mutiny" 10.29.87 (NBC); "Cheers" (series/recurring regular; episode "Bidding on the Boys") 11.19.87 to 11.12.92 (NBC); "Without Her Consent" (telefilm) 1.14.90 (NBC); "Unspeakable Acts" (telefilm) 1.15.90 (ABC); "Star Trek: The Next Generation" episode "First Contact" 2.21.91 (SYND.); "Wings" episode "Planes, Trains, and Visiting Cranes" 2.13.92 (NBC); "Cheers" episode "Is There a Doctor in the Howe?" 2.11.93 (NBC); "Cheers" episode "The Bar Manager, the Shrink, His Wife and Her Lover" 2.18.93 (NBC); "Wild Palms" (miniseries) 5.16.93 to 5.19.93 (ABC); "Frasier" episode "The Show Where Lilith Comes Back" 2.3.94 (NBC); "In a New Light" (special) 7.9.94 (ABC); "Frasier" episode "Adventures in Paradise" (Part 1 of 2) 11.15.94 (NBC); "Frasier" episode "Adventures in Paradise" (Part 2 of 2) 11.22.94 (NBC); "News Radio" episode "Friends" 11.14.95 (NBC); "Duckman" episode 3.23.96 (USA); "Pop Goes the Fourth" (special) 7.4.96 (A & E).

MOVIES: *Say Anything* (1989); *Green Card* (1990); *Penny Ante* (1990); *Pacific Heights* (1990); *Bugsy* (1991); *Malice* (1993); *The Paint Job* (1993); *Jumanji* (1995); *The Adventures of Pinocchio* (1996); *The Associate* (1996).

THEATRICAL PRODUCTIONS: *A Chorus Line* (1978–81); *West Side Story* (1981); *Dancin'* (1982); *Little Me* (1982); *Upstairs at O'Neal's* (1982–83); *Kicks* (1984); *The Road to Hollywood* (1984); *Just So* (1985); *Sweet Charity* (1985–87); *Waiting in the Wings: The Night the Understudies Take the Stage* (1986); *Showing Off* (1989); *Chicago* (1992); *Kiss of the Spider Woman* (1993); *Damn Yankees* (1994); *Pal Joey* (1995); *Chicago* (1996).

EMMY NOMINATIONS: Outstanding Supporting Actress in a Comedy Series, NBC ("Cheers," 1990–91); Outstanding Guest Actress in a Comedy Series, NBC ("Frasier" episode "Adventures in Paradise," Part 2, 1995).

AWARDS: Emmy: Outstanding Supporting Actress in a Comedy Series, NBC "Cheers," 1990–91); Tony: Best Supporting Actress in a Musical (*Sweet Charity*, 1986).

Rhea Perlman
(Carla Tortelli-LeBec)

Childhood and Family

On March 31, 1948, Philip and Adele Perlman welcomed the birth of their first child, Rhea. Born and raised in Brooklyn's Coney Island, New York, Rhea fondly remembers her unorthodox Jewish family—the family who pulled down the shades on Yom Kippur to eat instead of fasting, and parked their car around the corner to defy the tradition of not driving on the holiday. Rhea also has a younger sister, Heide (b. 1951), a television writer and producer, who worked on "Cheers" and "The Tracy Ullman Show."

The Perlman family emigrated from Poland in 1922 when Rhea's father was two years old. Phil subsequently worked as a salesman and manager for a mail order doll and toy parts company in New York. After retiring in 1986, Phil and Adele (a retired bookkeeper) packed up their Brooklyn belongings and moved to Los Angeles to be closer to their children.

Shortly thereafter, Rhea's father visited the "Cheers" set, and assistant director Thomas Lofaro offered Phil a role as an extra. Phil accepted and remained a bar regular until the series ended in 1993. Working as an extra actually sparked a second career for the one-time doll salesman. As a card carrying member of the Screen Actors Guild, Phil is enjoying bit parts (including appearances in three Danny DeVito films), and plans future appearances on other television shows.

Personal Characteristics

The 5'¼" actress is nothing like the bitterly ferocious barmaid she portrays on "Cheers"—in fact, just the opposite. In her youth, Rhea was shy and nervous, lacking self-confidence and atrociously fearful of trying anything new. Although still quite shy, Rhea is charmingly sweet, with a great sense of humor and a pleasant, laissez-faire outlook on life. For instance, after winning her third Emmy award, Rhea accidentally sat on the trophy, breaking a wing. Since her daughter Lucy liked the tattered statue, it is proudly displayed in her playroom among the other toys.

Rhea has strong moral and social beliefs and is not shy about vocalizing these views or exercising her social conscience. Rhea and her husband are actively involved in public awareness efforts concerning child day care, and in 1986 marched in a pro–day care rally at the governor's office in Sacramento. However, Rhea remains a very private woman. She strictly curtails the number of interviews she gives, and due to her lack of self-confidence is embarrassed to read or watch them. Although she has only watched a few episodes of "Cheers," Rhea is trying to observe more of her work to develop an appreciation of herself.

Acting—New York Years

Rhea had youthful dreams of becoming an actress, but because of her introverted personality, never anticipated attaining the goal. After graduating from high school in Brooklyn, Rhea enrolled in Hunter College in New York City. She quickly became bored with school and bypassed a college degree to pursue an acting career. Rhea remained in New York City and scrambled for Off Broadway roles (her first part was in the experimental play *Dracula Sabbat*). To support herself, the struggling actress accepted a variety of odd jobs—erasing book markings for a publishing company, performing allergy tests for a psychiatrist, and waiting tables. Rhea's real-life experience as a waitress ended in disaster when she spilled spaghetti on David Rockefeller's dining companion at the Rainbow Room in Manhattan.

In 1970 the 22-year-old novice of experimental theater watched a friend perform in the Off Broadway production *The Shrinking Bride*, in which Danny DeVito performed as a stable boy. After the show, Rhea dined with the cast and sat across the table from DeVito. It was love at first sight. She was captivated by his maniacal energy, and within two weeks they were living together.

For more than six years, Rhea and Danny lived and worked in New York City. Although they made ends meet, they were still struggling. Rhea worked odd jobs to support her boyfriend, and DeVito accepted any available job. He became convinced that Hollywood was the place for opportunity, and in 1976 persuaded his reluctant girlfriend to travel to Southern California. (They maintained their New York apartment for three more years just in case Hollywood did not work out.)

Acting—Hollywood Years

After the couple moved to Los Angeles, Rhea landed small parts in several television films. Her first recurring role was on the hit television series "Taxi," playing Zena Sherman, the girlfriend of despotic cab dispatcher Louie DePalma (played by her then boyfriend, Danny DeVito). Rhea appeared in four episodes of "Taxi" before being cast as a regular in the television series "Cheers." Despite only appearing in five "Taxi" episodes, for five years she watched and learned the comedic talents of the star-studded cast.

In 1982, the producers of "Cheers" were searching for fresh faces and unknown actors. Rhea was chosen for the role of the brazen, acerbic-tongued barmaid Carla Tortelli because cocreator James Burrows (who directed "Taxi") was impressed with her four episodic appearances on "Taxi." Rhea played the role of the foul-tempered waitress for 11 seasons, modeling the part after several tough-talking Brooklyn women she knew in her youth.

With her fiery temper and acrimonious disposition, Carla was an unlikely candidate to become one of television's most popular characters, but somehow it happened. In her freshman season, Rhea earned her first Emmy nomination as Outstanding Supporting Actress, and by the end of the series had garnered 10 nominations and four awards for her portrayal.

During her 11 years on "Cheers," Rhea had roles in five television movies and appeared in numerous television specials. Despite a prolific television career, which includes a plethora of guest appearances and 11 movies, Rhea had little impact on the silver screen. Her silver screen debut was a bit part in *Love Child* (1982), starring Amy Madigan and Beau Bridges, which involves a prison inmate, impregnated by a guard, who fights to keep her child. The movie received mixed reviews and had limited financial success.

Rhea's sophomore effort was a voice role in *My Little Pony: The Movie* (1986), an animated film about malevolent witches who besiege Ponyland. The other voice parts were performed by several noteworthy actors (Danny DeVito, Cloris Leachman, Tony Randall, Madeline Kahn). The movie earned mixed reviews and achieved moderate box office gains. Three years later Rhea appeared in *Enid Is Sleeping* a.k.a. *Over Her Dead Body* (1989), a comedy starring Elizabeth Perkins and Judge Reinhold which revolves around hiding a dead body. The movie earned lukewarm reviews and was a box office failure.

Despite appearances in four movies during the 1990s, Rhea has been relegated to mostly small supporting roles. In the oddball comedy *Ted and Venus* (1991), Rhea had a small role as the friend of a woman (Kim Adams) stalked by an obsessed poet (Bud Cort). That same year she had a minor part in *Class Act* (1991), a role-reversal comedy about an egghead and bully who are misclassified when they transfer from one school to another. A similar small role was awarded to Rhea in *There Goes the Neighborhood* (1992), a film about an entire neighborhood's attempt to unearth $8.5 million buried by a convict. All three films received mostly favorable scrutiny, but were not box office hits.

In *Canadian Bacon* (1995), starring John Candy and Alan Alda, Rhea is the female lead. This film satirizes the Persian Gulf War by having the United States invade Canada to boost the president's popularity. Rhea plays a law enforcement officer opposite Candy. The film was panned by critics and financially unsuccessful. The following year, Rhea had moderate box office success with costar DeVito in *Sunset Park* (1996) and *Matilda* (1996).

Relationships — Marriage

Rhea is married to the successful actor and director, Danny DeVito (born November 17, 1944, near Asbury Park, New Jersey, the youngest of Daniel and Julia DeVito's three children). They have three children, Lucy Chet (b. 1983; Chet was Devito's father's nickname), Gracie Fan (b. 1985), and Jake (b. 1987).

Rhea and Danny first met in 1970 and moved in together two weeks later. After cohabiting for over 11 years, they finally tied the knot on Thursday, January 28, 1982. On a rainy afternoon, the prospective bride could not decide between a sweat suit and an attractive T-shirt, so she rented an antique

Rhea Perlman

wedding dress. DeVito rushed home during a two-hour lunch break from "Taxi" for a rain-soaked garden ceremony performed by Ralph Pyle, a Los Angeles Philharmonic French horn player who doubled as a nondenominational licensed minister. For the wedding march, the happy couple chose a recording of "I'm in the Mood for Love" by Alfalfa (of Our Gang fame).

The couple's successful Hollywood marriage is laudable in an industry littered with crumpled relationships. One critical element of their success is unselfishness. They trade career experiences and discuss almost everything, and neither star is competitive about his or her career. For example, when Rhea was a struggling actress in Hollywood, she remained supportive and pleased by her husband's success on "Taxi." Moreover, they often consult one another to smooth out problematic scripts or perform a part to assess its comedic qualities. Filming obligations, however, have been extremely taxing on both spouses. For instance, when DeVito was filming *Jewel of the Nile* (1985), Rhea, Lucy, and infant Gracie traveled to bug infested Fez, Morocco, to be with him for one month.

Despite career obligations, Rhea treasures motherhood. Familial obligations are her first priority, and show business is secondary. When the children were younger, both parents were up at 7 a.m. to share baby duties. The children regularly accompany Rhea to the park and museum, and the family follows DeVito to movie locations whenever possible. DeVito even rejected a role in Ridley Scott's film *Legend* (1986), starring Tom Cruise, because Rhea and Lucy could not accompany him to London.

When DeVito is on location, he faithfully calls home at least three times a day. His hotel suites are brimming with family photographs and stacks of videotapes of Rhea and the kids engaging in daily activities. However, commuter parenting can be difficult on the children. Although Rhea worries about her children and the effects of their irregular, showbiz lifestyle, she realizes all she can do is love her children and spend as much time with them as possible.

Although their lifestyle may appear chaotic and in a state of constant flux, Rhea and Danny are virtual homebodies. They relax by watching television and movies, playing pool, or entertaining friends such as Michael Douglas and Tony Danza. They rarely have dinner parties, preferring simple gatherings with a few select friends. The vegetarian DeVito does most of the cooking (his specialties are red beans, brown rice and escarole) and even converted Rhea, the Hostess cupcake addict, to the discipline.

Their spacious six-bedroom Spanish-style Los Angeles hacienda resembles a Toys "R" Us showroom, with carved wooden frogs, a Haitian room divider decorated with fish-like creatures, paintings of horses, and prehistoric cave artwork. Creative toys for the kids are scattered across the floor, and an art gallery of the children's paintings and drawings decorates the walls. Rhea likes the house, not because it embodies Hollywood's idea of success, but since it is a short distance from the Griffith Park Observatory, Travel Town train museum, Los Angeles Zoo, and an area for horseback riding. Moreover, the happy couple rarely takes romantic getaway vacations. Their official vacations are usually spent with the extended family at their five-bedroom Malibu beach house overlooking the Pacific Ocean.

The Future

After "Cheers" ended, Rhea concentrated on familial obligations, and continues to emphasize this priority in her life. Now that "Cheers" is well into syndication and the hardest part of parenting is behind her, Rhea is redirecting her attention to her professional future. She currently stars in a CBS comedy series with Malcolm McDowell. The sitcom "Pearl" involves a blue collar widow who matches wits with a stern professor.

Rhea has recently finished costarring in two feature films with her husband, *Sunset Park* (1996) and *Matilda* (1996), and is primarily interested in finding roles that are fun or out of character, such as mentally unstable women or blustery old ladies. If her track record is any indication, Rhea will concentrate on her television series additional feature films with DeVito, and spending quality time with her family.

Acting Credits

The following is a comprehensive list of Rhea's television, movie and theatrical accomplishments.

TELEVISION: "Stalk the Wild Child" (telefilm) 11.3.76 (NBC); "I Want to Keep My Baby!" (telefilm) 11.19.76 (CBS); "Mary Jane Harper Cried Last Night" (telefilm) 10.5.77 (CBS); "Having Babies II" (telefilm) 10.28.77 (ABC); "Intimate Strangers" (telefilm) 11.11.77 (ABC); "Like Normal People" (telefilm) 4.13.79 (ABC); "Taxi" episode "Louie and the Nice Girl" 9.11.79 (ABC); "Taxi" episode "Louie Meets the Folks" 12.11.79 (ABC); "Angie" episode "Angie and Brad's Close Encounter" 1.14.80 (ABC); "Taxi" episode "Louie's Rival" 11.19.80 (ABC); "Taxi" episode "Louie's Fling" 11.5.81 (ABC); "Drop-Out Father" (telefilm) 9.27.82 (CBS); "Cheers" (series) 9.30.82 to 5.20.93 (NBC); "Taxi" episode "Zena's Honeymoon" 12.9.82 (NBC); "Taxi" episode "Celebration of Taxi" 3.23.83 (NBC); "Saturday Night Live" (host) 10.15.83 (NBC); "St. Elsewhere" episode "Cheers" 3.27.85 (NBC); "NBC All-Star Hour" (special) 9.16.85 (NBC); "NBC's 60th Anniversary Celebration" (special) 5.12.86 (NBC); "Amazing Stories" episode "The Wedding Ring" 9.22.86 (NBC); "The Tortellis" (series premiere) 1.22.87 (NBC); "Funny, You Don't Look 200!" (special) 10.12.87 (ABC); "Dangerous Affection" (telefilm) 11.1.87 (NBC); "Matlock" episode "The Network" 12.1.87 (NBC); "A Family Again" (special) 10.15.88 (ABC); "Wonder Works" episode "Two Daddies" (voice only) 5.8.89 (PBS); "The Last Halloween" (special) 10.28.91 (CBS); "Roc" episode "The Stan Who Came To Dinner" 1.19.92 (FOX); "Back to School '92" (special) 9.8.92 (CBS); "To Grandmother's House We Go" (telefilm) 12.6.92 (ABC); "A Place to Be Loved" (telefilm) 4.4.93 (CBS); "Shelley Duvall's Bedtime Stories" episode "Bootsie Barker Bites" 10.20.93 (SHOWTIME); "Spoils of War" (telefilm) 4.9.94 (ABC); "Sesame Street's All-Star 25th Birthday: Stars & Street Forever!" (special) 5.18.94 (ABC); "The Simpsons" episode "Fear of Flying" (voice) 12.18.94 (FOX); "Best of Taxi" (special) 12.19.94 (CBS); "The Critic" episode "Sherman, Woman and Child" 3.5.95 (FOX); "The Critic" episode "From Chunk to Hunk" 4.2.95 (FOX); "Pearl" (series) 9.14.96 to present (CBS).

MOVIES: *Love Child* (1982); *The Ratings Game* (1984); *My Little Pony: The Movie* (voice, 1986); *Enid Is Sleeping (Over Her Dead Body)* (1989); *Ted and Venus* (1991); *Class Act* (1991); *There Goes the Neighborhood* (1992); *Canadian Bacon* (1995); *Sunset Park* (1996); *Matilda* (1996); *Carpool* (1996).

THEATRICAL PRODUCTIONS: *Dracula Sabbat*.

EMMY NOMINATIONS: Outstanding Supporting Actress in a Comedy,

Variety or Musical Series, NBC ("Cheers," 1983); Outstanding Supporting
Actress in a Comedy Series, NBC ("Cheers," 1984–91, 1993).
AWARDS: Emmy: Outstanding Supporting Actress in a Comedy Series,
NBC ("Cheers," 1984–86, 1989).

John Ratzenberger
(Cliff Clavin)

Born on April 6, 1947, and raised in Bridgeport, Connecticut, John Dezso
Ratzenberger was the only son and middle child of Dezso Alexander and
Bertha (Grohowski). A child of Hungarian descent, John attended Catholic
school and attributes his sense of comedic timing to a grammar school nun,
Sister Regina. John foresaw a future in show business when he was able to make
his friends laugh without getting caught by the austere sister. Although the
actor was not known for his academic record, he certainly enlivened the classroom.

John's truck driving father made a strong impression on the young comedian. His father would interrupt dinner with a Jack E. Leonard impression—
cruising through the kitchen while twirling a hat as he exited the room. John
also recalls Sunday mornings, his father's only day off, because the elder
Ratzenberger would play a Louis Prima–Kelly Smith album so loudly it res-
onated throughout the house, waking everyone.

In addition to pumping gas in Bridgeport and graduating from high
school in 1965, John attended Sacred Heart University in his hometown.
While collaborating with a college classmate, they originated a two-man
improvisational act, "Sal's Meat Market," in which John wrote, directed, and
acted (frequently playing up to 15 characters per show). In 1971 the pair
impetuously crossed the Atlantic Ocean to tour Europe with the act. Fortunately, the troupe captured the attention of the Arts Council of Great Britain,
which awarded a monetary endowment to fund a continental tour—a veritable first for an American actor.

Their tour rarely lacked excitement. Once, the troupe was to perform for
the lunch crowd at a London pub, but nobody attended the show. John strolled
to the outside window ledge to attract an audience, and the death defying stunt
actually lured spectators upstairs to watch the remainder of the show.

The improvisational act lasted for roughly five years, and during the remainder of the decade John toured Europe individually and in the theater (though
he occasionally visited the United States). It was difficult for an American to
sustain a substantial acting career in England, so John had to supplement his

income through carpentry and, despite being acrophobic, working as a tree surgeon's assistant. However, when the option was either working or starving, John chose to perform menial tasks so he could continue pursuing his passion for acting. As for employment related to his discipline and avocation, John wrote for the British Broadcasting Corporation (BBC) and appeared in the movies *A Bridge Too Far* (1977) and *Yanks* (1979), which were filmed in Europe.

While visiting the United States in 1981, John successfully landed the role of Cliff Clavin, the "Cheers" blowhard postman. In fact, John practically created the role for himself. He originally auditioned for the role of Norm Peterson, but when his reading did not enthrall the producers, John suggested a know-it-all character for the bar. The creators were intrigued because they had overlooked such a character in the show's original concept.

By resurrecting a character he played in a European production, John engaged in a 10-minute rendition using office props to enchant the producers, who inevitably lapsed into interminable laughter. The producers agreed to sign him for seven episodes. Cliff was originally conceived as a security guard, but a few days before "Cheers" was aired the character was converted to a mailman. The producers contrived a postal carrier as a means of facilitating the introduction of information to the bar—he could obtain fascinating ideas by walking the mail route.

At times it appeared Cliff Clavin knew everything about nothing, and nothing about everything as he enlightened bar patrons with arcane facts. Surprisingly, John actually extemporized many of Cliff's obtuse, enigmatic observations, having acquired the knowledge from subscriptions to a variety of obscure technical magazines. The producers typically supplied a tidbit of information in the script and allowed John to use his improvisational skills to expound on trivia.

Having two sisters and always feeling comfortable around women, John found that the most challenging aspect of playing Cliff was successfully portraying a character intimidated by women. However, when he behaved moronically on-camera and uttered incomprehensible gibberish in the presence of beautiful women, he created one of the most humorous depictions of a chronically insecure male ever filmed. Moreover, the Clavin witticisms swiftly became a popular pillar on the series. Consequently, John's seven-episode contract was continually renewed, and after the first season he became a cast regular, remaining until the series' finale. John's successful portrayal of Cliff Clavin earned him two Emmy nominations for Outstanding Supporting Actor (1985-86).

Ironically, Cliff Clavin was a braggart with numerous retentive qualities, but was hailed nationwide by members of the postal profession (who ordained Ratzenberger as an honorary member of their organization). To date, John remains inordinately popular in his hometown of Bridgeport, where he once was named the grand marshall in the city's annual parade.

John Ratzenberger

In addition to portraying the infamous mailman for 11 years, John participated in a variety of other projects. He coauthored two teleplays, "Friends in Space" (1978) and "Scalped" (1979), and appeared in the plays *Curse of the Starving Class* and *The Connection*. In 1976 John made his film debut in *The Ritz*, and over the course of the next decade appeared in over 20 movies. However, the following decade was relatively lean for feature film roles, primarily due to John's voracious commitments to television movies, series guest appearances, and directorial endeavors. He appeared in over a dozen television episodes and movies, and had at least that many television directing credits.

In 1993, John was slated to star in the Fox network series "Locals," in which he played Jerry Hawthorne, a small town barber in Port Ellen, New York. The show involved eccentric inhabitants who proffered a challenge to outsider Mike Levine, a New York City cab driver, who ultimately married Jerry's sister. The pilot aired June 23, 1994, but no station offered to buy the series. John was a co-executive producer with "Cheers" alumni Mert Rich and Brian Pollack, and the song was composed by Craig Safan, who also penned the music for "Cheers."

The British did not forget John, either. They invited him to spend a five-month "Cheers" hiatus starring in the miniseries "Small World," a comedy based on the world of academia. In the series, John plays an American professor of English who travels extensively, delivering lectures on the "textuality" of the novel.

Despite having limited acting roles since "Cheers" expired, John has made some public service announcements and television commercials. In 1994 he appeared with Ed Begley, Jr., in a public service announcement promoting the use of mass transit. In television advertising, John used the image of know-it-all Cliff Clavin to familiarize consumers to products. This vogue accentuated the long-running advertisement campaign for Tropicana Twister juice drinks, in which John balks at the brand's deliciously daring flavor combinations by asserting that Twister Light is nothing less than "a menage à fruit."

As for John's personal life, he married Elizabeth Georgia Stiny on September 9, 1984, and they have two children, James John and Nina Katherine. John enjoys spending time with his wife and children (they especially like sailing together), and he is an avid reader. He also plays the banjo and does woodworking in his spare time.

John is active in a variety of professional and social organizations. He is a member of the American Federation of Television and Radio Artists (AFTRA), Screen Actors Guild, Writers Guild of America, the Directors Guild of America, and the British Actors Equity Association. As an ardent nature lover, John is active in Greenpeace, Wilderness Society, Natural Resources Defense Council, San Francisco Sierra Club, and Farmland Trust. Moreover, he originated Eco-Pak Industries in Kent, Washington, which is devoted exclusively to developing an ecologically safe Styrofoam packaging replacement made of lumber scraps and sawdust. Although John recently sold the ever-expanding company, he remains a consultant.

Besides advocating land conservation, John also practices philanthropy with his own land. In 1993, the Ratzenberger family donated 5 of their 16 acres in the Seattle area to Russian Orthodox monks who were departing after four years of unsuccessfully attempting to establish a monastery in the region. John and his wife generously bestowed the parcel rather impetuously after listening to a heartwarming valediction ceremony for the monks.

As for the future, John will continue directing for television, which has always been an interest (he directed several "Cheers" episodes and other television shows). With the swift demise of his prime-time pilot "Locals," John has considerably more time available to concentrate on a directorial career. Since acting is not a top priority, John is unlikely to have significant movie or television roles, but will undoubtedly accept numerous small supporting roles and guest appearances. For instance, he had a voice role in the animated movie *Toy Story* (1995) starring Tom Hanks and Tim Allen. Since familial obligations are very important, John will stay close to his home in between filming projects.

Acting Credits

The following is a comprehensive list of John's television, movie and theatrical accomplishments.

TELEVISION: "Twilight's Last Gleaming" (telefilm) 2.14.78 (CBS); "Goliath Awaits" (miniseries) 10.16.81 to 10.17.81 (OPT); "Code Red" episode "All That Glitters" 11.29.81 (ABC); "Cheers" (series) 9.30.82 to 5.20.93 (NBC); "Wizards and Warriors" episode "To the Rescue" 5.7.83 (CBS); "Magnum P.I." episode NA 10.18.84 (CBS); "St. Elsewhere" episode "Cheers" 3.27.85 (NBC); "The Love Boat" episode "A Day in Port" 9.28.85 (ABC); "Friday Night Videos" (guest host) 11.9.85 (NBC); "NBC's 60th Anniversary Celebration" (special) 5.12.86 (NBC); "Combat High" (telefilm) 11.23.86 (NBC); "The Tortellis" episode "Frankie Comes to Dinner" 2.4.87 (NBC); "Time Stalkers" (telefilm) 3.10.87 (CBS); "D.C. Follies" 3.12.88 (SYND.); "Going to the Chapel" (telefilm) 10.9.88 (ET); "Camp Cucamonga: How I Spent My Summer Vacation" (telefilm) 9.23.90 (NBC); "Wings" episode "The Story of Joe" 10.5.90 (NBC); "Nurses" episode "Illicit Transfers" 11.14.92 (NBC); "Blossom" episode "Sitcom" 5.3.93 (NBC); "Moon Over Miami" episode "Farewell My Lovelies" 10.6.93 (ABC); "Locals" (pilot) 6.23.94 (FOX); "She TV" 8.30.94 (ABC); "The Simpsons" episode "Fear of Flying" (voice) 12.18.94 (FOX); "Murphy Brown" episode "A Rat's Tale" 2.13.95 (CBS); "Sister, Sister" episode "Thanksgiving (Part 1)" 11.15.95 (WBN); "Sister, Sister" episode "Thanksgiving (Part 2)" 11.22.95 (WBN); "Caroline in the City" episode "Caroline and Richard's Mother" 4.25.96 (NBC).

MOVIES: *The Ritz* (1976); *Valentino* (1977); *A Bridge Too Far* (1977); *Twilight's Last Gleaming* (1977, U.S./Germany); *Warlords of Atlantis* (1978, Brit.); *Superman I* (1978); *The Bitch* (1979); *Arabian Adventure* (1979, Brit.); *Hanover Street* (1979, Brit.); *Yanks* (1979); *Superman II* (1980); *Motel Hell* (1980); *The Empire Strikes Back* (1980); *Ragtime* (1981); *Outland* (1981); *Reds* (1981); *Warlords of the 21st Century* (1982); *Gandhi* (1982); *Battletruck* (1982); *Firefox* (1982); *Protocol* (1984); *The Falcon and the Snowman* (1985); *Combat Academy* (1986); *House II: The Second Story* (1987); *Toy Story* (1995).

THEATRICAL PRODUCTIONS: *Curse of the Starving Class; The Connection.*

WRITING CREDITS: Teleplays: "Friends in Space" (coauthor, 1978); "Scalped" (coauthor, 1979).

DIRECTING CREDITS: "Cheers" episode "And God Created Woodman" 1.14.88 (NBC); "Sydney" episode NA 4.25.90 (CBS); "Down Home" episode "This Bug's for You" 4.28.90 (NBC); "Down Home" episode "Don't Rock the Boat" 3.30.91 (NBC); "Down Home" episode "Evian Spelled Backwards Is Naive" 4.27.91 (NBC); "Down Home" episode "Dream Boat" 5.4.91 (NBC); "Cheers" episode "Head Over Hill" 11.14.91 (NBC); "Cheers" episode "The King of Beers" 10.8.92 (NBC); "Cheers" episode "Norm's Big Audit" 1.14.93 (NBC); *Stuck* (1993); "Evening Shade" episode "Mama Knows Best" 5.9.94

(CBS); "Madman of the People" episode "Guys Just Wanna Have Fun" 10.13.94 (NBC); "Madman of the People" episode "Truths My Father Told" 1.12.95 (NBC).

EMMY NOMINATIONS: Outstanding Supporting Actor in a Comedy Series, NBC ("Cheers," 1985–86).

George Wendt
(Norm Peterson)

Childhood and Education

On October 17, 1948, George Wendt was born to a strict Catholic mother. His grandfather was a successful newspaper reporter whose claim to fame was using hidden photographic equipment to preserve the execution of Ruth Snyder (which is now encased in the Smithsonian Institution). Raised in a wealthy suburb on Chicago's South Side, George was a 165-pound teenager who loved basketball (and was a noted slam dunker). Despite majoring in shenanigans at a strict Jesuit prep school, he graduated in 1965 and attended Notre Dame University. After a few uneventful years, George was expelled for failing to attend class, missing final exams, and basic indolence. If beer guzzling and partying had been part of Notre Dame's curriculum, George would have been an honors student. He was only motivated to have fun. Yet somehow amidst his quest for amusement, George graduated in 1971 from the less prestigious Rockhurst College in Kansas City with a bachelor of arts degree in economics.

After college, George meandered aimlessly throughout Europe for two years. His primary jobs during this restful period were doing laundry, brushing his teeth, and writing postcards. However, since he rarely brushed his teeth, mailing a postcard gave him a real sense of accomplishment for the day! During a sojourn through Spain, George contemplated his mission in life and made a lengthy list of occupations he despised—scientist, doctor, teacher, businessman, and salesman—and in 1973 returned to Chicago without a career goal, but with a firm concept of the vocations to avoid.

Personal Life

George is intelligent, easygoing, and almost nothing like the "Cheers" character Norm Peterson. He considers himself wiser, less crude, and more

assertive than Norm, though their similarities include decidedly banal clothing and hairstyles (George is most comfortable in an Air Jordan T-shirt, shorts
and running shoes, and sporting a ragtag, no-frills hairdo).

George is the stereotypical slacker, just one of the guys. As for indoor
activities, he enjoys lounging on the couch, watching sports on television (especially the Chicago White Sox), drinking beer, male bonding, and listening to
his favorite musicians (Pearl Jam, Gutterball, Hole, Bob Mould). George has
an insatiable appetite for knowledge and avidly reads four newspapers a day
(which drives his wife crazy). As for outdoor recreational activities, he enjoys
loitering around San Francisco's La Rocca's Corner Bar when he is in town,
driving his BMW, swimming, and playing basketball.

George is also obsessed with running. When his weight reached an all-
time high in 1985 (a guarded secret), George consulted a fitness trainer to help
reduce the excess pounds. Since 1985 his daily routine has included laps on
the track of a private all-boys' school near his Studio City home. After two
years of daily running, George began logging the miles—a one-mile warm-up
walk, three nonstop miles at 10½ minutes per mile, two more miles of inter-
vals, and a half-mile cool-down walk. Despite his 5' 10", 250-pound frame
(which he strives to reduce to 225), the actor's calves are solid, and he moves
like a natural athlete.

George is a life-long jock, but granted, a large one, and has maintained
the athleticism of his youth. Woody Harrelson was particularly impressed
with George's basketball abilities, and they continue to play the game
together. George is equally adept as a sports announcer. One memorable highlight is when he joined play-by-play announcer Steve Stone to broadcast a
Chicago Cubs game as a celebrity fill-in for Harry Caray, the customary Cubs
announcer.

Acting—Early Years

After working on soda trucks, caddying, and eliminating every other
despicable employment opportunity, a career in comedy appeared to be one of
the few tolerable jobs remaining. Thus, after returning to his hometown in
1973, George called the Second City Theatre box office to inquire about being
accepted into one of their comedy improvisational workshops. He chose this
particular theater because of its reputation and his familiarity with the establishment (George spent his collegiate days frequenting Second City to avoid
studying). After an audition, he was accepted into a workshop.

Excited about the combination of nonchalance and performing, George
applied himself to a trade for the first time in his life. Soon there was an opening for a touring theater group, so he auditioned for and received a part. George
was focused and motivated, and worked harder than ever before, but loved it.

George Wendt

Despite staying at Second City for six years, success was elusive and struggling times lingered—one night George was actually booed off the stage. However, he persevered to hone his acting and comedy skills (though George does not consider himself a very good actor, and is more of a dry, understated comic than a stand-up).

While touring with the Second City troupe, George met his future wife, actress and screenwriter Bernadette Birkett. They became local celebrities, and their 1978 wedding was rather a coup among Chicago socialites. In 1980 they moved to Los Angeles with Second City cast members to develop a concept into a television series, but the pilot, "Nothing but Comedy," was not picked up for the season. Despite swiftly landing guest appearances on a multitude of successful television shows and earning bit parts in movies, this was a frustrating period in George's life. He went from the fast-paced, pressurized atmosphere of Second City to the decelerated, languid atmosphere of Hollywood where he worked two days and had a six-month hiatus.

George's career took a turn for the better when his appearance as an exterminator on "Taxi" brought him to the attention of director James Burrows and the Charles brothers (the triumvirate who created "Cheers"). When the trio was casting the new series, they remembered George and asked him to audition.

Acting—"Cheers"

In 1982, George competed against John Ratzenberger for the role of beer-guzzling loaf Norm Peterson, and landed the role of the archetypical patron who spends every night in a tavern drinking beer and talking fatuously. The producers were set on George from the start. Despite his prior commitment to the fledgling pilot series "Making the Grade" (which suffered a quick demise) and the fact that he would have been unavailable for the full season, the producers still offered George the part.

Norm's arrival at Cheers was met with a chorus of patrons shouting in unison, "Norm!" which inevitably preceded a classic one-liner. On a typical day and or night, Norm, with beer in hand, was seated complacently on the stool at the corner of the bar, watching life pass him by. Norm frequented Cheers to avoid going home to his never seen (but occasionally heard) wife, Vera.

George played the popular "Cheers" character Norm Peterson for the entire length of the series (1982–93). His portrayal of the indolent bar regular earned him six Emmy nominations for Outstanding Supporting Actor (1984–89), though he never won. Norm's indelible image as a beer-swilling lounge lizard helped solidify Wendt's television commercial contract to promote Meister Brau Light beer.

Acting—Movies and Television

In addition to working on "Cheers" for 11 years, George appeared in numerous feature films but was almost exclusively relegated to small supporting roles. In his freshman year of filming, George appeared in *My Bodyguard* (1980), which received positive reviews, and *Somewhere in Time* (1980), which was berated. Two years later, he appeared in a pair of movies that received mixed reviews, *Airplane II: The Sequel* (1982) and *Jekyll and Hyde: Together Again* (1982).

In 1984, George appeared in five movies that met with critical apathy and box office mediocrity. During the remainder of the 1980s he only appeared in three movies, but his roles were more substantial. George's first substantial role was a factory worker in *Gung Ho* (1985), starring Michael Keaton, who functions as a management-employee liaison when a Japanese firm purchases a United States automobile factory. The movie received moderate reviews, but was so financially successful that it became a television series, albeit a short-lived one.

In *House* (1986), starring William Katt, George plays a neighbor who becomes concerned when a horror novelist moves into his dead aunt's haunted house. The movie was actually praised, but the sequels paled in comparison. In the much forgotten movie, *Plain Clothes* (1988), George assists star Arliss

Howard in returning to a high school as an undercover cop to solve a teacher's murder.

By the end of the decade, George's acting credentials and expanded roles earned him top billing in *Never Say Die* (1990), an action thriller about investigative journalists caught in a web of international intrigue. Critics reacted contemptuously, and George wore the insignia of being miscast in an inept lead role capacity. His box office starring days faded fast with this movie, and his follow-up, *The Masters of Menace* (1990), was reviewed with similar derision, despite appearances by Dan Aykroyd, James Belushi and John Candy.

The film *Guilty by Suspicion* (1991), starring Robert De Niro, attacks the Cold War era House Un-American Activities Committee, which probed suspected communists in the film and theater industries. George plays De Niro's screenwriter pal, Bunny Baxter, who lacks backbone during the investigation and eventually sells out his friends. The movie had high hopes, but only met the expectations of a few critics.

In 1992, George landed a role in the Mel Gibson movie *Forever Young*, in which he plays Gibson's scientist friend who performs suspended animation experiments and helps freeze the hero aviator in 1939, after his lover is supposedly killed in an automobile accident. Despite theatrical success, the entire cast was criticized as being miscast, including George for abandoning his forte in comedy.

During the 11-year run of "Cheers," George had other television work, as well. He hosted "Saturday Night Live" and created the popular role of a Chicago super-fan whose comrades only know two subjects, "da Bears" and "da Bulls." In 1991 George returned to "Saturday Night Live," unannounced, to act in another sketch involving the super-fans, and joined the rest of the "Cheers" cast in surprising Kirstie Alley, who was hosting the show.

Acting—Post-"Cheers"

Since viewers so readily identified with George Wendt as plain old Norm Peterson, the guy permanently affixed to the corner barstool, NBC attempted to utilize his popularity by devising a television series, "Under the Hood" (loosely based on Tom and Ray Magliozzi and their Boston-based National Public Radio call-in show "Car Talk"). The show never materialized, so CBS purchased the pilot and agreed to 13 episodes. CBS revamped the entire show, from cast to concept to location, by hiring actor Pat Finn, comedically focusing on the relationship between an irresponsible younger brother and a mature older brother, and moving the show to Madison, Wisconsin. "The George Wendt Show" premiered on March 3, 1995, to give CBS a Wednesday night ratings boost and was promoted as *Wendts*day night comedy.

Despite initial ratings success, the show suffered a quick descent and was not renewed for a second season.

George continued his involvement in the theater. In *Wild Men!* (1993), an Off Broadway comedy by Second City graduates about male bonding, he plays an alcoholic commodities trader who gambles away his marriage, career, and net worth. Although Wendt was praised for his comedic energy, the play was labeled as redundant, unduly elongated, and sluggish.

Marriage and Family

In 1980, two years after their marriage, George and Bernadette moved their family to Los Angeles, where Bernadette helped develop the television series pilot "Nothing but Comedy." Although the pilot was never picked up, over the years Bernadette devised six more pilots (none of which were picked up), had a series of movie bit parts and television guest appearances, and a longer stint as Jackie Schumaker on "It's Garry Shandling's Show." Bernadette also appeared on "Cheers" in various capacities—as Tinker Bell and the voice (not face) of Vera Peterson—and made a guest appearance on "The George Wendt Show." George and Bernadette have a total of five children, three of whom are their own (Joshua, Andrew and Hilary) and two from her previous marriage.

In their Los Angeles home, cooking is an obsession with George (he especially loves to barbecue). Their home was renovated to emphasize the courtyard with an elaborate outdoor cooking facility. It serves as the focal point, enclosed on three sides by the family room, main kitchen, and pool house, while basking beneath the shade of a Chinese elm. The courtyard has all the essentials for the joys of cooking—stove, sinks, running water, dining area, and beer on tap.

The Future

George will continue pursuing movie roles, in a supporting actor capacity. He recently agreed to portray one of the Chicago super-fans in a Paramount movie adaptation of the "Saturday Night Live" skit on "da Bears." His future as a leading man in a television series is uncertain since CBS canceled "The George Wendt Show." Undoubtedly, George will be content with television guest appearances and minor telefilm roles, as he has in the past, and will continue pursuing a theatrical career.

Acting Credits

The following is a comprehensive list of George's television, movie and theatrical credits.

TELEVISION: "Avery Schreiber—Live from the Second City" (special, 1979); "Soap" episode NA 4.13.81 (ABC); "Taxi" episode "Latka the Playboy" 4.21.81 (ABC); "Making the Grade" (series) 4.5.82 to 5.10.82 (CBS); "Alice" episode "Monty Falls for Alice" 4.18.82 (CBS); "Cheers" (series) 9.30.82 to 5.20.93 (NBC); "M*A*S*H" episode "Trick or Treatment" 11.1.82 (CBS); "Garfield on the Town" (special) 10.28.83 (CBS); "St. Elsewhere" episode "Cheers" 3.27.85 (NBC); "Friday Night Videos" (guest host) 11.9.85 (NBC); "Twilight Zone" episode "The World Next Door" 10.18.86 (CBS); "The Tortellis" episode "Frankie Comes to Dinner" 2.4.87 (NBC); "Wings" episode "The Story of Joe" 10.5.90 (NBC); "Tales from the Crypt" episode "The Reluctant Vampire" 7.10.91 (HBO); "A Comedy Salute to Michael Jordan" (special) 9.20.91 (NBC); "Saturday Night Live" (guest appearance) 9.28.91 (NBC); "Roc" episode "The Stan Who Came to Dinner" 1.19.92 (FOX); "Seinfeld" episode "The Trip (Part 1)" 8.12.92 (NBC); "Bob" episode "Da Game" 2.5.93 (CBS); "The Edge" 4.11.93 (FOX); "Hostage for a Day" (telefilm) 4.25.94 (FOX); "The Simpsons" episode "Fear of Flying" (voice) 12.18.94 (FOX); "The George Wendt Show" (series) 3.3.95 to 4.12.95 (CBS); "Columbo: Strange Bedfellows" (telefilm) 5.8.95 (ABC); "The Building" episode NA 9.3.95 (CBS); "Bye Bye Birdie" (telefilm) 12.3.95 (CBS); "Good Company" episode "Day 1346: Friendship" 3.18.96 (CBS); "Comic Relief's American Comedy Festival" (special) 5.4.96 (ABC).

MOVIES: *My Bodyguard* (1980); *Somewhere in Time* (1980); *Airplane II: The Sequel* (1982); *Jekyll and Hyde: Together Again* (1982); *The Woman in Red* (1984); *Dreamscape* (1984); *Thief of Hearts* (1984); *Ratings Game* (1984); *Small Affair* (1984); *Fletch* (1984); *Gung Ho* (1985); *House* (1986); *Plain Clothes* (1988); *Never Say Die* (1990); *The Masters of Menace* (1990); *Guilty by Suspicion* (1991); *Forever Young* (1992); *The Little Rascals* (1994); *Man of the House* (1995).

THEATRICAL PRODUCTIONS: *Wild Men!* (1993).

DIRECTORIAL CREDITS: "Cheers" ep "Airport V" 2.25.88 (NBC).

EMMY NOMINATIONS: Outstanding Supporting Actor in a Comedy Series, NBC ("Cheers," 1984–89).

III. The Cheers Bar

Bar Facts

Located at 112½ Beacon Street, the business sign outside Cheers indicated the bar was established in 1895, but the actual year was 1889. (Carla had Sam change the year because she was into the science of numerology at the time, and 1895 was luckier than 1889.) When the bar first opened it was called Mom's, named after an aging ex–fan dancer who provided free room and board to attractive, newly arriving immigrants, (in other words, it was a brothel). Since 1970, the buildings adjacent to Cheers included a gym, book store, and bank. Even the interior of Cheers transformed during this time frame. The stairs to Melville's were initially on the other side of the wall, the original floor tiling was a ghastly green, and the 1970s paneling was replaced.

In 1976 Sam purchased Cheers from Gus O'Malley, who later moved to Arizona. O'Malley previously purchased the bar from another man named Gus, who was great at solving personal problems and died of a heart attack inside Cheers by table number 5. The one commonality among all the owners was having the same patron, Norm Peterson.

During Sam's tenure, the bar had three postal carriers: Walter Q. Twitchell, Tommy, and Larry. Cheers was closed on Christmas morning, had a maximum capacity of 75 persons, the office telephone extension was 221, and the balcony functioned as the smoking section. The interior decor had a wooden lady and wooden Indian (Tecumseh, whose belly was rubbed for good luck), and a moose named Dave. The countertop had Sam and Diane's initials engraved into it and a quarter varnished to the surface. The bar patrons were kept warm by a gray Little Diablo furnace (a Guatemalan, 55,000 BTU, full-duct, four-square model), and above the office copier hung the sign, "This machine is for copying documents, not your butt."

Other than a dartboard and jukebox, Cheers had a haunted Foosball table, a karaoke machine, Billiard Buddy Adaptor (a combination pool table, Ping-Pong table, knock-hockey and slot-clock track), and billiards tournaments on Sunday evenings. The bar acquired a mechanical bull in 1990 because it was the only useful piece of equipment the corporation could salvage from

119

a Texas company that went bankrupt. To increase business, Sam ordered a blood pressure machine, but G & S Amusements accidentally sent a slot machine (the Gametime 36X with 3 model sprockets and triple-action tumblers).

The price of tap beer ranged from $1.50 to $2.50, a shot of liquor was $2.50, the minimum drink order was $5.00, and Cheers patrons received a free drink on their birthday. The huge binder behind the bar housed Norm's bar tab and dated back to when he was referred to as the skinny guy at the end of the bar. Woody founded the *Cheers Newsletter*, and the first lead story was that Cheers never had a newsletter.

The only patron with a key to the front door of the bar was Norm. The Cheers mascot was a Dalmatian named Spotty, and the bar's best dart player was Sam. Although many weddings were scheduled to be performed by justice of the peace Harrison Fiedler, only two couples actually married in Cheers—Frankie and Janet, and Barry and Joanne. (Janet later caught Frankie cheating on her in the poolroom and shot him dead in the alley. His ashes were kept in an urn behind the bar.)

The patrons always yelled, "Norm!" when he entered the bar; however, the only exception was when he became wealthy with the Tan 'N' Wash business. When a corporation purchased Cheers in 1987, only Woody yelled, "Norm!" whereas everyone else shouted, "Reggie!" for their favorite yuppie patron. While Sam was tending bar in Mexico, the Cancun patrons yelled, "Pepe!" for a rotund Mexican bar regular. After Sam allowed an old baseball buddy (Tom Kenderson) to promote his coming-out-of-the-closet book at Cheers, the gang threatened to take their business to Clancy's. Their primary trepidation was Cheers being converted into a gay bar like Vito's Pub.

Cheers survived times of hardship, most notably the blaze of 1992 that gutted the bar after Rebecca placed a freshly extinguished cigarette into the office wastebasket. The cost of remodeling was not covered by insurance because Sam had a $25,000 deductible. The other notable tribulation was John Allen Hill's ownership of the bar's bathrooms and poolroom. Sam and Rebecca jointly purchased these essential bar components by paying $5,000 and $25,000, respectively.

Corporate Ownership

In 1987 Sam sold Cheers to the Lillian Corporation. A few months later, he returned to the bar, searching for employment as a bartender. However, corporate Cheers had two bartenders, Woody and Wayne, so to make room for Sam as a bartender (and save Woody's job), the Cheers gang devised the scheme, "Operation: Wayne Down the Dwain." As part of the plan, Wayne agreed to quit if a patron ordered a drink he could not make. When all the bar regulars ordered a screaming viking, Wayne quit in disgust.

As part of the corporate bar decor, the new manager, Rebecca Howe, opted for a more professional appearance by making the employees wear hideous lime-colored uniforms. Their attire was promptly discarded when Sam won a bet with Rebecca that he could persuade Carla to marry Eddie LeBec.

Daniel T. Collier (nicknamed Pinky) was CEO and chairman of the board of the Lillian Corporation. Rebecca was the first corporate manager of Cheers, and her supervisor was Evan Drake, a corporate vice president. Evan Drake had a butler, Greyson; a yacht servant, Lorenzo; a chauffeur for his Rolls Royce, Martin; and a daughter, Laurie. Drake accepted a position to head the corporation's Tokyo Division, and was replaced by Greg Stone, who was immediately replaced by Martin Teal (a graduate of Harvard University at age 18 and Wharton Business School at age 20). Teal hired his father, Dennis, as a personal assistant.

Cheers Employees

The multitude of Cheers waitresses (both permanent and temporary) included: Carla, Diane, Rebecca, Corrine (Hungry Heifer waitress), Cora (truck stop waitress), Annie Tortelli (Carla's daughter-in-law), Kelly Gaines (Woody's future wife), Lillian Huxley (British waitress), Laurie Drake (Evan's daughter), Annette Lozupone (Carla's sister), Cherry (fired because she kept removing her blouse), and Julie (quit because Sam slept with her sister). Waitresses who were mentioned but never appeared on the show included Didi, Karlene, Joanne and Angela. According to Sam, every waitress who terminated her employment was given a severance boink (or the cash equivalent, $1.14).

The various bartenders included: Sam, Coach, Woody, Carla, Diane, Rebecca, Norm (to qualify for the Cheers medical plan and a charity basketball game), Ramon (from Cancun), Wayne (corporate bartender), Harley (for Carla and Eddie's wedding reception), Frankie Lozupone (Carla's nephew), Henri (Frenchman), Earl (replaced Rebecca as manager), Kevin McHale (for a charity basketball game), Ken Charters (when Sam was a manager-host), Gus O'Malley (former owner of Cheers), and Malcolm Kramer (patron with only six months to live).

Other employees and hired workers included: Tiny (Cheers bouncer), Bernard (telephone repairman who propositioned Rebecca incessantly), Sy Flembeck (Cheers advertising agent), Don Santry (beer tap repairman and Rebecca's future husband), Elaine (harpist), Russell Boyd (pianist and Woody's cousin), Loretta Tortelli (singer), and Nick Tortelli and Frasier Crane (janitors).

Miscellaneous information about various Cheers employees included: Cheers' bouncer Tiny was paid minimum wage (Sam convinced him it was

$2.00 per hour), was able to move the plate in his head, and self inflicted wounds with a blow torch if he let himself down. Career waitress Lillian Huxley was an exceptional employee loved by all patrons, and her daughter, Carolyn, was a model for *British Vogue* magazine. Finally, Earl was the Cheers manager momentarily in 1990, and formerly a shortstop for the Chicago Cubs.

Cheers also had some employment turnover. First, Woody was fired in 1986 because Sam could not afford three bartenders after his manager-host idea failed. Since the new employee, Ken Charters, had a wife and three kids, Woody was the most expendable. When Ken quit to accept another position, Sam immediately rehired Woody. Second, when Woody won the Boston city council election, Carla became the new assistant bartender. Finally, when Rebecca was rehired as the Cheers manager in 1990, her first assignment was to fire the other manager, Earl.

Cheers Patrons

Phil was a member of the CIA, trained the Green Berets, and worked on the Manhattan Project. He served time in prison for robbing a Piggly Wiggly grocery store, and one drunken evening tried to join the Flying Wallendas (but quickly sobered from the height).

Gregg (later known as Paul Creypens) could sing the entire "Bonanza" theme song. Paul Creypens was a regular since 1982 but excluded from the Cheers gang's activities (he was even denied a beer tab). Born in 1948 in Honolulu, Hawaii, Paul was a mess cook in the navy, the Cheers physical fitness trainer in 1982, and subsequently became a tollbooth attendant (though he always dreamed of being an international jewel thief). He was also divorced (his wife left him).

Tom (also known as Barney, Tom Sherry, Tom Ballard, and Thomas Babson in various episodes) was the legal eagle who worked at the law firm of Sing and Kleckman and finally passed the attorney bar exam in 1986. His first case was representing Sam for a willful assault and battery charge brought by Diane. If Tom could have any woman in the world, he would choose Kim Basinger in *9½ Weeks* (1986).

Al was the elderly patron who thought the biggest big-wig of them all was Sinatra. The most fun he had since 1958 was fondling clothes in Diane's suitcase, and the last time he was called a screaming viking was on his honeymoon.

Miscellaneous information about the other regular Cheers patrons included: Pete owned an abundance of surveillance equipment because his wife slept around a lot, and thought Davy Crockett was the greatest American hero; Chuck (also known as Tim and Greg in earlier episodes) was employed as a janitor in a biology lab where they made mutant viruses; and

Barry was homosexual, but subsequently married a woman named Joanne (though it ended in divorce). Other miscellaneous bar regulars included Alan (also known as Mike in earlier episodes), Larry, Hugh, Steve, Mark, Jack, Joe and Tony.

The Cheers gang's favorite movie and theme song was *The Magnificent Seven* (1960), and they always cried when watching *It's a Wonderful Life* (1946). When they watched the National Cable Ace Awards the category the gang rated was, "The Most Impressive Display of Female Flesh in a Tight-Fitting Dress." The gang was captivated with Frasier's reading of *A Tale of Two Cities* by Charles Dickens, because he added carnage and modern flare. Moreover, they ate lunch every day at The Dip & Fry, went to the last night of business at the Twi-Lite Drive-in to watch the All-Night Godzilla Marathon, and missed the bathroom stuffing record by one person because Woody counted himself twice (Woody and me).

The first bar argument was naming the sweatiest movie ever made, and Sumner Sloane won by guessing *Cool Hand Luke* (1967). Other unique bar discussions included: the length of a whale's intestine (Cliff claimed it was over three miles long); the amount of skin a person sheds in a year (Cliff claimed it was over three pounds); fictional twins they would like to see kissing; the worst way to die; the best car song; the smartest animal; how much faster was the fax versus the mail; riddles about Cliff's brain; who was better, Grandpa on the "Munsters" or Uncle Festor on the "Addams Family"; if the Brady Bunch crashed in the Andes, who would be eaten first (Woody suggested the maid, but to first ask her for directions on the best way to prepare herself); why the Coyote wanted to eat the Roadrunner; why Casper the Friendly Ghost had friends at the end of each cartoon, but no friends at the beginning of the next; answering all the mysteries of Disneyworld; which television program the gang was watching when Norm had a cheese doodle stuck to the side of his mouth; if the Lennon sisters, the McGuire sisters and the Andrew sisters all came to a four-way stop, which would have the right-of-way; and former presidents with fish parts for their faces. As for bar trivia, the person who held the record for stuffing beer nuts up his nose was Jimmy "the Snorkel" Stevens.

Some of the interesting bar contests over the years: ugliest tongue contest; beard growing contest (Cliff won by attaching a fake beard with an industrial adhesive); who could identify the most anachronisms in the Gladiator Film Festival; whose breath smelled most like tuna (Norm won); biggest spit bubble; how long it would take John Allen Hill to make Sam go crazy (John Allen Hill won $200); tricks with digits exhibition (Lilith won by stuffing her fist in her mouth); when Rebecca would have sex, how good it would be, and what her partner would say to her the next day; who could get the most women's telephone numbers in one night; how poorly Sam batted in the major league; and whether Sam or Woody would be the first to get a kiss from Rebecca.

Not-So-Regular Patrons

The most infamous psychotic patron was Andy-Andy (Andy Schoeder), who was convicted of manslaughter for killing a waitress. Sam originally paid Andy $20 to date Diane, and she subsequently offered Andy a theatrical audition to perform Shakespeare's *Othello*. However, he attempted to strangle Diane during the scene and was sent to a state mental institute. After being released he had a new girlfriend, Cynthia, and told her a few lies, i.e., he owned Cheers; Sam was an ex-con flasher whom he helped by hiring as a bartender; Diane wanted to have his child; and he counseled Frasier for kleptomania. Andy supposedly left the country in 1985 but returned six years later strapped with dynamite and demanding to see Diane.

As for the many miscellaneous patrons: one of the most popular patrons was Fred because he bought a round of drinks whenever a sibling died; one of the most obnoxious patrons was New York Yankee fan Big Eddie, who ridiculed the Red Sox; the patron with the biggest lies was Thomas Hilliard, III (alias Eric Finch), who enthralled the gang with stories of being a spy and a poet, but was actually a multimillionaire who offered to purchase Cheers for $1 million; the eldest patron was Buzz Crowder, the last surviving member of the Fighting Double Deuce (22nd Brigade) from World War I; the most nerdy patron was Marshall Lipton, the "Ph.D from M.I.T.," who was a professor of Cybernetics at Massachusetts Institute of Technology, and devised a theory that the Boston Celtics always lost when the Van Allen belt was in a state of flux.

As for other patrons: the regular Cheers con man was Harry "the Hat" Gittes; the most religious patron was Kevin, who visited Cheers the night before entering a monastery; the most generous patron was Malcolm Kramer, owner of a chemical plant outside Chicago and a graduate of Harvard Business School, who bequeathed the Cheers gang $100,000 for entertaining him after he was told he only had six months to live; the cymbalist for the Boston Symphony was Misha, who visited Cheers between rests and counted beats so he knew exactly when to return; and the most silent patron was Sotto, the mime.

Various Bar Competitions

The Miss Boston Barmaid Contest was an annual event that commenced in 1939, and since 1976 the winning contestants had an average bra size of 38. Cheers' only victory was in 1983, when Diane overcame a facial tick. Carla competed in the 53rd annual contest to win the grand prize (a Mazda Miata convertible), and although she performed superbly, the judges crowned Shawnee Wilson as the winner because of her physical beauty and large breasts.

The longest running competition was whether Rebecca would finally have sex, how good it would be, and what her beau would say. Rebecca had sex with Robin in 1989, and Lilith won by having the closest guess (August 1992). Rebecca claimed the sex was fantastic, so Norm, Ken, David, and Cliff's mom won by having the closest guess ("very good"). Lastly, Robin said, "I love you," so Cliff won with the closest guess ("I'll respect you in the morning").

Other various competitions: Sam and Henri competed against one another to get the most women's telephone numbers, and the Frenchman won 10–9; Diane and Carla held a waitress contest to see who could get the most tips in one night, and Diane won by $1.00.

Gary's Olde Towne Tavern

Gary, a magna cum laude graduate in American literature from Princeton University, was a member of Sigma Ki fraternity, and the owner of Gary's Olde Towne Tavern (which was three blocks from Cheers). His tavern opened in 1983 (or 1984 in other episodes) and had three known bartenders, Gary, Matt, and Woody Boyd. Gary's biggest rival was Cheers, and when juvenile pranks were involved, Gary always retaliated within 24 hours. As for the Gary's Tavern–Cheers sports competitions, in 1986 Gary's win-loss record was 173-1 (they lost in bowling); however, in 1990 they also lost in basketball. (Gary's Tavern defeated Cheers in almost every sport, such as baseball, volleyball, softball, and tag football).

Cheers' bowling victory was memorable because Diane single-handedly won the match at Vic's Bowl-O-Rama, which commenced an annual tradition of the Cheers gang calling Gary's Tavern to brag about the victory. In 1988 Gary stole the bowling trophy, and when he returned it broken, bar wars began. Cheers' highlight prank was interrupting Gary's live satellite telecast of a boxing prizefight with a poetry reading. Norm and Cliff read "Ballad of the Dead Ladies" by Dante Gabriel Rossetti, a 19th century poet. However, Gary accomplished the supreme shenanigan by having the Cheers gang prank themselves. Gary generously offered to send Wade Boggs to Cheers to sign autographs, but the gang became suspicious, so they chased the Boston baseball legend outside and "pantsed" him.

The 1990 basketball competition was easily won by Cheers because they had Boston Celtics star Kevin McHale on their team. Despite wagering $5,000, Gary had the last laugh. Kevin McHale twisted his ankle during the game, and Woody tried to pop it into place. The next day the Celtics' team physician claimed McHale suffered a season-ending injury. When Sam offered $5,000 to conceal Cheers' involvement, Gary's "team doctor" accepted the bribe and Gary's Tavern received all the publicity by donating the money to an orphanage.

The bars also competed in the annual Bloody Mary Contest. Cheers won the competition in 1982 and 1983, and Gary's Tavern was victorious from 1984 to 1987 (because of their secret ingredient, black cardamom). In 1988 Cheers, ensuring that Gary's Tavern did not win, staged a phony contest so Gary would miss the actual event. Although it is unknown which bar won the contest, one thing is certain: Gary's Tavern did not win!

St. Patrick's Day marked another competitive event filled with pranks. The bars had an annual bet of $100 on who could get the most business that day. As usual, Gary's Tavern won the competition, as it had every year since opening; however, there were two memorable pranks. In 1990 Cheers accused Gary of stealing Tecumseh (the wooden Indian), so they shut down Gary's Tavern. After learning Rebecca had Tecumseh removed for refurbishing, the gang preempted Gary's retaliation by shaving their heads to spell out G-A-R-Y. Of course Sam wore a rubber cap because without his hair he would be just one of the guys! The ultimate insult came when Rebecca revealed that Gary's Tavern was closed for remodeling and the Cheers gang had shaved their heads for no legitimate reason.

The other memorable event was in 1993, when Sam agreed to increase the annual wager to include the losers traveling to the winner's bar and singing "Getting to Know You" in their birthday suits. After losing, Cheers was represented by Sam, Norm, Woody, Cliff, and Paul (because he insisted on being included in their activities).

Halloween was the other special occasion wrought with pranks. Naturally, Gary always prevailed with the best pranks, so in 1991 the Cheers gang vowed not to lose to him. To accomplish this task, the gang joined forces with Gary to play a prank on Sam by pretending Gary was dead. Although Sam was in disbelief (his eulogy was, "Get out of there, Gary"), he eventually fell for the gag. Sam later exacted revenge by starting a rivalry with the "new" owner of Gary's Tavern, Frank "The Angel of Death" Carpaccio, a mafia boss. As the seriousness of the pranks escalated, the Cheers gang (Woody, Carla, Norm and Cliff) entered a witness protection program and were abandoned on a deserted highway in North Dakota. Sam then called the highway telephone and said, "Gotcha!"

The only person capable of an effective prank against Gary was Harry "the Hat" Gittes. In 1993 he posed as a wealthy developer, Rutherford Cunningham, and purchased Gary's Tavern for $1 million to build a shopping center. Gary bulldozed his bar before the check cleared, and it bounced. Although outclassed, Gary was still able to embarrass the Cheers gang one last time by accusing them of bulldozing his bar (because Sam previously threatened to get Gary). As the Cheers gang kneeled and begged Gary not to call the police, he snapped a photograph of the groveling congregation.

Melville's

Melville's dress code required men to wear dinner jackets and women to wear taffeta (and have the correct change for the rest room). Vic was the maître d', Paul was the waiter, and the two hatcheck girls were Miss Kenderson and Vera Peterson. The busboy was Reuben, an undocumented alien who was soft and sweet with a voice like a nightingale, and his significant other was Melville's pastry chef. Melville's opened for lunch at noon, and all the eating scenes were in booth number five.

In 1990 Melville's was purchased by John Allen Hill, a successful restaurateur with a dining establishment in Manhattan eloquently called J.H. Cafe. His only daughter, Valerie, dated Sam, but only to infuriate her father. Carla became Hill's permanent one-night stand, and affectionately called him "The Bullet." She was also the only person to say, "I love you" to him. Hill had his share of insulting nicknames, such as John Cougar Mellonhead, Sweat Hog, Perverted Goat Boy, Road Kill, Bag of Bones, Zit Face, Bladder Polyp, Bullet Head, Hatchet Face, Package from Amityville, Pond Scum, Hairless King of the Snobs, Knobby-Headed Weasel, Bald and Wrinkled, and Evil Little Dwarf.

Hungry Heifer

The Hungry Heifer, owned by Sid Nelson, was considered a roadside landmark because it was the only building on the Eastern seaboard with a giant red-eyed, steam-snorting bull on the roof. Norm circulated a petition to have the restaurant preserved as an historical landmark. The Big Eaters' Circle was the Hungry Heifer's special dining club, and the busboy's name was Gus. (At Sid's insistence, Gus was the incendiary who razed the restaurant to cinders.)

Some of the Hungry Heifer's menu entrées were: Ton of T-Bone ($4.00 for 24 oz. of USDA Choice A bef (not beef)—a Hungry Heifer trademark for a processed, synthetic, meat-like substance); Loobster (lobster substitute); Surf and Turf (tuna fish sandwich with beef gravy); Carnivore Platter (steak dinner topped off with pork chops); Chef's Special Ribs (the cook made fun of your tie); Ribscapade (Wednesday night special); Chef's Tribute to Swine (Thursday night special); You Keep the Hoof night; and a 24 oz. steak for $1.99.

Cheers—Guest Celebrities

Cheers had its share of celebrity visitors. The various political figures included: Admiral William J. Crowe, Jr. (chairman of the Joint Chiefs of Staff); Michael Dukakis (governor of Massachusetts); Raymond L. Flynn

(Boston mayor); Gary Hart (1988 presidential candidate); Ethel Kennedy (was married to Robert); John Kerry (Massachusetts senator); and Thomas P. "Tip" O'Neill (former Speaker of the House of Representatives).

Several television talk show hosts appeared on the show: Johnny Carson (former late night talk show host); Dick Cavett; Arsenio Hall (former late night talk show host); and John McLaughlin (syndicated political round table participant). Some other television and film figures also appeared: Alex Trebek (host of "Jeopardy!"); Robert Urich (star of "Vega$"); Spanky McFarland ("The Little Rascals"); and Doc Severinsen (former regular musician on "The Tonight Show with Johnny Carson").

Noteworthy sports figures included Wade Boggs (Boston Red Sox); Mike Ditka (ex–Chicago Bears coach); Kevin McHale (Boston Celtics); and Luis Tiant (ex–Red Sox pitcher). The musical guests included Harry Connick, Jr., Bill Medley and Bobby Hatfield (the Righteous Brothers), and the 139th Street Quartet. The guest models were Kim Alexis (super model) and several *Playboy* playmates.

Miscellaneous Episodes

In the series pilot, the first person to walk through the front door of Cheers was a young boy who ordered a beer using the fake military I.D. of First Sergeant Walter Keller, born 1944 (making the boy 38 years old). For Cheers' 100th anniversary, Boston Mayor Raymond L. Flynn specially appeared to award a plaque, and officially declared "Cheers Day" to be celebrated on Saturday, November 4, 1989; the guest of honor was Mr. Weaver, a 106-year-old Bostonian.

Luis Tiant, ex–Red Sox pitcher, starred in a Field's Lite beer commercial, and was relieved by Sam after continually fumbling his lines. Czechoslovakian hockey star Tibor Svetkovic learned English by watching television commercials, and shared the same television agent (Lana Turner) as Sam Malone. As for television, the most frequently aired station was WLBD channel 13, whose newscast consisted of Joanne (anchor), Dr. Buzz (meteorologist), and Dave Richards (sportscaster).

Miscellaneous items of interest to Bostonians: the coldest day in Boston's history was January 12, 1981, and the Charles River was the best make out place in Boston.

Final Episode

When Diane returned to Boston in 1993, both she and Sam pretended they were married—Diane's husband was homosexual and a dog groomer, and

Sam's wife was Rebecca Howe. Rebecca claimed to be a corporate attorney specializing in products liability litigation for the law firm of Emerson, Lake and Palmer. Together she and Sam had four children (Sam, Jr., Darby, Newton, and Chelsea).

Diane and Sam reunited romantically, and Sam agreed to accompany her to California where he was going to work at a health club juice bar. When the airplane was detained, Sam reconsidered his decision and returned to Cheers, like Norm always knew he would. The last noteworthy act of the series was Sam adjusting a picture of Geronimo that hung on the balcony wall (signifying a tribute to Nicholas Colasanto).

IV. The Characters

Sam Malone

Childhood and Family

Born circa 1948, Samuel "Mayday" Malone also was known by the aliases, Lance Manyon and Honeyboy Wilson. Sam lived his entire life never being able to fulfill his parents' expectations. If he received a "B" on his report card, they wondered why it was not an "A"; and on Father's Day when Sam was about six years old he made his father breakfast in bed, but his dad merely complained the eggs were too dry and the toast too light.

The Malones were Catholic and proud of their Irish nationality. Sam's great grandfather emigrated to the United States from County Cork, Ireland, and immediately faced blatant employment discrimination—businesses hung NINA (No Irish Need Apply) signs. He was told to change his name, but refused because he was proud of the Malone surname.

Sam's mother believed boys should learn to care for themselves, so she taught the men in the family how to cook. As for his father, Sam once went over three years without speaking to him. The only time the elder Malone said he was proud of his youngest son was when Sam was hired as a corporate executive.

Despite a sibling rivalry with his older brother, Derek, Sam and he shared bunk beds and spent many nights talking about comic books, movies, records, and all the babes they would sleep with once they had their own bedroom. Sam eventually developed an inferiority complex because Derek was the favorite child and perfect in every way. Besides being a wealthy international lawyer, Derek was handsome, with curly blond hair and Windex-blue eyes, very talented (he sang operas, tap danced, and performed billiard trick shots), spoke four languages (including Spanish), flew his own plane, and traveled extensively.

Sam's socialization process included being taught to prove his manhood by the number of women with whom he had sex. Toward that end, he loved taking his pet dog for a walk because it was a great way to meet chicks. Apparently Sam did not become too emotionally attached to the pets because he was unsure whether his dog's name was Fluffy or Buffy, or whether one of these was the name of a woman he had met.

Sam's first oral report in school was on how maple syrup was made, and his only acting experience was performing in the play *How Boots Fooled the King*. Sam dropped out of high school after signing a baseball contract during his senior year. He was always embarrassed about this fact, and promised his parents he would earn a diploma. In 1985, Sam enrolled in night school and received a diploma by successfully completing a geography class. (He was receiving an "A" while sleeping with the teacher, Miss Alannah Purdy, and subsequently earned a "D" based on his knowledge of geography.) His education ended there. The furthest Sam got in college was halfway through the application.

Personal

Sam stood 6'3" tall, with brown pompadour hair and eyebrows that grew together like a big fuzzy caterpillar. He was attractive like Gary Cooper, and on a scale of 1–10, Sam rated himself a 12. He had a dimple on his buttock which was covered by bikini briefs (sometimes by boxers), and left one button on his shirt unfastened so he could scratch his belly. He lived by "The Ten Commandments of Sam Malone" (the two known commandments being, #3: thou shall not loan thy car; and #4: honor thy hair). Sam's doctor placed him on a bran diet, and in 1990 Sam had a gallstone the size of a golf ball.

Sam usually spent Thanksgiving with his old Army buddies. (He was never in the full-time military, only the reserves; but his buddies were.) His accountant from 1974 to 1984 was Sy, and thereafter it was Norm Peterson. Sam's attorney was Thomas Babson, who also doubled as his landscaper.

Sam's two hidden talents were his "bar slide" (a full glass of beer sliding along the bar and taking a 90-degree turn around the corner) and his sexual prowess. The two areas he prohibited anyone from touching were his business and certain private anatomical parts. The one thing Sam wished he could do was make his eyes vibrate like those of Randy Evans, a first baseman for the Cleveland Indians. (Another remarkable player, Johnny Driscoll, did handstand push-ups during spring training.)

As for cultural interests, Sam was not overly knowledgeable about the arts (despite Diane's arduous efforts to stimulate some interest). For instance, he never heard of revered New England artist Phillip Semenko, was not impressed with nonrepresentational artists, and thought French Impressionist Paul Cézanne's paintings looked like they were created while the artist was goofed on skunk weed. In contrast, Sam's favorite painting was the commercialized *Dogs Playing Blackjack*, and the one work of art he knew was Michelangelo's "Two Muscular Guys Touching Fingers" (actually "The Creation of Man").

Classical music concerts and the opera were two additional areas of disinterest. Sam preferred laser light shows and people being shot from cannons. Moreover, his knowledge (and interest) in books was limited. He thought *Man and Superman* by George Bernard Shaw was a comic book, and he read the book *Speak Out and Score* (a book on business success) because he thought it would be about picking up babes. In fact, Diane was shocked if he read a book without the words "naughty," "hot" or "throbbing" in the title. Sam's one impressive literary feat was reading *War and Peace* in five days.

Besides bicycling on his Schwinn, Sam had several hobbies, mostly related to the pursuit of women, such as sailing (babes on waves), skiing (melting snow bunnies), and his hair (babes love it). The sea always reminded Sam of the song "Popeye the Sailor Man," and in 1983 he nearly won the Boston Regatta (and captained Robin Colcord's boat in the 1989 event). One of Sam's less than successful maritime efforts happened in the Caribbean when he sailed his boat into an uncharted reef. As for skiing, Sam usually frequented the ski hills of Stowe, Vermont, and Sugarloaf, Maine. On his only skydiving jump he blew chow at 5,000 feet.

Sam enjoyed several indoor sports, too. He was Cheers' best dart player, and whipped Robin Colcord at darts, billiards and chess. As for arm wrestling, Sam had beaten every person in the bar except Jack Dalton (Diane's European boyfriend). Sam also enjoyed boxing and racquetball. He accompanied Harry "the Hat" Gittes to a Marvin Hagler prizefight in 1983, and defeated Woody at racquetball (though Sam suffered a hernia requiring surgery at Boston General Hospital). In addition, with Diane as his partner, Sam won a ballroom dancing trophy and was known for being as graceful as a bull swan.

For a very special occasion, Sam saved a box of fine Perfecto Cuban cigars that Reggie Jackson gave to him. Sam opened the cigars in 1993 to celebrate his return to Cheers (after abandoning the notion of living in California). Sam's most flattering award was being selected as one of Boston's 20 most eligible bachelors by *Boston* magazine.

Sam's philosophy of life was to service the queen bee. However, at age 45 he began realizing that his sexual compulsiveness prevented him from experiencing more meaningful aspects in his life, such as a serious relationship with a woman or having a son to carry on the Malone name.

Sam believed in a life after death where Snickers candy bars were served for breakfast. Sam had a reincarnation memory that he fought in the Civil War, and when he had a near death experience his *hair* flashed before his eyes.

Other miscellaneous information: Sam's mother was the only person who could order Sam to march; he did excellent impersonations of actor Gary Cooper; he used a Snoopy toothbrush; he chipped a tooth on a hard shell in a Melville's salad; he liked flower patterns on china because it was easier to hide food he disliked; Sam had chicken pox as an adult; he sought counseling from Connie Forsythe to deal with anxiety attributed to being mistreated by John Allen Hill; and he felt there were several activities every man must experience as part of his passage into manhood—betting with a bookie, going to a cathouse, urinating off a balcony, and mooning out of the back of a car.

Sam's Hair

According to Sam, good looks will open doors, but good hair will blow them off their hinges. He even had hair insurance (which required three estimates before he could make a claim). Sam first realized he was balding on August 12, 1989, and his biggest secret was wearing a toupee (i.e., a hair replacement system) to cover his pate. The only people who knew this secret were Carla Tortelli-LeBec and his stylist, Tony.

Great hair requires special treatment and care. The tools necessary to trim Sam's hair included sterile tungsten steel scissors, an English bone comb (including 36 to 39 tines), and a conditioner with a provitamin B-5, carotene complex. Sam also protected his precious hair with a shower cap whenever entering a wine cellar.

Personal Likes and Dislikes

The three things Sam most enjoyed in life were fun women, hot dogs (especially the rat parts), and game shows. His favorite color was blue, his favorite time of the day was 8:15 p.m., and he loved Froot Loops breakfast cereal. As for television and movies, Sam most enjoyed the Three Stooges (especially the early shows with Curly), he thought Jerry Lewis was a great comedian, and his favorite actor was Robert Mitchum (Sam watched every Mitchum movie made since 1972). Musically, Sam preferred rock 'n' roll, though he relied upon Johnny Mathis for romantic music. Sam also loved the smell of sawdust (it reminded him of childhood, when his father had a workshop).

Friends

When Sam was 19 years old, his best friend and minor league teammate was Buck, who taught him to hot-wire a car. One summer they hitchhiked along Route 66; however, their friendship faded once Buck was elected into the Hall of Fame. Sam also vacationed with his ex–Red Sox teammates. Every year on the weekend of George Washington's birthday (mid–February), they traveled to Stowe, Vermont, to melt a few snow bunnies.

Sam's closest and best friend was Coach. Since their days together in the minor and major leagues, Coach was very protective and helped solve Sam's personal problems, most notably his alcohol dependency. (Coach was the only person to confront Sam about his drinking problem.) After Coach's death, Rebecca became Sam's closest friend, though Paul Creypens helped solve Sam's personal problems. Carla was a friend since 1977, and knew more about Sam's baseball career than Sam did.

In contrast, Sam's biggest enemy was Gary, who brought out both the worst (in terms of pranks) and the best in him (in terms of respect). Gary had a way of unifying the Cheers gang toward one common goal—to get Gary! Despite the animosity between them, Sam realized he had a friend in Gary.

Sam's Automobile

Other than his hair, Sam's most cherished possession was his 1964 Corvette—rally red (also described as flame red) with a rag top, black interior and knock off hubs. The vehicle identification number was U510593947-D, and the gas mileage was 19 m.p.g. (highway) and 15 m.p.g. (city). Even the slightest scratch in the paint or chrome warranted a tow to an auto garage (he couldn't drive the car because it was disfigured). Sam's mechanic was Gordon (who kindly gave Sam a free radiator flush for his birthday), and his shammy boy was Philipe.

When his Corvette was stolen in 1992, Sam formed a victim support group for persons who had high performance vehicles stolen. Equally traumatic moments occurred when Sam had to sell the Corvette to purchase Cheers in 1989, and after getting it back, having to re-sell it to pay for remodeling the bar three years later.

In the first instance, Sam's newspaper advertisement read, "For Sale: Corvette. Meet Chicks." Each potential purchaser was subjected to several multiple choice questions to judge his compatibility with the car. Dennis Hammill was an interested buyer but failed the multiple choice test. Sam eventually sold the car to Lilith Sternin-Crane. His replacement vehicle was a passion beige Volaré (economical, but not a babe magnet). Women began laughing at him, so Sam begged Lilith to return the car (and offered an additional $1,000). Frasier eventually persuaded her to return the car.

The second time, Sam sold his Corvette to pay for Cheers' remodeling after the fire of 1992. Sam's neighbor, Kirby McFeeney, an avid collector of classic automobiles, purchased the car. Sam and Kirby first met at Sam's victim support group meeting. Sam reacquired the Corvette three months later when Kirby died and his widow, Susan McFeeney, a kindergarten teacher, had no use for the car (she liked her Volkswagen). Sam suavely persuaded her into selling it for less than fair market value ($10,000 over two years). However, Sam felt uncharacteristically guilty (scratching the paint three times in one week), and eventually agreed to pay fair market value for the car.

Baseball Career

The only baseball card Sam owned was one of himself. His baseball career began in February of his senior year of high school (circa 1966), when he received a contract. Since graduation was not until June, he decided to drop out of school to play for the Boston Red Sox minor league class A farm club in Pawtucket.

In 1972 he moved into the major league ranks as a right-handed relief pitcher wearing Red Sox uniform number 16. As one of the best groomed pitchers in the major league, Samuel "Mayday" Malone's best pitch was the hard slider. His teammates called it the "slider of death" because he usually gave up a three-run homer. As for another pitch, Coach taught Sam how to throw a knuckleball.

Sam's roommate was Red Sox catcher Tom Kenderson, whose favorite mixed drink was gin and tonic. Tom was a practical joker and a babe hound. Ironically, he later revealed his homosexuality in an autobiography titled *Catcher's Mask* (Sam was highlighted in chapters seven through nine), and promoted the book at a press conference and book signing at Cheers. Sam was shocked and dismayed by this revelation, but overcame his macho bravado to support Tom's decision.

Sam had several baseball superstitions and rituals. He never pitched to anyone named Reggie, Willie or the Bull (though he pitched to Reggie Jackson), and before every game he would rub Coach's head, who in turn would rub Sam's tummy. Before long, everyone in the stadium was watching two grown men rubbing each other, so they moved the ritual to the locker room, and eventually gave it up entirely.

Sam began drinking alcohol during his ball-playing days because he lost his curve ball and had an intense fear of losing. He handled the pressures of baseball by drinking alcohol and chasing women, and used to break out of a slump by drinking himself into a coma. Coach was the only person who really cared; he used to walk Sam back and forth across the clubhouse, pouring coffee down his throat to sober him up before a game, whereas Sam's roommate, Tom Kenderson, abandoned Sam when his drinking became too excessive.

Outside baseball, Sam's superstitions continued when he acquired a bottle cap to help him overcome the urge to drink alcohol. The talisman was from a bottle of beer—the last drop of alcohol he had. While experiencing withdrawals, he squeezed the bottle cap so hard that rigid marks became embedded in the palm of his hand and the cap eventually compressed. When Sam had the urge to drink, he would simply look at the bottle cap, and the horrifying flashbacks sedated the craving. (In 1982 Sam loaned the talisman to slumping Red Sox pitcher Rick Walker, who ultimately lost the bottle cap in Kansas City.)

Although Sam was well-liked, there was one player he despised—Coach's best friend, T-Bone Scorpageoni. Sam resented T-Bone for two reasons: T-Bone thought he was God's gift to mankind, and he once propositioned Coach's wife.

The baseball player who gave Sam the most problems was Frank Robinson (though Reggie Jackson hit nearly half his home runs off Sam's pitches). New York Yankee star Dutch Kincaid was the most prolific batter to face Sam. He hit 27 home runs in 27 at bats, and after every home run paraded around the bases doing his trademark "windmill" routine. Dutch's manager, Cap Richards, arranged Dutch Kincaid Day at Yankee Stadium, and his son, Billy, conned Sam into throwing a lame pitch so Dutch could hit a home run. Dutch was upset, and returned to Cheers to prove his batting prowess (and tagged Sam for 226 consecutive hits). In contrast, Sam was not very productive at the plate. Although claiming his highest batting average was .211, in reality Sam never hit better than .149.

The most inspirational moment in Sam's baseball career occurred on a hot August day in 1974 during a doubleheader against Cleveland. Coach Ernie Pantusso became the temporary manager when Johnson was thrown out of the game. With the bases loaded in the ninth inning, Sam walked a batter, and then Charlie Spikes stepped up to the plate. Coach approached the mound, but instead of pulling Sam out of the game, he said, "Go get 'em," and Sam did.

Sam most enjoyed the baseball fans, many of whom would wait outside the stadium and throw themselves at him. The most memorable fan was Marge Thornhill. She attended every home game at which he played, and sat behind first base in row five, screaming insulting remarks while he pitched. Sam savored the fame associated with being a baseball celebrity, and missed the public attention after his career ended. The most attention he received after retiring was when he was nearly hit by a truck.

Sam's greatest baseball memory was of a doubleheader against Baltimore in 1972. He saved both games with seven pitches, and faced Boog Powell twice. (Incidentally, in another episode, Sam was depicted as earning his first major league save on August 5, 1973, in a doubleheader against Baltimore.) In an equally memorable game, with the tying run on second, Sam struck out Cash, Kaline and Freehan.

Sam's most embarrassing moment occurred July 14, 1975, against the Baltimore Orioles. Although he pitched three innings and had a good game statistically, Sam was intoxicated at the time and thought the Oriole mascot was a huge mutant bird. He hurled a fastball and hit the feathered creature between the eyes, causing a concussion. The press crucified Sam, and it took him three years to live it down. (The game was subsequently aired on the Play Ball Channel, channel 58.)

The most lamentable moment in Sam's baseball career took place during an important night game at Tiger Stadium. He had not pitched in a while because of his drinking, so he stayed sober all day; it was toward the end of his career and Sam wanted to prove he still had the talent to be a major league pitcher. When the coach called, Sam chickened out by saying his arm hurt. He was afraid to go out on the mound.

Sam's baseball career lasted five years (circa 1972–77) until an elbow problem forced an early retirement (i.e., he drank himself out of baseball). The press mercilessly criticized Sam for his drinking, and he was further humiliated by being told he was cut from the team on his birthday. He quit drinking permanently two years later.

The most memorable ex–Red Sox player was Dave Richards. He described himself as the second biggest babe hound (second only to Sam), and was married to and divorced from Brenda. His bumper sticker read, "Honk if You're Horny." Dave had a television sports segment, "I on Sports" and a radio talk show. Two classic sign-offs were "Good night, and may the sports be with you" and "Good night, and remember, the world is full of winners and losers. Here's hoping you're one of them."

Baseball—Retirement

According to Sam, "a lot of people may not know this, but I happen to be pretty famous." Unfortunately, he was also vexed by being forgotten in the annals of baseball. In one incident, ex-teammate and friend Dave Richards asked Sam to interview for a "Where Are They Now?" television segment. Not only was Sam chosen as a last resort (John McEnroe, Gerry Cheevers, M. L. Carr, Jim Rice and Robert Parish had prior commitments, and Becky Bannerman, a junior high school gymnast, was on a field trip), but midway through the interview Dave canceled Sam in favor of John McEnroe.

In another incident, Sam donated his Red Sox jersey to a celebrity auction for a children's hospital. When nobody purchased the jersey, Sam feared the embarrassment of having it given away during the last 10 minutes of the show by a chimpanzee, Mr. Bo Bo, who drew names from a coconut. Despite efforts to purchase it—Diane paid $100, Sam paid $200, and the bar raised $116 and a voucher for a quart of buttermilk (courtesy of Norm's dairy clients, the Brubakers)—the jersey was returned for auction. Eventually, Bert Simpson bought the uniform for $300 to put the damn thing to rest. The entire ordeal made Sam feel like an ex-ex-baseball player. (He was also neglected when the Red Sox organization did not invite him to the alumni banquet in 1985.)

In 1992 Sam attempted a comeback for two reasons. First, the Boston Red Sox were in dire need of pitching personnel; and second, a former teammate and pathetic pitcher, Mitch Ganzell (nicknamed Mrs. Ganzell), was also making a comeback. After a tryout, Sam made the cut and was assigned to the Red Sox double A farm club in New Britain, Connecticut. He went on the road with the team, but did not enjoy reliving his youth.

His roommate, Slim, repeatedly called Sam "Maybe, Midday, and Monday" Malone, and the rest of the team were rowdy, obnoxious juveniles (as Sam had been in his youth). Sam quickly realized he did not appreciate their boisterousness—yelling, running around, towel snapping, pantsing new players, pillow fights, beer drinking, staying out all night, and patting guys on the butt. It was too much like the old days, and he had matured. Sam quit the team and returned to Cheers.

After retiring, Sam's only baseball glory was participating on various softball teams. He volunteered to pitch in a chamber of commerce charity softball game against the *Playboy* playmates, but took the game too seriously. He had 17 strikeouts (he counted 18), hit Babette in the head with a pitch when she crowded home plate, and celebrated the 7–0 win with victory laps after the game. In another softball event, Sam was hired as a corporate executive so he could pitch for the company's softball team (just in time for the playoffs). He replaced a legitimate corporate executive, Heppel, and even wore his predecessor's jersey (number 11).

Employment

Other than baseball, Sam had several occupations or employment opportunities. He was best remembered as the proprietor of Cheers (1977–87, 1990–present), but also worked as a bartender (1987–90) when Cheers was under corporate ownership. In 1987 he sold the bar to expunge the memory of Diane (who left Boston to finish writing a novel for publication), and used the proceeds to purchase a boat to circumnavigate the globe. After sinking the boat somewhere in the Caribbean (he hit a reef which was then named "No Brains Atoll" in honor of him), Sam returned to Cheers and was hired as a bartender (eventually earning $6.80 per hour and having the title "executive supervising bartender"). Sam's corporate connection was Vice President Greg Stone.

In 1989 Sam attempted to purchase a bar. Since Cheers was unaffordable, he bought another bar, Tim's Place, along the waterfront and intended to rename it Sam's Place. However, Robin Colcord persuaded Sam to abandon the idea, and helped rescind the loan. (Robin then bought the property and developed it into a high-rise resort.)

Sam also attempted a career as a television sportscaster when he relieved the vacationing Dave Richards. Despite the expectation of a permanent position, it never materialized because Sam's commentaries ranged from boring and noncontroversial to outrageous and ludicrous. For example, Sam gave commentaries on rooting for the home team and artificial grass versus natural turf (he was undecided), then created a rap song commentary about old athletes doing sports on television, and concluded with a ventriloquist act (with Little Sam).

His other television occupation was endorsing products. Sam's most noteworthy commercial was for Field's Lite Beer. In the commercial, Luis Tiant continued to botch the product slogan, and was relieved by Sam, who earned a save by saying, "You don't feel full with Field's, you just feel fine." Sam's agent, Lana Marshall, arranged the commercial but insisted on bartering sexual favors for commercial endorsements. When Sam ended the pleasure part of their relationship, she terminated the business part.

In the literary realm, Sam achieved limited success. First, Dick Cavett suggested that Sam prepare an autobiography highlighting his baseball career, his bout with alcoholism and the irony of owning a bar. Sam cajoled Diane into writing the manuscript, which was ultimately rejected by the publisher because the content was not controversial enough. Sam and Diane then rewrote the manuscript, highlighting Sam's libidinous behavior. (It is unknown whether the manuscript was ever published.) Second, a quasi-literary success occurred when Sam's self-originating quote ("What does a stuffed shirt know about blue collar poetry?") was included in Diane's research for a book. Finally, Sam's only known literary success came in 1986 when he submitted a poem to *Cysagy*, a small literary magazine. The poem "Nocturne" was accepted and published on page 37. He eventually confessed that the poem was derived from a love letter Diane had written to him. (The letters were wrapped with a red bow and stored in the bar's safe.)

Sam's final occupation was a two-week stint in 1988 as an eastern regional sales manager (he was hired so he could pitch for the corporate softball team). Sam had an office complete with a secretary, Mimi, and the requisite picture of himself on the desk. His first telephone call was to his father. After learning the real reason for his advancement, Sam confronted Evan Drake with an ultimatum: if Sam did not have legitimate executive talent, they should part ways. Later that day Sam returned to Cheers as a bartender.

In 1990 the Lillian Corporation offered to sell Cheers to Sam for $1.00 as a token of their appreciation for his averting a hostile takeover by Robin Colcord. Sam was elated by the offer but unable to garner the necessary financial backing to purchase the bar. Fortunately, other bar patrons donated their two-cents worth and he lowballed the corporation into selling the bar for $.85.

Thereafter, Sam was inundated by recent technological advances in business, so he hired Rebecca as the manager. In 1991 they became partners by jointly purchasing the bathrooms and poolroom from John Allen Hill (Sam paid $5,000 and Rebecca paid $25,000). The following year Rebecca destroyed the bar in a conflagration when her freshly extinguished cigarette ignited the office wastebasket.

Romance: Sammy Style

Sam's first sexual encounter was in the sixth grade (by then he had seen half the girls in his class in their underwear). He remembered this milestone because he could not get to the girl's house until the crossing guard showed up. Sam's second sexual encounter was with the crossing guard! (However, in another episode Sam claimed the crossing guard was his first sexual encounter.)

Sam's most treasured relationship device was his black book of women's telephone numbers. It contained all the important telephone numbers in his life—women he slept with (including Rebecca and his cleaning lady, Desiree Harrison) and his mother. Each woman was rated on a four-star scale (the first star was free, and the rest had to be earned). The book was so sacred that it was stored in a waterproof pouch and locked in a safe at night. Once, when Sam misplaced his black book, a pubescent teen, Timmy, used it to arrange dates, asking each woman to meet him at the roller rink wearing French-cut panties and a black leather miniskirt.

Other than the black book, Sam had a babe kit. The red plastic fold-down tote contained all the necessary components for a successful date—his first edition black book, a Members Only jacket, a picture of him and Elvis, and a special blend of cologne (combination of Old Spice, High Karate, and something to remove spots). Other than his babe kit accoutrement, Sam used jasmine-scented oriental oil for body massages.

Not surprisingly, Sam could not develop an intimate relationship with a woman, or even care about her until they did the one thing he most cared about—sleep together. He rarely spent an evening talking to a woman because he believed there was nothing to talk about—a guy did all his talking *beforehand*. When a romantic relationship was nearing the end, Sam had six prearranged breakup speeches (e.g., "I'm ashamed to be a man" or "I have a contagious skin disease and insanity runs in my family"), or he said, "I'll call you tomorrow" or gave her a fictitious telephone number. Until Diane came along, Sam never thought about morality and integrity in a relationship. Although women and sex were a significant interest in his life, Sam had at least one nonsexual interest—the Three Stooges.

Regarding Sam's dating ritual, there are three types of women he refused to date: married, underage, and comatose. As for romance, according to Sam, a man should only use the word "love" in tennis and *after* he paid for the hotel room. His best come-on line was, "Hey baby, what's your sign?"

As for Sam's intriguing love life, it was so prolific that his bed was located in the Smithsonian Institution. The strangest place he ever had sex was in the back of a car (it was on an assembly line), and he once made love to a woman who was about to marry another man (it was in the back of a limousine on the way to her wedding).

As for marriage, according to Sam, the one person who could not be trusted was a bride. Marriage changes women. After listening to the wedding vows they inevitably believe those solemn words. Sam was married once, but after a whirlwind romance it ended in disaster (his alcohol problem caused their inevitable divorce, prior to 1979).

Sam's many sexual conquests and one-night stands finally caught up with him. In 1993, after reflecting upon his fading youth and bachelorhood, Sam realized this lifestyle prevented him from experiencing a special and meaningful relationship. He decided to seek counseling for sexual compulsiveness under the guidance of Dr. Robert Sutton. Of course, one of his first actions was to proposition another patient, Rachel, for a date.

Other miscellaneous information regarding Sam's love life: he folded his socks before sex; salt air gave him extra stamina; he yearned for Jacqueline Bisset whenever he drank tequila; he never slept with Carla because he always thought she would be too much woman for him; he considered it a romantic gesture for a man and woman to have their buns tattooed; and he found the best way to win the heart of a woman was to take her to Cape Cod for a romantic evening.

Relationships—Diane

When they first met, Sam thought Diane was a twit and a snob but readily admitted she was his only true love. Their first kiss was in the fourth episode—depressed after Dave Richards canceled a television interview, Sam misinterpreted her encouraging words, "Go for it" as a prelude to a kiss. Diane was flattered by the show of affection, and despite hurling him onto the pool table, admitted finding him somewhat attractive.

Although they flirted with each other throughout the first year, they did not begin dating until 1983. In the interim, they arranged blind dates for one another. When Diane described and arranged the perfect date for Sam (intelligent, attractive, funny), he thought she was describing herself, and that *she* was his secret date for the evening. Accordingly, Sam planned to be her date. However, when Diane arrived with Gretchen, he rushed into the poolroom and paid a stranger, Andy-Andy, $20 to be Diane's date. As it turned out, Andy was convicted of manslaughter for killing a waitress, and the evening went downhill from there.

Despite an obvious physical attraction, Sam and Diane suppressed their feelings toward one another. They officially began dating when Diane rejected his brother, Derek. Diane was contemplating a serious relationship, and began arguing with Sam because he denied any feelings for her. They became sexually aroused by the intensity of the argument which culminated in a fervent embrace and kiss.

Despite their constant bickering, Sam insisted he never worked harder to maintain a relationship than he did with Diane. For example, when he was invited to dinner with Diane and two other intellectuals, Sumner and Barbara Sloane, he spent five days and nights reading the novel *War and Peace* to fit in conversationally. When they were not quarreling, Sam and Diane enjoyed vacationing at various New England resorts, such as the Sea Shadows Inn (room 5) in Marblehead, Massachusetts, and in a Pequots, Connecticut, resort (room 12).

Sam and Diane's relationship was best known for its confrontations. Throughout their years of dating they spent more time ruminating than executing, altercating than communicating, estranging than reconciling. In fact, making up was the cornerstone of their relationship. There were multiple instances of interminable feuding and relationship breakups, but only a few were particularly noteworthy.

After their breakup in 1984, Sam returned to the bottle and drank himself senseless. Debauchery and decadence ensued as he partied constantly with an endless string of one-night stands. Eventually, Diane and the Cheers gang convinced him to see psychiatrist Dr. Frasier Crane.

Sam suppressed his attraction toward Diane, but his romantic interest remained an attainable goal when Diane fortuitously revealed a mutual attraction. Once, while making love to Frasier, she inadvertently called out Sam's name. In another instance, Diane had a psychosomatic allergic reaction because of her feelings for Sam. Finally, as she prepared to leave for Europe with Frasier, Diane shared a passionate moment with Sam that was almost a new beginning; however, Sam wanted a no strings attached dalliance, whereas Diane yearned for commitment. Their constant expression and repression ignited their internal passions, and it was only a matter of time before they externalized their feelings.

Sam continued to date other women, but when his relationship with Boston city councilor Janet Eldridge failed, he proposed marriage to Diane. Notwithstanding her rejection of the offer, Diane returned to the bar the next day to accept the marriage proposal (unfortunately he had already withdrawn the question). Diane refused to believe he no longer loved her, and decided to work at Cheers until he proposed marriage again. Sam attempted to prove his apathy by flaunting his dates, but when she purposely spoiled a weekend retreat, they discussed their feelings and reaffirmed their sexual desires for one another. (However, once again, they did not resume dating because Sam wanted a one-night stand and Diane wanted commitment.)

Although Sam tried to convince Diane that he did not love her, he eventually proposed marriage two more times. The first time she rejected the proposal, he envisioned killing her and chased her six blocks until she tripped and fell. Sam was arrested, and the judge ordered him to propose marriage again or risk going to jail. Sam reluctantly proposed, and this time Diane accepted.

Sam and Diane's Weddings

The first scheduled wedding between Sam and Diane was in 1983 (Coach was selected as the best man). Diane proposed marriage to Sam to satisfy the terms of her father's will and prevent her mother's disinheritance. The wedding was canceled because their arguing was making a mockery of matrimony.

They also prepared to wed in 1987 with a brief engagement. The bachelor party was held at Cheers, where the gang rented X-rated movies from the Hot and Nasty Video Boutique and served Diane as the dessert inside the surprise cake. In addition to a bachelor party, Sam and Diane endured the more mundane ritual of wedding preparations. First and foremost was the engagement ring. Diane wanted a $5,200 ring from Barton & Lyle jewelers, but Sam could not afford it, so he purchased a wholesale ring for $1,200 from Norm's friend, Bruce. To conceal the truth, Sam spent a total of $8,640 (the real ring, $5,200; the bargain ring, $1,200; sterling silver corn cob holders, $290; four pink frocks, $950; and damage to his car, $1,000).

Sam and Diane received one wedding gift in advance of their nuptials. Frasier gave them a $1,500 marriage counseling session with the renowned Dr. Simon Finch-Royce, who concluded Sam and Diane were incompatible, and not only should they call off the marriage, but they should never see each other again.

The final arrangement was purchasing a home. Although Sam and Diane agreed to live in his apartment until they could afford a house, Diane found the perfect abode and made a down payment without Sam's knowledge. After finalizing the sale, Diane decided she could not live in the house because it was filled with the memories of the original owners, Bert and Lillian Miller. She then refused to sell it because each potential purchaser merely wanted to *live* there. After holding one final Christmas for the Miller family, Diane accepted the house.

Shortly before the wedding, Sumner approached Diane with the opportunity to finish a novel for publication. Sam did not want her to bypass this chance of a lifetime, but she insisted upon marriage. During the ceremony Sam said, "I do," but rescinded the words after the publisher offered Diane a sizeable advance to finish writing the novel. He convinced her to pursue the dream, and Diane vowed to return in six months. Sam realized this career opportunity would irreparably change their lives, and told her to have a good life.

Six years later Sam sent Diane a congratulatory telegram for winning a writing award, and invited her to Boston. Their seemingly innocuous prevarications about their lives were illuminated after Diane arrived unexpectedly at Cheers. Rebecca Howe role-played the part of Sam's wife, and they bragged about their four children (Sam, Jr., Darby, Newton, and Chelsea). Irrespective of their deceptions, Sam and Diane reunited and became engaged.

Sam made arrangements to begin a new life in California working at a health club bar serving nutritious beverages. As the plane prepared to depart, Sam realized he was only marrying Diane out of a fear of loneliness and reconsidered his impending commitment. Although Sam and Diane never married, Coach and Woody were the only persons who thought they should tie the knot.

Relationships—Sam's Harem

According to Sam Malone and Dave Richards, the following list revealed their best possible night of babe hunting: in terms of quantity, Minneapolis; in terms of quality, Chicago (July 4); in terms of both quantity and quality, Las Vegas. Sam had many romantic interludes, rendezvous and one-night stands, and slept with thousands of women. The list could be infinite, knowing Sammy's sexual exploits, but the following were his most notable sexual conquests.

Sam's most famous political romance was with Boston city councilor Janet Eldridge, who entered Cheers as part of a campaign stop. Despite publicly rejecting his dinner invitation, her campaign manager and press secretary, Phil Schumacher, gave Sam her private telephone number. They began dating, but everyone at the bar was concerned that Janet was using Sam to win the Irish vote, and that her feelings were not genuine. Janet later admitted this was her initial intention, but with the caveat that she had since fallen in love with him.

Janet appeared to be sincere, but then convinced Sam to fire Diane (under the guise of advancing her career). Janet's true intentions were to eliminate the competition for Sam's affection. After Sam was embarrassed during a press conference, Janet realized he still loved Diane. Despite losing Janet, Sam had the pleasurable memory of partnering with presidential candidate Gary Hart during a game of Trivial Pursuit.

Sam's most bizarre relationship was with Amanda Boyer, a sanitarium patient with an obsessive and irrational possessiveness toward men. Within days she brought her parents, Todd and Mona Boyer, to Cheers to meet her latest fiancé. Amanda threatened suicide when Sam tried to end the relationship, but ironically it was Amanda who ended it after Diane revealed that Sam (alias Ralph) was the person she spoke about in group therapy.

Notwithstanding Sam's lengthy resumé of sexual triumphs, there had only been one claim of paternity against him. A former lover, Denise, intimated that

Sam or one other man was the father of her 7 lb. 10 oz. child. Sam made a pact with God—if the paternity test was negative, he would give up sex for three months. The test was negative, and soon he had an irresistible urge for sweets (Sam's metaphor for sex).

He consulted a priest, Father Barry, about the secrets of celibacy and whether God would forgive him if he splurged on a big box of chocolates. He read the Bible for guidance and to find a loophole in his pact with God. He even tried taking cold showers, putting ice in his pockets, and foregoing oysters. Finally, after three weeks of abstention, Rachel Patterson happened along and tested his resolve. (They shared a wonderful romantic memory of a Vermont ski lodge, a roaring fire, baby oil and gravity boots; her perfume, Devastation, was equally irresistible.)

Sam and Rachel left Cheers for a hotel room, but to Sam's surprise the nightstand had a Bible in it! So they went to another hotel room, and once again there was a Bible in the nightstand. They inexorably traveled from hotel to hotel, but were unable to find a room without a Bible. Sam finally realized God was speaking to him through hotel nightstands. This convinced him to abstain from sex for the full three months.

Sam had several long-term, light-hearted relationships. The longest relationship involved an annual Valentine's Day date. Since approximately 1971, Sam and Lauren shared this special day at a cabin in Maine. Their 1991 encounter was probably the most memorable because Sam injured his back and they spent the entire evening *talking*. They subsequently agreed to a biannual date that included Arbor Day.

Sam's only other known long-term relationship was with Judy Marlow. It began in the late 1970s and was rekindled 15 years later. The interesting aspect to this tryst, metaphorically speaking, was that Sammy tried to pitch both games of a doubleheader—he attempted to date a mother, Judy, and her daughter, Laurie, simultaneously. Sam ultimately struck out because Laurie was engaged and asked him to give her away at the wedding. A similar feat took place when Sam dated the Henshaw triplets. Unfortunately, Sam was drinking heavily at the time, and later discovered the triplets were actually one person!

Sam dated at least four intelligent women. The first attempt was in 1982, in response to Diane's criticizing his endless string of busty and brainless bimbos. Sam wanted to prove he could date intelligent women, so he perused his black book and found Debra. Sam brought her to the bar to brag about attending a Mozart concert, but it was soon revealed they went to see *Star Wars*. Sam became depressed because he used to love going out with the type of women in his book, and now, because of Diane, all he could think about was how stupid they were.

Sam's second intelligent date was Claudia Mitchell. She was interested in Chinese tapestry and Indian cooking, and was unimpressed with Sam's adolescent come-ons and lack of refinement. They dated briefly but broke up because she preferred spending time with Diane.

Thirdly, Sam made a more diligent effort with *Boston Scene* magazine reporter Paula Nelson. Sam consulted with Diane about French Impressionist painters and other cultural topics, and then regurgitated the information in conversations with Paula. He loved the hot irony of using Diane's brain to get another woman's body.

The final intelligent woman that Sam dated was a friend of the Cranes, Dr. Sheila Rydell, a clinical psychologist and a fellow at Boston University. Sam prudently arranged a professional meeting with her, feigning impotence. She accepted his dinner invitation though the evening concluded early when Sam insisted upon Sheila's professional opinion. She diagnosed Sam as an aging lothario with massive insecurities, the fear of dying and the fear of living; without constant sex he would probably shrivel up like a dried anchovy and die. In sum, he was one sick cowpoke.

The only married woman Sam dated was Maxine, and upon discovering this fact, he ended the relationship. Maxine's husband, Marvin, was not forgiving and threatened Sam with a gun. Sam coaxed Marvin into relinquishing the weapon, and as Sam put the gun in his back pocket, it discharged, nicking his derrière. Sam received television coverage for his injury, but his version varied slightly from the truth. He claimed a band of armed marauders attacked him, and he was shot in the leg when giving a Bruce Lee karate kick to dislodge the gun from the leader's hand (which ultimately scared the others away). After seeing the television news report, Marvin returned to Cheers with another firearm, but this time Diane convinced him to spare Sam's life.

Sam dated one woman for revenge. He romanced Valerie Hill to infuriate her father (and Sam's antagonist), John Allen Hill. John bribed Sam not to date his daughter, offering the Cheers back room rent free and the use of his parking spot. Sam agreed, but quickly yearned for the forbidden fruit. When John finally accepted the relationship, Valerie dumped Sam because she was involved with him merely to upset her father.

Sam also dated the daughter of a waitress. When Diane departed for Europe, she was replaced by Lillian Huxley. Sam labored to arrange a date with Lillian's gorgeous daughter, Carolyn, a lingerie model for *British Vogue*, only to discover she despised sex.

Less-known dates include Miss Tennessee (a beauty pageant contestant); Julie (a dental hygienist who accompanied him for a weekend on Evan Drake's yacht); Erin (a young, attractive, athletic woman who exhausted Sam with constant exercise); Wanda Mendelson (Sam's all-night plumber—you had to go to her house to get your pipe fixed); Debbie (a radio contestant with whom Sam spent a weekend in Atlantic City); Miss Kenderson (hatcheck girl at Melville's); Alice Anne Volkman (Rebecca's college professor and author of a business success book); and another Julie (a Cheers waitress who broke up with Sam after discovering he slept with her sister).

Relationships—Rebecca

The last known official record of the number of times Sam unsuccessfully propositioned Rebecca was 4,659. However, he was close to attaining his goal on many occasions and used numerous schemes to trick her into sleeping with him. Sam was tenacious, and every day sealed an envelope with a signed and dated note that read, "Today is the day that I will sleep with Rebecca Howe."

In one noteworthy attempt to score with Rebecca, Sam feigned attending an embassy gathering and sleeping with Robin Colcord's other woman, Jean-Marie Bolièrre. Sam boasted having a sexual rendezvous in an elevator, and how the danger heightened their passion. Rebecca asked him to re-enact the encounter with her, and after tying him to the elevator railing and pulling his pants down around his ankles, she exited, sending Sammy to the hotel lobby.

One of Sam's devious plots pitted Rebecca against her sister, Susan Howe. Since Rebecca and Susan were very competitive, he arranged to date both women on the same night. However, the Howe sisters played a prank on Sam by having Rebecca pretend to shoot and kill Susan. As he attempted to hide the body, the entire Cheers gang appeared to reveal the antic. Sam nearly had a heart attack.

Although Sam's efforts to have his way with Rebecca failed repeatedly, he achieved success in 1990. Rebecca was depressed because her relationship with Robin appeared to be over, and realized Sam was the only man who ever cared for her. This emotional moment lead to a sexual interlude, though shortly after their dalliance, Robin returned to Cheers to reclaim his woman.

Sam actually considered marrying Rebecca at one time. In 1993 he was at a crossroad in his life—approaching middle age (45) and the prospect of being alone. Sam eloquently propositioned Rebecca by claiming if he did not find someone else in the next couple of years, she was at the top of a very short list. This was quite a switch from two years prior when he implemented Plan Z, i.e., pretending to be a homosexual to convince Rebecca that he did not love her.

Sam's Concept of Conception

In 1991 Sam began reflecting upon his life and fading youth, and the fact that he was alone—he had neither a woman to share his life nor a child to pass on the family legacy. His desire to procreate was precipitated while baby sitting and becoming emotionally attached to the Cranes' child, Frederick. Since Sam was not in love with any woman, he decided to search for a surrogate mother to bear his child, with no expectation of motherly involvement. However, the concept of incubating Sam's seed was not too appealing, and even his first choice, Carla (selected because of her childbirth experience), refused to go through pregnancy and delivery merely because Sam was feeling a little lonely.

While baby sitting Frederick at Cheers, Sam fell asleep as he watched the movie *Blue Hawaii* (1962). In his dream, Elvis spoke to Sam through the television and recommended giving Rebecca a chance at motherhood. Sam was hesitant, but after posing the question, she responded enthusiastically. Unfortunately, the goal of conception proved to be unattainable. They tried everything—basal body temperature method, reducing caffeine intake, and having Sam wear freon-based underwear. He even went to a fertility specialist, who concluded his sperm count was well within the normal range.

In addition to conception, Sam and Rebecca had to resolve the dilemma of naming the child. Sam wanted the child to have his last name because Howe sounded too much like a question. Sam envisioned having a son (Sam, Jr., a 25-game winner for the Red Sox) and a granddaughter (Samantha, who dated a boy with a degree in laser beam demolecularization).

After countless failures, they began arguing over their inability to conceive. During a romantic weekend in a luxurious hotel, Sam realized it would be disastrous to have a child when the parents are not in love and they mutually agreed to postpone parenthood.

Cheers

Circa 1976, Sam purchased Cheers. He was a drunk at the time, and after overcoming his alcohol dependency, retained the bar for sentimental reasons. To Sam, Cheers was the closest thing to home, and since he had no life insurance, the bar was his primary asset. Yearly taxes cost $2,000 to $3,000 (though in 1984 Norm finagled a $15,000 refund). Sam nearly lost the bar in 1985. In a bet with Eddie Gordon, Sam wagered the bar, claiming that he could marry Jacqueline Bisset within one year of the date of the bet. Sam located a woman of the same name living in Green Bank, West Virginia, who agreed to marry him. Faced with losing the bet, Eddie Gordon settled for a green olive with a pimento. (One other notable wager involved the Cheers football pool—Sam had not won since 1974.)

As for investments, Sam purchased $1,000 in stock shares based on a tip from Kelly Gaines' wealthy relative, Conrad Langston. Within a week he lost all his money and discovered the investment tip was from a member of the "Hard Luck Five," a group that had never made a sound venture.

In old age, Sam envisioned Woody owning Cheers. Woody and his son would run the bar, and his wife and daughter would wait tables. At the end of the night, they would take off their shoes and socks to total the receipts!

The combination to the Cheers safe was the same as the date of Sam's birth. Locked inside the safe were Diane's old love letters (wrapped in a red bow), a ticket to the 1980 boat show, three poker chips, a key, a toaster warranty, a whistle, a CC battery, and four paper clips.

As for some of the most memorable pejorative nicknames Sam acquired over the years, the list includes: Goof, Rapidly Aging Adolescent, 6'3" Bubble Gum Card, Butthead, Cucumber Brain, Bean Brain, Rat Lips, Broken Brow, Slime Ball, Sky King, Grumble Bunny, Fluffy, Pantywaist, Underpants, Mr. Groin, Dink, One Sick Cowpoke, and Wussy Little Fraidy Cat. The most complimentary sobriquets have been Magnificent Pagan Beast; Tall Hunk with the Rippling Rump; Mean, Tight, Specimen Hunk; and Passionate Macho Stud Horse.

Rebecca Howe

Childhood

Born in 1953, Rebecca was raised in San Diego, California. Her family nickname was Pooky (originated by her father) and she was the black sheep of the family. Despite burning down her playhouse, Rebecca's most notorious faux pas was accidentally shooting something off an aircraft carrier (one international incident and she was branded for life!).

Rebecca had a difficult childhood due to her parents' inordinately high standards. The Howes measured success according to wealth, happiness, and the undying devotion of Rebecca's father. Consequently, her greatest struggles in life were meeting the high expectations of her parents and competing with her successful siblings. Rebecca always wanted more supportive parents, like Brian Keith and Maureen O'Hara in *The Parent Trap* (1961). Her only fond childhood memory was running away to San Francisco, where she hung out with Grace Slick and learned the lyrics to "White Rabbit" by Jefferson Airplane.

As a child, Rebecca cherished animals, owning a cat and a pony. She loved her Persian cat, Princess, and was greatly saddened when her parents claimed that Princess had escaped through a window that was painted shut, i.e., they had put the cat to sleep. Rebecca's pony won first prize in a horse show, and was fed sugar cubes, chocolates, and Snickers candy bars. Of course,

Rebecca splurged on these treats too, and one day was told she could no longer ride the pony because she had "outgrown" it.

Family

Rebecca's father, Franklin E. Howe, was a naval captain known by the sobriquet "Brig" because he put so many sailors in jail. Since the Howe family moved frequently because of Franklin's occupation, they became very distrustful of neighbors. However, Franklin, on his own volition, once left the family for six months to find himself. He returned at peace with himself—you could see it in his eyes as he came roaring up the driveway. Despite his rugged exterior, Franklin loved to sew, and converted Rebecca's old bedroom into a sewing haven.

Rebecca's mother was an interior designer and a concert cellist, so Rebecca was especially knowledgeable about classical music. When she was two years old, she began turning the pages while her mother played, and in the process acquired considerable disdain for certain classical compositions, such as Mahler's 3rd Symphony. Rebecca hated being the daughter of a musician, because the food tasted like rosin, and every time she tried to sit on her mother's lap, she slipped through her legs.

Rebecca had three siblings, two brothers and a sister. One brother was an attorney, the other a surgeon, and her sister, Susan Howe, was an accomplished actress known for the horror film *Night of the Mutants* and for being crowned Miss San Diego in a hometown beauty pageant. Susan had one regrettable childhood memory—at age six she wet herself during her "I Am an American" speech at the Flag Day assembly. In their youth, Rebecca and Susan shared a bedroom and spent their time talking about boys, doing each other's hair, and dreaming about owning a ranch with horses.

Personal

Rebecca had chestnut-brown hair with auburn highlights, and had a tattoo and mole removed from her lower back as part of an automobile accident settlement with a plastic surgeon. Although this tattoo was removed, Rebecca may have had Sam's name tattooed on her derrière after losing a bet as to whether he would break the earnings record at a celebrity charity auction. Rebecca's most memorable fashion accessory was a pair of $32,000 diamond earrings on loan from Shreeve, Krump & Low jewelers which she planned to wear to the launching of "Old Ironsides" (USS *Constitution*).

Rebecca's biggest secret was the song that turned her knees to butter and made her lose all inhibitions ("You've Lost That Lovin' Feeling" by the Righteous Brothers). Her motto was "Just Do It," and she wanted her autobiographical movie to star Meryl Streep. Rebecca perceived herself as a bad person, but always thought she could become better by marrying a millionaire or having a baby.

Rebecca had several vices, including excessive eating and smoking. When she was depressed, Rebecca would eat ice cream (because that's what losers do!). When she was upset, she would eat Snickers candy bars and chain-smoke cigarettes. She made two attempts to quit smoking. In the first instance, using negative reinforcement, Rebecca vowed to do the most repugnant task imaginable, i.e., sleep with Sam. She failed to quit smoking, but Sam did not enforce the promise because Rebecca was not in the mood. In the other attempt, Sam sent Rebecca to Dr. Kluger's No Mercy Clinic. She outlasted the doctor, who eventually began smoking and sharing his woes, such as his desire to be an artist.

Rebecca was involved in one consumer protection issue. She appeared on "Consumer Patrol," urging viewers to boycott the Lady Baldy hair remover. However, Rebecca quickly modified her vituperation after learning Robin Colcord owned the company (LessCo Ventures) that produced the product.

Other miscellaneous information: in Boston, Rebecca lived in apartment number 5A and was superintendent of the building; her first European trip was visiting Italy sometime prior to 1987 (when she had a reputation for being cheap and slutty); her childhood rebelliousness included filling the salt shakers with sugar; after a beauty makeover by *Redbook* magazine, she emerged with blonde hair; and she hated having her picture taken because she became too tense, and pretty soon looked like something the cat coughed up!

Personal Likes and Dislikes

Rebecca was fond of animals and had numerous childhood pets. She was especially attached to Woody's Christmas ham—a piglet she named Snuffles. Rebecca decided to free the piglet from Christmas doom, so she released Snuffles in the woods. Ironically, the wise swine somehow made it back to Woody's parents' home in Indiana just in time for Christmas—the Boyds said Snuffles was delicious!

Besides her love for Snickers candy bars, Rebecca had other passions: her favorite television show was "Spenser: For Hire," and her dream car was a red Mercedes. In 1988 she purchased a base model, but when the expense of ownership became too burdensome she sold it to Frasier for $6,000.

Education

Rebecca was the first girl in her class to develop breasts, and the fattest girl in high school (though her sister once stated Rebecca had not been fat since age 12). At one memorable high school prom, Rebecca weighed 300 pounds, looked like a Goodyear blimp, wore an ugly dress, and was prescribed tetracycline (for acne).

In high school, Rebecca took Latin as a foreign language and wanted to take German but it conflicted with driver's education. Her most notable school activity was participating in drama, and she appeared in at least two productions: *The Bad Seed* and the sophomore class production of *South Pacific* (she played one of the nurses who washes Nelly Forbush's hair).

After graduating from high school at age 18, Rebecca attended the University of Connecticut, where she majored in marketing and appeared in the theatrical production *Hair*. Despite wearing braces, she earned the college nickname Backseat Becky. Her biggest shortcoming was indecisiveness, but she overcompensated by becoming a real suck up. During her senior year (in January 1977), Rebecca wrote a term paper titled, "Jimmy Carter: The Three Term President" for a class taught by her favorite teacher, Alice Anne Volkman (who authored the book *Speak Out and Score*). Rebecca received an "F" on the paper, failed the class, and suffered a nervous breakdown. Rather than being crushed by this setback, Rebecca's insatiable desire for success helped her persevere by retaking the course in the summer and earning a bachelor's degree. Rebecca continued working on the paper, and in 1989, resubmitted it to Ms. Volkman, who gave her an "A."

Executive Career

Rebecca began working for a major corporation in 1981, and two years later was hired as a junior executive for the Lillian Corporation. Her first raise was in 1987, and she slowly worked her way *down* the corporate ladder to manager of Cheers (which became her most productive business pursuit). During her reign as manager, Rebecca received a WOBBIE, a Women of Boston Business Award (a very prestigious award won by thousands of women), but failed to gain acceptance into the Boston League of Business Women because she was too self-involved and not community minded enough.

In the business world, Rebecca continued her college tradition of sucking up to persons in power. She frequently volunteered to organize parties for executives' children and corporate retirees. Rebecca also agreed to dog sit Buster (formally known as Sir Brownvann the Gallant from Fairhaven Manor), a prizewinning $10,000 Doberman pinscher owned by Mr. Sheridan, the vice president in charge of East Coast marketing, research and sales.

Despite brown-nosing executives, at least 36 people passed Rebecca on the corporate ladder. However, the 1989 promotion of 5'3" weasel Henry Weinberg to director of advertising prompted Rebecca to quit the corporation. She stormed into Vice President Anawalt's office, insulted him, and quit. Rather than accepting the resignation, Mr. Anawalt promoted Rebecca and tripled her salary. Unfortunately, moments later he was arrested for insider trading, and Rebecca lost her only corporate promotion.

Rebecca was terminated by the corporation twice. In 1988 she was fired by Vice President Greg Stone because the bar was more successful under Sam's management. Mr. Stone then rehired Rebecca as comanager, but only under limited conditions—she had to accept a slight pay cut, continue working on her master's degree, consult with Sam on major decisions, and wait tables during busy hours (under the direct supervision of Carla). Rebecca unwillingly accepted the offer because she needed a job to pay for the dream car (a base model Mercedes) she had recently purchased. Approximately one month later, Mr. Stone was fired, and his successor, Martin Teal, reinstated Rebecca as the sole manager of Cheers.

In 1990 Rebecca was terminated again. Although Robin Colcord used her secret password to obtain confidential corporate records, she was fired because the corporation never really cared for her work. After refusing to wait tables at Cheers, Rebecca accepted employment as Miss Miracle Buff (earning $6 per hour), demonstrating the indestructibility of Miracle Buff car wax at an auto show. Sam felt sorry for her, and rehired Rebecca as the manager of Cheers. The following year she was earning $7 per hour working in her managerial capacity.

Other Employment

Prior to her corporate aspirations, Rebecca once had a chance to land her dream job. Unfortunately, she became nervous and botched the interview. First, she complimented the interviewer's clothes, and then took it back so as not to appear a suck up. Then she offended him, and before long was singing "Knick-knack, Patty-wack." In the end, Rebecca lost her dream job at the House of Pancakes. As for other employment, if Rebecca could relive her life, she would have chosen a career in advertising (because of her exceptional communication skills) or engineering.

Romance, or Lack Thereof

Since the first day of puberty, Rebecca had several romantic fantasies she wanted to fulfill with her lover. These fantasies included: walking hand in hand along the beach, feeding the seagulls, skipping stones and burying her man in the sand up to his neck; a picnic in the park and paddle boat ride; going to the zoo; sitting in the seventh row at *The Phantom of the Opera*; and concluding the evening by making love. When her sweetheart, Robin Colcord, spent the day with Sam consumed by intense sports competitions, Rebecca fulfilled most of these fantasies with Woody Boyd.

Several past lovers stated that Rebecca was not very good in bed and she turned them off of girls. Despite a relatively inactive sex life, Rebecca was a pregnancy waiting to happen. A gynecologist reported Rebecca was as fertile as an Iowa cornfield, having fallopian tubes like fire hoses and fully stocked ovaries. Rebecca ovulated on the 12th of every month, and referred to her menstrual period as "Mr. Charlie."

Although she accepted very few dates, Rebecca was the object of infatuation on several occasions. Her admirers included Gino Tortelli, Carla's son, who sent Rebecca nude photos of himself taken in the mall photo booth, and Russell Boyd, Woody's cousin, who wrote her love songs and painted a mural of her on the wall in his hotel room. Rebecca also dated a skydiver named Bob Speakes.

Relationships—High School

Although Rebecca had several high school boyfriends, her sister usually enticed them away. Rebecca's most memorable beaux were Corky Passovak and Mark Newberger. Rebecca found it difficult to reminisce about her relationship with Corky Passovak (who also participated in high school drama), and cried every time she mentioned their date at the movies when he met an ex-girlfriend.

Mark Newberger, Rebecca's first love, was voted "Most Likely to Succeed" and participated in extracurricular activities (Glee Club, debate team captain, water polo champion, and head of the prom committee). Rebecca and Mark met during the high school theater production of *The Bad Seed*, and appeared together in the sophomore class production of *South Pacific* (Mark played the lead role of Emile de Becque). Both he and Rebecca had a crush on their high school Latin teacher, Mr. Vincent. Rebecca regretted not pursuing Mark romantically after high school, but at the time she wanted to go to college and be free. Although Mark was homosexual, he claimed Rebecca was the one girl who confused him about his sexuality.

Relationships—Men of Power

Although Rebecca found men's eyes physically appealing, her primary objective was dating men who could advance her career. She would readily abandon love and romance for a man of power and stature. For over three years she rejected numerous dates with corporate coworkers so she would be available if and when Vice President Evan Drake expressed an interest in her. Ironically, her continual rejection of men earned her a reputation as a lesbian. When Evan moved to Tokyo, Rebecca quickly expressed an interest in his replacement, Vice President Greg Stone.

The one exception to Rebecca's rule about dating men in power was Martin Teal (he was too young and incredibly short). Thus, to avoid dating him, Rebecca implored Sam to pose as her boyfriend. Much to her dismay, Sam refused to play along with the charade. Since she lacked the ability to say "no" to any man in power, Rebecca accepted Martin's dinner invitation. After one date, he proposed marriage and she passed out. A wedding seemed inevitable until Sam played the part of Rebecca's lover and interrupted the ceremony moments before the vows were spoken.

Rebecca was also attracted to wealthy, powerful businessmen. Other than Robin Colcord, her most notable pursuit was Walter Gaines (Kelly's father) and his $72 million estate. When he invited Rebecca to his mansion to listen to classical music, she misinterpreted the invitation as having romantic overtures. She began entertaining thoughts of love, and dreamed of becoming the next Mrs. Mr. Gaines (she did not know his first name). Upon her arrival at the Gaines estate, Rebecca realized she was invited as a mere domestic servant. Despite her disappointment, Rebecca subsequently rejected Mr. Gaines' sincere proposition for a date.

Relationships—Robin Colcord

Robin Colcord was a wealthy entrepreneur with numerous investments and properties—Colcord Foundation, Colcord Foundation of the Arts, Colcord Investments, Colcord Plaza on Fifth Avenue, and LessCo Ventures. To limit taxes, Robin earned $1 per year as CEO of his corporation. He lived in a penthouse guarded by the Triton 5000 laser security system. Miles chauffeured Robin's white limousine, Jonathan was the valet, and Howard was his secretary. During college Robin played the lead in Shakespeare's *Richard II*, and named his sailboat after the biblical Rebecca.

Rebecca first met Robin when he visited Cheers to thank her for a business idea. Rebecca had sent him various investment strategies, along with a photograph of herself, and suggested he sell his South End property. Instead, he redeveloped the land by building high-rise condominiums, an artificial lake, and a golf course. Robin showed his appreciation by giving her a necklace that was a small scale version of the high-rise with a diamond in each window—and there were a lot of windows!

Robin then invited Rebecca to spend three days visiting cities on the

West Coast, where she shopped and received a beauty makeover. Rebecca affectionately nicknamed Robin "Sweet Baby" (though at their wedding she confessed he was really her "Rich Baby"). One of the most trying events of their relationship was Rebecca's decision to sleep with Robin. She had concerns about being too forward, and whether she would perform satisfactorily. They finally consummated their relationship on the night of Carl Yastrzemski's Testimonial Dinner ($1,000 a plate). They began the evening arguing about Robin's insensitivity toward her feelings, which quickly evolved into a passionate kiss. He took Rebecca to Little Wally's Pup and Burger for a double-bacon chili burger, and later that evening they made love while listening to the song "You've Lost That Lovin' Feeling" by the Righteous Brothers (Robin had a disc jockey at a radio station he owned play it all night long). On this magical evening Robin spoke those three little words, "I love you."

Despite Robin's inadequacies in bed (he was a little quick, but then again, he was English!), Rebecca was in seventh heaven. He showered her with gifts, perhaps the most memorable being an antique oak desk. Robin intimated the desk had a surprise, and the hint was "ring." Naturally, Rebecca expected an engagement ring, and swiftly dismantled the desk with a chain saw. It was later revealed that "ring" referred to a circular tea cup stain on the top of the desk, which was created by George Bernard Shaw after writing the fifth act of *Man and Superman*.

As their relationship became more serious, Robin contemplated a permanent arrangement. While searching for a lifetime soul mate, he narrowed the field to three finalists—Jean-Marie Bolièrre (the chargé d'affaires at the French Consulate), Christine Davi (a ballerina), and Rebecca. Jean-Marie was the biggest challenge for Rebecca, but she knew Jean-Marie was out of the picture when Robin bought her a furnished house (each woman he discarded received this gift).

In 1990 Robin used Rebecca's password to access confidential corporate records with the intent to effectuate a hostile takeover of the Lillian Corporation, and as a result was convicted of insider trading and imprisoned in a minimum security prison. During his incarceration, Robin worked in the bakery (in charge of sticky buns) and picked up trash in the park. While he was in prison, Rebecca was particularly upset when Jean-Marie received recognition as the mystery femme for whom Robin Colcord gave up his fortune. Jean-Marie was on "The Arsenio Hall Show" and "Hollywood Squares." Robin eventually set the record straight about Rebecca being his true love, but she failed to receive the same notoriety as Jean-Marie.

In 1991, after dating for nearly two years, Robin selected Rebecca as his bride-to-be. Immediately prior to his release from prison, Robin sent her a single white rose and a card with the inscription, "Dear Rebecca, I'll be free on Monday. If you're free as well, will you care to join me in holy matrimony?" Rebecca enthusiastically accepted the proposal, and beseeched Lilith to be her matron of honor. However, at the bridal shower, Rebecca became intoxicated and confessed to Sam that she did not love Robin. Despite this revelation, the next morning she proceeded with the wedding.

Frasier was scheduled to sing at the wedding, but was quickly discharged from his duties when Bobby Hatfield of the Righteous Brothers arrived for the city hall ceremony. After Robin recited a beautiful poem, Rebecca said her vow: "I only loved you for your money." (The song "We've Got Tonight" jogged her memory that she did not love Robin.) Prior to his imprisonment, the value of Robin's estate was $200 million, but upon his release he was destitute. Later that evening Robin asked Rebecca whether she would love him if he had $6 million hidden in a money belt. Thinking he was bluffing, she boldly said "no." To her astonishment, he removed the money belt from the bottom of Rebecca's office desk drawer and walked out of her life.

Robin returned to Cheers two years later, a changed man. He relinquished the $6 million and took a vow of poverty. After leaving Boston, he walked through Europe, worked on a kibbutz (farm) in Israel, and joined the merchant marine. Despite being blessed by the pope, Robin resorted to stealing to supplement his meager lifestyle, and was imprisoned in Louisiana. Rebecca perceived Robin's return as another opportunity for wealth, so she pretended to love him, hoping the claim of poverty was another test of her affection.

During this visit, Robin also played a prank on the Cheers gang by convincing them there was another money belt hidden in the bar. After the gang ravaged the bar in a probing frenzy, Robin revealed the fiendish gag. His parting words were, "I never really cared for you. Ta!"

Relationships — Sam

Despite Sam's endless propositions and Rebecca's repeated denials of any physical attraction, she had erotic dreams about him. These subconscious desires were even more repulsive to Rebecca because she wanted rich, powerful men — men who owned blocks, not men who played with them! The last official record of the number of times Sam propositioned Rebecca was 4,659.

After three years of rejecting Sam, in 1990 Rebecca acquiesced after Robin left for Switzerland to avoid imprisonment. She finally realized Sam was the only man who ever cared for her. They shared an intimate moment in the Cheers office, but shortly after their dalliance, Robin returned to reunite with Rebecca. In 1993 Sam eloquently propositioned Rebecca by telling her that if he did not find a better woman in the next couple of years, she was at the top of a very short list. Not surprisingly, she was offended by the prospect of being his safety net.

Relationships—Don Santry

After the humiliating incident with Walter Gaines, Rebecca ventured on a depressing weeklong cruise (she stepped on a poison blowfish and her leg swelled like a bloated corpse). While vacationing she underwent intensive soul-searching, and decided to terminate her selfish pursuit of men with wealth and power by resolving to date only decent men. Toward that end, she accepted a date with plumber Don Santry (they met at Cheers while he was repairing the beer taps). Within two weeks Rebecca knew he was the right man for her, and began contemplating marriage. (She knew Don loved her and that she was the best thing to ever happen to him, because he said it with his eyes.)

Don was enamored with Rebecca, and quickly proposed marriage. Although her first three answers were "no," she finally accepted his proposal at Melville's. They immediately wed at city hall. Although slightly depressed about marrying a mere plumber, Rebecca also realized Don was too good for her. Her last concern was whether Don would receive a job with the city sewer department.

Cheers

As manager of Cheers, Rebecca was featured in a *Boston Globe* magazine article on women who ran pubs. Her picture turned out perfect, but it was placed in the obituary section and indicated she died in bed. The corporation was kind enough to send flowers and a condolence card which stated, "Dear Friends at Cheers: We mourn the loss of Rebecca Howe. At last her pain is over."

The one entertainment device Rebecca hated was Cheers' slot machine. She perceived the machine as a metaphor for life—everyone pulls the handle, some are winners and some are losers. Knowing she was a loser, Rebecca proved it by inserting 579 nickels in the machine without ever winning. In desperation, Sam paid Carla $20 to rig the slot machine to pay out with the next play. Rebecca was cajoled into playing one more time, but only won the nickel she inserted. Rebecca rejoiced because this proved she was not a loser—she was a break evener!

Rebecca once planned a Thanksgiving dinner for the entire Cheers gang. Fortunately, it was held at Cheers, and everyone was spared a grilled cheese sandwich entrée and an ambulance ride to the hospital (unlike the kids who attended the last Thanksgiving dinner she hosted).

At Cheers, Rebecca had her share of insulting sobriquets, such as Mrs. Granite Panties, Meat Grinder, Serving Wench, Screaming Boss Lady from Hell, Howitzer, Rebecca of Hornybrook Farm, and Tree-Hugging Dirt-Munching Druid.

Diane Chambers

Childhood

Diane's earliest recollection was of an in utero experience of a 4th of July concert her mother attended. She was born one month premature (circa 1954), and her parents were somewhat disappointed because they were hoping for a son. She received the nickname Muffin from her father (because she was sweet and toasty) and her wonderful sense of humor came from her mother's side of the family.

As an only child, Diane had a lonely youth. She was not close to anyone in her family—her father worked and her mother was incredibly social—so she relied upon her pet cat, Elizabeth Barrett Browning, to provide comfort and love. Elizabeth was Diane's closest friend and confidante, and was always reassuring, especially in times of sickness or when Diane's parents were fighting. Possibly the worst night of Diane's life was at age 12 when her parents separated. She contemplated throwing herself into the lake, but changed her mind because nobody would be there to care for Elizabeth. (Elizabeth died in 1983, but within four years was replaced with another pet cat.)

Diane compensated for a lonely childhood by becoming attached to her stuffed animals. She assigned personal names to each animal, and considered them her friends. Her dearest childhood pal was a hand puppet named Brian the Lion, and her other friends included Mr. Jammers (a giraffe), Freddy Frog Bottoms, Gary Gorilla, and Mr. Buzzer (a bee).

One of Diane's human friends was Heather Landon. She and Heather were friends since grade school, and best friends since the fourth grade (circa 1963). Diane and Heather referred to spaghetti as pascetti, and one of their favorite telephone pranks was pretending to be radio talk show hosts. They made telephone calls and asked, "For a trip to Hawaii, please name three cars that start with 'P'." When the person answered, for example, "Plymouth, Pontiac, and Porsche," the girls responded, "I'm sorry those cars start with gas," and hung up.

Since age seven, Diane's ultimate childhood dream was to become a ballerina. She had years of private lessons, and even auditioned at the Juilliard School. Her dream never reached fruition because on the very first step of her audition she fell and bloodied her nose. They refused to allow Diane to continue with the audition, and she never heard from them again.

Diane's childhood had its share of successes and setbacks. In high school she was voted "The Girl Most Likely to Marry Into Old Money," and one of her proudest moments was fighting singlehandedly to integrate her sorority, which discriminated against girls with poorly publicized coming out parties.

There were three particular instances when Diane felt horribly defeated and humiliated: when she failed to get the lead in the school play; when she was 17 and not asked to the junior prom; and when she was not elected cheerleader.

Diane was somewhat socially stunted because she always had her face in a book. She began reading the *New York Times* at age four, then went straight to the classics, and in fourth grade received the book *Being and Nothingness* from her mother. Diane won merit badges as a Brownie in the Girl Scouts, and spent a great deal of time mastering the fine points of Ping-Pong in the elaborate recreation room her father built for her.

Personal

In terms of physical appearance, the youthful Diane was a gawky girl with a facial tic which she controlled through meditation (she preferred a half-hour session before breakfast). She also conquered several unspecified phobias by confronting them. Her skin pigmentation was the color of Elmer's Glue (or what Restoration poets refer to as "alabaster skin"), and she avoided sunlight, due to her tendency to freckle. Diane had a swan-like neck, and flaxen hair that smelled wonderful because she used dandruff shampoo.

Diane loved going to Cape Cod in the winter, and always wanted to see Kansas City. Her favorite resorts included one at Pequots, Connecticut (room 12), and the Sea Shadows Inn (room 5, where she enjoyed clams oregano) in Marblehead, Massachusetts. One of her particularly unique habits was that she ate every pretzel in exactly three bites. Diane was a speed reader, and kept a personal journal to pen her deepest feelings. She hated female contests with every fiber of her being because they degrade women, and abhorred bachelor parties because they are juvenile, sexist rituals.

In 1982 Sam entered Diane in the Miss Boston Barmaid contest. She surreptitiously planned to win the contest so she could denounce it. Diane won, and as she prepared to give her condemnatory speech, the emcee announced several prizes she was to receive—a dozen roses, six months free dry cleaning, a food processor, and a $200 shopping spree—and when the grand prize was announced (a trip for two to Bermuda), in a rare act of spontaneity, Diane was overcome with excitement and forgot to denounce the contest. Diane's lack of spontaneity was due to spending all of her time analyzing every situation and talking about everything. Diane believed an unexamined life was not worth living.

Diane was very competitive (though she preferred the word intense), and always had to be on top. This was best illustrated in a Ping-Pong match between her and Sam. Diane was winning 20–19 and serving the ball. She conned Sam into setting down his paddle so they could overcome their competitiveness. As they exited the poolroom, she rushed back, served the ball, and proclaimed, "I win!" Although adept at this sport, Diane claimed Simon Says was her best game.

Socially, Diane was a bit of a slumber cat. Although she was a member of a cheese club, she despised most blue-collar activities—she never played billiards, never watched a pro football game (live or on television), and disliked miniature golf, sports arenas and amusement parks.

Despite Diane's disdain for sports, she participated in the Cheers football pool for approximately three weeks, until Sam banned her for winning too often. Sam was particularly upset about the "systems" Diane used for predicting the winning teams—the color of the players' uniforms (red beats blue, blue beats yellow, yellow beats mauve), which animal was more ferocious (a bear versus a dolphin), and cities with symphonies led by foreign-born conductors. She also wanted to test a theory about the most dominant state flower.

In the religious realm, Diane was not very committed. She prayed as a child, but this ritual lapsed for several decades. Her belief in God was unknown, though on one occasion she prayed to a deity for a sign to guide her actions. Diane once had a religious experience while watching a hummingbird hover next to a flower, finding it almost impossible to imagine that something could hang in midair so long. (Sam joked that she probably never saw one of his curve balls!)

Family

Diane's father, Spencer Chambers, was a wise and learned man who amassed a considerable fortune by the time of his death in 1973. He married a poor woman named Helen, who gave birth to his only offspring, Diane. Spencer and Helen had a disputatious marital relationship, and even though they separated briefly, they remained married until his death. Their frequent arguments may explain why he loved a good joke more than he loved his wife. When Spencer and Helen fought, Diane hid in her room and cuddled with her pet cat, Elizabeth.

Spencer was a good father. He loved Diane very much, and was always concerned about her well-being. In his last will and testament, he inserted a clause that would disinherit his wife if Diane did not marry within 10 years of his death. Spencer was concerned that Diane would never find a mate, though he made dating very difficult for her. He never tried to know Diane's boyfriends, and decided he did not like them based solely on bad posture or facial hair, and became especially upset when she brought home a utopian socialist.

Spencer was a businessman who traveled quite frequently. His business partner was Jack Meeken—Diane remembers sitting on Jack's lap and being tossed in the air as he asked, "Who's your favorite uncle?," to which she would playfully shrill "Uncle Jack! Uncle Jack!" Jack was also remembered for his pipe smoking and the unique scent of Peruvian blend tobacco he used.

Diane referred to her mother as "Mummy." Helen Chambers became a wealthy and eccentric socialite overly accustomed to money and social status— since marrying Spencer, her entire life revolved around these status symbols. In fact, Helen tried to prevent her own disinheritance by coercing Diane into proposing marriage to Sam, and even contemplated marrying the family chauffeur to avoid impoverishment.

Helen was overbearing, condescending, and extremely inconsiderate to persons in lower social classes. She treated her domestic servants with disdain—telling the family chauffeur, Boggs, that she only treated him with civility to prevent class warfare. Boggs was born in 1913 and employed by the Chambers family for at least 25 years. During that time he embezzled a small fortune from the Chambers estate, and then used his ill-gotten gains to woo Helen Chambers after her disinheritance in 1983. Helen even distanced herself from Diane. She spent very little time with her daughter and was not physically demonstrative with her. It was a Chambers family tradition on Thanksgiving for each member of the family to say thanks to those special people who had influenced his or her life.

Home Sweet Home

While working at Cheers, Diane lived in apartment "E." In 1987 she and Sam bought a house from Bert and Lillian Miller, an elderly couple that had lived there for 40 years. The house had three bedrooms, two and one-half bathrooms, a formal dining room, a huge fireplace in the living room, hardwood floors, a bay window, crown molding, and a large basement. The Millers had several children and grandchildren, including Mikey, Bert, Jr., Janey, Naomi, and David.

Intellectuals

Diane envied several persons for their intellectual and creative capabilities. She praised Dr. Simon Finch-Royce, a noted psychologist and renowned marriage counselor, as being the wisest man she knew. Dr. Finch-Royce was a practicing psychiatrist at London General Hospital and authored a marriage manual.

Diane lauded Dr. Sumner Sloane, a professor of world literature at Boston University (who was also her former employer, lover, and fiancé), as being the most brilliant man she knew. Dr. Sloane had an article published in *Harper's* in 1982, and went out of his way to employ Diane as a teaching assistant.

As for non-human intelligence, Diane credits the dolphin as being the smartest animal.

Personal Favorites

Diane's favorite type of music was classical (she loved Mozart), and her favorite opera was *Lucia di Lammermoor* by Gaetano Donizetti. As to popular music favorites, she liked the song "Our House" by Crosby, Stills, Nash & Young. Diane's favorite era was the Renaissance, her favorite Elizabethan poet was Christopher Marlowe and she thought French painter Georges Seurat (1859–91) was the finest naturalist of his time. Although her favorite name was Toby, Diane wanted to name her first child Emile.

Psychology and Personal Philosophy

Diane was an obsessive compulsive about neatness. Little things disturbed her, such as the organization of the pencil, pen and pad in her waitress apron. Prior to coming to Cheers in 1982, Diane received therapy from Dr. Graham, a clinical psychologist. In February 1983 she had daily counseling sessions, and in the summer of 1984 consulted with a therapist at Goldenbrook sanitarium in Connecticut. Diane's personal psychology espoused the tenets of Skinnerian behaviorism—the way to modify behavior was to change individual habits. Diane's personal philosophy espoused humanism. She believed there was something fine or noble about every human being. As part of her humanitarian goals, Diane wanted to be known as "the voice of her generation" in defending sisterhood.

In the world of politics, Diane was an uncontroverted liberal. She opposed the re-election campaign of Boston city council candidate Janet Eldridge, because Janet was an old-money conservative who favored big business over greatly needed social programs. For that reason, Diane supported Janet's opponent, James Fleener, and created the Fleener campaign slogan, "Whim with Jim." (She loved it because it sounded so Joycean.) Despite Diane's efforts, James Fleener was defeated by a landslide.

Diane expected Ted Kennedy to be president one day, and once flagged down Thomas "Tip" O'Neill, Speaker of the House of Representatives (at the time), to discuss her philosophy of life and government. Diane believed voting was the highest honor bestowed upon the citizenry and that the second highest honor was jury duty. Diane was the jury foreman in an attempted murder case. In the case, the husband, Bill Grand, attacked his wife, Sherry Grand, in the kitchen with a power saw. The other jurors thought he was innocent, but Diane insisted upon his guilt. The charges were eventually dropped when Bill and Sherry reconciled their differences.

Educational Development

Diane was bred and educated to walk with kings, and attended the most prestigious schools. She was always the brightest in her class—a legitimate "A" student. Diane was a member of a high school sorority, and attended Bennington College (an exclusive private college specializing in the performing arts). One of Diane's most memorable college party themes had the guests dress as their favorite Elizabethan poet. Diane went as Christopher Marlowe because she was deeply into *Dr. Faustus* at the time.

Diane hopped the pond to live in France after receiving a full scholarship to attend school at the Sorbonne. Upon her return to Boston, Diane attended Boston University for extensive educational training—she was close to having a master's degree in 37 majors, including art, art history, English, French, psychology (she had 26 units), pre-law, literature, poetry, anthropology, Indian studies (she could be pretentious when discussing Indian cooking), and Manchurian folk dancing. Diane also took classes in practical feminism, and completed six semesters of bowling because she needed the physical education credits and could read between frames. Diane was a member of the Phi Epsilon Delta sorority, and did not date Sigma Chi fraternity members.

Several college professors influenced Diane's academic development. Dr. Wendell Grant, her freshman creative writing professor, was instrumental in her success as an award-winning television screenplay writer (she mentioned him in her acceptance speech); Dr. Narsutis was her professor for graduate American literature; Sebastian DeWitt was her theater professor and a renowned drama coach; Dr. Lowell Greenspon assisted her in formulating a psychology paper for publication titled, "The Don Juan Syndrome in Modern Culture: An Analysis of Satyriasis," which used Sam as a case study. Sam's pseudonym was Trevor (though he wanted her to use Duke).

Diane also did a study on paranoia as a psychology experiment for her behavior sciences colloquium, and used the Cheers gang as unsuspecting subjects. Diane and a classmate, Irving, set out to prove paranoia can exist in a comfortable environment. Irving sat alone in Cheers for hours, observing everyone and taking notes. The study proved effective because the gang began accusing each other of wrongdoing.

When Diane revealed the experiment, the Cheers gang vowed revenge. Soon Diane became paranoid in anticipation of their vengeance, which caused her to unwittingly play a prank on herself. When the Boston public television station (WLBD) asked to film her poetry reading, Diane expected this to be the retaliation, so she clucked like a chicken in a poem titled, "Ode to a Cornish Hen." Unfortunately, the television program, "Boston's Working Poets," hosted by Martin Gallagher, was a legitimate show about part-time poets reading their work in their own habitats, and WLBD aired the "poem." Although Diane was embarrassed, she was more saddened by the fact that the gang did not take the time to retaliate—she still felt like an outsider. The gang then exacted revenge with the ol' bucket of water over the door gag. A drenched Diane joyously proclaimed, "I love you guys!"

Friends

Diane had very few friends during adulthood, which paralleled her lonely childhood. She maintained contact with two childhood friends: Heather Landon and Bennington College roommate Rebecca Prout. In 1983 Heather moved to Boston and began a friendship with Sam. Although her congeniality was initially mistaken as a sexual come-on, Diane and Heather reconciled this misunderstanding and reaffirmed their friendship.

Rebecca Prout was married to Elliot, who had a Ph.D. in ichthyology. Upon receiving the degree, Elliot ran off with one of his students during a squid expedition. His departure crushed Rebecca, so she decided to blot his memory with one night of unbridled, bestial pleasure—to burn at the stake of passion. Sam Malone fit the image of her dream man—tall, dark, strong, hairy arms, unintellectual, one-word sentences, and peasant stock—so she asked him to fulfill her desires. Sam willingly accommodated Rebecca's request, until she bored him with dismal Russian poems.

Rebecca's occupation involved translating Russian poems, and her favorite was "Another Christmas of Agony" by Mikhail Kheraskov:

> Misha the dog lies dead in the bog.
> The children cry over the carcass.
> The mist chokes my heart,
> covers the mourners.
> At least this year we eat.

Even this poem was not enough to help Rebecca overcome the depression caused by Elliot's departure.

Another one of Diane's friends was Gretchen, a graduate student working on her thesis in kinesiology (the study of physical movements) who lettered in three sports. Diane considered Gretchen to be bright, witty, attractive, and a perfect match for Sam. Diane arranged for Gretchen to be his blind date, but the pair only went out once.

Diane met another acquaintance as a patient at Goldenbrook sanitarium in Connecticut. Amanda Boyer was also a patient at the time, undergoing treatment for an excessive preoccupation and irrational possessiveness toward men.

Employment

Although Diane's parents were wealthy, she refused to accept their money. She did not want to be handed money on a silver platter, and promised her mother she would prove her self-worth.

As a college student, Diane tutored junior high students. One student, Stevie McDunna (Steve McNeese in the show credits), subsequently became a surgeon (and the treating physician for Sam's hernia injury). Diane also worked at the Third Eye Bookstore, and was a teaching assistant for Dr. Sumner Sloane from 1980 to 1982. In 1985 Diane interviewed with Professor Moffat for a teaching assistant position, and became a substitute teaching assistant at a Boston college in 1986.

Cheers

In 1982 Diane was abandoned at Cheers by her fiancé, Dr. Sumner Sloane. She was unemployed, had no job skills and nowhere to go, but realized her memorization skills qualified her for a waitress position. Her first memorized drink order was two vodka gimlets (one straight up, one blended rocks); Shiver's rocks and soda; Comfort Manhattan, hold the cherry; white wine spritzer with a twist; and one Bushmill Irish decaf, hold the sugar. Diane accepted Sam's offer of employment, and her first customers were tourists who could not speak English.

Diane worked at Cheers for five years, but left her employment six different times (five times voluntarily). Her first departure was three months after being hired, when she embarrassed a patron, alias Eric Finch, by proving he was a pathological liar. Diane realized she did not fit in with the crowd, so she quit. Her exodus was short-lived because Sam convinced her the best solution was to find Mr. Finch and apologize.

Diane's second departure was in 1983, when her employment interfered with her and Sam's relationship. She quit to find employment elsewhere, but returned dejected because every job offer had sexual strings attached. When she interviewed for a proofreading position at a small publishing company, the interviewer, Mr. Hedges, called Sam to ask whether he ever saw her naked! Diane was appalled at the behavior of male employers, but soon admitted a personal hypocrisy after realizing she accepted employment at Cheers because of her sexual attraction to Sam.

A year later Diane and Sam had a tumultuous argument over her defiance of an ultimatum not to pose for artist Phillip Semenko. Diane returned to Cheers three months later to help Sam control an alcohol problem (that resurfaced after their breakup). Coach convinced her to resume working as a cocktail waitress, but within the year left her employment a fourth time to spend six months in Europe with her new beau, Dr. Frasier Crane.

Diane's European sabbatical did not go as planned, and after leaving Frasier at the altar she entered a Boston convent. Sam asked her to return to Cheers, and this time her employment lasted approximately nine months, until Sam's girlfriend, Boston city councilor Janet Eldridge, convinced him to fire Diane. Diane subsequently found employment as a checkout clerk at Hurley's Market.

Shortly thereafter, Sam and Janet broke up, and he proposed marriage to Diane. After reconsidering her rejection of his proposal, Diane decided to work at Cheers until he proposed again. In this instance, Diane was not rehired—she merely entered the bar, picked up an apron, and began working. Despite being embittered by Diane's stinging rejection, Sam allowed her to work so she would observe all the women he was going to date.

Diane left her employment at Cheers for the last time in 1987. Sam proposed marriage again, and this time she accepted. Immediately prior to the wedding, Diane was given the opportunity to finish writing a novel for publication, and they mutually agreed to postpone the wedding so she could finish the book. (She was supposed to leave for six months but did not return for over six years.)

Diane's Muse

In the realm of intellectual endeavors, Diane flaunted her knowledge, especially of the arts—literature, painting, poetry, opera, classical music, etc. If she was not quoting famous authors or classic prose, she was actively pursuing the finer arts—jotting notes for a novel, practicing caricature sketches, or subjecting the gang to cerebral activities, such as television debates, operas, and mime performances.

In her educational pursuits, Diane continued to gravitate toward the arts. She took classes in mime, caricature drawing, ballet, Manchurian folk dancing, ballroom dancing (she and Sam won a trophy), poetry, literature (including Samoan literature), and film techniques. Several individuals influenced her life and love for the arts: Emily Dickinson, Buddha, Shari Lewis and Lambchop, Frank Lloyd Wright, and Jack London, to name a few.

Diane was also a literature aficionado, and praised the works of Jack London, Marcel Proust, John Donne, and John Keats. In contrast, Diane disliked the work of Count Lev Nikolayevich Tolstoy, especially his novel *War and Peace* because she considered it to be the most over-analyzed novel ever written. Even Ernest Hemingway's work was too pretentious for her liking.

Diane was a collector of rare books and antiques. Her pride and joy was a first edition of *The Sun Also Rises* autographed by "Papa Bear" Ernest

Hemingway. The inscription was simply, "Ernest Hemingway. Madrid, 1927." (She jokingly stated the inscription read, "Dear F. Scott: Boy that Zelda is one crazy chick!") Diane purchased the book for $500 and eventually sold it for $1,200 to Sam, who outbid Bruce Sayers.

Diane enjoyed the theater, in which she had been a student director and a performer in several plays. She appeared in *Romeo and Juliet* (when she was a child), *Tiny Alice* (during her enrollment at Bennington College), and played a waitress in *Bus Stop* (while attending Boston University). Diane enrolled in theater classes taught by professor Sebastian DeWitt, and even assisted Andy Schroeder, a.k.a Andy-Andy (Diane's young protégé), in performing the strangulation scene from *Othello* for an audition. Andy was infatuated with her and thought she was being unfaithful by kissing Sam, so he used his anger to perform the scene with precise authenticity and realism by attempting to strangle Diane. Diane's art interests also included an inexplicable love of dance. Ever since she was a child she wanted to dance. Despite her failings as a youngster, and bypassing this career to concentrate on being a novelist, she never lost her desire to perform ballet. She continued to enroll in dance classes throughout college and studied under the renowned Madame Likova. When Frasier changed Madame Likova's incisive criticism of Diane's performance to aggrandized laudation, Diane decided to audition for the Boston Ballet. Fortunately, Frasier told her the truth moments before her performance.

Diane had a similar adoration for movies. She proudly boasted about ruining the grading curve in her film techniques class, and insisted on directing Woody's home video *Manchild in Beantown* and *Manchild in Beantown Redux* (her edited version of the video). The video was intended to show Woody's parents that he lived in a safe, wholesome environment, but Diane's directorial debut failed to persuade Woody's parents, largely because her work was too derivative of Jean Luc Godard.

In the realm of painting, Diane felt honored when asked to pose for renowned New England artist Phillip Semenko. Semenko's creative inspiration came from making love to everything he painted, and his most famous painting, *The Harvard-Yale Football Game*, cost him three months in prison (though he still received Christmas cards from some of the guys). He asked Diane to pose because she had an ancient soul and an intense suffering; her eyes had the look of a strangling sparrow.

Diane also appreciated painting as an art form. She had a broad range of favorites, from the French Impressionists to New England's finest non-representational artists. Her broad knowledge of the arts was one reason Diane recognized and posed for Phillip Semenko. However, Diane did not appreciate commercial art, and particularly despised Sam's favorite painting, *Dogs Playing Blackjack*.

Diane's Writing

The written word was very special to Diane—she yearned to be recognized as a great poetess, world renowned novelist, and revered artist. She modeled her behavior after famous individuals in the expectation this would help her acquire the talents or skills of successful people. For instance, while working at Cheers, she used the bar as research for a novel by documenting "snippets of Americana" (the insightful quotes of patrons) to replicate the actions of Jack London. Diane's self-authenticating quote was, "How could I have known when I woke up this morning that I would meet a monk and a doughboy? Two men with one foot in heaven."

Diane enjoyed poetry, and was on speaking terms with the poetry editor of *Atlantic Monthly*. She even submitted a poem for publication to *Cysagy*, a new literary review (with a circulation of about 600) dedicated to publishing prose and poetry on the cutting edge. Diane received a form letter rejection stating her work was "not entirely without promise," and interpreted this as a "soon and inevitably to be published" letter. A few of Diane's unfinished poems included "A Hurricane of Wills," "The Death of a Shallow Man" and "A Bartender Dismembered." Diane even tried to enthrall Dick Cavett with two of her poems, "Ephemeral" and "Ephemeral II."

Diane diligently wrote novels, too. Her pen name was Jessica Simpson-Bourget, and she insisted on an "as told to" credit when she helped write Sam's autobiography. One of her favorite psychology papers was titled, "Hello, Jung Lovers." Diane's literary resumé included a novel nearly accepted for publication. In 1987 Dr. Sumner Sloane submitted one of her papers, *Your Casteism Conundrum*, to a publisher who was interested in expanding it into a novel. Diane spent nearly a year in Maine completing the manuscript which was ultimately rejected because it was too long (her agent suggested trimming a couple thousand pages and making it into a screenplay). She abandoned the book, and moved to Hollywood to write for television.

Although only attaining marginal success in Hollywood, everything changed in 1993 when one of her screenplays won a National Cable Ace Award for Best Writing in a Movie or Miniseries. The award was presented by model Kim Alexis and ex–Chicago Bears coach Mike Ditka. Her award-winning screenplay, *A Heart Held Hostage*, was based on the life of Carla Tortelli-LeBec. The story line was about a hardworking, resilient mother who beat the odds to raise her six children, but in the end went berserk and took out a couple of people with an ouzzi. (The ending cost Diane the humanitarian award.) Diane vowed her next screenplay would involve Sylvia Plath's tragic story.

Theory of Relationships

Diane firmly believed every woman had an image of Mr. Right, and should never settle for anything less. She described her ideal man as "very intellectual, and very well educated, perhaps even overeducated, if there was such a thing. Not particularly athletic, perhaps even clumsy, but charmingly so. Blond, blue-eyed, with a Byron-like innocence." (Sam thought she described herself.)

According to Diane, the most romantic gesture she had ever known was love at first sight. She was deeply touched when Coach experienced this with Irene Blanchard. Diane also believed carving lovers' initials into wood was another romantic gesture, and carved her and Sam's initials into the Cheers bar countertop. As for actual romance, Diane disliked ear nibbling because it sounded too much like a chipmunk.

In matters of amour, Diane was jealous about past lovers in her man's life. She thought it would be a marvelous gesture for Sam to destroy his black book of women's telephone numbers, and was disheartened that he did not discard the book after they began dating. When Sam refused to destroy the book, she became even more incensed and nearly ended their relationship over the ordeal. She was also quite upset with Sam because everywhere they went—to the market, to the movies, to get their blood test—Sam met an old flame.

Diane had many theories and beliefs about relationships. She believed a doctorate changed a man, and he was likely to abandon a current relationship to pursue other women. Diane also believed the opposite of love was indifference, not hate. Most surprisingly, Diane believed a person should not be totally honest in a relationship. For example, she claimed if Sam were to have a one-time only affair, she would not want to know.

Finally, Diane despised being treated as a sex object; she only wanted to be known for her intelligence and social grace. For example, she was dismayed when Sam referred to her as a "love bunny" on a radio talk show, and insisted that he make a formal apology on the air. Diane did not want to be grouped among his many nameless and faceless bimbos—she wanted to believe their dating relationship was special.

Relationships—Diane's Suitors

Diane had the opportunity to marry five different men: Dr. Sumner Sloane, Boggs (the Chambers' chauffeur), Dr. Frasier Crane, Jack Dalton and Sam Malone. The first four proposed to her once, and Sam proposed five times (i.e., over the telephone after breaking up with Janet Eldridge, on a boat anchored off the coast of Maine, at Cheers when she began crying, in a court of law when the judge ordered him to propose, and in 1993 before she returned to California).

Diane even proposed marriage to Sam once. In 1983 her mother was on the verge of disinheritance under the terms of her father's will if Diane did not marry within 10 years of his death (and the deadline was approaching). Diane asked Sam to consent to an immediate marriage and expeditious divorce to satisfy the terms of the will. Sam agreed but became concerned that Diane was taking the marriage vows too seriously when she chastised him for leering at a woman during the ceremony. As they began arguing, Diane's mother canceled the wedding.

SUMNER SLOANE. Diane had always been intimidated by Dr. Sumner Sloane, even though he was her employer, lover, and fiancé. Sumner was a professor of world literature at Boston University, and hired Diane as his teaching assistant. Soon their relationship developed into something meaningful, and Sumner proposed marriage. He was reading a book by William Butler Yeats, and Diane was reading a book by Marcel Proust, when he looked up to her and quoted a verse from the poem "The Bait" by John Donne, "Come live with me and be my love, and we will some new pleasures prove." Diane accepted, and they made arrangements for their wedding and honeymoon in Barbados.

Diane and Sumner stopped at Cheers for a celebratory glass of champagne en route to the airport. Sumner then suggested giving Diane his grandmother's antique gold wedding ring, so he left the bar (on two separate occasions) to retrieve it from his ex-wife, Barbara. When he failed to return, Diane called the airline to reschedule their plane reservations, only to discover Sumner and Barbara used the tickets to fly to Barbados.

One year later, Sumner appeared at Cheers to recapture Diane's heart. Although he and Barbara had separated, Sumner asked Diane to meet Barbara and himself for dinner. Diane reluctantly agreed, and Sam talked his way into a double date with three intellectuals. By the end of the evening, Sam concluded that Sumner was trying to woo Diane, and realized he and Diane did not belong together—she was merely slumming between Ph.Ds. Diane was faced with the decision to return to Sumner's arms or remain in Sam's. She chose Sam because he read *War and Peace* for her.

Sumner's persistence was apparent when he returned in 1987 and prevented Diane from marrying Sam. This time Sumner did not try to win her heart, but rather appealed to her intellect with a tempting book publication contract. Sumner submitted one of Diane's papers to Houghton Miflin Company (a Boston publisher), who was interested in having her finish it for publication. Sumner's plan was successful. Diane and Sam decided to postpone their wedding so she could finish writing the novel.

BOGGS. Diane's second marriage proposal was from Boggs, an elderly gentleman who was the Chambers' chauffeur for over 25 years. He proposed marriage to prevent Diane's mother from being disinherited under the terms of Spencer Chambers' will. Since there was never a romantic relationship between the two, she respectfully declined his kind and thoughtful proposal.

FRASIER CRANE. Diane's third suitor, Dr. Frasier Crane, used to make obscene telephone calls to her. They met at Goldenbrook sanitarium—he worked as a consulting psychiatrist, and she was a patient (though he was not her therapist). Diane voluntarily entered the sanitarium to regain her composure after a nervous breakdown caused by her and Sam's breakup. She remained at Goldenbrook for three months, and once was restrained to her bed for her own safety (for a week and a half, so she was told), when psychotropic drugs affected her sense of balance.

Diane and Frasier's first encounter was rather fortuitous. She and an elderly woman were playing croquet on the Goldenbrook front lawn when Diane accused the woman of cheating. The pair began wrestling on the ground when Frasier intervened to squelch the dispute (and removed a croquet mallet from Diane's hands as she prepared to strike her worthy opponent).

Frasier's mother, Hester Crane, had difficulty accepting Diane. She was concerned that Frasier's life and career would be ruined, and he would have a bad marriage with a pseudo-intellectual barmaid. To prevent this from occurring, Hester threatened Diane's life and then offered Sam money to become romantically involved with her.

Diane and Frasier had other relationship difficulties, such as her inability to accept his work commitments, especially the frequent out of town psychological seminars (multiple personality, fetish, and nerve ending seminars). There were further difficulties when Diane and Frasier decided to elevate their relationship to a higher plateau—cohabitation. At first Diane experienced an allergic reaction and blamed it on Frasier's puppy, Pavlov, so the dog was given to Sam (who renamed it "Diane"). When the irrefutable evidence proved Diane had a psychosomatic reaction due to her feelings for Sam, Frasier insisted he return Pavlov. Diane misinterpreted the argument as Frasier standing up and fighting for her, and her "allergy" miraculously vanished.

Part of the intrigue of Diane and Frasier's relationship occurred on Sunday, when they only spoke French. Diane loved this weekly escapade, but Frasier was not equally enamored. Moreover, he confessed that he never had a bit of fun in their relationship, especially on Sunday, and the only thing more egregious than her French pronunciation was her syntax.

Although Diane's relationship with Frasier was intellectually stimulating, she retained romantic feelings for Sam. Once, while making love to Frasier, Diane inadvertently called out Sam's name, and when Frasier asked Diane to accompany him on a six-month trip to Europe, she was reluctant to leave Sam. Although she agreed to accompany Frasier (because Sam maintained a facade of indifference), she and Sam shared a passionate moment before Diane departed for Europe. The rapture never blossomed because Sam wanted a one-night stand, whereas Diane wanted the commencement of a meaningful relationship.

While in Europe, Frasier unexpectedly proposed marriage to Diane at

Luigi's, an Italian restaurant. Diane immediately called Sam, hoping he would express his true feelings for her. When he failed to oblige, she accepted Frasier's proposal. The loving couple made arrangements to be wed at Dr. Marino's parents' estate in Florence, Italy. When their car broke down in a small Italian village, Diane suggested they wed immediately. At the altar, Frasier said his vows, and then the priest asked Diane if she would take Frasier as her husband. She looked around and asked Frasier if the priest was talking to her. When Frasier nodded yes, Diane left.

She began a spree of decadence across Europe—dancing on cafe tables, swimming in fountains, cavorting with counts and soccer players, and sunbathing nude. She later atoned for her behavior by entering St. Anselm's Abbey (located one hour outside Boston) and working as a servant for the Sisters of the Divine Severity.

JACK DALTON. During Diane's spree of decadence, she met Jack Dalton at the running of the bulls in Pamplona, Spain. His love of danger intoxicated her. Jack was an adventurist who unleashed Diane's impetuousness to do activities she previously had been too inhibited to attempt. Diane ultimately rejected Jack's marriage proposal because she had a secret love back in Boston. (When Sam overheard this, Diane claimed her secret love was Mickey Mantle!)

SAM MALONE—EARLY ATTRACTION. Diane's attraction to Sam was an endless theme that played throughout the show (even when she dated Frasier), and the continual repression of her true feelings for him was a thinly veiled facade. Diane admitted she began working as a cocktail waitress at Cheers partially due to her physical attraction to Sam. They flirted with each other through sexual metaphors and double entendres, and over the course of their relationship, he proposed marriage to her five times, but she only accepted twice (in 1987 and 1993).

Sam first kissed Diane one month after she was hired. He was depressed after a former teammate, Dave Richards, canceled a television interview, and at Diane's urging decided to "go for it." Diane was somewhat flattered by the kiss, but instinctively flipped him onto the pool table. (Diane learned this self-defense tactic in her practical feminism class.) This was also the first time Diane admitted that Sam was attractive—as she stated, "When the light strikes you in a certain way and your hair is combed right and I'm standing back a ways, you're sometimes somewhat unrepugnant."

SAM MALONE—DATING. Diane and Sam continued to suppress their attraction toward one another, and did not officially begin dating until the 1983 season premiere. What ultimately united the couple was Diane's rejection of Sam's brother, Derek. When Sam feigned indifference about her leaving for Paris with Derek, they became involved in a fiery dispute that lead to a passionate kiss and culminated in the consummation of their relationship.

SAM MALONE—RELATIONSHIP TENSIONS. Diane and Sam's tumultuous relationship was uncontrovertible. Difficulties arose when Sam first uttered those three special words, "I love you" after she gave him two tickets to a Marvin Hagler prizefight (purchased from Dr. Phil Kepler for $200). He was merely flippantly thanking her for the tickets, but she interpreted the words literally. After discussing their miscommunication, they decided to spend one week analyzing the depth of their relationship. After seven days they could not identify any reason for maintaining their relationship, yet continued dating (though Sam hinted that he actually did love her).

The next milestone of confrontation was Sam's desire to spend a ski weekend with his baseball teammates to melt a few snow bunnies. He concocted a story about having to attend his Uncle Nathan's funeral. Sam embarrassed himself by adding to the deception with additional acts of blatant dishonesty. Diane knew the truth and used emotional blackmail to keep Sam home for the weekend.

In another incident, Diane was livid upon discovering that Sam still had his black book of women's telephone numbers. Since they were dating, she found it offensive and a breach of the sanctity of their relationship for him to maintain any contact with his past sexual exploits. Diane was further incensed when Sam went to bed with another woman, Didi, even though nothing happened (because he thought of how much Diane meant to him). She broke up with him, but they reaffirmed their relationship when Sam openly expressed his feelings for her.

The most significant divisiveness between the couple occurred in 1984. Sam exalted himself for being selected one of Boston's 20 most eligible bachelors by *Boston* magazine. Diane was frenetic, and attempted to strangle him with a telephone cord. Sam attempted to make amends by having the renowned Phillip Semenko paint her portrait, but after arguing with Semenko, Sam forbade Diane to pose. She initially acquiesced to Sam's ultimatum, but could not resist this opportunity of a lifetime (and figured Sam would forgive her once he saw the finished product). When Diane revealed the truth, Sam was unforgiving, and they broke up.

SAM MALONE—THE BREAKUP. After the breakup between Diane and Sam, she entered a sanitarium, where she met and began dating Dr. Frasier Crane. Despite her newfound love, there remained an ever present sense that she and Sam would reunite. When Diane left Frasier at the altar, Sam tracked her down in a convent to explain that he tried to stop the wedding, he loved her, and they should have been married. Diane placed her faith in God to give her a sign, and ultimately returned to Cheers (though she and Sam did not resume dating).

SAM MALONE—THE REUNION. After Sam's relationship with Boston city councilor Janet Eldridge failed, he proposed marriage to Diane over the telephone. Diane insisted upon a romantic proposal, so Sam chartered a boat off the coast of Maine, chilled champagne and prepared a candlelight dinner.

He popped the question, only to have her reject him because of reservations that the proposal was a reaction to the failing of his relationship with Janet.

Diane reconsidered her rejection, and the next day entered Cheers to accept Sam's marriage proposal (however, he withdrew the question). Still believing Sam loved her, Diane decided to work at the bar until he proposed marriage again. Sam dated many women over the next several months, and when he adamantly denied any feelings of love for her, Diane began to cry. Sam was unable to resist her tears, and proposed marriage to her again, but she still said "no!"

Sam envisioned killing her, and actually chased her six blocks before she tripped and fell, bruising her thigh and wrenching her neck. Sam was arrested and jailed for willful assault and battery. The judge then ordered Sam to propose marriage one more time or risk going to jail. Sam reluctantly proposed, and this time Diane accepted. (She gave him the option to back out, but he insisted on going through with it.)

Diane and Sam began planning the wedding, starting with the engagement ring. When Sam learned the engagement ring of her choice would cost $5,200, he opted for a $1,200 ring from Norm's friend, Bruce. She also insisted on having the ring box so she could store it in her momento drawer between her French Club pin and her retainer. In the end Sam spent nearly $8,640 to conceal his deception, but Diane still learned the truth. The second critical wedding arrangement was to select a honeymoon destination. Diane chose Tibet, but assented to Sam's selection because he was inexorably determined to go to Disney World. Third, their names were placed with a bridal registry assistant, Penelope, and they ordered household necessities (monogrammed linen, fingertip towels, dust ruffles), registered for flatware, and selected china patterns (everyday china and Royale Doulton Carlisle fine china).

Immediately prior to their marriage, Diane went on a contemplative retreat for a spiritual catharsis. She made a sojourn to the Glade, a Buddhist monastery in Florida known for having the biggest Buddha east of the Mississippi.

As their wedding day approached, Sumner informed Diane that a publisher might be interested in one of her novels. Everyone at the bar wagered on whether Sam and Diane would say their vows, and Carla was the only person who cried during the ceremony. When the publisher offered Diane a sizeable advance to finish writing the novel, she agreed, and departed to Sumner's secluded cabin in Maine (down the road from Ted Koppel's cabin), vowing to return in six months.

SAM MALONE—THE FINAL REUNION. Six years passed before Diane returned. After she won a writing award, Sam sent a congratulatory telegram and invited her to Boston. When she arrived unannounced, both Diane and Sam tried to conceal a few fabrications they had told each other about their lives, most notably that they were married with children. Diane's "husband" was her dog groomer, Reed Manchester, an aspiring documentary filmmaker (she agreed to help him write a "Tales from the Crypt" episode). However, Reed's live-in lover of six years, Kevin (nicknamed Muffin), exposed their homosexual affair. Sam fabricated a marital arrangement with Rebecca Howe. Despite having their prevarications unveiled, Diane and Sam still reconciled and then resurrected their past relationship.

They decided to marry and move to California to start anew. As the plane prepared to depart, they reconsidered their decision and the adverse consequences it would have on their lives. Diane was apprehensive about Sam hindering her career aspirations. In the end they went their separate ways.

Analyzing Diane and Sam's Relationship

Diane frequently analyzed her and Sam's relationship, and found insight regarding their attraction toward one another. She admitted to being physically attracted to Sam, and even acknowledged an irresistible compulsion after their breakup. There was an undeniably fabulous sexual component to their relationship. In fact, physicality was the primary basis for being together because Diane and Sam had different backgrounds, ambitions, and dreams. But in defense of their union, they shared one common bond—the ability to be vulnerable to one another. Despite repeated illustrations of their incompatibility, they perpetually labored (albeit unsuccessfully) to make their relationship endure.

A primary reason for their incompatibility was the fact that their entire relationship was a contest of wills. Individually they aspired for power in their relationship—to have the upper hand—but never attained this goal because they were equally inflexible. The most predominant argument was who broke up with whom, and one frequently interjected personal insults to feel superior to the other—Diane criticized Sam's intelligence, and he preyed upon her aloofness and eccentricities. Each argument was a struggle to exert power, influence, and dominance over the other. This constant struggle for dominance was the ultimate pitfall in their relationship.

Diane's criticism of Sam's intelligence was not contemptuous nor apathetic toward his feelings. On the contrary, she was quite concerned about Sam's feelings, and often acted to protect his ego. When Sam donated his baseball jersey for a celebrity memorabilia auction, she purposely bought the unsold jersey to protect him from embarrassment. In another instance, Diane comforted Sam's ego after giving her honest psychological analysis of him.

Another reason for their failing relationship was Sam's disrespect for women. Diane claimed he was inconsiderate and insensitive, especially toward her feelings. For example, after their first night of making love, Diane wanted to spend the next day together, but Sam went to a football game instead.

When she invited Sam over for a seven course meal, he ate a burger beforehand. He gave Diane second-hand flowers for Valentine's Day, failed to visit her when she was ill, and gave her steak knives for Christmas. He also shrunk her one of a kind, hand-spun lambs wool sweater that was purchased in Ireland.

Sam acted so abominably in their relationship that Diane shared the experiences with a therapy group at Goldenbrook sanitarium (referring to Sam with the alias Ralph).

Relationships—Diane's Dates

Besides the many men who proposed marriage to Diane, she also had a myriad of other interested dating prospects, some for romance, some for fun, and others for vengeance.

Diane's most interesting date was Andy-Andy (a.k.a Andy Schroeder). Sam paid Andy $20 to go on a date with Diane, and he quickly revealed he was convicted of manslaughter and had spent ten years in prison for killing a waitress at Via Molano restaurant. He heard voices—the shrill of his mother—and dreamed his hands were claws. Diane had nightmares about Andy after he was released from the state mental hospital. He returned to Cheers to apologize to Diane (for trying to strangle her) and to introduce his fiancée, Cynthia.

Diane had several other unique dates. Walter Franklin was able to tell you instantly how many letters you used in a sentence, and Dennis Kaufman was a puppeteer who appeared at Cheers dressed in Renaissance garb.

Diane frequently dated men based solely on their physical appearance. She dated Herb Sawyer, president of the Boston accounting firm H.W. Sawyer & Associates, merely because he was physically attractive, but she spent the evening fending off his advances. In another instance, Diane tried to prove physical appearance was not important. She arranged a blind date with a man, Stuart Sorenson, who had inadvertently left his coat at Cheers, but she ultimately decided to end the relationship because he was not physically appealing. (Fortunately, Stuart ended the relationship first, after reconciling with an ex-girlfriend.)

As for an ideal man, Diane once dated Sam's brother, Derek Malone. He was a very talented and attractive international lawyer. For their first date they flew to Martha's Vineyard. Despite having the ideal relationship, Diane, wishing to remain with Sam, rejected Derek's offer to accompany him to Paris.

Diane also dated men of social stature. She once dated wealthy socialite Jordan Brundage, and bragged to the gang about accompanying him to dinner at The Cafe, a trendy Boston restaurant that was rather a coup among certain self-important and pretentious circles. Sam canceled her dinner reservation made three months in advance, and she spent the evening in the lobby waiting for a table to become available.

Diane nearly dated a political candidate. James Fleener, a candidate for the Boston city council, was impressed with Diane's dedication to his campaign, and decided to ask her out on a date. He reconsidered after Frasier intimated Diane had had a sex-change operation.

At other times Diane used men as pawns. When she worked as a substitute teaching assistant at a Boston university, a young college student, Lance Apollonaire, propositioned her to accompany him on a weekend retreat. Diane was physically attracted to the 6'2½" Adonis-like creature, but was more interested in flaunting Lance to make Sam envious. Diane also used Frasier and Derek Malone in similar capacities of invidiousness. She dated Frasier to mask her feelings for Sam, and went out with Derek to make Sam jealous.

Diane committed one incident of unfaithfulness while she was dating Sam. She revealed this innocent indiscretion when a "cursed" weight scale correctly predicted her infidelity with a fortune that read, "Deception in romance proves costly." When Diane confided that Sam did not satisfy all of her needs, they nearly ended their relationship.

Other dates with less specific background information include: Chad Stark, a cardiologist; Gregory, a doctor; David from the anthropology department; and a man named Brian.

Diane Playing Matchmaker

Diane was quite meddlesome in the relationships of others, and enjoyed arranging dates between couples. She not only arranged dates for Sam, Coach and Frasier, but also found a way to intervene in nearly every Cheers relationship, in one form or another.

In 1983 Diane arranged a blind date between Sam and Gretchen, but the evening lost its magic when he reciprocated by arranging for Diane to date an ex-con convicted of manslaughter. She also interfered with Sam's dating relationships when she characterized the women he dated as busty and brainless. He responded by dating every woman he knew to find some intelligent life out there.

Frasier was the victim of Diane's impertinence in two relationships. When he became engaged to marry Candi Pearson, Diane made every effort to dissolve their relationship before Frasier made the ultimate commitment. His other romantic relationship was Diane's only success as a matchmaker. After witnessing Frasier's acrimony toward Dr. Lilith Sternin, Diane worked the magic of makeup to expose the sensuous side of Dr. Sternin. Frasier was instantaneously aroused, as was she, and by the end of the day they were intimate.

Diane's role of cupid continued when she arranged a date for Coach. He was infringing upon Diane and Sam's privacy, so she arranged for Coach to date a bank teller, Katherine, and once helped build his confidence to pursue a neighbor, Nina, in his apartment complex.

Diane was even involved in Carla's relationships. When Carla conned Marshall Lipton into believing he was the father of one of her children, Diane persuaded her to confess the truth. Diane even prompted Carla to date Hank Zenzola, and tried to persuade her into reconciliation with her ex-husband, Nick, claiming he had changed for the better.

Diane intervened in the relationships of nearly every person in the bar. She interfered with Woody's love life by reuniting him with his Indiana girlfriend, Beth Curtis, and by convincing Woody not to cohabit with Coach's niece, Joyce Pantusso. Norm also fell victim to Diane's intrusive nature when she tried to prevent him from having an affair with a client, Emily Phillips. Cliff was spared from Diane's obtrusiveness—probably because he rarely had a relationship.

Cheers

When Diane first entered Cheers in 1982, everyone thought she was a snob (and their impression remained unchanged over the years). Sam thought she was a twit and a snob, and in retrospect, Diane even considered herself a "prissy little snot." Diane's only true friend at Cheers was Coach; he was like a father to her. With everyone else, however, she was an outcast excluded from their activities.

Diane and Carla were mortal enemies. There was no love lost between them, and Carla often served a generous helping of insults at Diane's expense. Despite their antagonistic demeanor, Diane did respect Carla's toughness and her ability to keep her head up despite all adversity. And they did have one common bond—they were both very competitive. Diane and Carla once had a waitress contest to see who could get the most tips in one evening. Diane miraculously won the contest by earning $1.00 more than Carla.

Some of the most memorable insulting nicknames Diane acquired over the years (mostly from Carla) include: Lizard Lips, Motor Mouth, Mullet Head, Gooseneck, Pencil Neck, Lady Fish Face, Vampira, The Stick (the most prevalent), The Stick Lady, Beanpole, Miss Chicken Parts, Miss Robin Dead Breast, Bone Butt, Rebecca of Skinnybrook Farm, Bleach Bag, Lady Dye Job, Goldilocks, Whitey, Pretentious Self-diluted Windbag, Snob, Squawk Box, Love Bunny (Diane found this derogatory), Dufus, and Cookie.

Carla Tortelli-LeBec

Childhood

Carla Maria Victoria Angelina Teresa Apollonia Lozupone was born in 1952 (with her two marriages she added the surname Tortelli-LeBec). Because of her stubbornness Carla was named after her grandmother's mule. Carla was nicknamed Muffin because her brothers once put yeast in her ears and tried to bake her face.

Carla was raised on Federal Hill, a rough section of town, and abused by her father. She had a pet Labrador retriever named Sparky, and as a teenager often frequented the Twi-Lite Drive-in. Nick Tortelli, who later became her first husband, was Carla's dancing partner on the television show "Boston Boppers." As part of a ritual before every show, they spat on each other's shoes for good luck. The teenage dancing sensations were a short-lived tandem because Carla's pregnancy disqualified her from appearing on the show.

Family

Of Italian descent, the Lozupones' only talent was making a curse come true. The family heirloom was a hocked silver wedding ring that had been passed down through the generations, but originated when Uncle Marigal gave it to Aunt Sophia.

Carla's grandfather Antonio lived in Naples before venturing to America. After deserting his family in 1921, Antonio had nothing but the shirt on his back and his lucky quarter. He hopped a freight train from Boston to Los Angeles and worked packing fruit until he earned enough capital to own a business selling candied peaches. He invested the profits in oil, and through frugal living and wise investments amassed an estate worth $20 million. He atoned for the prior desertion by bequeathing his entire estate to the surviving Lozupones in Boston. However, Antonio's illegitimate son, Paolo, suppressed the will, and within 10 years squandered the entire fortune on fast horses and loose women. When the will finally surfaced, the executor of the estate, Whitley Morris (Whitney in show credits), gave Carla the remaining inheritance—Antonio's lucky quarter.

Carla's viciousness was precipitated by having six older siblings, three of whom were named Annette, Angeline and Sal (and one of her sisters was known by the sobriquet No-neck). Carla was envious of one sister because she had Carla beat in every way—she was 5'2", her husband never had a drink before noon, and she was a beautician.

In addition, Carla and Annette were not very close, and only saw each other on special occasions—weddings, holidays, and stays of execution. In fact, the only other way to get them together would be to have Carla identify her sister's body. In 1983 Annette worked as a temporary waitress at Cheers while Carla gave birth to her fifth child. Annette appeared shy and introverted, but her actions demonstrated promiscuity and extroversion. While working, she dated every man who asked her out—including Cliff!

According to Lozupone family tradition, all the women in the family had to name one son with their father's first name and their mother's maiden name. Carla's father was named Benito Lozupone, and her mother's maiden name was Mussolini. Carla staunchly refused to abide by this tradition because she would have had to name one of her sons Benito Mussolini. To trick Carla into honoring the tradition, her mother feigned having the "death dream." Carla's son Gino eventually consented to the change (the family agreed to call him Gino for short).

The "death dream" notified a Lozupone of their imminent demise. The dream was always the same. At the funeral, when opening the casket on the table, you saw a person's feet (because you opened the wrong end), and after opening the other end you saw yourself with pennies over your eyes. This dream occurred fairly early in life because rarely did family members live past age 43.

Another family tradition involved respecting thy mother. The punishment for insulting a Lozupone mother was spending the night in the Murphy bed. One family aphorism: if you receive a single white rose, have someone else start your car. Finally, the Lozupones were known for having atrocious dental habits because they recommended brushing after every war.

Other family relatives of noteworthy importance cannot be forgotten. Cousin Santo was a private investigator who located Diane Chambers in a sanitarium and confirmed Vera Peterson was not having an affair. Carla's Cousin Tino swore to God that he would give up meat, and after eating a burger that evening his teeth fell out. Carla's nephew Frankie was probably the purest of the Lozupones (he worked as a temporary bartender at Cheers), and Zia was known as the hugger in the family. Carla's Uncle Joe accidentally invented the mixed drink "Leap Into an Open Grave" while making a car bomb, and her grandfather invented the mixed drink "I Know My Redeemer Liveth."

Personal

Carla was 5'¼" with brown eyes and frizzy dark chestnut hair (from her father's side of the family), and had no visible scars, tattoos or birthmarks (except the word "Hi" tattooed on her left thigh). She was raised in the strict Catholic faith, prayed to St. Jude, the patron saint of lost causes, and attended church every Sunday. Her telephone number was 555-7843, and if she ever wrote an autobiography, it would be titled, *I'm Greasing the Construction Workers.* Carla's phobias included needles, public speaking, and flying. She created a technique to alleviate the anxiety of public speaking by picturing the audience naked, with the exception of black socks. Carla's fear of flying (or fear of crashing) originated on her first flight when the plane hit turbulence and threw her and Nick all over the bathroom.

According to Carla, all great friendships begin with one small act of vengeance. Her two best friends were Sam and Woody, and she particularly admired Sam for being a selfish, egotistical pig. Carla's most cherished belief was that men are toe jam, and her secret to being so tough was always looking on the bright side of things. Even the death of a loved one had a bright side—"it ain't me!"

Music had many different effects upon Carla. "Unchained Melody" by the Righteous Brothers made her lose all self-control, and she became vigorously sprightly upon hearing "Shout" by the Isley Brothers. When she was depressed, nothing worked better than listening to Gene Pitney records.

Carla only asked for four things in life: fresh fish, ten cents off laundry detergent, volcanic boils all over her ex-husband's back, and the Red Sox in the World Series before she died. Philosophically, Carla believed if you cannot say something nice, say it about Diane; and the point of life was having children—creating life.

Carla always lived in an apartment that was too small for her family's needs, but in 1986 she found the perfect dwelling in size and price. Unfortunately, the Meadowview Acres residence was built on a 17th-century prison graveyard where hundreds of the worst murderers and cut-throats were executed. According to legend, they would rise from the dead and seek vengeance on anyone who lived there. Superstitious Carla was petrified to spend one night alone in the house, so Cliff volunteered to accompany her to break the curse. In the morning Carla realized the low price of the house was due, not to a curse, but to the fact that it was built at the end of an airport runway. She was ecstatic!

Other miscellaneous information: Carla could whistle with her fingers; made raspberry sounds with her armpit (wearing a tank top worked best); created blue sparks in her mouth with wintergreen Lifesavers; extra heavy barbecue sauce made her repeat like a Howitzer; and one of the most precious things she owned was a key chain made by her son Anthony during his first year at camp (she sold it to Cliff for $3).

Personal Likes and Dislikes

Carla's favorite meal was Chicken McNuggets, and her favorite hobby was drawing underarm hair on the models in *Vogue* magazine. Carla's most treasured artwork was an oil painting of her and Elvis, and naturally the best vacation she ever had was a trip to Graceland. Carla's favorite movie was *Lady and the Tramp* (she always cried when they ate the spaghetti), and her favorite bedtime story was *The Runaway Bunny* (she read it at least 1000 times and cried every time). Carla hated anchovies, but was fond of the smell of roast pig.

High School

Carla spent half her life in reform school at St. Clete's Correctional Institute for Wayward Girls, administered by Drusilla Dimeglio. Carla's closest high school compatriots were Kathy Settuducatto, Donna Guzzo, Mo McSweeney, and Roxanne Brewster. Carla once left teeth marks in Dimeglio's ankle and vowed revenge on the despised principal. Carla's day of vengeance arrived 20 years later when Dimeglio entered Cheers and did not recognize her former pupil. Carla implemented the vengeance she dreamed about as a teenager—to shave Dimeglio's head. When the opportunity arose, Carla moderately resisted the temptation and they actually became friends (but not before shaving half of Dimeglio's head).

At age 14, Carla became the most popular girl in school after singing the lead role in the choir while wearing nothing under her robe. Besides her popularity, Carla was known for one other thing—being pregnant. Her high school yearbook accurately predicted she would be pregnant the rest of her life. The three things Carla regrets about high school were never going to prom or homecoming, never having a slumber party, and never traveling to Fort Lauderdale for spring break.

Superstitions

Carla was very superstitious, and even used two palm readers, Madame Lavinda and Madame Lazora (Carla's spiritual advisor and psychic since the early 1970s). Madame Lazora's spiritual contact with the other side was Princess Cotia, a 17th-century Rumanian princess, who was hammered with spikes and burned at the stake, and still kept her sense of humor! Madame Lazora's first customer was Bob.

Madame Lazora's fraudulent psychic enterprise fleeced the public for numerous years, charging $50 per psychic session and $250 per 50-minute seance. Being a foreign resident and not having to pay taxes enabled Madame Lazora to purchase a Jaguar automobile with cash. Her hand-picked successor, Carla, was hesitant because she was not prophetically inclined. When Madame Lazora admitted being a charlatan, Carla was distraught but quickly recuperated after realizing how profitable the profession could be, especially after increasing the fee to $60 per psychic session.

Employment

Carla began working at age 15, and learned everything about waiting tables from a career waitress named Cora at a greasy spoon. Before accepting employment at Cheers, Carla worked at the Broken Spoke and has fond memories of the owner celebrating special occasions by having his way with her on the bar countertop.

Carla began working at Cheers in 1977, and held the titles senior waitress and managing director of waitresses. In 1993 she became the new assistant bartender to replace Woody (after he became a city councilor). She earned the most tips during the third trimester of pregnancy, and had an income of $500 per week (including tips) after taxes, though IRS auditor Donald Zajac estimated her gross income at $1.3 million. Carla made more money than a postal carrier, and Norm was the only customer who never gave her a tip (he never thought the service was good enough).

Sam was reluctant to have Carla tend bar because she frequently made lethal homemade mixed drinks which caused everyone to become intoxicated and ravage the place. In one incident, 12 patrons made a naked conga line winding out Cheers' front door. Despite being admonished, Carla prepared another lethal drink that lowered her inhibitions, and after a wild night of partying she had a one-night stand with Paul Creypens.

When Cheers closed for remodeling, Carla accepted a temporary waitress position at a competitor's establishment, Mr. Pubb's. Although she despised the embellished congeniality of the employees, Carla could not resist the high wages. Despite vowing to quit Cheers, she returned when she realized that the new trainee, Ellen, an anthropology major at Boston University and a poetess, was a Diane Chambers clone.

Relationships—General

According to Carla, every woman wants to be controlled by her man, and the two things women love doing the most are curing a guy of impotence and giving it to him again when he gets out of line! She considered going to bed with a man a good icebreaker, and once claimed she could win the heart of Rebecca's boyfriend, Don Santry, in 10 minutes (or in half the time by using jumper cables and a wet towel).

The longest Carla ever made a man wait for sex was until they were both undressed, and the wildest place she ever had sex was on a carousel at

LaGuardia International Airport (carousel D was best because it was the bumpiest). She refused to have sex on Elvis' birthday, and officially became a slut when she could not remember the name of the man with whom she had sex the previous night. When Carla enjoyed evenings of R & R, she was referring to spending time with Roy and Ralph!

Carla was attracted to goalies and catchers—men in masks, the grunts. She loved the sexiness of their scarred faces, missing teeth, and noses mashed to a meaty pulp. The most handsome man Carla knew was Robert Redford, and her butcher was the most handsome man she knew in Boston.

The image of Carla's dream man was someone confident, not cocky, and okay-looking but not a pretty boy. He would dress nicely in a burgundy leather jacket with cherry Lifesavers in the left pocket and a pack of Camels in the right. (He was trying to quit both, without success.) His nose was broken in all the right places, and he had a scar on his chin he refused to discuss. He cracked his knuckles all the time, which made Carla crazy. He spoke infrequently, but he did not need to say much. He falls for Carla real hard. She hurts him a few times, but he gets over it, and they eventually get married.

As for weddings, Carla's single most important superstition was that the bride and groom not see each other before the ceremony on the day of the wedding. As for her own wedding, Carla refused to be married on a Wednesday.

Carla did not have much success dating. Every man she ever liked ended up having something seriously wrong with him, and all the other men were geeks or those entering the geek-hood. According to Carla, you could not swing a dead cat without hitting some bum who once dumped on her. Carla's one regret was never having a date with Fabian.

Relationships—Nick Tortelli

Nick Tortelli was Carla's first love—a man to whom she could never say "no." She first saw Nick at Marc's Big Boy but never really noticed because he was so hairy. (Nick had been mistaken by many people as the bogus missing link exhibited at the Amsterdam World's Fair.) Over time Carla grew to love Nick's unique characteristics—the way he flexed the panther tattoo on his arm, the way the hair grew in his ears, and the way he drooled in bed. Their ideal date was eating burgers at White Castle and watching wrestling.

There were three things that could be said about Tortelli men. One, they draw women like flies; two, they treat women like flies; and three, their brains are in their flies. Despite Carla's unconditional love, Nick treated her like a dog. He cheated on Carla eight hours after they began dating; and then borrowed her car, sold it, and gave the money to his other girlfriend without even apologizing. Carla's vindication was to marry him. Actually, she was pregnant, so Nick proposed marriage: "Hey, Carla. I knocked you up and you know where I live, so I guess I have to." Nick hid the engagement ring in an X-rated soap on a rope, and scrubbed Carla raw for two hours before she found it.

Carla married at age 15 (though she once stated she was not stupid enough to be married at age 16). At Tortelli weddings, the men leave the fly of their pants unzipped as a sign of fertility. Nick and Carla's wedding day was especially memorable because Nick impregnated Carla's sister! Their marriage lasted 10 years and produced four children but ended in divorce, which was consistent with Nick's idea of fatherhood—when the egg split so did he. Although hesitant to annul Carla's marriage, the church acted promptly when Nick tried to sell the bishop his own watch. As a member of the high school class of 1962, 1963 and 1964, Nick also graduated from the Colletti Academy of TV Repair. While attending the academy, Carla financially supported him by waiting tables. After graduation, they divorced because Carla did not fit in with the other television repairmen's wives. He subsequently opened a television repair business, the Tortelli Television Hospital, and at one point business was so good that he had 10 employees, two of whom were American! In 1986 Nick moved to Las Vegas, where the business went bankrupt. His next entrepreneurial endeavor was Nick's Talent Emporium, an agency with only one client, his wife Loretta. Other novel business ventures included an orangutan act and the home slot machine, Flush & Win (though people had difficulty retrieving their winnings).

In 1984 Nick remarried and relished flaunting Loretta's beauty. He even enclosed a full-body nude photograph of the bride and groom in the wedding invitation sent to Carla. When Sam accompanied Carla to the wedding, Nick could not bear the thought of another man wanting her. At one point, he turned to Sam and Carla, threw the wedding ring at them and said, "Pay attention!" Nick was further enraged that Carla wore the same dress she wore when marrying him. Even after the wedding, en route to Hawaii for the honeymoon, Nick returned to Cheers and asked Carla to take him back. Carla stood firm in rejecting him. Despite winning this battle, she was depressed because Nick had someone to love, and her entire love life was a charade.

At this moment she and Sam kissed, but quickly discovered there was no spark between them. Sam subsequently confided he never pursued Carla romantically because she would be too much woman to handle. Despite being physically attracted to Sam, Carla admitted they could never marry because he was a babe hound—he would be checking out the bridesmaids during their wedding. Besides, she anticipated being the "other woman" in Sam's marriage.

When Loretta left Nick to pursue a singing career with the Grinning Americans, he became financially destitute because of a prenuptial agreement giving her the house and the business. Nick was hired as a janitor at Cheers, and used this opportunity to court Carla. Everyone recommended reconciliation because Nick appeared to have changed (he rented a room with a sink, clipped his toenails, joined the Young Men's Christian Support group, and contemplated a magazine subscription), so she tested his love (and he passed). After Carla finally agreed to take him back, Loretta allured Nick by urging reunification. Loretta was discarded by the Grinning Americans, but Nick's talent agency resurrected her singing career as a member of the Lemon Sisters.

Relationships—Eddie LeBec

Eddie's real name was Guy (pronounced Ghee, as in geek) Raymond LeBec. (He was called Eddie because Guy was a weenie name.) His other nicknames were Toothless Little Frog, Horny Little Frog, and Ice Eating Geek. Born in Alma, Quebec, Eddie's favorite picture was of his and Carla's twins, Jesse and Elvis. Carla and Eddie's special song was "O' Canada" (the Canadian national anthem).

Eddie's entire life revolved around ice skating. Despite having one bad eye, he was a career goalie drafted from the junior league in the fifth round by Toronto, where he spent one year. Eddie was traded to Winnipeg, then Calgary, and finished his career in Boston wearing jersey number 33. Eddie won at least one trophy, the Eastern League Comeback of the Year Award.

When Eddie was traded to Boston in 1987 he performed sensationally. His superstitious ritual before every game involved entering Cheers, ordering a club soda with no ice, two lime slices and a red straw. After finishing the drink he set a napkin on the rim of the glass, placed the red straws on top of the napkin, and made a cross symbol with his index fingers. Once Eddie and Carla began dating, he added one more detail to his ritual—a kiss. This began the infamous LeBec nine-game slump beginning after the Montreal Canadians game and ending with the Edmonton Oilers. After accepting responsibility for Eddie's misfortune, Carla terminated their relationship for the good of the team. When he discovered Carla's scheme, they reconciled but added a breakup skit to his hockey ritual.

Within one year he was cut by the Boston Bruins because the organization was implementing a youth movement. Eddie retired from hockey when no other team claimed him. After unsuccessfully searching for employment, he accepted a position as a penguin in the traveling ice show Wonderful World of Ice. Carla became jealous of the ice show headliner, Franzi Schrempf, despite the fact that Eddie did not have an affair with her. Eddie continued with the ice show until his death in 1989. In remembrance, Carla circulated a petition to have his jersey number retired, but settled for free season tickets to the Bruins games (which was all she really wanted in the first place).

As for romance, Carla and Eddie met at Cheers, but soon their relationship became stagnant. When a breakup seemed imminent, Carla announced the arrival of yet another child. Eddie was despondent, but after contemplating the options he proposed marriage. Carla accepted, which meant a marital union between the two most superstitious people in the world. To coincide with their superstitions, they had to be married on the next Saturday (eight days after Eddie proposed marriage) before 4:00 p.m., as long as their auras remained in the blue spectrum, there was no solar eclipse, and all the planets and constellations were in line. Otherwise they had to wait until the year 2042.

Despite a Catholic ceremony (allowed because her marriage with Nick was annulled), Carla and Eddie's wedding had a precarious start—the bride and groom saw each other immediately prior to the ceremony, Eddie broke a mirror (for seven years bad luck), Anthony and Annie moved into Carla's house, Anthony hated Eddie, Carla learned she was pregnant with twins, Eddie was cut by the Bruins, and his mother hated Carla. Despite Eddie's canceling the wedding, Sam reunited the couple, who were officially married by Father Barry at 4:01 p.m.

The wedding reception was held at Cheers and featured napkins of a hillbilly holding a shotgun and saying, "We don't want to get married, we have to." The wedding gift from Norm was discount silverware purchased from his friend Bruce, and Frasier caught the bridal bouquet. The honeymoon was supposed to be at a nice resort in Waikiki, but their plans changed when Eddie was cut by the Bruins. Instead of a honeymoon, Carla worked as a cocktail waitress at her wedding reception.

EDDIE'S BIGAMY. Eddie's deep, dark secret was being a bigamist. He married another woman, Gloria, after impregnating her during a tender moment in the front seat of a Toyota Corolla. Gloria was from Kenosha, Wisconsin, and met Eddie (nicknamed Pengy) when the ice show was in town.

Despite Eddie's bigamous relationship, he wrote a letter to Carla explaining everything. In the event of his death, Eddie had instructed an ice show companion, Gordie Brown, to deliver the letter to Carla. In the letter Eddie confessed the truth, but also explained that Carla was his true love and he only married Gloria because he wanted the child to have a father. Eddie died saving the life of Gordie Brown, and in the process was run over by the Zamboni ice machine.

The truth about Eddie's bigamy was first revealed at his funeral. The priest summoned Eddie's wife to step forward, and both Carla and Gloria came forth. Despite a major catfight, the wives eventually became good friends. They even agreed to share Eddie's estate—which at the time appeared to be nothing. Gloria shared the $100 she was bequeathed, but Carla was not as generous when she unexpectedly received $50,000 from an ice show life insurance policy. Carla concealed the newfound wealth, but the guilt from her chicanery was so overwhelming that she developed intractable shakes that subsided only after distributing half the proceeds to Gloria.

After Eddie's death, Carla refrained from dating for several months before going out with Red Sox player Darryl Mead (#43, batting .270). The evening was a disaster because she saw Eddie's face everywhere. Madame Lazora subsequently conducted a seance to convince Carla that Eddie's spirit was content with her dating.

Relationships—John Allen Hill

Carla and John Allen Hill commenced an antagonistic relationship by unremittingly insulting each other about defects in their personal appearances—a classic love-hate relationship in disguise. Ironically, Sam facilitated the ardent union by sending Carla to exact revenge against the man he loathed. Carla went to Hill's office and began insulting him; he reciprocated, and before long they were insulting each other against the file cabinet. (After sleeping with Hill, she gave him the affectionate nickname The Bullet.) Carla and Hill had a unique dating relationship—an endless string of one-night stands. There was no commitment and no expectation of permanency; however, Carla crossed the line when she said, "I love you." No one had ever said these words to him (not even his wife or daughter), so Carla's unexpected admission precipitated his heart attack. While Hill convalesced, they agreed to elevate their relationship to a plateau beyond the physical. After attempting to sustain a conversation, they recognized their incompatibility (except sexually) and decided to revert to their prior arrangement—a purely sexual relationship.

Relationships—Others

Carla always had an attraction toward baseball players. Besides Darryl Mead, she gave ex–Red Sox catcher Tom Kenderson her telephone number and a couple of quotes from past lovers. A low point in Carla's dating life was attempting to find a man by placing a personal ad in *Boston Scene* magazine. When there was no response, the Cheers gang created a fictitious bachelor to answer the ad (Mitch Wainwright, an international pilot and model). Carla fell in love with Mitch and began rejecting legitimate suitors, such as funeral director Vinnie Claussen, the father of seven children. The gang convinced Carla to go out with Vinnie, and on their first date Vinnie role-played Mitch, and Carla role-played Raven, a Las Vegas show girl. Carla also dated Phil, a tire distributor from Rhode Island. They shared a sexual rendezvous in Art's Hideaway Adult Motel.

After finding the perfect man, Henry "Hank" Zenzola, Carla discovered he had a heart condition that prevented him from performing activities that would get him too excited. Carla ended the relationship because she was so wild in bed she nearly killed guys with healthy hearts. She considered Hank the best lover she ever had because they never fought or cheated on one another.

Other than her husbands' marriage proposals, Carla did reject one remarkable suitor, Frasier's mentor, the renowned Dr. Bennett Ludlow. As with most of her dates, Carla became pregnant; but unlike most of her dates, Dr. Ludlow proposed marriage. Carla rejected the proposal because she was waiting to be swept away by her dream man, a man whom she had not met but wanted to remain available when she did.

Carla's most surprising date was her agreeing to accompany Cliff Clavin to the Gala Postman's Ball. Of course, she demanded a new dress, $100 and a VCR. After Cliff canceled the date, he had to give Carla a big screen television before she would agree to a blind date with Lewis. Although Lewis was a nerdy hippie, they instantly became friends in the back seat of Cliff's station wagon.

Children

Carla had a total of eight children, from eldest to youngest: Anthony, Serafina, Anne Marie, Gino, Lucinda (Luccia), Ludlow, and Jesse and Elvis (twins). Nick Tortelli was the biological father of the first five children. The first child pushed Carla and Nick into marriage, and the fifth occurred after their divorce. Ludlow was sired by Dr. Bennett Ludlow, and the twins were the progeny of Eddie LeBec.

The first four children were not breast-fed; they went straight to raw meat. Of those four, two were ugly, one was obnoxious, and the other was stupid (Carla's favorite). Two of Carla's daughters were expelled from St. Mathias' School for Girls, and the last four children were conceived out of wedlock. Unfortunately, since Carla gave birth so many times, she had fallen arches and her varicose veins were stripped twice.

Carla reached her sexual peak at age 12, and first became pregnant at age 15 (in another episode she was pregnant at age 16). She was most fertile during Indian summer, which was when all of her children were conceived, and lost all self-control when the temperature hit 95 degrees (at that point she even found Cliff Clavin sexually attractive). Carla used the LeMans method of childbirth—she screamed like a Ferrari, and her labor pains always coincided with Celtics home games (she feigned labor pains so she could leave work early to attend the games).

When Carla first discovered she was pregnant with Lucinda, she immediately seduced Marshall Lipton, the nerdy Ph.D. from M.I.T., for one night of wild passion (though she never touched him again). Despite convincing Marshall that he was the father, Carla's guilty conscience inevitably compelled her to reveal the truth (and Marshall refused to marry her).

Carla enjoyed taking her children to the petting zoo so they could slap the animals around. They reciprocated by giving her Drano and something for picking locks as Mother's Day presents. Carla extolled her children's skill of getting a person and a radio out of a late-model car in less than 60 seconds. A Thanksgiving tradition at Carla's home was to have the children wait on the curb at noon, and have their various fathers drive by to pick them up. Whoever was left spent the day with their mother.

Carla hired at least two baby-sitters: Miss Gilder (earning $6 per hour) and Anna Clasetti (who threatened to jump off the Route 93 overpass). On the day of Anna's suicide attempt, Carla had to leave work early because Anna was baby-sitting her children at the time. Others volunteered to baby-sit with similar success—Cliff was returned within hours, bound and gagged, whereas Sam and Rebecca lasted the entire evening; however, Rebecca was locked in the clothes dryer while it was running. Thus, it was not surprising that Carla's insurance company required each baby-sitter to sign a release of liability form before beginning their tour of duty.

ANTHONY. Carla's nicest child, Anthony, was conceived in a hotel room and born in 1969. His favorite beverage was root beer with immoderate amounts of sugar added. In 1984 Anthony was the basis of a custody dispute because Nick's wife, Loretta, was physically unable to bear children. (Nick later relinquished the custody battle.) The following year, at age 16, Anthony wanted to marry his girlfriend, Annie, but they needed parental permission. Carla offered consent but only if the young lovers could spend two weeks without having any contact. Knowing that all Tortelli men are scum, Carla expected Anthony to seek companionship with another woman, but he never left the house. As she was about to give consent, Anthony was mesmerized by Annie's cousin, Gabrielle, and refused to get married. Despite leaving the bar with Gabrielle, Anthony and Annie eventually married a few years later (and had sex a mere six times per day).

In 1987 the happy couple moved to Las Vegas to live with his father, but returned a year later when Nick's business went bankrupt and Anthony was unable to collect unemployment (he and Annie then moved in with Carla and her new husband, Eddie). Anthony also had a job as the assistant night manager at Burger Burger Burger, and in 1991 was in jail for some unspecified crime.

SERAFINA. Serafina was born in 1975 and married at age 18 because she was pregnant. She dated Pat McDugall, a retired police officer who received disability from a whiplash injury and was the father of her child. Despite an unplanned pregnancy, Carla was still proud because Serafina knew the identity of the father, and gave her blessings for their marriage ("You're never going to collect alimony by staying single"). Carla's advice was not to marry for love because she did, and Nick was the worst possible husband.

Notwithstanding her mother's advice, Serafina married Pat McDugall in a wedding ceremony at Melville's, and they held the reception at Cheers. Entertainment was provided by Captain Gus and his Polka Pirates, and the newlyweds' wedding presents included two sets of *Star Trek* steak knives, compliments of Woody and Kelly, and Nick and Loretta. (The gifts were unused and unwanted wedding presents each couple had received as a gift at their respective weddings.)

GINO. In 1975 Carla went into labor with Gino while watching Benny Hill—she was laughing so hard she began having contractions. Her proudest moment was Gino's decision to become a priest. Carla figured having a son in the priesthood was a free ticket out of hell, so she became blatantly sadistic and wreaked havoc on the Cheers gang. Gino promptly chose to forego the priesthood to become a male model because he did not want to waste his looks on the church. Finally, like all Tortelli men, Gino was proud of his sexuality, and had a crush on Rebecca Howe. He sent her nude photographs of himself (which were taken in the mall photo booth).

THE OTHER CHILDREN. On her first date, Anne Marie saw *101 Dalmatians* with Vito Raggazoni, but not before Carla interviewed, photographed, and fingerprinted the lad. Anne Marie had to repeat one grade three times. Lucinda inherited the "Tortelli Knuckles" and was unable to wear rings on her fingers. Ludlow (Lud) was the most intelligent Tortelli child because he had the genes of a Rhodes scholar, his father Dr. Bennett Ludlow. Lud was a regular Poindexter with no athleticism, had a pet boa constrictor named Mr. Tibbington, hated fish, and held his breath as a sales pitch. Finally, the twins, Jesse and Elvis, were conceived in the backseat of a Datsun hatchback.

Cheers

Carla arrived in Boston involuntarily and rather fortuitously—she was stripped, gagged, had her money stolen, and put on a bus with a one-way ticket to Boston. She became a waitress at Cheers in 1977, and took an instant disliking to one particular waitress—Diane Chambers. Carla knew Diane could not be trusted to keep a secret, and tested her resolve by confiding that Sam was the father of Gino (Carla's son). As Carla expected, the next day Diane disclosed the secret. In another instance, Carla wrote Diane's name on the men's bathroom wall ("for a good time call Diane Chambers") using the telephone number from an employment application. Carla interminably criticized Diane's hair color, particularly whether she was a natural blonde. As Diane was departing for Europe, Carla gave her a note with the helpful Italian phrase, "Excuse me, Mr. Pharmacist. Where do you keep the peroxide?"

Over the years Carla acquired a few derogatory nicknames, though considerably less offensive than the ones she dispensed, such as Twerp, Spaghetti Breath, Honey Bear (she considered this offensive), Velcro Top, Brillo Head, and Little Foul-mouthed Fright-wigged Rodent. John Allen Hill was the primary target of insolent terms, including Sewer Rat, Maggot, Hideous Gargoyle,

Shrike, Slattern, Sasquatch, Catcher's Mit, Phlegm Face, Yeasty Oil Slick, Manwich, and Sluttish Mole.

Woody Boyd

Childhood

On July 23, under the zodiac sign of Leo, Margaret and Edgil Boyd announced the birth of a boy they named Huckleberry Tiberius Boyd (more commonly known as Woody). Woody had a great relationship with his father—they went fishing, bowling, hung out together, and passed notes in class. However, Woody's childhood was not without trauma. When he was six years old his house burned down. He got out alive, but while running away fell into a well and almost died. Other life threatening incidents included: contracting smallpox (which was his first childhood disease); falling off a beanstalk (he cracked two ribs and punctured a lung); being trapped during a cave-in; and falling off a turnip truck and being dragged 300 yards down a gravel road into a rosebush. The fact that the roses smelled nice was his only fond memory of that event.

Woody had several pets as a child—a dog (Truman), a prize cow (Velveeta), and a prize pig (Maribel). Velveeta's claim to fame was giving birth to a two-headed calf. Woody took Maribel on the county circuit but lost the contest when he refused to suck up to the judges. It broke his heart. As for Maribel, Woody said she was good—with applesauce!

Family and Relatives

The Boyd family was not always known by this surname. Woody's great grandmother had the surname O'Leary, but changed it after an incident during which her cow knocked over a lantern and burned an entire city to the ground. The shame was so great that the family moved to Ohio and changed their name to Wilkens. Naturally, something horrific occurred there, so they moved to Indiana and changed their name to Boyd.

The Boyds were a poor rural family—Woody's father, Edgil Boyd, was a farmer by trade, and his wife, Margaret, was a housewife with career aspirations of being a drummer in a power trio (her hero was Ginger Baker of the rock group Cream). Margaret also took choir classes, and frequently gossiped over coffee, divulging family secrets for a piece of crumb cake. Woody's parents once ran off with the Pentecostal caravan for one year (and he was lucky they even returned). Woody's only sibling was an older brother, Tom, and their grandmother Meg was well-known for her famous chili made from an old family recipe (she obtained it from the old family down the street).

Woody had at least 12 uncles. Uncle Elmo injured his hand in a fireworks accident, Uncle Elroy used a plunger as a substitute for his prosthetic leg, and Uncle Fergie was the legendary beekeeper. Two other uncles included Uncle Henry and Uncle Elwood.

Three of Woody's uncles died. Uncle Ford was remembered as the inspiration for the name of Aunt Edna's Killer Fudge Brownies. The first time she made the recipe, he came running in from the field and was hit by a combine. He hung on for a few days, and in the end was praying to die. Uncle Orlo was remembered for two incidents. He shouldered the shameful secret of checking into a motel with a cream separating machine. In the other incident, he left Hanover to seek fortune and fame in the big city, but Terre Haute chewed him up and spit him out. Orlo returned to Hanover with his head between his legs—he was in a train accident on the way home! It was a tragic story because Uncle Orlo eventually drowned in a sitz bath. Uncle Spence's claim to fame was falling 20,000 feet out of an airplane and landing on the only pile of hay within a two-mile radius. He was not the luckiest man alive because he fell through the propeller first. One unspecified relative died by being buried alive in potatoes.

Uncle Skylar was remembered for hooking up the milking machine before an electrical storm—the cows never forgave him. Uncle Wayne was a master of getting women in the mood for romance—he gave them money, which worked like a charm. Back in Hanover, Uncle Jim frequently built fake houses made of sticks and canvas, and placed them on the railroad tracks. Then he hid in the bushes with a camera to take pictures of the engineer screaming.

Uncle Willy was the family cross-dresser. The deep, dark secret of the Boyd family was the reason why you never saw Uncle Willy and Aunt Mae in the same room at the same time. (Incidentally, Woody only mentioned four aunts: Mae, Edna, Lou and Lefty.)

As for more distant relatives, Woody had several memorable cousins. Cousin Skeeter lost a thumb in a mortar accident—big show-off; and Cousin Elmore wore a goofy hunting cap with deer antlers—BIG mistake! Woody's cousin, Russell Boyd, sojourned to Boston en route from Florida after being discarded by his girlfriend. He visited Cheers hoping to hit the big time like Woody did! Russell was eccentric by Hanover standards—he was always writing, painting and sculpturing rather than bettering himself by learning air conditioning repair and riding dirt bikes. Russell was hired as a pianist at Cheers, and quickly became obsessed with Rebecca, serenading her with love songs and painting a mural of her on the wall of his hotel room. When Rebecca ended the infatuation, Carla became his next target of affection.

Hometown

Woody's hometown was Hanover in Posey County, Indiana. The mayor of Hanover, Dwight Woemack, endured the shame of his wife eloping with old Mr. Smithers (a goat). Hanover had two claims to fame: it was the place mat capital of the world and the UFO capital of the world. There was an old saying in Hanover; "The pigs are smarter than the people." Of course, this saying was originated by the tourists. Even Hanover residents had a scapegoat; they thought everyone from French Lick, Indiana, was a doofus. (Everyone knew French Lick was the doofus capital of the world. Of course, everyone in French Lick thought the same of Hanover residents.)

Duck hunting was considered one of the manliest sports in Hanover. The guys did not actually go hunting, rather it was an excuse for them to get together and blow duck horns. Woody had a great duck call because he used a Good & Plenty box.

It was immoral to engage in premarital sex (the high school art teachers were the only couple to defy this tenet), and unwed pregnant women were stoned for their moral turpitude. Moreover, the man was the head of the household, and when he spoke, all of his *wives* listened.

In Hanover, everyone drank beer, and the old Hanover hangover cure was guaranteed to make you feel better. "First, put on your pajamas. Then take an aspirin with a cold glass of water, and then you vomit 'til your nose bleeds and heave until you see the angels."

Other miscellaneous information included: the Hanover Corn Parade was Hanover's version of the Rose Parade; in Hanover, bet welshers were rubbed in bacon fat and placed in the sty with Romeo the friendly hog; and a typical Hanover bachelor party involved dressing farm animals in women's clothing.

Personal

Woody was 6'0" and allergic to black cardamom. His most recent role model was Sam Malone, but prior to knowing Sam, it was St. Thomas Aquinas. In his spare time, Woody volunteered to cook and deliver meals to the elderly, participated in a walk-a-thon against illiteracy, manned the suicide hot line and recycled. Dr. Frasier Crane was the second smartest person Woody knew (second only to Cliff Clavin).

Woody was Lutheran, and originally a member of the Lutheran Church of Missouri Synagogue. At the insistence of his wife, Kelly, he became a member of the Evangelical Lutheran Church of America. Woody accepted Frasier's wise and learned advice—convert to Kelly's religion if he ever wanted to see her naked again!

As for leisure activities, Woody was involved in arm wrestling, sports trivia, poker, party games and bowling. Woody was the arm wrestling champion of Posey County, and in 1986 declared Jack Dalton (Diane's old flame) as the new champion after losing to the worldly adventurist. Woody was also the best poker player in the greater metropolitan Hanover area. Some of the poker prizes included chicken in a box, one-eyed rooster and possum on a pole. Woody also invented the Hanover game Hide Bob's Pants. Everybody loved the game (except Bob).

Woody was very adept at bowling, until "the tragedy." Although he won several trophies as a bowler, Woody quit the sport after maiming a maintenance repair man, Sully, in a fluke accident. Woody was picking up an 8-10 split when the bowling ball hit Sully between the eyes. Sully was unable to continue working as a maintenance man, and eventually became a clown at children's parties—even though he was not invited!

As for further Hanover experiences, Woody was shunned by the Amish, and was a member of a biker gang—he owned a Schwinn 3-speed with a banana seat! (However, in another episode he intimated being the only kid without a bicycle.) The only famous person he could impersonate was Dwight Woemack, the mayor of Hanover.

The one subject Woody knew was finances. He wisely memorized the serial numbers on all his paper currency, so if he lost any bills he would be able to identify them. He prayed to God every night, hoping he would never become rich. He buried his life's savings in his backyard, and stored the treasure map in his shoe.

Woody had difficulty comprehending the concept of death because most of the members of his family were maimed, not killed. He was once struck by lightning, and if reincarnated, Woody would like to return as the president of France because it would attract a lot of business for the bar.

Other miscellaneous information regarding Woody includes: he saved all his baby teeth, was a great chef, and a vocal stylist; he was always the banker in Monopoly; he chased rabbits in his dreams; he loved the "Ziggy" comic strip; he thought Jerry Lewis was a good comedian; the most attractive person he knew was Carla's butcher; and the traditional Boyd Halloween prank was the ol' bloody thumb gag.

Personal Likes and Dislikes

Woody's favorite color was blue, and his favorite painting was *Dogs on the Train* (comparable to Sam's favorite painting, *Dogs Playing Blackjack*). Woody's favorite food was Sno-balls because they are bite-size, and he loved Choco-Puffs cereal, especially the lick-and-stick tattoo books that he saved for special occasions.

Woody's favorite Christmas song character was Rudolph the Red-nosed Reindeer, and he loved the children's singer Nanny Gee. Woody attended her "1992 Tickle Tummy Tour" concert but sat in row YY (the second to last row in the balcony). Despite such a distant seat, Woody felt sorry for the poor slobs in row ZZ!

As for dislikes, the most disgusting thing Woody could imagine was someone coming in from the field, taking off their shirt, and exposing their sweaty, matted-down chest hairs. This may not appear disgusting, but then again, you never saw his grandmother!

Apartment

Woody shrewdly negotiated a 10-year lease for his apartment (#8) in Chinatown. The apartment was decorated with furniture from the interior of cars, and an old Farrah Fawcett poster hung on the wall. The best selling feature was that the apartment had cable television, though he subsequently became addicted to "The Home Shopping Channel" and purchased countless useless trinkets.

When Woody contemplated having a female roommate to share the housing costs, the primary concern was his ritual of undoing the top button of his pants after eating a good frozen meal. He eventually roomed with Terry Gardner, a dental hygienist from Indiana and the daughter of a minister. She lived with Woody for one day before revealing she had an extremely jealous husband, Cutter Gardner. Cutter was known for lifting a tractor off a guy's leg—and placing it on his throat. Woody escaped injury by claiming Cliff spent the night with Cutter's wife.

Education

Although it is unknown at what age Woody graduated from high school, he thought Rebecca's daddy must have pulled some strings for her to graduate at age 18. That may explain why Woody was able to pass notes to his father in class. Even more astonishing was the fact that Woody was the smartest student, and nicknamed Mr. Smarty Pants, Little Einstein, and Brainiac.

In high school, Woody was 100 pounds overweight and his girlfriend, Beth Curtis, was 50 pounds overweight. They earned the title, "The Couple Most Likely to Explode." In school politics, Woody once ran for class president, but was voted class clown!

Woody was involved in many extracurricular activities. He was the first alternate on the Hanover High boxing squad, but his greatest interest was the theater. Woody's first play was *Jack and the Beanstalk*, and he was also involved in the senior class production of *Hello Donald* (f.k.a *Hello Dolly*). His other memorable theater experience was with his drama teacher, who once invited Woody over to listen to music and wear a fancy dress.

After graduating from high school, Woody received a memory quilt created by all the women in his family. It encompassed each memorable childhood event—a piece of his baby blanket, first childhood disease, first play, and his house burning down. After high school Woody attended bartender school where he studied for years to become an ace mixologist.

Employment

Woody had many occupations: dog-sitting, baby-sitting, and clerking one summer at the Piggly Wiggly. He also aspired to become an author. One book in development involved a boy and his dog roaming the countryside, doing good deeds, and drinking beer. Regardless, his ultimate career choice was becoming a bartender in a big city. His dream came true on September 26, 1985, when he entered Cheers looking for a job. When Woody sent out resumés, Coach was the only person to respond. They became pen pals, and Woody eventually visited Cheers to meet the man. Woody learned of Coach's death after arriving at the bar, and since Cheers needed a barkeep, Woody was hired.

In 1992 Woody moonlighted part-time, working the graveyard shift (in a graveyard) digging the graves and burying the dead. He accepted the job to earn additional money to pay for Kelly's engagement ring, but only lasted a few days before becoming fatigued and delusional. His most memorable night was spent burying Mrs. Jane Vanderhoven, beloved wife and mother. Woody exhumed her body three times to ensure her mortality.

Acting Experience

Woody participated in many theatrical productions, such as *Jack and the Beanstalk, Hello Donald, Authors in Hell, An Evening with the Prophets, Cleopatra, Our Town, The Story of Snow, Twelve Angry Men* (1990), *Hair,* and *Arsenic and Old Lace.*

Jack and the Beanstalk was Woody's first taste of the theater. In the first act, he fell from the beanstalk and almost died. He was also involved in the senior class production of *Hello Donald* (f.k.a *Hello Dolly*), which was renamed because Donald Wexler was the only person who could sing the part. This production sparked Woody's desire for acting as an avocation.

When Woody moved to Boston he pursued his interest in acting more vigorously. He performed for the Boston Community Theater under the directorship of Lee Bradken and Grif Palmer (who was also the janitor at Carla's children's school). Although the beginning was rough, Woody progressively sought and attained more significant roles. He was a Mark Twain understudy in *Authors in Hell* (1987) and a Moses understudy in *An Evening with the Prophets* (1988). His first lead role was playing Marc Antony in *Cleopatra* (1989), and then he procured the lead role of George Gibbs in *Our Town* (1989). His other impressive role was the king of the flakes in *The Story of Snow* (1987).

Woody also had his share of anguish. His most humiliating experience was being the only person to disrobe during the nude scene in the production of *Hair* (1990). Ironically, Woody was cast for the part in *Hair* by impressing the directors with his "butt walk." On opening night the gang gave him a 17-jewel watch with a leather band (retrieved from the Cheers lost and found). Woody was very appreciative because he had lost a similar watch a month earlier! In *Arsenic and Old Lace* (1991) his performance was dubbed as weak and he received the ultimate insult when the newspaper misprinted his name as Woody Doyb.

Woody's acting credentials also included television appearances. His first exposure was volunteering as a crowd scene extra on "Spenser: For Hire" in 1988. Actually, only his plain white shirtsleeve appeared on the show, but he proudly bragged about meeting Robert Urich during the filming of the scene. Woody loaned his gloves to Robert Urich, and even accompanied him to a party after the filming. The gang refused to believe Woody, and relentlessly badgered him (joking that his shirt was dating Morgan Fairchild).

Woody's first television acting job was in 1990 playing a bartender in a commercial for Veggie-Boy (a vegetable juice consisting of water, broccoli, cauliflower and kale). His only line was "I like it!" The company quickly canceled production of the product because it had little marketable appeal.

Employment—Politics

Woody became a member of the Boston City Council by defeating three-term incumbent Kevin Fogerty in the district 3 election. Fogerty had a wife, Estelle, and two children (Hilary, age 11, and Joseph, age 8) who attended Fenwick Elementary School. Woody's campaign began as a joke and turned into an even bigger one! Frasier wanted to prove the voting public were like sheep and even a chimp could get 10 percent of the vote, so he chose Woody. When Fogerty was arrested for public intoxication, Woody's electability escalated.

Woody's poster slogan was "He's One of Us" and his campaign slogan was "Make a Change." Frasier became Woody's speechwriter, and the press lauded Woody's down-home, farm boy image. Boston newspaper reporter Holly Matheson misinterpreted his convoluted answers about a barn with rats as a metaphor for cleaning up crime in government.

When it appeared Woody might win the election, Frasier convinced him to withdraw from the race during an election debate. As Woody announced the withdrawal of his candidacy, Kelly announced she was pregnant. After this heartwarming display, Woody easily won the election.

Relationships—General

Woody was Hanover's official go-between to deliver love notes, and his naiveté was accentuated in the area of romance. He did not believe in premarital sex, and thought the sexual metaphor of getting a home run meant receiving a kiss. Woody proposed marriage twice: to Mary, an elderly widow (her ex-husband was Lloyd) and to Kelly Gaines. Woody was dressed like Mark Twain in preparation as an understudy for the play *Authors in Hell*, and thought Mary was falling in love with his elderly personage. He did not want to break her heart, so he proposed marriage. She rejected the offer because she was three times his age (she was old, not stupid).

Relationships—Beth Curtis

Woody moved to Boston because he wanted to see the world, and left behind his girlfriend, Beth Curtis, because she wanted to stay in Indiana. After discovering Woody had a girlfriend in Indiana, the Cheers gang had Beth fly to Boston for a visit. During their separation, Woody and Beth both lost a substantial amount of weight, and upon her arrival, they began eating incessantly. It was later explained (by the Cheers janitor at the time, i.e., Frasier) that they were subconsciously suppressing their sexual desires for one another by using food as a substitute. After realizing this truism, they consummated their relationship to satiate their sexual (and nutritional) appetites.

Despite overcoming their sexual inhibitions, Woody and Beth were unable to sustain a long-distance relationship. The following year Beth informed Woody that she was marrying another Hanover resident, Leonard Twilley. En route to their wedding and honeymoon in Niagara Falls, the prospective newlyweds visited Woody to ensure he was coping effectively. To prove he was unaffected by the news, he arranged a date with Sam's cleaning lady, Desiree Harrison. Naturally, the evening was calamitous, but everything worked out.

Relationships—Kelly Gaines

Woody's most serious relationship was with the daughter of a wealthy corporate executive. Kelly Susan Gaines (who changed her surname to Boyd in

1992) was born at 8:00 a.m., weighed 7 lbs. 3 oz., and had the cutest birth-
mark on her shoulder. Not surprisingly, her favorite precious metal was gold,
and she collected over 1000 Barbie dolls (along with a closet full of Barbie doll
body parts—in anger she removed the limbs of certain dolls).

Coming from a wealthy background, Kelly did not have a job until college, and only accepted a waitress position at Cheers because her sociology class
assignment required her to write about a past job experience. Norm and Carla
loved having Kelly as a waitress. Norm trained her to erase marks from his bar
tab, claiming each one represented a beer purchased in advance, and Carla
trained Kelly that each tip was intended for the head waitress. Kelly's naiveté
and sheltered life even prevented her from believing that subways exist.

Kelly's father insisted she attend college in Paris for one year. He actually wanted to separate her from Woody, in the hope she would find another
man during the European sabbatical. Kelly's Parisian roommate was Cindy
Ann, and her best friend was Henri, a photography instructor. Kelly subsequently invited Henri to America after she returned to Boston.

As for the Gaines family, they were members of the Evangelical Lutheran
Church of America. Kelly had at least one sister, and her grandmother
(known strictly as Grandmother Gaines) was the family matriarch, ruling
the Bostonian estate from Florida. Kelly's Aunt Martha thought she was
Eleanor Roosevelt, and liked Woody because she thought he was Winston
Churchill.

Kelly's father, Walter Gaines, had a net worth of $72 million and was vice
president of the Lillian Corporation. Although Walter was divorced, he and
his ex-wife, Roxanne, were originally attracted to one another by their common love of classical music. Roxanne, a dancer in her youth, had an inexplicable adoration for Woody. At a Gaines family gathering, she could not resist
propositioning him for sex and mauling him (attacking him on the couch,
putting her hand on his leg during dinner, and pinching his derrière during
the family photo).

Walter Gaines' brother, Richard, was married to Katherine (with whom
Walter had a torrid affair). Their rendezvous was nearly revealed when Woody
unexpectedly interrupted a sexual liaison on the floor of Walter's library.
Woody thought Walter was sweaty and breathless because he was exercising;
however, Walter was sure Woody knew of the indiscretion. After attempting
to bribe Woody with fishing trips, a boat (the SS *Silence*), and spending an
innumerable amount of time with him, Walter inadvertently revealed the
tryst. Unfortunately this revelation was overheard by the family butler, Hives,
who eagerly extorted Walter for his silence.

Another relative of noteworthy importance was Kelly's cousin, Monika.
As children, Kelly and Monika played together, and their favorite hiding place
was in the dumbwaiter. Monika married Dieter, an insanely jealous German,
and sexually propositioned Sam at Woody and Kelly's wedding.

The Gaines estate had two guard dogs (Hitler and Attila) for protection, a guest house that became Woody and Kelly's abode for a few months after their marriage, and an Australian couple who did the dishes.

KELLY'S DATING RELATIONSHIPS. Prior to dating Woody, Kelly dated Nash (a wealthy socialite, Princeton graduate, and member of the Ivy League boxing squad). Woody and Kelly first met when he was working as a bartender at the Gaines estate for a "Welcome Home from Europe" party in honor of Kelly. Nash became jealous of Woody and challenged him to a fight. One punch later, Woody was knocked out and Nash had bits of face in his pinky ring. Kelly felt sorry for Woody and they agreed to go on a date to make Nash jealous. Their memorable first date included a monster truck and tractor pull, and ended with Pac Man and dinner at Pizza by the Yard (where Woody had standing reservations).

Kelly had one other quasi-romantic relationship, with Henri, her friend and photography instructor in Paris. Kelly invited him to America, and Henri knew he wanted to stay once he laid eyes on that big lady in the harbor—not lady liberty, but Ki Ki. The suave Frenchman chaperoned Woody and Kelly's dates and insinuated with continuous banter he would steal Kelly away. Henri's master plan was staging his deportation to con Kelly into marrying him so he could acquire citizenship, have a quick divorce, and take half of her wealth.

Henri was the French version of Sam Malone. In France, Henri heard of the legendary Sam Malone via stewardesses. The strangest place Henri ever had sex was in the balcony of the Paris Opera during a performance. While in France, Henri was a photography instructor and bartender. As Henri's student, Kelly posed for photographs wearing sexy lingerie, and together they played the game he invented—shower rescue. His first job in the United States was working as a temporary bartender at Cheers while Woody was on his honeymoon.

Kelly's other romantic interest was Sam Malone. As she prepared to marry Henri, Sam interrupted the ceremony to convince her to renounce the wedding. Kelly misinterpreted his plea as a love confession, and admitted there had always been a spark between them.

KELLY DATING WOODY. Naturally the differences in social status and wealth hindered the relationship of Woody and Kelly, and the disdain of her father toward Woody provided additional strain. For her birthday, Woody initially bought *The Really Big Book of Dutch Humor*, until the Cheers gang convinced him to give her a special gift—one from the heart. Woody gave her "The Kelly Song," which he created and then performed at her birthday party:

> Kelly my darling you are my sunshine/When we're together I feel
> fine/Your smile is so lovely, your hair is so clean/You make me feel
> that the whole world is mine/Kelly, Kelly, Kelly, Kelly, Kelly, Kelly,
> Kelly, Kelly/Kelly, Kelly, Kelly, Kelly. K—E—L—L—Y/Why?/
> Because you're Kelly, Kelly, Kelly, Kelly, Kelly, Kelly Kelly,
> Kelly/Kelly, Kelly, Kelly, Kelly, Kelly, Kelly, Kelly of mine/Mine,
> mine, mine, mine, mine, mine, mine, mine/Mine, mine, mine, mine,
> mine, mine, mine, mine, mine.

After hearing the song, Kelly still expected a present. Woody was dejected, but sold everything he owned to buy her a diamond pendant.

Before Kelly left for Paris, Woody gave her a promise ring—a promise there would be an engagement ring forthcoming. The special ring was a family heirloom in the Boyd family (his father gave it to a woman in Iwo Jima during World War II). Kelly returned one year later, and although they remained in love, their relationship lacked physical intimacy (though they once made love while watching *Old Gringo*, but the whole row was snoring). They decided to consummate their relationship in a sleazy motel, but Carla eventually dissuaded them. Woody and Kelly decided to wait until marriage. Their sexual abstinence lasted three years, but ended only hours before their wedding because Woody could not resist watching Kelly model her trousseau. (After this sexual experience, Woody finally understood all the jokes the Cheers gang had told over the years.)

Woody first proposed marriage to Kelly in her bedroom as she prepared to depart for Europe. They planned to elope, but Woody felt reprehensible about the plan to purloin Kelly from her father, so they settled for a secret engagement. Eighteen months later, he proposed marriage to Kelly as she prepared to exchange wedding vows with Henri. Kelly accepted, but Woody insisted upon a prenuptial agreement—he did not want her to get half of his stuff! Kelly's father was equally concerned, and had Woody sign a power of attorney to prevent Woody from squandering the Gaines family fortune.

Woody budgeted $500 for Kelly's wedding ring, so Carla kindly offered to sell a "family heirloom" ring (i.e., junk jewelry). Woody selected Sam as his best man. One wedding dilemma was excluding people from the engagement party. Frasier wisely suggested eliminating the least desirable guests, so Woody immediately excluded the Cranes!

In the Cranes' wedding card Lilith wrote, "May you never forget the way your hearts leapt up when first you gazed into each other's eyes." She then placed the card on the wedding gift—a set of *Star Trek* steak knives. (It was the most useless wedding gift the Cranes had received, so they recycled it.) Carla's wedding gift was an astrological marriage chart, which ultimately presaged that their marriage would be ruinous. Norm and Cliff gave a used rubber wastebasket from Norm's kitchen.

The wedding ceremony was originally scheduled to be performed by Dr.

Chatfield, a minister, until he unexpectedly died moments before the ceremony. Kelly's Uncle Roger unequivocally refused to perform the ceremony because he was in the midst of a bitter divorce and abhorred marriages. However, while intoxicated he loved weddings, so the Cheers gang encouraged Uncle Roger to consume mass quantities of alcohol, and the wedding ceremony was successful. Unfortunately, the honeymoon cruise was curtailed when Woody and Kelly argued over their religious beliefs. The marriage appeared destined for demise until Frasier convinced Woody to convert to her religion. By 1993 Kelly was pregnant with their first child, and although the child's name was unknown, Woody always wanted to name his son Woody, Jr.

Cheers

When Woody moved to Boston to become a bartender in the big city, his father gave him some sound advice: "Never trust a man who can't look you in the eye. Never talk when you can listen. And never spend venture capital on a limited partnership without a detailed analytical fiduciary prospectus." This sound advice, however, did not protect Woody from being mugged ten times during the first two years he lived in Boston.

Boston's excessive street violence prompted Woody's father to summon his son back to Indiana. In response, the gang created a home video to prove Woody lived in a wholesome, stable environment with a strong support system. Woody's father tossed the video in the thresher, but allowed his son to stay in Boston because of a note he received from Al (the elderly bar patron) that simply stated, "Let your son choose his own path and it will always lead back to you."

Everyone in Hanover idolized Woody. They thought he sold his soul to the devil to hit the big time (i.e., becoming a bartender in the big city). Like many bartenders, Woody wanted to be remembered for inventing a mixed drink. He was going to name one of his concoctions "The Blue Boyd of Happiness." When he finally mixed a fantastic recipe, he forgot the ingredients.

Woody had a perfect attendance record, except for one day when he stayed home because of an illness. Although he began feeling better by midday and could have returned to work, he stayed home to watch the circus freaks on "Oprah." Since Woody never took a vacation, Rebecca compelled him to take a one-week trip to Venice and Florence, Italy. However, Woody never made it because he fell asleep at the airport terminal and missed the plane. He had so much fun at the airport he wanted to spend time at the bus depot! Woody was such a dedicated employee that he repeatedly won the Employee of the Month Award (primarily because Sam and Carla refused the plaque).

Woody's first European vacation was in London, compliments of the Gaines family. The young, impressionable Woody returned pompous and egocentric, and began castigating the Cheers gang about their callowness and narrow-minded views. He soon realized Kelly's wealth was changing him, so he insisted they each live on their own income.

At Cheers, the insulting nicknames conferred upon Woody were quite voluminous, and the most memorable included: Billy-Bob-Joe-Jim, Jethro, Gomer, Efuss, Festus, Howdy Doody, Dweeb, Cornmeal, Corncob, Cotton, Bumpkin, Hoof-in-mouth, Grain Brain, Hicksville, Tractor Boy, Farm Boy, Dirt-Eating Farm Boy, Nelly Bell, Baboon, Horseshoe, Doorknob, Woodman, Woodchuck, Woodwork, Woodhead, Woodpile, Wood Rot, Rhinestone Cowpie, Lonesome Cowpie, and Walking Disney Character (without the fur). Sobriquets that preyed upon Woody's interest in the performing arts included: Robert DeZero, Mark Twit and Oliver Twit.

Norm Peterson

Childhood

Norm was born in 1948, and his formal birth name was Hilary R. Peterson (Hilary was his grandfather's name, and the middle initial stood for Resourceful). His grandfather was a surgeon who once killed a man in a mishandled operation. As for Norm's father, he loved beer and was almost in the army. Norm's one regret in life was never saying, "I love you" to his father before he passed away. Norm mentioned having at least one brother (who was married).

As a child, Norm was the first in his class to develop breasts, had a Lionel train set, and was a member of the Boy Scouts (but quit after one week, when they mentioned something about a hike). As a teen, Norm frequented the Twi-Lite Drive-in until his concession stand tab became so enormous he had to avoid going there. Some of Norm's fondest childhood memories involved sitting next to his father in Boston Garden, watching his heroes play professional basketball. Norm's last childhood memory was having his appendix removed.

High School

Norm attended Dean Axton High School, took French classes, and was a member of the football and wrestling squads. In football, the coach told everyone to give the ball to Peterson and the team went on to have a successful season—Norm was the team's equipment manager. Wrestling was Norm's most successful extracurricular endeavor. Norm earned the nickname Moonglow after his shorts were accidentally pulled down by his opponent during a state wrestling tournament. This public exposure also captured the attention of his future wife, Vera Kreitzer. Norm's biggest wrestling rival and competitor for Vera's affection was Wally Bodell. Norm always defeated Wally (in both sports).

Norm and Vera were high school sweethearts. On their first date, she gave Norm flowers, candy and wine, and he reciprocated by giving her nothing. Norm's father disapproved of Vera because he heard she had loose morals, but it turned out she had loose *molars*. Vera's claim to fame was a reputation across the Midwest for giving the best hickeys. At the senior prom she gave Norm a hickey that lasted approximately 15 years (until Christmas 1981). After high school, Norm enlisted in the army (he was stationed at Fort Dix) and the Coast Guard (which is rather ironic because water made him seasick).

Personal

Norm was 5'10" with alabaster skin and had a nice pink aura. He wore a size triple E shoe, and had an American flag with the motto "God Bless the U.S. Postal Service" tattooed on his posterior (after a night of drunken debauchery he and Cliff visited Fred's Tattoo Parlor, but Norm received Cliff's brand by accident). Norm's personal best in bowling was breaking 200, and he last went to a gym in 1971. He owned a blue Honda Civic sporting the bumper sticker "Accountants Do it with Interest," and ended every correspondence with the phrase "And I hope the Red Sox win the pennant."

As for organizational membership, Norm belonged to the Knights of the Scimitar after Cliff used his clout to facilitate the other members' acceptance of him. Norm merely used the fraternal organization to develop business contacts, but was undeterred when the Knights prohibited dealings amongst members. However, he immediately terminated his membership when they banned beer at all organization functions. Norm's other membership was being a minister for the Church of the Living Desert. In the 1960s he sent $1 to a church advertising on the back cover of *Rolling Stone* magazine.

Norm had several friends, and since 1978 his best friend was Cliff Clavin. Other friends included Sid Nelson, owner of the Hungry Heifer; Bruce, known for selling jewelry and silverware at discount prices; and George Foley, an unemployed tree surgeon (though their relationship faded when it interfered with Norm and Cliff's friendship). Another important person was Sam Malone because he was like a brother to Norm.

Norm's biggest fear was being a failure. (When Carla stated he was a failure, Norm responded, "Then I've licked it!") The last time he cried was when

Vera said she was pregnant and it later turned out she wasn't. Unfortunately, she didn't tell Norm until *after* their wedding—he must have cried for a week!

One of Norm's lifelong dreams was to sail the South Pacific to Bora Bora, build a hut, and then send for Vera. In 1984 he had the opportunity to fulfill the dream after learning that a potentially fatal ailment was merely an X-ray flaw. Since he was given a second chance at life, Norm made all the arrangements to sail to Bora Bora, but at the last minute reconsidered. Fearing public humiliation, he hid in Sam's office for one week. Norm's other lifelong dream was to sing in a barbershop quartet, a dream he fulfilled in 1986.

Norm did an excellent impersonation of John Wayne, and believed Babe Ruth was the greatest American hero. When Cliff commented that the Bambino was a veritable eating and drinking machine—a glutton—Norm responded, "Who am I supposed to model my life after, Gandhi?" Not surprisingly, Norm's motto was "I came, I drank, I stayed." He even devised a form of currency (the letter "B" with a slash through it) representing the number of beers he charged to complete a project.

In his youth, Norm was politically involved. At age 12, he campaigned for John F. Kennedy in the 1960 presidential election by walking around wearing a poster board with the inscription "All the Way with J.F.K." After a three-decade hiatus from civic causes, Norm was prompted into action to circulate a petition to preserve the Hungry Heifer as an historical landmark.

According to Norm, the most important thing in life is love. It does not matter who or what you love, as long as you love it totally, completely, and without judgment. What Norm most loved was his barstool, and if there was a heaven he wanted his barstool—and God had better not be sitting on it either! Norm said that when he dies he wanted to be buried under the big plastic Little Wally at Little Wally's Pup and Burger restaurant.

Other miscellaneous information: according to Norm, the most sacred place in the world is Boston Garden; he thought the smartest animal was the ant because they built entire farms without blueprints; he was always the banker and race car in Monopoly; he was never very good at telling people bad news; he owned a dog as an adult; and thought the worst way to die was sliding down a razor bannister.

Birthdays

Norm spent his 36th birthday (in 1984) in the hospital after being hit between the eyes with a champagne cork that ricocheted off the Cheers bell behind the bar. Besides a battery of tests, the hospital removed a mole from his buttock. As a birthday gift, Sam paid $683 for the elective surgery and Vera gave Norm a health club membership (subtle hint). Amazingly, Norm used the membership by doing 25 in the pool every day—cannonballs, not laps.

Norm always wanted a beer for his birthday, and on the 43rd anniversary of his birth (in 1991), he received that very special gift from the Cheers gang. Sam gave him one of the best gifts—a Celtics team jacket and the opportunity to meet Kevin McHale. Cliff's gift was equally generous—he researched the historical significance of birthdays and uncovered a lot of interesting facts, and agreed *not* to share them with Norm.

Likes and Dislikes

Norm's two favorite eating establishments were the Hungry Heifer and Little Wally's Pup and Burger. The former was best to impress out-of-town guests, and the latter was best if you wanted to power down the animal fat. Although Norm never became a member of the Big Eaters' Circle at the Hungry Heifer, he had a high probability of acceptance because a member died every week or so.

Norm's favorite pizza ingredient was anchovies, he loved buttercream chocolates, and his favorite snack was Ho Ho's. On Tuesday evenings he accompanied Vera to Hurley's Market for free sausage samples, though the store restricted their dining to 12 links. Although Norm loved beer, he refused to drink bottled beer.

The Peterson Estate

Norm and Vera owned a home, but slept in separate rooms—she reposed in the bedroom and he slumbered on the couch in the living room. Norm still used the bedroom, but only to hide beer (in case of an emergency). As homeowners, Vera did all the upkeep, though Norm experienced particular disquietude when she called concerning two feet of water in the basement. Norm hastened home because it was one foot more than usual!

Cliff offered to buy the Peterson abode in an attempt to lowball his friend who was desperate to sell. Norm immediately accepted Cliff's purchase price and proclaimed, "At last, English-speaking neighbors!" The Petersons' next-door neighbors were Phyllis and Ron Henshaw.

Employment

As the proud owner of three suits and five ties, Norm had a multitude of occupations. Although his mother wanted him to become a matador, Norm's primary profession was accounting (he graduated 30th in his class). His job satisfaction was seeing the look on some old hag's face after saving her a couple hundred bucks on the short tax form.

Norm's first accounting position at H.W. Sawyer & Associates ended in 1982 after he physically accosted the firm's president, Herb Sawyer. Norm volunteered as party director and organized Roman Bacchanal Night, i.e., a toga party. One duty as party director was to arrange a date for the company president. When the female escort canceled, Diane reluctantly agreed to entertain Mr. Sawyer. Herb was expecting a promiscuous date, so he became more aggressive when Diane resisted his advances. Norm finally intervened by ejecting the company president from the bar.

Norm remained unemployed for six months until Derek Malone (Sam's brother) arranged a position at the prestigious accounting firm of Goldstein, Boreman & Cowacomie. Unfortunately, this employment was short-lived. Norm discovered the firm was cheating on taxes; however it was not a moral stance that led to his termination—he was fired after taking too long of a lunch break.

After nine months of unemployment, Norm accepted a position as a dishwasher at Melville's. Realizing his desperation, the Cheers gang persuaded Sam to hire Norm as a tax accountant for the bar. His calculations entitled Sam to a $15,000 refund, but Sam seriously doubted Norm's competence and surreptitiously retained another accountant. When Norm discovered the subterfuge, they engaged in a raucous argument. After rectifying their disagreement, Norm became Cheers' sole accountant for subsequent yearly tax returns.

With newfound confidence, Norm commenced self-employment in Norm Peterson, Inc., an accounting firm. Despite working out of the trunk of his car, Norm soon developed a clientele that included a dress boutique owner, Emily Phillips, and dairy farmers, the Brubakers. However, in 1985 he returned to the corporate world as an accountant for Talbert International, where he was promptly promoted to corporate killer (the guy who fires employees) by executive Mr. Hecht. The position was created because employees found it particularly humiliating to be fired by someone clearly and markedly superior to themselves, and it caused too much stress on the executives. A background check evinced that Norm had absolutely nothing in his life any employee could envy or resent, so he was offered the promotion.

The promotion was irresistible—a 300 percent raise, and if Norm did not accept the promotion he would have been fired. Needless to say, he accepted the position and proved to be the perfect candidate because he was particularly adept at doling out pity. His first termination was Billy Richter, who ended up feeling sorry for Norm rather than himself. When Norm inevitably became desensitized to the torment he was inflicting and no longer empathized with the terminated employees, he decided to quit.

The following year, Norm found another accounting position at some unspecified company. At one point he was in line for a promotion to accounts manager, competing against Morrison, who was sleeping with the boss' wife, Mrs. Reinhart. Norm contemplated revealing this juicy tidbit to ensure a promotion, but the Cheers gang (mostly Diane) persuaded him to take a moral stance and remain reticent. He ultimately lost the promotion because Vera did not fit in with the other executives' wives. Norm was offended and quit, but his most noble act was not informing Vera that she was the cause.

By the fall of 1986 Norm's occupational deviation turned to various entrepreneurial endeavors. After successfully advising a few clients on business investment ideas, he implemented a self-originating business venture, Tan 'N' Wash (a combination tanning salon and laundromat). The Cheers gang insisted upon being included in the investment, so Norm obliged. As business waned, the gang became apprehensive about losing their investments, and demanded Norm return their shares. Shortly thereafter, the business became successful and the gang became resentful. After making amends, Norm distributed dividend checks to everyone, claiming he never purchased their shares. As the gang joyously danced in the street, Norm was informed that a heavy snowfall had collapsed the roof of Tan 'N' Wash and there was no insurance.

After this entrepreneurial disaster, in 1987 Norm returned to the workforce as an accountant at Masterson, Holly & Dixon, where he occupied the former closet-sized storage office (room 2511), in conjunction with another accountant, Warren Thompkins. Norm took the initiative to prove he was a leader, and prepared a proposal to the board of directors. Fortunately for Norm, his office mate stole the idea and presented it to the board (which proved fateful). Thompkins concluded Norm was a moron, whereas Norm realized his niche in life was to remain an anonymous cog in the corporate machinery.

Within months Norm dabbled with a painting career (painting Rebecca's office and apartment, and Evan Drake's bedroom), worked as Santa Claus at Nagle's department store, and one year later in 1988, began interior decorating. While painting the interior of the Cranes' town house, he revealed a special aptitude for designing interiors. After successfully redecorating their residence, the Cranes arranged prospective clients, Kim and Robert Cooperman. To convince the Coopermans he was qualified to be an interior decorator, Norm feigned being homosexual. However, when Sam refused to role-play the part of Norm's lover, and Norm admitted he was straight, the Coopermans rescinded the contract. (When Norm agreed to perform the task for half price, they promptly rehired him.)

Six months later Norm formally organized a painting business, AAAA Painting, and hired Rebecca to do the marketing. The business logo was Carl Chameleon (because like a chameleon you, too, should change colors), and the slogan was "Thank you for making Four A Painting your foray into painting." Notwithstanding Rebecca's assistance, the business became so successful Norm hired three painters (Rudy, Scott and John). However, due to Norm's lack of managerial assertiveness, the employees began taking advantage of him. To remedy the problem, Norm created a fictitious company, K & P Painting, Inc., and business partner, Anton Kreitzer, whose purpose was to keep the employees in line. The painters responded accordingly, but when "Anton" pushed them too far, they revolted and quit.

Norm lingered as a quasi-painter for the next three years, doing odd jobs such as painting the Cranes' town house (again) and nursery, and his sister-in-law's nursery. However, in 1992 his dream job happened along. While sitting at Cheers, an interviewer solicited Norm to volunteer for a beer taste test. Norm was so adept at tasting, he was hired as the brewery's official taste tester. The dream job only lasted one week because he botched the final interview with the brewery president, Mr. Hoffmeyer. Norm received one check, payable to Norm Peter*man*, because Norm Peter*son* was still collecting unemployment!

Relationships—General

Norm only had sex with one woman in his life, Vera, who is also the only woman he ever loved. But, if he could have had any woman in the world, he would have chosen Jill Eichenberry ("L.A. Law") because she was attracted to short dumpy guys, like her husband, Michael Tucker ("L.A. Law"). Despite having several opportunities to be unfaithful, Norm declined the offers of all four women (Emily Phillips, Phyllis Henshaw, his secretary Doris, and Dot Carroll).

Norm's first opportunity was in 1983. Emily Phillips owned a dress shop boutique and was Norm's accounting client. Everyone except Diane encouraged him to have an affair, and he even accepted an invitation to Emily's apartment. Norm returned two hours later feigning exhaustion and proudly displaying a hickey (courtesy of a car vacuum). However, the truth was revealed when Emily informed everyone that Norm left to park the car and never returned.

Two years later, Norm's next-door neighbor, Phyllis Henshaw, became concerned her husband, Ron, was having an affair with Vera. They hired a private detective, Carla's cousin, Santo, to verify their suspicion. Although Ron and Vera contemplated having a sexual rendezvous, they decided against it. Irrespective of their spouses' fidelity, Phyllis propositioned Norm, but he respectfully declined because he loved only Vera.

In 1990 Norm rejected the advances of his secretary, Doris, who was inexplicably enamored with him. Unfortunately, business declined and Doris' employment had to be terminated, but this only escalated her obsession which manifested itself in her following Norm everywhere. The only means of ending the infatuation was to rehire Doris. Since Doris refused to go out with her own boss, that meant that Norm—as boss—was off the hook. In other words, to have uninterrupted beer drinking, Norm had to rehire Doris (despite business being slow), which was an inexpensive alternative considering he had to buy Vera a house!

Norm's final opportunity for a sexual perfidy was in 1993 with Internal Revenue Service agent Dot Carroll. While auditing his taxes she exposed Norm's attempt to defraud the U.S. government with fake calendars and receipts. Norm decided to flirt with her, and she responded favorably by arranging a rendezvous at the Ritz Carleton (room 147). Despite uncovering Norm's diabolical scheme to have Carla intervene as the jealous wife, Dot did not exact reprisals for his faithfulness.

Relationships—Vera

Although Vera resembled Ed Asner and had legs like scratching posts, she possessed a wonderful sense of humor and loved telling fat guy jokes. For example, "How many fat guys does it take to change a light bulb? Answer: You can't get a fat guy to change a light bulb. You can't even get him to come home on Christmas Eve!" Vera also had a low threshold for excitement. She went into a tizzy after cracking open a double-yolk egg.

Besides being a member of the Women's Auxiliary Club, Vera worked as a travel agent until being laid off in 1991. She was subsequently employed as a hatcheck girl for Melville's restaurant, but was fired after continuously watching Norm through a knothole in the floor. Vera was such a Tupperware fanatic that she wanted to be buried in one of the containers—just lower the casket into the ground, burp the corner, and she would be sealed fresh for eternity!

Vera's parents lived in one of those rectangular states, and her aunt lived in Springfield, Massachusetts. Since 1978 Norm spent all but two Thanksgiving celebrations at Vera's parents' house; however, he despised the ordeal because they had no beer or television, and the heat was set at 80 degrees. Vera had a sex fiend sister, Donna, and her cousin Natalie purportedly would date any man (but wisely rejected Cliff Clavin and his perverted telephone ice-breaker joke).

Norm proposed marriage to Vera at the Twi-Lite Drive-in, and they tied the knot on November 17, 1972 (or 1978, depending upon the episode), under the beguilement of Vera's pregnancy (she did not tell him until *after* the wedding). At their wedding, Vera refused to allow Norm to kiss her (though he did not try very hard), and Norm's father gave the traditional celebratory toast "Thank God I'm not paying for this!" Norm and Vera received a very special wedding gift from Cliff and Esther Clavin—a set of *Star Trek* steak knives.

The newlyweds spent their honeymoon in New Orleans, and on their wedding night, Norm threw himself at her mercy. He successfully avoided sex by begging and pleading, and telling her how wrong it was to force him to go though with it. Vera finally told Norm that if he could not get the job done she would have to hire a professional. He affectionately called their honeymoon suite "The Dead Zone." Norm and Vera consummated their marital union one week after their marriage, and during intimate moments they would think of baby names. Appropriately enough, carved in Vera's headboard were the words "I'm only doing this for charity."

Norm and Vera never had children because Norm couldn't—he looked at her and he just couldn't! Although Norm joked about Vera and could not remember her birthday or their anniversary, he remained faithful; fidelity was his sole measure of being a good husband. Nevertheless, if Norm ever saw her in bed with another man, he would buy a few pencils from the guy and send him on his way.

Long after the wedding vows were uttered, Norm's wedding ring remained as visible as ever—in the window of a pawnshop on Boyleston Street. Although not romantically inclined, Norm's wedding anniversary gifts were very innovative. Over the years, he gave Vera an ashtray, took her out for pizza on their tenth anniversary, and waved as she drove past the bar on their fifteenth anniversary.

Norm and Vera were not without their marital difficulties, and actually separated for four months (October 1983 to February 1984). During their separation, Norm lived at Cheers. On his first date as a bachelor he watched *Gandhi* with Arlene Horstley, a secretary at H. W. Sawyer & Associates. As for Vera, she remained in the Peterson homestead and dated Norm's high school rival, Wally Bodell. Norm and Vera eventually reconciled after a mutual friend arranged a blind date during which they went out with each other.

Cheers

The Cheers gang was like a family to Norm, and his trademark was having the patrons shout, "Norm!" as he entered the bar. Of course, the patrons at every establishment, Gary's Olde Towne Tavern, Nick's Bowl-O-Rama, Hungry Heifer, etc., yelled his name. Notwithstanding, in 1987 when the corporation purchased Cheers, only Woody yelled "Norm!" Prior to becoming a regular at Cheers, Norm used to frequent Vito's Pub but ceased his patronage when it turned into a gay bar.

Norm's regular seat was a barstool at the end of the bar, a place he occupied since the Ford administration. (He was particularly upset when a yuppie named Jeoffrey occupied his stool.) Previously he sat in the Cheers balcony, by the piano.

Norm's beer consumption was so invariable, a person could set his watch by it—87 sips of beer represented exactly two hours. Norm's love of beer was exemplified by his ritual of ensconcing full cans inside Cheers in case of an emergency. He had to tap into this hidden reserve only once, when Gary built a concrete wall around the beer taps (though Norm always expected the emergency would be a nuclear incident).

A typical evening for Norm was drinking beer at Cheers and then going home to consume a bucket of buffalo wings. In one incident, the morning after imbibing too many of Carla's highly intoxicating special mixed drinks, Vera made him breakfast in bed and called him "Mr. Two-time."

In one of Norm's luckier moments, he had Sam place a bet on black 17 on a roulette table in Atlantic City. The number paid on two consecutive turns and Norm became wealthy. Rather than paying his extremely large bar tab, he bought Sam a boat (the *Mayday Malone*) to replace the one that sank. Previously, when Norm's beer tab was $837 over his credit limit, Rebecca allowed him to paint her office to repay the debt.

Cliff Clavin

Childhood

Clifford C. Clavin, Jr., born an only child in 1947 (1949 in another episode), was breast-fed longer than most children. He was endowed with a recessive jumping gene from his mother's side of the family, and often wondered how his life would have changed had his mother married Carl Lewis (the track star). Cliff also had a wide derrière acquired from his father's side of the family, enabling him to bounce back after being pushed down. Cliff was taught to sew, knit, crochet, and petit-point (he was particularly proud of a self-made rug of John Wayne ascending into heaven) because his mother believed all boys should learn these skills.

Cliff described his childhood as idyllic—happy and problem free; he was well-liked, well-adjusted, and class valedictorian. Notwithstanding this appellation, as a child he was laughed off the playground. In eighth grade, Cliff wanted to attend the science fair, but he had a tapeworm (or ringworm) so he was unable to go. His mother used to tell him bedtime stories about gangrene, and when Cliff was unable to sleep, the two of them would role-play characters from *Peter Pan*—she dressed as Captain Hook and tied up Cliff, who in turn played Peter Pan (he was quite a crazy teenager). In adolescence, he had severe acne, and puberty was one long nightmare because his mother would not allow it in the house.

Cliff's favorite hiding place was the closet (because his mother used to lock him in there to teach him to be polite), and he used to love sliding down the bannister. Cliff's favorite tree, which he planted as a child, was an Elm named Elmer. One indelible childhood memory was being 10 years old and losing a Hopalong Cassidy watch in a cave at Cadillac Ranch in Merrimack Cavern. Over 30 years later, when he tried to locate the missing watch, his butt became lodged in one of the caverns.

Cliff attended a public high school and was a member of the prom decorating committee (which caused permanent crepe paper stains on his hands). The last time Cliff cried was at the junior prom. He was stuck with a pin while his mother attached a boutonniere, and he received a staph infection. Proms and dances were particularly depressing for Cliff because he yearned to be out on the floor; however, he never learned to dance because there was no one with whom to practice.

Cliff's high school sweetheart was Wendy Beaman, but it was his mother who accompanied him to the prom when his date failed to show. The entire experience was humiliating; Cliff was laughed at by the other kids, and then they pantsed him. As for the high school yearbook, when his mother saw improper inscriptions, she made him eat it. After high school Cliff attended college but never graduated.

Family

According to Cliff, through a genetic quirk the Clavins inherited two extra teeth, which was the only way to prove they were the rightful heirs to the Russian throne. The Clavins were often mistaken as royalty because of their fine-boned wrists, and in medieval times they were the royal taste testers. Cliff's grandfather was remembered for growing a thick beard (he died when Cliff was six years old), and in fact, facial hair was so predominate in the family that Cliff became the first Clavin not to grow a beard.

Clifford C. Clavin, Sr., abandoned the family when Cliff was nine years old. One of the few childhood memories Cliff had was slinking into his father's room to wear the turban which was part of the Knights of the Scimitar's fraternal raiment. Nearly 20 years later, Cliff was reunited with his father, who was a fugitive avoiding prosecution for real estate fraud. After sharing a very enjoyable day, he asked Cliff to accompany him to Australia. As Cliff contemplated calling the authorities, his father escaped through the bathroom window at Cheers, never to be seen again.

Cliff's mother, Esther Clavin, was born in 1929 with type "O" blood, and was in the USO on 42nd Street in New York City during World War II. Esther owned a cat, had a red convertible, and could work magic in a darkroom. While giving birth to Cliff, she was in labor for 72 hours because of his wide hips (in another episode it was 36 hours). One Mother's Day, she received steer manure, and one of the proudest moments in her life was in 1947 when she shook the hand of Bing Crosby.

After being deserted by her husband, Esther had very few gentlemen in her life. In 1986 she finally met the right man, Duncan "Fitz" Fitzgerald, a wealthy inventor from Michigan who designed the metal vapor input valve used in commercial and military jet engines. Anticipating newfound wealth, Cliff arranged a blind date between Esther and Fitz. They took an instant liking to one another and quickly planned a wedding. However, Esther insisted Fitz give his wealth to charity before they married. Although despondent about losing the potential riches, Cliff threw a low-budget bachelor party with Sam supplying the bar and the belly dancers. Fitz had the time of his life, and promised to take good care of Cliff financially. However, the celebration was short-lived because the deliriously exhausted Fitz died of a heart attack.

In 1993 Cliff placed Esther in a retirement home. Although hesitant at first, she became acclimated within a few days and before long was playing sports and being courted by fellow residents. (Esther's claim to fame was being named MVP in the softball tournament—she went 4 for 4 at the plate, but her hook slide into third base won the hearts of everybody.) Cliff was delighted, but quickly withdrew her from the retirement home after discovering the insurance would not cover the entire cost of her stay and he would be personally responsible for the remainder.

The two places Esther wanted to see before she died were Burbank, California, and Formosa. In 1992 she fulfilled half the dream by traveling to Burbank to see Cliff's joke delivered live on "The Tonight Show with Johnny Carson." Cliff and his mother also belonged to Club Med and loved watching the Home Shopping Channel.

Personal

Cliff had big ears, a cerebral cortex 8 percent larger than the average human's, and autumn-complexion skin (he took a quiz in *Redbook* magazine). Tattooed on his posterior was a big heart with the inscription "I love Vera" (he accidentally received a tattoo intended for Norm). Cliff prayed every night, wrote his thoughts in a journal (not a diary), and wore a shower cap to bed.

Cliff received an allowance until he was 30 years old, and was quite perturbed when his mother took him off the dole. His vengeance came a few years later when her pension fund went bankrupt. According to Cliff, "What goes around comes around," and when she came begging for money, he refused to give her any.

In the realm of athletics, Cliff obtained his knowledge of karate by taking classes at the *YWCA*. Although never competing in the Boston Marathon, he always registered for the event annually to get a free T-shirt. He would then wear the T-shirt outside the health club to impress women. Cliff's exercise routine was prehensile-isotomic-geometrics which involved muscle tension under constant constriction. He merely flexed a muscle for 60 seconds. The beauty of this regime was you never perspired, and could do it anytime, anywhere.

Cliff used shock therapy in a peculiar attempt to alter his acerbic personality. The notion materialized after no one visited him at New England Presbyterian Hospital (room 194) after appendectomy surgery. One session was held at Cheers, but the shock treatment proved ineffective due to Cliff's inability to control his deriding, insolent and caustic comments.

Cliff's trademark was wearing white socks—with jeans, a postal uniform, business suits, tuxedos, and even in the tanning booth (Clavin men have feet as sensitive as a baby's bottom). However, it is unknown whether white socks accompanied the kilt he wore when the Gala Postmans' Ball held their "Night in Glasgow" theme party.

In 1986 Cliff proudly became a member of the fraternal organization Knights of the Scimitar. As a child he dreamed of this honor, and even helped his best friend, Norm Peterson, to become a member. The one organization in which Cliff could not enlist was the Navy because of his asthma, so he joined the U. S. Postal Service (if he could not join the armed services, at least he could deliver draft notices to those who could). Despite never becoming a military enlistee, Cliff always carried a Swiss army knife (with tweezers and toothpick). According to Cliff, every soldier in the Swiss army owned one—that's why nobody messes with Switzerland!

Some of Cliff's special talents included memorizing the Dewey decimal system, doing impersonations of French Impressionist painter Paul Cézanne (1839–1906), and singing operas, such as the *Ave Maria*. He attempted to break the world records for walking backwards and riding a mechanical bull, but missed both by a few hours. However, he had a personal record of stuffing eleven Spanish peanuts up his nostrils.

Watching television was another hobby, though Cliff claimed he only inadvertently watched "Teatime with Brenda" while channel surfing between "Combat" and The *Playboy* Channel. His favorite television channel was the Weather Channel because he liked to watch meteorologist Dorothy Boysic and listen to her lateral lisp. Cliff had every episode of "The Little Rascals" on videotape (except "Good Eats" and "Captain Spanky's Showboat"), and had a childhood crush on Darla. Cliff first saw *The Love Bug* in 1969 at the Twi-lite Drive-in (the 22-year-old went with his mother and remembers wearing his pajamas).

Cliff had one near-death experience when his mother's Crock-Pot exploded. After this incident, he began growing a mustache. Cliff also had a reincarnation experience in which he lived in the Old West (and handled himself pretty well). As for death, Cliff planned on giving his belongings to his mother and contemplated cryogenics—having his head frozen until science found a cure for the ailment that killed him.

Other miscellaneous information: Cliff learned to like vegetables by walking around with them in his pockets; he lacked tidiness; he used to frequent the drive-in with his buddies; he was a clandestine bounty hunter tracking D. B. Cooper; he used postage stamps to bribe police officers; he insisted upon being the thimble in Monopoly; he thought the worst way to die was being eaten by rats.

Likes and Dislikes

Cliff loved Twinkies and hated anchovies. In addition to always ordering wing-dings for lunch, Cliff avoided food containing tryptophan (an amino acid) because it made him sleepy, and was allergic to chocolate (though graham crackers served as a comparable substitute). Naturally, his favorite charity was Save the Clavin Foundation.

Cliff's favorite television program was "Jeopardy!," and in 1990 he fulfilled a lifelong dream by becoming a contestant on the show. Cliff competed against a lawyer, Agnes Borsic, and a doctor and chief of neurosurgery at Boston General Hospital, Milford Reynolds. The categories on Cliff's dream board were civil servants, stamps from around the world, mothers and sons, beer, bar trivia, and celibacy. He accumulated $22,000, but bet and lost everything in the final round. The final category was movies. The answer was "Archibald Leach, Bernard Schwartz, and Lucille LeSoeur," and the question was "What were the real names of Cary Grant, Tony Curtis, and Joan Crawford?" Cliff responded, "Who are three people who have never been in my kitchen?"

Birthdays

Cliff had very few happy birthdays. As a child, when no children arrived for his birthday party, Cliff's mother insisted upon the clown entertaining her son despite his incessant crying and importuning the clown to stop. This incident precipitated a clown phobia which subsequently included clowns at the car wash. Cliff also had an equine phobia, of an unknown origin, which included the carousel horses in front of the supermarket.

As an adult, Cliff experienced similar attendance problems when only Norm showed up for his surprise birthday party. Cliff's mother even forgot to go, and she organized the party. For his 30th birthday, Cliff received a $5 bill with the inscription "Happy 30th birthday, Cliffybits. Sorry, I didn't have time to shop. Love, Mom."

The Clavin Homestead

Cliff lived with his mother for over 30 years out of loyalty—he was the man of the house after his father deserted the family. However, Cliff had his freedom—he had his own room and hot plate, and could stay out as long as he wanted (so long as he called by 10 p.m.). Besides, they had fun together. On Sunday afternoons they sang and danced to the Grinning Americans, a wholesome group of women who wore pullover sweaters and sang patriotic songs. Cliff and his mother also exhibited their singing talents by performing a duet of "Come On to My House" and "Volaré" on their eight-track tape answering machine.

The Clavin homestead consisted of three bedrooms, two baths, a fishnet over the patio, and a handmade lava rock fire pit in the backyard. One neighbor, Jim McNulty, never took down his Christmas lights, and another neighbor was in training for the world lightweight kick-boxing championship. The kick boxer had thunderous parties on school nights and an unkempt front lawn with automobile parts strewn everywhere (nothing Cliff could use). In 1987 Esther Clavin sold her home to developer William Cronin for $250,000. Cliff initially encouraged development, but after reminiscing about his childhood years, he chained himself to an interior post to prevent its demolition. Esther was stunned by his display of devotion for their home, and agreed to fight to save their residence. As they exited, the house collapsed, and Cliff delightfully proclaimed, "We got a quarter of a million dollars for this dump!"

After the sale of the residence, Cliff briefly resided with Norm and later purchased a condominium. Esther moved to Florida, but in 1990 (after losing money at the dog track) returned to Boston to elude creditors. Having finally gained independence, Cliff resisted her efforts to inhabit his condominium. Woody agreed to accommodate Esther, who in turn accepted him as the son she never had (Cliff remained the son she did have). When Esther began teaching Woody assorted trivia, Cliff became jealous and finally made amends by allowing his mother to move into the condominium.

Although the condominium was small, Cliff proudly exalted its superb location for using binoculars to scope out the dollies at the pool. Naturally, his residential living was not without turmoil. The manager, Mr. Cranston, nearly evicted Cliff for accusing a neighbor, Mr. O'Leary, of being Adolf Hitler. With a heart-touching speech, Esther convinced the other tenants to give Cliff one more chance.

Automobile

Cliff's eccentric automobiles included a Studebaker and a 1965 Chevrolet station wagon. He once contemplated selling the station wagon for an

Alfredo, a new Italian import, and distributed an advertisement containing a picture of a Cadillac with the caption, "Chevrolet, the Cadillac of station wagons." Cliff's station wagon had an eight-track tape player and a trip meter that only reset to 38.

Cliff's automobile proudly displayed the bumper sticker "Letter Carriers Do It on Foot," and the trunk was stocked with two cans of tuna and a raft (in case the polar ice caps melted) and pictures from his Florida vacation. Cliff also devised a unique method of cooking while driving as an efficient use of time and energy. Before leaving on a trip he placed vegetable kebobs and hobo steaks on the engine to cook.

Employment—General

Although Cliff ultimately became a postal carrier, he dreamed of becoming a trapeze artist—the first person in the history of the circus to do the quadruple flip. He became obsessed with this career after seeing the movie *Trapeze* (1956) starring Burt Lancaster and Tony Curtis. As a child, Cliff also considered being a spy but decided not to go into intelligence. (Carla retorted, "That seems only fair because none of it went into you.")

As a teenager, Cliff worked at a slaughterhouse and retained an indelible memory of the animals' eyes as they prepared to meet their demise. In 1988 he supplemented his postal income by selling $19.99 mail order shoes which were crafted by a Missouri cobbler who poured his heart into every sole. However, the shoes were defective and squeaked with every step.

Employment—U.S. Postal Service

Although Cliff never joined the circus, he proudly enlisted in the service— the U.S. Postal Service. He joined the force in 1974 (or 1979 in another episode) and was a member of the South Central Branch. According to Cliff, the most rewarding aspect of being a postman was seeing the eyes of an old hag get all misty when he delivered a Mother's Day card.

Cliff had many proud moments as a postal carrier. In 1984 he was named Honorary Mail Carrier of the Seminole Indians (he was lost in the Everglades for days before being found by the tribe). Two years later, the South Central Branch selected him as Postman of the Year, along with 267 other proud postal carriers in the greater Boston metropolitan area. As part of the honor, the winners were invited to the Gala Postmans' Ball. Diane accompanied Cliff to the prestigious event.

In 1991 he was selected to re-enact the first Boston mail delivery down the venerable Boston Post Road (Cliff was given the final leg of the journey from Ingham to the central post office). Since the initial mail delivery was by horseback, Cliff inauspiciously proclaimed himself an accomplished equestrian. The uncontrollable horse darted throughout Boston, and Cliff finally reached the postal destination three hours late. However, since the original 18th-century delivery was three weeks late, Cliff shaved a little time off the record!

Cliff also had the honor of training a new postal employee, Margaret O'Keefe. She specifically requested Cliff because of his exemplary employment record. (Cliff was not impressed, because women do not belong in the trenches delivering mail, rather they were better suited for sorting mail or selling stamps.) However, when she exhibited an inexplicable infatuation with him, he warmed up to the idea. After Margaret completed the postal training, Cliff gave her arch supports.

The final accolade was Cliff's promotion to assistant supervisor of sub-district A, grid L. He earned the promotion the old-fashioned way—sucking up to his supervisor, Marty Furman. Cliff originally bribed Furman with a box of steaks, but as the competition increased, he added a ham radio and built a family room onto his supervisor's house. The other promotion to which he aspired was being selected as postmaster general of the Ecopod. Despite all of his postal awards and accomplishments, Cliff's name remained synonymous with screwing up. When someone erred, the postal supervisor would tell him to get his head out of his Clavin.

The worst day to deliver mail was when the Sears and Spiegel catalogues were distributed simultaneously. It was a phenomenon that happened once every 27 years, when both marketing strategies were in the same equinox. Similarly, sore shoulders were not uncommon on the day book clubs mailed their orders; for instance; *War and Peace* weighs three and one-half pounds in paperback.

One postal menace was dog bites, but Cliff deterred canine attacks by bathing in bubble bath. In one incident, he was bitten by a dog owned by Madeline Keith. After threatening a lawsuit, he was seduced into signing a release of liability form. Unfortunately, Cliff's defenses weakened and he signed the release before receiving any physical gratification. Immediately after he signed the form, she checked her answering machine for messages and told Cliff an outlandish story of how her husband, a soldier missing overseas for years, returned to Boston. She exited the room, never to be seen again.

Another postal employee hazard was job-related stress. Discussions about the fax machine and private mail competition which affect the sanctity of the U.S. Postal Service were anxiety provoking topics and caused Cliff to develop a rash. After unwittingly ingesting medication beyond the prescribed dosage, he contracted a case of gynecomastia—male breast enlargement.

Cliff's postal nemesis was Walter Q. Twitchell. Cliff was particularly upset when Twitchell won a trip to Disney World during the 1987 postal food

drive. Cliff lost three years in a row, but the last defeat was the most painful—
he lost by one can. After discovering that Woody forgot to put two cans in the
bin, Cliff sprinted to the airport and chased the Orlando-bound plane down
the runway while throwing cans of food.

Cliff's postal pride compelled him to report a coworker (Lewis, a former
boxing champion) for stealing fragrance samples from magazines. Lewis was
terminated and asked Cliff to discover the informant's name. A few days later,
Cliff was prepared to reveal the snitch—Juan Torez! However, Lewis knew the
truth and graciously spared Cliff's life.

Notwithstanding bragging about being an exemplary employee, Cliff was
reprimanded at least twice. In one incident he was extremely ill, so Norm hos-
pitably finished Cliff's route. Norm was arrested for mail theft, and after considerable coaxing, Cliff divulged the truth and received a 30-day suspension.
In the other incident, Margaret O'Keefe seduced Cliff into lying about a postal
vehicle being stolen to mask their tryst at a motel. After she persuaded him
to reveal the truth, he was disciplined with a six-week reassignment to zone
19 (Rottweiler Ridge). Cliff had at least one celebrity on his postal route,
renowned New England artist Phillip Semenko.

Employment—Comedy

Other than being a postal carrier, Cliff had an affinity toward comedy, to
follow in the footsteps of the greatest comic genius of all time, Jan Murray.
Cliff was first published as a humorist when his daffy-nitions (humorous
definitions of words or phrases) were printed in the *Post Office Newsletter*. His
first published joke was, "Postal Increase: What happens to your feet *after* you
finish your route." Another daffy-nition was "Psychiatrist: A guy who shrinks
your head *and* your bank account." Cliff's infamous punch line was "What's
up with that?"

Cliff even planned a comedy act, "The Cock-eyed Mind of Cliff Clavin"
(the same as every other night except he had a microphone), and debuted on
open mike night at a comedy club. Although Lilith loved his comedy and was
his biggest fan, Cliff's act bombed. His comedic career was temporarily resurrected when it appeared that "The Tonight Show with Johnny Carson"
accepted one of Cliff's submissions. However, it was actually a rejection letter that Norm changed to boost Cliff's spirits. Cliff reacted ecstatically, and
flew his mother and Norm to Burbank, California, to watch Johnny Carson
deliver the joke.

When they arrived at the studio, Norm bribed the cue card person to
insert the joke into the monologue. (The cue card person only agreed because
the joke was sure to flop, and he was scheduled to be replaced when Jay Leno
took over the show.) The joke submitted was "Today is Doc Severinsen's

birthday. You know, Doc is so old, [audience: "How old is he?"] when he was a kid he never blew out candles on his birthday cake; they didn't have fire yet." When the joke flopped, Cliff went ballistic claiming Johnny Carson botched the joke. After Cliff was ejected from the studio by security guards, Esther saved the day by having Johnny redo the joke, emphasizing the word "have." The joke was so successful that she and Norm were invited onstage to sit with Johnny.

Clavin Witticisms

In the area of food, Cliff believed American cheese was one of the world's finest cheeses, and the first Thanksgiving involved ancient Egyptians and astronauts from a distant galaxy. As for natural phenomena, Cliff had a few theories about the Bermuda Triangle and earthquakes. According to Cliff, the Bermuda Triangle was actually a trapezedarhomboid (though his mother contended it was actually a rhombus). Moreover, California earthquakes were actually sonic booms from a project funded by the United States to tunnel to the center of the earth and build giant computers to control the planet's rotation.

In the animal kingdom, Cliff believed the smartest animal was the pig. Accordingly, if pigs had language and thumbs they could be part of the workforce. In fact, they could provide 20–30 years of loyal service, and at their retirement party you could eat them. According to Cliff, it was a little known fact that the rat was not the carrier of the bubonic plague; instead it was carried by an animal known as the bubon. Another highly significant animal (in Cliff's world) was the leech because it was a medical panacea. However, drug companies were covering up their medical benefits because leeches are free.

According to Cliff, the goal of life is comfortable shoes, since all great accomplishments in history have been made by people with accommodating footwear. Aristotle wore sandals, Confucius wore thongs, and Einstein wore loafers. Conversely, Hippocrates went barefoot, and his intellectual genius was shortened by a sharp pebble. If not for that pebble, the microwave could have been invented in the Middle Ages.

Cliff had a novel theory to predict the next president of the United States. According to his calculations, the numerical value of each letter in each of the presidents' last names was equally divisible into the year they were elected. In 1984 Cliff deduced that the name of the next president would be Yelnick McWawa. Despite an inaccuracy in the prediction, Cliff was kind enough to send an inaugural fruitcake to Ronald Reagan.

As for America, Cliff was banned from jury duty after suggesting the reinstatement of the guillotine, and he subscribed to *Soldier of Fortune* (owning every issue except the Christmas edition). Furthermore, he designed a submarine with wheels that would have revolutionized modern warfare, but if World War III were ever to occur, Cliff would be in a fully stocked, juiced-up and armed Winnebago heading for the Mexican border—he and the cockroaches would do just fine! Finally, the military song "Ballad of the Green Beret" instilled a strong sense of patriotism in Cliff.

Relationships—General

Cliff's secret to being a stud was not wearing underwear, and during heavy petting, many women considered his big ears an erogenous zone. Cliff first received the "birds and the bees" talk from Norm, and then took a refresher course from his mother when he was 44 years old. Despite these educational discussions, Cliff knew he was prepared for fatherhood because he owned a copy of *The Little Mermaid*. He also had two theories about relationships: women were attracted to married men because of the wedding ring, and the best way to get a woman was to fake a heart attack.

Whenever Cliff was with a beautiful woman, the patrons asked if she was a cousin (or had a mental illness). Part of Cliff's problem (in this area) was his inability to communicate with women. His speech became incomprehensible gibberish or he transposed words in a sentence. Another reason was his ice-breaker jokes. Cliff's favorite was making perverted and obscene phone calls to women ("What are you wearing? You wanna know what I'm wearing?"). He loved the joke because it always worked on his mother!

Of course, Cliff's limited dating experience did not inhibit fabrications of sexual exploits. He often bragged about his sexual prowess, claiming to be Chairman of the Broads and a Burnin' Hunk of Churnin' Funk; or that women wanted to be his love hostage or Dr. Feelgood's next patient. Other statements depicting his sexual abilities include: "she's looking for a booster shot of ole vitamin CC," "there's still a lot of postage left on this U.S. male," and "I'll try a little Acu-Clavin on her." As for his sexual potency, according to Cliff, "Clavin men never shoot blanks—we're breeders, spawners; my loins are brimming with vitality." He also claimed to give a box of dried figs to every woman he dumped.

Cliff fabricated a sexual liaison and bragged about receiving love letters from a woman he met while vacationing in Florida. The letters were from Lynnette Cayhill, the manager of the Orange Blossom Motel, threatening to sue Cliff if he did not return items he had stolen. Besides fabricated affairs, Cliff had his share of love infatuations. His obsession with Priscilla Presley involved a few hundred letters, and Cliff had special feelings for Darla (of "The Little Rascals"). Cliff's sexual loneliness included frequent calls to the Party Hot Line (555-PRTY) that linked studs and babes so they could discuss their wild adventures.

Cliff's first known date was with high school sweetheart Wendy Beaman. He wanted to go steady with her, but it never materialized because of a psychosomatic reaction. Whenever he tried to make a commitment to a woman, he became instantaneously blind in her presence. (This condition recurred when Cliff was faced with a commitment to Margaret O'Keefe.) However, this reaction did not occur when he contemplated proposing marriage to Carla's sister, Annette Lozupone, in 1983.

Relationships—Sally

Cliff's first legitimate girlfriend was Sally, a neighbor and employee at the Yarn Barn (also a cowinner of the Employee of the Month award). Cliff was embarrassed about her appearance, so they stayed home every evening ritualistically sitting on the couch and watching "Jeopardy."

After giving herself a beauty makeover, Sally was transformed into a seductive woman. Naturally, Cliff insisted upon going to Cheers so he could parade her around the bar. He quickly realized the problems associated with dating a captivating woman—other men were equally enticed, so Cliff had to continually fend off their advances. Sally loved the newfound attention and refused to return to her former appearance.

Relationships—Margaret O'Keefe

Margaret Catherine O'Keefe, Cliff's first love, provided his only serious relationship. She was originally Cliff's postal trainee in 1989, and had an inexplicable attraction to his manners and love of trivia.

Cliff's first sexual liaison was with Margaret in a motel on Route 6 outside zone 27. Margaret drove a postal vehicle to the motel, and the post office reported it stolen. She seduced Cliff so he would lie to their supervisors to conceal the tryst. When subsequently insisting they tell the truth, Margaret was terminated and moved to Canada to join the Canadian Postal Service. Cliff nearly accompanied her, but the Cheers gang persuaded him to stay by appealing to his sense of patriotism with the song "Ballad of the Green Beret."

Margaret returned to Boston later that year and asked Cliff to be her man. Faced with commitment, he became hysterically blind. However, once realizing the illness was psychosomatic, Cliff was able to overcome the disability by unequivocally declaring his commitment to Margaret. Although the blindness was cured, he immediately became paralyzed from the waist down.

In 1991 Cliff introduced Margaret to his mother. It was difficult to introduce his significant other to the woman he loved more than anyone else in the world (and even more difficult to determine which woman fit which appellation). Although Esther was initially despondent, she quickly befriended Margaret and, on Cliff's behalf, proposed marriage to her. Esther planned a wedding with a luau theme and chocolate cake. As for wedding gifts, Margaret's parents offered the prospective newlyweds a freezer full of meat, and Esther agreed to buy them a mobile home. Notwithstanding the wedding arrangements, Cliff stood up to his mother (for the first time in his life) and refused to marry Margaret.

Margaret not only robbed Cliff of his virginity, but she was also the only woman with whom he was intimate (a grand total of three times in his life). Margaret used one of these private moments to implicate Cliff in a paternity issue. Carla was furious because she specifically requested they promise not to bring any Clavins into the world. She begged Cliff to get fixed—she offered to pay for it and even offered to do it! Despite knowing he was not the biological father (the real father was a Canadian named Jerry), Cliff agreed to marry her. When Margaret called Jerry to tell him the good news, they decided to reunite, and she returned to Canada permanently.

Cheers

Initially, Cliff was not part of the Cheers gang, but became an integral member after whining long enough about wanting to be included. Although Cliff had his share of embarrassment, his most humiliating experience was an incident with a barroom bully, Victor Shapone, who was irritated by his prating verbosity. Shapone gave Cliff three options: fight, admit to being a coward and a liar, or leave the bar. Cliff chose the latter but subsequently returned to the bar to prove his manliness by breaking a board with his foot and a brick with his head. The gang was awestruck, and then he discretely asked Diane to take him to the hospital because he never had a karate lesson in his life.

Contacting political figures was another area that frequently caused problems for Cliff. He wrote Boston Mayor Raymond Flynn weekly, and was eventually arrested for the content of the letters. Although he did not write Boston City councilor Kevin Forgerty, Cliff was issued a restraining order to remain at least 50 feet from the politician.

Prior to participating in the Party Hot Line, Cliff did not need technology to be a party man in the 1970s. He was known to shed his clothes and go streaking after a night of wild partying at Cheers. Twenty years later, he had another taste of wild partying after consuming Carla's lethal mixed drink (though Cliff did not remember much after the wooden lady laughed at him and called him a half-man).

Regarding the Cheers gang, Cliff contemplated how certain members would die. Norm would die of a heart attack, Sam would be killed by a jealous husband, and Frasier, well, suffice it to say that it would not be a pleasant death. Carla was by far the cruelest toward Cliff. For one of his birthdays she made him eat a bug (that laid eggs in his stomach). Carla also made a prank telephone call to the police, claiming Cliff dismembered Margaret O'Keefe and put her in his freezer. Cliff's mom threw out a year's supply of Omaha steaks, trying to protect him.

Some of Cliff's finer moments (in his mind) included his wacky inventions. According to Cliff, he was the actual inventor of the Toilet Duck, though his original idea was the Toilet Goat. Other inventions were homegrown, such as the beetabaga (a vegetable hybrid of the beet and rutabaga), a squash depicting the Hawaiian Islands, and vegetables resembling famous public figures. He had a potato that looked like Richard Milhous Nixon, a squash that brought to mind June Lockhart, and an unknown vegetable that was the spitting image of George Schultz.

Frasier Crane

Childhood

In 1952 Frasier W. Crane was born in Seattle, Washington. He had a rather lonely childhood; teased and ostracized by peers, he was always the odd man out—the children would say, "You take the girl and we'll take Frasier." Thus, it is not surprising that his fondest childhood memory was being alone in the full-size submarine he built in his parents' basement during six painfully frustrating months of his adolescence.

Frasier's solitude was also perpetuated by his parents, who were never very close to him. His mother taught him birthdays were just like every other day, nothing special. On one memorable birthday Frasier received a bran muffin with a pat of oleo. At age eight, he began visiting a psychologist.

Frasier's favorite childhood snack was cinnamon toast and strawberry milk, and his favorite song was "All the Pretty Little Horses." As a child he attended various concerts, such as *Peter and the Wolf*, *The Nutcracker*, and *Swan Lake*. Frasier never had chicken pox, though he had an insect phobia (especially bees) and developed a phobia of animals because his mother would not allow him to have a pet. (However, in another episode he had a spider collection, and had a pet dog as an adult.)

Family

Frasier's grandfather was the first Crane to emigrate to the United States. Frasier's father, Martin Crane, was a research scientist who was always too busy with experiments to spend time with his son. Supposedly Martin died prior to 1982 (though in the television spin-off "Frasier," he was a retired police officer. Apparently, Frasier fabricated the death because he was upset with his father at the time). Martin was so attached to a pet owl (Plato), he had it stuffed and mounted after its demise.

Frasier's mother, Hester Crane, was a psychiatrist and died in the mid-1980s. Hester was overly protective of Frasier and even threatened to kill Diane if she continued dating her son. Hester and Martin had a healthy sex life, and often played Broadway cast albums to disguise their lovemaking.

Personal

Frasier was raised in the Episcopalian faith (though once stated he had no religious upbringing), and some of his idiosyncrasies include being obsessive-compulsive about neatness and having a dust allergy. When growing a beard, Frasier resembled Sigmund Freud; however, Sam thought he looked like the guy on the can of deviled ham. Frasier wore pinstriped boxer shorts and broke the crown of a tooth on a green marble that Carla put in his Martini glass. In 1986 he became a member of the Fraternal Order of the Caribou, a sporting lodge with only three other members, and his first drive-in experience was in 1993 when attending the Twi-Lite Drive-in on its last night of business for the All Night Godzilla Marathon.

Frasier did impersonations of Jimmy Stewart and John Wayne, and was a very adept downhill skier. Despite his athleticism, Frasier realized he had become corpulent and lethargic since entering the bar in 1984, so he hired a personal trainer, Richard. When Lilith could not keep her hands off Richard, he was fired and replaced by Sam Malone. Although Frasier was initially motivated to exercise, the novelty of physical fitness quickly dissipated. Frasier's other workout regimen was using a NordicTrack.

As for relaxation techniques, Frasier had two. After experiencing an excruciatingly painful headache, he resorted to acupuncture and acupressure from Dr. Lee, a sexy, Asian female. The other technique was yoga, in which Frasier lowered his heart rate until he appeared dead. (Lilith taught him this technique on their honeymoon!)

Although Frasier's entire life involved stability and complacency, he resented being characterized as a good boy. To prove otherwise, he ran with scissors in his hand, swam after lunch, petted strange dogs, crossed the street against the walk signal, and joined forces with a female biker, Ellen. Frasier gave her the nickname Viper, and referred to himself as Slash.

When coping with bad news Frasier envisioned the worst possible thing imaginable, which happened to be Lilith having an affair. He had a $1 million life insurance policy, and thought the worst way to die was to pass away alone, knowing you had never been loved.

Other miscellaneous information: Frasier had more educational degrees than Lilith; they had a joint checking account; his barber was Woody; he avoided driving a car at night because of nocturnal nervousness; and he was always the race car in Monopoly.

Personal Likes and Dislikes

Frasier loved Kit Kat candy bars, and preferred a wedge of lime in his beer. His favorite soft drink was Classic Coke, and when they announced its return, he danced around the bar in his underwear with swizzle sticks in his ears. Frasier treasured a $1,200 first edition *A Tale of Two Cities*, written by his favorite British author, Charles Dickens. His favorite figure from the Pre-Rafaelite Brotherhood was Dante Gabriel Rossetti. Frasier believed Aristotle was the greatest thinker of all time, and had all 13 episodes of *I, Claudius* on videocassette. Frasier's favorite classical music work was Mahler's 3rd Symphony, and he enjoyed singing karaoke (despite having no formal training). One of his favorite childhood toys was Sparkhead, and he disliked fish as a child (but eventually grew to like it).

The Crane Town House

The Cranes lived in town house number 13, and Tuesday was garbage night. They had a spacious living room directly below their bedroom, and when redecorating their residence, the Cranes hired Ivan, a famous Boston designer who programmed himself to dream about the space he was designing. Ivan was written about in every magazine from *Metropolitan Home* to *Better Homes and Gardens*, and had more awards on his shelf than Frasier had shelves. The Cranes despised the aloof designer, and subsequently hired Norm Peterson to redesign their dwelling.

Education

Frasier was an academic elite and Rhodes scholar. During college his stress relieving hobbies included fencing and chess. Ironically, the only person who consistently defeated him at chess was Woody Boyd. Frasier's broad education included mastering foreign languages (French, German and Chinese) and performing in the theatrical productions *Cyrano de Bergerac*, *Can-Can*, and *The Mikado*.

After his performance as the number two man in *Can-Can*, Frasier seriously considered abandoning psychology as a college major to pursue a degree in the performing arts. However, his father insisted he be a psychologist, and Frasier did not want to disappoint his father. Therefore, Frasier continued with his formal education until receiving a Ph.D. from Harvard University, and then entered the psychiatric profession.

Career

Frasier's philosophy of life was to heal the human condition, and as a psychiatrist he earned in excess of $60,000 per year. He specialized in the treatment of phobias and preached strict Freudian psychology. In addition, he was the on-call psychiatrist for the city of Boston, a consultant at Goldenbrook sanitarium, a prison counselor, and visited New England Presbyterian Hospital as part of his work. Frasier's career received a further boost in 1985 when he was offered a teaching position as a visiting scholar at the University of Bologna.

Frasier learned hypnosis from Dr. Messmer, and his mentor was Dr. Bennett Ludlow. To remain in constant contact with his patients, Frasier maintained a pager and carried a cellular telephone in his briefcase. According to Frasier, the difference between a psychiatrist and a psychic is the former can prescribe drugs!

Frasier's successful psychiatric practice led to a commercialized version of his therapy marketed through public seminars as "The Crane Train to Mental Well-being." He had 27 articles published in psychiatric journals, wrote a book on bad marriages, and won several awards, such as the Mildred Bergen Fellowship and a Fisk Foundation grant (involving a thesis on man's never-ending desire to work and strive toward accomplishment). He also prepared a paper titled "Ingmar Bergman: The Poet of the Subconscious" (discussing the psychological ramifications of his film work), and began writing the book *Nice Psychiatrists Who Marry Castrating, Shrew, Battle-ax, Harridan Fishwives.*

For over 20 years, he retained the same secretary, Mrs. McGrady, who was known for her blue hair. She was subsequently replaced by a 21-year-old temporary secretary, Shauna. As for psychiatrist fees, Frasier noted there was a 40 percent customary courtesy discount in the United States.

The most noteworthy psychological hypothesis that captivated Frasier was the "Inner Hairy Man" theory. It postulated that within each man is a hidden primal beast softened by years of civilization and sensitivity. Frasier discovered this theory on the television show "Sally Jessy Raphaël." He decided to find his inner hairy man by taking a primal journey with Sam, Norm and Cliff.

Political Involvement

Frasier gained political experience by working on two election campaigns. His first political experience was romantically motivated. When Diane wholeheartedly supported candidate James Fleener in the 1986 Boston city council election, Frasier immediately joined the campaign. Despite their efforts, Fleener lost the election and Frasier failed to win Diane's heart.

Frasier's other political involvement was Woody Boyd's Boston city council candidacy. Frasier initially launched the campaign as a psychological study of voter ineptitude in candidate selection. He hypothesized that even a chimp could get 10 percent of the vote, so he decided to have Woody run for election. Frasier handled the publicity and functioned as Woody's political speechwriter.

Friends and Colleagues

Interestingly enough, despite all of Sam's childish games and pranks, he was Frasier's closest friend. Many of Frasier's other friends were fellow students during his days of college and graduate study. At Oxford University, Frasier befriended Simon Finch-Royce, who subsequently became a prominent marriage counselor and a staff member at the London Psychiatric Hospital. During college they performed *The Mikado* (Frasier played Yum-Yum, and Simon played Pitty-Sing).

Another renowned acquaintance was Julian Weinstein. Frasier and Julian were medical school lab partners when Frasier dissected his first frog. Julian subsequently became a renowned heart specialist and quickly forgot Frasier. (When Frasier asked Dr. Weinstein to arrange dinner reservations at The Cafe, a trendy Boston restaurant, he could not recall Frasier's name.)

One of Frasier's psychologist friends, Dr. Lawrence Crandell, tested his theory of fidelity while touring to promote his book *The Forever Couple: The Joy of Loving One Person for the Rest of Your Life*, a best-selling marriage manual. His hypothesis proved invalid—he tried to seduce Rebecca and then Maria, a chambermaid.

Relationships—General

If Frasier could have any woman, he would choose Loni Anderson (John Phillip Sousa would kill for her set of oompahs). Frasier's first love was Diane Chambers, and Lilith Sternin was the first person to love him for something other than his brain.

According to Frasier, the perfect means of releasing sexual tension was playing the piano because no matter how badly you perform, a piano never laughs nor stomps out of the room refusing to let you play again for three days! After making love, Frasier would pout until the woman complimented his sexual performance (a simple "Thank you Conan" would suffice to satiate his ego).

Frasier proposed marriage to four women: Nanette Gutsman, Diane Chambers, Candi Pearson, and Lilith Sternin. Although all four accepted his marriage proposal, only two (Nanette and Lilith) tied the knot with him.

Relationships—Nanette Gutsman

Frasier and Nanette married at a youthful age, while he was a first-year medical student. The marriage lasted only a couple of months, but he fondly recalled the fervent passion exhibited in the short time they knew one another—how her pet cat (Bo Bo Black Paws) would lay on Frasier's back and purr wildly as he and Nanette were being intimate.

After the divorce, Nanette became a successful children's singer (Nanny Gee) and had two concert tours, "1992 Tickle Tummy Tour" and "Itsy Bitsy World." Her telephone number was 555-6792, and she smelled like gingerbread. Frasier and Nanette were reunited in 1992 after she spotted him in the audience during one of her concerts. She gave Frasier a lustful kiss, and then tried to win his heart. After a catfight with Lilith, Nanette discontinued pursuing her ex-husband.

Relationships—Diane Chambers

Frasier met Diane at Goldenbrook sanitarium in Connecticut. She was a voluntary patient regrouping from a nervous prostration caused by breaking up with Sam, and he worked as a consulting therapist (though he was not her treating physician). They met rather fortuitously. Diane was playing croquet with an elderly woman on the front lawn. They began arguing when Diane accused the woman of cheating, and after wrestling on the ground, Frasier intervened as Diane was preparing to strike the woman with a croquet mallet.

Frasier and Diane's relationship had many flaws. First, Diane's repressed love for Sam never extinguished. Early in their relationship, Diane inadvertently called out Sam's name while making love to Frasier. Frasier was distraught, and sought advice from Sam. To maintain anonymity, Frasier used the names Thor (Frasier) and Electra (Diane), but Sam easily deduced the true identity of the parties.

The second flaw in their relationship was Diane's lack of love for Frasier.

She openly admitted using Frasier to heal her broken heart caused by the breakup with Sam. Diane never felt a fiery passion with Frasier, and he failed to satisfy her hedonistic desires.

And finally, Frasier and Diane's relationship waned because they were too strong-willed and uncompromising. Frasier was probably the most compromising, but even he had limits. Frasier sacrificed his puppy, Pavlov, replaced all the furniture and sanitized his town house to accommodate Diane's allergy, but the sneezing and voice change became intolerable. In contrast, Diane was constantly upset about Frasier's work commitments and their lack of quality time together.

Despite their incompatibility, in 1985 Frasier proposed marriage to Diane at Luigi's restaurant in Italy. Diane tentatively accepted, and they planned to wed at the Marino estate in Florence. However, when their car broke down in a small Italian village, they arranged to marry immediately. As they stood at the altar, Frasier said his vows, and when the priest asked Diane if she would take Frasier as her husband, Diane asked Frasier if the priest was speaking to her. Frasier nodded yes, and she left.

Frasier's reputation, career and life were shattered; he quit the psychiatric profession, had low self-esteem and a drinking problem. He sought professional therapy from his mentor, Dr. Bennett Ludlow, and accepted a janitorial position at Cheers to censure Diane for ruining his life. Sam became Frasier's inspiration because he had been able to regroup his life after breaking up with Diane.

In retrospect, Frasier acknowledged that his relationship with Diane was a two-way street, and he was run over in both directions. He was blinded by her beauty and intellect, and only realized he was Diane's pawn nearly two years later when she admitted using him to blot the memory of her true love, Sam.

Frasier's depression continued for several months, so Sam and Diane created a scheme to cure the good doctor. Sam approached Frasier with symptoms of depression in the hope he would properly diagnose the problem and regain confidence in his abilities as a therapist. However, after their first session, Frasier unexpectedly concluded that Sam and Diane were still in love. Despite being told the truth about their conspiracy to fabricate depression symptoms, Frasier remained sanguine in his diagnosis and returned to the psychiatric profession.

Although Frasier never rekindled his romance with Diane, he was envious of others who possessed her. When Boston city council candidate James Fleener expressed interest in Diane, Frasier dissuaded any intrigue by insisting she had had a sex-change operation.

Relationships—Lilith Sternin

Frasier and Lilith began their inevitable union with a calamitous first date during which he appraised her as passionless, stoic and emotionally numb.

Their evening ended early with no expectation of a second date. In spite of this, Frasier continued expressing a romantic interest in Lilith by stalking her. He called her at all hours of the night and hung up when she answered, went through her mail, and sat in his car, watching her house at night.

Fatefully, they were scheduled to debate psychological issues on the local PBS television program "Psychology This Week" and were eager to demonstrate their intellectual superiority. Diane recognized the embittered asperity between Frasier and Lilith as sexual magnetism, and gave Lilith a beauty makeover. After she unveiled her new image on the television program, Frasier was awestruck. Their psychological discourse became entangled in sexual metaphors, and they concluded the broadcast by playing footsy. Notwithstanding their chagrin, personally and professionally, later that day they returned to Frasier's tastefully decorated town house to physically consummate their relationship.

Frasier and Lilith subsequently moved in together and referred to their cohabitation by the acronym POSSLQ (People of the Opposite Sex Sharing Living Quarters). In appreciation for Diane and Sam bringing the doctors together (though Diane deserved most of the credit), Frasier and Lilith arranged a dinner party for the foursome. The entire evening was catastrophic. Everyone but Sam was exasperated when secrets were revealed, and they took turns locking themselves in the bathroom.

On the one-year anniversary of the day they met, Frasier and Lilith exchanged gifts. He gave Lilith an antique Louis Quatorze armoire, and she gave Frasier a gray tie. He was gravely disappointed because he wanted a set of golf clubs. Shortly thereafter, Lilith gave Frasier an ultimatum: to marry or terminate their relationship. As he pondered the options available, the Cheers gang sadistically convinced Frasier that Rebecca had a love interest in him. Armed with a lady-in-waiting, he wrote Lilith a missive explaining they should see other people. Nonetheless, after realizing Rebecca did not even know he existed, Frasier rushed home to resuscitate his relationship with Lilith by explaining that Rebecca wanted him but he cast her aside. Lilith confronted Rebecca, discovered the truth, and then chastened Frasier by requiring him to formally discontinue the affinity.

Frasier and Lilith's relationship inevitably evolved into matrimony. Frasier's bachelor party was held at Cheers and featured a stripper, Karen, who turned out to be one of his patients. After several derogatory remarks about matrimony, Lilith gave Frasier the option to change his mind about their impending nuptials. Despite reservations, he went forth with the plans, and Sam was selected as the best man. The wedding gifts included a set of *Star Trek* steak knives courtesy of Norm and Vera, and an astrological chart from Carla that ultimately predicted their marriage would descend into a life of interminable embroilment.

On their one-month wedding anniversary, Frasier purchased an original

Tidwell painting titled, *Number 7*, but after ascertaining that Lilith despised this particular painter and painting, Frasier proffered his Mercedes. The most costly gift he ever gave was for their fifth wedding anniversary—he vowed not to quarrel with Lilith's mother during her Boston visit.

Lilith was equally generous in her gifts to Frasier. For his birthday she gave him an enlarged photograph of herself sprawled across a bearskin rug, wearing nothing but a business suit! (Privately she bestowed more revealing photographs taken by Henri.) As for sexual hang-ups: Frasier and Lilith scheduled appointments to make love, they never made love during daylight hours (Lilith refused to oblige), and she always undressed in the dark (Frasier asked her to).

Frasier and Lilith once yearned to abandon civilization to live in the wilderness. Lilith's impending motherhood prompted primal desires of returning to nature. She began sewing clothes, and vowed to eat only the food Frasier killed. Sam convinced them to spend one weekend at a cabin in Maine to test their commitment to a wilderness existence. After a few hours of cabin life (absent light, heat or food) the allurement vanished, but the ultimate inducement prompting Frasier and Lilith to return to their pretentious lifestyles was a newspaper review for La Porta's, a trendy Boston restaurant.

Lilith referred to Frasier by using various nicknames, such as Cinnamon Bear, Jelly Bear, Duckling, Fawn, Snowball, Dandelion, Darling, Darling Face, Dearest, Prometheus, Conan, My Steed, Tootsie Roll, and Frasier-Doodle.

Relationships—Others

After Lilith had an affair, separated from Frasier, and left with her lover to live in the Ecopod, Frasier had two opportunities at romance. In the first instance, his temporary secretary, Shauna, expressed an interest in dating the doctor. The Cheers gang convinced him to spend the evening with her, so he bought a toupee for the evening (fortunately Sam convinced him not to wear it). When Frasier went to Shauna's house for dinner, he was met at the door by Shauna and her parents. The evening worsened as Frasier discovered Shauna had used him as a pawn against her parents, who disapproved of her boyfriend, Rick. After a vehement family argument, Frasier spent the night playing Yahtzee with Shauna's parents.

In the other instance, Frasier was depressed after receiving a telegram which stated Lilith was requesting a divorce. The Cheers gang held a divorce party, and Rebecca offered condolences. After chauffeuring Frasier to his town house, they submitted to their feelings for each other and spent the night together. As they lay in bed (though never physically consummating), Lilith returned from the Ecopod to witness the tryst.

Cheers

Frasier first visited Cheers in 1984 to help Sam overcome his drinking dependency. Within a short period of time, Cheers became his support system and the patrons his primary source of companionship. As part of his initiation into the pack, the Cheers gang took Frasier snipe hunting. They went into the woods, and as the bagger (Frasier) stood in a clearing holding a gunnysack, the others (Cheers gang) went into the bushes to beat out the snipe, i.e., they went out for dinner and returned to Cheers for beers. Frasier spent two hours in the woods before deducing he was duped.

One of the gang's most significant errors was destroying Frasier's last will and testament. Carla accidentally burned the will after mistaking the envelope as containing Sam's fertility test results. During a "flash forward" scene, years later, after Frasier's death, the attorney read the contents of the will and promulgated, "Sam Malone's sperm count is well within the normal range." Lilith responded, "That damn bar!"

Frasier also had his share of dissension with the gang. The most emphatic tirade occurred when Norm and Cliff reported his credit card stolen. Sam was not privy to the antic, and cut Frasier's gold card in half. Frasier vowed never to return to Cheers. Norm and Cliff eventually divulged their machination so Frasier and Sam could propitiate their friendship.

When Frasier helped the Cheers gang by frequenting their enterprising new business, Tan 'N' Wash, he was burned by tanning bed number three (the Bahama Mama) because it had a faulty thermoregulator. Frasier was burned so severely that he described himself as impersonating a blood blister.

In one of Frasier's more mortifying moments, he accompanied Carla to a hockey game and was consumed by the controlled mayhem. When a spectator would not remove his hat, Frasier did it for him, so the man returned the hat with his fist. Frasier was arrested, but the subsequent charges were dropped, provided he underwent seven hours of psychological counseling.

Some of the debasing nicknames perpetrated upon Frasier included: Spineless Bastard, Wimpy, Neanderthal Husband, Dr. Death, Dr. Cyclops, Chrome Dome, Receding Hairy Man, Fat Head, Egghead, Silver Spoon Egghead, Dr. Von Ego, Pompous Twit, Snobby Know-it-all Windbag, Licentious Quack, and Compulsive Anal Retentive Chowderhead.

Lilith Sternin-Crane

Childhood and Family

Lilith was born in 1957 and began wearing her hair in a bun when she was three days old. The daughter of a Jewish family, Lilith was not very close to her relatives and had a very demanding mother, Betty Sternin. Lilith was never able to stand up to her mother and became very submissive in her presence; her childhood was filled with fear of her mother's scorn and contempt. Although Lilith's parents' occupations were unknown, her grandfather was a butter and egg man in New Jersey. Her great uncle was born in 1894, and would commence a rousing rendition of "Over There" whenever he saw Frasier (whom he referred to as "colonel").

One traumatic childhood memory was when Lilith's father asked her to close her eyes, and then left for two years. Lilith had at least one childhood friend, Dorothy Greenberg, who later moved to New York. Dorothy became a professional student specializing in the comuneros uprising in Paraguay during the 17th century.

In high school Lilith was a bad seed and never learned to drive because she was always too busy having fun! She eventually learned to drive two decades later, after convincing Sam to be her instructor. Sam quit after one lesson when Lilith gave a trucker the finger, gunned the car up to 80 m.p.h., and ran him off the road. The bumper sticker on the truck read, "Insured by Smith & Wesson." She then pushed her finger into the folds of the trucker's neck (thinking Sam could take him), and Sam sustained a bloody nose.

Personal

Lilith had cold, gray eyes, and one foot larger than the other (which necessitated left and right sock drawers). Her delicate constitution forbade her from consuming shallots, and she was allergic to strawberries. Moreover, Lilith loathed being photographed because the film was always overexposed, making her look as white as a ghost.

As for her personal interests, Lilith's favorite flower was the rose (her mother loved cascading lilies), she loved to bathe in Mr. Bubble, and her favorite hiding place was the balcony of Cheers. Moreover, Lilith's favorite Marx Brother was Zeppo (it cracked her up when he stood there with no expression on his face), and favorite figure from the Pre-Rafaelite Brotherhood was Christina Rossetti, the sister of Dante Gabriel Rossetti, a 19th-century poet.

Lilith knew the lyrics to "My Funny Valentine," and the one piece of music that turned her into a cheap tramp was "Che gelida manina" (roughly translated to "your tiny hand is frozen") from *La Bohème*. After watching a male stripper, Randy, at her bridal shower, Lilith was never able to listen to the song "Shock the Monkey" by Peter Gabriel without crying.

Lilith believed the best way to overcome the fear of aging was reliving your childhood and listening to heavy doses of CCR (Creedence Clearwater Revival, a 1970s rock group). She first experienced the death of a loved one when her favorite laboratory research rat, Whitey, died.

Other miscellaneous information: Lilith refused to have sex during daylight hours; she could hear a dog whistle; she refused to allow a Christmas tree in the house; and the words she will always cherish are "Lilith, I want to marry you anyway" (spoken by Frasier).

Some of the pejorative nicknames used in reference to Lilith include: Blimpy (referring to her pregnancy and being two weeks overdue), Madame Ovary, Brunhilda, Elvira, Death with Hips, Ice Cube in Heels, Morticia, and Chalk Face.

Career

Lilith worked as a research psychologist at Boston General Hospital earning $60,000 per year, and her professional accreditations include M.D., Ph.D., E.D.D. and A.P.A. She preached the psychological tenets of behaviorism and despised Sigmund Freud because his theories are outdated, unsupported by clinical data, sexist and superstitious. Lilith was a member of the Psychoanalytic and Social Therapeutic Practitioners Society, and her lab assistant was Otto.

In her research, Lilith worked extensively with rats, and she believed that the laboratory rats worshiped her as a goddess. She had two favorite rats: Whitey and Whiskers. After Whitey died, Whiskers (also known by the lab identification number 17A) became Lilith's favorite.

Lilith's clinical success culminated in the publication of the book *Good Girls, Bad Boys.* (The title was her editor's idea; she wanted *A Cross-sectional Study of Control Group Females with a Tendency Toward Self-destruction, Vis-à-vis Damaging Relationships with Members of the Opposite Sex.*) Lilith's research hypothesized that women are attracted to men who are bad for them because they represent danger. However, once outgrowing the "bad boy," they make mature decisions and eventually lead lives with upstanding, substantial men. Lilith promoted her book with a guest appearance on "Teatime with Brenda," hosted by Brenda Balzak on channel 13 at 3:30 p.m., on February 15, 1990. Lilith used Sam and Frasier to represent the "bad boy" and "good boy," respectively. While describing Sam's physical attraction, she became titillated and propelled herself at him. Although nothing ever came of the incident, Frasier was quite distraught.

Lilith also had success with a paper she wrote on sensory deprivation. She inadvertently locked her lab assistant, Otto, in the isolation chamber before leaving on a two-week vacation. What could have been a serious lawsuit turned into an award-winning paper!

Miscellaneous information regarding her career: Lilith had two more years of dream analysis experience than Frasier; she authored more books than Frasier; and she wrote more articles in a year than he read.

Relationships—Frasier Crane

Lilith and Frasier had their first meaningful social interaction when they went on a date. However, the evening was disastrous. Lilith ended the date early, and Frasier labeled her as passionless, stoic and emotionally numb. The closest they came to physical contact was Lilith slamming the car door on Frasier's hand. Although despising Frasier when they first met, Lilith subsequently admitted he was her first love (though Lilith's mother never outgrew her disdain for him). A few months later, they were reunited for a psychological debate on a local PBS program, "Psychology This Week." Since Lilith and Frasier were still embittered from their dating fiasco, they relished the opportunity to demonstrate their intellectual superiority.

Beneath the acrimony, Diane recognized the sexual attraction between them and gave Lilith a beauty makeover to soften and refine her rigid appearance. During the debate, Lilith and Frasier were excited to a sexual frenzy, and after a lengthy discussion using sexual metaphors, they ended the broadcast by playing footsy. Notwithstanding their embarrassment, they returned to Frasier's town house to express their feelings.

In their relationship, Frasier used various pet names to refer to Lilith, such as Sweet Potato, Peach Blossom, Blossom Bottom, Little Chopped Salad, Parsnip, Wild Asparagus, Pea Pod, My Sweet, Sugar, Sugar Pants, Peanut Butter Cup, Buttercup, Popsicle, Jelly Bean, Moon Pie, Marine Melon, Angel, Angel Face, Dear Heart, My Treasure, Cherub, Dove Bar, Little Starlet, Little Badger, and Firebrand.

Frasier proposed marriage to Lilith at Cheers, and she responded, "Yes, my steed. Yes." Although matrimony was inevitable, there were two incidents that nearly impeded their union. In the first, Frasier made disparaging remarks about marriage, so Lilith gave him the opportunity to rescind his proposal and cancel the wedding. The other vexatious moment occurred when Frasier asked Lilith to sign a prenuptial agreement. Aghast and dismayed by Frasier's request, Lilith retaliated by paying $2,000 for a romantic weekend with Sam (as part of a celebrity charity auction). Her plan worked. In a fit of jealous rage, Frasier stormed into the hotel room to reaffirm his love for Lilith (and forsook the notion of a prenuptial agreement).

As the wedding approached, Rebecca organized a bridal shower at Carla's house, purchasing napkins with the inscription "Matzeltov Sy and Effie Kupperman" (Rebecca received a discount price when Sy left town with his secretary). The women had a wild evening highlighted by a male strip show, and Lilith became so intoxicated she propositioned the stripper, Randy. The party ended early when the women engaged in a fistfight over which was better, mayonnaise or Miracle Whip. In addition to organizing the bridal shower, Rebecca was the maid of honor (even though they only knew each other a few months). The wedding reception was held at Cheers; however, since Lilith's mother was not able to attend the wedding or reception, on their fifth wedding anniversary she demanded Lilith and Frasier re-enact their wedding vows.

Lilith's closest Bostonian friend was Rebecca. On one occasion, Lilith transformed Rebecca's image into something more professional and businesslike. Although Rebecca remained unnoticed at the corporate meeting in Melville's, Lilith was offered a position as vice president of the eastern seaboard.

Relationships — Dr. Pascal

Lilith was involved in one other romantic relationship. After seven years of marriage, she found herself working side by side with researcher Dr. Louis Pascal. Lilith was attracted to Dr. Pascal (also known as Googie) primarily because he enabled her to act uncharacteristically spontaneous and uninhibited. He filled a void in Lilith's disciplined and regimented life. Although she tried to fill it with awards and accomplishments, Lilith eventually yearned for something else. Rebecca first discovered the adulterous relationship when Lilith was enthusiastically kissing Dr. Pascal in his Lexus. Lilith confessed the truth to Frasier and announced her desire for a trial separation.

Lilith and Dr. Pascal arranged to cohabit in the Ecopod (a self-contained, mile-wide subterranean environment beneath the desert floor that was to serve as a prototype for an eventual space station for human colonization—like the Biosphere, only on a larger scale). The plan was to have two humans occupy the Ecopod for one year, and Lilith was going to be part of this experiment. During her absence, Frasier was given custody of Frederick. Unfortunately, just moments after the lid to the Ecopod was sealed, Dr. Pascal revealed his claustrophobia, went insane, and invented an imaginary friend, Dr. Jaworski. (While she was there, Frasier provided prank telephone calls nightly.)

Lilith lived in the Ecopod for six months before escaping. However, the effects of living underground were indelible. Lilith insisted upon sleeping in the cellar (you can take the girl out of the Ecopod, but you can't take the Ecopod out of the girl!). Upon returning to Boston, she caught Frasier in bed with Rebecca. After considerable effort and persuasion, Lilith and Frasier were reconciled.

Children

Lilith and Frasier's only child was Frederick. He was born on November 2, 1989 (two weeks overdue), the same day as the 100th anniversary celebration of the opening of Cheers. Lilith experienced labor pains during the celebration and was accompanied to the hospital by Frasier and Sam. Since she had false labor pains, Frasier and Sam assisted another woman, Gail Aldrich, in the delivery room, and Lilith took a taxicab home. On the trip home, she went into labor again and gave birth in the backseat of the taxi (enduring the pain by biting down on the cab driver's foam rubber dice).

Frederick was one week old when he first visited Cheers, and returned the following day for a ceremonial bris (circumcision). Although the bris was originally scheduled at the Crane residence, Frasier kidnapped Frederick to save him from the knife. Lilith located the pair hiding in the Cheers office and reasoned with Frasier to allow the circumcision. The bris was performed by Dr. Levinson in the Cheers poolroom and also functioned as the entertainment for a corporate employee's retirement party.

Lilith opted to stay home to care for Frederick, but the Cranes also hired nannies, such as Torsten, a Swedish male, and a young lady to whom Lilith referred to as a 16-year-old bundle of breasts. Although Frederick was scheduled to attend a prestigious day care (Magic Hours Learning Center), he was not accepted because of an irascible confrontation between his parents at the conclusion of the admission interview.

Frederick's educational career suffered a further setback when his I.Q. test results showed he was average. Lilith and Frasier were despondent about this revelation and aghast that this was even conceivable, especially considering their stature and intelligence. Frasier ultimately blamed Lilith's inferior gene pool (i.e., the granddaughter of an egg and butter man from New Jersey).

When he was 11 months old, Frederick said his first word, "Norm!" His first concert was the Nanny Gee "1992 Tickle Tummy Tour"; his favorite song was Al Jolson's "Sonny Boy"; and his favorite book was *The Runaway Bunny*. Lilith forbade Frederick from playing with toys depicting violence.

At age 2, Frederick was nearly denied the ghoulish tradition to trick-or-treat on Halloween. Lilith despised the ritual of begging for non-nutritious treats from strangers, but conceded when the ritual was limited to Cheers. For his first Halloween experience, Frederick dressed as Spiderman (and Lilith dressed as Christina Rossetti, her favorite figure from the Pre-Rafaelite Brotherhood).

Ernie "Coach" Pantusso

Personal History and Family

Of Italian descent, Ernie Pantusso had two nicknames: Coach and Red. The former sobriquet was given by some guy named Barry because Ernie was a former coach in the minor and major leagues. Coach thought he was given the nickname because he never flew first class! The byname "Red" was given by his teammates because he had read a book.

Coach had at least three siblings—a sister and two brothers. His sister lived in Minnesota and was just like Coach. When Coach went to visit her, he asked to be picked up at the airport, and she drove to the *Boston* airport. Fortunately, that was what he meant! Coach's older brother was the artist in the family and extremely cruel. During their youth, he used to dunk Coach's head under water. Coach's baby brother lived in Reedsport, Oregon, with his family. His wife, Phyllis, was a calligrapher, and his daughter, Joyce, attended Boston University. When Joyce moved to Boston, she was escorted by the quaintly impressionable Woody Boyd. Ingenuousness gave way to lustfulness, and soon the lovebirds contemplated marriage or at least cohabitation. Sam and Diane eventually persuaded the youthful lovers merely to date.

Coach loved his grandfather's dog, but it died after falling down in the bathtub, and his grandfather deceased after being hit by a bus. Since 1978 Coach attended an annual family reunion in Ohio—he was accidentally sent an invitation and did not want to disappoint anyone. The family loved him so much they invited him annually, and inured him with the appellation "Uncle Whitey" (they were an African-American family).

Personal

Although good looking, Coach was no Harold Flynn (not Errol Flynn), a second baseman for the Chicago Cubs—good looks, no hit! Surprisingly, Coach retained his good looks despite having an unusual habit of banging his head on the bar when he was furious.

Coach was frequently conned by cardsharps and salespeople. An elderly patron, George Wheeler (alias Eddie "the Mole," Moley and Moleman in Phoenix; and Sid in Philadelphia), played gin with Coach daily. The friendly game cost Coach $8,000 before local con Harry "the Hat" Gittes concocted an elaborate ruse to cozen George in a poker match. Coach was also conned into purchasing land in Florida and buying the Old North Church in Boston (which he had a difficult time unloading to some unsuspecting soul). Finally, Ducky Hedges borrowed $50 and never repaid the loan.

Coach had a lengthy history of being absentminded, but pleasingly so. After forgetting to wear his winter jacket, he entered the bar shivering and concerned about having malaria. He also had a habit of forgetting his car keys in the bar. To remedy this, he kept the original set of keys in the car and carried an extra set of keys. True to character, he locked the keys in the car and then forgot the second set of keys at the bar.

Coach owned a station wagon when he was married, and despite having never been to Hawaii or Utah, he once traveled to Vermont to get a driver's license because he heard the test was easier! In addition, Coach had a special talent for consuming things that were not food, and had a personal record for going 11 consecutive days without starting a major fire.

Other miscellaneous information: Coach banked at Bay Harbor Savings and Loan; in guessing games he loved to answer "Julius Laroza"; his gallbladder was located in Providence, Rhode Island; and he always had a saying about the afterlife, "I hope there aren't a lot of stairs!"

Personal Favorites

Coach's lucky number was three, and his favorite time of day was 1:37 a.m. (though it was formerly 8:15 p.m.). Coach's favorite actor was Robert Mitchum, and since 1972 he watched every Mitchum movie with Sam. Coach knew every line to the movie *Thunder Road*, and just the thought of the movie *Fort Apache* made the hair on his arms stand straight up.

Education

Coach did not have a pleasant parochial education. He was compelled to either memorize the poem "A Birthday" by Christina Rossetti or have his knuckles smacked with rosary beads. Coach had difficulty memorizing "The Pledge of Allegiance" and despised his teacher, Mr. Spires, for the humiliation of having to deliver the pledge in front of his entire class in the school auditorium.

Coach never received a high school diploma because he skipped grades 9 through 12. In 1985 he enrolled in a night school geography class taught by Miss Alannah Purdy. After receiving an "A" on the final exam, he earned the highest grade in the class. It could have been Coach's unique studying technique that earned him such an honor. He set the material to music and substituted the original song lyrics with factual information about each country.

Coach tried to learn foreign languages, but had little success. His French tapes merely taught him to speak English with a French accent, and he only knew two Spanish phrases, meaning "How tall is my dentist?" and "Is that really your sister?" However, after a one-night crash course with Sam's brother, Derek, Coach learned to speak Spanish fluently.

Employment and Baseball

In his youth, Coach began working as a busboy, and subsequently enlisted in the Navy, being stationed in Pensacola, Florida. His dream was to play and coach baseball, and eventually become a bartender in a nice place. His dream came true.

Baseball

Donning jersey number 47, Coach played minor league ball for the St. Louis Browns and the Birmingham Barons. While playing for the Browns organization, he perfected his specialty—being hit by pitches (HBPs). He led the league in HBPs two years in a row, and held the record for the most HBPs in a career. Coach proudly exalted he must have been hit in the head with at least 100 fastballs (and never wore a helmet).

Coach was sent to the Birmingham Barons when an ultimatum went awry. The managers were going to send his best friend, T-Bone Scorpageoni, to the Barons, so Coach said, "If T-Bone goes, then I go." (Regardless, Coach had a good time in Birmingham.) T-Bone retired and moved to Phoenix, his final resting place. Coach's other teammates included Artie, Tom, Charlie, Lefty, and Scooter McGrath. Coach was particularly impressed with Topeka player Danny "the Blindman" Corelli a.k.a. "Fancy Dan." Fancy Dan was known as "the Blindman" because he sold venetian blinds during the off-season (Coach thought Dan was truly blind).

Coach had the opportunity to coach in the minor and major leagues. He coached for Pawtucket, the Red Sox minor league team, and eventually moved up the ranks to become third base coach for the Red Sox. He was Sam's pitching coach, and taught him to throw a knuckleball. Coach's most inspirational words to Sam were "Blow it, and I don't know you."

Coach loved the fans the most. His favorite fan was Rosie McGonigal. Prior to betting against the Celtics in 1983, she was the last sure thing he had. Coach also loved the players, particularly the practical jokes of Red Sox catcher Tom Kenderson. Tom put Coach's toothbrush in sweaty socks, placed dead animals in his locker, shaved his whole body, and once put an analgesic balm in his jock strap. Coach thought of Tom every time he had jock itch.

In the major league, the highest position Coach attained was third base coach. He was ultimately fired because he never said anything to the players when they made mental errors. As the head coach of a youth league team, the Titans, Coach became a tyrant obsessed with winning. Although his team was successful, earning the right to compete in the championship game, the players revolted and threatened to quit. Faced with the realization that he was turning into the type of person he loathed as a child, Coach returned to his usual affability.

Coach had another opportunity, to coach in the Venezuelan winter league. Eddie Fuentes tried to procure the position while Coach learned Spanish. Despite becoming fluent in Spanish, Coach was not hired. They loved his Spanish, but his *English* was the problem!

Relationships

Coach's only wife, Angela, passed away during their marriage, and the song "A Foggy Day" sung by Frank Sinatra always rekindled endearing memories of her. They were introduced through Wally Angells, and Coach knew he would marry Angela the moment he laid eyes on her because he was struck by "the thunderbolt" (an Italian phrase for love at first sight). Coach loved her so much he became insanely jealous and enraged when learning that T-Bone once made a pass at Angela. (Coach was able to forgive him, and later discovered T-Bone made passes at all the teammates' wives.)

Coach and Angela had one child, and selecting the baby's name resulted in the most tumultuous argument they ever had. Angela wanted Lisa, and although Coach liked the name Becky, he wanted the original name, Baby Girl Pantusso. Angela won the fight. Lisa adored Rocky Road ice cream and lived in Pennsylvania where she became a district manager for Omni, a company selling business suits door to door. Lisa remained single after rejecting her only suitor, Roy, an obnoxious Omni salesman who loved female full-contact karate. He was the top salesman in the New Jersey territory, and only proposed marriage to acquire the Pennsylvania sales territory. Lisa accepted the marriage proposal because she was concerned about becoming an old maid. Coach ultimately convinced her that she was beautiful and worthy of a special man in her life.

Prior to marriage, Coach had the perfect pickup line for alluring women in the stands. Whenever he saw an attractive woman, Coach would intentionally injure himself to gain her sympathy. He would lean into a pitch, dive face first into a bag, or take a real hard ground ball in the gut. Once, he was not in the game, so Coach caused a self-inflicted injury by throwing himself down the dugout steps. It worked every time.

Coach used the same suavity to gain the sympathy of Nina, an enchanting tenant who moved into his apartment building. Although Nina was much younger, Coach took Diane's advice and asked her for a date. When she rejected him, Coach did what he knew best—he threw himself down Melville's steps. It worked because she spent the evening nursing his injuries.

Coach was only struck by "the thunderbolt" twice in his life, with his first wife and with Irene Blanchard. The moment he laid eyes on Irene (in late 1984), Coach knew he was going to marry her. Coach wooed Irene and discovered they had so much in common: besides liking music and Italian food, she was a widow and he was a widower; she was a hairdresser, and he had hair; and neither of them had been to Utah. After dating for three weeks, he proposed marriage and she accepted. Coach asked Sam to be his best man.

Moments after the proposal, Irene won $2 million in the Massachusetts lottery. She immediately reneged on their wedding engagement. Coach waited patiently for her to get over the initial excitement of being affluent, and continued to organize their wedding. Irene eventually landed a wealthy European industrialist and moved to Carfu.

Sam and Diane arranged a blind date between Coach and Katherine, a bank teller. After a successful double date at an Italian restaurant, Coach walked her to the bus stop. (According to Coach, Katherine was nice but she did not fit in—she was like a fourth wheel!) Coach subsequently returned to the bus stop to speak with Katherine, and they began dating.

Cheers

Although Thursday was Coach's regular day off, he still worked (though he usually went a little slower).

Coach worked at Cheers until his death in 1985.

Coach began working at Cheers in 1977 and was adored by everyone, though Diane was especially enamored because he was the only person who appeared to care for her. She viewed him as her only true friend and a father figure. According to Coach, Diane was the smartest person he knew.

Coach's famous mixed drink was the Contikki Tikki. As a bartender, he inventoried the bar glasses by assigning personal names to each glass (two of the glasses were named Larry and Steve). Coach tried to make Cheers more classy by humming tunes into the receiver when he placed a telephone caller on hold.

Coach's barroom errors included being conned into purchasing useless products from various salespeople. For example, the Billiard Buddy Adaptor (an entertainment device that combined a billiard table, Ping-Pong table, knock-hockey table, and a slot-clock track) cost the bar $600. Coach also purchased 30 gross of cocktail napkins featuring a picture of two hunters, with one saying, "Did I hear a buck snort?" His final infamous purchase was an antique weight scale sold by a salesperson who was a cross between Abraham Lincoln and Adolf Hitler.

V. The Episodes

Season One: 1982–83

(NBC Thursday, 9:00–9:30 p.m. EST)
Season Regulars: Ted Danson (Sam Malone), Shelley Long (Diane Chambers), Nicholas Colasanto (Ernie "Coach" Pantusso), Rhea Perlman (Carla Tortelli), George Wendt (Norm Peterson).

Technical Credits: *Created by* Glen Charles, Les Charles and James Burrows. *Producers:* James Burrows, Glen Charles, Les Charles. *Co-Producers:* Ken Levine and David Isaacs. *Writers:* David Angell, Glen Charles, Les Charles, Ken Estin, Katherine Green, David Isaacs, Ken Levine, David Lloyd, Heide Perlman, Earl Pomerantz, Tom Reeder. *Director:* James Burrows. *Executive Script Consultant:* David Lloyd. *Associate Producer:* Tim Berry. *Directors of Photography:* John Finger, Kenneth Peach, A.S.C. *Art Director:* Ed La Porta. *Film Editors:* Andrew Chulack, Daniel T. Cahn, Robert A. Daniels, Douglas Hines, A.C.E. *Unit Production Manager:* Penny Adams Flowers. *First Assistant Directors:* Thomas Lofaro, Michael Stanislavsky. *Second Assistant Director:* Brian James Ellis. *Music by* Craig Safan. *Song:* "Where Everybody Knows Your Name." *Lyrics and Music* by Judy Hart Angelo and Gary Portnoy. *Sung by* Gary Portnoy. *Casting:* Stephen Kolzak. *Set Decorators:* Chuck Tycer, George Gaines. *Technical Coordinator:* Gil Clasen. *Script Supervisors:* Sonny Filippini, Gabrielle James, Doris Grau, Marge Mullen, Judy Redlin, Roberta S. Scelza. *Production Mixers:* John Hicks, James R. Wright. *Costume Supervisor:* Robert L. Tanella. *Women's Costumers:* Joyce Ann Unruh, Roberta Newman. *Makeup Artists:* Charlene Roberson, Brad Wilder. *Hair Stylists:* Charlotte Harvey, Marilyn Phillips. *Production Designer:* Richard Sylbert (#1). *Special Technical Advisor:* Harry Anderson (#19). *Music Editor:* Mary Morlas. *Sound Effects:* Ed Norton. *Main Title Design:* James Castle and Bruce Bryant. *Recorded by* Glen Glenn Sound. *Opticals:* Freeze Frame. *Assistants to the Charles Brothers:* Sharon Black, Mark Burman, Tony Colvin, Penelope Franks, Scott S. Gorden, Nancy Koppang, Glen Miller, Marsha Nadler, Mark Nardone, Diane Overdiek, Lana Repp Lewis, J.W. Smith, Lorraine Strode, Donna Wheeler, Alison E. Wrigley. *Executive in Charge of Production:* Richard Villarino. *Charles/Burrows/Charles Pro-*

ductions in Association with Paramount Television.

1. "Give Me a Ring Sometime"
(9/30/82). Diane Chambers and her fiancé, Sumner Sloane, enter Cheers to celebrate their wedding engagement en route to Barbados. Sumner leaves to retrieve his grandmother's antique gold wedding ring which happens to be on his ex-wife Barbara's finger. While waiting in solitude, Diane is entertained by the Cheers gang but unamused by their kindhearted, meddlesome nature. Sumner returns empty-handed, but quickly exits to visit Barbara one more time. When he fails to return, Diane discovers that Sumner and Barbara are on the flight to Barbados. Diane's life is shattered, so Sam kindly offers and she accepts a waitress position at Cheers.
Written by Glen Charles and Les Charles. *Directed by* James Burrows.
Characters: Michael McGuire (Sumner Sloane), John P. Navin, Jr. (Boy), Ron Frazier (Ron), Erik Holland (Customer), John Ratzenberger (Cliff).
Note: Michael McGuire subsequently appeared in "Empire" (as Edward Roland).

2. "Sam's Women" (10/7/82).
Diane is appalled by Sam's choice of women—busty and brainless—so he strives to find one intelligent woman in his harem. After failing to impress her with Debra, Sam becomes infuriated because he used to have fun with these women and now all he thinks about is how stupid they are. **Subtopic:** A patron, Leo, enters the bar to discuss a personal problem. Coach accepts the challenge which involves the homosexual relationship between Leo's Caucasian son, Rick, and an African-

American male, Ron. Using his ingenuous style of persuasion, Coach unwittingly convinces Leo to accept his son for who he is or risk losing him for good.
Written by Earl Pomerantz. *Directed by* James Burrows.
Characters: Donnelly Rhodes (Leo Metz), Donna McKechnie (Debra), Keenen Wayans (Customer #1), Jack Knight (Jack), Angela Aames (Brandee), John Ratzenberger (Cliff).
Note: Donnelly Rhodes may be remembered for his role in "Soap" (as Dutch). Keenen Wayans received the most notoriety for his television show "In Living Color," and his movie credits include *Star 80* (1983), *Eddie Murphy Raw* (1987), *I'm Gonna Git You Sucker* (1988), and *The Five Heartbeats* (1991). Angela Aames appeared in "B.J. and the Bear" (as Honey, a pistol packing mama) and "The Dom DeLuise Show" (as Penny).
Notable Quote: On Sam's dating a different woman every night:
DIANE: "He's overcompensating for feelings of inadequacy with an ostentatious display of hormonal activity."
NORM: "That's our Sammy!"

3. "The Tortelli Tort" (10/14/82).
An obnoxious Yankee fan, Big Eddie, visits Cheers and relentlessly ridicules the Red Sox. After Big Eddie harasses Sam about his drinking problem, Carla jumps on his back and repeatedly beats his head on the bar countertop. Eddie threatens a lawsuit but agrees to settle if Sam terminates Carla's employment. Sam seriously considers the proposal, but reconsiders when Carla agrees to undergo psychological counseling to control her temper. Sam convinces Eddie to give her a second chance; Eddie tests her resolve

by insulting various Boston sports franchises, and when she calmly accepts the insults, Eddie drops the lawsuit.

Written by Tom Reeder. *Directed by* James Burrows.

Characters: Ron Karabatsos (Eddie, Stephen Keep (Dr. Graham), Thomas Babson (Customer #1), Richard Mc-Gonagle (Customer #2), Paul Vaughn (Customer #3), Rex Ryon (Rough Looking Guy #1), John Fiedler (Fred), John Ratzenberger (Cliff).

Notable Quote: On Big Eddie teasing Sam about his alcoholism while playing baseball:

EDDIE: "Hey, what was it like pitching to two guys at the same time? Better yet, what was it like coming in with bases loaded, and so were you?"

4. "Sam at Eleven" (10/21/82). Dave Richards asks Sam to be a guest on the television sportscast segment "Where Are They Now?" Shortly after commencing the interview, Dave is notified that John McEnroe wants an exclusive interview, so Dave and his crew immediately pack up their equipment and exit the bar. Sam becomes depressed because this incident officially ended his baseball career. Diane offers consolation by sharing one of her painful childhood memories, but he is neither interested nor appreciative. **Subtopic:** Con man Harry "the Hat" quenches his thirst and supplements his income by preying upon the Cheers gang with various hat, coin, and card tricks.

Written by Glen Charles and Les Charles. *Directed by* James Burrows.

Characters: Fred Dryer (Dave Richards), Paul Vaughn (Customer #1), Eapen Mathai (the Recordist), Michael Mann (the Guy), Harry Anderson (Harry), John Ratzenberger (Cliff).

Note: Fred Dryer later starred in "Hunter" (as Rick Hunter, 1984-91). Harry Anderson is best remembered as the star of "Night Court" (as Judge Harold T. Stone), but also starred in "Dave's World" and the less successful "Our Time." His movie credits include the starring role in Disney's *The Absent-minded Professor* (1988).

Notable Quote: In response to Diane's flipping Sam onto the pool table after he kissed her:

DIANE: "It's a reflex. I learned it in a class—Practical Feminism."

SAM: "What was your final, crippling a Buick?"

5. "The Coach's Daughter" (10/28/82). Coach's daughter, Lisa, brings her fiancé, Roy, to Cheers. Roy is an obnoxious, outspoken door-to-door business suit salesman who quickly offends everyone. Disgusted with his mannerisms, the Cheers gang persuades Coach to speak with Lisa before she marries him. During their conversation, Lisa admits that Roy is insufferable and only marrying her for a company promotion. However, she is concerned about becoming an old maid. After a heart-to-heart discussion, Coach eventually convinces Lisa that she is special and worthy of someone better than Roy. **Subtopic:** Diane tries to captivate customers with her original caricature sketches, but her drawings prove to be lacking (mostly in resemblance).

Written by Ken Estin. *Directed by* James Burrows.

Characters: Allyce Beasley (Lisa Pantusso), Philip Charles MacKenzie (Roy), Tim Cunningham (Chuck), Jacqueline Cassel (Woman #1), Teddy Bergeron (Man #1), John Ratzenberger (Cliff).

Note: Allyce Beasley appeared regularly in "Moonlighting" (as receptionist Agnes Dipesto).

6. **"Any Friend of Diane's"** (11/4/82). Diane's Russian poet friend, Rebecca Prout, seeks solace after her husband, Elliot, elopes with another woman. To overcome her melancholy, Rebecca wants one night of uninhibited, bestial pleasure—to burn at the stake of passion with a simple, peasant-stock man. Although Sam willingly accommodates her request, Rebecca bores him with dismal Russian poems, so he escapes through a window. His unexpected departure makes her feel unattractive, so Sam and Diane pretend they had a lovers' quarrel to convince Rebecca that he only accepted her proposition to make Diane jealous. **Subtopic**: Norm tries to impress a client, Darrell Stabell, by abstaining from alcohol.

Written by Ken Levine and David Isaacs. *Directed by* James Burrows.

Characters: Julia Duffy (Rebecca Prout), Macon McCalman (Darrell Stabell), John Ratzenberger (Cliff).

Note: Julia Duffy may be best remembered for her roles in "Newhart" (as Stephanie Vanderkellen), "Designing Women" (as Allison Sugarbaker), and "Mommies" (as the irritating neighbor Barb). She also appeared in "The Doctors" (as Penny Davis, 1972–77) and "Love of Life" (as Gerry Brayley).

Notable Quote:

COACH: "How's life treating you, Norm?"

NORM: "Like he caught me in bed with his wife."

7. **"Friends, Romans, Accountants"** (11/11/82). Norm volunteers as party director for his accounting firm's annual get-together and organizes a toga party at Cheers. On party night, Norm is the only accountant wearing a toga, and his predicament escalates when the female escort cancels her date with the company president, Herb Sawyer. Norm solicits Diane to be Herb's date for the evening, and although reluctant, she agrees because Herb is attractive. Herb expects a promiscuous date, so when they are alone in the poolroom he begins mauling Diane. As she resists his advances, Norm intervenes to physically remove the company president from the bar, and in the process is fired from his job.

Written by Ken Levine and David Isaacs. *Directed by* James Burrows.

Characters: James Read (H.W. Sawyer), Kenneth Kimmins (Fred Wilson), Jonathan Terry (Accountant #1), Jim Hudson (Accountant #2), Peter Van Norden (Cymbals Player), Edie Berry (Accountant #3), John Ratzenberger (Cliff).

Notable Quote: Diane, responding to the Cheers gang teasing her:

DIANE: "You know, Sam, if I'm to serve both as a waitress and a butt of jokes, I think I should make more money."

CARLA: "Yeah, what does a good butt make in this town?"

8. **"Truce or Consequences"** (11/18/82). Carla and Diane continue their interminable feuding and elect to spend the evening together at Cheers to resolve their differences. For the occasion, Carla mixes a special drink, Leap Into an Open Grave, and when they begin to catch a buzz, she tests Diane's ability to keep a secret. Carla confides that Sam is the father of her then youngest son, Gino. Of course, Diane cannot keep a secret, and after speaking with Coach, realizes Carla lied. Diane is incensed with Carla's

intentional deception, and they engage in a heated argument. After Sam intervenes to mediate the dispute, Diane soon appreciates the absurdity of the lie.

Written by Ken Levine and David Isaacs. *Directed by* James Burrows.

Characters: Jack Knight (Jack), David A. Penhale (Customer #1), John Ratzenberger (Cliff).

Notable Quote: After Diane and Carla have a few peaceful moments together:

DIANE: "You know, I think we're coming together."

CARLA: "That's the open grave [a potent alcoholic drink]. Give it another 15 minutes and you'll be French-kissing the sump pump."

9. **"The Coach Returns to Action"** (11/25/82). Coach is physically attracted to Nina, a new tenant in his apartment building, but lacks the confidence to ask her for a date. When Nina visits Cheers, she adamantly rejects Sam's repeated propositions, which leads him to conclude she is undatable. Diane believes otherwise and begins building Coach's confidence until he agrees to ask Nina for a date. Nina respectfully declines his offer, but Coach still has one last trick up his sleeve. He resorts to an old technique he used in his ball playing days—intentionally injuring himself—and throws himself down Melville's steps. Nina takes the bait and spends the evening nursing Coach's injuries.

Written by Earl Pomerantz. *Directed by* James Burrows.

Characters: Murphy Cross (Nina), Bill Wiley (the Tour Guide), Keone Young (Tourist #1), Barry Cutler (Tourist #2), Eve Smith (Tourist #3), Julia Hendler (the Little Girl), John Ratzenberger (Cliff).

Notable Quote:

SAM: "What's up, Norm?"

NORM: "My nipples. It's freezing out there."

10. **"Endless Slumper"** (12/2/82). Red Sox pitcher Rick Walker consults Sam about how to break out of a slump. Sam recommends a good luck charm, such as his lucky bottle cap. Rick borrows the bottle cap, and his luck immediately changes for the better, whereas Sam experiences nothing but bad luck. After two weeks of misfortune, Sam confronts Rick about returning the talisman, and Rick confesses that he lost it in Kansas City. Sam is distraught because he has been having the urge to drink and needs the bottle cap to overcome the temptation. In a showdown with his battle against alcoholism, Sam resists the urge to drink and realizes his willpower, not the bottle cap, keeps him from drinking.

Written by Sam Simon. *Directed by* James Burrows.

Characters: Christopher McDonald (Rick Walker), Anne Haney (Miss Gilder), John Ratzenberger (Cliff).

Note: Christopher McDonald also appeared in "Good Advice" starring Shelley Long.

Notable Quote: On using meditation to break out of a pitching slump:

COACH: "What he [Rick Walker] needs to do is beef up his sex life. You know, see a little bit of the ladies. Take the edge off."

NORM: "He's right. Sammy here has taken off more edges than a carpenter."

11. **"One for the Book"** (12/9/82). A patron, Kevin, visits Cheers the day before entering a monastery. When alcohol lowers his inhibitions, he

passionately kisses Diane. Kevin begins doubting his life's calling, so Diane tries to reassure him to follow the path of the light. Kevin ultimately chooses the church after a "miracle" occurs—he put a quarter in a broken player piano and it began playing music. Coach subsequently confesses he had the piano fixed a few days earlier. **Subtopics:** A doughboy, Buzz Crowder, visits Cheers for a reunion with his World War I buddies, but soon realizes he is the only surviving member of the Fighting Double Deuce. Meanwhile, Diane documents bar quotes for a novel she is writing, which infuriates Sam because he is never quoted.

Written by Katherine Green. *Directed by* James Burrows.

Characters: Ian Wolfe (Buzz Crowder), Boyd Bodwell (Kevin), Jack Knight (Jack), Frank McCarthy (Mr. Phillips), John Ratzenberger (Cliff).

Notable Quote: On Kevin's entering the monastery:

KEVIN: "I have to take a vow of chastity. I also have to take a vow of silence."

NORM: "Yeah, if you're going to give up sex, you might as well give up talking. What fun is messing around if you can't tell the guys about it?"

12. **"The Spy Who Came in for a Cold One"** (12/16/82). A British patron (alias Eric Finch) impresses the Cheers gang by recalling outlandish stories of being a British counter-intelligence spy. However, Diane is not so easily fooled and spends the entire day exposing his lies. The moment she is convinced Finch is a pathological liar, she, too, succumbs to his charm when he claims to be a poet. After this falsehood is exposed, Finch confesses he is really multimillionaire Thomas Hilliard, III, and offers $1 million to purchase Cheers. Diane is outraged at the incessant prevarications and elaborate cons, and shreds the check in disgust. At that moment, a chauffeur enters the bar and confirms Mr. Hilliard's identity and wealth.

Written by David Lloyd. *Directed by* James Burrows.

Characters: Ellis Rabb (Eric Finch), Jack Knight (Jack), Robert Evan Collins (Chauffeur), Kurtis Woodruff (Sailor), John Ratzenberger (Cliff).

Notable Quote:
SAM: "What's new, Norm?"
NORM: "Most of my wife."

(NBC Thursday, 9:30–10:00 p.m. EST)

13. **"Now Pitching: Sam Malone"** (1/6/83). Sam meets a sexy sports agent, Lana, who is interested in using him as a spokesperson in various television commercials. Lana is well-known for her manipulation of male athletes by bartering television commercial contracts for sexual favors, and lures Sam by offering him an endorsement contract for Field's Lite Beer. He soon realizes the only way to continue receiving television commercial endorsements is to mix business with pleasure. Believe it or not, Sam objects to this arrangement, but it takes Diane and Coach to convince him to take a stand. When Sam ends the pleasure part of their relationship, Lana terminates the business part.

Written by Ken Levine and David Isaacs. *Directed by* James Burrows.

Characters: Barbara Babcock (Lana), Richard Hill (Tibor Svetkovic), Luis Tiant (Himself), Jan Rabson (Director), Paul Vaughn (Paul), John Ratzenberger (Cliff).

Note: Barbara Babcock won an Emmy for Outstanding Lead Actress in a Drama Series in "Hill Street Blues" (as Grace Gardner), and also appeared in "Lou Grant" and "Dallas" (as Liz Craig).

Notable Quote: Sam's TV agent, looking for a new spokesperson:

LANA: "Perhaps it's time for me to find a new face."

NORM: "Hey, my face is new."

LANA: "Good. You still have time to return it."

14. "Let Me Count the Ways" (1/13/83). Diane becomes despondent when her childhood cat, Elizabeth Barrett Browning, dies. Diane spends the day lamenting the loss, but reacts angrily when the Cheers gang is unsympathetic. Sam uses her emotional frailty as an opportunity for sexual advances, but Diane interrupts their kiss to analyze their emotions (which leads to yet another argument). **Subtopic:** A patron, Marshall Lipton, provides scientific evidence that the Boston Celtics will lose their next game. Sam and Coach bet against the Celtics and have difficulty concealing their euphoria when the team loses.

Written by Heide Perlman. *Directed by* James Burrows.

Characters: Mark King (Marshall Lipton), Jack Knight (Jack), Alan Koss (Alan), Steve Hanafin (Steve), John Ratzenberger (Cliff).

Notable Quote: On Diane's being envious of Carla's toughness:

DIANE: "What good could you possibly say about a loved one dying?"

CARLA: "It ain't me!"

15. "Father Knows Last" (1/20/83). Carla is pregnant (again) and formally announces that the child's father is the nerdy Ph.D. from M.I.T., Marshall Lipton. Diane finds this conjugal bond intriguing. Upon further investigation it becomes apparent that Marshall is not the biological father, and Carla is beguiling him into supporting the child. Appalled at this blatant deception, Diane intimates that Carla cannot escape her conscience and will be racked with guilt. Carla's conscience ultimately prevails, and she confesses that her ex-husband, Nick, is the actual father. When Marshall refuses to marry Carla, the Cheers gang decides to "adopt" the child by donating money and volunteering to play a fatherly role in its life.

Written by Heide Perlman. *Directed by* James Burrows.

Characters: Mark King (Marshall Lipton), Jack Knight (Jack), Herb Mitchell (Tom), Mary Ellen Trainor (Mary), John Ratzenberger (Cliff).

Notable Quote: Diane toasting Carla's pregnancy:

DIANE: "To the baby. With Marshall as the father, it's sure to have brains. With Carla as the mother, it's sure to have need for them."

16. "The Boys in the Bar" (1/27/83). Cheers hosts a book signing and press conference for Sam's old Red Sox roommate, Tom Kenderson. The book, *Catcher's Mask*, is the first public pronouncement revealing Tom's homosexuality. After serious soul-searching, Sam chooses to support Tom's revelation. However, the patrons are not as receptive and express concern that Cheers will transform into a gay bar. When Diane mentions that two homosexuals are in the bar, the gang becomes homophobic, eventually tricking three patrons into leaving Cheers. As it turns out, the three men are not gay, and Diane relishes the opportunity to expose the gang's ignorance and foolish intolerance.

Written by Ken Levine and David Isaacs. *Directed by* James Burrows.

Characters: Alan Autry (Tom Kenderson), John Furey (Larry), Michael Kearns (Richard), Kenneth Tigar (Fred), Lee Ryan (Bob), Jack Knight (Jack), Tom Babson (Barney), Wesley Thompson (Photographer), Shannon Sullivan (Reporter #1), John Bluto (Reporter #2), Harry Anderson (Harry Gittes), John Ratzenberger (Cliff).

Note: Kenneth Tigar also played the role of Dr. Lowell Greenspon in "Cheers" (#80).

Notable Quote: On homosexuals:

CARLA: "I'm telling you, if guys keep coming out of the closet there isn't gonna be anyone left to date, and I'm gonna have to start going out with girls. [looking at Diane as one of the girls to date] Yuck!"

DIANE: "Carla, you don't have to worry about me. I like my dates a little more masculine than you. Not much, but a little."

17. **"Diane's Perfect Date"** (2/10/83). Sam and Diane agree to find the perfect date for each other. After Diane describes his perfect date, Sam believes that she is surreptitiously planning to be his date, so he decides to be hers. When Diane introduces Gretchen, Sam rushes into the poolroom and pays the only available person, Andy-Andy, $20 to be Diane's date. Andy-Andy accepts the offer and openly reveals he was convicted of manslaughter for killing a waitress. As the hair-raising evening concludes, Sam apologizes to Diane and explains the misunderstanding. Knowing Sam is smitten with her, Diane tricks him into admitting it aloud. When Sam tries a similar ploy, she denies having any feelings for him.

Written by David Lloyd. *Directed by* James Burrows.

Characters: Derek McGrath (Andy), Gretchen Corbett (Gretchen), Doug Sheehan (Walter Franklin), John Ratzenberger (Cliff).

Note: Derek McGrath appeared in "Dallas" (as Oswald Valentine). Doug Sheehan appeared in "General Hospital" (as Joe Kelly) and "Knots Landing" (as Ben Gibson).

Notable Quote: Sam, getting ready for a date:

NORM: "Oh, Sammy. Watching you get ready for a date is like watching a great matador prepare for a bullfight."

CLIFF: "I hate that stuff. You know, who wants to see a guy manipulate and torment a poor unthinking creature like that?"

SAM: "Hey, I always buy them breakfast, don't I?"

18. **"No Contest"** (2/17/83). Sam enters Diane in the annual Miss Boston Barmaid Contest without her knowledge. Since she despises all female contests, Diane is outraged at being entered in the contest (much like you enter a heifer in a county fair). Although reluctant to participate, Diane decides to compete so she can win and denounce the contest. When her hidden agenda is revealed, Sam tries to sabotage the scheme by reminding Diane of her facial tick, but she overcomes this obstacle with a rousing speech which enables her to win. As Diane prepares to give her condemnatory speech, the emcee announces she has won a trip to Bermuda. In a spontaneous exhibition of delirium, Diane forgets to denounce the contest.

Written by Heide Perlman. *Directed by* James Burrows.

Characters: Speaker "Tip" O'Neill (Himself), Charlie Stavola (Emcee),

Tessa Richarde (Bonnie), Renee Gentry (Yvonne), Sharon Peters (Jocelyn), Paul Vaughn (Paul), Daryl Roach (Judge #1), James Shamus Sherwood (Judge #3), Bob Ari (Judge #2), John Ratzenberger (Cliff).

Note: Thomas "Tip" O'Neill was the Speaker of the House of Representatives at the time.

Notable Quote: In reference to the Miss Boston Barmaid finalists:

CLIFF: "None of those girls have what I'm looking for."

NORM: "What's that?"

CLIFF: "Low standards."

19. "Pick a Con ... Any Con" (2/24/83). An elderly gentleman named George befriends and then swindles $8,000 from Coach. The Cheers gang solicits the assistance of Harry "the Hat" to con George in a poker match. When Harry loses all of Sam's money, it is revealed that Harry and George were working together to hoodwink Sam. The gang then asks George to play Harry in one poker match for all the money. Coach volunteers to cheat, but when he inadvertently gives the signal (a scratch on the nose), George ends up losing $10,000 of his own money. Harry leaves the bar ecstatic (and wealthy), while George is seething with rage. After George leaves the bar, Harry returns to reveal that he and Coach staged the entire evening as an elaborate ruse to con George.

Written by David Angell. *Directed by* James Burrows.

Characters: Harry Anderson (Harry), Reid Shelton (George Wheeler), Alan Koss (Mike), Stephen D. Lee (Leo), John Ratzenberger (Cliff).

Note: Reid Shelton had a regular series role in the HBO hit "1st and Ten" (as head coach Ernie). Harry Anderson was the special technical advisor for this episode.

Notable Quote: On Diane's good mood:

SAM: "You're in a pretty good mood tonight."

DIANE: "Last night I was up until two in the morning finishing off Kierkegaard."

SAM: "I hope he thanked you for it."

20. "Someone Single, Someone Blue" (3/3/83). Diane's mother, Helen Chambers, discloses that she will be disinherited if Diane does not marry immediately. As the deadline approaches, Helen begs Diane to pick any man for a quick wedding (and divorce), so she chooses Sam. Naturally, he is concerned Diane will take the vows seriously, but agrees to help her mother. As the ceremony commences, Diane accuses Sam of leering at a woman. After a fiery dispute, her mother cancels the wedding. Helen becomes disinherited and is surprisingly propositioned by her chauffeur, Boggs. Although hesitant, Helen reconsiders when Boggs reveals he is wealthy after embezzling from the Chambers family for nearly a quarter century.

Written by David Angell. *Directed by* James Burrows.

Characters: Glynis Johns (Mrs. Helen Chambers), Duncan Ross (Boggs), Dean Dittman (Harrison Fiedler), Paul Willson (Gregg), John Ratzenberger (Cliff).

Notable Quote: Diane's mother, commenting on Sam's attractiveness:

HELEN: "Diane's told me about you. You're almost as handsome as she says you think you are."

21. "Showdown" (Part 1 of 2) (3/24/83). Sam's inferiority complex resurfaces when his eternally perfect brother, Derek, visits Boston. The Cheers gang is captivated by Derek's talents, and Diane is mesmerized by his charm and physical beauty. Diane admits her attraction to Derek, but only to make Sam envious. When Sam remains ambivalent about his feelings, Diane accepts Derek's invitation to fly to Martha's Vineyard. **Subtopic:** Coach has an opportunity to manage a baseball team in Venezuela, but needs to learn Spanish. Within a few hours, Coach becomes fluent in the language and owes all his success to Derek.

Written by Glen Charles and Les Charles. *Directed by* James Burrows.

Characters: George Ball (Derek), Deborah Shelton (Debbie), Alan Koss (Alan), Paul Vaughn (Paul), John Ratzenberger (Cliff).

Note: Deborah Shelton was a recurring regular in "Dallas" and appeared in *Body Double* (1984).

Notable Quote: On Carla's sex life:

CARLA: "I'm always falling for the guys I hate. My whole life has been the wrong man, at the wrong time, in the wrong place, with the wrong birth control device."

22. "Showdown" (Part 2 of 2) (3/31/83). Sam's brother, Derek, continues dating Diane, while Sam feigns indifference about his true feelings. When Derek invites her to accompany him to Paris, Diane contemplates a long-term relationship. However, before accepting Derek's offer, she confronts Sam, demanding some sort of commitment from him. When he refuses to oblige, Diane leaves the office but immediately returns to be with him. Upon re-entering the office, she hits Sam in the nose with the door—he was trying to stop her departure. Diane realizes he truly cares, but when he denies having any feelings for her, they begin another argument which inflames their passions.

Written by Glen Charles and Les Charles. *Directed by* James Burrows.

Characters: Lois de Banzie (Lady #1), Helen Page Camp (Lady #2), Alan Koss (Alan), Paul Vaughn (Paul), Peggy Kubena (Cindy), Tim Cunningham (Chuck), John Ratzenberger (Cliff).

Note: Lois de Banzie also played the role of a nun in "Cheers" (#70).

Notable Quote: Everyone, discussing Diane's love life with Derek:

CARLA: "You know, I'm sick of hearing about her. Ever since Lady Dye Job arrived, she gets all the attention. I mean, nobody cares about me anymore. Nobody asks what Carla's doing anymore."

CLIFF: "Carla, Carla. Come on now, be fair. You know, we weren't that interested in your life before she got here."

Season Two: 1983-84

(NBC Thursday, 9:30–10:00 p.m. EST)

Season Regulars: Ted Danson (Sam Malone), Shelley Long (Diane Chambers), Nicholas Colasanto (Ernie "Coach" Pantusso), Rhea Perlman (Carla Tortelli), John Ratzenberger (Cliff Clavin), George Wendt (Norm Peterson).

Technical Credits: *Created by* Glen Charles, Les Charles and James Burrows. *Producers:* James Burrows, Glen Charles, Les Charles. *Writers:* David Angell, Nick Arnold, Glen Charles, Les Charles, Ken Estin, Lissa Levin, David Lloyd, Heide Perlman, Earl Pomerantz, Tom Reeder, Sam Simon, Max Tash, Michael J. Weithorn. *Director:* James Burrows. *Associate Producer:* Tim Berry. *Executive Script Consultant:* David Lloyd. *Story Editors:* Heide Perlman, David Angell. *Director of Photography:* John Finger. *Art Directors:* Herman Zimmerman, Monty Elliot. *Film Editors:* Andrew Chulack, M. Pam Blumenthal. *Unit Production Manager:* Linda McMurray. *First Assistant Directors:* Thomas Lofaro, Randy Carter, Leonard R. Garner, Jr. *Second Assistant Director:* Brian James Ellis. *Music by* Craig Safan. *Song:* "Where Everybody Knows Your Name." *Lyrics and Music by* Judy Hart Angelo and Gary Portnoy. *Sung by* Gary Portnoy. *Casting:* Stephen Kolzak. *Set Decorators:* Lynne Albright, Anthony D. Nealis. *Technical Coordinator:* Gil Clasen. *Script Supervisor:* Gabrielle James. *Production Mixers:* Gordon Klimuck, James Wright. *Costume Supervisor:* Robert L. Tanella. *Women's Costumer:* Sandra Culotta. *Makeup Artist:* Bruce Hutchinson. *Hair Stylists:* Rebecca DeMorrio, Marilyn Patricia Phillips. *Music Editor:* Chips Swanson. *Sound Effects:* Sam Black. *Main Title Design:* James Castle & Bruce Bryant. *Recorded by* Glen Glenn Sound. *Opticals:* Freeze Frame. *Assistants to the Charles Brothers:* Janet Allen, Tony Colvin, Christine Connor, Marilyn A. Dustin, Penelope Franks, Marcia Friedman, Sheila Guthrie, Anthony Kinniebrew, Danny Lipsius, Glen Miller, Marsha Nadler, Diane Overdiek, Lana Repp Lewis, Brian H.

Sato, Richard P. Solomon, Todd Stevens, Lori Kay Wilson, Michael Zito. *Executive in Charge of Production:* Richard Villarino. *Charles/Burrows/ Charles Productions in Association with* Paramount Television.

23. **"Power Play"** (9/29/83). Resuming last year's cliffhanger, Sam and Diane's fiery dispute turns into a passionate embrace and kiss. Diane suggests sharing their emotions in a place where Sam has never been with another woman. When Sam is unable to find a virgin motel, they go to the only available place—Diane's apartment. While in her bedroom, Sam begins criticizing Diane for naming her stuffed animals, and an argument ensues. Sam is asked to leave, but returns later that evening demanding her submissiveness. Diane pretends to call the police to teach Sam a lesson, but they eventually settle the dispute and consummate their relationship.

Written by Glen Charles and Les Charles. *Directed by* James Burrows.

Characters: Alan Koss (Alan), Paul Vaughn (Paul).

Notable Quote: On the Hindu theory of reincarnation that if you do not lead a good life, you come back in a more lowly condition:

NORM: "Last time out I must have made a real ass out of myself."

24. **"Little Sister Don'tcha"** (10/13/83). Carla goes into labor with her fifth child, so her sister, Annette, works as a temporary waitress at Cheers. Annette appears very shy, but quickly reveals a dark side by accepting a date with every man who propositions her. After going on a date with Annette, Cliff immediately falls in love with her and contemplates proposing marriage. However, she does not even remember

Cliff's name, so Norm tactfully reveals Annette's sexual promiscuity. Cliff becomes irate and insults Norm, but they promptly reconcile their differences.

Written by Heide Perlman. *Directed by* James Burrows.

Characters: Rhea Perlman (Annette Lozupone), Paul Vaughn (Paul), Paul Willson (Tom), Jerry Prell (Customer).

Note: Rhea Perlman played the dual role of Carla and Annette.

Notable Quote: One reason Cliff dates infrequently:

CLIFF: "I have impossibly high standards for a woman."

NORM: "Yeah, she has to like you."

25. **"Personal Business"** (10/20/83). Carla protests when Diane receives preferential treatment, so Diane resolves the problem by quitting her job at Cheers. One week later she is on the verge of being hired as a proofreader, but the employer, Mr. Hedges, is only interested in asking Sam whether he ever saw her naked. Diane is appalled and disgusted because every job offer has sexual strings attached. After being rehired at Cheers, she and Sam mutually confess the only reason they have an employment relationship is because of their physical attraction toward one another. **Subtopic:** After a two-week separation, Norm struggles with the reality that his marriage may be over, and is dismayed because Vera already has a date.

Written by Tom Reeder. *Directed by* James Burrows.

Characters: Tony Brafa (Mr. Anderson #1), James Ingersoll (Mr. Anderson #2), Patrick Stack (Customer #1).

Notable Quote: On Diane's finding another job:

CLIFF: "So, what's going on here, Normy? You've been looking for months, and Diane goes out there and snags a job in a couple of weeks."

NORM: "Well, it's easier for girls. I mean, if God made me a woman, I would never be out of work."

CLIFF: "Well, yeah, as long as there are carnivals."

26. **"Homicidal Ham"** (10/27/83, 10:00–10:30 p.m. EST). Andy-Andy (a.k.a. Andy Schroeder) visits Cheers and purposely fumbles a robbery attempt so he can return to prison. Instead of calling the police, Diane offers him a second chance by developing an acting career, and arranges an audition with her theater professor. After one week of intensively rehearsing the strangulation scene from *Othello*, Andy falls in love with Diane and feels betrayed when he sees her kissing Sam. Diane tries to explain she only loves Andy as a friend, but he is unforgiving. Andy uses his rage to act the Shakespearean play with authenticity by attempting to strangle Diane for her unfaithfulness.

Written by David Lloyd. *Directed by* James Burrows.

Characters: Derek McGrath (Andy Schroeder), Paul Vaughn (Paul), Alan Koss (Alan), Severn Darden (Professor DeWitt).

27. **"Sumner's Return"** (11/3/83). One year after abandoning Diane at Cheers (in episode 1), Sumner returns to explain his actions. After being invited to dinner to meet his ex-wife, Barbara, Diane intimates she is romantically unattached. However, Sam insists upon having dinner with these intellectuals, and spends the next five days reading *War and Peace* to appear intellectual on at least one subject.

When Sumner arrives alone, Sam quickly realizes he planned the entire evening to win Diane's heart. At this crossroad, she is forced to choose between two suitors, and ultimately chooses Sam because he read *War and Peace* for her.

Written by Michael J. Weithorn. *Directed by* James Burrows.

Characters: Michael McGuire (Sumner Sloane).

Notable Quote: On Sumner visiting Cheers after a one-year absence:

SUMNER: "I know you're surprised to see me. But let me tell you, it's taken every ounce of courage I have to show my face in here today."

COACH: "Oh, come on. We get a lot of funny looking faces in here."

28. **"Affairs of the Heart"** (11/10/83). Carla vehemently resists the sexual come-ons of a patron, Hank Zenzola, but succumbs to his charm. Hank proves to be the perfect man, so she breaks up with him. Paradoxically, Carla is concerned Hank will dump her because she has fallen in love with him. Diane assists in reuniting the couple by allowing them to use her apartment to consummate their relationship. When Coach reveals Hank has a serious heart condition, Sam and Diane hasten to warn Carla, who then breaks up with Hank. **Subtopic:** Sam raises the price of tap beer, so Norm budgets his suds allowance to restrict his consumption.

Written by Heide Perlman. *Directed by* James Burrows.

Characters: Don Amendolia (Henry "Hank" Zenzola).

Notable Quote: Carla's concern about Hank having a heart condition:

HANK: "Maybe if we didn't get too wild [it would be safe to have sex]."

CARLA: "Are you kidding? I've

almost killed off guys with good pumps."

29. **"Old Flames"** (11/17/83). Dave Richards solicits Sam to go babe hunting. When Diane interrupts their escapade, Dave is shocked to learn Sam is dating the "human brain." To prove Sam is still a babe hound, Dave claims he can cause their breakup within 24 hours. When Dave reveals the existence of Sam's black book of women's telephone numbers, Diane's fury leads to their apparent breakup. Dave then arranges for Sam to date an attractive airline stewardess, Didi, but at the hotel room he resists the temptation. Diane views this negatively and officially breaks up with him. However, when Sam unequivocally declares his commitment to Diane, she reaffirms their relationship.

Written by David Angell. *Directed by* James Burrows.

Characters: Fred Dryer (Dave Richards), Elizabeth McIvor (Didi).

Notable Quote: Diane criticizing Sam's intelligence, or lack thereof:

DIANE: "Sam, if brains were money, you'd have to take out a loan for a cup of coffee."

30. **"Manager Coach"** (11/24/83). Coach accepts an offer to manage a little league baseball team, the Titans, and quickly becomes obsessed with winning. Despite earning the right to play in the championship game, the players rebel against Coach's tyrannical behavior and threaten to quit. Consequently, Coach modifies his Draconian managerial style after realizing he is becoming the type of person he always hated as a child. **Subtopics:** Norm remains unemployed, so Cliff generously offers a $500 loan but immediately has reservations about his act of

kindness. Meanwhile, Carla begins breast-feeding her child in the bar, which disturbs many of the patrons.

Written by Earl Pomerantz. *Directed by* James Burrows.

Characters: Herb L. Mitchell (Mort Sherwin), Elliott Scott (Peewee), Corey Feldman (Moose), Martin Davis (Tank), Paul Vaughn (Paul), Alan Koss (Alan).

Note: Corey Feldman began acting at age three. He has had extensive exposure in television commercials, a multitude of minor television roles (e.g., "Mork and Mindy," "Eight Is Enough," and "Alice"), and has attained mediocre success in motion pictures [e.g., *Meatballs 4* (1992) and *License to Drive* (1988)].

Notable Quote: After Sam told Diane to stop badgering him about Coach's obsessive desire to win:

DIANE: "Very well. And from now on there's a part of me that's hands-off to you."

SAM: "Just my luck, it will be one of the parts I care about."

31. **"They Call Me Mayday"** (12/1/83). Diane tries to enthrall Dick Cavett with her poetry, but he is more interested in Sam's autobiography. Diane assists Sam in writing a few sample chapters; however, the publisher ultimately rejects the manuscript because it lacks controversy—not enough sex or perversion. At Mr. Cavett's suggestion, Sam considers highlighting his sexual exploits, with Diane agreeing to rewrite the torrid affairs using a pseudonym. **Subtopic:** Norm competes against an old high school wrestling rival, Wally Bodell, who is attracted to Vera. When Wally begins pursuing her, he and Norm settle the dispute by wrestling (the winner gets Vera).

Written by David Angell. *Directed by* James Burrows.

Characters: Walter Olkewicz (Wally Bodell), Ed Quinlan (Bob), Dick Cavett (Himself).

Note: Walter Olkewicz played a role in the television show "Grace Under Fire."

Notable Quote: On Norm and Vera after they separated:

NORM: "Vera called this morning."

SAM: "Oh yeah. You guys gonna patch it up?"

NORM: "No. She just wanted to reach out and nag someone."

32. **"How Do I Love Thee, Let Me Call You Back"** (12/8/83). Diane purchases tickets to a Marvin Hagler prizefight and gives them to Sam. As a way of thanking her, Sam flippantly says, "I love you," but Diane takes these words seriously. When Sam tries to explain that the words were not meant literally, they agree to separate for one week to examine the depth and meaning of their relationship. Diane solemnly contemplates their relationship, while Sam parties with the Cheers gang. When she enters the bar to discuss their week-long contemplative hiatus, Sam is playing poker with the gang. After comparing notes, Sam and Diane realize there is no good reason why they should remain together, yet they continue dating.

Written by Earl Pomerantz. *Directed by* James Burrows.

Characters: Harry Anderson (Harry Gittes), Alan Koss (Alan), Kevin Rooney (Phil), Gerald Berns (Dave).

Notable Quote: On Sam frequenting a strip joint:

Sam: "That's the first time I've been in the combat zone sober. It just goes to show you, you can still have a good time without drinking, as long as you're surrounded by naked broads shaking their wallies in your face."

(New Time: Thursday, 9:00–9:30 p.m. EST)

33. **"Just Three Friends"** (12/15/83). Diane's childhood friend Heather visits Cheers, and Sam believes she is seducing him. Diane refuses to believe this, and Heather unequivocally denies any attraction. However, at a dinner party Diane begins having second thoughts about the purity of Heather's intentions, and misinterprets her overt friendliness as a sexual advance. Despite arguing, Diane realizes the error of her way, apologizes, and reaffirms her friendship with Heather. **Subtopic:** Coach locks an ornery attack dog in the office, and the only way to allay the dog's ferociousness is to feed him alcohol.

Written by David Lloyd. *Directed by* James Burrows.

Characters: Markie Post (Heather Landon).

Note: Markie Post previously appeared in "The Fall Guy" (as bail bondswoman Teri Michaels/Shannon, 1982–85), and had a successful role as defense attorney Christine Sullivan in "Night Court." She also costarred with John Ritter in "Hearts Afire" (as Georgie Ann Lahti).

Notable Quote: On Diane's introducing a friend:

Diane: "This is Heather Landon. My oldest friend."

Carla: "Meet her this morning?"

34. **"Where There's a Will..."** (12/22/83). A wealthy patron, Malcolm Kramer, visits Cheers after learning he only has six months to live. To lift his spirits, Sam allows Malcolm to work as a bartender for the night. Malcolm

thoroughly enjoys himself and as a show of gratitude bequeaths the Cheers gang $100,000 in a codicil to his will. The gang begins arguing over the distribution of the money, so Malcolm appoints Sam to distribute the proceeds. When the arguments persist, Sam uses a magic trick to create the illusion that he burned the will. Although the bickering stops, when Sam reveals the plan to keep the money for himself, Diane convinces him to burn the will once and for all.

Written by Nick Arnold. *Directed by* James Burrows.

Characters: George Gaynes (Malcolm Kramer), Alan Koss (Alan), Tom Babson (Tom), Tim Cunningham (Greg), Elizabeth Hill (Female Customer #1), Jacqueline Cassel (Female Customer #2).

35. **"Battle of the Ex's"** (1/5/84). Diane plans a romantic weekend, but the plans change when Carla receives a wedding invitation from her ex-husband, Nick Tortelli. As Nick flaunts his bride-to-be, Loretta, Carla becomes indignant and begs Sam to be her wedding date to make Nick envious. Sam reluctantly agrees, and the plan works perfectly. As the newlyweds prepare to leave for their Hawaiian honeymoon, Nick returns to Cheers begging Carla to take him back. She proudly rejects him, but begins crying because she has no one to love. In a moment of despair, she and Sam share their first kiss, and discover there is no spark between them.

Written by Ken Estin and Sam Simon. *Directed by* James Burrows.

Characters: Dan Hedaya (Nick Tortelli), Jean Kasem (Loretta), Allen Williams (Dr. Paul Kendall), Jacqueline Cassel (Customer #2).

Note: Dan Hedaya subsequently

starred as the character Nick Tortelli in "The Tortellis" (1987), which was a short-lived spin-off of "Cheers," and also appeared in "Hill Street Blues" and "Sister Kane." His movie credits include roles in *Wise Guys* (1986), *Running Scared* (1986), and *The Addams Family* (1991). Jean Kasem costarred as the character Loretta Tortelli in "The Tortellis," and married Casey Kasem (of "America's Top 40" fame).

36. **"No Help Wanted"** (1/12/84). The unemployment checks cease, so Norm resorts to washing dishes at Melville's. To help him out, the Cheers gang pressures Sam into hiring Norm as his accountant. Sam is averse to the idea but agrees. However, he begins doubting Norm's competence and hires another accountant to prepare his taxes. After Norm discovers Sam's subversive tactics, a fervid argument ensues which places their relationship at a crossroad. In this power struggle of friendship, Norm concedes first by groveling, crying, and begging for Sam's forgiveness. Sam then agrees to hire Norm as the Cheers accountant for the following tax season.

Written by Max Tash. *Directed by* James Burrows.

Characters: Barbra Horan (Becky Hawley), Rus Marin (Customer #1), Steve Giannelli (Customer #2), Hal Ralston (Customer #3).

Note: Max Tash wrote or directed the original "WKRP" episodes, and is a graduate of the University of Iowa.

Notable Quote:

COACH: "Can I draw you a beer, Norm?"

NORM: "Nah. I know what they look like. Just pour me one."

37. **"And Coachie Makes Three"** (1/19/84). After a nice dinner at her apartment, Diane senses that her and Sam's relationship is becoming monotonous. Before she can spice things up by slipping into sexy lingerie, Coach arrives, eager to watch a Robert Mitchum movie with Sam. Soon Sam and Diane are desperate for privacy because Coach spends every evening with them watching movies. They arrange the perfect blind date for Coach, but he claims that Katherine does not fit in. As a last resort, Sam and Diane explain their need for privacy. Although temporarily heartbroken, Coach meets with Katherine later that evening and they begin dating.

Written by Heide Perlman. *Directed by* James Burrows.

Characters: Eve Roberts (Katherine), Milda Dacys (Woman #1), Robyn Peterson (Woman #2).

Notable Quote: Sam and Diane, seeking privacy away from Coach:

DIANE: "There's only one solution to this problem. We have to tell Coach to stop hanging around us."

NORM: "Diane's right, Sam. If you don't want Coach hanging around, just tell him. It's the honest, ethical way to approach it…. Of course, if you want to make it easier on Coach, why don't you just rip out his heart and do a tap dance on it."

38. **"Cliff's Rocky Moment"** (1/26/84). A patron, Victor, is annoyed by Cliff's constant chatter, and vocalizes his intolerance when Cliff continues to enlighten patrons with witticisms. Victor is interested in a fight, so Cliff hires Lewis, a postal employee and ex-boxing champion, for protection. However, Lewis quickly realizes Victor is justified in despising Cliff, and refuses to provide protection. Cliff then claims to be a black belt in karate, but ultimately leaves the bar to avoid a

confrontation. He returns to prove his karate skills by breaking a board with his foot and a brick with his head. As the Cheers gang celebrates the astonishing feat, Cliff discretely asks Diane to take him to the hospital because he never had a karate lesson in his life!

Written by David Lloyd. *Directed by* James Burrows.

Characters: Peter Iacangelo (Victor Shapone), Sam Scarber (Lewis), Alan Koss (Alan), Elizabeth Hill (Liz).

39. **"Fortune & Men's Weights"** (2/2/84). Coach is conned into buying an antique weight scale, and the Cheers gang becomes enthralled with the fortunes dispensed with each weigh-in. When fortunes appear to come true, the patrons' entertainment quickly turns to trepidation that the scale is cursed. Even Diane is convinced when her fortune accurately predicts "deception in romance proves costly," and she divulges having secretly dated a man without Sam's knowledge. They break up and begin arguing over who was first to end the relationship. As the show ends, there remains a question as to whether they will continue dating. **Subtopic:** Norm has a blind date with Vera which ultimately resolves their marital problems.

Written by Heide Perlman. *Directed by* James Burrows.

Characters: Alan Fine (Deliveryman #1), Charles Champion (Deliveryman #2), Al Rosen (Al), Tim Cunningham (Greg).

Notable Quote: On Norm and Vera's getting back together and making love:

NORM: "We went back to what used to be our place and we kind of made love."

SAM: "Wait, you can't kind of make love, Norm."

NORM: "You don't know Vera."

40. **"Snow Job"** (2/9/84). Sam and his Red Sox buddies prepare to embark on their annual skiing pilgrimage (to melt a few snow bunnies), so he concocts a story about attending his Uncle Nathan's funeral. Unbeknownst to Sam, Diane knows about the ski weekend and uses emotional blackmail to persuade him to confess the truth and forego the ski weekend. Despite leaving and returning three times, Sam spends a cold weekend in Boston. **Subtopics:** Norm immediately befriends George Foley, which makes Cliff despondent because he is excluded from their activities. Meanwhile, Coach attempts a personal record for breaking the fewest bar glasses in a month, but misses the mark after slipping on a banana peel—those damn tropical drinks!

Written by David Angell. *Directed by* James Burrows.

Characters: James Gallery (George Foley), Gary Gershaw (Tommy).

Notable Quote: Norm's response after playing a game of pool with George:

NORM: "That guy is gooooood. He made me look like a big dope out there, Cliffy."

CLIFF: "Oh, yeah? What did he do, turn the lights on?"

41. **"Coach Buries a Grudge"** (2/16/84). After attending a funeral for his friend T-Bone Scorpageoni, Coach invites all of his ex-teammates to an honorary memorial service at Cheers. After overhearing that T-Bone made a pass at his wife many years ago, Coach expresses contempt for his friend and refuses to give the eulogy. He then decides to publicly crucify T-Bone, but ultimately responds by giving a heartfelt speech. When it is revealed that T-Bone made a pass at all the teammates'

wives, the honorarium turns into a lynch mob wanting to hang T-Bone in effigy. As everyone exits the bar, Diane sings a touching rendition of "Amazing Grace" to soothe the savage beasts.

Written by David Lloyd. *Directed by* James Burrows.

Characters: Fred Carney (Tom), Arthur Lessac (Art), Don Bexley (Charlie), Jack O'Leary (Lefty), Bob Lobel (Customer #1), Albert Rosen (Al).

Notable Quote: On T-Bone's making a pass at Coach's wife:

DIANE: "Coach. Come on, now. You have to find a way to put this behind you. Angela and T-Bone are both in heaven now."

NORM: "Let's hope he's not hitting on her up there."

42. "Norm's Conquest" (2/23/84). When Norm invites a new business client, Emily, to Cheers, everyone except Diane encourages him to have an affair. In the process of discussing Norm's options with the Cheers gang, Emily is disregarded and prepares to leave. Norm apologizes, and they agree to go to her apartment for dinner. Stormin' Norman is ready for love, and returns two hours later fatigued, with his clothes in disarray and a hickey on his neck! The gang listens to his exploits, but unbeknownst to Norm, Emily notified them that he went to park the car and never returned. After being humiliated and ridiculed by the gang, Norm admits that Vera is his only love.

Written by Lissa Levin. *Directed by* James Burrows.

Characters: Anne Schedeen (Emily Phillips), Alan Koss (Alan), Tim Cunningham (Tim), Steve Giannelli (Steve).

Note: Anne Schedeen is best remembered as a regular in the television hit "ALF" (as Kate Tanner, 1986-90), but was also in "Paper Dolls."

Notable Quote: Norm, lying about having an affair:

CLIFF: "What a pathetic display. I'm ashamed God made me a man."

CARLA: "I don't think God's doing a lot of bragging about it, either."

43. "I'll Be Seeing You" (Part 1 of 2) (5/3/84). Sam is immersed in self-laudation for being chosen by *Boston* magazine as one of Boston's 20 most eligible bachelors. Diane is disconcerted because he is not "available," and after a brief altercation they agree to begin their relationship anew by being totally honest with one another. Sam's attempt at honesty only infuriates Diane, so he tries to make amends by hiring Phillip Semenko to paint her portrait. The artist is captivated by Diane's suffering, but Sam, who despises Semenko, forbids her to pose (or their relationship is over). Despite the ultimatum, Diane poses for Semenko. **Subtopic:** Coach organizes the annual Cheers picnic, but the gang is not eager to participate.

Written by Glen Charles and Les Charles. *Directed by* James Burrows.

Characters: Christopher Lloyd (Phillip Semenko), Christopher Carroll (Ed), Steve Giannelli (Steve).

Note: Christopher Lloyd has won numerous Emmys and has been lauded for his diverse roles in the movie *Back to the Future* (1985, and its sequels in 1989 and 1990), and *The Addams Family* (as Uncle Fester, 1991). He also appeared in *One Flew Over the Cuckoo's Nest* (1975), *Mr. Mom* (1983) and *Who Framed Roger Rabbit?* (1988).

Notable Quote: Regarding Diane not trusting Sam:

NORM: "I know what you mean,

Sam. Once the trust goes out of a relationship, it's really no fun lying to them anymore."

44. "I'll Be Seeing You" (Part 2 of 2) (5/10/84). Despite Sam's ultimatum, Diane poses for revered artist Phillip Semenko. When the painting is finished, Diane expects Sam's forgiveness, but is met with animosity for disobeying a direct order. They have an acrimonious dispute, and after slapping each other several times, they end their relationship (again). Diane vows never to set foot in the bar if Sam does not prevent her departure; Sam's acquiescence signals the end of their

relationship. **Subtopic:** Coach uses the pathetic old man approach to persuade the gang into participating in the annual Cheers picnic.
Written by Glen Charles & Les Charles. *Directed by* James Burrows.
Characters: Christopher Lloyd (Phillip Semenko), Christopher Carroll (Ed), Steve Giannelli (Steve).
Notable Quote: Sam and Diane, arguing:
DIANE: "Do you know what the difference is between you and a fat-brained ass?"
SAM: "Nope."
DIANE:" The fat-brained ass would."

Season Three: 1984-85

(NBC Thursday, 9:00–9:30 p.m. EST)
Season Regulars: Ted Danson (Sam Malone), Shelley Long (Diane Chambers), Nicholas Colasanto (Ernie "Coach" Pantusso), Rhea Perlman (Carla Tortelli), John Ratzenberger (Cliff Clavin), George Wendt (Norm Peterson).
Technical Credits: *Created by* Glen Charles, Les Charles and James Burrows. *Executive Producers:* James Burrows, Glen Charles, Les Charles. *Producers:* Ken Estin and Sam Simon. *Writers:* David Angell, Peter Casey, Glen Charles, Les Charles, Ken Estin, David Isaacs, David Lee, Ken Levine, David Lloyd, Jim Parker, Heide Perlman, Tom Reeder, Elliot Shoenman, Sam Simon. *Director:* James Burrows. *Associate Producer:* Tim Berry. *Executive Script Consultant:* David Lloyd. *Executive Story Consultant:* Heide Perlman. *Executive Story Editor:* David

Angell. *Director of Photography:* John Finger. *Art Director:* Herman Zimmerman. *Film Editors:* M. Pam Blumenthal, Douglas Hines, A.C.E., Roger W. Tweten. *Unit Production Manager:* Linda McMurray. *First Assistant Director:* Thomas Lofaro. *Second Assistant Director:* Brian James Ellis. *Music by* Craig Safan. *Song:* "Where Everybody Knows Your Name." *Lyrics and Music by* Judy Hart Angelo and Gary Portnoy. *Sung by* Gary Portnoy. *Casting:* Lori Openden, C.S.A., Stephen Kolzak. *Original Casting:* Stephen Kolzak. *Set Decorator:* Lynne Albright. *Technical Coordinator:* Gil Clasen. *Script Supervisors:* Gabrielle James, Rosemary Dorsey. *Production Mixers:* Michael Ballin, Gordon Klimuck. *Costume Supervisor:* Robert L. Tanella. *Women's Costumers:* Sandra Culotta, Melissa Franz. *Makeup Artist:* Bruce Hutchinson. *Hair Stylists:* Marilyn

Patricia Phillips, Susan Germaine. *Music Editor:* Chips Swanson. *Sound Effects:* Sam Black. *Main Title Design:* James Castle and Bruce Bryant. *Opticals:* Freeze Frame. *Cameras and Lenses:* Panavision. *Assistants to the Charles Brothers:* Rick Beren, Leslie Brenner, Kelly Brock, Christine Connor, Marilyn A. Dustin, Mary Fukuto, Sheila Guthrie, Rebecca Helm, Sue Herring, Geraldine Leder, Mary Ann Leslie, Cary Matsumura, Diane Overdiek, Brian H. Sato, Debra Wanderer. *Executive in Charge of Production:* Richard Villarino. *Charles/Burrows/Charles Productions in Association with* Paramount Television.

45. "Rebound" (Part 1 of 2) (9/27/84). The breakup between Sam and Diane had serious consequences; Sam began boozing and babe hunting, and Diane had a nervous breakdown. After Diane spends three months in Goldenbrook sanitarium, Coach convinces her to return to Cheers to help Sam overcome his alcohol dependency. With the assistance of the Cheers gang, Sam agrees to meet with psychiatrist Dr. Frasier Crane. Naturally, Sam perceives Diane's return to the bar as a sign of her love for him; whereas Diane perceives Sam's drinking as a subliminal confession of his love for her.

Written by Glen Charles and Les Charles. *Directed by* James Burrows.

Characters: Kelsey Grammer (Frasier Crane), Duncan Ross (Boggs), Anita Elevi (Baton Twirler), Larry Harpel (Customer #1), Brian Burt (Customer #2).

Note: Kelsey Grammer later starred as the character Frasier Crane in the television spin-off "Frasier."

Notable Quote: Norm, attempting to impregnate Vera:

COACH: "Normy, it's Vera. She says to hurry home, her cycle is at its peak."

NORM: "Again? Her cycle has more peaks than the Adirondacks.... Even Secretariat got to wait until he was in the mood once in a while."

46. "Rebound" (Part 2 of 2) (10/4/84). After several counseling sessions, Frasier concludes Sam is capable of coping with his alcoholism. When Diane and Frasier reveal their romantic bliss, Sam also claims to have found the perfect woman, Julie, a waitress at Cheers. However, Julie quickly breaks off the relationship and quits after learning Sam slept with her sister. Knowing Diane is dating someone else, Sam intrepidly asks her to fill the recently vacated waitress position. Initially, she and Frasier resist the idea, but Coach uses ingenuity and psychology to convince them otherwise.

Written by Glen Charles and Les Charles. *Directed by* James Burrows.

Characters: Kelsey Grammer (Frasier Crane), P.J. Soles (Julie), Ethel Sway (Croquet Player), Larry Harpel (Customer #1), Brian Burt (Customer #2).

Notable Quote: On Sam's alcohol problem:

CLIFF: "Thank God I don't have an alcoholic personality."

CARLA: "You don't *have* a personality."

47. "I Call Your Name" (10/18/84). While being intimate with Frasier, Diane calls out Sam's name. Frasier is distraught and consults Sam for advice. Knowing Diane still wants him, Sam uses discreet badinage to annoy her, but Diane gets revenge. She arranges an intimate moment with Sam to confess her love. Sam reciprocates, and as they share a passionate embrace, Diane shouts out Frasier's name! **Subtopic:** Cliff reports a fellow postal worker, Lewis, for stealing fragrance samples from magazines. When Lewis asks Cliff to reveal the identity of the snitch, Cliff is prepared to confess that Juan Torez did it!

Written by Peter Casey and David Lee. *Directed by* James Burrows.

Characters: Sam Scarber (Lewis), Mitch Kreindel (Eddie), Erwin Fuller (Mr. Fancy Bottom), Kelsey Grammer (Frasier Crane).

Notable Quote: Frasier's banter, after having a beer:

FRASIER: "Thanks for the cold one, Sam."

SAM: "You're welcome, Frasier."

FRASIER: "The beer, I mean, not Diane."

48. "Fairy Tales Can Come True" (10/25/84). Cliff dresses as Ponce de León for the Cheers Halloween party, and falls in love with Tinker Bell. After a magical evening together, they arrange to meet at Cheers the following night to reveal their true identities. Cliff waits patiently, but Tinker Bell never arrives. She eventually calls to confess her insecurities, and when they finally meet, the timid pair share a dance. **Subtopic:** Frasier leaves town for another seminar, and suggests Sam and Diane attend a concert together.

Written by Sam Simon. *Directed by* James Burrows.

Characters: Bernadette Birkett (Tinker Bell), Alan Koss (Alan), Steve Giannelli (Steve), J. Alan Thomas (Jeff), Rebecca Soladay (Woman #1), Kelsey Grammer (Frasier Crane).

Note: Bernadette Birkett also played the role of Vera Peterson in a later episode of "Cheers" (#267).

49. "Sam Turns the Other Cheek" (11/1/84). Sam ends a relationship with a married woman, Maxine, but her jealous husband, Marvin, is not forgiving. He enters Cheers armed with a gun, and threatens Sam's life. Sam eventually persuades Marvin to relinquish the firearm, but it discharges, nicking Sam's derriere. After telling the Cheers gang he was shot while karate kicking an armed marauder, Sam's prevarication receives television coverage, which prompts Marvin to return with another pistol. However, this time Diane intervenes to save Sam's butt. **Subtopic:** Carla has a painful toothache and agonizes over going to the dentist.

Written by David Lloyd. *Directed by* James Burrows.

Characters: Carmen Argenziano (Marvin), Kim Lankford (Maxine), Mark Sawyer (Customer #1).

Note: Carmen Argenziano appeared in "Crime and Punishment" (as Lt. Anthony Batoli).

Notable Quote: On Carla's kids:

CARLA: "What a night. $200 in tips."

COACH: "What are you going to do with all that money?"

CARLA: "I'm going to spend it all on my kids."

COACH: "Good girl."

CARLA: "How many gunnysacks and one-way tickets do you think it will buy?"

50. "Coach in Love" (Part 1 of 2) (11/8/84). After meeting a Cheers patron, Irene, Coach is struck by "the thunderbolt" (love at first sight) and unequivocally declares he is going to marry her. While Coach sweeps Irene off her feet, Sam agrees to act as a decoy by entertaining her daughter, Sue. Coach successfully accomplishes his task, and after dating for three weeks, he proposes marriage. Irene accepts, and shortly thereafter is notified she won $2 million in the state lottery. **Subtopic:** Sam tries desperately to get a date with Sue and refuses to accept her incessant rejections.

Written by David Angell. *Directed by* James Burrows.

Characters: Bette Ford (Irene Blanchard), Ellen Regan (Sue Blanchard).

Notable Quote: On Diane's childhood hand puppet:

DIANE: "Brian the Lion was my dearest childhood pal."

CARLA: "Then being a grimy bar rag should be a step up."

51. "Coach in Love" (Part 2 of 2) (11/15/84). Winning the lottery irreparably changes Irene's life. She is no longer complacent with her old lifestyle, and has no room for Coach in her future. Irene begins mingling with wealthy socialites, and cancels the wedding. Coach refuses to believe she has changed, so he continues planning the wedding. As the special day nears, Coach still believes Irene will come to her senses, despite her engagement to a wealthy European industrialist. Coach's wedding day comes and goes, but Irene never shows.

Written by David Angell. *Directed by* James Burrows.

Characters: Bette Ford (Irene Blanchard), Ellen Regan (Sue Blanchard), Alan Blumenfeld (Customer #1), Jason Tatar (Customer #2).

Notable Quote: Diane's happiness with Frasier:

DIANE: "Sam. The day I met Frasier Crane, I stopped looking for Mr. Right."

SAM: "Yeah, that would discourage me, too."

52. "Diane Meets Mom" (11/22/84). Diane meets Frasier's mother,

Hester, for the first time, and although appearing jocular, Hester threatens to kill Diane if she continues dating Frasier. Hester is concerned about Frasier and does not want her brilliant son to ruin his career by marrying a pseudo-intellectual barmaid. When Frasier refuses to believe Diane, she confronts him with an ultimatum: choose whether he believes her or his mother. Frasier sides with Diane, and after Hester explains her actions, they seem to forgive and forget. However, as they prepare to leave the bar, Hester tries to bribe Sam to rekindle his romance with Diane.

Written by David Lloyd. *Directed by* James Burrows.

Characters: Nancy Marchand (Hester Crane), Tom Kindle (Phil Ryan), Larry Harpel (Larry), Kelsey Grammer (Frasier Crane).

Note: Nancy Marchand won critical acclaim and an Emmy for Outstanding Supporting Actress in "Lou Grant."

Notable Quote: On Norm's getting a mole removed from his butt:

LARRY: "I didn't know you were that [pause] vain. Who's ever gonna see your rear-end?"

NORM: "You're just about to, wise guy."

53. "An American Family" (11/29/84). Nick's wife, Loretta, is unable to bear children, so he tries to gain legal custody of his and Carla's son, Anthony. Carla is concerned because she is unable to say "no" to Nick, and does not want a court to prove she is an unfit parent. She reluctantly agrees to the change of custody, and quickly becomes distraught over losing her eldest son. When the Cheers gang convinces Carla to fight for legal custody, Nick attempts to persuade her by working his magic behind closed doors.

After a half-hearted attempt, Nick withdraws his request for custody.
Written by Heide Perlman. *Directed by* James Burrows.
Characters: Dan Hedaya (Nick Tortelli), Jean Kasem (Loretta Tortelli), Thomas Babson (Tom).
Notable Quote: On Carla seeking legal advice from Tom:
CLIFF: "Look, Carla. You're talking to a man who thinks affidavit is a Jewish wine."

54. **"Diane's Allergy"** (12/6/84). Diane and Frasier elevate their relationship to a higher plateau—cohabitation. However, Diane immediately develops an allergy, and blames Frasier's puppy, Pavlov, for her symptoms. Sam agrees to care for Pavlov (renaming her Diane), but the allergy persists. The lovebirds soon realize the allergy is a psychosomatic reaction caused by her unconscious feelings for Sam. Since Pavlov is not the problem, Frasier insists that Sam return the puppy. Sam refuses, and as they fiercely dispute custody, Diane believes they are fighting over her. Miraculously, this demonstration of love by Frasier is sufficient to cure her allergy.
Written by David Lloyd. *Directed by* James Burrows.
Characters: Cory "Bumper" Yothers (Ben), Kelsey Grammer (Frasier Crane).
Notable Quote: A kid visits the bar looking for Sam:
KID: "I'm looking for Sam Malone, ex–Red Sox player."
CARLA: "That's him over there behind the bar."
KID: [looking at Sam and Coach standing next to each other] "Boy, has he gotten old."
SAM: "Oh, no, no son. I'm Sam Malone."
KID: "I know."

55. **"Peterson Crusoe"** (12/13/84). Norm's life is in the balance when doctors intimate a spot on his X-ray may indicate a fatal ailment. When the X-ray result is negative, Norm decides to begin his life anew by fulfilling a lifelong dream of sailing to Bora Bora. For three weeks the Cheers gang receives letters from Norm postmarked from the tropical paradise. However, Norm never left Boston and is living in Sam's office. (He gave the letters to a sailor to mail from Bora Bora.) The gang is momentarily upset with Norm's cowardice, but after sharing personal dreams gone awry, they coax him out of the office.
Written by David Angell. *Directed by* James Burrows.
Characters: Howard Goodwin (Mark), Michael Griswold (Conrad), John Marzilli (Joe).
Notable Quote: On Cliff's dream of being a trapeze artist:
CLIFF: "When I was a lad I went to see the movie *Trapeze* with Burt Lancaster and Tony Curtis."
COACH: "No kidding, Cliffy. Did you sit between them?"

56. **"A Ditch in Time"** (12/20/84). Sam dates Diane's Goldenbrook sanitarium friend, Amanda, who is irrationally obsessive with men. Amanda promptly announces her and Sam's wedding engagement, and even invites her parents to Boston to meet her new fiancé. Whenever Sam tries to terminate the relationship, she threatens suicide. However, when Diane explains that Sam is the same man she mentioned in group therapy at Goldenbrook, Amanda immediately breaks up with him. Sam is stunned, and insists Diane explain why he was such a terrible boyfriend. She obliges, and the list goes on and on!

Written by Ken Estin. *Directed by* James Burrows.

Characters: Carol Kane (Amanda), David Wiley (Todd), Kate Williamson (Mona), Larry Harpel (Larry).

Note: Carol Kane has appeared in the movies *Jumpin' Jack Flash* (1986) and *License to Drive* (1988), and received acclaim for her role in "Taxi" (as Simka Gravas, Latka's girlfriend), winning Emmys for Outstanding Lead Actress (1982) and Outstanding Supporting Actress (1983).

Notable Quote: Regarding Amanda's state of mind if Sam dumps her:

DIANE: "Well, she could do something ghastly again."

SAM: "You, you don't mean...?"

DIANE: "Yes, she could try to kill herself."

SAM: "Oh, thank God. I thought I was in danger there."

57. **"Whodunit?"** (1/3/85). Frasier is anxious to spend time with his mentor, Dr. Bennett Ludlow, but Ludlow only wants to spend time with his new love—Carla! Frasier and Diane feel slighted when Ludlow is unavailable for their company, and are astounded when they discover he is always canceling on the nights Carla does not work. As the peculiar romance continues, Carla becomes pregnant with child number six. Ludlow proposes marriage, but Carla rejects the offer because she does not want to be married when her dream man comes along.

Written by Tom Reeder. *Directed by* James Burrows.

Characters: James Karen (Dr. Ludlow), Ernie Sabella (Stan), Kelsey Grammer (Frasier Crane).

Notable Quote: On Carla's being pregnant again:

DIANE: "Oh, Carla. When you

were in high school and you took hygiene, did you cut the 'how not to' lecture?"

CARLA: "I had to, I was *pregnant*."

58. **"The Heart Is a Lonely Snipehunter"** (1/10/85). Frasier feels like a social outcast among the Cheers gang, so Diane convinces them to include him in their activities. To initiate Frasier into the gang, they take him snipehunting—an age-old tradition where the initiating member (the bagger) waits in a clearing with a gunnysack while the others go into the bushes to beat out the snipe. In other words, the bagger is abandoned in the woods while the rest of the gang goes to dinner and then to Cheers for beers. A few hours later, Frasier returns to the bar dejected because he failed to catch any snipe. He then cons the gang into taking him snipehunting again, but this time he plans to abandon them!

Written by Heide Perlman. *Directed by* James Burrows.

Characters: Alan Koss (Alan), Tim Cunningham (Tim), Walter Smith (Customer #1), Kim Elliott (Customer #2), H.B. Newton (Customer #3), Kelsey Grammer (Frasier Crane).

Notable Quote: Cliff, trying to get himself invited on a fishing trip:

SAM: "Cliffy. You wanna go fishing with us?"

CLIFF: "Well, nah. That's okay, Sam. I don't want to infringe on you and Norm's good time."

NORM: "You're gonna have to if you want to come along."

59. **"King of the Hill"** (1/24/85). Sam agrees to pitch for the Boston Chamber of Commerce in a charity softball game against the *Playboy* playmates. Sam's competitiveness compels him to take the game too seriously and

he humiliates the Playmates—17 strike-outs in a 7–0 win. After discussing the game, Sam and Diane realize they are both too competitive, and illustrate it with a Ping-Pong match. On the game point, Diane and Sam mutually agree to lay down their paddles to overcome their competitiveness. As they exit the poolroom, Diane rushes back, serves the ball, and declares, "I win!"

Written by Elliot Shoenman. *Directed by* James Burrows.

Characters: John Hancock (Lenny), David Paymer (Reporter), Jeana Tomasina (Becky), Heidi Sorenson (Ginger), Ola Ray (Andrea), Larry Harpel (Larry), Steve Giannelli (Steve).

Note: Jeana Tomasina, Heidi Sorenson, and Ola Ray were actual *Playboy* playmates.

Notable Quote: Carla conversing with a *Playboy* playmate:

CARLA: "You know what bugs me about women like you? You take off all your clothes, you pose nude for a magazine, thousands of men see you naked. I have to go to them one by one. It's not fair."

60. **"Teacher's Pet"** (1/31/85). Sam enrolls in a geography night class to earn a high school diploma and aces it by sleeping with the teacher, Alannah Purdy. After a confrontation with Diane, Sam demands that his final exam grade be based solely upon his class performance. With Coach's assistance, Sam ultimately passes the class with a "D" (though his greatest satisfaction is embarrassing Diane when she fails to correctly name the state capitals of South Dakota and Oregon). **Subtopic:** Cliff is hypersensitive about the size of his ears and contemplates ear-tuck surgery.

Written by Tom Reeder. *Directed by* James Burrows.

Characters: regulars only.

Notable Quote: On Sam kissing his night class teacher:

COACH: "I saw them smooching in the parking lot. I was putting up a notice there on the bulletin board."

DIANE: "With probing tongue?"

COACH: "No Diane, with a thumb-tack and my thumb."

61. **"The Mail Goes to Jail"** (2/7/85). Cliff is ailing from a winter cold, so Norm volunteers to finish his postal route. When Norm is arrested for mail theft, Cliff confronts a serious dilemma—retain his employment or exonerate Norm. Cliff initially informs the police that Norm was stalking him, but finally reveals the truth and receives a postal reprimand. Norm is released from jail and only accepts an apology after Cliff agrees to stand on a barstool with his pants around his ankles while barking like a seal. **Subtopic:** Diane criticizes the Cheers gang's inability to fix the bar's furnace, and becomes stuck in the heating duct while attempting to do the dirty deed herself.

Written by David Lloyd. *Directed by* James Burrows.

Characters: Debi Richter (Bambi), Troy Evans (Cop), Nick De Mauro (Customer), Larry Harpel (Larry), Al Rosen (Al).

Notable Quote: Norm, volunteering to deliver the mail for Cliff:

NORM: "Let me drop these [letters] off for you, Cliffy."

CLIFF: "Ah, Norm. You're not trained. You're not qualified."

NORM: "What qualified? You drop them in a slot. A chimp could do it."

CLIFF: "They did a study at the University of Michigan. Chimps were 32 percent slower. [However] they were better at customer relations."

62. "Behind Every Great Man" (2/21/85). Sam tries to impress a *Boston Scene* magazine reporter, Paula Nelson, who is interviewing Cheers patrons for a story on Boston's dating scene. She is rather intelligent, so Sam uses Diane's knowledge of Impressionism to win the heart of Paula. Diane misconstrues Sam's newfound interest in the arts as a surreptitious means of rekindling their romance. She is thoroughly convinced after overhearing Sam make hotel reservations for the weekend in an effort to recapture the magic. Diane packs a suitcase for a romantic weekend, but at the last minute discovers Sam has another date.

Written by Ken Levine and David Isaacs. *Directed by* James Burrows.

Characters: Alison La Placa (Paula Nelson), Al Rosen (Al), Larry Harpel (Larry), George R. Wendt (George).

Note: Alison La Placa has appeared in "Tom," "The Jackie Thomas Show" (as Laura Miller), "The John Larroquette Show," and played the role of Linda Phillips in "Duet" and "Open House."

Notable Quote: Sam, trying to acquire knowledge about the arts:

SAM: "Guys. Does anybody remember anything that Diane has said about Impressionism?"

CARLA: "No. But I know she makes a bad first one."

63. "If Ever I Would Leave You" (2/28/85). Loretta has an opportunity to join the singing group The Grinning Americans, so she forsakes her marriage to Nick, taking the house and the business. Nick enters Cheers a shattered man and begs Carla to take him back. To prove he is a changed man, Nick accepts a janitorial position at Cheers. Despite the Cheers gang's urging her to take him back, Carla resists his frequent advances. When she eventually succumbs to his charm and agrees to give Nick another chance, Loretta returns to take him back. He immediately returns to her arms, crushing Carla in the process.

Written by Ken Levine and David Isaacs. *Directed by* James Burrows.

Characters: Dan Hedaya (Nick Tortelli), Jean Kasem (Loretta Tortelli), Steve Giannelli (Steve), Kelsey Grammer (Frasier Crane).

Notable Quote: On Carla not believing Nick wants her back:

NICK: "Here, I'm going to hold my hand over this flame until you believe my sincerity."

CARLA: "Go ahead, I happen to be fond of the smell of roast pig."

64. "The Executive's Executioner" (3/7/85). Norm has a reputation for leaving work early, so it is quite a surprise when his boss, Mr. Hecht, offers Norm a 300 percent raise and a promotion to corporate killer—the guy who fires employees. Norm has the option of accepting the raise and promotion or be fired. He wisely accepts the promotion; as he says, "I cannot be bought and I cannot be threatened, but you put the two together and I'm your man!" Norm is perfect for the job because he is good at pity, but eventually his tear ducts dry up, so he decides to quit.

Written by Heide Perlman. *Directed by* James Burrows.

Characters: Richard Roat (Mr. Hecht), Mark Schubb (Billy Richter), David Wohl (Phil Wagner), Raye Birk (Walt Twitchell), Warren Munson (John Parker), Randy Miller (Michael), Larry Harpel (Larry).

Notable Quote: After Cliff writes a spiteful letter to his neighbor:

CARLA: "Look Clavin, just think of this as your ticket out of Weenie Town."

CLIFF: "Carla, I made that trip a long time ago."

CARLA: "Yeah, but they threw you out at Dinkville."

65. "Bar Bet" (3/14/85). Twelve months earlier, a patron, Eddie Gordon, made a bet that Sam could not marry Jacqueline Bisset within one year. Sam was drinking tequila at the time, and wagered the bar that he could marry her. As the year deadline approaches, Eddie returns to collect on the bet. After considerable effort, the Cheers gang locates a Jacqueline Bisset in West Virginia and convinces her to visit Boston. Sam then works his magic, and she agrees to a quick marriage and divorce. When Eddie realizes he cannot win, he settles the bet for a green olive with a pimento.

Written by Jim Parker. *Directed by* James Burrows.

Characters: Michael Richards (Eddie Gordon), Laurie Walters (Jacqueline Bisset), Thomas W. Babson (Tom Sherry), Dean Dittman (Harrison Fiedler), Al Rosen (Al).

Note: Michael Richards subsequently became a successful supporting actor in "Seinfeld" (as Kramer). Laurie Walters is best known for her role as Joannie Bradford in the 1970s television hit "Eight is Enough" starring Dick Van Patten.

Notable Quote: Cliff, teasing Tom about never passing the attorney bar exam:

TOM: "You know, when I pass my bar exam, Cliff, you're gonna eat your words."

CLIFF: "Yeah, if I have any teeth left."

66. "Cheerio Cheers" (4/11/85). Frasier accepts a teaching position in Europe and asks Diane to accompany him. Diane is hesitant because she knows this will impede her and Sam's inevitable reunion. When Sam expresses no interest whatsoever, she accepts Frasier's offer. Cheers hosts a going away party for her and Frasier, and as the evening progresses, Sam and Diane become romantically involved. However, before rekindling their romance, Diane insists their intimacy lead to a future commitment. Sam's failure to commit to a relationship is sufficient justification for Diane to accompany Frasier to Europe.

Written by Sam Simon. *Directed by* James Burrows.

Characters: Kelsey Grammer (Frasier Crane).

Notable Quote: Sam, wishing Diane happiness on her European trip:

SAM: "Just because the two of us didn't travel well."

DIANE: "When did we ever travel?"

SAM: "Are you kidding me? We went through hell together."

DIANE: "Yes. Well, it helped you knew the language."

67. "The Bartender's Tale" (4/18/85). Sam searches for a waitress to replace Diane, but Carla rejects every attractive applicant. Sam is forced to hire Lillian Huxley, a career waitress, and someone with whom he will have absolutely no sexual involvement. However, Sam wants to date Lillian's very attractive daughter, Carolyn, and as he solicits Lillian's permission, she misconstrues his words as a love confession for her. Although intrigued by Lillian's self-proclaimed sexual prowess (two husbands died in bed very happy), Sam decides to date Carolyn, who rather ironically despises sex! **Subtopic:** Diane and Frasier enjoy their European vacation.

Written by Sam Simon. *Directed by* James Burrows.

Characters: Lila Kaye (Lillian), Camilla More (Carolyn), Rhonda Shear (Sydney), Brynja Willis (Brenda), Gregory Snegoff (Bellboy), Tim Cunningham (Tim), Kelsey Grammer (Frasier Crane).

Notable Quote: On Carla's interviewing a waitress:

CARLA: "Have you had any experience serving the public?"

SYDNEY: "You mean dressed?"

68. "The Belles of St. Clete's" (5/2/85). Carla seeks vengeance on her old high school principal, Drusilla Dimeglio, and summons her childhood friends to collaborate on the revenge. Carla always fantasized about shaving Drusilla's head, but her friends refuse to participate in the scheme. Despite having an opportunity to implement the dastardly deed, Carla somewhat resists the temptation. In the end, she becomes friends with Drusilla—but not before shaving half of her head. Subtopic: Cliff brags about a sordid affair while vacationing in Florida, but Norm discovers Cliff's "love letter" is actually from a motel manager threatening a lawsuit if Cliff does not return certain stolen items.

Written by Ken Estin. *Directed by* James Burrows.

Characters: Camila Ashland (Drusilla Dimeglio), Kate Zentall (Kathy Settuducato), Catherine Paolone (Donna Guzzo), Marsha Warfield (Roxanne Brewster), Ellen Gerstein (Mo McSweeney), Alan Koss (Alan), Thomas W. Babson (Tom), Tim Cunningham (Tim), Steve Giannelli (Steve), Larry Harpel (Larry), Kelsey Grammer (Frasier Crane).

Note: Marsha Warfield is best known for her role as Roz Russell in the television hit "Night Court" starring Harry Anderson, but she also hosted the daytime talk show "Marsha Warfield" (1990–91) and appeared in "Anything for Love."

Notable Quote: On Cliff's possibly having an affair in Florida:

NORM: "Why don't you guys believe that Cliff had a little affair in Florida? I believe him. I mean, she could have been drunk, blind, just out of prison!"

69. "Rescue Me" (5/9/85). While in Europe, Frasier proposes marriage to Diane. Before responding, she telephones Sam, hoping he will talk her out of it. When he continues to feign ambivalence, she accepts Frasier's proposal. Sam subsequently reconsiders and flies to Italy to stop the wedding. In the meantime, Diane and Frasier are stranded in a small Italian village, and decide to marry immediately. The season finale ends on this cliffhanger of whether Diane and Frasier were married, or if Sam reclaimed her for himself.

Written by Ken Estin. *Directed by* James Burrows.

Characters: Martin Ferrero (the Waiter), James V. Christy (Dan Corelli), Dan Galliani (the Priest), Susan Kase (the Stewardess), Kelsey Grammer (Frasier Crane).

Notable Quote: Sam contemplates stopping Diane and Frasier's wedding:

SAM: "I gotta do this. It's not for me. It's not for Diane. It's for Frasier. I mean, nobody deserves to be married to that woman."

Season Four: 1985-86

(NBC Thursday, 9:00-9:30 p.m. EST) **Season Regulars:** Ted Danson (Sam Malone), Shelley Long (Diane Chambers), Rhea Perlman (Carla Tortelli), John Ratzenberger (Cliff Clavin), Woody Harrelson (Woody Boyd), George Wendt (Norm Peterson).

Technical Credits: *Created by* Glen Charles, Les Charles and James Burrows. *Executive Producers:* James Burrows, Glen Charles, Les Charles. *Producers:* Peter Casey and David Lee, Heide Perlman, David Angell. *Writers:* David Angell, Peter Casey, Andy Cowan, Cheri Eichen, Norm Gunzenhauser, Kimberly Hill, David Lee, David Lloyd, Heide Perlman, Tom Reeder, Susan Seeger, Tom Seeley, Bill Steinkellner, Phoef Sutton, Miriam Trogdon, David S. Williger. *Directors:* James Burrows, Thomas Lofaro. *Co-Producer:* Tim Berry. *Executive Script Consultant:* David Lloyd. *Executive Story Consultants:* Cheri Eichen and Bill Steinkellner. *Director of Photography:* John Finger. *Art Director:* Herman Zimmerman. *Edited by* Andy Ackerman. *Film Editors:* M. Pam Blumenthal, Doug Hines, A.C.E. *Unit Production Manager:* Linda McMurray. *First Assistant Directors:* Thomas Lofaro, Brian James Ellis. *Second Assistant Directors:* Brian James Ellis, Leonard R. Garner, Jr. *Music by* Craig Safan. *Song:* "Where Everybody Knows Your Name." *Lyrics and Music by* Judy Hart Angelo and Gary Portnoy. *Sung by* Gary Portnoy. *Casting:* Randy Stone. *Original Casting:* Stephen Kolzak. *Set Decorator:* Lynne Albright. *Technical Coordinators:* Bill Fraley, Don Bustany. *Script Supervisors:* Gabrielle James,

Doris Grau. *Production Mixer:* Michael Ballin. *Choreographer:* Tad Tadlock (#89). *Costume Supervisor:* Robert L. Tanella. *Women's Costumers:* Sandra F. Culotta, Sharon Swenson. *Makeup Artist:* Bruce Hutchinson. *Hair Stylist:* Marilyn Patricia Phillips. *Music Editor:* Chips Swanson. *Sound Effects:* William H. Angarola. *Main Title Design:* James Castle and Bruce Bryant. *Opticals:* Freeze Frame. *Cameras and Lenses:* Panavision. *Assistants to the Charles Brothers:* Rick Beren, Leslie Brenner, Tonya Cannon, Peter Chakos, Christine Connor, Mary Fukuto, Land Courtney Hay, Rebecca Helm, Sue Herring, Margi Lintz, Carol Navratil, Diane Overdiek, David Reid, Rachelle Ricks, Danielle Veerman, Barry Zajac. *Executive in Charge of Production:* Richard Villarino *Charles/Burrows/ Charles Productions in Association with* Paramount Television.

70. **"Birth, Death, Love, & Rice"** (9/26/85). Sam arrives at Cheers and recounts past events. After arriving at the Marino Estate in Florence, Italy, he was thrown in jail and then purchased by a local landowner to replace an ox that died. Sam escaped and returned to Boston but failed to stop Diane and Frasier's wedding. Meanwhile, Frasier's life was shattered after being left at the altar, and Diane went on a spree of decadence. When visiting Cheers, Frasier confides that she is atoning in a nearby Boston convent, so Sam pays a visit to convince Diane to return to Cheers. **Subtopic:** Woody Boyd debuts as the naive farm boy hired to replace Coach, who died earlier that year (on the show and in real life).

Written by Heide Perlman. *Directed by* James Burrows.

Characters: Alan Koss (Alan), Larry Harpel (Larry), Lois de Banzie (Sister Marie), Patricia Huston (Sister Catherine), Arnold F. Turner (Customer), Kelsey Grammer (Frasier Crane).

71. "Woody Goes Belly Up" (10/3/85). The Cheers gang secretly arranges for Woody's Indiana girlfriend, Beth Curtis, to visit Boston. The moment Woody and Beth lay eyes on one another they have an irresistible urge to eat (they are using food to suppress their sexual desires). Although Diane tries to teach them better eating habits, Woody and Beth quickly realize having sex is the best solution. As the episode ends, Diane and Sam discuss their past sexual relationship, and soon suppress their sexual desires by devouring everything in sight! **Subtopic:** Frasier is still depressed over losing the love of his life, Diane, so he quits the psychiatric profession and becomes a janitor at Cheers.

Written by Heide Perlman. *Directed by* James Burrows.

Characters: Amanda Wyss (Beth), Liz Keifer (Lisa), Al Rosen (Al), Sean E. Markland (Waiter), Kelsey Grammer (Frasier Crane).

Notable Quote: On Woody and Beth's substituting food for sex:

FRASIER: "In short, food became your substitute for sex."

NORM: "Vera became mine!"

72. "Someday My Prince Will Come" (10/17/85). When an overcoat is forgotten at Cheers, Diane envisions her dream man while fantasizing about the owner of the cashmere garment. After considerable cajoling from Sam and Carla, Diane impetuously arranges

a blind date with the owner, Stuart. After dating for one week, Diane and Stuart appear to be compatible, but she ultimately decides to terminate the relationship because he is not physically attractive. Diane quickly realizes the hypocrisy of her behavior—preaching that inner beauty is all that matters, when in actuality she, too, succumbs to physical attractiveness.

Written by Tom Seeley and Norm Gunzenhauser. *Directed by* James Burrows.

Characters: Frank Dent (Stuart Sorenson).

Notable Quote: Diane, claiming that looks are unimportant:

DIANE: "If my face were transposed on another soul, would it matter?"

CARLA: "To the poor sap who got it, it would."

73. "The Groom Wore Clearasil" (10/24/85). Carla's 16-year-old son, Anthony, asks permission to marry his girlfriend, Annie. Carla reluctantly agrees to give parental consent, but only if Anthony abstains from seeing Annie for two weeks. Carla expects his eyes to wander, but he stays home the entire time. However, as Carla prepares to sign the marriage consent form, Anthony becomes attracted to Annie's cousin, Gabrielle, and postpones the marriage. **Subtopics:** Diane interviews for a teaching assistant position and insults the professor when attempting to elicit why Sumner Sloane recommended her so highly. Meanwhile, Cliff proudly displays a homegrown potato resembling Richard Nixon.

Written by Peter Casey and David Lee. *Directed by* James Burrows.

Characters: Timothy Williams (Anthony), Mandy Ingber (Annie), Sherilyn Fenn (Gabrielle), Al Rosen

(Al), John Ingle (Professor Moffat), Craig Berenson (Customer).

Note: Mandy Ingber was a regular cast member in the short-lived television spin-off "The Tortellis" (1987). Sherilyn Fenn appeared in "Twin Peaks" (as Audrey Horne) and several movies, the most notable being *Fatal Instinct* (1993) and *Boxing Helena* (1993).

Notable Quote: In reference to Carla's son being in love with Annie:

CLIFF: "Ah, don't be so hard on him, Carla. You know, men will do some pretty strange things to have a girl by their side."

CARLA: "In your case, inflate one."

74. **"Diane's Nightmare"** (10/31/85). Diane dreams that Andy-Andy, a.k.a. Andy Schroeder, is released from the state mental hospital and hiding in the Cheers cellar. On a dark, stormy night, the electricity fails, and one by one the Cheers gang enters the cellar, never to return. When she awakens, Andy actually visits the bar to introduce the gang to his fiancée, Cynthia. Despite the minor white lies Andy told Cynthia—he owns the bar, Sam is a reformed flasher, Frasier is a kleptomaniac, and Diane wanted to have his child—the gang acts out the charade to convince Cynthia that Andy is an upstanding citizen.

Written by David Lloyd. *Directed by* James Burrows.

Characters: Derek McGrath (Andy Schroeder), Nancy Cartwright (Cynthia), Tim Cunningham (Tim), Kelsey Grammer (Frasier Crane).

Notable Quote: After awakening, Diane wonders if it was a dream:

DIANE: "Oh, Sam. This may be a silly question. But you don't have a velvet smoking jacket, do you?"

SAM: "Hey, come on. I'm smoking in any jacket."

75. **"I'll Gladly Pay You Tuesday"** (11/7/85). Sam loans Diane $500 to purchase a rare Hemingway book, but becomes upset when she subsequently wastes her money on luxuries without repaying the debt. Diane senses the hostility and gives him the book as collateral. Sam is supposed to place the book in the office safe, but instead takes it home. While reading the book in the tub, he accidentally drops it in the bathwater and the book is ruined. When Diane wants the book returned so she can sell it to an interested buyer, Sam bids $1,200 to prevent her from knowing the truth. Diane finds Sam's interest in literature sexually arousing, but still demands payment in accordance with his last bid.

Written by Cheri Eichen and Bill Steinkellner. *Directed by* James Burrows.

Characters: William Lanteau (Mr. Sayers), Eve Glazier (Little Girl), Steve Giannelli (Steve), Alan Koss (Alan), Rick Andosca (Guy).

Notable Quote: On Cliff's walking backwards to break the world record:

NORM: "I know you guys think that Cliff's pretty weird. But I'll say this much, he'll probably never reproduce."

76. **"2 Good 2 Be 4 Real"** (11/14/85). In a desperate search for a man, Carla places a personal ad in the newspaper. Out of concern for her depression and desperation, the Cheers gang creates a fictitious beau, Mitch Wainwright, to answer the ad. Carla immediately falls in love with Mitch, and begins rejecting legitimate suitors such as funeral director Vinnie Claussen. The gang eventually confesses the

truth and convinces her to date Vinnie. **Subtopic:** Diane asks a mime, Sotto, to entertain the Cheers patrons, but when he is more irritating than entertaining, Norm and Cliff eject him from the bar.

Written by Peter Casey and David Lee. *Directed by* James Burrows.

Characters: Don Lewis (Sotto, the Mime), Michael Alaimo (Vinnie Claussen), Jack F. Gallagher (Customer).

Notable Quote: Regarding not allowing a mime to work in the bar:

SAM: [to Diane] "From now on, nobody works in this bar that wears more makeup than you do."

77. "Love Thy Neighbor" (11/21/85; approx. 9:40–10:10 p.m. EST). Norm's neighbor, Phyllis Henshaw, suspects her husband is having an affair with Vera, and convinces Norm to hire a private investigator, Santo Carbone, to confirm or deny the allegation. Santo determines Vera and Ron contemplated a tryst but did not follow through. Despite this revelation, Phyllis seriously considers a sexual liaison with Norm. Although tempted, Norm faithfully rejects her proposition because he does not cheat on his wife. **Subtopic:** When Sam refers to Diane as a love bunny during an interview on Dave Richards' radio talk show, she demands a formal retraction and apology on the air.

Written by David Angell. *Directed by* James Burrows.

Characters: John F. Dryer (Dave Richards' Voice), Miriam Flynn (Phyllis Henshaw), Ernie Sabella (Santo Carbone), Carolyn Ann Clark (Woman), Richard Young (Frank), Frank Czarnecki (Jack).

78. "From Beer to Eternity" (11/28/85). After losing in baseball, the Cheers gang challenges Gary's Tavern to a bowling match. Things look dismal when Cheers' ace bowler Woody Boyd refuses to participate because of "the tragedy"—he once maimed a bowling alley maintenance man in a freak bowling accident. The gang still participates and is losing resoundingly until Diane reveals bowling is one of her hidden talents. Despite her single-handedly winning the bowling competition for Cheers, Sam remains despondent because this was the first time Cheers defeated Gary's Tavern in any sports competition, and he needed a woman to do it for him.

Written by Peter Casey and David Lee. *Directed by* James Burrows.

Characters: Joel Polis (Gary), Alan Koss (Alan), Tim Cunningham (Tim), Steve Giannelli (Steve), Jack Kosslyn (Bill), Kim Waltrip (Woman).

Notable Quote: Carla, threatening Gary during the bowling contest:

CARLA: "Back off, buster, or I'll put vaseline in your finger holes."

GARY: "Just try to touch my ball."

CARLA: "I was talking about your nose."

79. "The Barstoolie" (12/5/85). Cliff's father unexpectedly visits Cheers 30 years after abandoning his family. Cliff is apprehensive at first, but after one day of male bonding the Clavin men become buddies. Unfortunately, Cliff's dream of having a father figure is shattered when his dad reveals he is moving to Australia to avoid prosecution for real estate fraud. While Cliff contemplates calling the authorities, the elder Clavin escapes through the bathroom window at Cheers. **Subtopic:** Sam dates an intelligent woman, Claudia, who immediately befriends Diane and eventually breaks up with Sam because she finds his relentless come-ons unappealing.

Written by Andy Cowan and David S. Williger. *Directed by* James Burrows.

Characters: Dick O'Neill (Mr. Clavin), Claudia Cron (Claudia).

Note: Dick O'Neill is best remembered for his recurring regular role as Charlie Cagney (Chris Cagney's father) in "Cagney & Lacey," and had many acting roles in shows such as "Falcon Crest," "Dark Justice" and "Empire."

Notable Quote: Sam, anticipating sex after his date with Claudia:

SAM: "Claudia's been a tough nut to crack, but tonight's the night she's gonna be enjoying all the rides in Sammy's magic kingdom."

DIANE: "She's in for a Mickey Mouse evening with Goofy as her guide."

80. **"Don Juan Is Hell"** (12/12/85). Diane prepares a psychological case study on the Don Juan syndrome, using Sam as her subject. The thesis is so remarkable that Diane's professor, Dr. Lowell Greenspon, allows Sam to speak to the class. Midway through the presentation Diane explains to Sam that the paper is not flattering. When Sam responds dejectedly, she recants the denigrating remarks to avoid hurting his feelings, and claims to have changed the facts to support her thesis. As Diane attempts to prove Sam can have a nonsexual relationship with a woman, the demonstration ends early when they become sexually aroused.

Written by Phoef Sutton. *Directed by* James Burrows.

Characters: Kenneth Tigar (Dr. Lowell Greenspon), Stephen Minor (Barry), Rafael Mauro (Reporter), Tim Cunningham (Tim).

Notable Quote: Sam, inviting Dr.

Lowell Greenspon (Diane's psychology professor) to the bar for his class presentation:

LOWELL: "I don't think some of the members would mind coming by for a drink afterwards. It would give them a chance to meet the clinical case in the flesh."

SAM: "Oh, I'm not gonna promise that. We'll just see how the evening goes."

81. **"Fools and Their Money"** (12/19/85). After several weeks of success in the Cheers football pool, Woody decides to bet his life savings ($1,000) with a bookie. Despite agreeing to place the bet, Sam keeps the money to protect Woody from making a foolish mistake. Naturally, the parley comes through, and he would have won $10,000. Although he admits being upset with Sam, they eventually settle their disagreement by singing "Home on the Range." **Subtopic:** Frasier is still embittered that Diane ruined his life and career, so he spends all of his time correcting her grammar.

Written by Heide Perlman. *Directed by* James Burrows.

Characters: Arthur Taxler (Frank), Paul Willson (Paul), Al Rosen (Al), Kelsey Grammer (Frasier Crane).

Notable Quote: Diane, trying to explain that Sam did not place the bet:

DIANE: "Woody. I want to speak metaphysically."

WOODY: "And you need money for the language lessons. No problem."

82. **"Take My Shirt ... Please"** (1/9/86). Sam donates his Red Sox jersey to a celebrity memorabilia auction on public television. Initially, the jersey fails to sell, so Diane purchases it to protect his image and ego. Sam tells her to return it, and when the jersey

fails to sell again, he pretends to be an elderly woman purchasing it. Diane catches him in the act, so the jersey is returned to the auction one more time. Finally, a viewer, Bert Simpson, purchases the garment for $300 to put the damn thing to rest. **Subtopic:** Norm entertains boring clients, the Brubakers, and solicits Cliff's conversational skills to retain their business.

Written by David Lloyd. *Directed by* James Burrows.

Characters: Robert Symonds (Mr. Brubaker), Frances Bay (Mrs. Brubaker), Patrick Cronin (Bert), Earl H. Bullock (Announcer).

Notable Quote: What Sam likes most about public television:

SAM: "I especially like the two guys that talk about the day's events."

DIANE: "MacNeil-Lehrer?"

SAM: "No, no. Bert and Ernie. [pause] Oh, wait a minute, unless that's their last names."

83. **"Suspicion"** (1/16/86). Diane and a fellow psychology student, Irving, conduct a paranoia study using the Cheers gang as unsuspecting subjects. Irving creates an atmosphere of paranoia, and when Diane discloses the study, the gang vows revenge. Soon Diane becomes paranoid, and when a PBS show wants to film her poetry reading, she expects this to be the act of vengeance. Diane responds by clucking like a chicken, and to her dismay, the "poem" is aired. Despite the embarrassment, Diane is more upset because the gang did not take the time to exact revenge. However, vindication comes with the ol' bucket of water over the door gag, and a drenched Diane rushes out of the office, joyously proclaiming, "I love you guys!"

Written by Tom Reeder. *Directed by* James Burrows.

Characters: Hamilton Camp (Martin Gallagher), M. C. Gainey (Irving), Joseph Paz (Customer), Kelsey Grammer (Frasier Crane).

84. **"The Triangle"** (1/23/86). Frasier is still depressed and drinking heavily, so Sam and Diane devise a plan to boost his confidence as a therapist and convince him to return to the psychiatric profession. When Sam fakes symptoms of depression, Frasier concludes the cause is Sam's subconscious love for Diane. For Frasier's benefit, Sam and Diane feign being in love, but when they cannot mutually agree on the best way to word the affair, they begin arguing. Although Frasier witnesses their contention and is told the truth, he remains confident with the diagnosis and returns to the psychiatric profession.

Written by Susan Seeger. *Directed by* James Burrows.

Characters: Al Rosen (Al), Kelsey Grammer (Frasier Crane).

Notable Quote: Frasier, looking at a beer:

FRASIER: "Now there's a head I can shrink."

85. **"Cliffie's Big Score"** (1/30/86). Cliff wins the Postman of the Year award and invites Diane to the Gala Postman's Ball. She declines because of a very important Cheese Club meeting, so he asks Carla, who accepts, but only if he gives her money, a dress and a VCR. When Diane subsequently accepts Cliff's invitation, he arranges a blind date, Lucas, for Carla. After the ceremony, Carla becomes very friendly with Lucas in the backseat of Cliff's station wagon. At this moment, Cliff inadvertently reveals that Diane was his first choice as a date, so Carla convinces him to make sexual advances

toward Diane. When Cliff makes the attempt, Diane abandons him on a deserted highway.

Written by Heide Perlman. *Directed by* James Burrows.

Characters: Timothy Scott (Lucas), Al Rosen (Al).

Notable Quote: Carla's evening with Diane, Cliff and a weird hippie:

CARLA: "I can see this is gonna be a laugh a minute. An evening with the stick, the nerd, and door number three."

86. "Second Time Around"
(2/6/86). Frasier sinks into another state of depression, this time because of his dating life, or lack thereof. When his first date with Dr. Lilith Sternin is disastrous, Sam asks a friend, Candi Pearson, to entertain Frasier. After one date, Frasier and Candi announce their wedding engagement. Diane leads the assault to convince him that marrying Candi would be catastrophic, both personally and professionally. After considerable effort and discussion, Frasier realizes he is only attracted to Candi's uninhibited nature and they are totally incompatible, so he cancels the wedding.

Written by Cheri Eichen and Bill Steinkellner. *Directed by* Thomas Lofaro.

Characters: Jennifer Tilly (Candi Pearson), Bebe Neuwirth (Dr. Lilith Sternin), Lou Fant (Justice of the Peace), Kelsey Grammer (Frasier Crane).

Note: Jennifer Tilly starred in the Fox television series "Key West" (as Savannah) and appeared in "Shaping Up."

Notable Quote: On Frasier's being dumped by Lilith shortly after Diane left him at the altar:

CARLA: "That poor yutz. Even the trash only gets dumped once a week."

87. "The Peterson Principle"
(2/13/86, 9:30–10:00 p.m. EST). Norm and another employee, Morrison, are finalists for a promotion. When a colleague reveals that Morrison is sleeping with the boss' wife, Norm contemplates using this information to solidify his promotion. He ultimately makes the ethical choice of not revealing the sexual rendezvous, and loses the promotion because his wife, Vera, does not fit in with the other executives' wives. Norm is offended and quits. However, his most noble act is not telling Vera that she cost him the promotion. **Subtopic**: Frasier shows slides of his and Diane's European vacation, and cannot control the wisecracks about how she tore out his heart.

Written by Peter Casey and David Lee. *Directed by* James Burrows.

Characters: Daniel Davis (Mr. Reinhardt), Chip Zien (Jeif Robbins), Adam Carl (Vito), Kelsey Grammer (Frasier Crane).

Notable Quote:

SAM: "What's happening, Norm?"

NORM: "It's a dog-eat-dog world, and I'm wearing Milkbone underwear."

88. "Dark Imaginings" (2/20/86).
Sam tries to prove his youthfulness by competing against Woody in racquetball. In a Pyrrhic victory, Sam suffers a hernia injury that requires surgery. To conceal the "old man's" injury, Sam informs the Cheers gang he is going skiing and then secretly admits himself into a hospital. While convalescing, he contemplates his fading youth and copes with the fear of aging. To track Sam's location, sleuthhound Diane follows a trail of paw prints on the nurses he constantly fondled. After offering consolation, Diane's efforts prove fruitful because

Sam quickly attempts to allure her into his hospital bed.

Written by David Angell. *Directed by* James Burrows.

Characters: Thomas Callaway (Jack Turner), Deborah Dalton (Nurse Louise), Pamela Bach (Bonnie), Tim Dunigan (Doctor McNeese), Christine Dickinson (Joan), Lisa Vige (Judy), Jeré Fields (Nurse Brenda), *139th Street Quartet*: Peter Neushul (Baritone), Larry F. Wright (2nd Tenor), Douglas M. Anderson (1st Tenor), James Kline (Bass); Kelsey Grammer (Frasier Crane).

89. "Save the Last Dance for Me" (2/27/86). When the "Boston Boppers" television show announces a dance competition reunion, Carla and Nick agree to enter as partners. However, the partnership is short-lived, as they begin arguing over who was a better dancer when they were teenagers. They mutually agree to change partners—Nick chooses Loretta, and Carla selects Sam. Although the new dancing partners perform admirably, the arrangement proves ineffective as both pairs are disqualified. Carla and Nick then reunite for one dance to prove they are the best dancing couple, and actually win first place.

Written by Heide Perlman. *Directed by* James Burrows.

Characters: Dan Hedaya (Nick Tortelli), Jean Kasem (Loretta Tortelli), Hal Landon, Jr. (Floyd Panjeric), Nick Dimitri (Eddie Gsznyk), Sinara Stull (Cheryl Koski).

Notable Quote: Carla, ecstatic about winning a dance contest:

CARLA: "It was like I was transported back in time. I wasn't a tired old woman with six kids. I was a fresh young teenager with *two* kids!"

90. "Fear Is My Co-Pilot" (3/13/86). One of Diane's many European lovers, Jack Dalton, whom she entertained after leaving Frasier at the altar, arrives unexpectedly and asks Diane to accompany him on an adventurous trip. After refusing because she enjoys the comfort and security of her stable, mundane lifestyle, Jack convinces Diane and Sam to take a plane ride. While airborne, Jack uses a yoga technique to lower his heart rate as if he were dead. As Sam and Diane confront their inevitable demise, they confess their love to one another. Although Jack explains he wanted them to face death so they could enjoy life, Sam challenges Jack to a fight and ends up with a black eye.

Written by Cheri Eichen and Bill Steinkellner. *Directed by* James Burrows.

Characters: Joseph Whipp (Jack Dalton), Kelsey Grammer (Frasier Crane).

Notable Quote: On Jack Dalton's always performing dangerous stunts:

JACK: "Some people say that I have a death wish. Far from it! I have a life wish."

CLIFF: "Oh? So does Normy... He wishes he had one!"

91. "Diane Chambers Day" (3/20/86). The Cheers gang plans another evening of watching *The Magnificent Seven*, and once again Diane is excluded. After Diane expresses feelings of anger and disappointment because she still feels like an outsider, Frasier suggests the gang spend one evening entertaining Diane by doing everything she enjoys (including attending the opera). Diane is overcome with emotion, and as the evening concludes, she becomes irresistibly attracted to Sam (thinking he organized the entire evening). At the risk of losing one night of passion, Sam confesses that Frasier planned everything. Diane finds this display of honesty even more irresistible, and although they do not become intimate, they do begin dating.

Written by Kimberly Hill. *Directed by* James Burrows.

Characters: Tom Harrison (Dennis Kaufman), Jacqueline Cassel (Jackie), Doris Grau (Corrine), Al Rosen (Al), Kelsey Grammer (Frasier Crane).

Notable Quote: Sam, inviting Diane back to his apartment:

DIANE: "My heart is saying 'yes'. My mind is saying 'no'."

SAM: "Why don't you let some other part of your body break the tie for you?"

92. **"Relief Bartender"** (3/27/86). When an ex–Red Sox player, Don Talbert, opens two new bars in Boston, Sam devises a marketing strategy to increase business—becoming a manager-host. Sam hires a new bartender, Ken, but when the marketing idea fails he is faced with the dilemma of firing one of the bartenders. Since Ken has a wife and family to support, Sam decides to fire the unattached Woody Boyd. After the termination is complete, a patron offers Ken a better job, so he resigns from Cheers. Although Sam convinces Woody to return, the wise Hoosier insists upon a wage increase.

Written by Miriam Trogdon. *Directed by* James Burrows.

Characters: Tony Carrierro (Ken Charters), Patricia Veselich (Mrs. Charters), Judith Barsi (Child #1), Edan Gross (Child #2), Kim Robinson (Andrea), Madgel Dean (Mrs. Benfer), Paul Eiding (Fred), Jack M. Lindine (Caribou #1), Terrence Beasor

(Caribou #2), Kelsey Grammer (Frasier Crane).

Notable Quote: In reference to Sam's ordering the waitresses around:

DIANE: "I'll buy the bullets if you'll pull the trigger."

CARLA: "Shooting is too quick. I want him to suffer. Why don't you start dating him again."

93. **"Strange Bedfellows"** (Part 1 of 3) (5/1/86). When Boston city councilwoman Janet Eldridge uses Cheers as one of her campaign stops, Sam boldly asks her out. Despite publicly declining the invitation, Janet privately offers her personal telephone number. Soon they begin dating. Although Sam basks in the limelight as a celebrity at political functions, Diane suspects Janet is only using him to bolster her electability. **Subtopic:** Diane campaigns for Janet's opponent, James Fleener, and Frasier agrees to provide assistance, hoping the time with Diane will rekindle their romance.

Written by David Angell. *Directed by* James Burrows.

Characters: Kate Mulgrew (Janet Eldridge), Max Wright (Jim Fleener), David Paymer (Phil Schumacher), Brad Burlingame (Brian), Carolyn Ann Clark (April), Michael G. Hagerty (Decker), Charles Walker (Reporter #1), Lawrence Lott (Reporter #2), Tim Cunningham (Tim), Paul Willson (Paul), Kelsey Grammer (Frasier Crane).

Note: Kate Mulgrew appeared in "Ryan's Hope," "Man of the People" and recently, "Star Trek: Voyager," but may be best known from "Mrs. Columbo" (as Kate Columbo/Callahan). Her movie credits include *A Stranger Is Watching* (1982) and *Throw Mama from the Train* (1987). Max Wright appeared regularly in "ALF" (as

Willie Tanner, 1986–90), and "Buffalo Bill" (as the nervous station manager Karl Shub).

Notable Quote: James Fleener's campaign slogan:

CARLA: "'Whim with Jim'?"

DIANE: "It's very Joycean."

CARLA: "If that means stupid, I agree."

94. "Strange Bedfellows" (Part 2 of 3) (5/8/86). Sam continues dating councilwoman Janet Eldridge, who feels threatened by Diane. Janet convinces Sam to fire Diane, under the guise of freeing her from a dead-end waitress position with a friendly shove out of the nest. Diane overhears the conversation and decides to quit instead. After Diane rescinds the resignation, Sam fires her, and she finds employment as a checkout clerk at Hurley's Market. **Subtopic:** Norm thinks his sister-in-law, Donna, is a sex fiend, and fears being alone with her while Vera is out of town visiting an ill aunt.

Written by David Angell. *Directed by* James Burrows.

Characters: Kate Mulgrew (Janet Eldridge), Max Wright (Jim Fleener), Senator Gary Hart (Himself), Kelsey Grammer (Frasier Crane).

Notable Quote:

WOODY: "Hey, Mr. Peterson. Can I pour you a beer?"

NORM: "Well, okay Woody. But be sure to stop me at one. Ah, make that 1:30."

95. "Strange Bedfellows" (Part 3 of 3) (5/15/86). Janet Eldridge holds a press conference at Cheers, and Diane purposely disrupts the proceedings by embarrassing Sam. Janet protects her political career and image by breaking up with Sam, and despite reassurances, she has a legitimate concern he still has feelings for Diane. After losing two women (Diane and Janet) in the same day, Sam picks up the telephone, dials a number, and proposes marriage to one of the two women. The season ends on the cliffhanger of which woman received the marriage proposal. **Subtopic:** Norm becomes distraught as he spends time with his oversexed sister-in-law, Donna.

Written by David Angell. *Directed by* James Burrows.

Characters: Kate Mulgrew (Janet Eldridge), David Paymer (Phil Schumacher), Steve Giannelli (Steve), Alan Koss (Alan), J.J. Wall (Reporter #1), Lawrence Lott (Reporter #2), Sheila Scott-Wilkinson (Reporter #3).

Notable Quote: On a possible marriage between Janet Eldridge and Sam:

JANET: "Haven't you ever thought about you and me tying the knot?"

SAM: "Ah, now you told me you didn't go for that kinky stuff."

Season Five: 1986-87

(NBC Thursday, 9:00–9:30 p.m. EST)

Season Regulars: Ted Danson (Sam Malone), Shelley Long (Diane Chambers), Rhea Perlman (Carla Tortelli), John Ratzenberger (Cliff Clavin), Woody Harrelson (Woody Boyd), Kelsey Grammer (Frasier Crane), George Wendt (Norm Peterson).

Technical Credits: *Created by* Glen Charles, Les Charles and James Burrows. *Executive Producers:* James Burrows, Glen Charles, Les Charles. *Producers:* Peter Casey, David Lee, David Angell. *Co-Producer:* Tim Berry. *Writers:* Jeff Abugov, David Angell, Peter Casey, Glen Charles, Les Charles, Chris Cluess, Andy Cowan, Cheri Eichen, Kimberly Hill, David Isaacs, Stuart Kreisman, Janet Leahy, David Lee, Ken Levine, Joanne Pagliaro, Heide Perlman, Tom Reeder, Bill Steinkellner, Phoef Sutton, David S. Williger. *Directors:* James Burrows, Tim Berry, Thomas Lofaro. *Executive Script Consultant:* Bob Ellison. *Executive Story Consultants:* Cheri Eichen and Bill Steinkellner. *Story Editors:* Janet Leahy, Jeff Abugov, Phoef Sutton. *Creative Consultant:* Tom Tenowich. *Director of Photography:* John Finger. *Art Director:* Dahl Delu. *Edited by* Andy Ackerman. *Unit Production Managers:* Thomas Lofaro, Linda McMurray. *First Assistant Directors:* Thomas Lofaro, Brian James Ellis, Susan Norton. *Second Assistant Directors:* Brian James Ellis, Susan Norton, Lisa Marmon, Sheila Stewart. *Music by* Craig Safan. *Song:* "Where Everybody Knows Your Name." *Lyrics and Music by* Judy Hart Angelo and Gary Portnoy. *Sung by* Gary Portnoy. *Casting:* Jeff Greenberg, C.S.A. *Original Casting:* Stephen Kolzak. *Set Decorator:* Lynne Albright. *Technical Coordinators:* Bill Fraley, Rick Beren. *Script Supervisor:* Gabrielle James. *Production Mixer:* Michael Ballin. *Costume Supervisor:* Robert L. Tanella. *Women's Costumer:* Sandra Culotta. *Makeup Artist:* Bruce Hutchinson. *Hair Stylists:* Marilyn Patricia Phillips, Michele Payne. *Music Editor:* Chips Swanson. *Choreographer:* Julianne Wilson (#107). *Sound Effects:* Edward F. Suski. *Editing Facilities:* Laser Edit,Inc.*Main Title Design:* James Castle and Bruce Bryant. *Cameras and Lenses:* Panavision. *Assistants to the Charles Brothers:* Rick Beren, Benzion Bergman, Peter J. Chakos, Christine Connor, Mary Fukuto, Sheila Guthrie, Sue Herring, David Lesser, Lori A. Moneymaker, Carol Navratil, Diane Overdiek, David Reid, Penny Segal, Danielle Veerman, Barry Zajac. *Executive in Charge of Production:* Richard Villarino. *Charles/Burrows/Charles Productions in Association with* Paramount Television.

96. **"The Proposal"** (9/25/86). Sam proposes marriage to Diane, but she withholds the answer pending a more romantic and memorable proposal. In a chartered boat anchored off the coast of Maine, Sam pops the question again, but she says, "No," believing the proposal is merely a reaction to being dumped by Janet. He abandons Diane at sea, but later that evening, she returns to Cheers to say "Yes." Unfortunately, Sam already withdrew the question, so Diane decides to work at Cheers until Sam changes his mind and they are inevitably united in holy matrimony.

Written by Peter Casey and David Lee. *Directed by* James Burrows.

Characters: regulars only.

Notable Quote: On romancing women:

WOODY: "My uncle Wayne was a master of putting women in a romantic mood."

SAM: "What did he do?"

WOODY: "Give them money— worked like a charm."

97. **"The Cape Cad"** (10/2/86). When Sam arranges a romantic getaway with another woman, Diane is ireful, so she arrives at the Cape to sour the mood. The weekend worsens when

his date, Vicki, has to leave early because her grandmother is ill. Sam continues the charade as if Vicki were present, but Diane knows the truth and uses this opportunity to embarrass him. In the end, they discuss their relationship and express a mutual interest in one another. However, they remain apart because Sam wants a one-night stand, whereas Diane wants a commitment. **Subtopic:** Carla's cat gives birth at the bar, so she unloads the litter by giving away a kitten with every beer purchase.

Written by Andy Cowan and David S. Williger. *Directed by* James Burrows.

Characters: Brenda Strong (Vicki), Willie Garson (Waiter), Don Perry (Hotel Manager), Sid Conrad (Husband), Kathryn White (Wife).

Notable Quote: Diane, continuously telling Sam that he loves her:

SAM: "I see what you're doing. You're trying to plant a little seed in my brain."

DIANE: "Oh, don't be silly. I know of nothing that grows in solid rock."

98. **"Money Dearest"** (10/9/86). With the expectation of instant riches, Cliff arranges a blind date between his mother, Esther, and a wealthy inventor, Duncan "Fitz" Fitzgerald. When Esther and Fitz announce their wedding engagement, Cliff arranges an expensive bachelor party at a fancy hotel to celebrate their impending marriage (and his newfound wealth). At Esther's insistence, Fitz agrees to leave his money to charity. Cliff becomes angry, but throws a low budget party at Cheers after realizing his selfishness. After a wild night of partying with belly dancers, Fitz suffers a heart attack and dies. **Subtopic:** When the girls celebrate Esther's bridal shower, Esther and Carla spend the entire evening trying to abandon Diane.

Written by Janet Leahy. *Directed by* James Burrows.

Characters: Frances Sternhagen (Esther Clavin), Richard Erdman (Duncan Fitzgerald), Paul Willson (Paul), Thomas W. Babson (Tom Ballard).

Note: Frances Sternhagen appeared in "The Doctors," "Love of Life" (as Mrs. Krakauer), and "The Golden Years" (as Gina Williams), and her notable movie credits include *Starting Over* (1979), *Independence Day* (1983), and *Raising Cain* (1992).

99. **"Abnormal Psychology"** (10/16/86). Frasier is scheduled to appear on a local psychology talk show, but reconsiders when his debate competition is a former date, Lilith Sternin (from episode #86). They ultimately agree to debate one another to reveal their intellectual superiority. Diane interprets their antagonism as sexual attraction, and gives Lilith a beauty makeover. When Lilith appears on the talk show, Frasier is sexually aroused (as is she), and after a lengthy discourse laced with sexual metaphors, they begin playing footsy. Despite the public humiliation, they cannot control their passion and begin dating. **Subtopic:** Woody plans a fishing expedition with Norm and Cliff, who reluctantly acquiesce when they run out of excuses for not going.

Written by Janet Leahy. *Directed by* James Burrows.

Characters: Bebe Neuwirth (Lilith Sternin), Richard Herkert (Moderator), Steve Giannelli (Steve), Alan Koss (Alan), Tim Cunningham (Tim).

Notable Quote: In reference to Lilith's personality:

FRASIER: "You know, you perplex me."

LILITH: "Oh?"

FRASIER: "Yes. Normally people of your limited physical appeal make up for it with an actual personality."

100. "House of Horror with Formal Dining Room and Used Brick" (10/30/86). Carla searches for a new residence and takes Cliff's advice on an inexpensive home on his postal route. Unfortunately, the house was built over a 17th-century prison graveyard and is cursed. Carla fears the supernatural and is afraid to move in. To allay her fear, Norm and Cliff agree to spend one night with Carla to prove the house is not haunted. Norm chickens out, but Cliff remains with Carla, and they actually spend a peaceful night together, eating pizza, dancing and talking. As the morning sun rises, Carla discovers that her house is not haunted. Instead, the home was inexpensive because it was built at the end of an airport runway.

Written by David Angell. *Directed by* James Burrows.

Characters: regulars only.

Notable Quote: Sam, perusing his black book to find an intelligent woman:

SAM: "There's got to be somebody in here with a brain. I mean, I don't even care if she's good looking. [pause] You got a sister, Frasier?"

101. "Tan 'N' Wash" (11/6/86). Norm's new business idea, Tan 'N' Wash, is a combination laundromat and tanning salon. After revealing the investment concept to the Cheers gang, everyone except Woody insists upon being included in the endeavor. When the business starts off slow, the gang begins whining and complaining until Norm agrees to buy their shares. Shortly thereafter, the business flourishes. The gang is envious and resentful of Norm's newfound wealth, and give him the cold shoulder. After they apologize, Norm surprises them with dividend checks because he never took them out of the business. As they joyously celebrate in the street, Norm is informed that the roof collapsed at the Tan 'N' Wash and the business was not insured.

Written by Cheri Eichen and Bill Steinkellner. *Directed by* James Burrows.

Characters: Paul Willson (Paul), Steve Giannelli (Steve).

Notable Quote:

PAUL: "Hey, Norm. How's the world been treating you?"

NORM: "Like a baby treats a diaper."

102. "Young Dr. Weinstein" (11/13/86). Diane brags about having dinner reservations at The Cafe, a trendy Boston restaurant, so Sam tries to use his clout to get a reservation. When this fails, he surreptitiously cancels Diane's dinner reservation and then arrives at the restaurant impersonating the renowned heart specialist Dr. Julian Weinstein. The charade works. However, Sam feels sorry for Diane, so at the end of the evening asks the maître d' to serve her. They dine together, but when he finds himself short on funds, Diane gets revenge by refusing to pay for his meal. **Subtopic:** Woody tries desperately to invent a mixed drink, and after numerous unsuccessful attempts finally comes up with a great combination but cannot recall the ingredients.

Written by Phoef Sutton. *Directed by* James Burrows.

Characters: Kristi Somers (Darlene), Dennis Robertson (Dr. Fisher), Barry Laws (Maître d'), Joseph Kell

(Waiter), Julian Barnes (Claude), Josh Clark (Jordan), Paul Lukather (Mr. Morton), Melinda Cordell (Mrs. Morton), J.J. Wall (Customer).

Notable Quote: Woody invents a mixed drink and asks Sam to taste it:

WOODY: "Hey, Sam, you want to try my new drink?"

SAM: "Woody, I can't touch that stuff. I'm an alcoholic.... Yeah, I drank myself out of baseball and a marriage."

WOODY: "Gee that's hard to believe."

SAM: "Well, that's true. Right, gang?"

[Cheers gang makes comments on what a drunk Sam was.]

WOODY: "No, I believe you were a drunk, Sam. I just didn't know you were married."

103. **"Knights of the Scimitar"** (11/20/86). Cliff brags about becoming a member of his father's fraternal organization and solicits the Cheers gang to become members. Norm is the first candidate, and agrees to join the fraternal order with the expectation of establishing business contacts, but soon discovers that soliciting business with fellow members is prohibited. He willingly accepts this rule, but quits moments after initiation, when beer is banned at all organization functions. **Subtopic:** A young college student, Lance Apollonaire, is interested in dating Diane, so she flaunts him to make Sam envious. Sam feigns apathy, but as Diane prepares to leave for the weekend, he intervenes by giving her a passionate kiss.

Written by Jeff Abugov. *Directed by* James Burrows.

Characters: J. Eddie Peck (Lance Apollonaire), Stephen Vinovich (High Sultan), Raye Birk (Walt Twitchell), Bill DeLand (Foley).

Note: J. Eddie Peck also appeared in the soap opera "The Young and the Restless."

Notable Quote: Regarding Diane's making Sam jealous:

CARLA: "Oh, come on. She's just trying to make you jealous, and you're suckin' it up like a Hoover Deluxe."

104. **"Thanksgiving Orphans"** (11/27/86). The Cheers gang decides to celebrate Thanksgiving at Carla's house. The holiday is filled with television sporting events, but when Norm's gargantuan turkey takes forever to bake and the meal is continuously delayed, everyone becomes irritable. After a few food items are innocently tossed, the entire ensemble descends into a raucous food fight. Mayhem ensues as everyone participates in (and wears) the culinary delights. **Subtopic:** Diane brags about receiving an invitation for Thanksgiving dinner at her professor's house. After realizing she was invited to work as a domestic servant, she spends the holiday with the Cheers gang.

Written by Cheri Eichen and Bill Steinkellner. *Directed by* James Burrows.

Characters: regulars only.

105. **"Everyone Imitates Art"** (12/4/86). Even though her poem is rejected by a publisher, Diane perceives the letter as a harbinger that she is inevitably a soon-to-be-published author. To prove she received a condescending form letter, Sam submits a poem which is ultimately published. Diane toils endlessly to prove he is guilty of plagiarism, and after being totally humiliated and embarrassed, Sam confesses he submitted one of her poems (from a love letter she had written to him). Diane is upset at first but then deeply touched that he saved her

letters. **Subtopic:** Carla goes on an Elvis pilgrimage—a vacation at Graceland.

Written by Heide Perlman. *Directed by* James Burrows.

Characters: Michael Holden (Customer).

Notable Quote: Diane, discussing a poem that was published in Sam's name:

DIANE: "Listen to this dribble. 'I fly through a puckish arena, where echoes dance, where echoes dance, where echoes dance.' [She pauses, with a curious look on her face.] This sounds familiar."

NORM: "Well, you said it three times."

106. **"The Book of Samuel"** (12/11/86). Woody's Indiana girlfriend, Beth, announces her engagement to another man, Leonard Twilley. En route to Niagara Falls for their wedding and honeymoon, Beth and Leonard stop in Boston to visit Woody. In an effort to prove he is coping without her, Woody uses Sam's black book to find a companion for the evening. When one woman, Desiree, is listed as "the best," Woody asks her to meet him at Cheers. To Woody's surprise, she is old, unattractive and dressed in rags, but then again Desiree is the best *cleaning lady*. Woody takes her to dinner but eventually confesses the truth.

Written by Phoef Sutton. *Directed by* James Burrows.

Characters: Amanda Wyss (Beth Curtis), Katherine McGrath (Desiree Harrison), John Brace (Leonard Twilley), Pamela A. Hedges (Tina Wilson), Barbara Chase (Woman), Steve Giannelli (Steve), Tim Cunningham (Tim).

Notable Quote: On Woody's Hanover girlfriend marrying someone else:

WOODY: "Well, when Beth gets here, I want to show her I have someone else, too. There's one thing I can't stand, it's that look of pity in her eyes."

DIANE: "I'm sure she's far too wrapped up in her own happiness to have time to pity you."

107. **"Dance, Diane, Dance"** (12/18/86). Diane takes a ballet class because it has always been her dream to become a ballerina. When she performs badly, Frasier changes the instructor's acrimonious critique of her dancing to laudatory praise. The raving review convinces Diane to pursue her lifelong ambition. Although the Cheers gang attempt to stop her numerous times, they do not have the heart to destroy her dream. As she stands onstage in preparation for an audition, Frasier finally confesses the truth (and she discretely exits before embarrassing herself). **Subtopic:** Cliff considers selling his babe-mobile (the station wagon) to buy an Italian import.

Written by Jeff Abugov. *Directed by* James Burrows.

Characters: Marilyn Lightstone (Leeza), Dan Gerrity (Choreographer).

Notable Quote: Diane, praising her terrible dancing (as they watch it on videotape):

DIANE: "Ever since I was a child, I wanted to dance so badly."

NORM: [laughing behind her back] "Look's like you got your wish."

108. **"Chambers vs. Malone"** (1/8/87). Diane enters Cheers with an intuitive feeling that Sam will propose marriage to her that day. After spending the day mocking Diane's intuition, Sam admits he once loved her, but not anymore. Diane is crushed, and as she

begins crying, Sam gets on one knee and proposes marriage. When Diane says, "No," Sam envisions himself on death row for killing her. He chases her down the street, and after she slips and falls, Sam is jailed for willful assault and battery. The judge orders Sam to propose marriage again or go to jail. Sam pops the question (again), and this time Diane accepts. **Subtopic:** Thomas Babson finally passes the attorney bar exam, and his first case is representing Sam on the willful assault and battery charge.

Written by David Angell. *Directed by* James Burrows.

Characters: Tom Troupe (Judge William E. Grey), Thomas W. Babson (Tom Babson), Glen Vernon (Priest), Michael Keys Hall (Assistant D.A.), Hugh Maguire (Hugh), Peter Schreiner (Pete), Mark Arnott (Mark), Patrick De Santis (Joe), Jack Ritschel (Warden), Lance E. Nichols (Bailiff).

Notable Quote: On intuition:

DIANE: [to Woody] "Do you believe in intuition?"

WOODY: "No. But I have this strange feeling that some day I will."

109. **"Diamond Sam"** (1/15/87). Sam and Diane announce their wedding engagement and shop for a ring. Sam realizes he cannot afford $5,200 for the ring Diane desires, so he pays $1,200 for a bargain ring from Norm's friend, Bruce. Despite every effort to conceal the truth from Diane (and spending over $3,000 as part of the cover-up), Sam eventually buys the expensive ring. When Diane discovers that Sam purchased junk jewelry, she discards the ring. Unbeknownst to her, Sam switched the rings, so she actually discarded the expensive one.

Written by Tom Reeder. *Directed by* James Burrows.

Characters: Al Rosen (Al).

Notable Quote: On Carla's reaction when Sam and Diane become engaged:

FRASIER: "Fascinating. She's experiencing denial."

WOODY: "What does that mean, Dr. Crane?"

FRASIER: "Well simply put, it means that the human mind blocks out that which it cannot emotionally accept."

WOODY: "What does that mean, Dr. Crane?"

FRASIER: "It means that you don't understand this and you never will."

110. **"Spellbound"** (1/22/87). Loretta discovers that her husband, Nick Tortelli, is having an affair, and solicits advice from Carla and Diane. To assist Loretta in her quest for independence, Sam hires her to sing at Cheers. Nick perceives Sam's kindness as an attempt to win Loretta's heart, so he reciprocates by attempting to win Diane's heart. Nick caters a candlelight dinner to Cheers, but when his efforts are wasted on Diane, he tries to woo Carla, and then Loretta. After three failed attempts to win the heart of three different women, Nick goes home alone.

Written by Kimberly Hill. *Directed by* James Burrows.

Characters: Dan Hedaya (Nick Tortelli), Jean Kasem (Loretta Tortelli).

Notable Quote: Nick, making a pass at Diane:

NICK: "Say the word, blondie, and we can happen."

DIANE: "I'd rather be the love toy of a Greek army battalion."

NICK: "Who wouldn't? But dreaming gets you nowhere."

111. **"Never Love a Goalie"** (Part 1 of 2) (1/29/87). Carla meets Eddie

LeBec, the hottest goalie in the NHL, who in turn expresses a mutual interest by inviting her to a hockey game. Soon they become a hot item, but once they officially begin dating, he hits a major losing streak. Carla becomes concerned that she is jinxing Eddie and causing his slump. **Subtopics:** Diane is picked for jury duty in an attempted murder case, and can't resist telling the Cheers gang the juicy details of the trial. Meanwhile, Frasier accompanies Carla to a hockey game for research purposes, and winds up in jail for fighting. The charges are dropped, but he has to undergo psychiatric counseling.

Written by Ken Levine and David Isaacs. *Directed by* James Burrows.

Characters: Jay Thomas (Eddie LeBec), Mark Arnott (Mark), Deanna Oliver (Deanna), Hugh Maguire (Hugh), Steve Giannelli (Steve).

Note: Jay Thomas' most memorable roles were costarring with Susan Dey in "Love and War" (as Jack Stein) and as a recurring character in "Murphy Brown" (as Murphy's fiancé, Peter). He also had a recurring role in "Mork and Mindy" (as Remo Da Vinci) and "Married People."

Notable Quote: Carla, evading jury duty:

CARLA: "They tried to get me once, but I got off because I got a good excuse. I'm the sole support of six children."

DIANE: "I suppose they felt that anyone who hadn't mastered birth control isn't smart enough for jury duty."

112. "Never Love a Goalie" (Part 2 of 2) (2/5/87).

After realizing she jinxed Eddie and caused his losing streak, Carla decides to break up with him for the good of the team. After receiving his walking papers, Eddie has a great game and the losing streak ends. After the game, he realizes the rationale behind the breakup. Carla and Eddie then reconcile their relationship but make one change in Eddie's pregame ritual—breaking up before every game. **Subtopic:** Diane continues jury duty in the attempted murder case, but the charges are dismissed. Shortly thereafter, the defendant, Bill Grand, and the victim, Sherry Grand, visit Cheers, and Diane helps fan the flames of dispute between the couple.

Written by Ken Levine and David Isaacs. *Directed by* James Burrows.

Characters: Jay Thomas (Eddie LeBec), Brent Spiner (Bill Grand), Suzanne Collins (Sherry Grand), William B. Jackson (Juror #1), Laura Waterbury (Juror #2), Linda Hoy (Juror #3), Hawthorne James (Juror #4), John Fleck (Bailiff), Mark Arnott (Mark), Steve Giannelli (Steve).

Notable Quote: On slumps:

CLIFF: "Hey, I'll tell you an interesting thing about slumps, too. Statistics show that they can be grouped into four categories. Sixty-five percent physical, seventeen percent emotional, fifteen percent psychological, and three percent dental."

113. "One Last Fling" (2/12/87).

The Cheers gang throws Sam a bachelor party, and he expresses concern about having the same woman for the rest of his life. Diane overhears this revelation (while hiding in the cake) and grants him a 24-hour flesh binge—a sexual catharsis to eliminate his physical desires for other women. Sam loves the idea, before realizing that Diane also has one day of sexual *carte blanche*. He spends the entire 24 hours in his car watching Diane's apartment in anticipation of her dating another man. Unbeknownst to Sam, Diane is down the street watching him. **Subtopic:** Carla goes to traffic school after receiving a speeding ticket.

Written by Cheri Eichen and Bill Steinkellner. *Directed by* James Burrows.

Characters: Tim Holland (Rick), Peter Schreiner (Pete), Mark Arnott (Mark), Tim Cunningham (Tim), Steve Giannelli (Steve), Larry Harpel (Larry), Alan Koss (Alan), Hugh Maguire (Hugh).

114. "Dog Bites Cliff" (2/18/87, Wednesday, 8:30–9:00 p.m. EST). Cliff is bitten by a dog on his route and contemplates a lawsuit. The dog owner, Madeline Keith, uses her charm and sexuality to persuade him to settle. Cliff is aware of Madeline's plan but relishes the opportunity to date an attractive woman. However, the temptation becomes too great when Madeline invites Cliff to a hotel. As they lay in bed moments before physical consummation, Cliff signs a release of liability form. Once the form is signed, Madeline creates an outlandish story to exit the hotel room. **Subtopic:** Diane leaves for a contemplative retreat at a Buddhist temple in Florida to purify her thoughts before marrying Sam.

Written by Joanne Pagliaro. *Directed by* James Burrows.

Characters: Anita Morris (Madeline Keith), Steve Giannelli (Steve).

Notable Quote: As Cliff is in bed with Madeline Keith, he calls Sam:

CLIFF: "Sam, can I make a small confession?"

SAM: "Sure."

CLIFF: "I'm scared."

SAM: "Well Cliff, if it's any consolation, I've seen her and I'm scared for you."

115. "Dinner at Eight-ish" (2/26/87). Frasier and Lilith decide to live

together, and invite Sam and Diane to dinner because they were the matchmakers. As the night progresses, Diane, Frasier and Lilith begin revealing secrets about their past, and one by one become angry and take turns locking themselves in the bathroom. Sam is the voice of reason in this episode, and the only person who is not offended by the revealed secrets. In the end, Frasier locks Diane and Lilith in the bathroom, so he and Sam can go upstairs to watch *I, Claudius*. **Subtopic:** Cliff agrees to baby sit Carla's kids, but within hours he is returned to Cheers bound and gagged.

Written by Phoef Sutton. *Directed by* James Burrows.

Characters: Bebe Neuwirth (Lilith Sternin), Zetta Whitlow (Jill), Doris Grau (Corinne), Al Rosen (Al).

Notable Quote: Cliff contemplating baby-sitting Carla's kids:

CLIFF: "Obviously she doesn't think that I can handle her kids. Yeah, but my guess is that they will settle down once they're confronted with a strong male authority figure."

NORM: "Are you bringing your mother?"

116. "Simon Says" (3/5/87). Sam and Diane have a marriage counseling session with Frasier's friend, the renowned marital expert Dr. Simon Finch-Royce. When Dr. Finch-Royce concludes that Sam and Diane are incompatible, she desperately tries to prove the doctor's conclusion is inaccurate. After four visits to his hotel room in one evening, Dr. Finch-Royce is so furious he guarantees that Sam and Diane's relationship will be an epochal success.

Written by Peter Casey and David Lee. *Directed by* James Burrows.

Characters: John Cleese (Dr.

Simon Finch-Royce), Ray Underwood (Busman).

Note: John Cleese won an Outstanding Guest Performance Emmy (1987) for his role in this episode. He is best known for his comedy success in "Monty Python's Flying Circus" (1969–74), "Fawlty Towers" and the movies *Monty Python and the Holy Grail* (1975), *Monty Python's Life of Brian* (1979), *Monty Python's The Meaning of Life* (1983), and other noteworthy films such as *Time Bandits* (1981) and *A Fish Called Wanda* (1988).

Notable Quote: Regarding Dr. Simon Finch-Royce's marriage books:

NORM: "Doc, hi. I'm Norm Peterson. I have to tell you that my wife is a big fan of yours, sir. Yeah, she reads all of those marriage improvement books."

SIMON: "Great. Have they helped?"

NORM: "Well, they've helped me. It gives her something to do in bed."

117. "The Godfather: Part III" (3/19/87, 9:30–10:00 p.m. EST). When Coach's niece, Joyce Pantusso, visits Boston to attend college, Sam is supposed to look after her. He arranges for sweet, innocent Woody to be Joyce's escort, but within one week they announce their wedding engagement. When Sam begs them not to marry, they decide to live together; when Diane begs them not to live together, they agree to merely date. After all this effort, Sam and Diane decide that children are too difficult, and resolve never to have sex again (though their pact only lasts a few seconds). **Subtopic:** Lilith and Frasier celebrate the one-year anniversary of the day they met. He desperately wants golf clubs, and is bitterly disappointed after receiving a gray tie.

Written by Chris Cluess and Stuart Kreisman. *Directed by* James Burrows.

Characters: Cady McClain (Joyce Pantusso), Joe Colligan (Jack), Al Rosen (Al).

Notable Quote: Frasier, discussing the purchase of an armoire for Lilith:

FRASIER: "You know, I think when you're trying to express your affection for your mate, old wood says it best."

WOODY: "What do I say?"

FRASIER: "I was talking about the armoire."

WOODY: "Oh, I never say that. I don't even know what an armoire is."

118. "Norm's Last Hurrah" (3/26/87). Norm gets another accounting job, and Diane convinces him to be a leader by proposing an idea to the board of directors. Diane supports him all the way, but Norm's office sharing colleague, Warren Thompkins, steals the proposal and delivers it to the board. The proposal proves to be incomplete and insufficiently researched, and is ultimately rejected. Thompkins is upset because he has to share an office with a moron, and Norm concludes he is content being an anonymous cog in the corporate machinery. **Subtopic:** Sam and Diane decide where to spend their honeymoon.

Written by Andy Cowan and David S. Williger. *Directed by* Thomas Lofaro.

Characters: Tegan West (Warren Thompkins), Neil Zevnik (Supervisor), Jeff Robie (Office Boy), Ron Davis (Board Member).

Notable Quote:

WOODY: "Hey, Mr. Peterson. What do you say to a cold one?"

NORM: "See you later, Vera. I'll be at Cheers."

119. "Cheers: The Motion Picture" (4/2/87). Woody's father believes Boston is dangerous and corrupt, and orders Woody to return to Indiana. The Cheers gang decides to make a home video to prove Woody lives in a safe environment with supportive friends. The video is a failure, but Diane sends her edited version anyway. As Woody prepares to leave for Hanover, he receives a telephone call from his parents telling him to remain in Boston. Apparently, a patron, Al, sent a note to Woody's parents which convinced them to let their son stay in Beantown. **Subtopic:** Cliff grows another famous vegetable and this one looks like George Schultz.

Written by Phoef Sutton. *Directed by* Tim Berry.

Characters: Doris Grau (Corinne), Al Rosen (Al).

120. "A House Is Not a Home" (4/30/87). Diane unexpectedly purchases a house without Sam's consent. Nevertheless, he is pleased to be the owner. After meeting Bert and Lillian Miller, the elderly couple who were the prior owners, Diane decides that she cannot live in the house because it is filled with the Millers' memories. When she refuses to sell the house, Sam and Diane resolve the dilemma by inviting the Millers over for one last Christmas celebration. When Sam refuses to allow the Millers one last Easter and asks them to leave, Diane agrees to move in because he claimed the house for them. **Subtopic:** Woody works on the *Cheers Newsletter*.

Written by Phoef Sutton. *Directed by* James Burrows.

Characters: Billie Bird (Lillian Miller), Douglas Seale (Bert Miller), Stephanie Walski (Naomi), Marc Smollin (David), Stefanie Mason (Annie), Lou Bonacki (Man), Penny Krompier (Mom).

Note: Billie Bird appeared in "Benson" and "It Takes Two," but is best known for her role in "Dear John" (as Mrs. Philbert, the sex-crazed elderly group member).

Notable Quote: Cliff, responding to some women controlling men:

CLIFF: "That's pathetic. You will never catch a woman of mine leading me around by the nose."

CARLA: "No, but you might catch her sunning herself on a rock."

121. "I Do, Adieu" (5/7/87). As Sam and Diane make final preparations for their wedding ceremony, Sumner intimates that she has an opportunity to finish one of her novels for publication. After careful consideration, Diane decides to forego the novel and insists upon marrying Sam immediately. As they are in the midst of saying their vows, Diane is notified that the publisher will give her a huge advance to finish the novel. Sam withdraws his "I do" and convinces Diane to chase after her dream. Diane agrees to leave for six months and vows to return to be wed. (Despite her reassurances, Sam knows that she is leaving for good.)

Written by Glen Charles and Les Charles. *Directed by* James Burrows.

Characters: Michael McGuire (Sumner Sloane), Walter Addison (Justice of the Peace), Steve Giannelli (Steve).

Notable Quote: The Cheers gang, betting on whether Sam and Diane will marry:

FRASIER: "I'll get in on that action. You see, I believe that the words 'I do' are not in her vocabulary."

Season Six: 1987-88

(NBC Thursday, 9:00–9:30 p.m. EST) **Season Regulars:** Ted Danson (Sam Malone), Kirstie Alley (Rebecca Howe), Rhea Perlman (Carla Tortelli), John Ratzenberger (Cliff Clavin), Woody Harrelson (Woody Boyd), Kelsey Grammer (Frasier Crane), George Wendt (Norm Peterson).

Technical Credits: *Created by* Glen Charles, Les Charles and James Burrows. *Executive Producers:* James Burrows, Glen Charles, Les Charles. *Producers:* Peter Casey, David Lee, David Angell. *Writers:* David Angell, Peter Casey, Glen Charles, Les Charles, Jeffrey Duteil, Cheri Eichen, Susan Herring, David Isaacs, David Lee, Ken Levine, David Lloyd, Bill Steinkellner, Phoef Sutton. *Teleplay by* Rod Burton (#160). *Story by* Rick Beren (#160). *Directors:* James Burrows, Thomas Lofaro, Tim Berry, Andy Ackerman, John Ratzenberger, Michael Zinberg, George Wendt. *Co-Producer:* Tim Berry. *Executive Script Consultants:* Cheri Eichen, Bill Steinkellner, Bob Ellison. *Creative Consultant:* David Lloyd. *Executive Story Editor:* Phoef Sutton. *Associate Producer:* Mary Fukuto. *Director of Photography:* John Finger. *Art Director:* Dahl Delu. *Edited by* Andy Ackerman, Linda Henry. *Unit Production Manager:* Linda McMurray. *First Assistant Directors:* Thomas Lofaro, Brian James Ellis. *Second Assistant Directors:* Brian James Ellis, Elizabeth Ward. *Music by* Craig Safan. *Song:* "Where Everybody Knows Your Name." *Lyrics and Music by* Judy Hart Angelo and Gary Portnoy. *Sung by* Gary Portnoy. *Casting:* Jeff Greenberg, C.S.A. *Original Casting:* Stephen Kolzak. *Set Decorators:* Laura Richarz,

Rick Gentz, Lynne Albright. *Technical Coordinator:* Bill Fraley. *Script Supervisors:* Gabrielle James, Bonnie Prendergast. *Production Mixer:* Pete San Filipo, Sr. *Costume Supervisor:* Robert L. Tanella. *Women's Costumer:* Cheryl Beasley Blackwell. *Makeup Artist:* Bruce Hutchinson. *Hair Stylist:* Marilyn Patricia Phillips. *Music Editor:* Chips Swanson. *Sound Effects:* David Scharf. *Editing Facilities:* Laser Edit, Inc. *Main Title Design:* James Castle, Bruce Bryant, Carol Johnsen. *Cameras and Lenses:* Panavision. *Assistants to the Charles Brothers:* Rick Beren, Christine Connor, Peter J. Chakos, Ahuva Fogel, Marni Gaylord, Nicholas Grad, Sheila Guthrie, Sue Herring, Lori A. Moneymaker, Carol Navratil, David Reid, Danielle Veerman, Barry Zajac. *Executive in Charge of Production:* Richard Villarino. *Charles/Burrows/Charles Productions in Association with* Paramount.

122. **"Home Is the Sailor"** (9/24/87). The postponement of Sam and Diane's wedding prompts him to sell Cheers and buy a boat to circumnavigate the globe. When the boat sinks, he returns to Cheers, looking for employment as a bartender. Bar manager Rebecca Howe is resistant, but her boss, Evan Drake, insists that she hire Sam to attract business. To make room for Sam, Rebecca contemplates firing Woody, so the Cheers gang concocts a plan to have the other bartender, Wayne, quit. Although the plan works, Rebecca is not amused and fires Sam. However, he suavely convinces her to give him a second chance. **Subtopic:** Carla is pregnant (again) and tells Eddie that he is the father. After

considerable thought, Eddie proposes marriage and she accepts.

Written by Glen Charles and Les Charles. *Directed by* James Burrows.

Characters: Jay Thomas (Eddie LeBec), Jonathan Stark (Wayne), Al Rosen (Al), Michael Tulin (Customer), Tim Cunningham (Tim), Steve Giannelli (Steve), Alan Koss (Alan).

Note: Jonathan Stark cowrote several "Cheers" episodes.

Notable Quote: Sam, convincing Rebecca to hire him as a bartender:

SAM: "Having a sports celebrity in the bar is great for business. I mean, you take a look at your major places in Atlantic City. They have your Willie Mays, your Mickey Mantle..."

REBECCA: "It seems the critical difference here is that I've heard of those people."

SAM: "Wait a second here. A lot of people may not know this, but I happen to be quite famous."

123. "'I' on Sports" (10/1/87). Sam agrees to be a temporary television sportscaster to cover for Dave Richards, but has to hide the employment from Rebecca because of a company policy against moonlighting. When his sports commentaries are not interesting or controversial enough— rooting for the home team and artificial grass versus natural grass—Sam spices things up by doing a sports rap. Unfortunately, his sportscaster career ends abruptly when he does a ventriloquist act with a wooden dummy, Little Sam. Although Rebecca discovers Sam's moonlighting, she does not terminate his employment at Cheers.

Written by Ken Levine and David Isaacs. *Directed by* James Burrows.

Characters: Fred Dryer (Dave Richards), Catherine MacNeal (Jo-

anne), J. Stephen Coyle (Dr. Buzz), Hugh Maguire (Hugh), Lenny Garner (Stage Manager).

Notable Quote: A channel 13 news report by the anchorwoman:

JOANNE: "And Keller is scheduled to be executed on Friday. I guess he won't be around for the Patriots-Buffalo game this Sunday."

124. "Little Carla, Happy at Last" (Part 1 of 2) (10/15/87). Carla and Eddie's superstitions make it difficult to coordinate their wedding plans. However, when he denounces the occult, they begin experiencing bad luck—Carla finds out she is pregnant with twins, Anthony and Annie return from Las Vegas to live with Carla, Anthony hates Eddie, and Eddie's mother hates Carla. Although Eddie and Carla appear to be able to handle all the adversity, his mother's irrational response prompts Eddie to cancel the wedding.

Written by Cheri Eichen and Bill Steinkellner. *Directed by* James Burrows.

Characters: Jay Thomas (Eddie LeBec), Timothy Williams (Anthony Tortelli), Mandy Ingber (Annie Tortelli), Janet Brandt (Mama LeBec).

125. "Little Carla, Happy at Last (Part 2 of 2) (10/22/87). Sam works overtime to get Carla and Eddie married, and even bets Rebecca he can do it. Sam eventually convinces the prospective bride and groom to consummate their nuptials, and the wedding reception is held at Cheers. Even though the newlyweds' bad luck continues, Carla is finally convinced their misfortune is not related to superstition, but rather to her pathetic life. **Subtopics:** Rebecca spends the evening waiting for Evan Drake to attend

the wedding reception, and is disappointed when he does not show. Meanwhile, Norm and Cliff search for an inexpensive wedding gift to give Carla and Eddie.

Written by Cheri Eichen and Bill Steinkellner. *Directed by* James Burrows.

Characters: Jay Thomas (Eddie LeBec), Timothy Williams (Anthony Tortelli), Mandy Ingber (Annie Tortelli), Janet Brandt (Mama LeBec), Ron Husmann (Bandleader).

126. "The Crane Mutiny" (10/29/87). Lilith gives Frasier an ultimatum: either they get married or their relationship is over. After Frasier expresses doubts about marriage, the Cheers gang insinuates that Rebecca is hot for him, so he leaves Lilith a note stating they should see other people. By the time Frasier realizes Rebecca does not even know he exists, Lilith has read the note. To save face, Frasier claims Rebecca lusted after him, but he turned her down. After discovering Rebecca has no love interest in him, Lilith purposely embarrasses Frasier by requiring him to end his "relationship" with Rebecca.

Written by David Angell. *Directed by* James Burrows.

Characters: Bebe Neuwirth (Lilith Sternin), Ralph Peduto (Bob), Tim Cunningham (Tim), Alan Koss (Alan).

Notable Quote: Frasier, having second thoughts about marriage:

NORM: "I know of plenty of women—they find you attractive."

FRASIER: "I know you're just being nice. But you see, I'm not really trying to shop around. I mean, Lilith Sternin is a good woman—strong, durable, reliable."

NORM: "She would make one hell of a radial tire, actually."

127. "Paint Your Office" (11/5/87). Rebecca generously offers Norm the chance to paint her office to reduce his huge bar tab. While painting, he is exposed to her personal side when she reveals an emotional attachment to her boss, Evan Drake. Rebecca perceives Norm as caring and compassionate, so she asks him to paint her apartment. He accepts, and allows Sam to accompany him as a painting assistant. Sam is hoping for the opportunity to witness Rebecca's personal side (horizontally), but when that notion fails, they spend quality time getting to know each other personally, not intimately.

Written by Peter Casey and David Lee. *Directed by* James Burrows.

Characters: regulars only.

Notable Quote:

WOODY: "What's going on, Mr. Peterson?"

NORM: "Let's talk about what's going *in* Mr. Peterson."

128. "The Last Angry Mailman" (11/12/87). Cliff encourages the sale of his childhood home to developers, but his mother, Esther, is hesitant. After reminiscing about the good times they had, Esther persuades Cliff to resist commercial development. However, she willingly sells the house when offered $250,000, so Cliff tries to save his residence by handcuffing himself to an interior beam. After convincing his mother to fight to save their home, it collapses. **Subtopic:** Frasier learns an interesting tidbit about Rebecca's college days—her nickname was Backseat Becky. Rebecca tries endlessly to explain the origin of the sobriquet, and finally pays Carla for a story sufficient to appease the Cheers gang.

Written by Ken Levine and David Isaacs. *Directed by* James Burrows.

Characters: Frances Sternhagen

(Esther Clavin), Kevin Dunn (Jim McNulty), Don Sparks (William Cronin), Tim Cunningham (Tim), Hugh Maguire (Hugh).

Notable Quote: Discussing Rebecca's nickname "Backseat Becky":

CARLA: "Wood, she likes to do her cushion pushin' on four wheels."

WOODY: "Miss Howe? Really? You know back where I come from we used to say something about girls like that."

CARLA: "What?"

WOODY: "Let's date 'em."

129. "Bidding on the Boys" (11/19/87). Cheers hosts a celebrity auction, and Sam works his way into the lineup. Rebecca is eager to surpass last year's charitable donations, so she bets Sam that he cannot be auctioned for $1,600. It appears bleak, but Lilith saves the day by purchasing Sam for $2,000. During their romantic weekend, Lilith sexually taunts Sam, who privately arranged for Frasier to barge into the hotel room and express his love for her. The plan has flaws, but it works. **Subtopics:** Lilith purchases Sam at the celebrity auction to infuriate Frasier for suggesting she sign a prenuptial agreement. Meanwhile, Woody is auctioned and purchased by a scary looking woman.

Written by David Lloyd. *Directed by* Thomas Lofaro.

Characters: Bebe Neuwirth (Lilith Sternin), Sharon Barr (Connie), Gary Beach (Emcee), Alan Koss (Alan), *Auction Bidders*: Shawn Gibson, Eli Guralnick, Terri Hanauer, Terri Hoyos, Roxanne Mayweather, Carolyn Pemberton, May Quigley, Kim Sebastian, Sheila Shaw, Cyndi Strittmatter.

Note: Sharon Barr also played the role of IRS agent Dot Carroll in

"Cheers" (#260), and appeared in "Max Headroom" (as Lauren, 1987).

Notable Quote: Frasier's distress that Sam might steal Lilith's heart:

SAM: "Would you stop that, now. You're my friend. I'm never gonna take a woman away from you."

FRASIER: "What about Diane?"

SAM: "And didn't God punish me with a vengeance?"

130. "Puddin' Head Boyd" (11/26/87). Woody works as a Mark Twain understudy, and while wearing the same type of clothes Samuel Clemens wore, he befriends an elderly widow, Mary. They have a wonderful time together, but Woody suspects Mary is falling in love with his Mark Twain character. He tries to break up with her, but when Mary expresses her pleasure with his company, he proposes marriage. Mary declines because she is well aware of Woody's age. **Subtopic:** Frasier and Lilith return from a Caribbean cruise gloating about losing weight on the vacation. As it turns out, they became seasick and spent the entire week vomiting and sleeping.

Written by Cheri Eichen and Bill Steinkellner. *Directed by* James Burrows.

Characters: Bebe Neuwirth (Lilith Sternin), Anne Pitoniak (Mary), John Paragon (Grif Palmer), Brigitte (Circus Girl).

Notable Quote: An elderly woman, discussing her poor vision:

MARY: "I'm blind as a bat without glasses."

WOODY: "I've never seen a bat with glasses."

MARY: "That's funny."

WOODY: [chuckling] "Yeah, I can imagine."

131. "A Kiss Is Still a Kiss" (12/3/87). Rebecca is still lusting after

Evan Drake, and makes a scene at his house party by kissing him. Evan orders Rebecca to leave the party but subsequently apologizes. Sam wisely uses this incident to trick Rebecca into kissing him passionately. He persuades Evan that Rebecca's earlier kiss was an attempt to make Sam jealous. However, after Rebecca shows her affection with a fervid kiss, Sam is convinced she is sexually attracted to him because no one can fake that kind of passion. Rebecca proves Sam wrong by kissing Frasier so fervently that he passes out! **Subtopic:** Frasier is upset when a colleague refutes one of his papers.

Written by David Lloyd. *Directed by* James Burrows.

Characters: Tom Skerritt (Evan Drake), Harry Anderson (Harry "the Hat"), Tom Ohmer (Assistant #1), Christian J. LeBlanc (Assistant #2).

Note: Tom Skerritt has a considerable movie credit portfolio, including *Alien* (1979), *Top Gun* (1986), *Poltergeist III* (1988), *Big Man on Campus* (1989), *Poison Ivy* (1992), and *A River Runs Through It* (1992). In addition, he won an Emmy as Outstanding Lead Actor in 1993 (as Jimmy Brock) in "Picket Fences."

Notable Quote:
SAM: "How's life treating you?"
NORM: "It's not, Sammy. But that doesn't mean you can't."

133. **"My Fair Clavin"** (12/10/87). Cliff has a new condominium and a girlfriend, Sally. He is embarrassed about her physical appearance, so they spend every night at home watching "Jeopardy!" When a makeover transforms Sally into an incredibly attractive woman, Cliff takes her to Cheers to brandish her beauty. However, after fending off other men's advances, Cliff becomes jealous and asks Sally to

revert to her former appearance. Sally refuses to accommodate his request because she is pleased with her new image and relishes the attention. **Subtopic:** Rebecca promises to sleep with Sam if she fails to quit smoking, and although he catches her lighting up, Sam does not enforce the pact.

Written by Phoef Sutton. *Directed by* James Burrows.

Characters: Karen Akers (Sally), Philip Arthur Ross (Philip), Steven Robert Ross (Steven), John Allen (Jeff).

Notable Quote: Cliff, giving a tour of his new condominium:
CLIFF: [Standing by a window looking out] "Did you notice the pool on your way in? So when summer rolls around and all those girls are out there in their French-cut bikinis, I don't have to tell you where I'll be."
NORM: "Standing right here with a pair of binoculars."
CLIFF: "That's right."

133. **"Christmas Cheers"** (12/17/87). It's Christmas Eve at Cheers, and everyone except Sam is giving Rebecca a present, so he desperately searches for a last-minute gift. A stewardess agrees to sell him earmuffs but accidentally gives him $500 diamond earrings. Rebecca adores the jewelry and invites Sam over to her place later that night. Sam decides not to take back the earrings (thinking he is going to get lucky), only to find out she is having a Christmas party at her apartment for *all* the Cheers employees. **Subtopic:** Cliff tries to win the postal food drive for a trip to Disney World, but loses by one can. When Woody claims he forgot to put two cans in the bin, Cliff chases the Orlando-bound plane down the runway while throwing cans of food at it.

Written by Cheri Eichen and Bill Steinkellner. *Directed by* James Burrows and Thomas Lofaro.

Characters: Jayne Modean (Tracy), Harry Frazier (Kris), Donavon O'Donnell (Santa #1), Hal Havins (Santa #2), Joseph V. Perry (Santa #3), Vincent Lucchesi (Vincent), Al Rosen (Al), Roger Keller (Shopkeeper), Catherine MacNeal (Newscaster).

Notable Quote: Woody, conversing with his mother about Christmas dinner:

WOODY: "Are you making the stuffing bone-dry, the way I love it? Well, can't you freeze some and mail it to me? [pause] No, not the gravy, that would be stupid. [rolling his eyes, and in a sarcastic tone to Sam and Carla] My mother."

134. **"Woody for Hire Meets Norman of the Apes"** (1/7/88). Woody is a crowd scene extra during the filming of "Spenser: For Hire" and actually meets Robert Urich. When the episode airs, everyone doubts the authenticity of his story because all that is televised is Woody's plain white shirtsleeve. Woody tries to prove he was on the show and met Robert Urich, but nobody believes him. **Subtopics:** When Norm demands payment for painting Cliff's house, he and Cliff exchange barbs which culminates in their using a chimpanzee metaphor to mock their respective professions. Meanwhile, Cheers hosts a book club meeting, and the members become drunk and rowdy, demanding male dancers to entertain them.

Written by Phoef Sutton. *Directed by* Tim Berry.

Characters: Paddi Edwards (Sylvia), Betty Vaughan (Laura), Tim Cunningham (Tim), Hugh Maguire (Hugh), Peter Schreiner (Pete), Robert Urich (Himself).

Note: Robert Urich has consistently been a highly coveted leading man in television shows, though his greatest successes were probably "Spenser: For Hire" and "Vega$" (as Dan Tanna). His other television roles include "American Dreamer" (as Tom Nash), "Soap" (as Peter Campbell), "S.W.A.T." (as Officer Jim Street), and "Tabitha" (as Paul Thurston). His movie credits include *The Ice Pirates* (1984) and *Turk 182* (1985).

135. **"And God Created Woodman"** (1/14/88). Corporate CEO Daniel Collier hires Rebecca to cater a party at his house with Sam and Woody as bartenders. When Rebecca breaks a very expensive vase, she fears losing her job. Woody graciously takes the blame, and Mr. Collier is so impressed with the display of honesty that he befriends Woody. The next day, however, Mr. Collier does not remember any of the events from the prior evening. When he confronts Rebecca about the vase, she again fears losing her job, so Sam takes the blame. Once again, Mr. Collier is impressed with the display of honesty and befriends Sam. **Subtopic:** Cliff sells mail order shoes to the Cheers gang, but all the shoes squeak.

Written by Jeffrey Duteil. *Directed by* John Ratzenberger.

Characters: Peter Hansen (Daniel Collier), Judde Mussetter (Linda), Tim Cunningham (Tim), Hugh Maguire (Hugh), Peter Schreiner (Pete), Al Rosen (Al).

136. **"A Tale of Two Cuties"** (1/21/88). At Evan Drake's insistence, Rebecca hires Laurie, a new waitress of his choosing. This leads Rebecca to conclude Laurie is Evan's lover. Rebecca's curiosity leads to envious rage, and she eventually punches Laurie. Evan

enters the bar immediately after the incident and reveals Laurie is his daughter. **Co-topic:** Carla's daughter-in-law, Annie, accepts a temporary waitress position at Cheers (while Carla is in labor with twins). Annie's infatuation with Sam makes her husband, Anthony, insanely jealous, so Sam solves the Tortelli tirade by having Anthony hired as an assistant manager at Burger Burger Burger.

Written by Cheri Eichen and Bill Steinkellner. *Directed by* Michael Zinberg.

Characters: Tom Skerritt (Evan Drake), Mandy Ingber (Annie Tortelli), Timothy Williams (Anthony Tortelli), Bobbie Eakes (Laurie), Paul Willson (Paul).

137. **"Yachts of Fools"** (2/4/88). Evan is still under the impression that Sam and Rebecca are dating, so he invites them for a weekend on his yacht. This is the perfect opportunity for Sam to impress Julie, a dental hygienist he has been dating for three days. Julie is introduced as Sam's sister, and she immediately becomes obsessed with Evan's wealth. Meanwhile, Rebecca does not bring a "sibling" because she wants to use this opportunity to confess her love to Evan. Both of their plans fail when Evan and Julie pair up. Although Evan confesses that nothing happened, Sam quickly discovers Julie is also romantically interested in Evan's servant, Lorenzo.

Written by Phoef Sutton. *Directed by* Thomas Lofaro.

Characters: Tom Skerritt (Evan Drake), Dorothy Parke (Julie), Tom Astor (Lorenzo), Eddie Frierson (1st Customer), Dominic Hoffman (2nd Customer).

138. **"To All the Girls I've Loved Before"** (2/11/88). When Frasier makes several derogatory remarks about marriage, Lilith wonders if he is serious about a permanent commitment. She gives him the option of canceling the wedding or calling her later that evening to reaffirm the wedding plans. The Cheers gang throws a bachelor party, but the mood sours when the stripper, Karen, turns out to be one of Frasier's patients. Meanwhile, at the bridal shower, Lilith lusts after the male stripper, Randy, when she does not receive the message that Frasier called to reaffirm the wedding plans. Upon her arrival at Cheers, Lilith expresses her love for Frasier, and he reciprocates. The wedding is on!

Written by Ken Levine and David Isaacs. *Directed by* James Burrows.

Characters: Bebe Neuwirth (Lilith Sternin), Karen Witter (Karen), Deke Anderson (Randy), Hugh Maguire (Hugh), Thomas W. Babson (Tom), Alan Koss (Alan), Peter Schreiner (Pete), Steve Giannelli (Steve).

Notable Quote: Rebecca, throwing Lilith a bridal shower:

REBECCA: "What kind of shower do you think? Kitchen, linen?"

CARLA: "Look at who she's hitching up with. Better make it marital aids."

139. **"Let Sleeping Drakes Lie"** (2/18/88). Norm is hired to paint Evan's bedroom, so Rebecca accompanies him to see the house. When Evan returns early, she is forced to hide in the bedroom closet. After several unsuccessful attempts to help her escape unnoticed (leaving the bedroom closet partially open, fabricating a story about killer bees from Mexico, and another involving a lifelong dream to carry a wealthy man across his front lawn), the Cheers

gang finally helps her escape through the bedroom window. **Subtopic:** Frasier brags about two beautiful patients he counseled that day, one of whom has a love obsession for dancers. When one of Frasier's female patients enters Cheers, Sam pretends to be a dancer to turn her on. When all his efforts fail, it is revealed he is dating Frasier's other patient—the pyromaniac—and she is alone in Sam's apartment!

Written by David Lloyd. *Directed by* James Burrows.

Characters: Tom Skerritt (Evan Drake), Cec Verrell (Jennifer McCall), Jay Bell (Greyson).

Notable Quote: On Frasier's attractive patient obsessed with men who dance:

FRASIER: "This woman has her passions inflamed by men who dance ....What's even more bizarre is that she will catapult herself compulsively into the arms of any man in tights or tap shoes. Fascinating fixation. [pauses, then looks at his watch] Oh, I have to go, I'm sorry. [rushes to door]

SAM: "Where are you going?"

FRASIER: "My ballet class!"

140. **"Airport V"** (2/25/88). Carla vehemently refuses to visit Eddie while he is traveling with the ice show because of her fear of flying. Although Frasier counsels her to overcome the phobia, by the time the actual flight session ends, Frasier develops a phobia about flying. **Subtopic:** A Boston critic, Murray Treadwell, includes Cheers in his review of establishments, and is attracted to Rebecca. She seriously contemplates sleeping with him for a good review, and after dating him, Cheers receives a spectacular review. Despite her repeated denials, everyone (including Evan Drake) thinks Rebecca slept with him.

Written by Ken Levine and David Isaacs. *Directed by* George Wendt.

Characters: Jay Thomas (Eddie LeBec), Peter Elbling (Murray Treadwell), Robert Starr (Passenger #1), Carol Navratil (Passenger #2), Pete Gonneau (Passenger #3), Michelle Davison (Flight Attendant), Al Rosen (Al), Peter Schreiner (Pete), Thomas W. Babson (Tom), Cooper Neal (Customer).

141. **"Sam in the Gray Flannel Suit"** (3/3/88). Evan Drake hires Sam as a corporate executive, which happens to coincide with the corporation qualifying for the softball play-offs. Sam is oblivious to this fact and enjoys the perks of executive stardom. Rebecca is suspicious about this sudden inexplicable corporate promotion, and quickly discovers the truth. She is anxious to humble Sam with the bad news, but feels guilty when he expresses pride in having an executive position. After being told the truth, Sam takes a stand to retain his dignity. Despite losing the corporate promotion, he returns to Cheers as a bartender.

Written by Cheri Eichen and Bill Steinkellner. *Directed by* Tim Berry.

Characters: Tom Skerritt (Evan Drake), Pamela Bowen (Mimi), Vincent Howard (Heppel), George Shannon (Burns).

142. **"Our Hourly Bread"** (3/10/88). Cheers is losing money, so Rebecca holds a raffle to promote the bar, with the grand prize being a Caribbean cruise. Business booms, but on the night of the raffle, Woody errs and declares two grand prize winners. Rebecca settles the problem by awarding two grand prizes—a cruise and an original Tidwell painting that was originally Frasier's anniversary gift to

Lilith. **Subtopics:** Frasier and Lilith celebrate their one-month wedding anniversary. When she expresses a disliking toward the artist Tidwell, Frasier offers his Mercedes as a gift. Meanwhile, the Cheers employees try to convince Rebecca to give them raises, but they only receive titles.

Written by Susan Herring. *Directed by* Andy Ackerman.

Characters: Bebe Neuwirth (Lilith Sternin), Thomas Ryan (#99), Ron Boussom (#66), Eric Menyuk (Larry the Mailman), Al Rosen (Al), Hugh Maguire (Hugh), Peter Schreiner (Pete).

Notable Quote: Woody's ecstacy after receiving a title instead of a raise:

WOODY: "Wait until I tell my folks. To think I came in here asking for a stupid little raise, and now this. I just hope it doesn't go to my head."

REBECCA: "That's what's nice about you, Woody. Nothing ever goes to your head."

143. **"Slumber Party Massacred"** (3/24/88). Carla invites Sam to dinner so her family can practice their social skills and manners. When Anthony announces Annie is pregnant, Carla becomes depressed because she is too young to be a grandmother. She goes into hibernation, so the Cheers gang tries helping Carla relive her childhood with a slumber party and singing oldies songs. Nothing seems to elevate her spirits until Cliff bends over and splits his pants. **Subtopic:** Lilith's childhood friend, Dorothy Greenberg, bores Frasier with her dismal conversations about 17th-century Paraguay.

Written by Phoef Sutton. *Directed by* James Burrows.

Characters: Bebe Neuwirth (Lilith Sternin), Jay Thomas (Eddie LeBec), Elizabeth Ruscio (Dorothy), Mandy Ingber (Annie Tortelli), Timothy Williams (Anthony Tortelli), Cynthia Songe (Cherry), Hugh Maguire (Hugh), Peter Schreiner (Pete), Michael Nowell (Customer #1), Noreen Hennessy (Customer #2), Torrey Hanson (Customer #3).

Notable Quote: Discussing slumber party antics:

LILITH: "According to my patient, when the first person falls asleep the others take her underwear, dip it in water, and then put it in the icebox for an hour to freeze solid."

CARLA: "Or they could let you wear it for ten minutes."

144. **"Bar Wars"** (3/31/88). On the third anniversary of their bowling victory against Gary's Tavern, the Cheers gang calls Gary to brag. The celebration ends early when the bowling trophy is stolen (and then returned broken). The bars exchange pranks, but Gary is so impressed with the Cheers prank of interrupting his live satellite telecast to read poetry, he agrees to have Wade Boggs sign autographs at Cheers. Gary's generosity makes the gang suspicious, so when a guy enters the bar claiming to be Wade Boggs, the gang chases him down the street and "pants" him. Unfortunately, the guy was in fact Wade Boggs. Gary played the ultimate ruse, having the Cheers gang play a prank on themselves.

Written by Ken Levine and David Isaacs. *Directed by* James Burrows.

Characters: Bebe Neuwirth (Lilith Sternin), Robert Desiderio (Gary), Wade Boggs (Himself), Tom Rosqui (Jensen), Greg Collins (Exterminator #1), Phil Morris (Exterminator #2), Al Rosen (Al), Tim Cunningham (Tim), Steve Giannelli (Steve), Alan Koss (Alan).

Note: Robert Desiderio appeared in "Knots Landing" (as Melcher).

Notable Quote: After Rebecca agreed to date Gary because he was cute:

SAM: "Cute? You think Gary's cute?"

REBECCA: "Yeah. He's got a real cute face and a nice body. He looks kind of like an athlete."

SAM: "Hey. What am I?"

REBECCA: "Jealous."

145. **"The Big Kiss-Off"** (4/28/88). Woody is infatuated with Rebecca, and after admitting an attraction to her, he is teased incessantly. Sam claims he has a better chance of getting lucky with Rebecca, so he and Woody bet to see who can get a kiss from her first. Woody's best attempt is having Rebecca rehearse a kissing scene from a play, but he is sidetracked when Sam claims the bar is out of vermouth. Sam tries numerous tricks (including choking and enlisting in the military), but nothing works. When Carla reveals the bet, Rebecca arranges to have Sam and Woody kiss each other, with the entire Cheers gang witnessing the passionate moment.

Written by Ken Levine and David Isaacs. *Directed by* James Burrows.

Characters: Carol Francis (Caroline), Al Rosen (Al), Alan Koss (Alan), Hugh Maguire (Hugh), Peter Schreiner (Pete).

146. **"Backseat Becky, Upfront"** (5/5/88). Evan Drake accepts a new corporate position in Tokyo, so Rebecca arranges a going away party at Cheers. Although Rebecca misses several opportunities to confess her love, Sam locks Evan's chauffeur, Martin, in the Cheers closet so she can drive Evan to the airport. Just before confessing her love, Evan tells Rebecca to pick up his girlfriend who is accompanying him to Japan. After three years of waiting for Evan, Rebecca finally realizes she has lost him forever, and crashes the limo into a 7-Eleven convenience store.

Written by Cheri Eichen and Bill Steinkellner. *Directed by* James Burrows.

Characters: Tom Skerritt (Evan Drake), Ron Barker (Martin), Vincent Howard (Heppel), Al Rosen (Al), George Shannon (Burns).

Season Seven: 1988-89

(NBC Thursday, 9:00–9:30 p.m. EST)

Season Regulars: Ted Danson (Sam Malone), Kirstie Alley (Rebecca Howe), Rhea Perlman (Carla Tortelli-LeBec), John Ratzenberger (Cliff Clavin), Woody Harrelson (Woody Boyd), Kelsey Grammer (Frasier Crane), George Wendt (Norm Peterson).

Technical Credits: *Created by*

Glen Charles, Les Charles and James Burrows. *Executive Producers:* James Burrows, Glen Charles, Les Charles. *Supervising Producers:* David Angell, Peter Casey, David Lee. *Producers:* Cheri Eichen and Bill Steinkellner. *Writers:* Cecile Alch, Tom Anderson, David Angell, Rod Burton, Peter Casey, Cheri Eichen, David Isaacs,

David Lee, Ken Levine, David Lloyd, Patricia Niedzialek, Dan O'Shannon, Brian Pollack, Tom Reeder, Mert Rich, Bill Steinkellner, Phoef Sutton. *Directors:* James Burrows, Andy Ackerman. *Co-Producers:* Tim Berry, Phoef Sutton. *Creative Consultant:* David Lloyd. *Executive Script Consultant:* Bob Ellison. *Executive Story Editors:* Brian Pollack and Mert Rich. *Associate Producer:* Mary Fukuto. *Director of Photography:* John Finger. *Art Director:* Dahl Delu. *Edited by* Andy Ackerman, Sheila Amos. *Unit Production Manager:* Linda McMurray. *First Assistant Director:* Thomas Lofaro, Brian James Ellis. *Second Assistant Directors:* Brian James Ellis, Teresa Pfiffner. *Music by* Craig Safan. *Song:* "Where Everybody Knows Your Name." *Lyrics and Music by* Judy Hart Angelo and Gary Portnoy. *Sung by* Gary Portnoy. *Casting:* Jeff Greenberg, C.S.A. *Original Casting:* Stephen Kolzak. *Set Decorator:* Laura Richarz. *Technical Coordinator:* Rick Beren. *Script Supervisor:* Gabrielle James. *Production Mixer:* Robert Crosby. *Costume Supervisor:* Robert L. Tanella. *Women's Costumers:* Cheryl Beasley Blackwell, Mira Zavidowsky. *Makeup Artist:* Bruce Hutchinson. *Hair Stylist:* Marilyn Patricia Phillips. *Music Editor:* Chips Swanson. *Sound Effects:* David Scharf. *Editing Facilities:* Laser Edit, Inc. *Main Title Design:* James Castle, Bruce Bryant, Carol Johnsen. *Cameras and Lenses:* Panavision. *Assistants to the Charles Brothers:* Peter J. Chakos, Christine Connor, Ahuva Fogel, Sheila Guthrie, Sue Herring, Lori A. Moneymaker, Carol Navratil, David Reid, Kerstin Robbins-Fares, Russ Sherman, Rich Stangl, Danielle Veerman, Barry Zajac. *Executive in Charge of Production:* Richard Villarino. *Charles/Burrows/Charles Productions in Association with* Paramount.

147. "How to Recede in Business" (10/27/88). The new corporate vice president, Greg Stone, makes a managerial change at Cheers by firing Rebecca and promoting Sam. After successfully persuading Stone to rehire Rebecca, Sam expects a show of appreciation from her (horizontally). She is appreciative and agrees to one date. During dinner, but before the night of passion commences, Rebecca learns there are certain conditions she must accept before returning as manager (i.e., a pay cut, consulting Sam on major decisions, completing her MBA degree, and waiting tables under the direct supervision of Carla). Rebecca is appalled and quits, but quickly returns because she needs a job to pay for the Mercedes she just purchased.
Written by David Angell. *Directed by* James Burrows.
Characters: Brian Bedford (Greg Stone), Peter Schreiner (Pete), Al Rosen (Al), Robert Pescovitz (Paul), Tim Cunningham (Tim).
Notable Quote: Rebecca, rejecting Sam's offer for a date after her heartthrob, Evan Drake, left for Tokyo:
REBECCA: "Men. You are all alike. Nothing but users and takers and big, stupid jerks who don't even know you exist, and then go running off to Japan with someone else."
SAM: "That is such a cliché."

148. **"Swear to God"** (11/3/88). Sam is informed by a past lover, Denise, that he may be the father of her child. Realizing he is not ready for fatherhood, Sam makes a pact with God to abstain from sex for three months if he escapes paternity. When it is determined he is not the father, Sam has difficulty keeping his vow of celibacy, especially when Rachel Patterson returns. They go to a motel, and

Sam is astounded to find a bible in the nightstand. They go from motel to motel, but cannot find a room without a bible, which leads Sam to conclude God is speaking to him through motel nightstands. This "miracle" convinces him to forego sex for the entire three-month period.

Written by Tom Reeder. *Directed by* James Burrows.

Characters: Eric Christmas (Father Barry), Kim Johnston Ulrich (Rachel), Shanna Reed (Suzanne).

Note: Shanna Reed also appeared in "Major Dad."

Notable Quote: On redirecting sexual energy:

FRASIER: "And best of all, Sam. No matter how badly you perform, a piano never laughs. Never stomps out of the room and refuses to let you play again for three days. Well, I'm off to Lilith."

149. **"Executive Sweet"** (11/10/88). Rebecca rejects Sam (again), but this time her rationale is that she only wants to date men who can advance her career. When Greg Stone is fired, Rebecca's new boss, Martin Teal, expresses an interest in dating her. Although Martin can advance her career, he is not physically attractive, so Rebecca avoids dating him by pretending to be Sam's girlfriend. Sam cannot resist this opportunity, so he "breaks up" with Rebecca to force her into dating Martin. After one magical date, Martin proposes marriage and Rebecca passes out. **Subtopic:** Woody stores 4,000 bees in Rebecca's office and has difficulty keeping them in the hive.

Written by Phoef Sutton. *Directed by* James Burrows.

Characters: Alex Nevil (Martin Teal), Gerald Hiken (Dennis), Nathan

Purdee (Delivery Man), David Schall (Chauffeur).

Notable Quote: Rebecca's decision only to date men who can advance her career:

REBECCA: "I have wasted too much time. I'm not getting any younger, and I've made the decision to only date men who can help my career."

SAM: "You know, they have a name for women like that."

REBECCA: "Yeah, vice president."

150. **"One Happy Chappy in a Snappy Serape"** (11/17/88). Rebecca tells her boss, Martin, she cannot marry him because she is still in love with Sam. Martin wisely offers, and Sam immediately accepts, a one-month bartender position in Cancun, Mexico, leaving Rebecca free to marry Martin. Sam loves Cancun so much he refuses to return to Boston, so Rebecca goes to Mexico and threatens him with a gun to force him to return. Sam refuses, but eventually feels guilty and flies to Boston to stop Rebecca and Martin's wedding. **Subtopic:** Carla lusts after the Mexican bartender, Ramon, who temporarily replaces Sam.

Written by Cheri Eichen and Bill Steinkellner. *Directed by* James Burrows.

Characters: Alex Nevil (Martin Teal), Gerald Hiken (Dennis), Fred Asparagus (Pepe), Marco Hernandez (Ramon), Loren Farmer (Tourist).

151. **"Those Lips, Those Ice"** (11/24/88). Carla becomes insanely jealous when a sexy German skater, Franzi Schrempf, joins the ice show and expresses an interest in Eddie. When tabloids write about Franzi's new lover, Carla suppresses her violent rage and attempts to regain Eddie's love by becoming the perfect wife—

satisfying his every desire, including being the hostess for a poker party at their house. Of course, the charade of kindness quickly ends when she finds out Eddie never touched Franzi. **Subtopic:** Frasier has a dilemma when he is unable to access his new cellular telephone because it is locked in his briefcase, and he forgot the combination.

Written by Peter Casey and David Lee. *Directed by* James Burrows.

Characters: Jay Thomas (Eddie LeBec), Isa Andersen (Franzi Schrempf), Alan Koss (Alan), Hugh Maguire (Hugh), Stuart K. Robinson (Customer), Charles Noland (Hockey Buddy #1), Andy Saylor (Hockey Buddy #2).

Notable Quote: Sam, speaking with sexy German ice skater Franzi Schrempf:

SAM: "We were just wondering now that you're here in Boston, what are your plans?"

FRANZI: "Well, while I'm here I would like to wear blue jeans, see a Tom Cruise movie, and eat a Big Mac."

SAM: "Oooh, sexy, dumb, *and* a cheap date."

151. **"Norm, Is that You?"** (12/8/88). Frasier and Lilith fire a renowned interior decorator, Ivan, when his designing concepts intrude upon the habitability of their home. Norm inadvertently reveals a knack for interior decorating and is hired to redecorate the Crane town house. After seeing his fantastic work, the Cranes arrange to have Norm design Kim and Robert Cooperman's town house, though the Coopermans are hesitant because they want their designer to be "stylish" (i.e., gay). Norm tries to fit their image, and everything is going fine until Sam refuses to play the part of his lover. Norm is then forced to confess he is straight!

Written by Cheri Eichen and Bill Steinkellner. *Directed by* James Burrows.

Characters: Bebe Neuwirth (Lilith), Jane Sibbett (Kim Cooperman), George Deloy (Robert Cooperman), B.J. Turner (Ivan), Craig Branham (Todd), Al Rosen (Al).

Notable Quote: Norm, after losing a decorating job because he is not gay:

NORM: "But the point is. I think you should judge people for *what* they do, not *who* they do."

153. **"How to Win Friends & Electrocute People"** (12/15/88). Cliff is admitted to the hospital for appendectomy surgery and becomes depressed when nobody from Cheers visits. He decides to undergo shock therapy to alter his personality, and holds one electrifying session in the bar. As expected, Cliff is unable to control his rude comments and is shocked repeatedly. After discontinuing the session, Cliff confesses the scheme to the gang, and they apologize for their insensitivity. **Subtopics:** Rebecca is featured in an article about women who run pubs, but her picture winds up in the obituaries. Meanwhile, Sam teaches Lilith how to drive, and the first driving lesson is the last when an outraged truck driver punches Sam in the nose.

Written by Phoef Sutton. *Directed by* James Burrows.

Characters: Bebe Neuwirth (Lilith), Robert Benedetti (Dave), Steve Bean (Reporter), Hugh Maguire (Hugh), Al Rosen (Al), Edward A. Wright (Mr. McManus), Shirley Prestia (Nurse), Andrew Lowery (Delivery Boy), Alan Koss (Alan), Peter Schreiner (Pete).

Notable Quote: In reference to Sam's teaching Lilith how to drive:

LILITH: "How do you think I'll do?"

SAM: "I've never had a woman in a car who didn't do great."

LILITH: "Wonderful. You teach me to drive, [and] I'll help you with your sense of humor."

154. "Jumping Jerks" (12/22/88). Woody, Norm and Cliff brag about their masculinity, and are forced to prove their mettle when a skydiving instructor, Bob Speakes, offers to take them up. Immediately before jumping, they reconsider their decision, but go back to the bar bragging about the jump. When Rebecca implies she is turned on by skydivers, Sam decides to jump, too. On the second jump, they again chicken out but return to the bar boasting about the adventure. Now Rebecca wants the sky kings to jump one more time while holding a Cheers banner. On the third jump, Woody dives first, and the entire gang follows suit. Sam expects this daredevil feat to win Rebecca's affection, but she is not impressed that he blew chow at 5,000 feet.

Written by Ken Levine and David Isaacs. *Directed by* James Burrows.

Characters: J. Kenneth Campbell (Bob Speakes), Thomas Sanders (Otto), Hugh Maguire (Hugh), Peter Schreiner (Pete).

Notable Quote: On Rebecca's idea to promote Cheers by having the gang skydive while holding a Cheers banner:

NORM: "Whoa, hold on a second. Are you talking about taking a pure sport such as skydiving, and tainting it for commercial gain?"

REBECCA: "Come on. A thing like that could have a tremendous impact."

NORM: "Hey, so could I."

155. "Send in the Crane" (1/5/89). Rebecca organizes a children's party for the corporate executives' brats and hires Woody to perform a clown act. He cancels after earning a part in a play, so Frasier fills in. Frasier does admirably, until the trick handkerchief drops his clown pants and exposes his (not so private) private parts. **Subtopic:** Sam attempts the feat of a lifetime—dating a mother, Judy, and her daughter, Laurie, simultaneously. He begins to subconsciously regret his actions, but decides to go for it anyway. Despite his efforts, Laurie only wants "Uncle Sammy" to give her away at her impending wedding.

Written by David Lloyd. *Directed by* James Burrows.

Characters: Bebe Neuwirth (Lilith), Sandahl Bergman (Judy), Chelsea Noble (Laurie), Patricia Morison (Mrs. Ridgeway), Peter Schreiner (Pete).

Note: Chelsea Noble played the part of Mike Seaver's girlfriend in "Growing Pains" (and is also Kirk Cameron's real-life wife).

Notable Quote: Sam, trying to date a mother and daughter at the same time:

FRASIER: "Sam, you're trying to date your girlfriend's daughter. Now, isn't there a little voice in the back of your mind trying to tell you something?"

SAM: "Little voice?"

FRASIER: "Your conscience?"

SAM: "Well, yeah, as a matter of fact I do hear this little voice, but it's not coming from the direction of my *brain!*"

156. "Bar Wars II: The Woodman Strikes Back" (1/12/89). The pranks continue as Cheers tries to find the secret ingredient in Gary's famous Bloody Mary mix. When their efforts fail, Woody quits Cheers and begins working as a bartender at Gary's Olde Towne Tavern. The change of employment is part of a prank to trick Gary into believing there is a change in the starting time of the contest, but twice he foils their plan. Gary is finally fooled when Carla's neighbor poses as the contest judge and declares Gary the winner. (The plan was to have Gary absent when the official judge showed up later that day.) Although the official winner is not declared, one thing is for sure, it is not Gary's Tavern.

Written by Ken Levine and David Isaacs. *Directed by* James Burrows.

Characters: Bebe Neuwirth (Lilith), Joel Polis (Gary), Robert O'Reilly (Ed Fogerty), Greg Collins (Greg), Vincent Pantone (Vince), Time Winters (Customer), Tim Cunningham (Tim), Alan Koss (Alan).

Notable Quote: On Cliff's career choice:

CLIFF: "I actually considered a career as a spy when I was young. But in the end I decided not to go into intelligence."

CARLA: "That seems only fair—none of it went into you."

157. "Adventures in Housesitting" (1/19/89). As a means of corporate advancement, Rebecca volunteers to dog sit a prize Doberman, Buster, owned by corporate vice president Mr. Sheridan. Since she is all alone in Mr. Sheridan's mansion, Sam concocts a plan to frighten Rebecca so he can spend the evenings protecting her. When Buster accidentally escapes, Woody finds another Doberman (an attack dog named Satan) to fool Mr. Sheridan until Buster is located. Of course, the plan is not perfect, but it is effective, and Buster returns unscathed. **Subtopic:** Frasier is nervous about

delivering a speech, so he uses Carla's tension relieving technique to overcome his anxiety.

Written by Patricia Niedzialek and Cecile Alch. *Directed by* James Burrows.

Characters: Bebe Neuwirth (Lilith), Michael Currie (Mr. Sheridan), Tim Cunningham (Tim), Alan Koss (Alan).

Notable Quote: After another attempt by Sam to proposition Rebecca:

REBECCA: "A man and a woman can be together in an evening without ending up rolling on the floor."

SAM: "Well, I know that's true with some people, but sweetheart, we're good looking."

158. "Please Mr. Postman" (2/2/89). Cliff's new postal trainee, Margaret O'Keefe, is sexually attracted to him, so they decide to share an evening of passion in a motel. When Margaret fails to return a postal vehicle, which is later found at the motel, they cover up their sexual liaison by claiming the vehicle was stolen. Margaret begins to feel guilty about their deceitfulness and insists they confess the truth. Consequently, Margaret is fired and joins the Canadian Postal Service, whereas Cliff is reprimanded and nearly accompanies her across the northern border. **Subtopic:** After a conversation about sexual stimuli, Sam tries to guess Rebecca's favorite song—the song that releases her sexual inhibitions.

Written by Brian Pollack and Mert Rich. *Directed by* James Burrows.

Characters: Annie Golden (Margaret O'Keefe), Howard Mungo (Policeman).

Notable Quote: Cliff, saying goodbye to Margaret as she leaves for Canada:

MARGARET: "But Cliff. It will be so terrible. I'll be so cold and alone. Who will keep me warm?"

CLIFF: "You'll do fine, Margaret. Women have that extra layer of fat."

159. "Golden Boyd" (2/6/89, Monday, 10:00–10:30 p.m. EST). Rebecca organizes a party for a corporate executive's daughter, Kelly Gaines, and has Sam and Woody tend bar at the gathering. Woody's naiveté and jocularity amuses the guest of honor but enrages her boyfriend, Nash. Woody and Nash arrange to fight at Cheers, and Woody is knocked out with one punch. He retaliates by asking Kelly for a date. She is hesitant but accepts the invitation as a way of making Nash jealous. The innocent, one-time-only date becomes more serious when they realize a mutual attraction. Woody and Kelly officially begin dating.

Written by Cheri Eichen and Bill Steinkellner. *Directed by* James Burrows.

Characters: Jackie Swanson (Kelly), Tyrone Power, Jr. (Nash), Richard Doyle (Mr. Gaines), Gary Bergher (Mr. Howell), Vaughn Armstrong (Mr. Osborn), Josef Rainer (Mr. Drysdale).

Note: Jackie Swanson's first role was in Prince's "Raspberry Beret" video (1985), for which she earned approximately $35.

Notable Quote: Woody, serving drinks to a group of wealthy people at a party:

NASH: "Dad has favored me with the option of going up on the Hill to page or being a clerk. So what do you think?"

WOODY: "Excuse me for interrupting. But I'd go with the clerk job. I had a blast the summer I clerked at the Piggly Wiggly."

NASH: "I'm sure you did, but I was talking about being a *legal* clerk."

WOODY: "Oh, this was all on the up-and-up."

160. "I Kid You Not" (2/16/89). Frasier and Lilith contemplate reproduction, so they spend time with Carla's child, Lud, to determine if they are suited for parenthood. When the Crane's begin monopolizing Lud, Carla becomes concerned about losing her child. However, after an embarrassing incident in a fancy restaurant, Frasier decides he never wants to be a father. At that moment Lilith informs him she is pregnant. **Subtopics:** Woody is tired of using the city bus, so he borrows Sam's Corvette to take Kelly on a date. Meanwhile, the Cheers gang teases Rebecca about sleeping with Sam because she rode in his car.

Teleplay by Rod Burton. *Story by* Rick Beren. *Directed by* James Burrows.

Characters: Bebe Neuwirth (Lilith), Jarrett Lennon (Ludlow), Jackie Swanson (Kelly), Peter Henry Schroeder (Maître d'), Charles Tachovsky (Waiter), Peter Schreiner (Pete).

Notable Quote: In regard to Carla's nerdy child:

CLIFF: "Looks like Carla's got herself a real Poindexter, there, eh? Yeah, it's sad to say that kids who are unaccepted by their peers really never learn how to get along with people in the big grown-up world."

NORM: "Why is that, Cliffy? Because they keep boring everyone and driving them crazy with long speeches filled with meaningless statistics."

CLIFF: "Yeah, yeah. Sixty-three percent of them live lives of quiet desperation."

NORM: "And how about those people who sit next to them?"

161. **"Don't Paint Your Chickens"** (2/23/89). Rebecca becomes irate when she is bypassed for another corporate promotion and decides to prove her worth by marketing Norm's painting business. (He is blackmailed into agreeing because Rebecca is threatening to collect his bar tab.) When Norm is hired for one painting job, Rebecca decides to quit the corporation. She confronts and insults a corporate executive, Mr. Anawalt, but he likes her initiative and offers her a promotion and raise. Moments later he is arrested for insider trading, and Rebecca loses her corporate advancement. **Subtopic:** Sam tries to keep pace with an attractive athletic woman, Erin, but terminates their relationship after becoming physically exhausted.

Written by Ken Levine and David Isaacs. *Directed by* James Burrows.

Characters: Stefan Gierasch (Mr. Anawalt), Lisa Aliff (Erin), Sarah Marshall (Mrs. Rosenbush), Ralph Meyering, Jr. (FBI Agent Adams), Peter Schreiner (Pete), Steve Giannelli (Steve), Tasia Valenza (Customer), Richard Epcar (Security Guard), Mark Legan (FBI Agent Thompson).

162. **"The Cranemakers"** (3/2/89). Frasier and Lilith are overwhelmed with the joy of impending parenthood and decide to abandon civilization to live in the wilderness. Sam convinces them to try one weekend in a cabin first. After only a few hours without heat or electricity, Frasier and Lilith are tempted by a newspaper review of a trendy Boston restaurant and promptly return to their pretentious lifestyle. **Subtopic:** The corporation requires Woody to take a vacation, so Rebecca arranges a trip to Italy. Despite missing the plane, he has a great week vacationing in the airport terminal.

Written by Phoef Sutton. *Directed by* Andy Ackerman.

Characters: Bebe Neuwirth (Lilith), James R. Winker (Whitney Morris), Peter Schreiner (Pete), Michael Holden (Customer).

Notable Quote: After Frasier and Lilith announce their decision to live in the wilderness:

NORM: "You guys want these pretzels?"

FRASIER: "No thank you. From now on I only eat what I kill."

NORM: "Then I suggest you kill about a half dozen beers and lighten up."

163. **"Hot Rocks"** (3/16/89). Rebecca is invited to a celebrity event, and she accessorizes with a pair of $32,000 diamond earrings on loan from a local jewelry store. When the earrings are misplaced, she accuses the Chairman of the Joint Chiefs of Staff, Admiral William J. Crowe, Jr., of being the thief. In desperation, Rebecca agrees to sleep with Sam if he can find the jewelry. Sam re-enacts the crime and locates the missing earrings in an empty water glass. Opportunity knocks, but when Rebecca expresses her repulsion at the thought of sleeping with him, Sam does not require her to fulfill the promise.

Written by Ken Levine and David Isaacs. *Directed by* James Burrows.

Characters: Admiral William J. Crowe, Jr., Chairman of the Joint Chiefs of Staff (Himself).

Notable Quote: In reference to Rebecca's wearing a sexy, low-cut dress:

REBECCA: "Well, I might just dress this way all the time. It makes me feel all at once desirable and businesslike."

CARLA: "You got a point. About a half a dozen guys asked me how much you charge."

164. "What's Up Doc?" (3/30/ 89). Sam is attracted to Frasier's sexy psychologist friend, Dr. Sheila Rydell, but after her unequivocal rejection, he decides to approach her on a professional level by faking impotence. Sheila sees through the charade, but succumbs to his charm and agrees to a date. When Sam insists upon her professional opinion of him, she obliges by opining he has massive insecurities and his whole life revolves around sex (in short, he is one sick cowpoke!). Sam becomes depressed, but quickly cheers up when Rebecca points out he has at least one interest other than sex—"The Three Stooges."

Written by Brian Pollack and Mert Rich. *Directed by* James Burrows.

Characters: Bebe Neuwirth (Lilith), Madolyn Smith Osborne (Dr. Sheila Rydell).

Note: Madolyn Smith Osborne subsequently played the role of an attorney in the movie *The Super* (1991) starring Joe Pesci.

Notable Quote: Discussing home videos:

CLIFF: "Ma had our home movies converted to tape. There's a great one of me all dressed up as Peter Pan. Ma is Captain Hook. She's tying me up. [chuckling] It's great."

NORM: "What, Halloween?"

CLIFF: "No, no. It's a little game we used to play to help me sleep. You know how crazy teenagers are."

165. "The Gift of the Woodi" (4/6/89). Woody's girlfriend, Kelly Gaines, celebrates her birthday, so Woody gives her a very special present—a song, a kiss, and says, "I love you." After Kelly receives this gift, she still expects a "real" present. Woody contemplates breaking up with her

because their lifestyles are too incompatible, but ultimately resolves the dilemma by spending all of his money to purchase a tiny pendant with crushed diamonds. When Kelly finally realizes Woody cannot afford the gift, she rejects the present. **Subtopics:** Rebecca believes her attractive image is hindering her career, so she consults Lilith for fashion advice. Meanwhile, Cliff tries to market his latest vegetable idea—the beetabaga.

Written by Phoef Sutton. *Directed by* James Burrows.

Characters: Bebe Neuwirth (Lilith), Jackie Swanson (Kelly), Bruce French (John), Richard Doyle (Mr. Gaines), Vaughn Armstrong (Uncle Val).

Notable Quote: In reference to Woody's anger:

WOODY: "What's the use. I don't care anymore."

SAM: "Don't be bitter."

WOODY: "I'm not bitter, Sam. I'm just consumed by a gnawing hate that's eating away at my gut until I can taste the bile in my mouth. [pause] Does anyone have a tic tac?"

166. "Call Me Irresponsible" (4/13/89). Carla and Eddie have their second wedding anniversary, and she expects a shower of presents from her husband. When it appears he may have forgotten, the Cheers gang secretly orders flowers, but Carla figures out their plan. When she realizes no presents are forthcoming, Carla sends flowers to herself, but the gang discovers that Eddie is not the sender. Just before midnight Carla receives a telephone call from her husband explaining that he wanted to surprise her by flying to Boston but the ice show prevented his departure. Carla is appeased, though it appears Sam may have called to remind Eddie about the anniversary.

Written by Dan O'Shannon and Tom Anderson. *Directed by* James Burrows.

Characters: Bebe Neuwirth (Lilith), Jay Thomas (Eddie), Ann Guilbert (Marge), Fredric Cook (McGuiness), Michael G. Hawkins (Deliveryman #1), Herb Caen (Deliveryman #2), Mark Arnott (Mark), Tim Cunningham (Tim), Steve Giannelli (Steve), Peter Schreiner (Pete).

Note: Ann Guilbert previously appeared in "The Dick Van Dyke Show" (as Millie Helper) and starred in "The Fanelli Boys" (as Theresa Fanelli).

167. **"Sisterly Love"** (4/27/89). When Rebecca's sister, Susan, visits Cheers, it is revealed the Howe sisters have not spoken for years because Susan always stole Rebecca's boyfriends. Sam uses their sibling rivalry to date both women—by pretending to be Rebecca's boyfriend, and then telling Rebecca that Susan is interested in dating him. The plan seems to work, until Rebecca catches Sam and Susan together in the Cheers office. Rebecca grabs a gun from her office desk drawer and shoots Susan several times. As Sam tries to hide the body, the Cheers gang surprises him and reveal the sisters staged the "killing" to teach Sam a lesson.

Written by David Lloyd. *Directed by* James Burrows.

Characters: Bebe Neuwirth (Lilith), Marcia Cross (Susan Howe), Richmond Harrison (Phil).

Note: Marcia Cross subsequently appeared in "Melrose Place."

Notable Quote: Carla, discussing Rebecca's attractive family:

CARLA: "Man, it's not fair. All the chicks in that family are loaded with great faces, hair, bods. What did my family get?"

WOODY: "Well, look at the bright side, Carla. It probably takes them hours to get ready every morning, whereas you look the same with or without makeup, and your hair practically combs itself."

168. **"The Visiting Lecher"** (5/4/89). Frasier's friend Dr. Lawrence Crandell makes several passes at Rebecca, but the Cheers gang refuses to believe her. Rebecca attempts to have Crandell admit the truth, and asks Sam to verify the confession by eavesdropping from the hotel closet. As they arrive at the hotel, Crandell is in the process of serenading a chambermaid with a violinist. When Crandell's wife, Valerie, unexpectedly arrives, she demands an explanation. As Rebecca reiterates his sexual advances, the facts become even more convoluted (and Crandell's infidelity remains Rebecca's unbelievable secret).

Written by David Lloyd. *Directed by* James Burrows.

Characters: John McMartin (Dr. Lawrence Crandell), Joanna Barnes (Valerie), Fabiana Udenio (Maria), Nicholas Miscusi (Zoltan).

Notable Quote: Dr. Lawrence Crandell, testing his theory of celibacy:

LAWRENCE: "And I'm glad to say, after ten months of celibacy I can now pronounce my principles sound."

SAM: "Whoa. After ten months of celibacy I couldn't even pronounce my name."

Season Eight: 1989-90

(NBC Thursday, 9:00–9:30 p.m. EST)
Season Regulars: Ted Danson (Sam Malone), Kirstie Alley (Rebecca Howe), Rhea Perlman (Carla Tortelli-LeBec), John Ratzenberger (Cliff Clavin), Woody Harrelson (Woody Boyd), Kelsey Grammer (Frasier Crane), George Wendt (Norm Peterson).

Technical Credits: *Created by* Glen Charles, Les Charles and James Burrows. *Executive Producers:* James Burrows, Glen Charles, Les Charles. *Co-Executive Producers:* Cheri Eichen, Bill Steinkellner, Phoef Sutton. *Producer:* Tim Berry. *Co-Producer:* Andy Ackerman. *Writers:* Tom Anderson, Elias Davis, Cheri Eichen, Sue Herring, David Isaacs, Ken Levine, David Lloyd, Rob Long, Dan O'Shannon, Brian Pollack, David Pollock, Mert Rich, Dan Staley, Eugene B. Stein, Bill Steinkellner, Phoef Sutton. *Teleplay by* Cheri Eichen, Bill Steinkellner, Phoef Sutton (#194). *Story by* Bill Steinkellner (#194). *Directors:* James Burrows, Andy Ackerman. *Creative Consultants:* David Lloyd, Ken Levine and David Isaacs. *Executive Script Consultant:* Bob Ellison. *Executive Story Consultants:* Brian Pollack and Mert Rich. *Executive Story Editors:* Dan O'Shannon and Tom Anderson. *Associate Producer:* Mary Fukuto. *Director of Photography:* John Finger, Howard Block. *Art Director:* Dahl Delu. *Edited by* Andy Ackerman, John Randle, Sheila Amos. *Unit Production Manager:* Linda McMurray. *First Assistant Director:* Brian James Ellis. *Second Assistant Directors:* Steven Pomeroy, Roger Mills. *Music by* Craig Safan. *Song:* "Where Everybody Knows Your Name." *Lyrics and Music by* Judy Hart Angelo and Gary Portnoy. *Sung by* Gary Portnoy. *Casting:* Jeff Greenberg, C.S.A. *Original Casting:* Stephen Kolzak. *Set Decorator:* Laura Richarz. *Production Supervisor:* Ahuva Fogel. *Technical Coordinator:* Rick Beren. *Script Supervisor:* Gabrielle James. *Production Mixer:* Robert Crosby, C.A.S. *Costume Supervisor:* Robert L. Tanella. *Women's Costumer:* B.J. Rogers. *Makeup Artist:* Bruce Hutchinson. *Hair Stylist:* Marilyn Patricia Phillips. *Music Editor:* Chips Swanson. *Sound Effects:* David Scharf. *Editing Facilities:* Laser Edit, Inc. *Main Title Design:* James Castle, Bruce Bryant, Carol Johnsen. *Cameras and Lenses:* Panavision. *Assistants to the Charles Brothers:* Libby Applebaum, Danielle Bodenhorn, Jessica Budin, Christine Connor, Nicholas Grad, Sheila Guthrie Nevil, Sue Herring, Georgyne Lalone, Tony Martinelli, Lori A. Moneymaker, Jessica L. Nagler, Mark Nasser, Carol Navratil, Eddie Pardella, David Reid, Kerstin Robbins-Fares, Russ Sherman, Rich Stangl, Barry Zajac. *Charles/Burrows/Charles Productions in Association with* Paramount.

169. "The Improbable Dream" **(Part 1 of 2)** (9/21/89). Rebecca has erotic dreams about Sam and hates herself because she wants a man who owns blocks, not one who plays with them. She confides in the Cranes, but Sam overhears the conversation and devises a plan to have Rebecca enact her dreams. When she is asleep in the office, he arranges to intervene in the middle of a dream so Rebecca will not know whether it is a dream or reality. The plan fails, but Rebecca realizes that maybe she should settle for Sam. As they begin to start a relationship, millionaire Robin Colcord enters the office, so Rebecca immediately casts Sam aside.

Written by Cheri Eichen and Bill Steinkellner. *Directed by* James Burrows.

Characters: Bebe Neuwirth (Lilith), Roger Rees (Robin Colcord), Tony DiBenedetto (Tony), Peter Schreiner (Pete).

Note: Roger Rees has appeared in the movies *If Looks Could Kill* (1991), *Stop! or My Mom Will Shoot* (1992), and *Robin Hood: Men in Tights* (1993).

Notable Quote: In reference to Frasier's putting a wedge of lime in his beer:

CLIFF: "It's yuppie nouveau to have a little fruit floating in your beer."

NORM: "Call me old-fashioned, Cliff, but the only thing I like floating in beer is my *liver*."

170. "The Improbable Dream" (Part 2 of 2) (9/28/89). Rebecca and Robin go on their first date, a three-day trip to the West Coast, and everyone is gossiping about the happy couple. Rebecca is on cloud nine, and Sam realizes he is envious because he cares for her. When Sam is finally convinced of his feelings, he confronts Rebecca, but before he can speak his piece, Robin walks in and tells her he cares for her deeply. Rebecca melts because she has waited a long time to hear a man say those words. Once again, Sam misses an opportunity to win the heart of Rebecca.

Written by Cheri Eichen and Bill Steinkellner. *Directed by* James Burrows.

Characters: Bebe Neuwirth (Lilith), Roger Rees (Robin Colcord), Al Rosen (Al), Webster Williams (Miles), Valerie Hartman (Marie).

Notable Quote: Sam, upset that Rebecca is dating Robin:

SAM: "It doesn't seem fair, does it? I've spent three years loosening the cap on that peanut butter jar, and right now she's sticking to the roof of somebody else's mouth."

171. "A Bar Is Born" (10/12/89). Sam realizes he hates his life and a change is necessary. He buys another bar, Tim's Place, along the waterfront, but Robin Colcord convinces him not to go through with the plan, and kindly agrees to make a few phone calls to rescind the contract. Shortly thereafter, Robin enters Cheers bragging about the profit he will make on the property he purchased—the same property he convinced Sam not to buy. Robin stole Sam's business idea and purchased the property to build a high-rise. **Subtopic**: Rebecca consults Carla about techniques to spice up a romantic evening with Robin.

Written by Phoef Sutton. *Directed by* James Burrows.

Characters: Roger Rees (Robin Colcord), Tony DiBenedetto (Tony), Alan Koss (Alan).

Notable Quote: In reference to Rebecca's receiving a watch from Robin, and being teased about not going to bed with him:

SAM: "When is your rich boyfriend coming back?"

REBECCA: "In about a week."

SAM: "Oh good. That will give you time to make up excuses not to go to bed with him."

REBECCA: "I want to go to bed with him. I'm just waiting for the right time."

SAM: "Well, maybe that's why he gave you the watch."

172. **"How to Marry a Mailman"** (10/19/89). Margaret O'Keefe returns to Boston and asks Cliff to be her man. Cliff reveals a psychosomatic illness that causes him to go blind whenever he is faced with commitment to a woman. Sam tries to help, but Cliff can only be cured when he willingly commits to Margaret. After agreeing to be her man, Cliff's blindness is cured, but he becomes paralyzed from the waist down. **Subtopic**: Rebecca is offered a free plastic surgery of her choice to settle an automobile accident claim against a plastic surgeon. The Cheers gang wants her to get a breast enhancement, but she decides to have a mole and tattoo removed from her lower back.

Written by Brian Pollack and Mert Rich. *Directed by* James Burrows.

Characters: Bebe Neuwirth (Lilith), Roger Rees (Robin Colcord), Annie Golden (Margaret O'Keefe), Webster Williams (Miles).

173. **"The Two Faces of Norm"** (10/26/89). Norm's painting business is booming, so he hires three painters. Norm quickly realizes he is not boss material when his employees begin taking advantage of him. To facilitate productivity, Norm creates a fictitious business partner, Anton Kreitzer, to handle employee discipline. Things improve dramatically until Norm pushes the employees too far. They quit and eventually unmask Norm's dual personality. **Subtopic**: Sam desperately wants to buy Cheers, so in an effort to save money he sells his Corvette and purchases a Volaré. When women begin laughing at him, Sam begs Lilith to return his Corvette.

Written by Eugene B. Stein. *Directed by* Andy Ackerman.

Characters: Eric Allan Kramer (Rudy), Cynthia Stevenson (Doris), Rob Moran (Dennis Hammill), Gordon Hunt (Gordon), Mark Knudsen (John), J.C. Victor (Scott), Jacqueline Alexandra Citron (Jennifer), Kristen Amber Citron (Veronica).

Note: Cynthia Stevenson also appeared in "Empty Nest" (as Amy, Harry Weston's niece), "Bob" (as Patricia McKay), hosted "My Talk Show" (as Jennifer Bass), and starred in "Hope & Gloria."

Notable Quote:

WOODY: "Hey, Mr. Peterson. Got room for a beer?"

NORM: "Nah, but I am willing to add on."

174. **"The Stork Brings a Crane"** (11/2/89). Lilith is two weeks overdue with the birth of her child and goes into labor at Cheers. She is rushed to the hospital but diagnosed with false labor pains. While waiting at the hospital, Frasier and Sam assist another woman, Gail Aldrich, in the delivery room. Lilith is discharged, and on the ride home gives birth in the backseat of a taxicab. **Subtopic**: Cheers celebrates its 100th anniversary, and Rebecca plans an entire day of events with celebrities and entertainment. Naturally, nothing goes as planned, and the entire day is a disaster.

Written by David Lloyd. *Directed by* Andy Ackerman.

Characters: Bebe Neuwirth (Lilith), Victoria Hoffman (Gail Aldrich), Mayor Raymond L. Flynn (Himself), Monty Ash (Mr. Weaver), Laura Robinson (Nurse), Raymond Hanis (Cameraman), Peter Schreiner (Pete), Michael Ennis (Doctor), Robin Krieger (Mayor's Aide), Seib (Mayor's Aide), *139th Street Quartet*: Doug Anderson, Jim Kline, Peter Neushul, John Sherburn.

Notable Quote: On Cheers' 100th

anniversary, featuring a 106-year-old man, Mr. Weaver:

REBECCA: "The reason Mr. Weaver is our guest of honor today is because he used to live in this neighborhood. Do you get it? He was here when Cheers opened [in 1889]."

NORM: "Big deal. I'm always here when Cheers opens."

175. "Death Takes a Holiday on Ice" (11/9/89). Carla receives a telephone call that Eddie died while saving the life of a fellow ice show employee, Gordie Brown. At the funeral it is revealed Eddie had another wife, Gloria, and the entire ceremony becomes a barroom brawl. After the mayhem, Carla tries to cope with Eddie's bigamy, and both wives try to discern which one of them was Eddie's true love. The answer is revealed when Gordie Brown delivers a note written by Eddie which explains his bigamy and unequivocally declares Carla as his true love.

Written by Ken Levine and David Isaacs. *Directed by* James Burrows.

Characters: Anne De Salvo (Gloria), Eric Christmas (Father Barry), Kevin Conroy (Darryl Mead), Thomas Haden Church (Gordie Brown).

Note: Thomas Haden Church subsequently became a regular on the television show "Wings" (as Lowell Mather).

176. "For Real Men Only" (11/16/89). When the Cranes plan a Jewish circumcision ceremony for Frederick, not only does the Cheers gang avoid the event, but Frasier also kidnaps the infant and hides in Rebecca's office. After further discussion, i.e., Lilith's insistence, Frasier acquiesces to the circumcision, which is performed in the Cheers poolroom. **Subtopics:**

Rebecca organizes a corporate retirement party which ultimately features Frederick's circumcision as the entertainment. Meanwhile, Carla circulates a petition to have Eddie's jersey number retired. When the Bruins balk at the idea, she drops the petition in exchange for free season tickets.

Written by David Pollock and Elias Davis. *Directed by* James Burrows.

Characters: Bebe Neuwirth (Lilith), Michael Currie (Mr. Sheridan), Jay Robinson (Larry), Rick Podell (Dr. Levinson), Michael Holden (Joe), Gilbert Girion (Will), Melanie Kinnaman (Tanya).

177. "Two Girls for Every Boyd" (11/23/89). Woody has the lead role in the community theater play *Our Town*, but has difficulty acting the intimate scenes with costar Emily. When the director considers finding a new leading man, Woody quickly learns to ad lib the part. **Subtopic:** After spending the day bragging about their manliness, the Cheers gang decides to hold a beard-growing contest. Everyone successfully grows facial hair except Cliff, whose beard is pathetically reminiscent of a wolf man. In response, he opts for an industrial adhesive to attach a fake beard, and wins the contest.

Written by Dan O'Shannon and Tom Anderson. *Directed by* James Burrows.

Characters: Bebe Neuwirth (Lilith), Jackie Swanson (Kelly Gaines), Lisa Kudrow (Emily), Jeffrey Richman (Lee Bradken), Ebbe Roe Smith (Ron), Peter Schreiner (Pete), Mark Kubr (Torsten).

Note: Lisa Kudrow appears in "Mad About You" (as Ursula) and costars in "Friends" (as Phoebe Buffay).

Notable Quote: On women being attracted to beards:

CLIFF: "Women can't resist a thick crop of jaw hair. It goes back to Androcles."

NORM: "Wasn't Androcles the guy who pulled the thorn out of the lion's paw?"

CLIFF: "That's what he told his wife when she found scratches on his back."

178. "The Art of the Steel" (11/30/89). Rebecca plans a romantic evening by waiting nude in Robin's penthouse to surprise him when he comes home. When he is delayed, Sam delivers the message personally and sees Rebecca in all her glory. As she escorts him to the elevator, the laser beam security system is accidentally activated, trapping them in Robin's penthouse. They spend the night talking, and escape the next morning when the maid deactivates the alarm. **Subtopic:** The Cheers gang plays Monopoly to teach Woody the concept of economics, but the entire game is marred by cheating and other self-serving antics.

Written by Sue Herring. *Directed by* James Burrows.

Characters: regulars only.

Notable Quote: In reference to spending an evening talking to a woman:

REBECCA: "You're trying to tell me that with all those thousands of women you supposedly slept with, you never stayed up and talked with one of them?"

SAM: "What's to talk about? A guy does all his talking *beforehand*."

179. "Feeble Attraction" (12/7/89). Norm's dwindling workload forces him to release his secretary, Doris, from her employment. He writes a letter of recommendation for Doris, which is misconstrued as a love confession. She reciprocates by admitting her love for Norm and begins following him everywhere. He quickly realizes the only way to be assured privacy is to rehire her. **Subtopic:** When Robin gives Rebecca a desk, he intimates there is a secret in the desk and provides the hint "ring." Rebecca destroys the desk with a chain saw while looking for an engagement ring, but the actual surprise is the ring-shaped stain on the top of the desk.

Written by Dan O'Shannon and Tom Anderson. *Directed by* Andy Ackerman.

Characters: Cynthia Stevenson (Doris), Michael Holden (Joe), John Pappas (Phil), Peter Schreiner (Pete).

Notable Quote: Norm, hiring Doris so she won't follow him around:

FRASIER: "You mean to tell me you're going to pay that girl week after week just to stop following you and watching your every move, interrupting your beer drinking?"

NORM: "Come on, Fras, this is nothing. I bought Vera a *house*."

180. "Sam Ahoy" (12/14/89). Sam, Carla and Norm agree to pilot Robin's sailboat in the annual regatta. During the race, Norm discovers a bomb in the refrigerator (placed by someone eager to kill Robin). They barely escape alive, and when Robin returns to Cheers, his only concern is liability. He attempts to have Sam sign a release of liability form, but Sam is appalled at Robin's insensitivity, and insists upon some showing of compassion. Sam rejects $60,000 in exchange for Robin's fake sentiment. When Carla and Norm learn of the payoff Sam declined, they chase after Robin to renegotiate a settlement.

Written by David Lloyd. *Directed by* James Burrows.

Characters: Roger Rees (Robin Colcord), Tim Cunningham (Tim), Patrick Maguire (Security Man), Stephen Burks (Aide).

Notable Quote: Sam, searching for a crew to sail Robin's boat:

SAM: "All right, I have to get me a crew here, don't I? Well, say there Carla, you're used to being around sailors, aren't you?"

181. "Sammy and the Professor" (1/4/90). Rebecca's favorite college professor, Alice Anne Volkman, visits Boston after writing the successful business book *Speak Out and Score*. Sam seeks her advice on how to buy Cheers, but the only business they discuss is between the sheets. Rebecca believes the sexual liaison probably means something special to Alice, and insists Sam return to her hotel to clear the air. He accommodates, but they only steam it up again. Rebecca is appalled and stands up to Alice by calling her a slut. **Subtopic:** Carla is audited by the IRS, and her plan to bury the agent in fake receipts could entomb Carla in jail.

Written by Brian Pollack and Mert Rich. *Directed by* James Burrows.

Characters: Alexis Smith (Alice Anne Volkman), Stack Pierce (Donald Zajac), Dietrich Bader (Waiter).

Notable Quote: In regard to Carla's being audited:

CARLA: "I'm getting audited. Next stop, prison. What am I going to do?"

CLIFF: "Probably make license plates."

182. "What Is ... Cliff Clavin?" (1/18/90). Cliff fulfills the dream of a lifetime by becoming a contestant on "Jeopardy!" He earns $22,000 in categories tailor-made to his inane knowledge, but loses it all in the final round. Cliff creates a spectacle on television and wallows in self-pity. When Alex Trebek visits Cheers and pretends he is contemplating quitting "Jeopardy!", Cliff's ego is redeemed when he persuades Alex to return to the game show. **Subtopic:** Sam misplaces his black book and becomes frenetic after receiving several telephone calls from irate women, so Rebecca assists him in catching the pubescent teen, Timmy, who is using the book to arrange dates.

Written by Dan O'Shannon and Tom Anderson. *Directed by* Andy Ackerman.

Characters: Alex Trebek (Himself), Greg E. Davis (Timmy), Bernard Kuby (Earl), Johnny Gilbert (Himself), Peter Schreiner (Pete), Audrey Lowell (Agnes Borsic), William A. Porter (Milford Reynolds), Steven Rotblatt (Stage Manager).

Note: Alex Trebek hosts the game show "Jeopardy!" Johnny Gilbert has a long history of hosting and emceeing game shows, such as "Beat the Odds" and "Fast Draw" in 1968-69.

183. "Finally!" (Part 1 of 2) (1/25/90). Robin is invited to Carl Yastrzemski's Testimonial Dinner and hires Sam for a baseball tutorial session. On the way to the dinner, Robin taps Sam's baseball knowledge while Rebecca sits idle in anger. When she and Robin begin a heated argument, it transforms into a passionate moment in his limousine, so they abandon Sam by the side of the road. The next morning, Rebecca arrives at the bar jubilant because she finally did it—she slept with Robin. The Cheers gang celebrates this event by having a burger at Little Wally's Pup & Burger, but as they are leaving Sam catches Robin with another woman.

Written by Ken Levine and David Isaacs. *Directed by* James Burrows.

Characters: Roger Rees (Robin Colcord), Bill Medley (Himself), Gail O'Grady (Laura Walton), Crystal Carson (Ingrid), Alan Koss (Alan), Webster Williams (Miles).

Notable Quote: Sam, once again propositioning Rebecca:

REBECCA: "Oh, Sam. You never stop."

SAM: "Oh, I'm sorry. It's in my genes."

REBECCA: "And that's where it's going to stay."

184. "Finally!" (Part 2 of 2) (2/1/90). By pretending there is a fire, Sam escorts Rebecca out of the restaurant to prevent her from seeing Robin with another woman. The next day, Robin offers Sam the chance to own Cheers in exchange for his silence. Sam rejects the offer and tells Rebecca the truth about Robin's infidelity. She accuses Sam of lying, but later that evening catches Robin with a ballerina. When Rebecca gives Robin an ultimatum, he claims she is one of three finalists in his quest for a wife. Although upset, Rebecca is pleased to hear she is in the lead.

Written by Ken Levine and David Isaacs. *Directed by* James Burrows.

Characters: Roger Rees (Robin Colcord), Bill Medley (Himself), Valerie Karasek (Christine Davi), Gilbert Girion (Will), Alan Koss (Alan), Carol Robbins (Elaine).

Notable Quote: Discussing Robin Colcord:

FRASIER: "The man is absolutely nothing more than a rich, spoiled, narcissistic philanderer. And I hate myself for envying him so."

185. "Woody or Won't He?" (2/8/90). Woody is invited to the Gaines estate to meet Kelly's mother, Roxanne, and spends the entire evening fending off her sexual advances. Although Kelly claims her mother is merely being friendly, Roxanne attacks Woody on the couch, puts her hand on his leg during dinner, and pinches his derriere during the family photo. **Subtopics:** Cheers installs a mechanical bull in the poolroom, and Cliff goes for the world record for the longest continuous ride. Meanwhile, Sam tends bar at a Gaines family party and loses $1,000 after acting on an investment tip from "The Hard Luck Five."

Written by Brian Pollack and Mert Rich. *Directed by* Andy Ackerman.

Characters: Jackie Swanson (Kelly), Melendy Britt (Roxanne Gaines), Bill Geisslinger (Conrad Langston), Richard Doyle (Mr. Gaines), Robert Gallo (Phil), Mark Arnott (Mark), Alan Koss (Alan), Peter Schreiner (Pete), Kevin Joseph Klein (Photographer), Kevin McDermott (Fireman), D. David Morin (Mechanic).

Notable Quote: In reference to Cliff's riding a mechanical bull:

CARLA: "How do you like that? For once the bull is throwing Clavin around."

186. "Severe Crane Damage" (2/15/90). Lilith authors the book *Good Girls, Bad Boys*, and appears on a local television talk show with Sam and Frasier to illustrate the bad boy and good boy, respectively. After describing Sam's physical attractiveness, she becomes enticed by the bad boy and thrusts herself upon him. In response, Frasier decides to prove he, too, is a bad boy by teaming up with a biker chick, Viper. When Frasier is forced to make a choice, he stays with Lilith. **Subtopic:** Cliff takes medication for work-related anxiety and becomes concerned when he learns the drug causes male breast enlargement.

Written by Dan O'Shannon and Tom Anderson. *Directed by* Andy Ackerman.

Characters: Bebe Neuwirth (Lilith), Phyllis Katz (Brenda Balzak), Lorelle Brina (Viper). *Talk Show Ladies*: Donna Fuller, Marsha Kramer, Marti Muller, Audrey Rapoport, Mark Arnott (Mark), Peter Schreiner (Pete).

Notable Quote: On Frasier's baldness, as he prepares to be on television:

FRASIER: "I just want to head to the men's room and check my hair."

CARLA: "Oh, I already checked— it's not in there."

187. "Indoor Fun with Sammy & Robby" (2/22/90). Rebecca convinces Robin to forego working for one day so they can fulfill her romantic fantasies. While visiting the bar, Robin is consumed by various sports competitions (darts, billiards, and chess), so Rebecca spends the day fulfilling her fantasies with Woody. Sam defeats Robin at darts and billiards, but has to use a computer program to compete at chess. Sam actually wins the match without the artificial intelligence, and since they bet one week's salary on the chess match, Sam wins a shiny penny (Robin earns $1.00 per year as CEO of his corporation, so one penny represents his after-tax income).

Written by Phoef Sutton. *Directed by* Andy Ackerman.

Characters: Roger Rees (Robin Colcord), Mark Arnott (Mark), Tim Cunningham (Tim), Peter Schreiner (Pete).

188. "50-50 Carla" (3/8/90). Carla befriends Eddie's other wife, Gloria, and they agree to share his estate. When Carla unexpectedly receives $50,000 from Eddie's life insurance policy, she conceals the windfall from Gloria. However, Gloria acts so nice during her stay that Carla's overwhelming sense of guilt causes her to relinquish half the proceeds. **Subtopics:** Woody is in the musical *Hair*. He tries to prepare for the nude scene by dressing scantily at Cheers, and on opening night he is the only actor to strip.

Written by David Lloyd. *Directed by* James Burrows.

Characters: Roger Rees (Robin Colcord), Anne De Salvo (Gloria), Steve Devorkin (Murray), Michael Holden (Joe), Peter Schreiner (Pete).

189. "Bar Wars III: Return of Tecumseh" (3/15/90). Thinking Gary stole the wooden Indian by the front door, the Cheers gang closes down Gary's Tavern on the busiest day of the year (St. Patrick's Day). When they learn Rebecca had Tecumseh revarnished, the gang tries to preempt Gary's retaliation by playing a prank on themselves (i.e., shaving their heads and having their picture printed in the newspaper). They later find out Gary's Tavern had been closed for months for remodeling, and Sam wore a rubber mask instead of shaving his head. **Subtopic:** Frasier and Lilith recreate their first romantic liaison.

Written by Ken Levine and David Isaacs. *Directed by* James Burrows.

Characters: Bebe Neuwirth (Lilith), Robert Machray (Fire Marshall), Tim Donoghue (Tucker), Peter Schreiner (Pete), Alan Koss (Alan), Phil Therrien (Deliveryman).

Notable Quote:

SAM: "What are you up to, Norm?"

NORM: "My ideal weight, if I were eleven feet tall."

190. "Loverboyd" (3/29/90). As Kelly prepares to depart for Paris to attend school, Woody gives her a promise ring. As she is packing, he sneaks into her bedroom and they agree to elope. Just before leaving to tie the knot, Kelly's father gives a heartwarming talk about how special she is to him. Woody overhears the conversation while hiding in the closet, and changes his mind about eloping because he feels guilty about stealing Kelly away from her father. **Subtopic:** Norm is the designated driver and goes the entire evening without drinking, primarily because Carla notified every bar.

Written by Brian Pollack and Mert Rich. *Directed by* James Burrows.

Characters: Jackie Swanson (Kelly), Richard Doyle (Mr. Gaines), Tony DiBenedetto (Tony), Trish Ramish (Chambermaid), Steve Giannelli (Steve).

Notable Quote: Rebecca persuading Woody not to elope:

REBECCA: "I once was deeply in love with a boy that my parents did not approve of, and I thought about eloping. But fortunately, I came to my senses. I mean, can you imagine what would have happened to me if I had married him?"

WOODY: "Yeah. Maybe you'd be happy now, instead of whining and being dumped on your whole life."

191. "The Ghost and Mrs. Le-Bec" (4/12/90). Carla tries to enter the dating scene for the first time since Eddie's death, but she sees his face everywhere. After her spiritualist, Madame Lazora, conducts a seance, Carla's fears dissipate, allowing her to date Darryl Mead, the Red Sox player who leads the league in tight-fitting pants. **Subtopics:** Rebecca appears on

the television show "Consumer Patrol" to complain about the Lady Baldy hair remover, but regrets her actions after discovering Robin owns the company that manufactures the product. Meanwhile, Frasier is upset when Lilith admits she would date other men if he predeceased her.

Written by Dan Staley and Rob Long. *Directed by* James Burrows.

Characters: Bebe Neuwirth (Lilith), Georgia Brown (Madame Lazora), Kevin Conroy (Darryl Mead), Michael Rupert (Dennis).

Notable Quote: Regarding Carla's psychic being a fraud:

FRASIER: "Carla, this psychic business is just a crutch to avoid reality. I mean, it's very easy for people to get hooked on this hocus pocus, and, well, before you know it this woman will be holding your hand once a week, charging you $100 an hour, and filling your mind with all sorts of confusing jargon."

CARLA: "And how is that different from you?"

FRASIER: [thinking for a second] "Well, ah, I can prescribe drugs."

192. "Mr. Otis Regrets" (4/19/90). Rebecca is envious of Robin's other woman, Jean-Marie, so she asks Sam to attend a gathering at the French consulate to spy on her. The event is canceled, but Sam feigns having sex with Jean-Marie (knowing Rebecca would be curious about Jean-Marie's sexual secrets). Although Rebecca asks him to demonstrate Jean-Marie's erotic ways, unbeknownst to Sam, she knows the party was canceled. When they re-enact a hotel elevator love scene, she ties him to the rail, undresses him, and then sends the elevator to the lobby. **Subtopic:** Woody

has a female roommate, Terry Gardner, but after one night she returns to her jealous husband, Cutter Gardner. When Cutter searches for the man that spent the night with his wife, Woody implicates Cliff.

Written by Ken Levine and David Isaacs. *Directed by* Andy Ackerman.

Characters: Bebe Neuwirth (Lilith), Christine Cavanaugh (Terry Gardner), Eric Bruskotter (Cutter Gardner), Colin Wells (Eric), Barry Zajac (Barry), Tony DiBenedetto (Tony), Peter Schreiner (Pete).

Notable Quote: Regarding Rebecca's envy toward Jean-Marie:

FRASIER: "Rebecca, I must tell you this is not a healthy relationship you're in—I mean, stuck in a run-off with another woman for Robin Colcord's affections, it's demeaning. [looking at a picture of Jean-Marie] Although it's nothing compared to what I'd do to have this exquisite creature grind her heel into my forehead. My God!"

193. **"Cry Hard" (Part 1 of 2)** (4/26/90). Rebecca is furious with Robin because he continues to date other women. In a rare decisive moment, she confronts him with an ultimatum, and Robin responds by asking her to cohabit. While moving into his mansion, Rebecca discovers he is receiving confidential corporate records by using her secret password. Rebecca intends to report him to the authorities, but just before meeting with the corporate board of directors, Robin arrives and proposes marriage. She willingly accepts and Robin shreds the evidence. To protect Rebecca from being implicated in the scandal, Sam reports Robin's illegal actions to the corporation.

Written by Dan O'Shannon and Tom Anderson. *Directed by* James Burrows.

Characters: Roger Rees (Robin Colcord), Jonathan McMurtry (Jim Montgomery), Edna Bodnar (Receptionist).

Notable Quote: Norm, doubting Cliff's statement that dust is mostly dead skin:

NORM: "Frasier, straighten him out, okay? What happens to old dead skin?"

FRASIER: "Apparently it sits on barstools and drinks beer all day."

194. **"Cry Hard" (Part 2 of 2)** (5/3/90). Robin is indicted for insider trading and flees the country to avoid prosecution. Rebecca is heartbroken, but becomes further depressed when she is fired. Sam tries to hide the fact he turned Robin in, but the truth is revealed when the corporation sells him the bar for $.85. Sam hires Rebecca as a waitress and she finally realizes Sam is the only man who ever really cared for her, so she decides to begin a romantic relationshipwith him. Shortly thereafter, Robin returns to Cheers to be with the woman he loves and unexpectedly witnesses the tryst. The season ends on the cliffhanger of whether Sam and Rebecca actually slepttogether, and if she will reunite with Robin.

Teleplay by Cheri Eichen and Bill Steinkellner and Phoef Sutton. *Story by* Bill Steinkellner. *Directed by* James Burrows.

Characters: Jonathan McMurtry (Jim Montgomery), Ron Canada (Agent Munson), Peter Schreiner (Pete), Michael Holden (Joe), Christopher Darga (Christopher), James Nardini (James).

Notable Quote: Discussing Robin's impending criminal trial:

ROBIN: "I've got a meeting with

counsel to discuss my defense strategy. [to Rebecca] I can't have you be the bride of a convict."

FRASIER: [to Norm] "If he goes to jail, *he'll* be the bride of a convict."

Season Nine: 1990-91

(NBC Thursday, 9:00–9:30 p.m. EST)

Season Regulars: Ted Danson (Sam Malone), Kirstie Alley (Rebecca Howe), Rhea Perlman (Carla Tortelli-LeBec), John Ratzenberger (Cliff Clavin), Woody Harrelson (Woody Boyd), Kelsey Grammer (Frasier Crane), George Wendt (Norm Peterson).

Technical Credits: *Created by* Glen Charles and Les Charles and James Burrows. *Executive Producers:* James Burrows, Glen Charles, Les Charles, Cheri Eichen, Bill Steinkellner, Phoef Sutton. *Producer:* Tim Berry. *Co-Producers:* Andy Ackerman, Brian Pollack, Mert Rich, Dan O'Shannon, Tom Anderson, Larry Balmagia. *Writers:* Tom Anderson, Larry Balmagia, Cheri Eichen, Sue Herring, David Isaacs, Ken Levine, Rob Long, Dan O'Shannon, Brian Pollack, Mert Rich, Dan Staley, Bill Steinkellner, Phoef Sutton. *Teleplay by* Phoef Sutton, Bill Steinkellner, Cheri Eichen (#197). *Story by:* Bill Steinkellner (#197). *Directors:* James Burrows, Andy Ackerman. *Creative Consultants:* David Lloyd, Ken Levine, David Isaacs. *Executive Script Consultant:* Bob Ellison. *Story Editors:* Dan Staley, Rob Long. *Associate Producer:* Mary Fukuto. *Casting:* Jeff Greenberg, C.S.A. *Original Casting:* Stephen Kolzak. *Director Of Photography:* John Finger, Alan Walker. *Art Director:* Dahl Delu. *Edited by* Andy Ackerman, Sheila Amos. *Unit Production Manager:* Linda

McMurray. *Associate Director:* Nancy Heydorn (#202, 203). *Stage Managers:* Brian James Ellis, Steven Pomeroy. *Research:* David Reid, Cheryl Dolins, Renee Duenas, Sheila Guthrie, Scott Krager, Steve Nevil, David Rossi, Rich Stangl (#202, 203). *First Assistant Director:* Brian James Ellis. *Second Assistant Director:* Steven Pomeroy. *Music by* Craig Safan. Song: "Where Everybody Knows Your Name." *Lyrics and Music by* Judy Hart Angelo and Gary Portnoy. *Sung by* Gary Portnoy. *Set Decorator:* Laura Richarz. *Production Supervisor:* Ahuva Fogel. *Script Supervisor:* Gabrielle James. *Post-Production Coordinator:* Peter J. Chakos (#202, 203). *Costume Supervisor:* Robert L. Tanella. *Costumers:* Sherry Thompson, Sharon Taylor-Sampson. *Technical Coordinator:* Rick Beren. *Technical Director:* John Field (#202, 203). *Production Mixer:* Robert Crosby, C.A.S. *Video:* Randy Johnson (#202, 203). *Makeup Artist:* Bruce Hutchinson. *Hair Stylist:* Marilyn Patricia Phillips. *Cameras:* Ken Dahlquist, Rocky Danielson, Tom Dasbach, Kieran Hughes, Brian Pratt, John Repczynski, Marvin Shearer, Mark Warshaw, Larry Woodside (#202, 203). *Music Editor:* Chips Swanson. *Sound Effects:* David Scharf. *Editing Facilities:* Laser Edit, Inc., Laser-Pacific. *Baby Casting:* Dennis Gallegos, Ann Wilkinson (#220, 221). *Main Title Design:* James Castle, Bruce Bryant, Carol Johnsen. *Cameras and

Lenses: Panavision. *Assistants to the Charles Brothers:* Sheila Amos, Danielle Bodenhorn, Peter J. Chakos, Christine Connor, Cara Coslow, Cheryl Dolins, Rachel Donahue, Renee Duenas, Sheila Guthrie, Jane Henning, Sue Herring, Scott Krager, Joseph E. Lotito, Emily Miller, Mark Nasser, Carol Navratil, David Reid, Russ Sherman, Rich Stangl, Barry Zajac. *Charles/Burrows/Charles Productions in Association with* Paramount.

195. "Love Is a Really, Really, Perfectly Okay Thing" (9/20/90). Robin returns to Cheers and catches Sam and Rebecca dressing in the office. Rebecca still wants to date Robin, so she and Sam explain that nothing happened, and Sam tries to be noble by refraining from telling the Cheers gang he actually slept with Rebecca. When Rebecca finally allows him the privilege of bragging, nobody believes Sam because he waited too long to tell them (and they cannot believe that Rebecca was good in bed). **Subtopic:** Rebecca and Robin resume dating, and Robin is sent to prison without bond pending the outcome of his trial.

Written by Phoef Sutton. *Directed by* James Burrows.

Characters: Roger Rees (Robin Colcord), Eric Christmas (Father Barry), Edmund Gaynes (Bartender), Christopher Abraham (Customer).

Notable Quote: Sam, explaining why he did not brag about sleeping with Rebecca:

SAM: "It's just that I thought that I'd be betraying our friendship. I never really had a friend before."

REBECCA: "You have lots of friends."

SAM: "No, no. I never *had* a friend before."

196. "Cheers Fouls Out" (9/27/90). The rival bars duke it out on the basketball court. Gary thinks he has two ringers, but Cheers coasts to victory with Boston Celtics star Kevin McHale (despite twisting an ankle). When a man claiming to be the Celtics' team doctor declares that Kevin's twisted ankle is a season-ending injury, the Cheers gang pays him $5,000 not to implicate them. Gary, who used the doctor as part of a prank, ends up receiving all the praise when he donates the money to charity.

Written by Larry Balmagia. *Directed by* James Burrows.

Characters: Bebe Neuwirth (Lilith), Roger Rees (Robin Colcord), Kevin McHale (Himself), Joel Polis (Gary), James Hornbeck (Doctor).

Notable Quote: Kevin McHale, viewing an X-ray with a hairline fracture:

KEVIN: "Let me take a look at it. [reading the X-ray.] It says adult male gorilla. That's not me. Could be Lambeier."

197. "Rebecca Redux" (10/4/90). Rebecca quits her waitress job at Cheers and accepts employment as Miss Miracle Buff demonstrating car wax at an auto show. When Sam and Woody accidentally see her working and witness her humiliation, Sam agrees to rehire her as the manager of Cheers. **Subtopic:** Sam's frustration with the bar computer forces him to hire a manager, Earl, who turns out to be the perfect employee, loved by everyone. Unfortunately, Sam chooses loyalty over competence and rehires Rebecca as the manager of Cheers (her first assignment is to fire Earl).

Teleplay by Phoef Sutton and Bill Steinkellner and Cheri Eichen. *Story by*

Bill Steinkellner. *Directed by* James Burrows.

Characters: Bryan Clark (Earl), Perry Anzilotti (Promoter), Randy Pelish (Customer), Timothy Fall (Car Show Patron), Tony DiBenedetto (Tony), Peter Schreiner (Pete), Stanley Bennett Clay (Deliveryman #1), Paul Cira (Deliveryman #2).

Notable Quote: In reference to Cheers' new manager, Earl:

SAM: "This is our new manager. This is Earl. Earl used to play shortstop for the Cubs."

NORM: "All right! One of us!"

Earl: "You guys from Chicago?"

CARLA: "Nah, they're all losers."

198. "Where Nobody Knows Your Name" (10/11/90). With Robin's recent imprisonment, the press begins scrutinizing his private life, so Rebecca tries to conceal her identity as his lover. When Jean-Marie goes public that she is Robin's lover and receives all the publicity and notoriety, Rebecca is embittered with jealous rage. Sam convinces Robin to set the record straight with the press, and when he does, Rebecca still receives no publicity. **Subtopic:** It is Indian summer, and Carla is at her most fertile time of the year. She tries desperately to control her attraction to men, which includes Fraiser and Cliff.

Written by Dan O'Shannon and Tom Anderson. *Directed by* Andy Ackerman.

Characters: Roger Rees (Robin Colcord), Arsenio Hall (Himself), Catherine MacNeal (Joanne), Ron Ulstad (Sherman), Paul Willson (Paul).

Notable Quote: Regarding Carla's fertility during Indian summer:

CARLA: "Every time I've conceived a kid it's been during Indian summer. I cannot let any man touch me, talk to me or see me, or I'll be shooting out kids like a Pez dispenser."

199. "Ma Always Liked You Best" (10/18/90). Cliff's mom, Esther, returns to Boston, but Cliff, content with his independence, forbids her to live in his condominium. When Woody accepts her as a roommate, Esther adopts him as her new son, making Cliff extremely jealous. As Woody and Cliff fight over Esther, she settles the problem by agreeing to share her love with both "sons." **Subtopic:** Construction outside Cheers is disrupting business, so Rebecca decides to build a rear entrance. When Norm becomes lodged between the iron bars in the window, the jaws of life are required to remove him.

Written by Dan O'Shannon and Tom Anderson. *Directed by* Andy Ackerman.

Characters: Frances Sternhagen (Esther Clavin), Rocky LaPorte (Jeff), John Posey (Lars), Paul Willson (Paul), Peter Schreiner (Pete), Ken Foree (Policeman #1), James F. Dean (Policeman #2).

Notable Quote: Cliff's mother, Esther, adopting Woody as her new son:

ESTHER: "I've found a wonderful companion in Woody. He's like the son I never had."

CLIFF: "Well, what about me?"

ESTHER: "You're the son I *did* have."

200. "Grease" (10/25/90). Norm tries to preserve the Hungry Heifer as an historical landmark by circulating a petition for an injunction to prohibit its demolition. The restaurant owner, Sid, wants to sell the restaurant, so he asks Norm to torch the place. When Norm refuses, Sid solicits the busboy to do it. **Subtopic:** Carla parades her body to tease and sexually frustrate the prison inmates (one of whom is Robin Colcord) who are picking up trash in the park across the street from Cheers. Meanwhile, Sam teases Rebecca about Robin being a prisoner.

Written by Brian Pollack and Mert Rich. *Directed by* James Burrows.

Characters: Sheldon Leonard (Sid Nelson), John Patrick Reger (Guard).

Notable Quote:

SAM: "It's a little early in the day for a beer, isn't it, Norm?"

NORM: "So float a corn flake in it."

201. "Breaking In Is Hard to Do" (11/1/90). Rebecca plans a sexual rendezvous with Robin while he is in prison. As Carla diverts the attention of the guards and other inmates, Rebecca takes Robin into the bushes. Robin is tempted but resists because he will soon be eligible for parole. **Subtopic:** Frasier and Lilith are depressed after discovering their child, Frederick, is average. Frasier blames Lilith for having inferior genes. While discussing how to facilitate Frederick's educational development, they argue over which one of them should forego their career to stay home with the child.

Written by Ken Levine and David Isaacs. *Directed by* Andy Ackerman.

Characters: Bebe Neuwirth (Lilith), Roger Rees (Robin Colcord), Clive Rosengren (Doug Aducci), John Boyle (Prison Guard), Edward Penn (Prisoner), Paul Willson (Paul), Philip Perlman (Phil).

Notable Quote: Rebecca, writing a love letter to Robin during work:

SAM: "How are you going to get work done if all you do is think about sex?"

REBECCA: "I don't know, Sam. How do you do it?"

SAM: "I'm a boy. It's my job."

202. "Cheers 200th Episode Celebration" (Part 1 of 2) (11/8/90, 9:00–9:30 p.m. EST). In a panel discussion with the entire cast of characters, John McLaughlin is the moderator, while the actors converse about the characters they portray and reminisce about past episodes.

Written by Cheri Eichen, Bill Steinkellner and Phoef Sutton. *Directed by* James Burrows, Andy Ackerman.

Characters: Ted Danson (Sam), Shelley Long (Diane), Rhea Perlman (Carla), George Wendt (Norm), John Ratzenberger (Cliff), Kelsey Grammer (Frasier), Woody Harrelson (Woody), Bebe Neuwirth (Lilith), Kirstie Alley (Rebecca), Roger Rees (Robin), John McLaughlin, James Burrows, Glen Charles, Les Charles, Phoef Sutton, Cheri Eichen, Bill Steinkellner.

203. "Cheers 200th Episode Celebration" (Part 2 of 2) (11/8/90, 9:30–10:00 p.m. EST). In a panel discussion with the entire cast of characters, John McLaughlin is the moderator, while the actors converse about the characters they portray and reminisce about past episodes.

Written by Cheri Eichen and Bill Steinkellner and Phoef Sutton. *Directed by* James Burrows, Andy Ackerman.

Characters: same as Part 1.

204. "Bad Neighbor Sam" (11/15/90). Melville's new owner, John Allen Hill, is pompous and condescending, and Sam takes an immediate disliking to the restauranteur. Hill conveniently reveals that he owns Cheers' poolroom and bathrooms, and uses this as leverage to take advantage of Sam.

Soon Cheers becomes inundated with Melville's yuppie clientele and is inevitably transformed into something Diane would have liked! As the tension escalates (as well as Sam's blood pressure), Sam eventually goes ballistic. **Subtopic:** Although upset because Kelly allowed a man to take sexy photographs of her, Woody is pacified when Frasier apprises him that an elderly priest was the photographer.

Written by Cheri Eichen and Bill Steinkellner. *Directed by* James Burrows.

Characters: Bebe Neuwirth (Lilith), Keene Curtis (John Allen Hill), Carl Mueller (Jeffrey), Sandy Edgerton (Hilary), Tamara Mark (Martha), Philip Perlman (Phil), E.E. Bell (Bradley), Aileen Fitzpatrick (Mrs. Armstrong), Fred Slyter (Patron).

Notable Quote: On Sam's anger toward John Hill:

SAM: "Nobody messes with Sam Malone, least of all some hairless king of the snobs."

WOODY: [to Frasier] "Wow, that was a real shot at you from out of nowhere, huh, Dr. Crane?"

205. **"Veggie-Boyd"** (11/22/90). Woody plays the part of a bartender in a television commercial promoting Veggie-Boy vegetable drink. His line is "I like it," but when he tastes the product, he hates it. Woody is wrought with guilt for being a liar and promoting a product he despises, so Frasier hypnotizes him to like it. However, the company decides to stop producing the beverage, and Woody panics because he cannot live without Veggie-Boy! **Subtopic:** Sam buys trivia napkins for the bar, and they are an instant success. Cliff becomes jealous and upset, so the Cheers gang decides to alternate between Cliff and the napkins every other day.

Written by Dan Staley and Rob Long. *Directed by* James Burrows.

Characters: Bebe Neuwirth (Lilith), Tom Everett (Director), Debbie Gregory (Jill), John Cervenka (Technician), Philip Perlman (Phil), Michael Holden (Joe), Tony DiBenedetto (Tony).

Notable Quote: A trivia napkin question:

FRASIER: "What civilization was the first known to brew beer?"

TONY: "Early Greece."

SAM: "Ancient Rome."

NORM: "Old Milwaukee."

206. **"Norm & Cliff's Excellent Adventure"** (12/6/90). Norm and Cliff decide to spice up their day by playing pranks on the Cheers gang. They overstep the bounds when reporting Frasier's gold card as stolen. Sam refuses to honor the card and cuts it in half, so Frasier vows never to return to Cheers. Norm and Cliff try to make amends, but when all else fails, they admit their dastardly deed. Norm and Cliff ultimately pay for their fun when Sam forces them to surrender their credit cards to Woody. **Subtopic:** Woody is addicted to the Home Shopping Channel and begins purchasing all sorts of useless items.

Written by Ken Levine and David Isaacs. *Directed by* James Burrows.

Characters: Bebe Neuwirth (Lilith), Tom Klunis (Heinrich), Paul Willson (Paul).

Notable Quote: Regarding the Home Shopping Channel:

CLIFF: "Ma loves it. She's always watching it. She's always saying, 'If I had a rich son, he would buy me this. If I had a rich son, he would buy me that.' Who do you think bought her the TV in the first place?"

NORM: "You, Cliff?"

CLIFF: "No. But if I find the guy, I'm going to shove that clicker down his throat."

207. **"Woody Interruptus"** (12/13/90). Kelly returns from France accompanied by her photography instructor, Henri, who is determined to steal her heart. Woody becomes concerned, so he and Kelly plan an evening in a sleazy motel to physically consummate their relationship. However, nothing goes as planned because they are too self-conscious. Carla rushes to the hotel and succeeds in convincing them to wait. **Subtopic:** The Cheers gang exchanges pranks with each other, and they all revolve around Cliff's plan to have his head frozen after he dies.

Written by Dan Staley and Rob Long. *Directed by* James Burrows.

Characters: Jackie Swanson (Kelly), Anthony Cistaro (Henri), Michael Keenan (Dr. Eckworth), Douglas MacHugh (Night Manager), Paul Willson (Paul), Tony DiBenedetto (Tony).

Notable Quote: Discussing premarital sex:

WOODY: "What do you think about premarital sex, Mr. Peterson?"

NORM: "Well, Wood. There's an old saying, why buy the cow when you can get the milk for free. Then of course, you get married and you wake up one day and realize, oh my God, I've married a *cow*."

208. **"Honor Thy Mother"** (1/3/91). Carla's mother fakes having the "death dream" in an attempt to trick Carla into following the family tradition of re-naming one of her sons. Carla sternly resists because she would have to name one of her sons Benito Mussolini. She eventually allows Gino to change his name (they will call him Gino for short), and he eagerly agrees because the real Benito Mussolini was known as "Il Duce." Sam is appalled at the tactics of Carla's mother and calls her a bad parent. Following Lozupone family tradition, Sam is forced to spend the night in the Murphy bed for insulting Carla's mother.

Written by Brian Pollack and Mert Rich. *Directed by* James Burrows.

Characters: Bebe Neuwirth (Lilith), Sada Thompson (Mama Lozupone), Keene Curtis (John Allen Hill), Oceana Marr (Zia), Josh Lozoff (Gino), Carol Ann Susi (Angeline), Randy Pelish (Sal).

Note: Sada Thompson is probably best known for her role as Kate Lawrence in the television show "Family" (starring Kristy McNichol), for which she won an Emmy for Outstanding Lead Actress (1978).

209. **"Achilles Hill"** (1/10/91). When Sam becomes interested in dating John Allen Hill's daughter, Valerie, Hill agrees to relinquish his parking spot and give Sam the poolroom and bathrooms rent-free, if Sam promises not to date her. Sam agrees but then yearns for the forbidden fruit and decides to break the agreement. Ironically, when Hill finally accepts the dating arrangement, Valerie breaks up with Sam because she only dated him to upset her father. **Subtopic:** A haunted foosball table is retrieved from the Cheers basement, and soon everyone who plays the game turns into an evil person.

Written by Ken Levine and David Isaacs. *Directed by* Andy Ackerman.

Characters: Keene Curtis (John Allen Hill), Valerie Mahaffey (Valerie Hill), Eric Christmas (Father Barry).

Note: Valerie Mahaffey appeared

in "The Powers That Be" (as Caitlyn) and received an Emmy as Outstanding Supporting Actress for her role in "Northern Exposure" (1992).

210. "The Days of Wine & Neuroses" (Part 1 of 2) (1/24/91). Robin is financially destitute and on the verge of being released from prison. In preparation for his release, Robin proposes marriage to Rebecca, who willingly accepts. At the bridal shower she becomes intoxicated, and while conversing with Sam, confesses she does not love Robin. Moreover, not only does Rebecca not want to marry him, but also indicates that she really wants Sam. **Subtopic:** The Cheers jukebox is replaced with a karaoke machine, and the gang is captivated with the entertainment device, especially Frasier, who has found his true calling in life.

Written by Brian Pollack and Mert Rich. *Directed by* James Burrows.

Characters: Bebe Neuwirth (Lilith), Calvin Jung (Walter), Paul Willson (Paul), Shad Willingham (Deliveryman), Kristine Knudson (Woman).

Notable Quote: Rebecca, depressed about her impending marriage:

SAM: "Sweetheart, I can understand the temptation [to drink]...I'm a recovering alcoholic."

REBECCA: "I'm just not ready for commitment."

SAM: "Doubt is part of any relationship. I was divorced."

REBECCA: "You know, I drink for a couple of days and *you* were an alcoholic. I have a little bit of trouble with a relationship, and *you* were divorced. Do you retain water in the middle of the month, too, Sam?"

211. "Wedding Bell Blues" (Part 2 of 2) (1/31/91). The day after her intoxicating bridal shower, a sober Rebecca enters Cheers, eager to marry Robin. Sam tries everything to jog her memory of the previous night, when she expressed a lack of love for Robin. Finally, while Rebecca and Robin are at the altar, the song "We've Got Tonight" triggers her memory. Rebecca admits she only loved Robin for his money and calls off the wedding. Later that evening, Robin gives her a second chance, claiming to have $6 million in a hidden money belt. Expecting a bluff, she boldly rejects him again. Robin then removes a money belt from the bottom of the office desk drawer and leaves Cheers without her.

Written by Dan O'Shannon and Tom Anderson. *Directed by* James Burrows.

Characters: Bebe Neuwirth (Lilith), Roger Rees (Robin Colcord), Bobby Hatfield (Himself), Ray Stricklyn (Ed), Paul Willson (Paul), Ron Abel (Jonathan), George Case (Security Guard).

Notable Quote: In reference to Rebecca's impending wedding:

REBECCA: "You guys, I have my new wedding dress, and now all I need is something old, something borrowed, and something blue."

CARLA: "How about Norm's liver?"

212. "I'm Getting My Act Together & Sticking It in Your Face" (2/7/91). After Robin's departure, Rebecca slides into a deep depression, locks herself in the office for two days, and then travels to San Diego to reassess her life. Sam tries to persuade her to return, but fears his message may be misconstrued as an expression of his love for her. When Rebecca responds that she is eager to see him, Sam goes to no end to prove he does not love her—even pretending to be a homosexual. **Subtopic:** Frasier entertains the Cheers gang by reading Charles Dickens novels, but has to add carnage and modern flare to make the books more appealing.

Written by Dan Staley and Rob Long. *Directed by* Andy Ackerman.

Characters: Bebe Neuwirth (Lilith), Jeff McCarthy (Leon), Paul Willson (Paul), Jan Gan Boyd (Stewardess).

Notable Quote: Frasier enlightens the Cheers gang with Charles Dickens' novels:

FRASIER: "[That] puts me in mind of a novel by my favorite British author. You know who I mean. I'll give you a hint, Charles…?"

NORM: "In Charge?"

FRASIER: "Are you people really this ignorant? Or do you just do this to torture me?"

NORM: "Sometimes the two just go hand in hand."

213. **"Sam Time Next Year"** (2/14/91). Sam has celebrated Valentine's Day in the same fashion for the past 20 years—by going to a cabin in Maine to meet Lauren. However, this year Sam feels the effects of aging after injuring his back. He tries his best to perform for her, but when the truth is revealed, they spend the entire night talking. **Subtopics:** Frasier and Lilith bring two socially dysfunctional groups to Cheers, but they refuse to interact. As Frasier and Lilith demonstrate games of physical interaction, they become sexually aroused and promptly end the session. Meanwhile, Rebecca becomes depressed about not receiving a Valentine's Day card.

Written by Larry Balmagia. *Directed by* James Burrows.

Characters: Bebe Neuwirth (Lilith), Barbara Feldon (Lauren Hudson), Michael Dukakis (Himself), Roger Eschbacker (Jules), Gibby Brand (Adam), Don Took (Edward).

Note: Barbara Feldon is best known for her role in "Get Smart" (as Agent "99," 1965–69), but she also hosted the weekly magazine and documentary show "Special Edition" (1977) and was a former winner on "The $64,000 Question" for her knowledge of Shakespeare.

Notable Quote: Sam enters the bar:

SAM: "Any messages?"

CARLA: "Oh yeah, one of your old baseball buddies called. Dutch Kincaid."

SAM: "I'll be damned, I wonder what he wants."

NORM: "Probably another home run." [Sam served up a home run pitch to Dutch each time the two met on the diamond—a total of 27 during their careers.]

214. **"Crash of the Titans"** (2/21/91). When John Allen Hill decides to sell the Cheers poolroom and bathrooms, Sam and Rebecca become eager bidders, which requires them to do special favors for the owner. To win the good graces of Hill, Rebecca offers the ultimate gift, her body, but Sam counteroffers with twins. When Sam cannot compete with Rebecca's cash flow, they decide to be business partners and share the expense of purchasing the poolroom and bathrooms. Hill sells it for $30,000 (Sam pays $5,000 and Rebecca $25,000).

Written by Dan Staley and Rob Long. *Directed by* James Burrows.

Characters: Bebe Neuwirth (Lilith), Keene Curtis (John Allen Hill), Jeremiah Morris (Harry), Paul Willson (Paul), Philip Perlman (Phil) Tony DiBenedetto (Tony), Peter Schreiner (Pete), Adele Baughn (Hope), Anadel Baughn (Joy).

215. "It's a Wonderful Wife" (2/28/91). Vera is hired as the hatcheck girl at Melville's, which does not please Norm because she spends all her time watching him through a knothole in Melville's floor. John Allen Hill ultimately fires her, but when he adds a few insults, Norm defends Vera's honor. **Subtopic:** Lilith wants to give Frasier a special birthday present, and her wild side is exposed when Henri takes a few sexy photographs of her lying on a bearskin rug wearing nothing but a business suit! She gives Frasier the formal shots, but then discretely shows him more revealing photographs.

Written by Sue Herring. *Directed by* James Burrows.

Characters: Bebe Neuwirth (Lilith), Keene Curtis (John Allen Hill), Anthony Cistaro (Henri), Heather Lee (Miss Kenderson), Peter Schreiner (Pete), Tony DiBenedetto (Tony).

Notable Quote: After Lilith gives Frasier a portrait of her lying on a bearskin rug in a business suit:

LILITH: "It's a gag gift."

CARLA: "If you wanted us to gag, you should have taken a nudie."

216. "Cheers Has Chili" (3/14/91). While Sam is away, Rebecca converts the poolroom into a tea room and claims she can make $500 in one night. Business is slow until she starts selling Woody's homemade chili. Out of concern that Rebecca might attain her goal, Sam tries to sabotage her success by calling the health inspector. However, after realizing he should share her accomplishment, Sam kindly buys the last bowl of chili to put her over $500. Unfortunately, the gas hot plate explodes and destroys the tea room. **Subtopic:** Cliff is addicted to the Weather Channel because of an infatuation with the meteorologist's lateral lisp.

Written by Cheri Eichen and Bill Steinkellner and Phoef Sutton. *Directed by* Andy Ackerman.

Characters: Bebe Neuwirth (Lilith), Robert Machray (Fire Marshall), Peter Schreiner (Pete), Stanley Bennett Clay (Albert).

Notable Quote: After Lilith only orders tea from the menu:

REBECCA: "Just pig out. Order some strawberry tarts."

LILITH: "Strawberries make me break out."

REBECCA: "Well, at least that will put a little color in your face."

217. "Carla Loves Clavin" (3/21/91). The rules have changed for the Miss Boston Barmaid Contest, and this year contestants are judged for their talent, not bust size. Carla enters to win the grand prize (a new Mazda Miata), but has to be especially nice to Cliff, who is a contest judge. Cliff takes full advantage of Carla's special treatment of him, and only when the contest begins does she discover he is not a judge. She uses all of her animosity to perform spectacularly, but the real judges still award first place to a large-busted woman, Shawnee. **Subtopic:** As Norm delays painting Rebecca's office, she becomes increasingly upset with his indolence.

Written by Dan Staley and Rob Long. *Directed by* James Burrows.

Characters: Dante Di Loreto (Emcee), Nathan Davis (Mr. Quincy), Jessie Scott (Shawnee Wilson), Paul Willson (Paul).

Notable Quote: Woody, encouraging Carla to try out for the Miss Boston Barmaid's Contest:

WOODY: "Carla. Are you going to try out for this contest?"

CARLA: "I don't think so."

WOODY: "Well, you heard Sam. It's not about looks this year."

218. **"Pitch It Again Sam"** (3/28/91). Sam agrees to pitch against his baseball nemesis, Dutch Kincaid, in an event honoring the Yankees star. Sam has every intention to strike out Dutch, but is conned by Billy, a boy pretending to be Dutch's grandson who begs Sam to let his grandfather hit a home run. Sam obliges, but when he tells this heart-wrenching story to the Cheers gang, they do not believe him. Dutch then returns to Cheers to prove Sam cannot strike him out. **Subtopic:** Cheers adopts a lost puppy, Spotty, as their mascot, and Woody becomes emotionally attached to him. When three firemen claim ownership, they are conned into allowing Woody to keep the puppy.

Written by Dan O'Shannon and Tom Anderson. *Directed by* James Burrows.

Characters: Michael Fairman (Dutch Kincaid), Henry Woronicz (Cap Richards), Zachary Benjamin (Billy), James Ellis Reynolds (Fireman Jim), Peter Kevoian (Fireman Peter), Michael Cannizzo (Fireman Mike), Joel Anderson (Ballplayer), Victoria Barrett (Victoria), Leanne Griffin (Leanne).

219. **"Rat Girl"** (4/4/91). Lilith experiences the death of a loved one when her favorite lab rat dies. Frasier discovers the corpse in her purse and discards it into the garbage. Lilith is furious, and her vehement animosity is openly displayed during an interview with a private day care facility. The Cranes wanted Frederick to be enrolled in this prestigious school, but their unruly behavior nixes the deal. **Subtopics:** Sam has difficulty comprehending rejection from a woman, Paula,

who is dating Paul Creypens. Meanwhile, Rebecca begins eating healthy foods and tries to convert the Cheers gang.

Written by Ken Levine and David Isaacs. *Directed by* James Burrows.

Characters: Bebe Neuwirth (Lilith), Paul Willson (Paul), Beth Toussaint (Paula), Cheryl Lynn Bruce (Administrator), Andre Miripolsky (Administrator), Peter Schreiner (Pete).

Notable Quote: Lilith and Frasier arguing:

FRASIER: "What did you tell them about me?"

LILITH: "I described you in terms which were positively glowing, which is the way I'd like to see you in hell."

220. **"Home Malone"** (4/25/91). Sam volunteers to baby sit Frasier and Lilith's son, Frederick. The unexpected happens, as Sam is locked out of the house twice in an attempt to retrieve Frederick, who locked himself in the bathroom. **Subtopic:** Kelly works as a waitress at Cheers so she can write a paper on a past work experience. Her ditsiness reaps financial rewards for Carla and free beer for Norm.

Written by Dan O'Shannon and Tom Anderson. *Directed by* Andy Ackerman.

Characters: Bebe Neuwirth (Lilith), Jackie Swanson (Kelly), Anthony Cistaro (Henri), Christopher and Kevin Graves (Frederick Crane), Paul Willson (Paul), Peter Schreiner (Pete), Philip Perlman (Phil), Gary Lee Davis (Construction Worker #1), Norm Compton (Construction Worker #2), Steve Hulin (Construction Worker #3).

Notable Quote: Norm, schooling Kelly on how to find a job:

CLIFF: "You know, Norm. For a guy who's unemployed, you sure know a lot about getting work."

NORM: "Well, Cliff. I know a lot about water, but you don't see me drinking it."

221. "Uncle Sam Wants You" (5/2/91). Sam spends all his time at the Crane residence playing with Frasier and Lilith's son, Frederick. When Sam's obsession interferes with their privacy, Frasier tells Sam, "I made him, so I get to keep him!" and suggests that he have his own child. Sam begins searching for a woman who will agree to incubate his seed, give birth, and then disappear. His first choice is Carla but even she rejects him. Finally, in a dream, Elvis suggests that Sam give Rebecca a chance. Sam asks, she accepts, and they leave the bar eager to begin conception.

Written by Dan Staley and Rob Long. *Directed by* James Burrows.

Characters: Bebe Neuwirth (Lilith), Pete Willcox (Elvis), Christopher and Kevin Graves (Frederick Crane), Tress MacNeille (Daria), Paul Willson (Paul).

Season Ten: 1991-92

(NBC Thursday, 9:00–9:30 p.m. EST)

Season Regulars: Ted Danson (Sam Malone), Kirstie Alley (Rebecca Howe), Rhea Perlman (Carla Tortelli-LeBec), John Ratzenberger (Cliff Clavin), Woody Harrelson (Woody Boyd), Kelsey Grammer (Frasier Crane), Bebe Neuwirth (Lilith Sternin-Crane), George Wendt (Norm Peterson).

Technical Credits: *Created by* Glen Charles, Les Charles and James Burrows. *Executive Producers:* James Burrows, Glen Charles, Les Charles, Cheri Eichen, Bill Steinkellner, Phoef Sutton. *Supervising Producers:* Dan O'Shannon and Tom Anderson. *Producer:* Tim Berry. *Writers:* Tom Anderson, Cheri Eichen, David Isaacs, Ken Levine, David Lloyd, Rob Long, Tracy Newman, Dan O'Shannon, Daniel Palladino, Dan Staley, Jonathan Stark, Bill Steinkellner, Kathy Ann Stumpe, Phoef Sutton. *Directors:* James Burrows, Tom Moore, Rick Beren, John Ratzenberger. *Co-Producers:* Dan Staley and Rob Long. *Creative Consultants:* David Lloyd, Ken Levine and David Isaacs. *Executive Script Consultant:* Bob Ellison. *Associate Producer:* Mary Fukuto. *Casting:* Jeff Greenberg, C.S.A. *Original Casting:* Stephen Kolzak. *Director of Photography:* John Finger. *Art Director:* Dahl Delu. *Edited by* Robert A. Bramwell, Peter J. Chakos. *Unit Production Manager:* Linda McMurray. *First Assistant Director:* Brian James Ellis. *Second Assistant Director:* Steven Pomeroy. *Music by* Craig Safan. *Song:* "Where Everybody Knows Your Name." *Lyrics and Music by* Judy Hart Angelo and Gary Portnoy. *Sung by* Gary Portnoy. *Original Songs:* Craig Safan, Cheri Eichen and Bill Steinkellner (#237). *Set Decorator:* Laura Richarz. *Production Supervisor:* Ahuva Fogel. *Script Supervisor:* Gabrielle James. *Costume Supervisor:* Robert L. Tanella. *Costumer:* Sharon Taylor-Sampson. *Post-Production Supervisor:* Peter J. Chakos. *Technical Coordinators:* Rick Beren, Jim Buck. *Production Mixers:* Robert Crosby, C.A.S., Richard Wachter. *Music Editor:* Chips Swanson. *Makeup Artist:*

Bruce Hutchinson. *Hair Stylist:* Marilyn Patricia Phillips. *Sound Effects:* David Scharf. *Editorial Facilities:* Laser-Pacific Media Corporation. *Sound by* Larson Sound. *Main Title Design:* James Castle, Bruce Bryant, Carol Johnsen. *Cameras and Lenses:* Panavision. *Assistants to the Producers:* Jeff Clinkenbeard, Cara Coslow, Renee Duenas, Susie Freeman-Johnson, Michael Grizzi, Jane Henning, Sue Herring, Scott Krager, Mairead Lee, Brian Lovell, Emily Miller, David Pavoni, Jeffrey Pfefferle, David Reid, Rich Stangl, Barry Zajac. *Charles/ Burrows/Charles Productions in Association with* Paramount.

222. **"Baby Talk"** (9/19/91). Sam has reservations about conceiving a child because he now realizes his entire life will change irreparably. Rebecca tries to allay his fears by discussing the purity of conception, but Sam concentrates on thoughts of passion. Their private consultation with trained professionals fails to help—Frasier advises Sam to think naughty thoughts, while Lilith recommends that Rebecca continue vocalizing pure thoughts. The misinformation and miscommunication ultimately impede their evening of conception. **Subtopic:** Woody is in charge of Cheers, but has difficulty finding a location for patrons who enjoy smoking.
Written by Dan O'Shannon and Tom Anderson. *Directed by* James Burrows.
Characters: Bruce Wright (Bowler).

223. **"Get Your Kicks on Route 666"** (9/26/91). Frasier is captivated by the "inner hairy man" theory of masculinity, so the Cheers gang (Frasier, Sam, Norm and Cliff) take a road trip to discover their inner primal beast.

When Sam falls asleep behind the wheel and crashes the car, the gang is left stranded in the desert. After several unsuccessful attempts to fix the car and get help, they contemplate their mortality. As dawn breaks, Norm greets them from a golf cart because he spent the night in a nearby motel. **Subtopic:** While the Cheers gang is on their primal journey, Lilith and Rebecca crave Carla's nephew, Frankie, who is temporarily working at Cheers.
Written by Dan O'Shannon and Tom Anderson. *Directed by* James Burrows.
Characters: Anthony Addabbo (Frankie), Paul Willson (Paul).
Notable Quote: Discussing the physical attractiveness of Carla's nephew:
LILITH: "Carla, surely as a woman you can see how your nephew might be considered desirable?"
CARLA: "Sure. You start thinking like that and you end up with Woody's family."

224. **"Madame La Carla"** (10/ 3/91). Spiritualist Madame Lazora contemplates retirement and solicits Carla as her successor. When Carla doubts whether she has the gift of foretelling the future, Madame Lazora admits being a charlatan, thereby shattering Carla's existence. However, the power of money has healing ways, and when Carla realizes the profit potential of this endeavor, she gladly accepts the reins. **Subtopic:** Woody's theatrical performance in *Arsenic and Old Lace* is criticized as weak, so he tries to improve by writing down his feelings. Although his performance improves, he is fired when the other actors read his honest but disparaging comments about them.
Written by Phoef Sutton. *Directed by* Tim Moore.

Characters: Georgia Brown (Madame Lazora), Jeffrey Richman (Lee Bradken), Jim Brochu (Bob), Barry Zajac (Barry), Peter Schreiner (Pete).

Notable Quote: Carla's spiritualist, Madame Lazora, enters the bar:

MADAME: "I sense the tortured anguish of many lost souls screaming for release."

NORM: "That's probably me. I had kielbasa for breakfast."

225. "The Norm Who Came to Dinner" (10/10/91). While Norm is painting the Crane town house, Frasier insists on climbing the ladder to finish the job. Unfortunately, the clumsy Crane falls off the ladder and onto Norm. Feeling responsible for Norm's back injury, Frasier urges him to stay for a couple days to recuperate. Norm's convalescence ultimately attracts the rest of the Cheers gang for nightly parties. Lilith becomes incensed when everyone refuses to leave, so Norm attempts counseling her on being light-hearted. **Subtopic**: Carla cons Rebecca into carrying an egg around for three days to prove she will be a good parent.

Written by Dan O'Shannon and Tom Anderson. *Directed by* Tim Moore.

Characters: Paul Willson (Paul), Philip Perlman (Phil), Peter Schreiner (Pete).

226. "Ma's Little Maggie" (10/17/91). Cliff introduces his girlfriend, Margaret O'Keefe, to his mother, Esther. At first, Esther is despondent about losing her son to another woman, but soon develops an affinity toward Margaret. Esther even proposes marriage to Margaret (on Cliff's behalf), but he stands up to his mother for the first time in his life by refusing to get married. **Subtopic**: Rebecca be-

comes concerned because she is still without child, and begins monitoring and regulating Sam's life to facilitate conception, i.e., no caffeine and wearing frozen underwear.

Written by Tracy Newman and Jonathan Stark. *Directed by* James Burrows.

Characters: Frances Sternhagen (Esther Clavin), Annie Golden (Margaret O'Keefe), Paul Willson (Paul).

Notable Quote: Cliff, introducing his mother to his girlfriend, Margaret:

CLIFF: "The only real hurdle is Ma. Oh yeah. It's very traumatic when the woman you love more than anything else in the world meets your significant other."

NORM: "Which would be which?"

CLIFF: "*Now* you see my problem."

227. "Unplanned Parenthood" (10/24/91). Sam and Rebecca decide to baby-sit Carla's kids to determine whether they will be good parents. Carla's rambunctious little monsters have a field day with the prospective parents, including stuffing Rebecca in the clothes dryer while it is running. Irrespective of these annoyances, she and Sam remain undeterred about their desire to have a child. **Subtopic**: Woody wants to introduce Kelly to his parents, but cannot afford plane fare to Indiana. Instead, he shoots a home video with Cliff (and then Frasier) functioning as the intolerable director.

Written by Dan Staley and Rob Long. *Directed by* James Burrows.

Characters: Jackie Swanson (Kelly), Leah Remini (Serafina), Josh Lozoff (Gino), Jarrett Lennon (Ludlow), Philip Perlman (Phil), Paul Willson (Paul), Risa Littman (Anne Marie), Thomas Tulak (Jesse), Danny Kramer (Elvis), Sabrina Wiener (Lucinda).

228. "Bar Wars V: The Final Judgment" (10/31/91). The Cheers gang unites with one common goal: not to be embarrassed during the Halloween pranks against Gary's Olde Towne Tavern. When Gary enters Cheers claiming to have a heart condition, Sam doubts his veracity and continues with the hologram prank (which ultimately causes Gary to die of a heart attack). Sam expects this to be a gimmick, but as the evidence becomes so overwhelming (a funeral and burying the casket), he is finally convinced of Gary's death. At this moment, Gary reappears to scare Sam, and the gang admits their involvement in the ruse. **Subtopic:** Frederick Crane enjoys his first Halloween by trick-or-treating at Cheers.

Written by Ken Levine and David Isaacs. *Directed by* James Burrows.

Characters: Robert Desiderio (Gary), Rick Cramer (Matt), Paul Willson (Paul), Philip Perlman (Phil), Christopher and Kevin Graves (Frederick).

Notable Quote: Regarding a Cheers Halloween prank on Gary:

CLIFF: "What would you do, Norm, if you saw Carla's disembodied head floating over the bar?"

NORM: "What I always do. Call a cab and go home."

229. "Where Have All the Floorboards Gone?" (11/7/91). Norm celebrates his 43rd birthday and is introduced to Boston Celtics basketball star Kevin McHale. Soon Kevin becomes captivated with bar trivia and obsessed with determining the number of bolts in the floor of the Boston Garden. When his game suffers, the Cheers gang tries to solve the mystery to save the Celtics' basketball season. **Subtopics:** Lilith gets a perm, and Frasier cannot contain his laughter. Meanwhile, as Woody and Kelly exchange gifts on their third anniversary of dating, he becomes distressed after giving her a dinky key chain and receiving a $300 camera.

Written by Ken Levine and David Isaacs. *Directed by* James Burrows.

Characters: Kevin McHale (Himself), Lynn McHale (Herself), Philip Perlman (Phil), Paul Willson (Paul), Glen Ordway (Himself), Tim Cunningham (Tim).

230. "Head Over Hill" (11/14/91). Sam wants revenge on John Allen Hill, so he sends Carla to fight the evil little dwarf. Carla accepts the challenge and goes for the throat, but winds up getting another part of his anatomy (i.e., they end up sleeping together). Sam feels betrayed, and Carla feels like a traitor, but she cannot contain her attraction for The Bullet (Hill). **Subtopic:** Cliff has the career opportunity of a lifetime when he is chosen to re-enact the first Boston mail delivery. However, during the final leg of the journey, he is unable to control the equine and becomes lost in the city.

Written by Dan Staley and Rob Long. *Directed by* John Ratzenberger.

Characters: Keene Curtis (John Allen Hill), Paul Willson (Paul), Jordan Lund (Barker #1), Ken Magee (Barker #2), Philip Perlman (Phil), Peter Schreiner (Pete).

Notable Quote: John Allen Hill, informing Sam not to use the Dumpster:

CARLA: [talking to Hill] "You can't order us around like that. Sammy can do anything he wants with his trash."

HILL: "Yes, I see today he's dressed it up in an apron."

231. "A Fine French Whine" (11/21/91). Henri stages his deportation to trick Kelly into marriage so he can

become a U.S. citizen (and get half of her money). Kelly agrees, but Woody is not receptive to the idea. Woody rushes to the courthouse to stop the wedding, and just before Kelly and Henri say their vows, the truth is revealed. **Subtopic:** Frasier agonizes over a painful headache and allows a sexy oriental doctor to perform acupuncture and acupressure to relieve the pain.
Written by Dan Staley and Rob Long. *Directed by* James Burrows.
Characters: Jackie Swanson (Kelly), Anthony Cistaro (Henri), Sonje Fortag (Bride), Jeff Heston (Groom), Paul Willson (Paul), Peter Foxon Miller (Tour Guide), Nancy Arnold (Dr. Lee), Ron Ray (Justice of the Peace #1), Bill Gratton (Justice of the Peace #2).
Notable Quote: Henri, reminiscing about his arrival in America:
HENRI: "I will miss this great country. I have been in love with it ever since I got my first glimpse of that big, beautiful woman in the harbor."
CLIFF: "Oh yeah, lady liberty."
HENRI: "She told me her name was Ki Ki."

232. **"I'm Okay, You're Defective"** (12/5/91). Rebecca and Sam visit a fertility specialist to determine the reason for their inability to conceive a child. Sam resists visiting the doctor because he does not want to know if his equipment is defective. When the results arrive, he does not have the willpower to open the envelope. **Subtopics:** Frasier contemplates his mortality while preparing a last will and testament. Meanwhile, the Cheers gang searches for a gross image that will make Norm lose his taste for beer. The winning image is Paul Creypens toweling off after a shower.

Written by Dan Staley and Rob Long. *Directed by* James Burrows.
Characters: Paul Willson (Paul), Julie Lloyd (Receptionist), Donald Hotton (Lawyer), John Serembe (Man at Clinic), Rob Neukirch (Adult Frederick), Philip Perlman (Phil).
Notable Quote: Rebecca, asking Sam to see a fertility specialist:
SAM: "Do you know why we are not conceiving? It's because you are too mean to me."
REBECCA: "I'm not mean. I'm perfectly nice. I just think you're shooting blanks, pal.... Here, just take the card, and if you want to call the doctor then fine, if you don't that's fine too. I mean it...."
SAM: "I can't make this call."
REBECCA: "Your fingers don't work, *either?*"

233. **"Go Make"** (12/12/91). Sam and Rebecca continue arguing over their inability to conceive and decide to spend a romantic weekend in a hotel. The weekend convinces them not to have a child—Sam decides love is necessary to unify the familial bond, and Rebecca concludes she wants a traditional family arrangement. **Subtopic:** Norm, Cliff and Frasier agree to take the Polar Bear Club plunge into the Atlantic Ocean in the middle of winter. However, Frasier is the only one foolish enough to actually go through with it and becomes deathly ill.
Written by Phoef Sutton. *Directed by* James Burrows.
Characters: Ric Coy (Little Sam), Gerry Gibson (Dad), Sharon Case (Bride), Stephen Preusse (Groom), Paul Willson (Paul).
Notable Quote: On the devotion of mailmen:
WOODY: "Aren't you going to finish your route, Mr. Clavin?"

CLIFF: "Are you kidding? There's too much snow and sleet out there. Besides, it's getting a little dark."

234. "Don't Shoot ... I'm Only the Psychiatrist" (1/2/92). Frasier encourages his low self-esteem group to interact with bar patrons. The group finds a common bond with the Cheers gang as they exchange stories ridiculing Frasier. Although humiliated and disconcerted, when the therapy group extols Frasier's effective therapy session, he revels in his accomplishment. **Subtopics:** Woody trims Sam's hair, but has to shave a section to retrieve a piece of gum. Sam wears a cap to mask the deformity and refuses to speak to Woody. Meanwhile, Carla celebrates Elvis' birthday and awaits some sign from the King (which is provided by John Allen Hill). *Written by* Kathy Ann Stumpe. *Directed by* James Burrows. *Characters*: Keene Curtis (John Allen Hill), David A. Levy (Derek), Steve Nevil (Lester), Harvey Evans (Syd), Paul Willson (Paul), Michael Holden (Joe), Philip Perlman (Phil), Richard Doran (Deliveryman).

235. "No Rest for the Woody" (1/9/92). Woody begins moonlighting in a graveyard to help pay for Kelly's engagement ring. Multiple employment causes him to become fatigued, especially after he disinters the same corpse three times to ensure its mortality. A combination of sleep deprivation and exhaustion takes its toll as Woody begins hallucinating that Kelly's grandmother is the corpse he exhumed. **Subtopics:** The Cheers furnace needs fixing, and Carla spends the day caging Rebecca behind the wall that houses it. Meanwhile, Sam is required by law to give his employees

group medical coverage, so he hires Norm as a bartender to qualify under the plan. *Written by* Tracy Newman and Jonathan Stark. *Directed by* James Burrows. *Characters*: Celeste Holm (Grandmother Gaines), Jackie Swanson (Kelly), Richard Doyle (Mr. Gaines), Sy Richardson (Gordon), Paul Willson (Paul), Marc Epstein (Waiter). *Note*: Celeste Holm also appeared in "Falcon Crest." *Notable Quote*: Woody, purchasing Kelly's engagement ring:
CLIFF: "So, Woods, how much did the ring set you back?"
WOODY: "Well, they say when you buy an engagement ring you're supposed to spend the equivalent of six months' salary. But it looked kind of naked without a diamond on it."

236. "My Son, My Father" (1/16/92). When Carla's son Gino decides to be a priest, Carla believes she is entitled to a "Get Out of Hell Free" card which gives her *carte blanche* to be vicious. She is obtrusively diabolical to everyone, until Gino abandons the priesthood to become a male model. Carla then atones for her behavior as God seeks vengeance. **Subtopics:** Cliff pursues a career in comedy by performing on amateur night at a comedy club, but his illustrious vocation ends that evening. Meanwhile, Sam chips a tooth on Melville's seafood and threatens to sue John Allen Hill, who ultimately gets revenge by faking a similar incident with a rock in Cheers' pretzels. *Written by* Dan Staley and Rob Long. *Directed by* James Burrows. *Characters*: Keene Curtis (John Allen Hill), Josh Lozoff (Gino), Paul

Willson (Paul), Philip Perlman (Phil), Neal Lerner (Emcee).

Notable Quote: Cliff's desire to be a comedian:

CLIFF: "All my life I kind of wanted to be a stand-up comedian. How's this for an idea? Comedy night at Cheers. Seven nights a week, six shows a night—'The Cock-eyed Mind of Cliff Clavin'.'"

FRASIER: "So you're saying it would be just like any other night, except for the mike."

237. "One Hugs, the Other Doesn't" (1/30/92). Frederick attends his first concert, where the singer, Nanny Gee, is revealed as Frasier's first wife. As Frasier sits in the audience with his family, Nanny Gee approaches and kisses him fervently. Lilith becomes incensed with jealousy because Frasier never mentioned a prior marriage. Nanny Gee agrees to perform a special concert at Cheers for Frederick's birthday and then admits her desire to win Frasier's favor. Lilith remains disconcerted, and when the tension rises betweenthe women, a catfight ensues. Nanny Gee acquiesces but leaves Frasier with a helpful tune which recites her telephone number.

Written by Cheri Eichen and Bill Steinkellner. *Directed by* James Burrows.

Characters: Emma Thompson (Nanny Gee), Christopher and Kevin Graves (Frederick), Paul Willson (Paul), Thomas Tulak (Jesse), Danny Kramer (Elvis), Edward Joseph Derham (Kid on Norm's Stool), Jonathan Daniel Harris (Kid at Food Table), Jennifer Williams (Mother).

Note: Emma Thompson also appeared in the movies *Dead Again* (1991), *Much Ado About Nothing* (1993), and *Remains of the Day* (1993), and won an Oscar for her performance in *Howard's End* (1992).

238. "A Diminished Rebecca with a Suspended Cliff" (2/6/92). Woody's cousin, Russell Boyd, moves to Boston after his girlfriend ends their relationship, and is hired as a piano player at Cheers. Russell becomes obsessed with Rebecca, serenading her with love songs and painting a mural of her in his hotel room. When Rebecca finally convinces him to end this fixation, Russell redirects his infatuation toward Carla. **Subtopic:** Cliff resists the new postal regulation requiring all mail carriers to wear different uniforms, and is tricked by his postal nemesis, Walt Twitchell, into wearing an outrageous costume.

Written by Dan O'Shannon and Tom Anderson. *Directed by* James Burrows.

Characters: Harry Connick, Jr. (Russell Boyd), Raye Birk (Walt Twitchell), Paul Willson (Paul), Jim Norton (Henderson).

Notable Quote: Cliff resists wearing a new postal uniform:

CLIFF: "As far as I'm concerned, it doesn't exist. This is the uniform that made me want to become a postal worker. And this is the uniform I'm sticking to."

CARLA: "You wouldn't have that problem if you washed it once in a while."

239. "License to Hill" (2/13/92). Sam entrusts Rebecca to supervise the bar while the Cheers gang holds a poker party in the poolroom. After being notified that the bar's liquor license has expired, Rebecca saves Cheers from losing it permanently by giving away free drinks and serving non-alcoholic beverages. When Sam learns about her actions, he chastises

Rebecca for her idiocy but then realizes he is at fault for allowing the liquor license to expire. **Subtopic:** Woody acts obnoxiously while taking everyone's money in the Cheers poker party.

Written by Ken Levine and David Isaacs. *Directed by* James Burrows.

Characters: Keene Curtis (John Allen Hill), Paul Willson (Paul), Philip Perlman (Phil), Stephen Rowe (Agent #1), Frank M. Schuller (Agent #2), Lenny Citrano (Customer #1), Nancy Stephens (Customer #2), Robert Gossett (Customer #3), Ralph P. Martin (Customer #4).

Notable Quote: Woody, winning at poker and being obnoxious:

FRASIER: "Woody. Your obnoxious, gloating behavior is not making you any friends."

WOODY: "Well, boo hoo, Dr. Crane, I can buy new friends."

240. **"Rich Man, Wood Man"** (2/20/92). Woody returns from Europe, behaving like an arrogant, wealthy socialite. After realizing the astounding metamorphosis he has experienced, Woody questions whether he and Kelly should continue dating. To save their relationship, Kelly tries to live in Woody's poverty-stricken world. The dilemma is resolved when Woody concludes they should each live on their own income. **Subtopic:** Frasier makes a stern attempt at physical fitness by hiring a personal trainer. Sam eventually becomes his trainer, but the fitness craze fades rapidly.

Written by Daniel Palladino. *Directed by* James Burrows.

Characters: Jackie Swanson (Kelly), Jarrett Lennon (Ludlow), Vili Kraljevic (Richard).

241. **"Smotherly Love"** (2/27/92). Lilith's mother, Betty Sternin, pressures Frasier and Lilith into renewing their wedding vows on their fifth wedding anniversary. Lilith is unable to say "no" to her mother, but when that special day arrives, she finally finds the strength to stand up to her mother. **Subtopic:** Rebecca makes several subtle (but unsuccessful) attempts to prompt Norm into paying his bar tab. However, his failure to pay the debt after winning a large sum of money on the roulette wheel provokes Sam to scold Norm for his irresponsibility.

Written by Kathy Ann Stumpe. *Directed by* James Burrows.

Characters: Marilyn Cooper (Betty Sternin), Wes Stern (The Stranger), Rebecca Staab (Debbie), Fredd Wayne (Dr. Bramwell), Paul Willson (Paul).

Notable Quote: Lilith, discussing her relationship with her mother:

LILITH: "My behavior is solely to please my mother. Why does she always try to turn me into something I'm not?"

CARLA: "Maybe deep down she always wanted a girl."

242. **"Take Me Out of the Ball Game"** (3/26/92). When a lame ex-Red Sox pitcher, Mitch Ganzell, attempts a comeback by trying out with the Red Sox farm club, Sam decides to relive his glory days. Sam makes the farm club but quickly realizes he has outgrown the baseball days and no longer enjoys joking around with the guys. **Subtopic:** Lilith entrusts Frasier to care for her favorite lab rat, Whiskers, while she is out of town. When Whiskers disappears, Frasier spends two days training another rodent to replace Whiskers (and deceive Lilith).

Written by Kathy Ann Stumpe. *Directed by* James Burrows.

Characters: John Finn (Mitch Ganzell), Anthony Starke (Slim), Paul Willson (Paul), Philip Perlman (Phil), Lance Slaughter (Teammate #1), Michael Wiseman (Teammate #2).

Notable Quote: Discussing who should manage Cheers while Sam is gone:

NORM: "Wait a minute. Carla's been here the longest. If anyone should take over, it's Carla."

CARLA: "Oh, no, no, no. Not me. I'm the kind of person that doesn't like responsibility."

NORM: "What are you talking about? You have eight kids."

CARLA: "Well, I wouldn't if I were responsible."

243. "Rebecca's Lover ... Not" (4/23/92). When an old high school flame, Mark Newberger, moves to Boston, Rebecca immediately falls in love with him and attempts to rekindle their romance. She plans a romantic evening at her apartment, and finds out (the hard way) that Mark is gay. However, the revelation does not prevent her from trying to convert him. **Subtopics:** Sam's Corvette is stolen, so he forms a victim support group to cope with the anguish. However, when the car is recovered, he quickly disbands the group. Meanwhile, Kelly spends time with the Cheers gang to get to know Woody's friends better.

Written by Tracy Newman and Jonathan Stark. *Directed by* James Burrows.

Characters: Harvey Fierstein (Mark), Jackie Swanson (Kelly), Kirby Tepper (Tom), Peter Keleghan (Kirby), Ben Mittleman (Policeman), Philip Perlman (Phil), Paul Willson (Paul), Joel Fredericks (Sam II), Jana Robbins (Alice), Barry Zajac (Barry).

Note: Harvey Fierstein subsequently appeared in *Mrs. Doubtfire* (1993).

Notable Quote: Kelly, fraternizing with the Cheers gang:

WOODY: "So what do you guys talk about?"

KELLY: "Oh, the usual. How the Celtics need a point guard, the Sox need pitching, the fact that there's an exact replica of the Earth on the other side of the sun that we can never see."

WOODY: "Wow, really? The Sox need pitchers?"

KELLY: "Well, on *this* Earth."

244. "Bar Wars VI: This Time It's for Real" (4/30/92). When a new owner, Frank "The Angel of Death" Carpaccio, purchases Gary's Tavern, the Cheers gang decides to start a rivalry. As the pranks escalate, the police insinuate Mr. Carpaccio is a mafia boss, so everyone except Sam enters a witness protection program and is bused to a deserted highway in North Dakota. At the highway telephone, Sam calls to remind them of their Halloween prank (in episode #228) and says, "Gotcha!" (Sam took out a 10-year loan to pay for this elaborate ruse.) **Subtopic:** Rebecca is selected by *Redbook* for a beauty makeover and luxuriates in her newfound image.

Written by Ken Levine and David Isaacs. *Directed by* Rick Beren.

Characters: Harry Guardino (Frank Carpaccio), Senator John Kerry (Himself), J.C. Quinn (Carmichael), Bari K. Willerford (Hanson), Larry Brandenburg (Cop), Paul Willson (Paul), Larry Paulsen (Fashion Photographer), Cleto Augusto (Police Photographer).

Note: Harry Guardino has had a prolific acting career. He appeared in "Perry Mason" (as Hamilton Burger) and "Get Christie Love" (as police captain Casey Reardon, 1974-75). The most successful movies in which he appeared are *Dirty Harry* (1971) and *Any Which Way You Can* (1980).

Notable Quote: In reference to learning from our mistakes:

FRASIER: "As that famous prankster Santayana once said, 'Those who do not learn from history are condemned to repeat it'."

WOODY: "You got that right, Dr. Crane. Back in high school I was condemned to repeat history three times. By the way, the same thing goes for mathematics."

245. **"Heeeeeere's Cliffy"** (5/7/92). Cliff is despondent that no television show will accept the jokes he submits, so Norm converts a rejection letter from "The Tonight Show with Johnny Carson" into an acceptance letter. When Cliff takes his mother, Esther, and Norm to Hollywood to watch the show in person, Norm bribes the cue card person to insert the joke in the monologue. The joke flops, and after expressing his indignation, Cliff is escorted to a security office. Esther helps Johnny Carson make the joke a success, and she and Norm are invited onstage. **Subtopic:** While Sam and Woody install a satellite dish on the roof of Cheers, they have a philosophical discussion about marriage, life and death.

Written by Ken Levine and David Isaacs. *Directed by* Rick Beren.

Characters: Frances Sternhagen (Esther Clavin), Joshua Mostel (Cue Card Guy), Paul Willson (Paul), Nicolas Mize (Security Guard), Angel Harper (Audience Member), Johnny Carson (Himself), Doc Severinsen (Himself).

Notable Quote: Cliff, thinking that Johnny Carson bought one of his jokes:

CLIFF: "Yeah, when my joke hits the airwaves, I'm going to start a new career. Yep. It's going to be Cliff Clavin, Jokemeister, Dr. of Ha Ha, Funny Man. Yeah, I'm [going to] be hanging around a whole new group of friends—Oscar and Emmy."

246. **"An Old Fashioned Wedding"** (Part 1 of 2) (5/14/92, 9:00–9:30 p.m. EST). Woody and Kelly consummate their relationship just hours before their wedding ceremony and are unable to keep their hands off each other. The Cheers gang not only works endlessly to prevent Mr. Gaines from seeing Woody and Kelly together, but they also continue making the necessary preparations for the special event. Meanwhile, other problems surface when the food caterer quits after a dispute with Rebecca, and the minister, Dr. Chatfield, dies moments before the ceremony is scheduled to begin.

Written by David Lloyd. *Directed by* Rick Beren.

Characters: Jackie Swanson (Kelly), Richard Doyle (Mr. Gaines), Colleen Morris (Monika), Daniel Gerroll (Chef Maurice), Richard Merson (Dr. Chatfield).

Notable Quote: Searching for a minister for Woody and Kelly's wedding:

REBECCA: "Don't you have an uncle who's a minister?"

KELLY: "Yes. Uncle Roger. But it didn't seem right to ask him—he's going through a terrible divorce right now. Apparently he got tired of coming home and finding his wife in bed with Hives."

REBECCA: "Well, that's pretty insensitive."

WOODY: "Hives was their butler."

247. **"An Old Fashioned Wed-**

ding" (Part 2 of 2) (5/14/92, 9:30–10:00 p.m. EST). The Cheers gang tries to conceal the death of the minister, Dr. Chatfield, while recruiting Kelly's intoxicated Uncle Roger to perform the ceremony. When he is sober, Uncle Roger hates weddings, so the gang provides him with plenty of alcohol to lift his spirits. At the same time, the gang continues to separate the bride and groom to prevent Mr. Gaines from witnessing this breach of wedding tradition. Cheers performs all the catering duties (because the original caterer quit), but in the end, everything comes together and the marital union is complete.

Written by David Lloyd. *Directed by* Rick Beren.

Characters: Jackie Swanson (Kelly), Milo O'Shea (Uncle Roger), Richard Doyle (Mr. Gaines), Colleen Morris (Monika), Mark Voland (Dieter).

Notable Quote: On speaking German:

SAM: "Anybody speak German?"
NORM: "Just the basics, Sam. Löwenbräu, Michelob, bratwurst."

Season Eleven: 1992-93

(NBC Thursday, 9:00–9:30 p.m. EST)

Season Regulars: Ted Danson (Sam Malone), Kirstie Alley (Rebecca Howe), Rhea Perlman (Carla Tortelli-LeBec), John Ratzenberger (Cliff Clavin), Woody Harrelson (Woody Boyd), Kelsey Grammer (Frasier Crane), Bebe Neuwirth (Lilith Sternin-Crane), George Wendt (Norm Peterson).

Technical Credits: *Created by* Glen Charles, Les Charles and James Burrows. *Executive Producers:* James Burrows, Glen Charles, Les Charles, Dan O'Shannon, Tom Anderson. *Co-Executive Producers:* Dan Staley and Rob Long. *Producer:* Tim Berry. *Writers:* Tom Anderson, David Angell, Peter Casey, Glen Charles, Les Charles, Fred Graver, Sue Herring, David Isaacs, David Lee, Tom Leopold, Ken Levine, David Lloyd, Rob Long, Dan O'Shannon, Rebecca Parr Cioffi, Heide Perlman, Dan Staley, Kathy Ann Stumpe. *Directors:* James Burrows, John Ratzenberger, Rick Beren. *Co-Producer:* Tom Leopold. *Story Consultant:* Kathy Ann Stumpe. *Executive Story Consultants:* Rebecca Parr Cioffi, Kathy Ann Stumpe. *Story Editors:* Fred Graver, Sue Herring. *Creative Consultants:* David Lloyd, Ken Levine and David Isaacs. *Executive Script Consultant:* Bob Ellison. *Associate Producer:* Mary Fukuto. *Casting:* Jeff Greenberg, C.S.A. *Original Casting:* Stephen Kolzak. *Director of Photography:* John Finger. *Art Director:* Dahl Delu. *Edited by* Robert Bramwell, Peter. J. Chakos, Michael Wilcox, Ron Volk. *Unit Production Manager:* Linda McMurray. *First Assistant Director:* Brian James Ellis. *Second Assistant Director:* Steven Pomeroy. *Music by* Craig Safan. *Song:* "Where Everybody Knows Your Name." *Lyrics and Music by* Judy Hart Angelo and Gary Portnoy. *Sung by* Gary Portnoy. *Set Decorator:* Laura Richarz. *Production Supervisor:* Ahuva Fogel. *Script Supervisor:* Gabrielle James. *Costume Supervisors:* Brett Barrett, Sharon Taylor-Sampson. *Technical Coordinator:* Rick Beren. *Production Mixer:* Robert Crosby, C.A.S. *Music Editor:* Chips Swanson. *Makeup*

Artist: Bruce Hutchinson. *Hair Stylists:* Marilyn Patricia Phillips, Dianne Pepper. *Sound Effects:* Randal S. Thomas, M.P.S.E., Joe Johnston. *Sound by* Larson Sound. *Main Title Design:* James Castle, Bruce Bryant, Carol Johnsen. *Cameras and Lenses:* Panavision. *Assistants to the Producers:* Pat Barnett, Cara Coslow, Vito Cupoli, Rosie Dean, Cheryl Dolins, Steven Dry, Sylvia Grant, Michael Grizzi, Jane Henning, Sue Herring, Mike Kopple, Brian Lovell, Emily Miller, Jeffrey Pfefferle, David Reid, Rich Stangl, Lynn Stevenson, Andrew Trossman, Rebekka Vieira, Barry Zajac. *Charles/ Burrows/Charles Productions in Association with* Paramount.

248. **"The Little Match Girl"** (9/ 24/92). Rebecca decides to change her life in a positive manner and starts by quitting smoking. Knowing Rebecca's luck, it is not surprising that her last cigarette ignites the paper in Sam's office trash can and causes substantial fire damage to Cheers. Sam is devastated. When he cannot obtain a loan to pay for the remodeling, he sells his Corvette. Rebecca finally confesses she accidentally torched the bar, and Sam fires her. He eventually rehires Rebecca because she gave him a chance when he needed it most (in 1987 she hired Sam after he sank his boat).
Written by Dan Staley and Rob Long. *Directed by* James Burrows.
Characters: Jackie Swanson (Kelly Boyd), Keene Curtis (John Allen Hill), Robert Machray (Fire Marshall), Amanda Carlin (Ms. Kurland), Peter Keleghan (Kirby), Peter Kevoian (Fireman).

249. **"The Beer Is Always Greener"** (10/1/92). Sam prepares for Cheers' grand reopening celebration, but loses all of his regular customers to another bar, Mr. Pubb's, because he cannot compete with the ten big screen televisions and free hors d'oeuvres. Carla temporarily accepts a waitress position at Mr. Pubb's, and after seeing her first paycheck, readily quits her employment at Cheers. However, when she is assigned to train a Diane clone, Ellen, Carla returns to Cheers, insisting that Sam promise never to go to Mr. Pubb's again. **Subtopic:** Woody and Kelly spend their honeymoon fighting over religious beliefs but settle their differences when Woody converts to her religion.
Written by Tom Leopold. *Directed by* James Burrows.
Characters: Jackie Swanson (Kelly Boyd), Glenn Shadix (Bernard), Matthew Glave (Bartender), Julia Montgomery (Ellen), Rosa Nevin (Gwen), Paul Willson (Paul), Alan Koss (Alan), Tim Cunningham (Tim), Philip Perlman (Phil), Spencer Beglarian (Customer).
Notable Quote: After Cliff's mailbag burned in the Cheers fire:
FRASIER: "Cliff, was that undelivered mail?"
CLIFF: "Oh, yeah it was, Doc. Oh my sweet lord, what a catastrophe. I mean, there could be letters from mothers to sons in there, social security checks, wedding invitations. Well, there's only one thing left for me to do now."
FRASIER: "What's that, Cliff?"
CLIFF: "Get up early tomorrow and stage a jeep accident."

250. **"The King of Beers"** (10/ 8/92). Norm participates in a beer taste test. When he proves to have exceptional taste buds, he is hired by a brewery as the official taste tester. The dream job only lasts one week because

Norm embarrasses himself and the brewery president, Mr. Hoffmeyer, in the final employment interview. **Subtopic:** Cheers is accidentally shipped a slot machine, and Rebecca becomes depressed because she cannot win. Carla finally rigs the entertainment device to pay out, and Rebecca is overjoyed when she breaks even.

Written by Dan O'Shannon. *Directed by* John Ratzenberger.

Characters: Cliff Bemis (Mike), Cameron Thor (Marketing Analyst), Paul Willson (Paul), Joe Costanza (Ray), Bradford English (Chuck), William Long, Jr. (Mr. Hoffmeyer), Mirron E. Willis (Deliveryman).

Notable Quote: Regarding Rebecca's losing continuously at the slot machine:

NORM: "Rebecca. Has it ever occurred to you that maybe the reason you always lose is because you think you're going to lose?"

REBECCA: "Don't give me that crap. I tried that positive thinking stuff, and I knew it wouldn't work and sure enough it didn't."

251. "The Magnificent Six" (10/22/92). Henri and Sam compete to see who can get the most women's telephone numbers in one night. Sam initially resists the competition, but when Cliff and other bar losers accept the challenge, he jumps in to do it for America! Sam loses the contest, but wins something more special—an evening with three women who do *everything* together. **Subtopic:** Sam forces Rebecca to undergo treatment to quit smoking. She enters Dr. Kluger's No Mercy Clinic, but instead of being cured, she out-smokes the doctor and receives a diploma by default.

Written by Sue Herring. *Directed by* James Burrows.

Characters: Anthony Cistaro (Henri), Eddie Jones (Dr. Kluger), Sondra C. Baker (Jane), Jennifer Gatti (Laura), Jeri Gaile (Marie), Leilani Jones (Jessica), Patricia Clipper (April), Maria Pecci (Shirley), Tim Cunningham (Tim), Alan Koss (Alan), Philip Perlman (Phil).

252. "Do Not Forsake Me, O'My Postman" (10/29/92). Margaret returns to Boston to tell Cliff he is the father of her child. Cliff cannot even recall having sex, but proposes marriage anyway, and she accepts. Despite discovering he is not the father, Cliff still agrees to marry Margaret. However, the celebration is short-lived when she decides to return to Canada to give the real father, Jerry, a second chance. **Subtopic:** Rebecca hires an advertising representative, Sy Flembeck, to create a jingle for the bar, and is upset when he tailors new lyrics to old nursery rhyme tunes.

Written by Ken Levine and David Isaacs. *Directed by* James Burrows.

Characters: John Mahoney (Sy Flembeck), Annie Golden (Margaret O'Keefe), Derek McGrath (Andy-Andy), Cameron Watson (Ad Executive), Paul Willson (Paul), Tim Cunningham (Tim), Jack Kenny (Tom), Leland Orser (Mark), Steve Giannelli (Steve).

Note: John Mahoney is best known for his role as Martin Crane (Frasier's father) in the television show "Frasier," though he also appeared in "Lady Blue" and "The Human Factor," and the movies *The Manhattan Project* (1986) and *Say Anything* (1989).

Notable Quote: On Margaret's not knowing who is the father of her child:

MARGARET: "I'm sorry I was gone for so long. I went out and had some pizza and ribs, ice cream and pickles, and chocolate."

CARLA: "Maybe it's Norm's kid."

253. "Teaching with the Enemy" (Part 1 of 2) (11/5/92). Rebecca catches Lilith steaming up the car windows with another man, Dr. Pascal, and has difficulty keeping the affair a secret after promising to give Lilith time to explain everything to Frasier. When Frasier is told the truth, he becomes very upset and struggles to accept her infidelity. **Subtopic:** Cheers hires a bouncer, Tiny, but the gang feels uncomfortable because of his girth and psychotic tendencies, so they find a way (albeit a cruel one) to get Tiny to quit.

Written by Tom Anderson. *Directed by* James Burrows.

Characters: Don Gibb (Tiny), Larry Brandenburg (Cop), Barry Zajac (Barry), Philip Perlman (Phil), Michael Buckman Silver (Customer).

Note: Don Gibb also starred in HBO's program "1st and Ten."

Notable Quote: Rebecca, catching Lilith with another man:

LILITH: "What you saw was me saying goodbye to him."

REBECCA: "Well, then he must be hard of hearing—you had his ear in your mouth."

254. "The Girl in the Plastic Bubble" (Part 2 of 2) (11/12/92). Lilith announces she is separating from Frasier to live in the Ecopod with her lover, Dr. Pascal. Frasier maintains custody of Frederick, but when the pain of Lilith's departure is too much, he threatens suicide as a means of forcing her to remain by his side. Frasier is eventually coaxed off the building ledge (he never intended an actual suicide), but their marriage is beyond

repair. Lilith continues with her plan to leave him.

Written by Dan O'Shannon. *Directed by* James Burrows.

Characters: Peter Vogt (Louis Pascal), Brian Smiar (Sergeant Rainer), Tim Cunningham (Tim), Patrick Shea (Police Officer).

Notable Quote: On Lilith's leaving for the Ecopod:

LILITH: "Well, I'm off. I don't know what the future holds. Whatever happens, I only hope I can realize my full potential. To acquire things the old Lilith never had."

CARLA: "Like a body temperature?"

LILITH: "That's very good, Carla! Incidentally, I've taken your little wisecracks for a few years now, you hideous gargoyle. And if you ever open that gateway to hell you call a mouth in my direction again, I'll snap off your extremities like dead branches and feed them to you at gunpoint."

255. "Ill-Gotten Gaines" (11/19/92). Woody accidentally catches Kelly's father, Walter Gaines, having an affair—Walter was rolling on the floor with his sister-in-law, Katherine Gaines. Actually, Woody thinks Mr. Gaines is exercising, but Walter assumes Woody is playing dumb in order to blackmail him. Walter befriends Woody and showers him with gifts to buy his silence. When the truth is revealed, Woody vows not to blackmail Walter, but the butler, Hives, who overhears the conversation, is not as scrupulous. **Subtopic:** Cheers hosts Thanksgiving dinner for the gang and uses Melville's restaurant to supply the necessities.

Written by Fred Graver. *Directed by* James Burrows.

Characters: Keene Curtis (John Allen Hill), Jackie Swanson (Kelly

Boyd), Richard Doyle (Mr. Gaines), Robert Cornthwaite (Hives), Sondra Currie (Katherine), Christopher and Kevin Graves (Frederick), John Valentine (Richard), Thomas Tulak (Jesse), Danny Kramer (Elvis), Sabrina Wiener (Lucinda).

Notable Quote: Walter Gaines, explaining the purpose of a power of attorney:

WALTER: "Let me put it in Hanover-ese, Woody. You know how a turkey when it feeds at the trough will eat until it dies? Well, these forms give me the right, now that you're feeding at the Gaines trough, to pull your head away if I think you're going to choke."

256. "Feelings ... Whoa, Whoa, Whoa" (12/3/92). Carla tells John Allen Hill she loves him. Hill is shocked to hear these words for the first time in his life and has a heart attack. Carla initially feigns indifference about his hospitalization, but realizes she caused the attack by sharing her feelings. While Hill is convalescing, they decide to elevate their relationship to something more meaningful than just sex, but quickly discover they are incompatible (except in bed). **Subtopic:** Cliff accuses his neighbor of being Adolf Hitler, and while gathering evidence to prove it, he is nearly evicted from his condominium.

Written by Kathy Ann Stumpe. *Directed by* Rick Beren.

Characters: Keene Curtis (John Allen Hill), Jackie Swanson (Kelly Boyd), Erick Avari (Mr. Cranston), Paul Willson (Paul), Tim Cunningham (Tim), Philip Perlman (Phil), Eric A. Payne (Customer).

257. "Daddy's Little Middle-Aged Girl" (12/10/92). Rebecca's father,

Franklin Howe, visits Boston and orders her to return to San Diego. She initially resists his request but then decides to comply with her father's wishes. Franklin's ultimate plan is for Rebecca to stand up for herself, but when that fails, he is forced to increase her allowance to keep her in Boston. (As it turns out, Rebecca found out about the plan from her mother, and they agreed to split any increase in allowance.) **Subtopic:** Woody and Kelly move out of the Gaines guest house and into Woody's apartment, but when Kelly's furniture occupies every square inch of the place, they begin searching for a house.

Written by Rebecca Parr Cioffi. *Directed by* James Burrows.

Characters: Robert Prosky (Franklin Howe), Jackie Swanson (Kelly Boyd), Ethel Kennedy (Herself).

Note: Robert Prosky appeared in "Hill Street Blues" (as Sgt. Stan Jablonski, 1984–87), and in the movies *Christine* (1984), *Green Card* (1990), and *Far and Away* (1992).

Notable Quote: Discussing Franklin Howe's retirement:

REBECCA: "Oh, Daddy, you work so hard. When are you going to get to retire?"

FRANKLIN: "Apparently when they wrap a flag around me and slide me off the ship."

258. "Love Me, Love My Car" (12/17/92). Sam discovers that Kirby McFeeney, the owner of his Corvette, has died, so he provides companionship to the widow, Susan, to convince her to sell the car for a low price. The plan works perfectly until Woody reveals the scheme to Susan. Sam feels guilty and begs for Susan's forgiveness. After considerable effort, she forgives him, and they become friends. **Subtopic:**

Rebecca becomes emotionally attached to Woody's Christmas ham (a piglet named Snuffles), and sets the pig free in the woods. The piglet finds its way back to Woody's parents' house in Hanover, Indiana, and they later report that Snuffles was delicious!

Written by David Lloyd. *Directed by* James Burrows.

Characters: Dana Delany (Susan), Shane Sweet (Shane), Toni Elizabeth White (Toni), Amanda Costello (Amanda).

Note: Dana Delany is best known for costarring in "China Beach" (as Lt. Colleen McMurphy), winning an Emmy for Outstanding Lead Actress in a Drama Series (1989). She also starred in the flop "Sweet Surrender" (1987), and appeared in "As the World Turns" (as Hayley Wilson) and "Love of Life" (as Amy Russell).

Notable Quote: Discussing Woody's piglet:

REBECCA: "He's so cute. Oh, he's shivering. Should we cover him with something?"

WOODY: "Well, not really. Maybe with some honey glaze and a little pineapple sauce."

259. "Sunday Dinner" (1/7/93). Frasier's temporary secretary, Shauna, expresses interest in him, so they plan a special evening at her house. Unbeknownst to Frasier, Shauna lives with her parents! After an uncomfortable dinner, the evening worsens as Shauna leaves with her boyfriend, Rick, and Frasier is left playing Yahtzee with her parents. **Subtopic:** Cliff and Norm are hired to videotape a family gathering at Cheers. When the batteries die, they pretend to videotape the gathering and miss the most unbelievable, once in a lifetime events.

Written by Fred Graver. *Directed by* James Burrows.

Characters: Kristen Cloke (Shauna), David Froman (Dad), Marilyn Rockafellow (Mom), Jonathan Emerson (Peter), Toby Ganger (Todd), Charles Esten (Marine), Colin Drake (Grandpa), Ruth Engel (Grandma), Paul Willson (Paul), Laura Gardner (Party Guest #1), George Milan (Party Guest #2), Richard Danielson (Rick), Christopher and Kevin Graves (Frederick), Tim Cunningham (Tim), Alan Koss (Alan).

260. "Norm's Big Audit" (1/14/93). Norm is audited by the Internal Revenue Service, so he buries the agent with fake receipts and altered calendars. When IRS agent Dot Carroll recognizes the deception, Norm flirts to persuade her not to report the indiscretion. Dot willingly accepts and invites him to her hotel room. However, faithful Norm cannot go through with it, so he summons Carla to visit the hotel, pretending to be his outraged wife. **Subtopic:** Sam tries to prevent the Cheers gang from watching a rerun of a 1970s baseball game in which he pitched. Apparently, Sam was drunk that night and thought the Oriole mascot was a huge mutant bird, so he nailed it between the eyes with a fastball.

Written by Tom Leopold. *Directed by* John Ratzenberger.

Characters: Sharon Barr (Dot Carroll), Paul Willson (Paul), Tim Cunningham (Tim), Steve Giannelli (Steve), Alan Koss (Alan).

Notable Quote: In reference to Norm's IRS tax audit:

CARLA: "I've known you for a long time and I consider you a friend. I just want you to know I have connections who might be able to make it a little bit easier for you."

NORM: "People in the IRS?"
CARLA: "No. Prison."

261. "It's a Mad, Mad, Mad, Mad Bar" (1/21/93). Robin returns to Boston penniless, but retains his sense of humor by playing a prank on the Cheers gang. Robin intimates he may have hidden a second money belt with $6 million somewhere in the bar. The gang subsequently destroys Cheers searching for the multi-million dollar prize. Robin then reveals there was no money belt; the prank was intended to teach the gang about the evils of money (and that he never really liked them). **Subtopic:** Rebecca pretends to love the "new" Robin, hoping his claim of impoverishment is merely a test of her love.
Written by Rebecca Parr Cioffi. *Directed by* James Burrows.
Characters: Roger Rees (Robin Colcord), Robert Machray (Fire Captain).
Notable Quote: Carla, thanking her children for kidnapping the fire captain:
CARLA: "Thanks kids. Now wipe down the car, ditch it, and get right to bed—it's a school night."

262. "Loathe and Marriage" (2/4/93). Carla's daughter, Serafina, is pregnant and announces her wedding engagement to a retired police officer, Pat McDougall. The wedding ceremony is held at Melville's and the reception at Cheers. Although Carla is irate when Serafina's father, Nick, arrives unannounced and uninvited, Serafina insists that he stay. The Tortellis eventually reconcile their differences, and the wedding is a success. **Subtopic:** Nick tries to convince wedding guests to invest in an orangutan act.

Written by Ken Levine and David Isaacs. *Directed by* James Burrows.
Characters: Keene Curtis (John Allen Hill), Jackie Swanson (Kelly Boyd), Leah Remini (Serafina), Josh Lozoff (Gino Tortelli), Dennis Cockrum (Pat McDougall), Barry Zajac (Barry), Jean Kasem (Loretta Tortelli), Dan Hedaya (Nick Tortelli).
Notable Quote: In preparation for Serafina's wedding:
HILL: "Oh, Ms. Tortelli, there you are. An hour behind schedule, I see. You are as prompt as you are lovely.... I'm here to remind you that this wedding must be over by 11:30 on the dot. That's when I open for lunch."
CARLA: "You open for lunch at noon."
HILL: "I know your family. They leave at 11:30. At 11:31 the Orkin man arrives."

263. "Is There a Doctor in the Howe?" (Part 1 of 2) (2/11/93). Frasier receives a telegram announcing that Lilith wants a divorce. To cheer him up, the Cheers gang throws a divorce party at the bar. Rebecca drives Frasier home and consoles him. Although she admits having no real physical attraction to Frasier, Rebecca agrees to sleep with him. Naturally, the gang interrupts Frasier's sexual rendezvous, and just before consummation, Lilith walks in to catch him and Rebecca in bed together. **Subtopic:** Woody experiences the effects of alcohol, which makes him obnoxious and offensive.
Written by Kathy Ann Stumpe. *Directed by* James Burrows.
Characters: Paul Willson (Paul), Tera Hendrickson (Audrey), Bebe Neuwirth (Lilith), Tim Cunningham (Tim), Alan Koss (Alan), Peter Schreiner (Pete).

264. "The Bar Manager, the Shrink, His Wife & Her Lover" (Part 2 of 2) (2/18/93). Dr. Pascal arrives in Boston to compel Lilith to return to the Ecopod. When she refuses, he uses a gun to persuade her and holds the rest of the gang hostage at Cheers. Lilith stands her ground and tells Pascal that she does not love him. He eventually listens to Frasier's rational words and relinquishes the firearm. Lilith then asks for Frasier's forgiveness and they reconcile their marriage.

Written by Kathy Ann Stumpe. *Directed by* James Burrows.

Characters: Bebe Neuwirth (Lilith), Keene Curtis (John Allen Hill), Peter Vogt (Dr. Louis Pascal), Paul Willson (Paul).

Notable Quote: Regarding your spouse having an affair:

SAM: "What would you do if you walked in and found Vera with another man?"

NORM: "Well, I'd probably buy a couple of his pencils and send him on his way."

265. "The Last Picture Show" (2/25/93). The Cheers gang experiences all the nostalgia associated with outdoor theaters by attending the Twi-Lite Drive-in on its last night of business (for the All-Night Godzilla Marathon). Their primary task is parking the car in a location where Cliff will never find them, but in the process the car gets damaged and stripped. **Subtopic:** When the former owner of Cheers, Gus, visits Boston, he is allowed to manage the bar for one night. Gus is overbearing and the employees hate him, but the bar earns a fortune under his tutelage.

Written by Fred Graver. *Directed by* James Burrows.

Characters: Pat Hingle (Gus O'Malley), Michael Winters (Security Guard), Nick Oleson (Man at Drive-in).

Notable Quote: Sam introduces Gus, the former owner of Cheers:

SAM: "I bought this place from Gus."

WOODY: "Sam, you've been had. You already own this bar."

GUS: "[to Woody] You must be Coach's boy."

266. "Bar Wars VII: The Naked Prey" (3/18/93). Cheers and Gary's Tavern compete in the annual St. Patrick's Day bet, but this year they up the ante. Sam has his usual success and loses resoundingly. The bet requires the loser (the Cheers gang) to go to the winner's bar (Gary's Tavern) and sing "Getting to Know You" in the nude. Harry "the Hat" provides revenge by posing as a wealthy developer who purchases Gary's Tavern for $1 million. However, Gary unwittingly bulldozes the bar before the check clears—yes, it does bounce. **Subtopic:** Rebecca tries to get accepted into a prestigious women's organization, but is rejected because she is too self-involved.

Written by Ken Levine and David Isaacs. *Directed by* James Burrows.

Characters: Harry Anderson (Harry "the Hat"), Robert Desiderio (Gary), Paul Willson (Paul), Maurice Roeves (Sean), Jayson Kane (Watch Salesman).

267. "Look Before You Sleep" (4/1/93). Sam's apartment is infested with silverfish, so he plans to spend the night with a stewardess, Julie. Unfortunately, Julie cancels and Sam accidentally locks his keys and wallet in the bar. The spare keys to the bar were lost, and every hotel room is occupied

due to a Shriners' convention. One by one he solicits the Cheers gang for a place to sleep. After exhausting all his options, Sam ends up spending a sleepless night with Cliff.

Written by Rebecca Parr Cioffi. *Directed by* James Burrows.

Characters: Frances Sternhagen (Esther Clavin), Peter MacNicol (Mario), Keene Curtis (John Allen Hill), Bernadette Birkett (Vera), Gordon Clapp (Shriner), Deirdre Imershein (Julie).

268. "Woody Gets an Election" (4/22/93). After listening to a politician spout platitudes, Frasier tries to prove even a chimp can get 10 percent of the vote in a Boston city council election, so he puts Woody on the ballot. When Woody's competition, Kevin Fogerty, is arrested for public intoxication, the Cheers gang unites to campaign for a victory. When it appears Woody might win the election, Frasier has second thoughts about his study on the voting public. He convinces Woody to withdraw, but the public still votes Woody to victory.

Written by Dan O'Shannon, Tom Anderson, Dan Staley and Rob Long. *Directed by* James Burrows.

Characters: Jackie Swanson (Kelly Boyd), Spanky McFarland (Himself), Philip Baker Hall (Kevin Fogerty), Peri Gilpin (Holly Matheson), Clarke Gordon (Chief Justice), Paul Willson (Paul), LaTanya Richardson (Moderator), Stephen Parr (Fogerty's Aide), Jerry Penacoli (Newscaster).

Note: Peri Gilpin later played the role of Roz in the television show "Frasier." Spanky McFarland was the star of "The Little Rascals."

Notable Quote: Frasier, making 300 posters to advertise Woody's candidacy:

FRASIER: "There is no need to go crazy. I only need to get ten percent of the eligible vote."

CLIFF: "Well, in that case, why don't you just put them up on Carla's headboard?"

269. "It's Lonely on the Top" (4/29/93). Carla prepares one of her lethal mixed drinks, and everyone but Woody pays the price the next morning, especially Carla. She remembers sleeping with someone, and is sickened to discover it was Paul Creypens. Sam convinces Paul to remain silent and further consoles Carla by telling her everyone has skeletons in their closet. To prove it, Sam removes his toupee. **Subtopic:** Norm and Cliff get their buttocks tattooed after drinking Carla's lethal mixed drink, and the next morning discover they were given each other's tattoo.

Written by Heide Perlman. *Directed by* James Burrows.

Characters: Jackie Swanson (Kelly Boyd), Paul Willson (Paul), Philip Perlman (Phil).

Notable Quote: Carla, distraught after sleeping with an unknown patron:

CARLA: "Hey, Sammy. You don't think any less of me, do you?"

SAM: "Well, let's see who it is first."

270. "Rebecca Gaines, Rebecca Loses" (Part 1 of 2) (5/6/93, 9:00–9:30 p.m. EST). Rebecca thinks Kelly's father, Walter Gaines, is interested in dating her when she is invited to his house for an evening of classical music. Rebecca immediately falls in love with him (and his money), but is particularly distraught when she arrives at the Gaines estate and is expected to work as a bartender. **Subtopic:** Cliff is furious with his mother, Esther, and when he decides to do something drastic, the Cheers gang suspects that he killed her. *Written by* David Lloyd. *Directed by* James Burrows.

Characters: Frances Sternhagen (Esther Clavin), Jackie Swanson (Kelly Boyd), Richard Doyle (Mr. Gaines), Robert Cornthwaite (Hives), Paul Willson (Paul), Calvin Remsberg (Baritone).

Notable Quote: Discussing Rebecca's fondness for classical music (and her weight problem):

WALTER: "Obviously, when you worked at the house, I failed to appreciate your depth."

CARLA: "Not to mention her width."

271. **"Rebecca Gaines, Rebecca Loses" (Part 2 of 2)** (5/6/93, 9:30–10:00 p.m. EST). Rebecca is depressed because she was merely invited to the Gaines estate as a domestic servant. When she becomes intoxicated on wine, Sam rushes to the mansion and convinces Walter Gaines to invite Rebecca to sit with him during the concert. He obliges, but has her physically removed from the house when she repeatedly interrupts the performance. **Subtopic:** The Cheers gang investigates Esther's disappearance and concludes Cliff killed his mother. Eventually it is revealed she was placed in a nursing home. However, her stay is brief, and Esther returns to Cliff's condominium when his insurance does not cover all the costs. *Written by* David Lloyd. *Directed by* James Burrows.

Characters: Frances Sternhagen (Esther Clavin), Richard Doyle (Mr. Gaines), George Hearn (George), Robert Cornthwaite (Hives), Paul Willson (Paul), Calvin Remsberg (Baritone), Renata Scott (Party Guest).

272. **"The Guy Can't Help It"** (5/13/93). After returning from a vacation, Rebecca decides to date decent men, and commences by dating Cheers' beer tap repairman, Don. She is immediately infatuated with Don, and after a few dates is ready to marry him. Sam tries to convince Rebecca that she is settling, and maybe she should wait for him instead. **Subtopic:** Sam agrees to seek therapy after realizing he has a sexual compulsiveness problem. His first order of business in therapy is to proposition another patient for a date. *Written by* David Angell, Peter Casey and David Lee. *Directed by* James Burrows.

Characters: Tom Berenger (Don), Sharon Lawrence (Rachel), Paul Willson (Paul), Gilbert Lewis (Dr. Robert Sutton), Bradford Bancroft (Group Member #1), Steve Kehela (Group Member #2).

Note: Tom Berenger appeared in the movies *Looking for Mr. Goodbar* (1977), *Butch and Sundance: The Early Days* (1979), *The Big Chill* (1983), *Eddie and the Cruisers* (1983), *Someone to Watch Over Me* (1987), *Major League* (1989), and *Major League 2* (1994), to name a few, and also was featured in "One Life to Live" (as Tim Siegel, 1975–76).

Notable Quote: Discussing Rebecca's age:

FRASIER: "And if the bloom is not off your rose just yet, you can certainly hear pruning shears approaching."

273. **"One for the Road" (Part 1 of 3)** (5/20/93, 9:22–10:00 p.m. EST). As the Cheers gang watches the National Cable Ace awards, they witness Diane winning an award. Sam kindly sends a telegram congratulating her, and when she calls to thank him, they both lie about their personal lives.

Sam casually invites her to Boston for a visit, never expecting her to accept. **Subtopic:** Rebecca continues to date Don, the plumber. After rejecting his three marriage proposals, Rebecca becomes depressed because she may have lost the only decent guy she ever dated.

Written by Glen Charles and Les Charles. *Directed by* James Burrows.

Characters: Tom Berenger (Don Santry), Mike Ditka (Himself), Kim Alexis (Herself), Paul Willson (Paul), Steve Giannelli (Steve), Alan Koss (Alan), Tim Cunningham (Tim), Shelley Long (Diane Chambers).

274. "One for the Road" (Part 2 of 3) (5/20/93, 10:00–10:30 p.m. EST). Diane arrives in Boston with her husband, Reed, and Sam asks Rebecca to play the part of his wife. As both Sam and Diane act out their lies, it is revealed neither is married, nor do they have any children. Despite these lies, Sam and Diane rekindle their romance and become engaged to be married. **Subtopic:** While Rebecca is pretending to be Sam's wife, and dining at Melville's (with Sam, Diane and Reed), Don proposes marriage to Rebecca, and this time she joyously accepts.

Written by Glen Charles and Les Charles. *Directed by* James Burrows.

Characters: Tom Berenger (Don Santry), Jackie Swanson (Kelly Boyd), Mark Harelik (Reed Manchester), Anthony Heald (Kevin), Paul Willson (Paul), Mitchell Lichtenstein (Waiter), Tim Cunningham (Tim), Steve Giannelli (Steve), Alan Koss (Alan), Shelley Long (Diane Chambers).

Note: Mark Harelik is remembered for his recurring regular role in "Wings" (as Davis, Helen's boyfriend).

275. "One for the Road" (Part 3 of 3) (5/20/93, 10:30–11:00 p.m. EST). Sam prepares to leave for California to begin a new life with Diane. He says goodbye and tells the Cheers gang to get their own lives—he is no longer their life support system. When the plane is delayed, Sam and Diane reconsider their impending nuptials. Sam decides to stay in Boston, while Diane returns to California, and they mutually agree to cancel the wedding. When Sam returns to the bar, the gang forgives and forgets, and everyone philosophizes about the meaning of life. **Subtopic:** Rebecca begins celebrating her new life with Don. Although married to a mere plumber, she realizes he is too good for her.

Written by Glen Charles and Les Charles. *Directed by* James Burrows.

Characters: Shelley Long (Diane Chambers).

Notable Quote: On Sam's moving to California:

WOODY: "So, Sam. What are you going to do about the bar?"

SAM: "Well, I thought I'd let Rebecca run it for a while, and afterwards I'll sell what's left for kindling."

Appendix: Emmy Nominations and Awards

(an asterisk before the entry indicates that "Cheers" won the award)

1982-83 Season (Awarded September 25, 1983)

1. *Outstanding Comedy Series: James Burrows, Glen Charles, Les Charles, Producers; Ken Levine and David Isaacs, Co-Producers
2. Outstanding Lead Actor in a Comedy Series: Ted Danson
3. *Outstanding Lead Actress in a Comedy Series: Shelley Long
4. Outstanding Supporting Actor in a Comedy, Variety or Music Series: Nicholas Colasanto
5. Outstanding Supporting Actress in a Comedy, Variety or Music Series: Rhea Perlman
6. *Outstanding Directing in a Comedy Series: James Burrows, "Showdown, Part 2" (#22)
7. Outstanding Writing in a Comedy Series: Ken Levine and David Isaacs, "The Boys in the Bar" (#16)
8. Outstanding Writing in a Comedy Series: David Lloyd, "Diane's Perfect Date" (#17)
9. *Outstanding Writing in a Comedy Series: Glen Charles and Les Charles, "Give Me a Ring Sometime" (#1)
10. Outstanding Art Direction for a Series: Richard Sylbert, Production Designer; George Gaines, Set Decorator, "Give Me a Ring Sometime" (#1)
11. Outstanding Achievement in Music and Lyrics: Judy Hart Angelo and Gary Portnoy, Composers and Lyricists; Pilot Song: "Where Everybody Knows Your Name"
12. Outstanding Film Editing for a Series: Andrew Chulack, "Endless Slumper" (#10)
13. *Outstanding Individual Achievement—Graphic Design and Title Sequences: James Castle & Bruce Bryant, "Showdown" (#21)

1983-84 Season (Awarded September 23, 1984)

14. *Outstanding Comedy Series: James Burrows, Glen Charles, Les Charles, Producers
15. Outstanding Lead Actor in a Comedy Series: Ted Danson
16. Outstanding Lead Actress in a Comedy Series: Shelley Long
17. Outstanding Supporting Actor in a Comedy Series: Nicholas Colasanto
18. Outstanding Supporting Actor in a Comedy Series: George Wendt
19. *Outstanding Supporting Actress in a Comedy Series: Rhea Perlman
20. Outstanding Directing in a Comedy Series: James Burrows, "Old Flames" (#29)
21. *Outstanding Writing in a Comedy Series: David Angell, "Old Flames" (#29)
22. Outstanding Writing in a Comedy Series: Glen Charles and Les Charles, "Power Play" (#23)
23. Outstanding Writing in a Comedy Series: David Lloyd, "Homicidal Ham" (#26)
24. *Outstanding Film Editing for a Series: Andrew Chulack, "Old Flames" (#29)
25. Outstanding Live and Tape Sound Mixing and Sound Effects for a Series: Gordon Klimuck, Production; Thomas Huth, Post-production; Sam Black, Sound Effects; Douglas Grey, Pre-production, "No Help Wanted" (#36)

1984-85 Season (Awarded September 22, 1985)

26. Outstanding Comedy Series: James Burrows, Glen Charles, Les Charles, Executive Producers; Ken Estin and Sam Simon, Producers
27. Outstanding Lead Actor in a Comedy Series: Ted Danson
28. Outstanding Lead Actress in a Comedy Series: Shelley Long
29. Outstanding Supporting Actor in a Comedy Series: Nicholas Colasanto
30. Outstanding Supporting Actor in a Comedy Series: John Ratzenberger
31. Outstanding Supporting Actor in a Comedy Series: George Wendt
32. *Outstanding Supporting Actress in a Comedy Series: Rhea Perlman
33. Outstanding Directing in a Comedy Series: James Burrows, "Cheerio, Cheers" (#66)
34. Outstanding Writing in a Comedy Series: Peter Casey and David Lee, "I Call Your Name" (#47)
35. Outstanding Writing in a Comedy Series: Glen Charles and Les Charles, "Rebound, Part 2" (#46)
36. Outstanding Writing in a Comedy Series: David Lloyd, "Sam Turns the Other Cheek" (#49)
37. *Outstanding Live and Tape Sound Mixing and Sound Effects for a Series:

Douglas Grey, Pre-production; Michael Ballin, Production; Thomas Huth, Post-production; and Sam Black, Sound Effects, "The Executive's Executioner" (#64)

1985-86 Season (Awarded September 21, 1986)

38. Outstanding Comedy Series: James Burrows, Glen Charles, Les Charles, Executive Producers; Peter Casey and David Lee, Heide Perlman, David Angell, Producers; Tim Berry, Co-Producer
39. Outstanding Lead Actor in a Comedy Series: Ted Danson
40. Outstanding Lead Actress in a Comedy Series: Shelley Long
41. Outstanding Supporting Actor in a Comedy Series: John Ratzenberger
42. Outstanding Supporting Actor in a Comedy Series: George Wendt
43. *Outstanding Supporting Actress in a Comedy Series: Rhea Perlman
44. Outstanding Directing in a Comedy Series: James Burrows, "The Triangle" (#84)
45. Outstanding Writing in a Comedy Series: Peter Casey & David Lee, "2 Good 2 Be 4 Real" (#76)
46. *Outstanding Sound Mixing for a Comedy Series or a Special: Michael Ballin, Robert Douglass, Douglas Grey, and Thomas J. Huth, "Fear Is My Co-Pilot" (#90)
47. Outstanding Editing for a Series, Multi-camera Production: Andy Ackerman, "Birth, Death, Love, & Rice" (#70)
48. Outstanding Editing for a Series, Multi-camera Production: Douglas Hines, A.C.E., "The Triangle" (#84)

1986-87 Season (Awarded September 20, 1987)

49. Outstanding Comedy Series: James Burrows, Glen Charles, Les Charles, Executive Producers; Peter Casey and David Lee, David Angell, Producers; Tim Berry, Co-Producer
50. Outstanding Lead Actor in a Comedy Series: Ted Danson
51. Outstanding Supporting Actor in a Comedy Series: Woody Harrelson
52. Outstanding Supporting Actor in a Comedy Series: George Wendt
53. Outstanding Supporting Actress in a Comedy Series: Rhea Perlman
54. *Outstanding Guest Performer in a Comedy Series: John Cleese, "Simon Says" (#116)
55. Outstanding Directing in a Comedy Series: James Burrows, "Chambers vs. Malone" (#108)
56. Outstanding Writing in a Comedy Series: Janet Leahy, "Abnormal Psychology" (#99)
57. Outstanding Editing for a Series, Multi-camera Production: Andy Ackerman, "Cheers: The Motion Picture" (#119)

58. *Outstanding Sound Mixing for a Comedy Series or a Special: Michael Ballin, Bob Douglass, Doug Grey, Thomas J. Huth, "The Proposal" (#96)

1987-88 Season (Awarded August 28, 1988)

59. Outstanding Comedy Series: James Burrows, Glen Charles, Les Charles, Executive Producers; Peter Casey and David Lee, David Angell, Producers; Tim Berry, Co-Producer
60. Outstanding Lead Actor in a Comedy Series: Ted Danson
61. Outstanding Lead Actress in a Comedy Series: Kirstie Alley
62. Outstanding Supporting Actor in a Comedy Series: Kelsey Grammer
63. Outstanding Supporting Actor in a Comedy Series: Woody Harrelson
64. Outstanding Supporting Actor in a Comedy Series: George Wendt
65. Outstanding Supporting Actress in a Comedy Series: Rhea Perlman
66. Outstanding Directing in a Comedy Series: James Burrows, "Backseat Becky, Upfront" (#146)
67. Outstanding Writing in a Comedy Series: Glen Charles and Les Charles, "Home Is the Sailor" (#122)
68. *Outstanding Editing for a Series, Multi-camera Production: Andy Ackerman, "The Big Kiss-Off" (#145)
69. Outstanding Sound Mixing for a Comedy Series or a Special: Pete San Filipo, Sr., Thomas J. Huth, Doug Grey, Bob Douglass, "The Last Angry Mailman" (#128)

1988-89 Season (Awarded September 17, 1989)

70. *Outstanding Comedy Series: James Burrows, Glen Charles, Les Charles, Executive Producers; Cheri Eichen and Bill Steinkellner, Producers; David Angell, Peter Casey, David Lee (Supervising) Producers; Tim Berry, Phoef Sutton, Co-Producers
71. Outstanding Lead Actor in a Comedy Series: Ted Danson
72. *Outstanding Supporting Actor in a Comedy Series: Woody Harrelson
73. Outstanding Supporting Actor in a Comedy Series: George Wendt
74. *Outstanding Supporting Actress in a Comedy Series: Rhea Perlman
75. Outstanding Directing for a Comedy Series: James Burrows, "The Visiting Lecher" (#168)
76. Outstanding Sound Mixing for a Comedy Series or a Special: Robert Crosby, Production Mixer; Sam Black, Robert Douglass, Thomas J. Huth, Re-recording Mixers, "Jumping Jerks" (#154)

1989-90 Season (Awarded September 16, 1990)

77. Outstanding Comedy Series: James Burrows, Glen Charles, Les Charles, Executive Producers; Cheri Eichen and Bill Steinkellner, Phoef Sutton, Co-Executive Producers; Tim Berry, Producer; Andy Ackerman, Co-Producer
78. *Outstanding Lead Actor in a Comedy Series: Ted Danson
79. Outstanding Lead Actress in a Comedy Series: Kirstie Alley
80. Outstanding Supporting Actor in a Comedy Series: Kelsey Grammer
81. Outstanding Supporting Actor in a Comedy Series: Woody Harrelson
82. *Outstanding Supporting Actress in a Comedy Series: Bebe Neuwirth
83. Outstanding Supporting Actress in a Comedy Series: Rhea Perlman
84. Outstanding Guest Actress in a Comedy Series: Georgia Brown, "The Ghost and Mrs. LeBec" (#191)
85. Outstanding Guest Actress in a Comedy Series: Alexis Smith, "Sammy and the Professor" (#181)
86. Outstanding Directing in a Comedy Series: James Burrows, "The Improbable Dream, Part 1" (#169)
87. Outstanding Writing in a Comedy Series: Ken Levine and David Isaacs, "Death Takes a Holiday on Ice" (#175)
88. *Outstanding Sound Mixing for a Series or a Special: Robert Crosby, Jr., C.A.S., Production Mixer; Thomas J. Huth, C.A.S., Sam Black, Bobby Douglass, Re-recording Mixers, "The Stork Brings a Crane" (#174)

1990-91 Season (Awarded August 25, 1991)

89. *Outstanding Comedy Series: James Burrows, Glen Charles, Les Charles, Creators-Executive Producers; Cheri Eichen and Bill Steinkellner, Phoef Sutton, Executive Producers; Tim Berry, Producer; Andy Ackerman, Brian Pollack, Mert Rich, Dan O'Shannon, Tom Anderson, Larry Balmagia, Co-Producers
90. Outstanding Lead Actor in a Comedy Series: Ted Danson
91. *Outstanding Lead Actress in a Comedy Series: Kirstie Alley
92. Outstanding Supporting Actor in a Comedy Series: Woody Harrelson
93. *Outstanding Supporting Actress in a Comedy Series: Bebe Neuwirth
94. Outstanding Supporting Actress in a Comedy Series: Rhea Perlman
95. Outstanding Guest Actor in a Comedy Series: Sheldon Leonard, "Grease" (#200)
96. Outstanding Guest Actress in a Comedy Series: Frances Sternhagen, "Ma Always Liked You Best" (#199)
97. Outstanding Guest Actress in a Comedy Series: Sada Thompson, "Honor Thy Mother" (#208)
98. *Outstanding Directing in a Comedy Series: James Burrows, "Woody Interruptus" (#207)

99. Outstanding Informational Special: "Cheers 200th Anniversary Special," James Burrows, Glen Charles, Les Charles, Creators-Executive Producers; Cheri Eichen, Bill Steinkellner, Phoef Sutton, Executive Producers; Tim Berry, Producer; Andy Ackerman, Brian Pollack, Mert Rich, Dan O'Shannon, Tom Anderson, Larry Balmagia, Co-Producers (#202–203)
100. Outstanding Editing for a Series, Multi-camera Production: Andy Ackerman, "The Days of Wine and Neuroses" (#210)
101. Outstanding Editing for a Series, Multi-camera Production: Sheila Amos, "Rat Girl" (#219)
102. Outstanding Sound Mixing for a Comedy Series or a Special: Robert Crosby, Jr., C.A.S., Production Mixer; Sam Black, Thomas J. Huth, C.A.S., Robert Douglass, Re-recording Mixers, "The Days of Wine and Neuroses" (#210)

1991-92 Season (Awarded August 30, 1992)

103. Outstanding Comedy Series: James Burrows, Glen Charles, Les Charles, Creators-Executive Producers; Cheri Eichen and Bill Steinkellner, Executive Producers; Dan O'Shannon and Tom Anderson, Supervising Producers; Tim Berry, Producer; Dan Staley and Rob Long, Co-producers
104. Outstanding Lead Actor in a Comedy Series: Ted Danson
105. Outstanding Lead Actress in a Comedy Series: Kirstie Alley
106. Outstanding Supporting Actor in a Comedy Series: Harvey Fierstein
107. Outstanding Supporting Actress in a Comedy Series: Frances Sternhagen
108. Outstanding Individual Achievement in Directing in a Comedy Series: James Burrows, "An Old Fashioned Wedding" (#246–247)
109. Outstanding Individual Achievement in Editing for a Series, Multi-camera Production: Robert Bramwell, Peter J. Chakos, "An Old Fashioned Wedding (#246–247)
110. Outstanding Individual Achievement in Sound Mixing for a Comedy Series or a Special: Robert Crosby, Jr., C.A.S., Production Sound Mixer; Robert Douglass, Sam Black, Thomas J. Huth, C.A.S., Re-recording Mixers, "Bar Wars VI: This Time It's for Real" (#244)

1992-93 Season (Awarded September 19, 1993)

111. Outstanding Comedy Series: James Burrows, Glen Charles, Les Charles, Creators-Executive Producers; Dan O'Shannon, Tom Anderson, Executive Producers; Dan Staley and Rob Long, Co-Executive Producers; Tim Berry, Producer
112. *Outstanding Lead Actor in a Comedy Series: Ted Danson

113. Outstanding Lead Actress in a Comedy Series: Kirstie Alley
114. Outstanding Supporting Actress in a Comedy Series: Rhea Perlman
115. Outstanding Guest Actor in a Comedy Series: Tom Berenger, "One for the Road" (#273–275)
116. Outstanding Guest Actress in a Comedy Series: Shelley Long, "One for the Road" (#273–275)
117. *Outstanding Individual Achievement in Editing for a Series, Multicamera Production, Robert Bramwell, "One for the Road" (#273–275)
118. Outstanding Individual Achievement in Directing in a Comedy Series, James Burrows, "One for the Road" (#273–275)

Index

68; screenplay 71; sex addiction 67,
73; substance abuse 70; theater 65,
70–71; violence 65, 67, 69; writing
71, 75
Harrington, Pat, Jr. 35
Harris, Jonathan Daniel 342
Harrison, Desiree 141, 201, 291
Harrison, Richmond 315
Harrison, Tom 285
Harry "the Hat" *see* Gittes, Harry
Hart, Gary (senator) 128, 145, 286
Hart Angelo, Judy: awards and nomi-
nations 357; song concept 4; song
credits 249, 259, 267, 277, 287, 297,
307, 316, 326, 336, 346
Hartman, Valerie 317
Harvard Alcohol Project 3
Harvard Business School 124
Harvard University 93, 121, 231
The Harvard-Yale Football Game 169
Harvey, Charlotte 249
Hatcheck girl 147, 213, 334
Hatfield, Bobby 128, 158, 332
A Hatful of Rain 34, 37
Haury, Lauren 39
Havins, Hal 302
"Hawaii Five-O" 35, 37
Hawkins, Michael G. 315
Hawley, Becky 264
Hawn, Goldie 72
Hay, Land Courtney 277
Headache 229, 340
Heald, Anthony 356
Health club membership 208
Hearn, George 355
A Heart Held Hostage 170
"Hearts Afire" 263
Hecht, Mr. 210, 274
Hedaya, Dan 263, 271, 274, 284, 292,
352
Hedges, Ducky 243
Hedges, Mr. 167, 260
Hedges, Pamela A. 291
Hello Again 86, 91–92
Hello Dolly 199
Hello Donald 199
Helm, Rebecca 268, 277
Helper, Millie 315
Helpmates 45
Hemingway, Ernest 168–69
Hendler, Julia 253

Hendrickson, Tera 352
Hennessy, Noreen 305
Henning, Jane 327, 337, 347
Henri (Kelly's friend): America, arrival
to 202, 331, 340; competition against
Sam 125, 348; deportation 203,
339–40; occupations 121, 202–3, 236,
331, 334; relationships, Kelly 202–4,
331; romantic relationships 203,
339–40; sexual exploits 203, 348; *see
also* Cistaro, Anthony
Henry, Linda 297
Henshaw, Phyllis 209, 212, 280
Henshaw, Ron 209, 212, 280
Henshaw triplets 146
Hepburn, Katharine 4, 9, 77
Heppel (corporate employee) 139, 304,
306
Herkert, Richard 288
Hernandez, Marco 308
Hernia 133, 167, 283
Herring, Sue: assistant to producers
268, 277, 287, 297, 307, 316, 327,
337, 347; editer 346; technical credits
268, 277, 287, 297, 307, 316, 326–27,
337, 346–47; writer 305, 320, 334,
348
Heston, Jeff 340
Heydorn, Nancy 326
Hibernation 305
Hickey 207, 212, 266
Hicks, John 249
High Sultan 290
"The Highway Honeys" 25, 33
Hiken, Gerald 308
Hill, Benny 193
Hill, Elizabeth 263, 265
Hill, John Allen 120, 127, 141: entre-
preneurial endeavors 127, 329; family
127; heart attack 190, 350; nicknames
127, 190; relationship to Carla 127,
190, 193, 339, 350; relationship to
Sam 123, 134, 147; *see also* Curtis,
Keene
Hill, Kimberly 277, 285, 287, 292
Hill, Richard 254
Hill, Valerie 127, 147, 331
"Hill Street Blues" 7, 15, 254, 264,
350
Hilliard, Thomas, III 124, 254
Hines, Douglas 249, 267, 277, 359